Preface

This tutorial is intended to provide both the beginning and the experienced manager with the materials they need to develop a thorough understanding of the basic theories, tools, techniques and skills of software management. It is introductory in that I do not assume that the reader has had extensive experience in the field. I have not attempted to gather herein all the knowledge a practicing manager might need to be totally effective; that, perhaps, would be too ambitious. Most managers take years to develop the skills, knowledge, and abilities required to successfully manage the delivery of an acceptable software product on time and within budget. Rather, I have tried to furnish my readers with a framework for organizing knowledge in a way that will make it both useful and usable.

The tutorial framework is centered around the five basic functions of management: planning, organizing, staffing, directing, and controlling. I discuss these functions along with the importance of software in the Introduction. Papers amplify important management theories, tools, and techniques and discuss ways of getting the job done. I treat both commercial and military systems and provide several case studies to serve as learning aids. I also provide a special section on the subject of software productivity to fill the void left by most textbooks on the subject. Finally, I have provided an annotated bibliography referring the reader to other useful texts to round out the volume.

During the four years since the publication of the second edition of this tutorial, considerable progress has been made in the field of software management. This progress is reflected in the improved quality of the papers included within the volume. These papers are more specific in their recommendations and more applicable to the problems managers face in today's software development projects.

As in the second edition, let me stress that management is both a discipline and an art: a discipline in that a body of knowledge exists to inform and guide management practice and an art in that there are no foolproof rules for applying this knowledge so as to reap its full benefits. Managers must develop their own judgment and common sense to use this knowledge successfully to accomplish goals through the use of people. My primary goal in this tutorial is to help readers cultivate this judgment.

I acknowledge the helpful suggestions offered by my colleagues and students and by the IEEE Computer Society Editorial Board. Last, but not least, I thank my wife and family for their patience and understanding. This edition is dedicated to all contributors.

Donald J. Reifer

Table of Contents

Part I: Introduction

"Under any social order from now to Utopia a management is indispensable and all enduring . . . the question is not: 'Will there be a management elite?' but 'What sort of elite will it be?'"

—Sidney Webb

The nine papers selected for this introductory section provide insight into the challenges associated with software management and the framework selected to use to study ways to deal with them.

The first three papers discuss the software industry and provide the reader with insight into how companies like IBM and Apple plan to capitalize on their software capabilities to continue to maintain their high growth rates now and in the future. These papers illustrate how rapidly software has grown in importance. Software is no longer viewed as just a service industry. Instead, software is viewed by major corporations as a product that can be sold by itself or to lever hardware sales. These papers show that software affects the corporate balance sheet and is an indispensable element of corporate strategies leading to profit and loss.

The fourth paper (Glaser) describes project management practices used by industry to manage the timely development of software products and discusses the challenges of today's projects and the practices used by many companies to overcome them. The paper stresses the concept that project management practices can work and that acceptable software systems can be delivered on time and within budget.

The fifth paper (Reifer) is a rewrite of an introduction prepared especially for this tutorial volume and provides the reader with an overview of the fundamental concepts of management. It describes how these concepts relate to the organizational framework of this tutorial, which revolves around the management functions of planning, organizing, staffing, directing, and controlling. The paper reinforces the message that software can be managed by using classical approaches and provides the reader with a road map for using this tutorial.

The sixth and seventh papers describe the software life cycle as viewed from two different vantage points—development and acquisition. Gibson and Nolan characterize the classical development life cycle, in which an organization's data processing group works with in-house users to develop and deploy an application system. In contrast, Driscoll portrays the military life cycle in which software is typically acquired contractually from an external source. Both these papers convey process models used in other papers within the volume.

The eighth and ninth papers describe lessons learned in software project management. Keider, in "Why Systems Fail," characterizes unsuccessful projects, while Farbman, in "Myths That Miss," identifies management myths. Both papers provide insight into problems that can be avoided if one learns from other's experiences.

1

SOFTWARE: THE NEW DRIVING FORCE

WITH COMPUTERS BECOMING MORE ALIKE, THE ACTION SHIFTS TO PROGRAMS

SHOPPING FOR SOFTWARE: TO WIN SPACE ON CROWDED RETAIL SHELVES, PRODUCERS TURN TO SOPHISTICATED MARKETING TACTICS

Raw power. That is what sold computers in the early days. Salesmen would fire off strings of statistics—how many millions of instructions per second a machine could handle, how many bytes of data it could store, how many bits it could process at a time.

But hardware is no longer where the action is. Computers are becoming remarkably similar—in many cases they are turning into off-the-shelf, commodity products. Now the computer wars are being fought on a new battleground: software—the instructions that tell computers how to do everything from processing payrolls to playing video games. "Hardware is getting less and less distinguished," says Jon A. Shirley, president of Microsoft Corp., a Washington State company that writes software for personal computers. "Software is what's leading the industry."

A key reason for the change in emphasis is an overwhelming demand from customers for packaged software that will let them apply computer power to a broad range of new tasks. Increasingly, corporations are finding they do not have the resources to write the programs they need. As a result, most companies have stopped writing their own software and are instead buying standard software packages (page 92).

'A TREMENDOUS CRY.' So far, producers have been unable to keep up with the need, and there has been a severe shortage of software able to take advantage of the power of the latest machines. "We're getting the hardware [we need from the industry], but software has not moved out at the same rate," says Robert J. Metzler, vice-president of First Computer Services, the data processing arm of First Union National Bank in Charlotte, N.C. "There's a tremendous cry in the industry [for software]." The flood of personal computers pouring into small businesses and homes has created an even faster-growing new market.

The booming demand for new and better programs has quickly turned software into big business. As recently as three years ago, software was still a cottage industry, with sales totaling just $2.7 billion annually. This year—according to estimates by Input, a California market research firm—sales are expected to top $10 billion.

With the industry growing that fast, several once-small software companies have become sizable corporations. Management Science America Inc. (MSA), for example, the largest independent software supplier, quadrupled in size during the past three years, topping $145 million in sales in 1983. Trying to capture some of the soaring market, thousands of new companies have entered the software business in recent years; by one count there are more than 3,000 software companies now.

While over the long term a shakeout is probably inevitable, the near-term outlook for most of these companies ap-

ANDREW POPPER

3

pears extremely bright. "The upside potential has barely been tapped," says Robert M. Freeman, senior analyst at Input. He expects the market to keep growing by a dizzying 32% a year, topping $30 billion in 1988. Software sales of that magnitude would amount to half of the $60 billion hardware business expected for the same year; today, revenue from software is equal to only 27% of the value of all the computer hardware sold (chart).

Sales of software for personal computers—the fastest-growing part of the software industry—should rise by an astounding 44% annually over the same five years. "We're finally at the point

which tell a computer how to carry out specific tasks such as accounting, payroll, or word processing.

But those distinctions are blurring:

□ **Consolidation.** International Business Machines Corp., to move faster into applications software, in November placed all its software efforts into a single, entrepreneurial unit—the same type of organization it used to launch the highly successful Personal Computer.

□ **Acquisitions.** To provide a full complement of software for their computers, makers such as Hewlett-Packard, Burroughs, and Prime Computer are rushing to buy applications software companies. Other manufacturers, including

□ **New players.** To grab a piece of the action, publishers and other communications companies outside the computer business—including CBS, Dow Jones, Dun & Bradstreet, McGraw-Hill, and Simon & Schuster—are licensing programs they then sell through their own distribution channels. "It's a very fragmented industry, but the potential is absolutely huge," says Richard W. Young, president of Houghton Mifflin Co.

□ **Japan's drive.** To catch up with their U.S. rivals, Japanese computer makers are launching major software development efforts. Perhaps the best evidence of just how important software has become is the drive by Japan's Ministry of

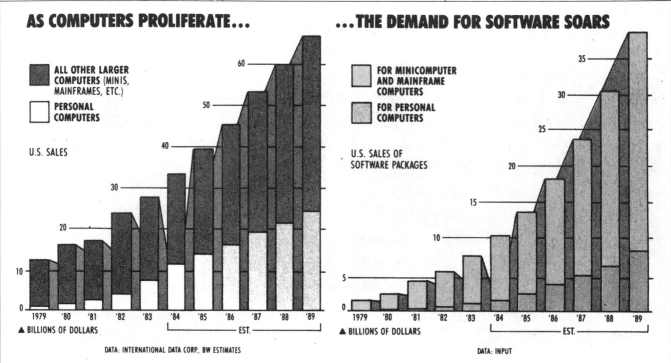

AS COMPUTERS PROLIFERATE...

ALL OTHER LARGER COMPUTERS (MINIS, MAINFRAMES, ETC.)

PERSONAL COMPUTERS

U.S. SALES

▲ BILLIONS OF DOLLARS — EST. —

1979 '80 '81 '82 '83 '84 '85 '86 '87 '88 '89

DATA: INTERNATIONAL DATA CORP., BW ESTIMATES

...THE DEMAND FOR SOFTWARE SOARS

FOR MINICOMPUTER AND MAINFRAME COMPUTERS

FOR PERSONAL COMPUTERS

U.S. SALES OF SOFTWARE PACKAGES

▲ BILLIONS OF DOLLARS — EST. —

1979 '80 '81 '82 '83 '84 '85 '86 '87 '88 '89

DATA: INPUT

where software applications are going to be a big moneymaker," says Jack M. Scanlon, vice-president of the Computer Systems Div. of AT&T Technologies Inc. But with the promise of such rapid market growth has come a feverish competition that is beginning to restructure the entire industry.

Until recently, nearly all software companies concentrated on a particular niche and fit neatly into one of three distinct market segments (table, page 76) that were divided along the same lines for both mainframe and personal computers. Systems software, which handles basic housekeeping operations such as controlling the printer and memory, was supplied primarily by the computer makers. They were joined by independent software companies in providing utility software, which, among other things, helps programmers write programs. And a host of other independent software companies competed in the third market: applications packages,

Honeywell, Sperry, and Digital Equipment, are setting up joint ventures with software suppliers. Says Roger T. Hobbs, vice-president for software products and services at Burroughs Corp.: "The demands for software are increasing so rapidly that it is impossible for the manufacturer to keep up."

□ **Expanding product lines.** Software companies are expanding product lines to maintain their competitive edge. Those that supply programs mostly for large mainframes—MSA, Cullinet Software, and Computer Associates International, for example—are snapping up personal computer software houses. And companies that specialize in systems software for personal computers—among them, Ashton-Tate, Digital Research, and Microsoft—are adding general-purpose applications software to their product lines. "Today you have to have a broad line," says Terry L. Opdendyk, president of VisiCorp. Otherwise, "the vendor is increasingly vulnerable to competition."

International Trade & Industry to change the law to boost Japan's fledgling software industry (page 96).

One result of many of these trends is that mergers and acquisitions in the industry are at an all-time high. Last year there were 146 acquisitions, valued at more than $1 billion—up 130% from 1982—reports Broadview Associates, a New Jersey company handling such transactions. And this frantic pace of activity is turning the software business into a hot investment area (page 94).

To compete successfully amid all the turmoil, software suppliers are struggling to formulate new strategies. One common focus is advanced design—especially the development of software aimed at making computers easier to use (page 93).

But just as important to the success of new software as advanced design is marketing. "You need a great product and great marketing," insists David S. Wagman, chairman of Softsel Computer

A QUICK GUIDE TO SOFTWARE—AND WHO SUPPLIES IT

Suppliers for large computers

Software companies: American Management Systems, American Software, Anacomp, ASK Computer Systems, Comserv, Hogan Systems, Informatics, Information Science, Integrated Software Systems, Management Science America, McCormack & Dodge (Dun & Bradstreet), Policy Management Systems, Shared Medical Systems, Technicon, Timberline Systems, University Computing (Wyly), Walker Interactive Products

Hardware makers: IBM, Sperry

Software companies: Applied Data Research, Artificial Intelligence, Cincom Systems, Computer Associates, Comshare, Cullinet Software, Informatics General, Information Builders, Johnson Systems, Mathematica, Pansophic Systems, Software AG, University Computing (Wyly)

Others: AT&T

Hardware makers: Burroughs, Digital Equipment, Honeywell, IBM, NCR, Sperry

Software companies: Applied Data Research, Computer Associates, Pansophic Systems

Others: AT&T

APPLICATIONS SOFTWARE

These programs turn the computer into something useful because they set up the system to handle a specific task. They can be for general-purpose applications, usable by a wide variety of companies, performing such jobs as general ledger accounting, payroll, and word processing. Other packages tailor the computer to the needs of a specific industry, such as banking, insurance, hospitals, manufacturing, or retailing

UTILITY SOFTWARE

These products are the middlemen between operating systems and applications software, and ensure that the applications programs are written and run efficiently. These include: compilers, which turn programs into code that computers understand; data base management systems that act as electronic librarians to keep track of data; and, for now, only on personal computers, "windows" and integrated "environments" that permit users to do more than one task at a time

SYSTEMS CONTROL SOFTWARE

These are the "housekeeping" programs that manage the operation of the computer's various components, such as printers and memories, so that they work smoothly together as the applications software performs its tasks. These products include operating systems, communications monitors, and network control programs

Suppliers for personal computers

Hardware makers: Apple, IBM

Software companies: Computer Task Group, Digital Research, Eduware, Information Unlimited Software (Computer Associates), Informatics General, Lotus Development, MicroPro, Peachtree Software (MSA), Safeguard, SEI, Sorcim, Software Publishing, Spinnaker, VisiCorp

Publishers: CBS, Dow Jones, Dun & Bradstreet, McGraw-Hill

Hardware makers: Apple, IBM

Software companies: Ashton-Tate, Condor Computing, Digital Research, Microsoft, Quarterdeck, Software Publishing, Stoneware, VisiCorp

Others: AT&T

Hardware makers: Apple, IBM

Software companies: Digital Research, Microsoft, Softech Microsystems

Others: AT&T

Products Inc., an Inglewood (Calif.) software distributor. "For a while it was either/or in this business, but now you absolutely must have both."

Nowhere is the new attention to marketing more noticeable than in the hotly competitive personal computer business. To reach the millions of personal computer users, software companies are spending huge amounts to introduce and advertise their products. Industry watchers have dubbed this obsession with splashy promotion "the Lotus syndrome"—a reference to the more than $1 million that Lotus Development Corp. spent over a three-month period in 1983 to launch its first product, the highly successful 1-2-3 package. "Lotus advertised so much that companies are going to be forced to step up their advertising just to be heard above the noise," says David E. Gold, a San Jose (Calif.) computer consultant.

ON A SHOESTRING. Advertising, in fact, has grown so important to software success that it has become one of the biggest barriers keeping out new companies. "The cost of technology development is dwarfed by the marketing cost; the ante has really been upped," says Rodney N. Turner, vice-president for sales at Ashton-Tate, a Culver City (Calif.) software company best known for its dBase II package. It takes as much as $8 million to launch a new software product today, he estimates. Ashton-Tate, by contrast, was founded on a shoestring—$7,500.

Any personal computer program must be carefully packaged and promoted. "It has to look good and has to be well supported by national advertising," maintains retailer Gregg E. Olson, a salesman at Mr. Software in Boulder, Colo. "A company that wants to sell to us has to have all their marketing elements in place to establish credibility with us and our customers."

Even companies that write software for the large minicomputers and mainframes are plowing more money into marketing. While programs for the larger systems, unlike those for personal computers, do not require heavy consumer advertising, says Martin A. Goetz, senior vice-president at Applied Data Research Inc., his company still boosted its 1984 advertising budget by 60% over last year, to about $2 million.

This emphasis on marketing comes chiefly from the need to reach a different, far broader group of potential customers. "Ten years ago, [our customer] was the data processing department, and if you had a product, you sold it to the technicians," says Robert D. Baskerville, group vice-president for product management at Computer Sciences

THE BEST-SELLING PROGRAMS
APPLICATIONS SOFTWARE

Name	Supplier	Price	Task
For personal computers:			
WordStar	MicroPro International	$495	Word processing
PFS:Write	Software Publishing	$125-$140	Word processing
1-2-3	Lotus Development	$495	Spreadsheet, graphics, and file management
Multiplan	Microsoft	$275	Spreadsheet
VisiCalc	VisiCorp	$250	Spreadsheet
VisiTrend/Plot	VisiCorp	$300	Draws graphs
PFS:Graph	Software Publishing	$125-$140	Draws graphs
General Accounting	BPI Systems	$195-$595	Standard accounting functions
Peachtree Accounting Software	Peachtree	$395	Standard accounting functions
For large computers:			
Human Resource System	Information Science	$50,000-$100,000	Personnel and payroll
MSA Human Resource System	Management Science America	$80,000-$130,000	Personnel and payroll
MSA General Ledger System/FICS	Management Science America	$50,000-$100,000	General ledger accounting
Policy Management System	Policy Management Systems	*	Insurance policy management

UTILITY SOFTWARE

Name	Supplier	Price	Task
For personal computers:			
dBase II	Ashton-Tate	$700	Data base management
PFS:File	Software Publishing	$125-$140	Data base management
Microsoft Basic	Microsoft	$350-$600	A compiler for writing Basic programs
Visi On	VisiCorp	$95	An integrated 'environment'
For large computers:			
Total	Cincom Systems	$95,400	Data base management
Mark IV	Informatics General	$78,000-$98,000	Data base management
ADABAS	Software AG	$106,000 and up	Data base management
System 2000	Intel Systems	$50,000-$100,000	Data base management
Focus	Information Builders	$66,000-$120,000	Data base management

SYSTEMS CONTROL SOFTWARE

Name	Supplier	Price	Task
For personal computers:			
Apple DOS	Apple Computer	Free with machine	Apple II and III operating system
CP/M	Digital Research	$150	Operating system for 8-bit computers
Concurrent CP/M-86	Digital Research	$350	Latest version of CP/M for 16-bit computers with windowing environment
MS/DOS	Microsoft	**	Operating system for IBM Personal Computer
For large computers:			
CA-Dynam	Computer Associates	$24,750	Disk and tape catalog management
CA-Sort	Computer Associates	$4,500-$7,500	Sorts and combines files
DATAMANAGER	Manager Software Products	$8,100	Keeps track of data in data base
SyncSort	SyncSort	***	Sorts and combines programs

*Price varies widely depending on size of installation and type of computer **Purchased through computer maker
***Leases for $6,200 a year on a three-year contract

DATA: INTERNATIONAL COMPUTER PROGRAMS INC., BW

Corp. in El Segundo, Calif. Today, he notes, a software company has "to sell to end users, and you have to emphasize more than the technical capability—you have to really sell the benefit."

Software marketing now means beginning with detailed product planning, so that a program will better meet the needs of customers. Before Wyly Corp. even began a $20 million program to diversify into applications software, for example, it brought in all its salesmen from the field to tell programmers what customers wanted—something most software companies had never done. "With modern software development techniques, you can produce almost perfect code, but if you don't understand the market, it could still be useless," says Ron W. Brittian, Wyly's vice-president for research and development.

Critical, too, is a reputation for good service and customer support. "To grow from a startup into a large software company is not so easy anymore; it's a question of distribution and of educating the customer in how to use the product," says Anthony W. Wang, executive vice-president at Computer Associates International Inc. Toward this end, his company recently installed a $250,000 television studio—costing $200,000 or more a year to run—to make training videotapes for its software customers.

READABLE INSTRUCTIONS. As competition heightens and customers become more demanding, companies selling personal computer software are providing a level of customer support far greater than anything they offered even a year ago. MicroPro International Corp., for example, has plowed $2.5 million into develop-

ing computer-aided instruction and retail-support aids for its software, which includes the best-selling WordStar. The company is also hiring journalists and other nontechnical writers to produce more readable instructions for today's less sophisticated customers. "A product is not a product until you have computer-aided instruction, it's not a product until you have video instruction, it's not a product until you have honest-to-God understandable language [in the manual]," says H. Glen Haney, president of MicroPro.

Establishing a marketing presence is especially critical to companies that provide personal computer software, because they must win space on already crowded retail shelves. Computer retailers are reluctant to take on new software without feeling confident it is a

'A LOT OF PEOPLE ARE WATCHING FOR US TO FALL DOWN'

Lotus Development Corp. is trying to do something that has proven to be next to impossible for personal computer software companies: follow up its first software package, a smash hit, with a second program just as successful. Witness VisiCorp, which is currently struggling to repeat its runaway success with VisiCalc, the electronic financial spreadsheet (page 88). "A lot of people are watching for us to fall down," admits Mitchell D. Kapor, Lotus co-founder and president.

Lotus has been a trend-setter from its beginning in April, 1982. In its first six months, the Cambridge (Mass.) company raised nearly $5 million in venture capital, a level of financing unheard of for a software company at that time. Then, to launch its pioneering product, dubbed 1-2-3, Lotus wowed the industry with an unprecedented ad campaign that cost more than $1 million over a three-month period. The integrated program combines financial-analysis spreadsheets, graphics, and data file management in a single floppy disk that sells for $495.

SECOND SUCCESS? Lotus sold 110,000 copies of 1-2-3 in its first nine months on the market, making the program one of the best-selling personal computer programs ever. Lotus racked up 1983 revenues of $53 million, ranking the company among the top five independent suppliers of personal computer software. "We think we've got a major competitive lead," says Kapor.

With just this one product under its belt, Lotus went public last October and sold more than 2 million shares to an enthusiastic market at $18 a

share—banking more than $41 million. Today the company's shares are trading in the mid-30s.

On Feb. 14, Lotus announced what it hopes will be its second hit: a $695 package called Symphony. This product adds three new features to 1-2-3's existing capabilities: word processing, a more sophisticated data management system, and the ability to communicate with other computers. The company plans to begin shipping Symphony early this summer.

But Lotus could have trouble matching the takeoff of 1-2-3: Several startups—including Ovation Technologies Inc. and Softrend Inc.—have announced plans to market integrated software packages with features similar to Symphony's. At the same time,

Lotus will soon be competing with suppliers of mainframe software—such as Cullinet Software Inc.—which are bringing out their own versions of Symphony-like software.

Kapor remains confident, however, that Symphony will be another hit. He will not say exactly how much Lotus plans to spend, but he concedes that the company will lay out even more money to launch Symphony than it did to introduce 1-2-3. It is also augmenting its retail sales with a team of its own salespeople who will sell directly to more than 150 of the largest U.S. companies. Despite the well-planned marketing effort, Kapor acknowledges the real test for Symphony will be user reaction. "The best marketing weapon is a superior product," he says.

winner. "Unless we're absolutely convinced that it's a great program, we'll wait to see how other channels of distribution do with it," says John H. Rollins, national manager for Sears Business Systems Centers, the computer retailing arm of Sears, Roebuck & Co.

One group trying hard to enter the software business may have an edge: the traditional book publishers. Because they already sell books to computer stores, the publishers "provide ready-made distribution channels," says Input's Freeman. Agrees William M. Graves, president of MSA: "There is a tremendous similarity in the microcomputer business and publishing."

'EIGHT DIFFERENT VENDORS.' No matter how they distribute their products, software companies are finding that they must offer a broader range of products than ever before. "The strategy is to offer a complete solution," asserts Robert N. Goldman, president of Cullinet.

"If a customer ends up with eight different vendors, none of the software works together." Cullinet, for instance, is augmenting its data base management software with such applications as general ledger accounting and manufacturing control programs.

Broadening a software line also helps a supplier leverage the large amounts of money spent on establishing a reputation and brand recognition. VisiCorp, which gained market fame with its hit program VisiCalc, is trying to expand its applications software with its family of Visi On integrated software. Similarly, Microsoft is plunging into such applications software as word processing and financial analysis to build on its reputation as a supplier of personal computer operating systems.

The trend toward comprehensive offerings will force small companies to target well-defined market niches. There will continue to be demand for special-

ized packages designed for the needs of a particular industry or profession. "There will be several very large software companies," contends John P. Imlay Jr., chairman of Management Science America., "but there will be literally hundreds of small companies, with under $100 million [in sales], that have specialized market niches."

Perhaps the most fundamental change in the software industry is the blurring distinctions between the suppliers. No longer can they be neatly divided into companies that make basic systems software and those that write programs for specific applications.

Moreover, the top mainframe software companies are rushing to market with software for personal computers. And vendors serving only the personal computer market are joining with suppliers of mainframe software. VisiCorp, for example, recently teamed up with Informatics General Corp. to offer VisiAnswer, a program that allows a user of an IBM Personal Computer to retrieve information from an IBM mainframe data base. These changes resulted in large part from the growing number of customers linking personal computers to large mainframe systems.

WOOING THE SPECIALISTS. As the emphasis in the data processing industry shifts to software—and as software companies strengthen their sales, service, and distribution—the big-system makers, too, are scrambling to do more to provide their customers with software. "In the old days, our customer wrote his own application [software]," notes Jon Tempas, vice-president for software products at Sperry Corp.'s Computer Systems operation. Today, he says, "there's an increased expectation for hardware suppliers to provide the complete solution." That means the equipment makers will need to provide more of their own software. Sperry, for example, now writes 95% of the software it sells for its computer line.

Most of the big-system companies, however, are turning to software specialists for help, since much of the demand is for applications software finely tuned to specific industries. "I don't think there's any hardware manufacturer that can—or should—provide all the software," says John E. Steuri, general manager of the Information Services Business Unit, IBM's new independent software group. "We'll be more and more dependent over time on software developed outside the company." For example, in January IBM began marketing with Comshare Inc. specialized software to help executives make decisions.

The pressure to team up with independent software companies is especially

---

'ONE DAY WE COULD GIVE AWAY HARDWARE TO SELL SOFTWARE'

Hewlett-Packard Co. was one of the first major computer makers to recognize that to keep its equipment sales growing, it would have to move strongly into software. "As a hardware maker alone, we couldn't survive," says Edward R. McCracken, general manager of HP's business development group.

Like most established hardware makers, the Palo Alto (Calif.) company until five years ago had provided the basic operating-system software to run its machines—but little more than that. So HP set out to discover its customers' needs and to write the applications programs to meet those needs.

This quickly became a three-pronged effort: HP acquired three specialty software houses, hired a staff of market researchers from such companies as General Mills Inc. and Heublein Inc., and spent more in research and development of applications software. That funding mushroomed to 15% of HP's 1983 computer R&D budget—or $38 million—up from less than 3% in 1980.

BRISK SALES. Over the past two years, HP has also tripled the number of outside software companies that are writing applications programs for its computers. There are now 500 cooperating software houses. Explains McCracken: "You can't do everything yourself."

HP will not break out software revenue figures from those of its overall computer business, which hit $2.4 billion last year. But McCracken admits HP is losing money on software it sells

as it plows more money into R&D. Nonetheless, he expects that software will eventually become a bigger—and profitable—part of HP business. In fact, jokes McCracken: "It's possible one day we could end up giving away the hardware to sell the software."

strong among makers of personal computers. "Without an adequate software base, a microcomputer dies," says Eugene W. Helms, vice-president for business development at Texas Instruments Inc.'s Data Systems Group. So TI is recruiting software suppliers to adapt their best-selling programs for its Professional Computer. Perhaps the most extensive effort to sign up independent software companies was made recently by Apple Computer Inc., which courted more than 100 companies to write software for its new Macintosh computer.

The California company was successful in signing up more than 80 of them.

Companies that do not move quickly to develop a broad line of software will have trouble keeping up. Consider Tymshare Inc., a computer time-sharing company. As computer prices began to drop precipitously, more and more of Tymshare's customers stopped renting computer time and purchased their own machines. Tymshare did not have any software packages to sell to its former clients. "We used to look at software as simply an in-house tool that we needed

to offer time-sharing," says one Tymshare executive. That attitude, he admits, "came back and bit us in the rear end." In 1983 the California company lost $1.7 million while sales fell 3% to $288 million. Now it is engaged in a major effort to expand into applications software, through internal development and by licensing packages from other companies.

With most software companies trying hard to move in the same direction, everyone will face stiffer competition. Already, prices for personal computer software are sliding wherever similar programs have proliferated—in electronic spreadsheets and word processors, for example. And a big battle is under way among suppliers of the various "windowing" software packages—software "environments" that permit the users of personal computers to display several tasks at once. VisiCorp has been forced to slash the price of its Visi On environment package from $495 to $95. "The consumer is going to force the prices down simply by demand," asserts Alvin B. Reuben, executive vice-president at Simon & Schuster Inc.'s electronic publishing division.

'FEELING THE PINCH.' As prices fall, the opportunity for a newcomer to jump in and grab quick and easy profits will all but disappear. The cost of developing and marketing new programs is mushrooming just when margins are shrinking. VisiCorp successfully launched VisiCalc in 1978 with a $500 budget. But the California company has spent more than $10 million developing its latest product, the Visi On environment. Product life is also getting shorter as new products come out faster. As a result, says Softsel's Wagman, "the stakes have gotten higher and much riskier from a development point of view."

For many companies, the risks will ultimately prove fatal. "There are companies out there that are already feeling the pinch of increased costs, new product announcements, and a changing marketplace," warns consultant Gold. Industry watchers predict that some big-name failures will occur within the next 18 months. By the end of the decade, many experts expect the software industry to have consolidated its thousands of suppliers into a few major players.

For those that make it, the future is promising. The demand by the growing army of computer users for easier-to-use software to handle an exploding variety of tasks will drive the industry to create software with far more capabilities than anything available today. "The only limit," says Stuart A. Walker, vice-president of marketing at Knoware Inc., "is the limit of new ideas."

PRODUCT VARIETY 'GIVES US A STRENGTH NO ONE ELSE HAS'

When John P. Imlay Jr. took the helm of Management Science America Inc. in 1971, the Atlanta software company was losing money on sluggish sales of just $2 million a year. MSA had just one product, a general-ledger accounting package, so Imlay began to expand the product line, by pursuing both internal development and acquisitions.

In doing so, Imlay has turned MSA into the country's largest independent software company. Sales have grown at a breakneck clip of 45% a year since 1972, hitting $145.2 million in 1983. During the past five years, earnings have grown tenfold, hitting $10.8 million last year.

MSA's product line now includes not only its own financial and personnel software but also manufacturing-systems software purchased from Xerox Corp.'s Arista group in 1982 and order-processing software developed by

Computeristics Inc., a Hamden (Conn.) company that MSA acquired in June.

While those mainframe products still provide the lion's share of revenues, Imlay is pinning MSA's growth on what he calls "the magnificent revolution": microcomputers. He moved into software for these machines in 1981 by buying Peachtree Software Inc. Last year, he added Edu-ware Inc., an education software company. Since 1981, MSA's microcomputer software sales have jumped a hefty 130%, to $21.7 million, in 1983.

But the best is yet to come, says 47-year-old Imlay, now MSA chairman. He predicts the software company will have 1984 sales of $195 million and hopes for sales of $500 million to $1 billion by the end of the decade. Any software company striving for $1 billion in sales, Imlay contends, must have a wide range of products. "If we're going to sell one [product to a customer], we're going to go back and sell 19 more. That gives us a strength no one else has."

9

VISICORP'S PLAN TO REVERSE ITS RICHES-TO-RAGS STORY

VisiCorp started the personal computer revolution in corporate offices with its VisiCalc, an electronic spreadsheet for financial analysis. Many people, in fact, credit VisiCalc with turning the Apple II computer into a best-seller. More than 600,000 copies of the program have been sold since it was introduced in 1979, powering VisiCorp growth faster than most entrepreneurs can even imagine: After just four years, sales of the privately held San Jose (Calif.) company topped $43 million in 1983, nearly half of them from VisiCalc.

Suddenly, however, the company finds itself in big trouble. It is fighting off attacks in both the courts and the marketplace—attacks that threaten VisiCorp's growth and perhaps its survival as an independent company. Roy E. Folk, a former VisiCorp marketing director, says that the company logged a $2.5 million pretax loss in its 1983 third quarter and incurred further heavy losses in the final period. "I can't imagine how VisiCorp can withstand many more quarters of multimillion-dollar losses," he says.

END OF THE LINE. The company's difficulties underscore the challenges facing personal computer software businesses that rely on a narrow product line. "VisiCorp has been deriving half its revenues from VisiCalc, and VisiCalc has come to the end of its product life," declares David E. Gold, a California software industry consultant. Until 1982, VisiCorp had not even revised VisiCalc. Since then it has introduced only two minor new versions. Meanwhile, competitors flooded the market with spreadsheet programs that outperformed VisiCalc and quickly ate into its sales. The hottest of these competitors is Lotus 1-2-3 from Lotus Development Corp. It is outselling Visi-Calc 2 to 1, according to a December retail survey by Future Computing Inc., a Texas market researcher.

VisiCorp may even lose its only bread-and-butter product. The company owns only the marketing rights to VisiCalc—the program itself belongs to Software Arts Inc., the Wellesley (Mass.) software company responsible for writing it. Last summer, VisiCorp sued Software Arts for $60 million, charging that it had failed to live up to its agreement to supply enhancements and new versions of the VisiCalc program.

But on Feb. 3, Software Arts an-

CHAIRMAN FYLSTRA: CAN HIS NEW SERIES OF SOFTWARE OFFSET VISICALC'S SLUMP?

nounced that it was ending its marketing agreement with VisiCorp and taking back exclusive rights to VisiCalc. It is charging that VisiCorp deliberately undercut sales of VisiCalc (on which Software Arts receives a royalty of 36% to 50% of revenues) to push VisiCorp's new "windowing" software package, Visi On, whose revenues VisiCorp does not share. VisiCorp lost the first round on Feb. 10 when a federal district court in Boston refused to issue a preliminary injunction prohibiting Software Arts from selling VisiCalc.

While the legal battle grinds on, Daniel H. Fylstra, VisiCorp chairman, paints a bright picture of the company's future—even if it loses the revenues from VisiCalc. He concedes that VisiCalc accounted for 50% of revenues in early 1983 but claims that "it's nowhere close

to 50% today." The company's big seller now, Fylstra says, will be Visi On and a series of applications software designed to work with it. Visi On is one of several new so-called environment packages that split the computer screen into sections, or windows, each displaying a different task and able to swap data with another (BW—Nov. 21). Visi On, Fylstra predicts, will return VisiCorp to profitability in 1984. "The fundamentals of our business have never been stronger," he says.

Still, skeptics wonder if Visi On will ever be as successful as Flystra expects. Many of them believe that VisiCorp has made some irrevocable marketing errors with its new product family. First, the company announced Visi On in late 1982, promising to begin shipping products in the summer of 1983. But it was late—shipments did not start until December. This delay discouraged dealers and gave competitors such as Lotus Development and Microsoft Corp. a chance to catch up. "Certainly one year was too long between the announcement and the product," says Thomas B. Towers, president of Knoware Inc., a Cambridge (Mass.) software company, and a former VisiCorp executive.

BIG TROUBLE. Critics also believe that Visi On was overpriced. It was introduced at $495, but initial sales were so weak that the price was slashed to $95 late last month. VisiCorp could be in real trouble unless the program starts selling well at the new price. The losses "don't put the company in jeopardy, but the failure of Visi On could," says Edward M. Esber, a Dallas consultant and former VisiCorp marketing vice-president.

Fylstra counters that December shipments of Visi On were close to a monthly revenue record for the company and that dealer acceptance is now good. He also notes that VisiCorp is the first company to market such a windowing environment for owners of International Business Machines Corp.'s Personal Computer model XT—and is three to six months ahead of potential competitors such as Microsoft, Lotus, and IBM itself.

At the same time, Fylstra strongly denies reports circulating in the industry that VisiCorp is trying very hard to raise additional capital and may even be looking for a buyer. "We have a strong balance sheet with no debt," he claims.

VisiCorp is laying the foundation for expansion, he says, through projects such as its joint venture with Informatics General Corp., a Woodland Hills (Calif.) software developer, to supply software linking IBM PCs to mainframes. "Well before the end of 1984," he vows, "everyone will see the full results of what we've set out to do. They'll conclude that many of our bets were right."

SOFTWARE MOVES TO CENTER STAGE IN THE OFFICE

One of the main reasons software has become so highly visible is that the computer has moved from the back room into the office. Programs of the past, buried inside corporate data processing centers, primarily handled clerical and accounting tasks, such as turning out payrolls and keeping track of accounts receivable.

Today's computer handles a rapidly increasing variety of management tasks—employing information as a competitive marketing weapon, for example. That trend, coupled with the explosion in the

Nowhere is this increasing importance more obvious than in corporate data processing budgets. Balay estimates that Gulf spends about half of its annual data processing budget to write its own software and to buy packages from independent suppliers.

At Aetna, half of the 4,000 people on the data processing staff are programmers. And Alperin says that 4% of the $237 million that Aetna spent on information processing last year went to purchase packaged software. Moreover, individual owners of personal computers

computer users are compromising—buying more ready-to-run software packages than ever before. "There has been a turnaround from five or six years ago," says James T. Manion, sales vice-president at ASK Computer Systems Inc. Few computer users write all their own programs anymore, he says.

ROAD MAPS. But while users sacrifice some uniqueness by buying a software package, that disadvantage is often outweighed by the time and money saved. A package can cut the time it takes to get a system up and running by more than half, figures Mayford L. Roark, executive director of systems at Ford Motor Co. He also estimates that buying a program from an outside vendor can cut development costs by 30% to 75%. "It's almost impossible to think of a function you might want to do on a computer that you can't find several software packages for," says Roark.

Where a custom solution to a problem is required, companies often find they can save time by modifying a standard software package for their own use. That is what Aetna did when it needed software to offer a new type of life insurance called universal life, which features flexible premiums. That allowed the company to match its competitors' universal life offerings quickly.

With such a variety of software available, companies are finding that writing their own programs from scratch makes about as much sense as drawing their own road maps for their salesmen. "In the past there was very little software available, and people almost routinely designed a customized solution," says John M. Hammitt, vice-president for corporate information management at Pillsbury Co. Now, "companies are forced to do a better job of evaluating the make-or-buy decision."

SOPHISTICATED BUYERS. U.S. corporations bought 50% more software packages last year than in the previous year, says International Data Corp., a market researcher. Such purchases, along with software services, now account for more than 8% of the average data processing budget, up from 6% in 1980, IDC says. Similarly, purchases of personal computer software packages soared 74% last year to top $1 billion, according to market researchers at California's Input.

The customers' new attitude toward software is beginning to alter fundamentally the way that computer systems are sold. "We're selling to a much more sophisticated consumer base than in the past," points out Elizabeth M. R. Hall, product manager at Information Science Inc., a Montvale (N. J.) software company. From now on, adds Honeywell's Douglas, "Software looms as a much more important factor in [a user's purchase] decision than hardware."

"OUR PLANT IS OUR DATA PROCESSING SYSTEM," SAYS AETNA LIFE'S ALPERIN

use of personal computers by executives, has given new prominence and importance to software in U.S. corporations. "The programs that we install to do our company's business are analogous to the tools an auto maker puts in place to manufacture auto parts," says Jeffry A. Alperin, an assistant vice-president in the Information Systems Support Dept. at Aetna Life & Casualty Co. "Our plant is our data processing system."

GETTING AN EDGE. Since the same computer hardware is available to everyone, it is the software that often gives a company a competitive edge. At oil companies, "software is now helping drive the search for oil and gas," says Michael C. Balay, general manager of information technology at Gulf Oil Corp. "You can have the same [seismic] information, but a unique software package may help you better interpret the data."

are no different from large corporations: Over the life of a computer, its owner will spend $2 on software for every $1 spent on hardware, according to industry estimates.

But users are finding it increasingly difficult to produce their own programs. Writing software is still a time-consuming process, and users find that while they want to employ their computers to handle more applications, they do not have enough programmers, time, or money to write all of the necessary software in-house. In fact, at many companies users must now wait as long as 18 months for new programs to be written. "The end users are demanding faster development of solutions," declares Richard R. Douglas, group vice-president for the U.S. Marketing & Services Group of Honeywell Inc.

To come up with this software faster,

THE DIFFICULT PATH TO THE EASY-TO-USE COMPUTER

AT AN IBM "USABILITY LAB," A VOLUNTEER TRIES OUT SOFTWARE AS RESEARCHERS LOOK ON FROM BEHIND ONE-WAY MIRRORS

Computing used to be the solitary domain of a priesthood of programmers. The arcane languages that they employed to command their giant mainframe systems were shrouded in such complexity that few laymen could understand, much less control, these behemoths. But the inexpensive yet powerful personal computer is changing all that.

Millions of nontechnical users are now running computers. These new operators, however, refuse even to read an instruction manual, let alone memorize the cryptic commands of the priesthood. Their aversion, coupled with the dramatic slide in the cost of computer power, has created a revolution in the way software is written. Today, making a program simple to control and easy to use is just as important as what the program actually does. Says Jeanne M. Baccash, a software engineer at American Telephone & Telegraph Co.'s Bell Laboratories: "There's a whole new thrust to reach a market that doesn't know or care what it means to 'boot a system' [start a computer]."

These efforts to make software simpler are crucial if the information processing industry is to continue its fast growth. "Rapidly advancing technology has left consumers, trainers, and computer salesmen behind," says Terry L. Opdendyk, president of VisiCorp. "How to spread the word of how to use the products is the key limiting factor [to the industry's growth]."

To make computers easier for novices to use, the industry is concentrating on development work in three key areas:

□ **Man-machine communications.** To reduce the number of commands that a user must memorize and type into a computer to get it to work, the latest software enables users to communicate with the machine in new ways. Some of these techniques are relatively simple, such as establishing menus to show users what commands are available to choose from. The most elaborate methods, used on such machines as Apple Computer Inc.'s new Macintosh, replace commands with an array of tiny icons or pictures—for example, a file folder to indicate filing. To tell the computer what to do, users point to the appropriate picture on the screen by moving a pointing device called a mouse over a desktop.

□ **Data exchange.** Early programs were built to accomplish tasks, such as calculating financial forecasts, with only the data located within the user's own computer. But users have grown more sophisticated and now want to get data stored in other machines—say, the corporation's central mainframe system. This ability is starting to show up in programs such as Informatics General Corp.'s Answer/DB, which extracts selected data from a mainframe computer and sends it to personal computers in a spreadsheet format for immediate use.

□ **Artificial intelligence.** This embryonic method of programming, which enables software to mimic human thought more closely, might one day be the easiest approach to use. It is starting to show up in programs such as Artificial Intelligence Corp.'s Intellect and Microrim Corp.'s CLIO, which let a user ask a computer for data with English sentences rather than esoteric commands.

Most programmers are ill-equipped to figure out how office workers and other nontechnical users best handle computers. So companies are bringing in professionals from disciplines as far afield as education and psychology to help in the design of man-to-machine communications. AT&T, for example, had a staff of psychologists survey about 400 computer users to help it decide how to add

12

BILLY GRIMES

commands to its Unix operating system.

Designing easier-to-use software also requires new development techniques. For instance, International Business Machines Corp. now tests its new software in "usability labs." In these labs, volunteers try to use IBM software while researchers with video cameras watch from behind one-way mirrors. "In the long haul, those that have easy-to-understand software will be the successful companies," says John E. Steuri, general manager of IBM's Information Services Business Unit.

A lot of discussion is going on in research circles over how best to use menus, pictograms, and other techniques to help both computer novices and experts. The type of coaching that a neophyte computer user requires becomes annoying once the user has learned to use the software. So designers want "to make sure the user is not presented with extraneous information when he has to decide what to do next," says Brian K. Reid, a Stanford University electrical engineering professor. MicroPro International Corp., for one, is trying to solve this problem by using a time-delay activator. If a user types in a command less than two seconds after being asked for it, the program assumes the user is proficient and skips over the menu listing of options. Users who take longer are given the benefit of directions from a menu.

DIVIDED SCREEN. Researchers are also struggling with the problem of how to standardize commands. Each computer program now uses different commands to accomplish the same function. An early attempt to solve this problem is the "environment" or "windowing" software packages for personal computers that are now coming to market. These packages—products such as Microsoft Corp.'s Windows and VisiCorp's Visi On—divide the computer screen into segments, each of which shows a different task (BW—Nov. 21). Common functions are performed the same way in each window.

The large amount of this kind of innovative software now being developed to make personal computers easier to use is also forcing the mainframe software companies to follow suit. "Mainframe vendors have been forced to make software easier, because users have been spoiled by micros," says David Ferris, an industry consultant.

For example, Information Builders Inc. has developed a version of its Focus data base management software that can run on an IBM Personal Computer. But the PC version, called PC-Focus, "has more features than the mainframe product because after using a personal computer customers have come to expect

more," says Gerald D. Cohen, president of the New York company. One of the PC-Focus features is called TableTalk. Each time a user moves from one step to another in the course of retrieving information from a data base, the computer automatically presents him with a menu of the appropriate choices.

'PUSHED ASIDE.' Another software challenge is to find simpler ways to exchange data between programs. In most cases, swapping data between a large mainframe and a personal computer is difficult because the two units use different formats for storing their data and different commands for retrieving them. The problem is similar to that of a person who is trying to communicate with 10 people, each of whom speaks a different language, explains Robert J. Spinrad, director of systems technology at Xerox Corp. "I could either learn all nine other languages," he says, "or we could all learn a common one—say, Latin."

But software vendors are not waiting until everyone in the industry agrees on what common language all computers should learn. In the past year a host of vendors, including Cullinet Software, Informatics General, and Cincom Systems, have announced products that link personal computers to large mainframes. Such capabilities will be a requisite for any software in the marketplace, says President Frank H. Dodge of McCor-

mack & Dodge Corp. "If mainframe software doesn't allow that link," he adds, "it's going to be pushed aside pretty rapidly."

Some experts think the ultimate mechanism for exchanging data is the use of sophisticated file-management software, often called data base management systems. These large programs index information and then store it in such a way that it can be retrieved using a variety of names—much the way a library card catalog lists the same book by author, subject, and title. By providing this uniform filing structure, a data base system simplifies the exchange of data.

What may soon make computers even easier to use is artificial intelligence software. Some companies are already working on AI programs that will eventually be able to remember an individual's habits in using the computer. The first AI applications from Microsoft—expected within the next year—will be likely to use these rudimentary pattern-recognition techniques in tutorial programs that teach novices how to operate software. These programs will adjust the level of tutorial difficulty by determining the proficiency of the student running the program. Says Microsoft Chairman William H. Gates: "Just as humans take actions based on past experience without having to be told again and again, so will software."

FINALLY, A FLOOD OF VENTURE CAPITAL

DUN & BRADSTREET'S WEISSMAN SAYS SOME COMPANIES EXIST ONLY TO LURE FUNDING

The software industry is finally getting its share of investment money. Some 90 software companies raised more than $180 million last year, according to *Venture Capital Journal*. As recently as 1980, only 18 software companies were able to attract venture capital. And about 20 software companies went public last year, double that of 1982. "Software is now an established part of the investment spectrum," says Alfred R. Berkeley, managing director of Alex. Brown & Sons Inc., a Baltimore investment banking firm.

Investors are turning to the software business in increasing numbers, partly because computer hardware no longer seems such a sure bet. Well-publicized failures such as Osborne Computer Corp. have made investors wary. "There were so many problems last year on the hardware side of the business that venture capitalists have become much more excited about software," says Thomas J.

Gregory, president of Ovation Technologies Inc., a software startup that just raised $5 million.

Conventional wisdom says software companies should be better able to weather an industry shakeout because they do not have the large inventories or fixed assets that hardware companies have. As a result, "you never go out with a bang because you can always scale back and make money," contends Fred Gibbons, president of Software Publishing Corp. "Hardware companies fail hard; software companies fail soft."

Venture capitalists are warming to software because they find it easier today than five years ago to grasp just what these products do. "Venture capitalists have always had a lot of trouble understanding software," asserts Jacqueline C. Morby, a general partner at TA Associates, who has overseen many of the Boston venture firm's more than 15 software investments. "It took them a long time to realize how big the market is."

For now, venture funds are flowing freely. "In essence, we can select the kinds of investors we want," says John R. Rowley, president of Digital Research Inc., which is closing a $20 million round of financing. At the same time, the stock market has responded positively to software producers. According to Alex. Brown, software stocks have performed 4.6 times as well as Standard & Poor's composite index of 500 stocks since the company began tracking them in 1979.

UNREALISTIC PRICES. The question remains: How long will the investors' love affair with software last? Some venture capitalists claim that the best opportunities have already passed. Morby says TA Associates is putting on the brakes. "We've not stopped looking at them, but we're certainly going to be very careful," she says.

Such a slowdown may seem overdue to some critics. So much money is available, they say, that even undistinguished startups find it easy to secure financing. "Some of these companies are there only to fulfill the need for venture capitalists to participate in the marketplace," complains Robert E. Weissman, executive vice-president of Dun & Bradstreet Corp. The easy availability of financing is elevating the prices of the good companies to unrealistic levels.

But no matter what software stocks do over the next few months, the capital markets should remain available to good companies for some time. Says Berkeley of Alex. Brown: "The fourth or fifth company in a niche market might not be able to get funding—but there will be even more money available for the successful companies who get in first."

JAPAN'S PUSH TO WRITE 'WORLD-CLASS' SOFTWARE

Japanese computer makers, virtually unknown a decade ago, are now household names—Hitachi, Fujitsu, NEC, Toshiba, and Mitsubishi. As the second-largest group of computer companies in the world—after the U. S.—they exported $2.7 billion worth of computers last year. But in their single-minded determination to build and export hardware that is faster and less expensive, the Japanese have given short shrift to software development. "Hardware manufacturers have been lazy about developing software," acknowledges Hisao Ishihara, managing director of the Japan Software Industry Assn. But now, he

> 'The Japanese are as dedicated to computers as they were to autos and shipbuilding'

points out, "that is suddenly changing."

Faced with the twin problems of rapidly falling hardware prices and the growing percentage of computer budgets being spent on software, Japanese hardware makers are scrambling to shift their resources into software development. Three years ago, for example, Hitachi Ltd.'s Computer Div. spent just 10% of its research and development budget on software. This year, even though software will account for about 10% of its computer revenues, Hitachi will spend 30% of its R&D money on software. "These days, more and more of the value added in information processing comes from the software," says Toshimitsu Kaihatsu, head of Toshiba Corp.'s Software Management Dept.

SETTLING UP. The Japanese are also keenly aware that to continue to be competitive internationally in computers they must now start developing world-class software. "We have to sell more overseas if we want to recover our software development costs," comments Shoichi Ninomiya, general manager of Fujitsu Ltd.'s Information Processing Group. His company now spends close to $100 million a year—more than one-third of its R&D budget—to develop software for

its mainframe computers. But almost all of that software is now sold to Japanese customers.

Until now, software has been the biggest handicap the Japanese have had in selling their equipment abroad—especially in the office and personal computer markets. This point was driven home in 1982 when International Business Machines Corp. sued Hitachi, one of the largest Japanese exporters of computers, charging the company with copying IBM software and reselling it with Hitachi's machines. Hitachi agreed in an out-of-court settlement to pay IBM between $2 million and $4 million a month in software license fees and agreed to let the U. S. computer giant inspect all new Hitachi products before they go on the market to ensure that they do not infringe any IBM copyrights. To avoid a similar lawsuit, Fujitsu has also agreed to pay IBM many millions of dollars and promised not to copy the U. S. company's software, although it would not disclose the details of its agreement.

BRIDGING THE GAP. Because of language and cultural differences, software written in Japan is obviously difficult to export. Not only must instruction manuals be translated, but often the programs have to be completely rewritten. Japanese accounting rules, for example, are different from those in the U. S., so accounting software written in Japan is useless in the U. S. This shortage of programs has severely limited the export potential of Japanese home and personal computers.

Japan's software industry is also held back by the preference of Japanese buyers for custom software rather than the standard software products that U. S. customers are increasingly buying (page 92). As a result, an independent Japanese software industry has been slow to develop. And the computer manufacturers' efforts to develop all the software themselves have been crimped by the large sums they must invest to improve methods of getting information into the computer and processing it, using Japanese *kanji* characters.

But it would be dangerous to write off the Japanese as competitors in world-class software. "The Japanese are as dedicated to computers as they were to autos and shipbuilding," says John P. Imlay Jr., chairman of Management Science America Inc. "If U. S. companies do

TOSHIBA'S KAIHATSU: "WE HAVE TO HAVE PRODUCTIVITY DOUBLE THAT OF THE U. S."

not innovate and supply quality products and customer support, the Japanese could make inroads."

Already, Japan has a big chunk of the U. S. market for the simplest type of software, that written for video games. Cultural differences are not a barrier to the export of such hit games as Pac-Man. The fast-growing software markets for engineering and scientific applications—which manipulate schematic drawings and numbers rather than words—are other areas where Japanese software could be sold overseas with little modification.

BANKS AND AIRLINES. The Japanese have also demonstrated their technical ability by creating powerful supercomputer software and sophisticated banking and airline reservation systems. "People are misreading the capability of the Japanese when they say Japanese can't build good software," maintains Joseph C. Berston, president of Comstute Inc., a software consulting firm based in Japan.

Indeed, Japanese companies may actually have some advantages over their U. S. rivals. Because of the legendary

thoroughness of Japanese workers, "the finished product here is better, more reliable, and easier to maintain," says consultant Berston. Labor costs are also lower for Japanese software makers. Well-educated, highly disciplined Japanese programmers are paid an average of about $10,000 a year. Their U. S. counterparts can expect a starting salary twice that—from $19,000 to $25,000, according to a survey by Robert Half International Inc., a personnel agency.

In addition to that salary differential, the Japanese claim their programmers are 10% to 15% more productive than their U. S. counterparts because of Japanese investments in program-development aids. To widen that margin, they are now building software factories that give their programmers access to even more sophisticated tools. Toshiba recently completed a factory that employs 3,000 software engineers to develop industrial software. Now the company is building a second software factory that will employ 2,000 more programmers. "To overcome Japan's language problem and compete with the U. S.," says Toshi-

ba's Kaihatsu, "we have to have productivity double that of the U. S."

NEC Corp., which already spends a significant portion of its annual $400 million software budget on productivity tools, says it will use its productivity and quality advantages to crack the U. S. market. It has hired U. S. software engineers to analyze the needs of U. S. computer users. The resulting lists of requirements are then fed into computers at NEC's Japanese software factories, where programmers write the software. In this fashion, NEC has already started developing commonly used business applications, says Yukio Mizuno, an NEC vice-president.

GOVERNMENT HELP. Perhaps the best illustration of the importance the Japanese now attach to software is the move by the Ministry of International Trade & Industry (MITI) to back the industry. MITI has set up several research laboratories to work on software, including a lab that is developing the so-called fifth-generation computer and software. That lab is budgeted to receive $23 million in MITI support this year. The ministry is also giving low-interest loans and tax breaks to software developers.

MITI hopes to boost its fledgling software industry further with a proposed revision in the copyright law. The ministry is pushing to allow Japanese companies to save money and programming time by making it legal for them to copy portions of existing software products without the permission of the original developers. Industry observers say the law, if passed, would help the Japanese leapfrog U. S. software companies by enabling them to copy popular U. S. programs and incorporate them into Japanese software products.

But even with MITI's help, it will be a long time before Japan's software industry catches up with its U. S. competitors—if it ever does. In 1982, the latest year for which figures are available, software sales in Japan were only $1.4 billion—just one-quarter of the total U. S. software sales that year. Although these sales are growing by 25% a year, Japan's software companies complain that their domestic clients are still far more willing to spend money on new hardware than to invest in software. But while their progress may be slow, Japanese computer companies are confident they will be a strong future force in the booming worldwide software business. "We don't want to copy IBM [software]," says Ishihara of the Software Industry Assn. "We want to beat IBM." ◾

TOSHIO SAKAI

COVER STORY

The Colossus That Works

Big Blue uses salesmanship and innovation to bestride the computer world

IBM. Three of the most famous letters in American business. For years the International Business Machines Corp. towered over the office-equipment industry. Then in the 1970s, besieged by Government antitrust charges and challenged by ambitious new rivals, the giant seemed to be staggering, and those three famous letters lost a bit of their luster. Was IBM's dominance in jeopardy?

Not a chance. Under the direction of John Opel, 58, who became chief executive officer in January 1981, the firm has been acting like its brashest competitors—entering new markets, chasing the latest technology, trimming organizational fat and selling more aggressively than ever. In 1982, IBM had profits of $4.4 billion on sales of $34.4 billion, making it the most profitable U.S. industrial company. Says Stephen McClellan, author of an upcoming book on the computer industry: "In the 1970s, IBM was a battleship in mothballs. Today it is a fleet of killer submarines."

Nowhere was the company's lean new stance more evident than in the way it plunged into the personal-computer market in August 1981. Tackling the mass market for computers for the first time, the company broke many of the traditions that had made it so successful in the past. Yet its new machine, the Personal Computer, generally known simply as the PC, has done nothing less than transform the industry. IBM has already captured 21% of the $7.5 billion U.S. market for personal computers, a staggering feat in so short a time, and is virtually tied with pacesetter Apple Computer, which had a four-year head start.

Big Blue, as IBM is nicknamed for the corporate color it puts on many products, is a mighty competitor in a range of products from electric typewriters that sell for $800 to data-processing systems that can

HARTMANN—MAGNUM

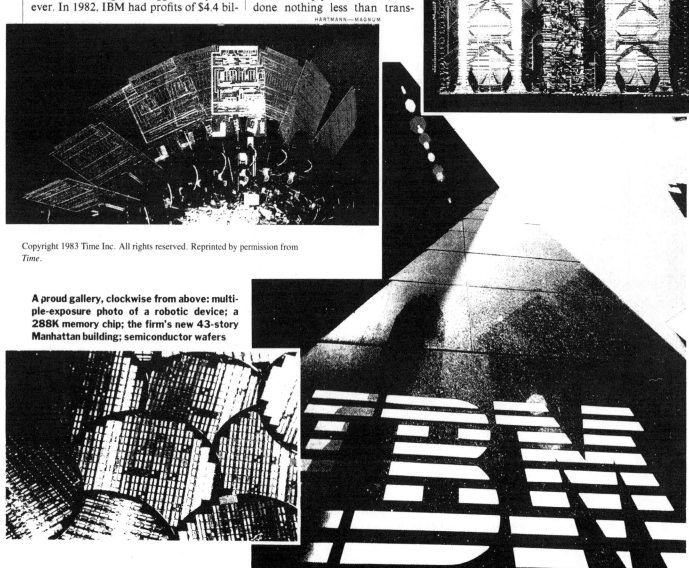

A proud gallery, clockwise from above: multiple-exposure photo of a robotic device; a 288K memory chip; the firm's new 43-story Manhattan building; semiconductor wafers

cost more than $100 million. It commands some 40% of the worldwide market for computing equipment and produces some two-thirds of all mainframe computers, which are big and medium-size business machines. So great is IBM's pre-eminence that rivals often seem to be running in a different race. Digital Equipment, the No. 2 computermaker, has less than one-fifth of IBM's sales. Says John Imlay Jr., chairman of MSA, an Atlanta-based software company: "IBM is simply the best-run corporation in American history."

At a time when American business sometimes seems to be slipping, IBM's triumphs have served as a reminder that U.S. industrial prowess and know-how can still be formidable. Struggling U.S. steel and automakers have been severely hurt by Japanese and European imports, but Big Blue's competitiveness is unquestioned. The company is the leading computer firm in virtually every one of the some 130 countries where it does business. "IBM is like your papa," says a Swiss computer-marketing specialist, "because it's so big and it's always there." Even in

HARTMANN—MAGNUM

Chairman John Opel at his stand-up desk; an instructor during a management training class; staff members eating lunch outside the cafeteria at the Armonk headquarters

HANK MORGAN

Japan, which has six major domestic computermakers and restricts access to its markets, IBM is easily the dominant producer of large computers and is fighting Fujitsu for the overall title. Last year IBM sold $1.9 billion worth of equipment in Japan to Fujitsu's $2.1 billion.

For all of its success, IBM has been rethinking some of the ways it does business. In a dramatic departure from its traditional practices, IBM built the PC largely from parts bought from outside suppliers and is selling it through retail

outlets like Sears and ComputerLand, as well as its own sales network. The company has begun offering discount prices and introducing new products at an accelerated rate. Last December IBM spent $250 million to acquire 12% of Intel, a leading computer-chip maker based in Santa Clara, Calif. In June IBM paid $228 million for a 15% stake in Rolm, also of Santa Clara, a major producer of telecommunications equipment. IBM plans to use Rolm to help create the so-called electronic office. Says Ulric Weil, a top computer analyst for Morgan Stanley & Co.: "We're watching a total transformation of the corporation."

In June IBM Chairman Opel announced that 1983 results were outstripping last year's. That helped push up the price of IBM stock, a leader in the eleven-month-old Wall Street bull rally. After years of hardly moving, IBM shares have nearly doubled in price since the rally started, climbing from 62¼ last August to close last week at 121.

Traditionally, IBM has been so deep in talent that its alumni have gone on to staff laboratories and executive suites throughout the computer industry. "Almost everybody in the business seems to be a former IBMer," observes William Easterbrook, an ex-IBM manager in Copenhagen who now watches the computer industry for Kidder, Peabody, a Wall Street securities firm. Illustrious former employees include Gene Amdahl,

founder of Amdahl Corp. (1982 sales: $462 million), which makes large computers; Joe M. Henson, president of Prime Computer (1982 sales: $436 million), a major producer of minicomputers; and David Martin, president of National Advanced Systems, the computer unit of National Semiconductor. Former employees usually speak highly of Big Blue. Says Flavil Van Dyke, president of Genigraphics, a computer-graphics firm: "I still look back fondly at IBM and try to run my company by IBM standards."

Customers of IBM often speak with that same kind of devotion. Some have been known to refuse to see salesmen from rival firms. Says James Marston, vice president for data processing with American Airlines: "You can take any specific piece of hardware or software and perhaps do better than IBM, but across the board IBM offers an unbeatable system." IBM buyers range from Government agencies like the National

HARTMANN—MAGNUM

Aeronautics and Space Administration, which directs space-shuttle missions with Big Blue equipment, to firms as diverse as Bank of America and Coca-Cola.

Longtime industry observers view the loyalty of some customers as a natural outgrowth of the attitudes that IBM drills into its workers from the day they arrive. "IBM creates an environment that is unique because of its strong set of beliefs and principles," says Martin. "It is almost overwhelming how it affects employees and rubs off on customers."

IBM's strong corporate culture is the lengthened shadow of Thomas Watson Sr., a charismatic executive who joined the Computing-Tabulating-Recording Corp. in 1914, renamed it International Business Machines in 1924, and

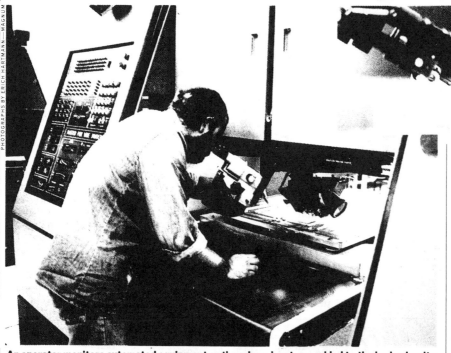

PHOTOGRAPHS BY ERICH HARTMANN—MAGNUM

An operator monitors automated equipment as tiny wires, inset, are added to the logic circuits

ran it until a month before his death in 1956. Watson was a visionary who believed above all in his company.

Under Watson, IBM had rules for practically everything. Employees were told what to wear (dark business suits, white shirts and striped ties) and what to drink (no alcohol, even when off the job), and were urged in signs posted everywhere to THINK. Aspiring executives usually started out in sales and marketing and were transferred so frequently that they took to joking that IBM stood for "I've Been Moved." Observes Gideon Gartner, chairman of the Gartner Group, a computer-research firm: "If you understand the Marines, you can understand IBM."

Many of the Watson-instilled codes remain in effect today, though in a softened form. All IBMers are subject to a 32-page code of business ethics. Sample warning from the blue-covered rulebook: "If IBM is about to build a new facility, you must not invest in land or business near the new site."

IBM salesmen can now drink at lunch, but if they do they are warned not to make further business calls that day. Male IBMers, who make up 80% of the 8,500-member U.S. sales force, must wear suits and ties when meeting prospective customers, although their shirts no longer must be white. Still, a neat and conservative appearance remains the IBM style. "I don't think I've ever seen an IBMer in a pink shirt or an outlandish tie," says Joseph Levy, a vice president for International Data, a Massachusetts-based computer market-research firm. The THINK signs have largely vanished, but the old admonition remains the title of the company's employee magazine.

IBM has combined Watson's stern

codes with a deep and genuine concern for the welfare of employees, who number 215,000 in the U.S. with an additional 150,000 abroad. The company has often fired workers, but it has never laid anyone off to cut costs; instead it retrains and reassigns them. The company's salaries and perks are widely regarded as among the most attractive in the industry. New employees are expected to spend their working lives with the firm, and regularly go through intensive training programs to upgrade their skills. "We hire with a career in mind," says Edward Krieg, director of management development. Although some overseas IBM plants are

Technicians track silicon-wafer production

Investments in the '70s led to current growth.

unionized, the firm has never had a union vote in any U.S. facility.

The generous fringe benefits extend to recreation. The company provides memberships for less than $5 a year in IBM country clubs in Poughkeepsie and Endicott, N.Y. There, employees can play golf, swim and participate in numerous other sports.

Watson was especially adept at motivating workers and inspiring loyalty. He personally commissioned a company songbook and led employee gatherings in numbers like *Ever Onward*.* The song was belted out with gusto during get-togethers of the IBM 100% Club, made up of members who have met 100% of their sales goals for the previous year.

Watson was succeeded by his son Thomas Watson Jr., who served as chief executive officer from 1956 to 1971. A powerful executive in his own right, the younger Watson had helped persuade his father to steer IBM into the computer age. After retirement, Thomas Watson Jr. was U.S. Ambassador to the Soviet Union under President Carter.

More than anything else, it was IBM's awesome sales skills that enabled the company to capture the computer market. Although it now seems hard to believe, IBM did not introduce the first commercial computer. Remington Rand did that in 1951 with a computer called Univac, which became the name of the firm's computer division. But Big Blue knew far more about winning customers than did Univac. IBM, whose major products at the time included calculators and tabulators, recognized that potential buyers might be frightened by the cost and complexity of computers. When the company entered the market in 1952, it set a high priority on dispelling customer fears. Buyers were promised that IBM service engineers would keep a close watch over the machines and quickly fix any glitches. The salesmen were so knowledgeable and thoroughly trained that their very presence inspired confidence. Univac representatives, by contrast, were seen to dwell on technical details that customers could barely follow.

The race was over by 1956. IBM had won a staggering 85% of the U.S. computer market, even though its machines were

*Sample lyric: "Our products are known/ In every zone/ Our reputation sparkles like a gem/ We've fought our way through/ And new fields we're sure to conquer too/ For the ever-onward IBM."

considered to be technically inferior to Univac's. Years later a Univac executive would lament, "It doesn't do much good to build a better mousetrap if the other guy selling mousetraps has five times as many salesmen."

The Univac episode helped give rise to the belief that IBM's real strength is in selling while its technical prowess often lags. Says Kenneth Leavitt, president of CGX Corp., a Massachusetts-based maker of high-performance display terminals: "IBM tends to be a step behind in technology but very good at marketing. There are all sorts of new technologies that IBM doesn't have the expertise to get."

Such claims naturally make IBMers bristle. "This is a shibboleth cultivated by certain Wall Streeters," declares Paul Low, manager of the IBM plant in East Fishkill, N.Y. "Nobody who peeks inside any of our 29 laboratories could fall for that nonsense." Company spokesmen like to point out that IBM spent $3 billion on research, development and engineering last year, an amount that exceeds the total revenues of many of its rivals. The firm has also taken the offensive in a new ad-

detail. "IBM will listen to almost anybody," says Joseph Levy of International Data, which analyzes computer-market trends. "It is one of our best customers." Big Blue subscribes to virtually every major computer market-research service and has a worldwide intelligence-gathering network that includes economists and market analysts.

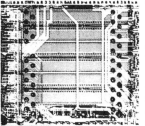
The heart of a new machine

The company takes equal pains in keeping the skills of its personnel up to date. Last year, for example, IBM invested more than $500 million on employee education and training. Most new IBMers spend much of their first six weeks in company-run classes, and managers are required to take at least 40 hours of additional instruction a year. The classwork often focuses on actual business case studies, in the manner of the Harvard Business School.

The IBM management formula worked so well that the company in the 1960s came to be known as Snow White

Recalls former IBM Chairman Frank Cary, Opel's predecessor: "The suit was a tremendous cloud that was over the company for 13 years. It couldn't help influencing us in a whole variety of ways. Ending it lifted a huge burden from management's shoulders." Jeffrey Zuckerman, special assistant to Antitrust Division Chief William Baxter, concurs: "We believe IBM must have been deterred from competing as aggressively as it otherwise would have."

Whatever the reason, IBM's momentum slowed markedly in the 1970s, a period Cary called "a time of planning and consolidation." The company entered the decade with a 60% share of the computer market and emerged with a still impressive but slimmed-down 40%.

Though IBM was growing at a respectable annual rate of 13%, the computer industry was expanding even faster. One challenge came from the Route 128 area around Boston, where Digital Equip-

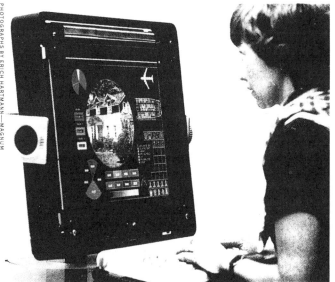

PHOTOGRAPHS BY ERICH HARTMANN—MAGNUM

Wonders of the laboratories: a worker aligns televised chips, left; a mixture of neon and argon gases makes the display screen glow

Despite a reputation for being better salesmen than scientists, the firm's employees have been awarded more than 11,000 patents.

vertising campaign that boasts of the more than 11,000 patents IBM inventors have acquired over the past 25 years.

Actually, IBM is skilled at blending both marketing and technical considerations. That goes a long way toward explaining how so huge a company has kept its edge in an industry where key breakthroughs are often made by blue-jeaned engineers working out of their garages.

What IBM seeks, above all, is products that sell. "They have tried to understand what the customer wants," says Stuart Madnick, a professor of management-information systems at M.I.T.'s Sloan School. "Often the customer didn't need or want the more advanced technology that others have produced. In many companies the technology has grown faster than the market can absorb."

IBM evaluates buyers' needs in fine

while its competitors were derisively dubbed the Seven Dwarfs. The dwarfs (Burroughs, Univac, NCR, Control Data, Honeywell, General Electric and RCA) dwindled to five when GE and RCA quit the computer business in the 1970s, and the others are now collectively referred to by their first initials as the BUNCH.

IBM's very success, however, almost backfired against the company. The Johnson Administration on its final working day in office, Jan. 17, 1969, opened a massive antitrust case, accusing the company of monopolistic and anti-competitive practices. The federal suit dragged on endlessly—at a cost to IBM of several hundred million dollars in legal fees—until the Justice Department abruptly dropped it in January 1982, declaring that the case was "without merit."

ment and other firms launched the minicomputer. Such machines were smaller and cheaper than the large ones IBM offered, but still performed a wide range of data-processing functions. Revenues of Digital Equipment, the leading maker of minis, have climbed from $265 million to about $4 billion over the past ten years.

Another challenge came from California's Silicon Valley, where the microprocessor, or computer-on-a-chip, was developed. The tiny devices packed thousands of circuits onto a postage-stamp-size silicon chip and gave rise to the microcomputer. Apple recognized the potentially vast appeal of personal computing, and its sales jumped from less than $1 million to $582 million between 1977 and 1982.

By the start of the 1980s, however, IBM had begun to move in new directions, and the dismissal of the lawsuit helped to accelerate the process. The most notable example was in the personal-computer field. Although IBM had been monitoring the market for years, it refused to jump in until it began seeing personal computers appear in offices and became convinced that there was enough demand to make their entry pay off. "There's no particular challenge to building a personal computer other than to build one that someone wants," says Cary.

The task of overseeing the creation of the PC fell to a twelve-member group in Boca Raton, Fla., led by Philip Estridge, a division vice president. The team was first assembled in July 1980 and told to develop a competitive and easy-to-use machine within a year. "Twelve-hour days and six- or 6½-day weeks were commonplace," recalls Estridge. The members made some key moves along the way that help account for the PC's enormous popularity. The planners decided, for example, to build the PC around a 16-bit microprocessor rather than an 8-bit one, which was at that time the industry standard. This move permitted the PC to run faster and handle more complex programs. Says Estridge: "We chose to up the power of the machine so that it could be used without too many changes for the next decade or so."

The group broke with tradition by setting up a so-called open-architecture scheme that makes the PC's technical specifications available to other firms. The idea was to permit outside companies and individuals to write software or build peripheral equipment for the PC and thereby expand its appeal.

The project, however, did not always unfold smoothly and without flaws. Early users discovered that the machine misplaced decimals in certain calculations, but the problem was quickly solved. Also, some owners complained that the keyboard had been poorly designed.

But those problems did not impede sales. "Within just a few months," says Morgan Stanley's Ulric Weil, "the IBM PC was *the* standard for the personal-computer market." Orders for the machine, which has a starting price, with standard accessories, of about $3,200, have been pouring in so fast that some buyers have had to wait several months to get one. Last year IBM sold an estimated 200,000 PCs, and this year sales of 800,000 or more are projected. In June, the Travelers Insurance ordered 10,000 PCs, to be delivered over the next two years. New companies with names like Compaq Computer and Eagle Computer have sprung up making machines that are modeled on the PC.

The explosive growth of the IBM entry has set up a confrontation with Apple Computer. Executives of the California-based company, which introduced a fully assembled personal computer in 1977, profess not to be worried. They even greeted the PC the day after it was announced with ads that read "Welcome IBM. Seriously. Welcome to the most exciting and important marketplace since the computer revolution began 35 years ago." Whatever the intent of the message, some IBMers found it condescending.

Apple Chairman Steven Jobs claims that IBM has expanded the personal-computer market and that his company's share of it has gone on growing at the expense of weaker rivals like Tandy, which owns Radio Shack. Says he: "Apple has a higher market share than IBM, and we intend to keep it." Indicative of how serious Apple considered the challenge was its decision to hire Pepsi-Cola President John Sculley, a marketing expert, to serve as Apple's president and chief executive. "This is not a bruising fight for market share between Apple and IBM," says Sculley. "It's a sorting out of who the major participants will be."

Some observers are far less confident about Apple's prospects. Gene Amdahl knows IBM from the perspective of a rival and a former 13-year employee. Says he: "IBM waits until some brash young companies develop a market to the point where it's interesting, and then they take it over. In Apple's case the shooting isn't over yet, but I think it's clear how the war will come out."

Plain Vanilla, but Very Good

When he was growing up in the 1930s in Jefferson City, Mo., then home to 23,000 people, his schoolmates called him Johnny. Slightly large hands and feet gave him a strong backstroke on the high school swimming team, recalls Boeing Chairman T.A. Wilson, a freestyler on the same squad. Johnny's father "Gump" ran a local hardware store. Years later, when the boy began making it big in business, a reporter for the local newspaper went out to see Gump and asked whether he was surprised by his son's success. "No," said Gump, "I always knew Johnny was a good boy."

Good as gold, almost. As chief executive officer of IBM, John Opel earned a handsome $1.3 million last year. He also owns $4 million worth of his company's stock.

Compared with the Thomas Watsons, father and son, Opel appears almost bland. "Plain vanilla," says one member of the IBM board, "but good plain vanilla." Says a middle-level executive: "With Tom Watson, you knew stories about him. With Opel, there are no vibes. You just know, in a business sense, exactly what his goals and objectives are."

In his simple but elegant office at IBM's headquarters in Armonk, N.Y., the only mildly unusual feature is a stand-up desk that Opel uses in addition to a standard one. He receives visitors with a correctness that is so smooth it can be mistaken for real easiness. But Board Member William Coleman, a Secretary of Transportation in the Ford Administration and now a Washington lawyer, says Opel is noted more for his strength than for his charm. Says Coleman: "He's tough. You can tell instantly when you're rubbing him the wrong way or when you've stayed beyond your time."

While IBM's stern dress code has been eased, Opel still follows the old one. His shirts are white oxford cloth and as buttoned down as the man. His ties are impeccable and subdued, his shoes standard-issue corporate cordovans: no buckles, tassels or other frills.

John Opel achieved the top post by molding himself to be just what the company wanted, because that is exactly what he too wanted. Opel sees himself as something of an interchangeable part of the firm. "I'm a product of the culture of IBM, of the way we do things," he says.

Starting with the firm straight out of the University of Chicago School of Business in 1949 as a salesman in Jefferson City, Opel was soon being shifted around with dizzying frequency; he has held 19 different jobs. His career picked up fast in 1959, when he was chosen to be an administrative assistant to Thomas Watson Jr., then president, for one year. Following that, Opel began serving in a wide variety of posts, ranging from manufacturing to press relations.

Opel today gives visitors and colleagues a sense of self-containment, but he admits to having had a wicked temper. Once when he could not get a flat tire off his Chrysler because he was turning a lug the wrong way, he became so enraged that he bashed in the side of the car. "I don't get angry the way I used to," Opel says.

WRIGHT STUDIO

The chairman on the 1940 team

Division Vice President Estridge, leader of the group that developed the Personal Computer

The tradition-breaking product has done nothing less than transform the industry.

In fact, IBM's aggressive new posture poses a threat to virtually the entire computer industry. "IBM is creating a dangerous situation for competitors in the marketplace," says computer-industry observer Gideon Gartner. Among those most at risk are makers of so-called plug-compatible computers that run IBM software but sell for less. Such firms thrived during the 1970s, when IBM was slow in delivering equipment. Now, however, a burst of IBM price cuts and new models could badly hurt them.

That has already happened to Mag-nuson Computer Systems (1982 sales: $18.4 million). The San Jose–based maker of medium-size computers prospered in the late 1970s when IBM failed to ship a rival system on time. But IBM fought back in 1981 by slashing prices and introducing a new model. Then, last October, IBM announced two additional computer models and cut prices again. "There was no question. That was the fatal blow," declares Magnuson President Charles Strauch. The company, which has chopped its work force from more than 640 employees to about 100 over the past

18 months, filed bankruptcy papers in March.

Other firms have also been hit hard. Like Magnuson, Storage Technology enjoyed a big jump in business in 1981 when IBM ran into technical difficulties introducing a new memory device. The Colorado-based company, which makes high-performance memory equipment, gained some 300 customers because of IBM's troubles. However, when Big Blue brought out an improved new line last year, Storage Technology's profits dropped to $64.7 million, from $84.2 million in 1981. Says Jesse Aweida, who co-founded Storage Technology after 13 years with Big Blue: "IBM used to be active in only certain areas of the computer business. Now it wants to be active in the whole business."

One big reason for IBM's clout is the major investments it began making in the late 1970s to upgrade manufacturing facilities. IBM executives point to that drive to cut production costs, launched under Cary, as a foundation of the company's current strength, because it has made the firm extremely cost-competitive. IBM has pumped some $10 billion into capital improvements since 1977. The Boca Raton line that turns out the PC is so highly automated that a personal computer can be assembled in ten minutes of worker time.

The plants use some of IBM's most advanced technology. An engineer in the firm's La Gaude, France, laboratory can

---

But the old intensity, just barely noticeable beneath the perfect manners, can still be useful. "People know that I mean what I say and that I don't suffer fools," he says.

John Opel is a lot more than just a corporate man, but he guards his privacy as closely as his company protects its secrets. He bridles at revealing much about his background or family, plainly believing that such matters are his own business. He fought with the U.S. Army on Okinawa in World War II and was wounded in the foot by a piece of shrapnel. He and his wife Carole have three daughters and two sons. He drives himself to work in a six-year-old car whose make he will not divulge and lives in a house he will not describe beyond noting that it is "big enough to accommodate five children."

Opel spends much of his non-IBM time with his wife. Three mornings a week they are up at 5:30 and drive 20 miles to do aerobic and exercise-machine workouts "at a place where they don't know me." The Opels fish together, go to the opera together and watch birds together. They also work together to protect their privacy. On the rare occasion when a reporter calls him at home, Carole Opel answers politely and promises to bring her husband to the phone. But then she sets down the receiver without ever telling him. Callers get the message.

Some IBM board members were worried about this almost obsessive penchant for privacy when Opel was being consid-

Says he: "I'm a product of the culture of IBM"

ered for chief executive. They were concerned that he would have trouble handling relations with the board and the public and within the company. Says one board member, former Pennsylvania Governor William Scranton: "He is very possibly the brightest chief executive I've ever dealt with. But he did have some difficulty expressing himself." Yet former Du Pont Chairman Irving Shapiro, another board member, says that this has not turned out to be a problem. Says he: "The beautiful thing is that Opel has come out of his shell."

During his years of rising through the corporate ranks, Opel was often frustrated by IBM's centralized management. "No matter what I had in my jurisdiction, I typically felt I was more competent to deal with it than anyone else. And that wasn't conceit, it was just simple laws of nature," says Opel. That experience left him with a desire for decentralized decision making. He now tries to force corporate policymaking down and out, retaining at headquarters only what is necessary for overall planning and control. "You have to have people free to act, or they become dependent," he says. "They don't have to be told; they have to be allowed." In pursuit of that goal, Opel established seven Independent Business Units, which operate much like small companies within IBM. One of the first products created by Opel's brainchildren: that bountiful beauty, the IBM Personal Computer.

—*By John F. Stacks*

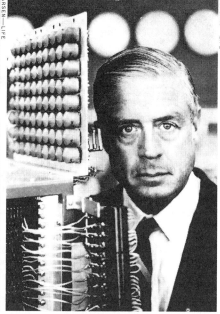

The Watsons, father and son: Thomas Sr. in August 1947 addressing a company convention; Thomas Jr. in 1957 with one of the early machines

Rules, principles and intelligent management have built an overwhelming corporate culture that often begins to affect customers as well.

transmit his computerized design information for a new chip via satellite to the IBM facility in East Fishkill, where the chip is actually manufactured. The chip will be floated through tubing on air from one manufacturing station to another and then tested by robotically controlled equipment.

IBM is also the world's largest producer of logic and 64K RAM memory chips, and installs its entire output in its own machines. The company, moreover, can produce at the same plant far denser 256K RAM chips, which Japanese firms are also developing. IBM could start making the chips ahead of the Japanese, perhaps by early next year.

In line with its new aggressiveness, IBM has been cracking down hard on those who would steal its secrets. It cooperated with the FBI last year in a sting op-

eration that nabbed employees of Hitachi and Mitsubishi Electric, two Japanese competitors, for trying to buy confidential IBM information. IBM then brought a separate civil suit against Hitachi, which pleaded guilty to conspiracy charges last February and was fined $10,000. The criminal case against Mitsubishi is still pending.

IBMers claim to be unruffled by Japanese competition. "I think I'll be physically ill if I hear one more time that the Japanese are coming," says Paul Low, manager of the East Fishkill plant. "That's not to say that they're not formidable rivals, because they are, but we're ahead." All six of the major Japanese makers of large computers together have less than 2% of the U.S. market for business computers.

Many outsiders believe that IBM is more concerned about the Japanese than

it professes. Says Magnuson Computer's Strauch: "I'm sure IBM's basic concern is the Japanese. It is almost certain that what happened to us was a message to the Japanese that if they have any thought of entering the market with a low-to-medium-range mainframe, they had better be prepared to compete at an extremely low cost." Apple's Jobs believes that IBM's investments in Intel and Rolm are at least partially intended to strengthen IBM's ability to compete with Japan.

The struggle between IBM and its Japanese competitors is most intense in Japan, where IBM lost its No. 1 position to Fujitsu in 1979. IBM Japan, the company's wholly owned subsidiary, is fighting back. "They are becoming surprisingly aggressive," says Yuji Ogino, managing director of IDC Japan, a unit of International Data. IBM Japan, which employs 13,000 Japanese workers, has been slashing prices and launching new marketing drives in a bid to win back its overall lead. Admits a spokesman for a rival Japanese firm: "IBM is an enormous competitor."

At the same time that it has been fighting vigorously for market share, IBM has been forming cooperative agreements with the Japanese. In one, IBM and Matsushita Electric Industrial teamed up to produce a personal computer that converts Japanese phonetic symbols into Chinese characters or Kanji. Typewriters have not been widely used in Japan, partly because, with so many different characters, a typical machine must be packed with about 3,000 Kanji. The new machine, which ranges in price from $4,100 to $12,700, has a keyboard of only 45 phonetic symbols plus the Latin alphabet. More than 15,000 of the machines have been ordered, and there is at least a two-month wait for delivery.

If striking similarities exist between

Testing the cables on a bank of early equipment in 1955 at a plant in Poughkeepsie, N.Y.

Salesmen were so knowledgeable and well trained that their presence inspired confidence.

IBM and Japanese companies, the reason is that Big Blue was the model for some Japanese business techniques. For example, IBM developed "quality circles" some 20 years ago. The circles, small teams of workers that get together to discuss ways to improve output and solve production problems, have been widely adopted in Japan and are often cited as a reason for productivity gains there. Both IBM and Japanese executives stress harmonious employee relations, and both place a high priority on becoming the most modern, cost-efficient manufacturer of the products they turn out.

Foreign operations are vital to IBM. Overseas business accounted for 45% of IBM's gross income in 1982 and 37% of the company's profits. IBM hires mainly local employees at its international locations. There are only 125 Americans among some 1,000 managerial and technical employees in the Paris headquarters of IBM's European, Middle Eastern and African operations. Says Hans-Olaf Henkel, a vice president in the Paris office: "Europeans like IBM not because it is American, but because it is IBM. It promotes from the inside, and the majority of senior positions are held by nationals of the country."

IBM executives concede that despite its wide-ranging successes, the company has its weaknesses and has made some major mistakes over the years. Despite increased efforts to recruit women and minorities, there are still few of either in management ranks. Only 3,089 of IBM's more than 29,000 managers are women. IBM policies, moreover, can seem high-handed, especially toward women. In December 1981, a California jury awarded $300,000 to an IBM marketing manager who quit after the company objected to her romantic relationship with a former employee who had joined a rival firm. She resigned when her boss, fearing a conflict of interest, tried to transfer her to another division. IBM is appealing the jury verdict.

Some employees find the firm slow to capitalize on opportunities in spite of steps to decentralize decision making. "IBM has more committees than the U.S. Government," complains one insider. To increase its flexibility, IBM has set up 15 small ventures within the company since 1981. These explore new business opportunities in such fields as robotics, specialized medical equipment and analytical instruments. The new units are independently run, but they can draw on IBM resources. This seems to provide IBM with the benefits of both a large company and a small one. Says Robert Burgelman, an assistant professor of management at Stanford University's Graduate School of Business: "If IBM can integrate these new ventures into its culture, the company is going to be an enormously dangerous competitor in most of the emerging areas of high technology."

IBM stumbled badly when it set out to produce an office copier in the 1970s. Executives first turned down a chance to buy a process that Xerox later used with great success, and then introduced a balky model. Admits Cary: "If you're asking was it a mistake to ship so many copiers before they were really reliable to sell, yes it was a mistake." The company was forced to suspend deliveries until the problems were solved.

IBM, in addition, has not broken into the market for so-called supercomputers, which are used mainly for scientific research. The company launched supercomputer projects in the 1950s and 1960s, but could not produce a design that executives believed would be profitable. IBM has since abandoned the specialized field to Control Data and Cray Research.

Opel is bullish about the future of IBM, and he is very optimistic about the outlook for the whole industry. He notes that while people have limited demands for commodities like shoes and automobiles, they seem to have an insatiable appetite for information. Says he: "I have yet to hear somebody say they could not use more information. Hence the demand for information processing, though perhaps not infinite, is enormous."

What will be coming next out of the IBM laboratories to satisfy that demand? Opel is clearly not ready to sit back and relax despite his company's achievements. Says he: "We've got an enormously successful operation. Therefore you could be complacent; you could play it safe and not change. All the natural forces in the business pressure you in that direction." But one sign that the pace of the past two years will continue will be the arrival of a home computer, which IBM originally code-named "peanut." This will sell for about $700 and could reach stores in late fall. The machine, fully compatible with the PC, will come with a built-in disc drive and cartridge slot for software. "It will offer the best performance on the market for its price," asserts Clive Smith, a computer watcher with the Yankee Group, a Cambridge, Mass., research firm.

IBM is also developing a raft of exotic technologies. These include Josephson Junction and quiteron switching devices that operate in trillionths of a second at temperatures that approach absolute zero (−459.67° F). Says one IBMer: "There's

BIG BLUE'S MARKET SHARE
Percent of units installed

72% — ☐ Mainframe Computers

38% — ☐ Small Business Computers

21% — ☐ Personal Computers

4% — ■ Minicomputers

35% — ☐ Typewriters

Source: International Data Corp

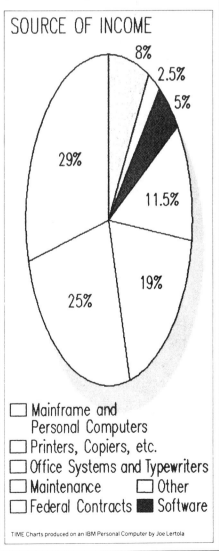

SOURCE OF INCOME

8%
2.5%
5%
29%
11.5%
25%
19%

☐ Mainframe and Personal Computers
☐ Printers, Copiers, etc.
☐ Office Systems and Typewriters
☐ Maintenance   ☐ Other
☐ Federal Contracts   ■ Software

TIME Charts produced on an IBM Personal Computer by Joe Lertola nothing, literally nothing, noteworthy in the field that IBM doesn't have its fingers into."

The biggest future payoff for IBM is likely to come in the field of office automation. The key to the so-called paperless office will be computerized networks that shuttle messages between computer terminals, telephones and other office equipment. All can then be consolidated into a "work station" atop a desk. "The world of the future is centered on powerful work stations," says Lewis Branscomb, IBM's chief scientist.

Last month IBM showed that it was determined to become a leader in developing the automated office by agreeing to acquire 15% of Rolm. That company's advanced PBX system, a type of computerized switchboard, can be used to direct the flow of voice and data traffic between work stations. The investment will enable the two firms to work out ways to link IBM computers with the Rolm PBX.

In fact, IBM has long been deeply involved in telecommunications. In 1975, the company bought a one-third interest in Satellite Business Systems, which transmits voice and computer data. IBM is seeking partners for communications ventures in Europe. In March 1982, it won an $18 million contract to upgrade the British telephone system, and it is installing a computer-driven telephone information service in West Germany.

IBM's moves into telecommunications will put it squarely in competition with American Telephone & Telegraph, now the world's biggest company. An extended battle between the two giants seems inevitable in the area where computers and communications overlap to create the Information Age. Once the separation of A T & T from its regulated telephone units goes into effect next January, the company will be able to use its Bell Laboratories and Western Electric facili-

ties to develop products to compete directly with IBM. A T & T through the new American Bell is expected to introduce computers next year, and it already has the capability of offering a wide range of data-processing services similar to those IBM provides.

In that upcoming clash of the titans and the continuing fight for the world computer market, IBM will be tough to beat. Its resources—human, technological and financial—are enormous. Its ability to combine salesmanship and service with research and innovation is unmatched in the U.S., perhaps anywhere. At a time when the rallying cry "Small is beautiful" can be heard even in business circles and when some critics charge that large corporations are inherently inflexible, IBM has shown how to be a successful colossus. —*By John Greenwald. Reported by Bruce van Voorst/New York, with other bureaus*

Softening a Starchy Image

A mustachioed little clown with an undersize jacket and oversize trousers to symbolize IBM's first computer aimed at the mass market? That hardly fits IBM's stuffy old image, but when the company needed an advertising campaign for its new personal computer 2½ years ago, it turned to one of the 20th century's most enduring and endearing characters: Charlie Chaplin's Tramp. Says Charles Pankenier, director of communications for the PC: "We were dealing with a whole new audience that never thought of IBM as a part of their lives." Industry insiders estimate that the firm has spent $36 million in one of the largest ad campaigns ever mounted for a personal computer.

Manufacturers of personal computers have been using readily recognizable people for some time to make the slightly intimidating machines seem warmer and more empathetic. Apple has Dick Cavett for its commercials, Texas Instruments recruited Bill Cosby, Commodore has William Shatner, and Atari just hired Alan Alda. None of these living celebrities, however, has had the impact of the Tramp. The character has starred in three widely seen television commercials, plus more than 20 print ads. He has won numerous advertising-industry awards.

Chaplin once explained that he created the character in 1915, after an accidental meeting with a hobo in San Francisco. The Tramp's resurrection was only slightly less serendipitous. IBM's advertising agency, the Madison Avenue firm Lord, Geller, Federico, Einstein, was looking for someone, or something, that would attack the problem of computer fright head on. The agency was talking about using the Muppets or Marcel Marceau, the

mime, when, according to Creative Director Thomas Mabley, the idea for the Tramp "sort of walked in and sat down."

Some officials at both the company and the agency were afraid that the floppy character was not in keeping with IBM's starched white-collar image. The question of whether the Tramp represented antitechnology sentiment, as epitomized in the most famous scene from one of Chaplin's best-known movies, *Modern Times*, was also raised. In the scene, Chaplin gets caught in the giant gears of a factory. But both the agency and IBM eventually concluded that the character, in Pankenier's words, "stands fear of technology on its head and would help the PC open up a new technological world for the non-technician."

Chaplin's enduring, endearing Tramp

The company obtained rights from Bubbles, the Chaplin family company that licenses use of the actor's image, to use the Tramp. To cast the part, the agency interviewed some 40 candidates in New York City and 20 on the West Coast. The winner was 5-ft. 6-in. Billy Scudder, 43, who has been doing Tramp impersonations since 1971. Says he: "Nobody tires of the little Tramp. He creates instant sympathy."

The commercials are elaborate Madison Avenue extravaganzas. In one 60-second spot, which symbolizes the problems of inventory control in a small business, the Tramp stands at the intersection of two assembly lines in a bakery. He comes a cropper when the fast-moving line spews cakes onto the floor after he tries to jam a giant-size one into an economy-size box. Taping the sequence required 30 takes—and 150 layer cakes.

The Tramp campaign has been so successful that it has created a new image for IBM. The firm has always been seen as efficient and reliable, but it has also been regarded as somewhat cold and aloof. The Tramp, with his ever present red rose, has given IBM a human face.

Apple's New Crusade

Deborah Wise and Catherine Harris

APPLE'S NEW CRUSADE

A BOLD PLAN TO TAKE ON IBM IN THE OFFICE

They shouted, they screamed, they jumped, they danced. More than a thousand salespeople hooted with delight as Apple Computer Inc. kicked off a spirited sales meeting on a balmy Hawaiian Monday in late October with a none-too-subtle jab at giant rival International Business Machines Corp., alias Big Blue.

As an Apple-ized version of *Ghostbusters*, last summer's top-40 hit song, pulsated in the background, the image of a perplexed businessman was projected on a giant screen above the milling throng. He was trying, without success, to master his IBM Personal Computer. As his frustration mounted, green slime started oozing out of the machine. "Who ya gonna call?" shouted the video. The audience erupted: "Bluebusters!"

RELIGIOUS FERVOR. Apple's two ranking Bluebusters, Chairman Steven P. Jobs and President John Sculley, are launching an all-out offensive in the office market. Their goal: to slow the IBM Personal Computer juggernaut. Apple, the premier maker of personal computers for homes and schools, is going great guns to turn its sleek, 10-month-old Macintosh into a true office machine. It hopes to sell the computer to managers who do not need heavy-duty, financial analysis tools by convincing them that it is the only viable alternative to the harder-to-use IBM PC, now the industry standard.

IBM's 100-or-more competitors are having to face the fact that if they are to succeed, their personal computers will have to work with programs written for the IBM PC. Mac, however, does not run IBM software. So, to compete, Apple will have to promote Mac's better graphics capabilities and its greater ease of use.

The near-religious fervor that Jobs and Sculley bring to their quest to crack the office market is not surprising. Businesses will buy fully two-thirds of the $14.5 billion worth of personal computers expected to be sold this year. If Apple cannot capture a healthy share of these sales over the next few years, its phenomenal growth rate will slow, and

the company will lose the star quality that made it a Silicon Valley legend. "We must remain a leader or slip quietly into the darkness of mediocrity," intoned the 45-year-old Sculley to the masses gathered in Hawaii.

MADCAP WORKAHOLICS. After 18 months at Apple, Sculley's speech rings with the same evangelical zeal of 29-year-old Jobs, who co-founded Apple. At first, industry experts were skeptical that Sculley would even survive Apple's peculiar organization and culture. The youthful-looking Sculley was a pin-striped East Coast marketer who had climbed quickly through the ranks of PepsiCo Inc. to become president of its domestic operations and a primary contender for the top spot (page 148). The Cupertino (Calif.) company's unorthodox culture—a mixture of entrepreneurial disdain for traditional authority and madcap "workaholism"—hardly seemed like his style. In addition, Apple's brash young chairman had a history of temperamental outbursts. His bluntness once provoked a colleague to give him a *Miss Manners* book to teach him discretion. "I am not a discreet person," Jobs is said to have replied.

Sculley, who is also chief executive officer, has silenced the doubters. He and Jobs have a healthy respect for one another, and their skillful teamwork is propelling Apple forward on its Bluebuster course. If this dynamic duo succeeds in carving out an office franchise, Jobs is sure that fast-growing Apple has "the chance to become the second-largest computer company [in the entire industry] by the 1990s." That move would put the eight-year-old company—whose sales have just reached $1.5 billion for the year ended Sept. 28—ahead of such giants as Digital Equipment Corp., now No. 2, and Burroughs Corp.

But Apple is no shoo-in to be the new No. 2. Although it has successfully wooed the education market and has won more than a million households with its seven-year-old pioneer, the Apple II, Apple has failed miserably in its at-

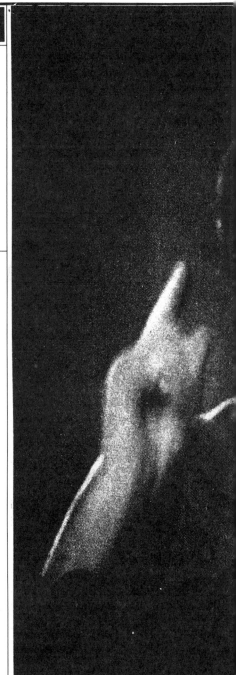

PRESIDENT SCULLEY ADDRESSES A SPIRITED S

tempts to attract business people with two more powerful personal computers, the Apple III and Lisa. IBM, meanwhile, jumped into the market late and rode roughshod over the competition. Despite a successful 1984, Apple has not been able to stop the erosion of its market share. This year, IBM expanded its slice of the market (for personal computers retailing for $1,000 to $10,000) from 30% in 1983, to 35%, while Apple's share shrank from 21% to 19%.

The Macintosh, which is so easy to handle that many people do not even bother to read the instruction manual, is currently a corporate outcast because it is not IBM-compatible. Computer makers far larger and more established than Apple—Texas Instruments, Hewlett-Pack-

G IN HAWAII: "WE MUST REMAIN A LEADER OR SLIP QUIETLY INTO THE DARKNESS OF MEDIOCRITY"

ard, and Digital Equipment, to name just three—have all tried hard, yet failed to buck the IBM-compatible trend. But Sculley is undeterred. "We want to be a clear alternative to IBM. We are not content to exist on the edge of a corporate giant," he declares.

FOLK HEROES. Apple's image as an irreverent, hip young company could also scare off plenty of potential corporate customers. Businessmen may marvel at the oft-told stories of how two young college dropouts (Jobs and Stephen G. Wozniak) turned the basic microchip into a consumer product and played a major role in starting the personal computer revolution. But buying computers from such entrepreneurial folk heroes may be another story. BUSINESS WEEK informal-

ly polled a group of managers at medium-to-large businesses recently to gauge their attitudes toward an Apple vs. IBM faceoff, and almost by rote, most purchasing agents and data processing professionals repeated the clichéd axiom: "No one ever got fired for buying IBM."

Nonetheless, considerable support has built up among enthusiastic users, software writers, and computer dealers for just the kind of IBM alternative offered by Apple. "Apple will never get in the front door. It will have to infiltrate," maintains Esther Dyson, publisher of a respected industry newsletter.

So far, Apple has had little success in reaching the middle managers it so desperately seeks. Early Mac buyers have tended to be innovators, experimenters,

software developers, and gadget freaks intrigued by the computer's whiz-bang features, such as an easy-to-use "mouse" pointer and its ability to generate and display high-quality graphics. Apple's new 65-person national accounts team, set up to woo large corporate customers, has so far produced only one major win: Peat, Marwick, Mitchell & Co. The Big Eight accounting firm has already installed more than 4,500 Macs. Concedes Apple Executive Vice-President William V. Campbell: "A lot of [corporate] accounts have not accepted that we have a serious office product yet."

Apple is using guerrilla tactics to break down the corporate world's brick wall of resistance. To circumvent the traditional data processing department and get its machine to the huge pool of middle managers, Jobs and Sculley have revved up a $100 million advertising program. They have also launched a new, imaginative "Test Drive A Mac" promotion: Any potential customer with a credit card can go to a computer store and check out a Macintosh equipped with business software for 24 hours.

Jobs's and Sculley's strategy to make it on IBM turf will truly test the company's mettle. As part of the effort, it will:
□ **Introduce the Macintosh Office.** In January, Apple will announce a lineup of of-

fice products that will turn the Macintosh into a complete office system. Deliveries will start later in the year. The package will include a low-cost, local-area communications network that will link together all Macintosh units in an office, a high-speed laser printer that will produce correspondence-quality text, and a memory device that will permit Macintoshes in an office network to share data stored in a common file.

To fit into the IBM world, Apple is promising to deliver a communications product that will allow Macintoshes in a

network to exchange data with IBM computers. Apple will also sell a special device that can be plugged into an IBM PC so that it can become part of an Apple network. Corporate buyers say that such features could give Apple a real boost in the office market. "When [Apple] has the ability to communicate with the IBM world, they become viable," says Paul E. Anders Jr., manager of information systems planning for Chrysler Corp.
□ **Speed Mac software development.** No matter how well designed or powerful a computer is, no one will buy it if it has

HOW SCULLEY WON HEARTS AND MINDS

After joining PepsiCo Inc. in 1967, John Sculley headed straight for the loading dock. The company put him to work at its Pittsburgh bottling plant to learn the soft-drink business from the ground up, and the slightly built management trainee responded with a zeal that was to become his trademark: He lifted weights every night at the local YMCA so that he could hoist the heavy cases of Pepsi Cola during the day. "That wasn't required for the job, but he wanted to make good—he wanted to get a total background," recalls Charles V. Mangold, a PepsiCo senior vice-president who was Sculley's supervisor at the time.

When Sculley signed on as president of Apple Computer Inc. 18 months ago, he tackled his job with the same drive. Recruited by the Cupertino (Calif.) personal computer maker primarily for his consumer marketing expertise, Sculley spent many an arduous hour learning the basics of personal computer technology. Today he can discuss the nitty-gritty of hardware design with the best Apple engineers. And soon he will be just as conversant on the software side: Sculley recently hired a 25-year-old software whiz to teach him all about programming.

EVANGELICAL. This kind of dedication has helped the 45-year-old Sculley fit into the corporate mold at Apple, where many employees see their work as an evangelical calling to bring computers to the masses. Sharing this vision was essential in winning the respect and wholehearted support of Apple employees—particularly that of the often-mercurial Steven P. Jobs, chairman and co-founder.

"When Sculley arrived he was analyzed under a microscope," acknowledges Joanna Hoffman, overseas marketing head for Apple's Macintosh

computer. "But he has managed to blend in well." Indeed, listening to Sculley's own Applespeak these days confirms that he has become a convert: "At Apple," he declares, "we have a chance to change society."

In day-to-day operations, however,

new products, and proved that he could work alongside the 29-year-old Jobs. "Without Sculley, [Apple] would have been a disaster," says Michele S. Preston, computer analyst at New York's L. F. Rothschild, Unterberg, Towbin.

"[I knew] my going to Apple would

JOBS AND SCULLEY: "WE SPENT A LOT OF TIME . . . GETTING TO KNOW EACH OTHER"

Apple's intense but low-key president has had to face the challenge of turning the computer maker around and steering it into the corporate market. When Sculley arrived in May, 1983, the company was fast losing ground to International Business Machines Corp. in the personal computer market. When the Apple III and Lisa—two machines that Apple had hoped would give it an entrée into the business marketplace—ran up against IBM's Personal Computer, it was no contest.

Sculley moved fast: He reorganized Apple's entire operation, fired several top managers, launched two successful

never work unless Steve and I had a good relationship," Sculley says. Their relationship has turned into something that is sometimes fatherly, other times brotherly. They complete each other's sentences, share jokes, and obviously enjoy one another's company.

THE COURTSHIP. Jobs relentlessly pursued Sculley for four and a half months before the PepsiCo executive agreed to join Apple. To make sure the chemistry was right, the two men spent long periods of time together, discussing a broad range of interests and ideas. During several consecutive weekends in Manhattan, they walked no programs to run. To get outside developers going, Apple must convince them that a large number of the machines will be sold, creating a large market for their programs.

□ **Sign up large customers.** The Apple national-accounts team is busily wooing a flock of large corporate buyers, going so far as to fly them to its Cupertino headquarters and then lay out its future product strategies. Apple has already placed a handful of Macs in more than 50 companies, including Honeywell Inc. and H. J. Heinz Co., and is counting on some of these highly visible companies eventually to become major Mac customers. Apple needs them. "You can't expect small business to buy what big business rejects," Sculley notes.

□ **Improve dealer relations.** Keenly aware of how important its relations with retailers are—retail stores currently sell 80% of all personal computers—Apple in October completely replaced its network of manufacturer's representatives, who acted as the middlemen between the computer maker and its retailers, with its own 350-person sales force. The Apple force is designed to support dealers and train their salespeople. Some dealers fear that Apple's sales force will turn into a direct-selling tool, but others hope it will help Apple stop the discounting done by some retailers, which brings on price wars and lower profit margins.

□ **Form strategic alliances.** In 1985, Apple expects to make distribution and technology agreements with several other major companies. Such relationships would be a big plus to Apple in selling national accounts. Reports of alliances with Wang Laboratories Inc. and American Telephone & Telegraph Co. have been strongest, but none of the companies will comment. In November, Apple selected Xerox Corp. to market its products in some Latin American countries.

Will Jobs and Sculley succeed in their

for hours through Central Park and the museums around it.

Sculley had developed a strong interest in technology at an early age: When he was 14 he applied for a patent on a color television tube, only to find that another company had patented roughly the same idea just weeks before. But electronics figured only briefly into the many conversations that Jobs and Sculley held, since the soft-drink marketer was not up to speed on personal computers.

Instead, Sculley talked to Jobs about baroque and classical art. In turn, Jobs spoke of music and poetry. "We just spent a lot of time in blue jeans getting to know each other," says Sculley. On one trip, the two executives drove around IBM headquarters in Armonk, N. Y., just to see the home of their giant rival. "I hired someone I could learn from," says Jobs, to which Sculley adds: "There are a lot of things Steve is learning from me, and a lot of things I am learning from him."

Sculley's relationship with Jobs is, in many ways, reminiscent of his friendship with mentor Donald M. Kendall, PepsiCo chairman and stepfather of Sculley's first wife, Ruth. The two men first met when Sculley, then 19, was dating Ruth. Later, Kendall was instrumental in Sculley's decision to switch from graduate work in architecture to business school. When Sculley joined PepsiCo after divorcing Ruth, the two men remained close. However, Sculley says, "Kendall and I separated our friendship from the business. He was running the company; I was running a division. [At Apple,] Steve and I are running the business together."

Of course, "together" does not always mean in agreement. In January, Sculley forced Jobs to merge Apple's Lisa and Macintosh divisions, even though Jobs wanted to delay the controversial move until Macintosh was launched. "He was right," Jobs is now quick to acknowledge.

The merger painfully eliminated duplicate jobs and created morale problems, but Apple lacked the resources to staff two groups selling computers that basically use the same technology and are aimed at the same market. "It was very painful, but we've lived through it," says Jay Elliot, Apple's human resources manager.

REPORT CARD: SCULLEY'S FRESHMAN YEAR AT APPLE

COURSE	GRADE*	COMMENTS
Product launchings	A	Introduced two successful computers, Macintosh and IIc
Management reorganization	A	Consolidated five divisions into two
Financial performance	A	Record earnings for the quarter ended Sept. 28, up 600%; 1984 sales up 54%
Stock market performance	C	Stock prices in 1983 fell from a high of 63¼ to a low of 17¼. Now Apple is trading at around 25
Long-term strategy	B+	Strategy for moving Macintosh into the office is sound, but Apple must deliver on time

*GRADED BY BUSINESS WEEK

Sculley has adapted to the California lifestyle just as quickly as he has to Apple's corporate culture. His day begins at 4:30 a.m. with a 5-mi. run. He often arrives at Apple before dawn and leaves after the dinner hour. At work he has abandoned suits and ties in favor of corduroys, topsiders, and open-collar shirts.

'A ROMANTIC.' Still fascinated by architecture, Sculley is also rethinking the East Coast tradition of the corner office—although he has one at Apple. He is helping design a new headquarters where public spaces, not executive offices, have the windows. At a company where performance rather than position brings the rewards, says Sculley, "we want to translate our management concepts into design."

Running Apple now takes up so many hours each day that Sculley has little time for anything else. At PepsiCo he was a board member of Keep America Beautiful and the Soft Drink Assn. He also served as a trustee of the State University of New York and lectured weekly at his alma mater, the University of Pennsylvania's Wharton School. Although he still keeps his 40-ft. yacht, he rarely sails it out of the harbor. When Sculley does break away for an evening, his idea of a good time is discussing Soviet-American relations with PepsiCo's Kendall, or dropping in on art dealers in San Francisco.

"I am a romantic who got sidetracked into business," declares Sculley, who now lives with his third wife 20 minutes from his Cupertino office. He expects to remain at Apple for several years, but he hopes one day to embark on his own artistic project in writing, painting, or some form of technological visual arts. For now, though, Apple, with its spirit of creativity—and bizarre collection of talent—seems an ideal way station for a self-styled Renaissance man who successfully builds businesses, yet, one senses, dreams of creating cathedrals.

By Deborah Wise in San Francisco

TABLE BY BRIAN McDONALD/BW

APPLE EMPLOYEES SPORTING BLUEBUSTERS T-SHIRTS: A NOT-SO-SUBTLE JAB AT THEIR GIANT RIVAL

grand plan? One or two years ago, most industry observers would have answered with an unequivocal "No." The company had failed in its drive to enter the business market by botching two important product introductions. The first Apple III machines off the production line in late 1980 didn't work, and while these problems were fixed quickly, the computer never really regained market momentum. Then, last year, all the excitement over Apple's pricy Lisa computer, a sophisticated $10,000 machine introduced in January, fizzled by June, when the company finally shipped the first models. To top it off, sales of the company's flagship product, the Apple II, began to slow.

But today, the chances for success seem much brighter. The newly reorganized Apple is on a roll. The company has succeeded in selling more than 200,000 Macs since January, and it has launched a smaller, portable version of the Apple II, called the IIc, which contributed to record sales of 113,000 Apple IIs in September, breaking the previous monthly high of 110,000 units shipped last December. Quarterly net earnings, which had been running low during the past year because of major investments in product development, factories, and marketing, rebounded from a low of $5.1 million, to $31 million in the quarter ended Sept. 28.

Sculley, convinced that no other manufacturer can now compete with Apple's Macintosh technology, figures that Apple has two years to make Mac a success in the business market. Industry analysts give Apple from six months to several years. But everyone agrees that if Apple is to have any chance, it must deliver the Macintosh Office on time. In the past, Apple has been notorious for missing its product deadlines. The promised Mac-to-IBM communications link, for example, was scheduled to be shipped this year. Now it has slipped to 1985.

Apple can ill afford to be too cocky about its technology. Even though the IBM PC family is far more complex than Mac, many software developers are writing programs that make them just as easy to operate. IBM is also moving aggressively by doing voluminous advertising and fire-sale pricing to grab even more of the personal computer market. **SOFTWARE GUSHER.** Given such IBM tactics, Apple will have to win strong support from software writers and computer dealers if it is to succeed in the office market. A year ago, for every Apple software package that hit the market, five programs were written for the IBM PC. Software developers were hesitant to devote their resources to Apple until they knew for sure that Mac would receive widespread market acceptance and until the arrival of a more powerful version of the computer—irreverently called Fat Mac—that had the capacity to run sophisticated business software.

Apple has now started to ship Fat Mac, which Jobs and Sculley hustled out in October, three months ahead of schedule, resulting in an outpouring of more than 100 new programs since Septem-

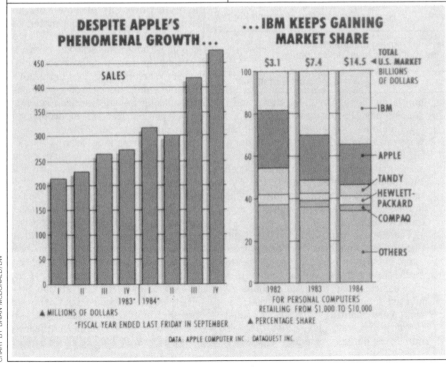

DESPITE APPLE'S PHENOMENAL GROWTH...

SALES

▲ MILLIONS OF DOLLARS

*FISCAL YEAR ENDED LAST FRIDAY IN SEPTEMBER

...IBM KEEPS GAINING MARKET SHARE

$3.1 $7.4 $14.5 ◄ TOTAL U.S. MARKET BILLIONS OF DOLLARS

IBM

APPLE

TANDY

HEWLETT-PACKARD

COMPAQ

OTHERS

1982 1983 1984

FOR PERSONAL COMPUTERS RETAILING FROM $1,000 TO $10,000

▲ PERCENTAGE SHARE

DATA: APPLE COMPUTER INC DATAQUEST INC

CHART BY BRIAN MCDONALD/BW

ber. "The next generation of interesting software will be done on Mac, not the IBM PC," predicts William H. Gates, chairman of Microsoft Corp. and one of Mac's original software supporters.

Even Lotus Development Corp., whose best-selling Lotus 1-2-3 integrated business software was a major factor in spurring sales of the IBM PC, has announced a new integrated business program for Mac. Called Jazz, the $595 software package will provide a Mac user with word processing, electronic spreadsheet, easy information retrieval, communications, and graphics. Scheduled for shipment in February, Jazz could help

THE YOUTHFUL TEAM TURNING OUT MACINTOSH RUNS A $1 BILLION DIVISION

boost Macintosh sales significantly.

News of this software gusher does not seem to have reached potential customers, however. To get the word out, Apple's sales force is busily training dealers in how the new programs work. And BusinessLand Inc., a national chain of 54 stores, recently began selling nine business programs with Mac as a package. "Since then, our [Mac] sales have grown exponentially," claims Vice-President Enzo Torresi.

Apple is even getting help inadvertently from IBM in winning over software developers. IBM's recent introduction of 31 of its own personal software products for the IBM PC sent shock waves through the software community. Independent developers, who saw the IBM move as encroaching on a major segment of their market (BW—Oct. 22), are now looking a lot more favorably at Apple, which scrapped plans to set up its own software division. "Apple's success is in the best interest of independent

vendors because it presents us with a target of opportunity," says Fred M. Gibbons, Software Publishing president.

Computer dealers, too, are wary of stiffening competition from IBM's sales force, which often undercuts dealers' prices for lucrative major accounts. Retailer relationships with Apple have not always been the smoothest, because of product discounting—Mac is now being offered for $1,795 in some markets, $400 less than its suggested retail price. But Apple is trying hard to hold down such selling, and dealers are supporting the company as an alternative to IBM.

"Apple is not out to compete with us," explains Norman Dinnsen, president of ComputerLand of San Diego. Adds retailer Anthony P. Morris, president of Morris Decision Systems Inc. in New York: "I'm not making much money selling Apples, but I like to see a good alternative to IBM."

Several large business-oriented chains, too—including BusinessLand, Sears Business Systems, and the Genra Group—have all recently started stocking Macintoshes. Their decision to carry Apple products shows just how much more competitive Apple has become. "Fiscal 1984 was a life-and-death struggle," admits Sculley, who came west from PepsiCo in May, 1983, to take over as Apple president. "[When I got here] my strategy was to get Apple through the [personal computer] shakeout," he says. At the time, Sculley promised a period of austerity—along with heavy investment in research and development, marketing, and distribution. "We are going to sacrifice short-term gains for

long-term health," he said a year ago.

Sculley managed to bring discipline to the erratic company without breaking Apple's spirit and without alienating Jobs or the Apple rank and file (page 148). To raise money needed for investment in the future, he cut the profit-sharing program, terminated several unprofitable operations, froze hiring, fine-tuned sales, fired several top executives, and reorganized management.

'FOR THE MASSES.' "John was faced with the formidable task of trying to bring some order [to Apple]," says Albert A. Eisenstat, Apple's general counsel. To do that, Sculley replaced Apple's five divisions, including centralized manufacturing and marketing for all products—with two decentralized divisions formed around the company's two main product lines. Del W. Yocam, a six-year Apple veteran, was named to run the Apple II Div., which is responsible for the Apple IIe and IIc computers. And Jobs took over the Macintosh Div., which also includes the new Lisa line.

Assigning Jobs to lead the Macintosh Div. surprised almost no one. From the beginning, Apple's temperamental chairman was the driving force behind the product on which Apple is staking its future. Three years ago, Jobs was ousted from the Lisa group after he continuously protested the way that product was evolving. Convinced that Apple should not have been developing a high-priced business machine, he stormed off to work on his own visionary product, the Macintosh—a low-cost, easy-to-use computer "for the masses."

Strategically, Jobs's headstrong move was counterproductive in that it inhibited the development of a coherent product line. Although the Mac design was similar to Lisa's, it could not run Lisa software. But time has borne out Jobs's conviction: Apple shipped more Macintoshes in its first 100 days on the market than Lisas in the past 12 months.

Today, under Jobs's tutelage, the Mac team—the same bright, hustling bunch of 24- to 35-year-olds who worked 90-hour weeks in the beginning to develop the machine—runs a division with an annual sales rate exceeding $1 billion. The Mac Div. has 600 employees now, out its fast growth has not changed its off-beat spirit. Its offices cluster around an octagonal foyer where a grand piano shares space with Jobs's BMW motorcycle ("I believe people get ideas from seeing great products," Jobs says). Two large speakers blast out rock music at night and play classical during the day. "We're an eclectic bunch, slightly unorthodox, self-motivating, and excited about products," declares Joanna Hoffman, Mac's 29-

year-old director of international sales.

Now, Apple's internal organizational goal, as Steve Jobs explains it, is to "Mac-ize" the rest of the company. He and Sculley want to keep its management layers as flat as possible while the company grows into a multibillion-dollar corporation. With only 5,800 full-time employees (1,200 temporary workers are hired on a seasonal basis), Apple's sales-per-employee ratio is a potent $300,000, up from $245,000 one year ago. By contrast, Intel Corp. has the same revenues, but employs three times as many people.

LESS INTIMIDATING. Keeping Apple lean seems to be working. The company has emerged from its turnaround with two successfully launched new products, the Macintosh and the IIc. And Sculley reinstated profit-sharing during a parking-lot beer-bash at Cupertino headquarters on Oct. 22. Analysts now expect sales to swoop past $2 billion in fiscal 1985.

Apple also seems to be having some success in the field. It has succeeded in getting Mac onto the desks of managers at several large companies. For example, Honeywell Inc.'s Aerospace & Defense Div. uses Macintosh and Lisa computers for a program to teach computer-assisted project planning to 40- to 60-year-old executives. Judith C. Simmons, director of information services, picked Apple computers because they were less intimidating than IBM-compatible machines. "It's helping to improve productivity, and so far, as many as 100 managers have decided to buy Macs," she says. The same holds true at Peat Marwick. Says Richard D. Webb, the partner in charge of its computer project: "There is no question it would have taken significantly more time [to train the people] on the IBM PC."

Apple's rivals in the business world— which include such majors as Data General, Burroughs, and Sperry—still do not consider the Mac a real challenger because it is not IBM-compatible. "We haven't seen many forays by Apple into the serious business place," says Herbert M. Shanzer, the vice-president who heads Data General Corp.'s Desktop Computer Div. No one is counting Apple out, however. "They've got good products, and they're a good company," says Edwin F. Carlson, a Burroughs Corp. vice-president. "We're not going to just step aside and let [Apple] in."

So just how good are Jobs's and Sculley's chances with Mac in the office market? Pretty darn good. Unless something cataclysmic happens, of course, IBM will continue as the No. 1 supplier of personal computers to large corporate customers. But its continuing success does not automatically mean failure for Apple and Macintosh. "IBM is always the safe choice," notes Jan B. Lewis, an industry analyst for InfoCorp. "But a lot of people want an alternative, and Apple is the best . . . alternative to IBM." Macintosh has already distinguished itself from the rest of the personal computer crowd. If Jobs and Sculley can come out on time with the rest of the products that turn Mac into a true office machine, then it could succeed handsomely.

By Deborah Wise in San Francisco and Catherine Harris in New York, with bureau reports

QUOTATIONS FROM CHAIRMAN JOBS

JOBS: "HAVING FUN"

In just eight years, 29-year-old Steven P. Jobs has propelled Apple Computer Inc., the Silicon Valley company he co-founded with Stephen G. Wozniak, into a billion-dollar corporation. With Apple's success, the brash young college dropout has become one of the nation's wealthiest corporate moguls—and one of its most eligible bachelors. And with fame and fortune has come a public forum for his outspoken, sometimes arrogant, opinions.

LEADERSHIP: "You have to set doable goals, but you still have to have a very lofty vision. You need a well-articulated vision that people can follow."

LARGE CORPORATIONS: "Go back 10 years. Polaroid and Xerox would have been on everyone's list of the 10 best-managed companies. How did they lose their way when they became multibillion-dollar corporations? When you start growing like that, you start adding middle management like crazy. . . . People in the middle have no understanding of the business, and because of that, they screw up communications. To them, it's just a job. The corporation ends up with mediocre people that form a layer of concrete. We're trying to keep Apple as flat as possible."

APPLE AS A ROLE MODEL: "Apple can be a model for the new corporation. In the past, power came from tradition—your position in the company, the number of people you had working for you, hard work, and longevity. Now longevity is not significant . . . and the young hotshots don't need to have people working for them."

COMPUTER INNOVATION: "If Apple falters, innovation will cease. We will go into a 'dark ages' in computing."

CORPORATE HEROES: "If we had living national treasures, Edwin H. Land [inventor of the Polaroid camera] would be one. He's someone who spent the majority of his life creating." (Also on Jobs' list are Chrysler Chairman Lee A. Iacocca, Federal Express Chairman Fredrick W. Smith, and William R. Hewlett, who co-founded Hewlett-Packard Co.)

IBM: "I believe that as a society, we have made a large mistake in not breaking up IBM. If there were a way I could participate in a public dialogue about [splitting up the company] . . . I would do it."

LIFE AT APPLE: "I'm having more fun now than I've ever had."

JOHN SCULLEY: "I like spending time with him—he's really smart. He's someone I can learn from."

POLITICS: "I am not political. I am not party-oriented. I am people-oriented. I was not inspired by either candidate [in the recent Presidential election]."

PERSONAL INTERESTS: "I like films and romances."

ROMANCE: "[I like] young, superintelligent, artistic women. I think they're in New York rather than Silicon Valley."

TURNING 30: "I'm apprehensive. For the first time, mortality is less an intellectual abstraction and a historical curiosity."

Managing Projects in the Computer Industry

George Glaser
Los Altos, California

Computer professionals tend to place a higher value on technical than management skills — an understandable, but shortsighted, view for those who want their work to bear fruit.

Computer professionals work on projects throughout their careers. Whatever the individual job—from the most junior trainee to the most senior manager—projects are a way of life.

Projects are as varied in their characteristics—duration, staff requirements, scope, and complexity—as in their objectives.

Unfortunately, project success varies as well. In the computer industry, the track record has been spotty, at best. Objectives are missed and schedule and cost targets overrun with distressing regularity and, at times, with equally distressing results. Once—in the infancy of the industry—these occurrences may have been excusable and even acceptable, but today we cannot afford frequent project failures.

The focus of this article is the management of large and complex projects. To understand what constitutes a successful project, we need to examine current project management practices (including a look at why projects often go awry) and what exactly is involved in the project management task. To this end, the article presents recommendations for project planning, for the use of project management tools, for the use of project management tools,

and for planning and conducting project review meetings. Specific reference is made to two large-scale sample projects: the design, construction, and start-up of a semiconductor wafer fabrication plant and the introduction of a family of high-performance peripheral devices.

An overview of project management practices

Not everyone has the motivation, inclination, or disposition to be a project manager any more than everyone is well suited to be a technical specialist. But, just as competent project managers must have some level of understanding and appreciation for the technology they manage, so must competent technical specialists have some level of understanding and appreciation for the management principles that apply to their work as computer professionals.

Examples of projects the computer professional is likely to encounter include

- researching the frontiers of computer technology;
- developing and implementing new application systems;

- designing, manufacturing, and marketing new hardware and software products; and
- planning, staffing, and equipping new or expanded computing facilities.

Knowing how to manage such projects is a critical skill for the computer professional. Yet project management skills must be scarce, since so many projects in the computer industry fail to achieve their objectives.

Why is this so? First, because computer professionals tend to place a higher value on technical skills than on management skills—an understandable attitude in a profession rooted in technology, but a short-sighted view for those who want to see their work bear fruit. The *real* economic value of computer technology stems from its effectiveness in meeting the needs of others. Both technical and managerial skills are needed to make that happen.

The second reason for the shortage of project management skills is that few individuals have the background and experience to teach such skills. In the academic community particularly, those dedicated to teaching the hard sciences are often openly disdainful of such "soft" subjects.

As a result, because few, if any, project managers receive formal training in the subject, most must acquire their skills on the job. All too often, this training proves to be very expensive indeed, both for hapless project managers who get into trouble and for the enterprises that must bail them out.

Fortunately, certain proven principles of general management apply to project management as well, and these principles *can* be taught. So there is help available if we can learn how to use it. First, though, we need to understand what distinguishes a project from on-going management. A project typically is distinguished by the following:

- a specific objective, such as to implement a new sales order entry system;
- a specific time period, such as to be operational by May 1, 1985;

- a budget for capital expenditures and operating expenses, such as a cost not to exceed $235,000; and
- an ad-hoc team, a team of individuals—some of whom are assigned part-time because of their skills and/or particular organizational relation to the task at hand—for example, two analysts, three programmers, and the manager of sales order entry (half-time).

These elements, in and of themselves, are not enough to make project management particularly difficult. Quite the contrary: a project with a straightforward objective, a realistic due date, an adequate budget, and proper staffing should be relatively routine for a competent manager.

Unfortunately, such ideal circumstances are rare in practice; more often, one or more of the following occur:

- Project objectives are poorly defined and/or understood, even by members of the project team.
- Project deadlines are dictated by external events or imposed arbitrarily by administrative fiat.
- Project budgets are based on naive estimates by inexperienced managers.
- Project staffing is determined more by availability than ability.

The outcome of projects launched under such circumstances is easily predicted. Managing a well-planned and well-staffed project is challenging enough; with fuzzy objectives, an unrealistic schedule, an inadequate budget, and weak staffing, project managers would need a miracle to succeed.

Yet projects with these weaknesses are launched every day. In fact, projects are routinely launched under circumstances that even *further* increase the chance of failure. For example,

- *Overly ambitious objectives.* Setting ambitious project objectives is often effective in motivating the project team to do their best. However, when project objectives force team members to stretch *beyond* their capabilities, motivation drops. Often this approach is

taken by companies trying to catch up with their competition. But trying to regain lost ground by embarking on a naively ambitious recovery course invites disaster.

- *Crash schedules.* Crash schedules, like ambitious objectives, can motivate a competent, well-managed project team to achieve truly outstanding performance. But when schedules are so tight that deadlines are missed consistently, the team may become so frustrated that they will "cheat" to create the impression that they are on schedule, perhaps by overstating progress or skipping important tasks altogether—both causing the project to fall even further behind schedule and even shorter of its objectives.

- *Cross-functional scope.* When multiple functional organizations must work together to reach a shared project objective, exceptional demands are placed on project managers, especially when they do not have formal authority over "outsider" members of the project team. The manager needs a high level of management skill *and* the political clout to go with it. Occasionally, a particularly capable manager will successfully substitute personal charm and diplomacy for political clout, but more often success depends on clout rather than charm.

- *Technological complexity.* Projects that depend on technological breakthroughs for their success present special management problems. Because such projects explore "uncharted territory," the manager may not be able to identify the detailed steps to be taken and, therefore, cannot realistically assess progress. Despite the high risk of failure, such projects are common in the computer industry. A few are successful, largely because survival is a strong motivator, but typically casualties are high.

No single one of these presents an insurmountable obstacle. However, they are often found in combination, sorely testing the skills of the project manager.

The project management task

Given that the management of projects is a demanding undertaking, what can be done to enhance the prospect for a successful outcome?

There is no short answer to this question, but the likelihood of any project's success is strongly influenced by the management philosophy (corporate culture, if you will) of the enterprise. If an organization is characterized by a high level of professionalism—a "can-do" attitude, careful planning, disciplined adherence to schedules and budgets, a sense of teamwork among organizational subunits, and a cadre of energetic and conscientious managers—it is well equipped to take on demanding projects. Organizations that fall significantly short in one or more of these basic strengths are playing in a high stakes game with poor cards.

Launching a project. The most opportune time for planning and organizing a project is, of course, at the time it is started. Enthusiasm is high, the outlook for success seems bright, the need for a plan of action is generally acknowledged, and the project team is eager to go to work. Moreover, at this time, the cost per day of planning is low because the number of people involved is relatively small and the atmosphere is relatively crisis-free. Later, the cost per day of slippage is substantially higher because the team and/or the operating facility is fully staffed, and the capital investment is high.

Each case has unique details, but the basic steps for launching a project are similar for a wide variety of circumstances. Guidelines are summarized in the box at right.

Project management philosophy. Every organization has a management philosophy—explicit or implicit—that governs the way it carries out day-to-day affairs. Ideally, all philosophies

take advantage of management strengths and compensate for management weaknesses, although some philosophies are more effective than others. So it is with project management. Every organization has a project management philosophy, whether explicit or not, whether effective or not. To be effective, such a philosophy must be tailored to the organizational, political, and economic realities of the organization and must be consistent with its general management philosophy.

No project management philosophy, of course, can guarantee the success of any project, no matter how noble its objectives or how diligently it is applied. It can, however, materially improve the prospects for success, *provided* all project participants accept the philosophy and it is administered in a consistent and disciplined manner.

When is an explicit statement of philosophy warranted? A project that involves a large number of tasks and complex organizational interrelation-

---

Guidelines for launching a project

Every project is unique in its management requirements, but certain steps can be taken at the time the project is launched to improve the prospects for a successful outcome. To that end, the following guidelines are offered:

1. Establish a realistic project objective, setting forth in detail what will be accomplished if the project is successful.

2. Appoint a competent project manager whose administrative, technical, and political skills are commensurate with the task.

3. Set up a project organization at the appropriate level and establish the appropriate communications links among all elements of the organization that must play a role in the project's success.

4. Staff the project with the proper mix of technical and administrative skills. Avoid, whenever possible, part-time assignments so that the individuals who are working on the project can devote their full attention to it.

5. Identify key project milestones that, when achieved, will demonstrate definitive progress toward the ultimate project objective.

Note: This step, plus Steps 6-11 below, may require several iterations before a satisfactory plan, schedule, and budget can be developed and approved.

6. Plan the project in detail, identifying all tasks that must be completed to reach each milestone.

7. Assign each task to an individual or to a specific organization so that responsibility for its completion is unambiguous.

8. Estimate the *time* required to complete each task. It is essential that the time estimate for each task be made by the individual or organization that bears the responsibility for completing it.

9. Estimate the *cost* of completing each task (or groups of tasks); again, these estimates should be made by the responsible party.

10. Produce a project schedule and time-phased budget (using critical-path or similar network techniques when the size of the project warrants).

11. Distribute the plan, schedule, and budget to all responsible parties and confirm their "ownership" of the tasks assigned to them.

12. Review the project schedule and budget regularly. At each review meeting, ask for reaffirmation of plans and schedules for the forthcoming period. On large, complex projects, make project reviews formal; take minutes to document key decisions and follow-up assignments.

13. Update project plans and schedules after each review meeting and distribute them as noted previously.

14. Manage the project!

---

ships would be a likely candidate. Consider the following case based on the recently completed start-up of a semiconductor-wafer fabrication plant:

- The project cost over $100 million.
- A number of organizational units were involved, including corporate facility planners and designers, R&D staff, outside architects and building contractors, and the line management that was to operate the new plant.
- The project manager, although a well-known and respected individual within the company, was managing a project of this size for the first time; furthermore, the key individuals reporting to the project manager had not worked together as a team before. In fact, several of them were new employees, hired specifically for this project.
- The site for the new plant was approximately 1000 miles away from the corporate offices where funding decisions were made and where most of the detailed product and process planning took place.

Together, these facts argued for a formal management approach and led to the adoption of the project management philosophy shown in the box at left. The facility was completed, equipped, and staffed on time.

Project plans and schedules. Seasoned project managers, well aware of the risks they face, look for ways to reduce their exposure to delays and cost overruns. Their most valuable ally is a detailed project plan to use in tracking progress.

A detailed project plan specifies what tasks need to be completed and in what order, what end-products or deliverables result, which individuals or organizations are responsible, and the estimated "time-to-complete." Using this detailed plan, managers can develop a similarly detailed schedule to indicate the date each task can start and the date it must be completed.

Identifying the tasks that make up a project is demanding and time consuming. For large, complex projects, such as those that span several years and that have a company-wide scope, developing an initial plan may take the project team several months of concentrated effort.

A good way to get started is to define major project milestones that, when reached, signify important progress toward the project's objective (see box above right). The milestones, in turn, can be used to identify tasks that precede and follow them. Note that the list in the box includes milestones for development engineering, manufacturing engineering, test engineering, customer engineering, production management, and marketing—all of

---

A sample project management philosophy

A semiconductor plant start-up

1. Make plans comprehensive and detailed. Gross plans only lead to gross blunders and gross overruns.

2. Have one—and only one—project plan and supporting schedule. This does not rule out subsidiary plans that are maintained in greater detail than what the project manager needs, but plans that are independent of the project manager's plans are inherently dangerous.

3. Report progress in detail against the plan. For each task, be prepared to report time to completion; avoid the use of "percentage complete," a particularly beguiling, but more often than not misleading figure.

4. Consider time estimates as commitments of the person who makes them. On the other hand, those responsible for tasks are encouraged to revise time estimates (upward, if necessary) whenever they encounter difficulties so that schedules are realistic at all times.

5. Urge forthright reporting of bad news. To slip a schedule is a sin, but to conceal a slippage—or to fail to reveal an anticipated slippage—is a grievous sin.

6. To avoid getting bogged down in detail, focus project reviews on activities that are now critical or that soon will be.

7. Make project review meetings formal, with a written agenda, careful preparation beforehand—and diligent follow-up afterwards—and select someone with a strong hand as chairman.

8. Hold project review meetings on a regular basis; adjust their frequency as the tempo of the project demands.

9. Make attendance at project review meetings mandatory for organizations designated as "critical" at each stage of the project. Furthermore, ensure that every organization is represented by an individual who can commit it to deadlines or revised cost objectives. Messengers bearing bad news but not responsible for it are not acceptable replacements for those in charge.

10. Report progress on all tasks scheduled for completion in the period just ended. Look ahead to the forthcoming period to reaffirm that scheduled commitments will be met. When it is known in advance that an activity scheduled for completion in the upcoming period will be behind schedule, develop and present alternative plans. These plans should, to the extent possible, minimize or offset any adverse effect on other activities by, for example, reallocating resources. At a minimum, warn others affected by the slippage in advance.

11. Ensure that capital expenditure tracking includes amounts already spent, amounts committed, and amounts necessary "to complete." Accounting should anticipate—not merely document—expenditures.

which influence the development of project plans.

For projects of the size just cited, critical-path (or similar) networking techniques are essential in developing and maintaining plans and schedules. (These techniques are discussed in more detail later in the section on project management tools.)

Accountability for results is critical to any management process. Accountability, however, comes only after responsible managers have endorsed the project plans and schedule. This endorsement is key, since it carries with it an implied commitment to the tasks and dates contained within. Until such commitments are obtained, the plan is little more than a project manager's "wish list" and can hardly be expected to be binding on other parties. Once the plan is formally adopted, however, individuals (or organizations) can be held accountable for completing specific tasks and meeting approved schedule targets.

Plans and schedules drawn up at the project's outset can quickly become obsolete as events unfold. To keep them current, they must be regularly reviewed and, when necessary, revised. Such changes should always be approved by the project manager, and such approval should not be lightly given, since casual and frequent schedule slippages obviously should be avoided. Nonetheless, it is better to slip a schedule and meet the revised dates than to cling to an unrealistic one, knowing that the team will not be able to meet it. Certain characteristics that distinguish a sound project plan from others are set forth in the box below right.

Project reviews. The enthusiasm for planning that accompanies a new project is often short-lived. Typically, there is an initial flurry of activity: task lists are created, time estimates are made, critical-path networks are drawn, Gantt charts are prepared for management, and budget requests are energetically presented. Once the project is approved and the funds authorized, however, the "plans" serve little purpose other than to decorate the

walls of the project manager's office. No further planning takes place until the project (and, presumably, the project manager) is in hot water, at which time the exercise is repeated with no greater conviction or commitment than when the project was initiated.

The best way to keep plans (and planning) alive is through a disciplined, i.e., regular and rigorous, review process. While format and content will differ just as project managers' management styles differ, project reviews are critically important in the management of any project.

Review meetings satisfy several objectives:

- to interject general management awareness, concern, and support.

Typical project milestones
The introduction of a new product

Marketing requirements defined	Test plans developed
Functional specifications released	Spare parts ordered
Performance specifications released	Manufacturing process instructions issued
Design review(s) completed	Manufacturing prototypes built
Engineering prototypes built	Field-support plans developed
Design validation test completed	Customer engineering documentation released
Engineering drawings released	
Beta-site test completed	Customer engineering training initiated
Product pricing finalized	
Product announced	Product validation test complete
Critical-part vendors qualified	First customer shipment
Long-lead parts ordered	Manufacturing cost review(s) completed
Hard tooling ordered	

Characteristics of a sound project plan

1. *Comprehensiveness.* Its scope covers *all* aspects of the project, including those that are the responsibility of support organizations.

2. *Uniqueness.* It is the only approved overall plan for the project. Subplans for lower level managers can, of course, be useful (even necessary) in certain situations, but independent plans, i.e., plans that are developed and executed independently of the official project plan, are a common cause of schedule slippage and other difficulties that result from poor communication and coordination.

3. *Attention to detail* Every significant task in the project is identified, and its logical sequence and relation to other tasks is explicitly stated.

4. *Clarity.* Every task is assigned to one and only one individual or

organizational unit, and its deliverables (or other conditions for satisfactory completion) are crisply defined so that progress can be assessed realistically; "fuzzy" claims of completion are often used to imply progress when, in fact, little real progress has been made.

5. *Authority.* It has been endorsed by the line management of each of the individuals or organizational units participating in the project. Time estimates, as a result, represent commitments by those responsible for completing individual tasks.

6. *Currency.* It is reviewed and updated on a regular and disciplined basis (and revised when necessary) so that it represents *the* project schedule at all times.

- to reaffirm the correctness and completeness of current plans and schedules;
- to anticipate potential problems and to assign responsibility and deadlines for their resolution;
- to foster cooperation and communication among the individuals and organizations involved; and
- to create a sense of enthusiasm, cohesiveness, and importance.

Note that "reporting on accomplishments of the previous period" is omitted from these objectives. Often, such recitations are not only a waste of time but also (worse yet) a smokescreen for avoiding discussion about what should have happened but did not.

Also absent is any suggestion that review meetings should be used to admonish those who missed deadlines. There is a proper time and place for confronting the nonperformer, but most would agree that public floggings have not proven effective in behavior modification. When schedules slip, the first order of business is to identify the implication of the slippage on the

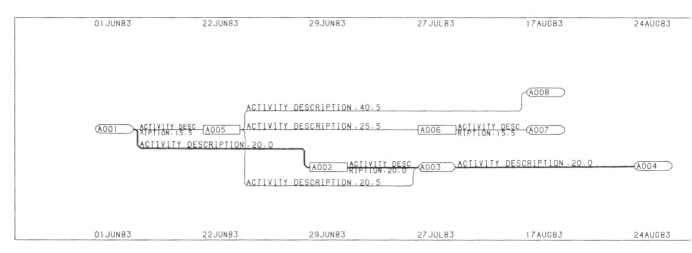

Figure 1. EN2 network. Used with permission of Systonetics, Inc.

ACTIVITY NAME	ACTIVITY DESCRIPTION	ACTIVITY CODE	PCT CMP	ORG DUR	EARLY START	EARLY FINISH	LATE START	LATE FINISH	TTL FLT
11	PROGRAM PLANNING	11	0	6	SON26APR83	SON03MAY83	26APR83	03MAY83	0
22	EDM PROCUREMENT	22	0	32	26APR83	08JUN83	10MAY83	22JUN83	10
211	EDM ANALYSIS	211	0	15	04MAY83	24MAY83	17MAY83	06JUN83	9
212	EDM SPECIFICATIONS	212	0	18	04MAY83	27MAY83	12MAY83	06JUN83	6
213	EDM DRAWINGS	213	0	24	04MAY83	06JUN83	04MAY83	06JUN83	0
214	EDM BREADBOARDS	214	0	24	04MAY83	06JUN83	04MAY83	06JUN83	0
51	STE DESIGN AND DEVELOPMENT	51	0	24	04MAY83	06JUN83	04MAY83	06JUN83	0
121	PDR	121	0	3	07JUN83	09JUN83	07JUN83	09JUN83	0
23	ASSEMBLY (EDM)	23	0	12	09JUN83	24JUN83	23JUN83	08JUL83	10
31	QUAL DESIGN & DEVELOPMENT	31	0	20	10JUN83	07JUL83	10JUN83	07JUL83	0
52	STE PROCUREMENT	52	0	28	10JUN83	19JUL83	29JUL83	06SEP83	35
24	TEST (EDM)	24	0	6	27JUN83	04JUL83	11JUL83	18JUL83	10
32	QUAL PROCUREMENT	32	0	32	08JUL83	22AUG83	29JUL83	12SEP83	15
41	FLT DESIGN	41	0	4	08JUL83	13JUL83	08JUL83	13JUL83	0
122	CDR	122	0	3	14JUL83	18JUL83	14JUL83	18JUL83	0
42	FLT PROCUREMENT	42	0	40	19JUL83	12SEP83	19JUL83	12SEP83	0
53	STE ASSEMBLY	53	0	16	20JUL83	10AUG83	07SEP83	28SEP83	35
54	STE TEST	54	0	5	11AUG83	18AUG83	29SEP83	06OCT83	35
55	STE DELIVERY	55	0	1	19AUG83	19AUG83	02NOV83	02NOV83	53
33	QUAL ASSEMBLY	33	0	18	23AUG83	15SEP83	13SEP83	06OCT83	15
431	FLT NO. 1 ASSEMBLY	431	0	18	13SEP83	06OCT83	29SEP83	24OCT83	12
34	QUAL TEST	34	0	12	16SEP83	03OCT83	07OCT83	24OCT83	15
123	FDR	123	0	3	04OCT83	06OCT83	28OCT83	01NOV83	18
432	FLT NO. 2 ASSEMBLY	432	0	16	04OCT83	25OCT83	04OCT83	25OCT83	0
35	QUAL DELIVERY	35	0	1	07OCT83	07OCT83	02NOV83	02NOV83	18
441	FLT NO. 1 TEST	441	0	5	07OCT83	14OCT83	25OCT83	01NOV83	12
451	FLT NO. 1 DELIVERY	451	0	1	17OCT83	17OCT83	02NOV83	02NOV83	12
442	FLT NO. 2 TEST	442	0	5	26OCT83	01NOV83	26OCT83	01NOV83	0
452	FLT NO. 2 DELIVERY	452	0	1	02NOV83	02NOV83	02NOV83	02NOV83	0

SYSTONETICS, INC.
PUTTING PROJECT MANAGEMENT
AT YOUR FINGERTIPS
NETWORK MSH1 / RCF NAME GANT
UP TO 50 CHARACTER PROJECT DESCRIPTION
UP TO 50 CHARACTER REPORT TITLE
RUN DATE 26MAY83 / DATA DATE 26APR83
UP TO 50 CHARACTERS OF TITLE BLOCK NOTATION
PROPRIETARY PRODUCT OF SYSTONETICS, INC.

Figure 2. Sample Gantt bar chart. Used with permission of Systonetics, Inc.

project completion date, then to focus on what can be done to recover the time lost.

How often review meetings should be held depends on the nature and length of the project. For a project of six months or more, formal reviews at the top management level should be held at least monthly. Reviews at the project-team level should be held at least biweekly. A decision-level spokesman for every organizational unit should attend so that revisions to plans and schedules can be adopted on the spot. A formal agenda should be prepared and distributed in advance, and formal minutes listing issues identified and actions taken should be recorded and circulated as a confirming document to those directly responsible and as an information document to others.

To repeat, review meetings are vital to the success of any project. They are the best—and often the only—mechanism for maintaining credibility of plans and schedules and for instilling a sense of teamwork and commitment vital to success.

Project management tools. A number of software tools are available to aid the project manager and members of the project team in carrying out their responsibilities.

Such tools have been developed for both large mainframes and for personal computers. They vary substantially in cost (from $200 for a small system for a personal computer to $100,000 for a stand-alone system with extensive graphics capability), the size of project network they can process (from a few dozen tasks to many thousands), their architecture (batch/remote-batch/timesharing/on-line interactive), and the flexibility of their progress reporting and report generation.

These tools typically provide one or more of the following complementary capabilities: time analysis, resource analysis, and cost analysis.

Time analysis. Using the critical-path (or PERT) method, time-analysis tools calculate a time schedule for a network of project tasks. The process usually consists of the following steps:

- Individual tasks, each with its estimated time to completion, are interconnected in a network to reflect the predecessor/successor relation among them.
- For each task, a "can start" date is calculated, indicating the earliest possible start date according to the scheduled start dates for each of the task's predecessors.
- A "must complete" date for each task is then calculated according to the scheduled start dates for each of the task's successors and the target completion date for the overall project.

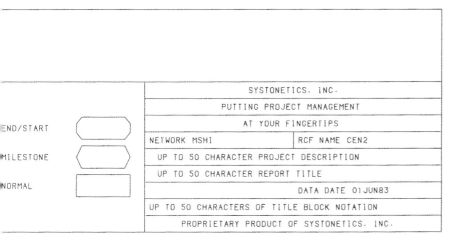

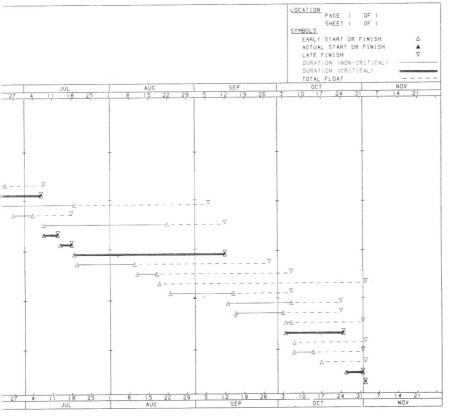

- The difference between the calculated time *available* to complete a task and the estimated time *required* to complete it—its *float* or slack time—is then calculated. If the float is zero, the task is said to be "critical," since any delay in completing it will cause a delay in completing the final task of the project.

Knowing the scheduled start and completion dates for each task in a project is fundamentally important in managing it. Knowing the float time for each task is fundamentally important in distinguishing between tasks that literally pace a project and those that allow greater scheduling flexibility.

Most time-analysis tools also provide for a variety of selecting, sorting, and reporting options so that customized schedules can be prepared,

for example, for responsible organizations, levels of management, types of resources, and time periods.

Resource analysis. The number and type of available resources—such as programmers, final test stations, and bulldozers—often determine when an individual task can start and the time needed to complete it. Project management software with resource-analysis capabilities can be used to produce a schedule that takes these constraints into account.

Cost analysis. Tools with cost-analysis capabilities are used to compute direct costs, on the basis of resource requirements and resource rates, and to summarize costs in various ways, by time period and organization, for example.

In addition to these analytical capabilities, certain project manage-

ment tools include graphics capabilities for drawing network diagrams (Figure 1), plotting Gantt (bar) charts (Figure 2), and graphing other types of project data, such as period costs (Figure 3). Almost all of them can be used to produce Gantt charts and relatively crude network diagrams on a line printer; still others can be used to produce both bar charts and network diagrams on a dot-matrix printer, although for projects with more than 100 tasks, printing delays become excessive; the most powerful tools can readily produce a wide variety of graphics output for very large projects (thousands of activities) on high-speed flat-bed or drum plotters.

Project management tools make the job of the project manager easier, and for projects comprising more than a few dozen tasks, they are essential. But neither one alone nor all of them together are effective in the hands of

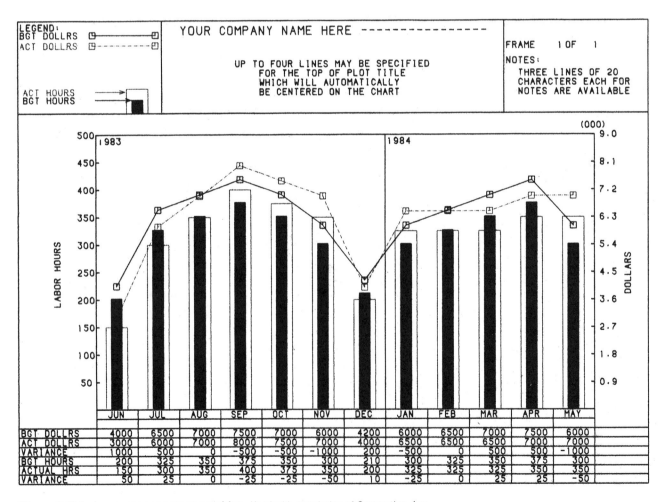

Figure 3. Tabular *xy* management graphics. Used with permission of Systonetics, Inc.

an inexperienced project manager or an undisciplined organization. Such tools are often acquired with the naive assumption that powerful tools can compensate for weak management skills—an assumption equivalent to believing that a mediocre artist can create classic sculpture if the chisel is sharp enough. Management tools can, in fact, do more harm than good if they are applied without adequate understanding of their limitations or without proper concern for the organizational and managerial issues that seem inevitably to accompany large projects.

What project management tools *will* do is relieve project managers of the more onerous clerical tasks and allow them to focus on the more challenging—administrative, technical, and political—aspects of the job.

For a project to succeed, the right people must complete the right tasks at the right time. This doesn't happen by accident. It happens because objectives have been stated crisply, obstacles to achieving them (including time and resource constraints) have been identified and realistically evaluated, detailed plans have been developed, and realistic schedules have been adopted.

Planning and managing a project in this way is hard work—and at times, even painful. Yet it is far less painful to plan at the outset of a project—and to manage carefully as it progresses—than it is to explain to our superiors why we are behind schedule and over budget, and to our team members why their hard work on a foundering project hasn't advanced their careers or gotten them a raise.

Managing a successful project, on the other hand, can be an exhilarating and rewarding experience. Those who make the investment in time and effort required to plan and manage their projects well can expect to realize a handsome payoff from that investment. □

Annotated bibliography

Argelo, S. M., "Pitfalls in Automation Projects," in *Beyond Productivity: Information Systems Development for Organizational Effectiveness,* M. A. Bemelmans, ed., North-Holland, Amsterdam, 1983, pp. 241-252.

Proceedings of the IFIP WG 8.2 Working Conference on the title subject.

Brooks, F. P., Jr., *The Mythical Man Month: Essays on Software Engineering,* Addison-Wesley, Menlo Park, 1975.

The *classic* book on the management of software engineering by the man who led the development of IBM's OS/360. Described by the author as "a belated answer to Tom Watson's probing questions as to why programming is hard to manage." Required reading for all project managers and those who aspire to the role.

Gall, J., *Systematics,* Quadrangle Press, New York, 1975.

A "valuable contribution to our understanding of organized failure," this book examines the pitfalls of systems analysis projects. Full of wise and wry comments on projects that got out of hand.

Glass, R. L., *The Universal Elixir and Other Computing Projects which Failed,* Computing Trends, Seattle, Wash., 1977.

A collection of short anecdotes about computer projects that failed and why they did so.

Kidder, T., *The Soul of a New Machine,* Avon Books, New York, 1982.

A Pulitzer-Prize-winning story about the development of Data General's Eclipse MV8000 computer (then called Eagle). Focus of the book is largely on the challenges faced by the project team and on the demands imposed on them by themselves and by the corporate culture in which they worked.

Metzger, P. W., *Managing a Programming Project,* Prentice Hall, Englewood Cliffs, N. J., 1973.

According to the author, a book that is "short on pure theory and long on practical 'how-to-do-it' advice." "The Definition Phase," chapter 2, contains a number of useful suggestions on project planning and management.

Quist, A. B., *Excuse Me . . . What Was That?,* Dilithium Press, Beaverton, Oreg., 1982.

A book "full of anecdotes about things that should've worked but didn't and things that did work but for all the wrong reasons." The author notes that "someone may actually derive wisdom from what is offered here, probably by accident." Humorous and insightful.

Reynolds, C. H., "What's Wrong with Computer Programming Management?" in *On the Management of Computer Programming,* G. F. Weinwurm, ed., Auerbach Publishers, Princeton, N. J., 1970, pp. 35-42.

Shelly, G. B., and T. J. Cashman, *Business Systems Analysis and Design,* Anaheim Publishing, Fullerton, Calif., 1981.

Chapter 10, "Project Management, Scheduling and Control," describes the use of Gantt charts and Pert (critical-path method) networks for systems analysis and design projects. Includes case studies.

Weinwurm, G. F., "The Challenge to the Management Community," in *On the Management of Computer Programming,* G. F. Weinwurm, ed., Auerbach Publishers, Princeton, N. J., 1970.

A pragmatic book on techniques for the management of computer programming projects by a series of respected and seasoned practitioners.

George Glaser is president of George Glaser, Inc., a consulting firm specializing in the management of technology-based companies and large-scale projects. He has consulted for corporate and institutional top management clients in both the US and Europe for 20 years. His previous positions include founder and president of Centigram Corporation, a supplier of voice response systems; 12 years as a member of the staff of McKinsey & Company, Inc., an international management consulting firm; product planner and manager for the Computer Products Division of Ampex Corporation; and a staff member in the Field Test and Business Data Processing Divisions of Sandia Corporation.

Glaser received a BSEE from the University of Notre Dame and subsequently studied business administration at the University of New Mexico. He is the US delegate to IFIP and one of its vice presidents. Previously, he was president of AFIPS and chairman of its Board of Directors. He also served as national chairman of ACM's Business Data Processing Group. He holds Centigram's US patent for continuous speech recognition apparatus.

Glaser's address is 15 Parsons Way, Los Altos, CA 94022.

The Nature of Software Management:
A Primer

Donald J. Reifer
TRW Systems

Reprinted from *Tutorial: Software Management* (First Edition) by D.J. Reifer, 1979, pages 2-5. Copyright © 1979 by The Institute of Electrical and Electronics Engineers, Inc.

Eighteen fundamental principles of management can be applied by software managers to help them plan, control, organize, staff, and direct their activities and personnel more effectively. These principles are based upon the fundamental premise that systems engineering and management methods, tools, and techniques can be applied logically and beneficially to the problem of producing large software systems products within schedule and budget.

Beauty and the beast

Producing a large software system is fraught with all the problems inherent in any highly labor-intensive activity. A large workforce must be assembled and organized into a cohesive team whose sole purpose is to produce an engineering product within the limits of time and budget. Plans must be made, and controls must be established. People must be trained, and they must be motivated to accomplish achievable goals that the entire team has agreed upon. Eventually, the workforce must be shifted to new work as the present task draws to completion.

Software management therefore consists of all the technical and management activities required to implement an acceptable solution to a validated user's need within an agreed-upon amount of time and with agreed-to resources. It involves decision-making and people. It is social, political, and technological. It has five constituent parts:

(1) Planning

(2) Controlling

(3) Staffing

(4) Organizing

(5) Directing

Software management cannot be accomplished by novices using recipes. Its practice requires skill, knowledge, understanding, and the ability to survive pressure. It is challenging, and it is frustrating. It is, indeed, beauty and the beast.

Taming the beast

An animal trainer must understand the nature of his beast before he attempts to tame it and train it. So must we.

Software is big business in American government and industry. The National Bureau of Standards estimates that annual federal spending on software has exceeded $5 billion. It also estimates that the accumulated federal investment in software has exceeded $25 billion.[1] Similar investments are found in industry. Many large commercial firms estimate that they spend as much as six percent of their gross sales annually on data processing services.[2] Most of this investment goes toward producing large inventories of software for in-house use by individual corporations.

Management's track record in producing quality software on schedule and within budget has not been impressive. A recently released General Accounting Office report is extremely critical of current management practices within federal agencies.[3] A similar report critical of industrial practices as seen through the Air Force's eyes, has also been released.[4]

Setting the stage

From our past successes and failures, we can glean guiding principles of software management that can serve us in building success into our future efforts. These principles are descriptive and predictive, but not prescriptive. They provide us with a logical framework within which to build an ordered body of knowledge.

We must bear in mind that the notions of accuracy and definitiveness that apply to the physical sciences do not apply to software management practices. Software management theory (the existing body of formalized knowledge) is still young and depends to a large degree on informal and unstructured application by its practitioners. In addition, software management is still more an art than a science, and its principles must therefore be inexact in their application to the software development process.

Modeling the process

Producing software involves more than just writing programs. A software system product must be specified, designed, fabricated, tested, and documented in a disciplined fashion.[5] It must be integrated with other products and with the hardware, and it must be demonstrated to be operational in a specific environment. Development involves a series of interrelated, time-phased activities called a life cycle. Two different life-cycle models are described in Part I of this tutorial. In this paper, however, we direct our attention not at these engineering tasks but, rather, at the management activities—planning, organizing, staffing, directing, and controlling—that must be performed in parallel with them to ensure successful completion of the system.

Planning: foretelling the future

Planning is the primary function of management, but lack of planning has been one of the major causes of failure within our industry.

Plans are either strategic or tactical.[6] Strategic plans identify major organizational objectives and govern the acquisition, use, and disposition of resources to achieve those objectives. Tactical plans deploy resources to achieve strategic objectives. Plans help managers decide in advance what will be done, when it will be done, how it will be done, and who will do it. This discussion leads us to the three principles of planning:

Principle 1: The Precedence Principle. Planning logically takes precedence over all other managerial functions.

Principle 2: The Effective Planning Principle. Plans will be effective if they are consistent with the organization's policy and strategy framework.

Principle 3: The Living Document Principle. Plans must be maintained as living documents or they quickly lose their value. Plans serve as the foundation for control. When they are not updated, control is severely impeded.

The most basic management plan is a budget. It establishes financial plans or technical plans (or both) in numerical terms. Technical budgets can be established to control software resource utilization (size and time); financial budgets can be established to control costs. Both types of budgets should be used during development as standards against which progress is measured.

It seems that nobody ever has time to plan. Software people tend to rush toward implementation without sitting back and spending time deciding what they are going to do and how. If software managers are to recognize and reverse this tendency, they must be taught the value of early planning and be motivated to devote time to it.

The following five planning steps, when completed, represent the actions necessary to implement the first three principles of planning:

1. A software development organization should establish a set of software development and management policies and a long-range business plan. The policies should describe configuration management, quality assurance, documentation, and other standards that will be used in developing software. These plans should be created by a management team with assistance from the rank and file. The plans should be communicated throughout the organization in a manner that leaves little doubt that they will be understood.

2. Before any new work is authorized, the responsible manager should develop a business plan. This plan should describe the job to be done, its constraints, an organization to do it, and the reasons why upper management should allocate resources to it.

3. Once the work is authorized, a project plan should be created to define the scope of the work to be done. This plan deploys resources and technology to achieve the objectives stated in the business plan. This plan also breaks the work into achievable tasks and provides the estimates (schedule, cost, size, timing, etc.) required to price the job.

4. Additional plans may be required, depending on the size of the job and the number of different organizations involved. These plans should be consistent with one another and should define interfaces with a minimum of overlap. Configuration management and test plans serve as examples.

5. Plans should be maintained as living documents. It is the manager's job to ensure that they are updated periodically.

Organizing: creating the shell

Managers create organizations to make it possible for people to work together efficiently in accomplishing mutually agreed-upon goals. Most software managers function within an existing organizational shell. They have very little control over the basic way in which their business enterprise is organized. Instead, they concentrate on making the internal functioning of their people effective. The structure they create makes it possible for everyone to know who is to do what and who is responsible for which results. This structure expedites communication by keeping the number of levels in the organization at a minimum. It distinguishes among project, line, and staff responsibilities. Most importantly, it ensures that one's authority is commensurate with one's responsibility. This discussion leads us to the three principles of organization:

Principle 4: The Early Assignment Principle. Make *one* person responsible for software as early in the life of the project as possible. Ensure that he or she occupies a high enough position within the hierarchy to successfully compete for resources (dollars, people, etc.). Make this person accountable for the final results.

Principle 5: The Interface Principle. The efficiency of an organization is inversely proportionate to the number of interfaces it has to maintain during the performance of a job.

Principle 6: The Parity Principle. A software manager's responsibility for action should be no greater than that implied by the authority delegated to him.[7]

Any project should be organized to expedite the accomplishment of goals and reduce risk. Because software is a key risk area in the development of most computer-based systems, the organization should be structured to make software development highly visible and easily controlled.

The primary contribution of a software manager who is named early will be to make plans and estimates realistic. All too often, a software organization must perform according to unrealistic schedules and budgets devised by people who haven't the foggiest idea of what they mean.

Software production is a labor-intensive activity. Communication problems dominate. If you can limit the number of times a fact has to be comunicated, you can limit the errors in translation.

Software production is heavily dependent on requirements generated by other sections of an organization. Software people have little or no control over these requirements, yet they are often blamed for outside factors not under their control. A software manager should be responsible only for that which he has authority to control. If a project needs to control a multidisciplinary team, working groups should be established to work out the problems, and a responsible manager should be designated to make decisions.

Staffing: acquiring the talent

The shortage of skilled manpower in the software field makes the retention and effective utilization of personnel a key management chore. Organizations are as good as the people who populate them. A manager must people his organization with the right talent. He must nurture this talent and effectively utilize it. He must weed out the "dead wood." He must also continually cultivate new managers. This leads us to the three principles of staffing:

Principle 6: The Quality Principle. Using a few experienced people for critical tasks (such as design) is often more effective than using larger, unskilled teams. An experienced software engineer is "worth his weight in gold."

Principle 7: The Personnel Development Principle. An open commitment to personnel development often pays dividends. Better trained technical and managerial personnel can effectively cope with tomorrow's problems instead of today's.

Principle 8: The Dual Ladder Principle. Promotion should be possible up either a technical or a managerial career path.

Software people are a very mobile population. The market is always wide open for good people, and their loss often impacts project performance drastically because they are hard to replace. Retaining good people is a primary responsibility of management, and one way to do it is to make sure the interesting work is spread out and that people are not too overloaded.

Software development is a high-technology discipline. New advances to the state of the art make continuous updating of technical skills mandatory. Companies that are reluctant to send their personnel to classes or to set up in-house instruction only hurt themselves.

As in other scientific disciplines, good technical performers are often promoted to management positions. This is frequently a mistake, because the skills that make one a good software engineer are often different from those that make one a good manager.[8] Good software managers must be developed. A useful development approach is to make the aspiring manager an assistant before sending him out on his own. Dual career paths, in the spirit of chief programmer[9] or democratic teams, is a promising approach, too.

Directing: leading the way

Managers must get things done through other people. They must communicate their goals to their subordinates, and they must motivate them to achieve those goals. These tasks are often difficult because software people tend to be highly creative and individualistic. They rebel against authority, but authority must be established. Communications and mutual trust must be developed in order for direction to become effective. This leads us to the three principles of direction:

Principle 10: The Motivation Principle. Interesting work and the opportunity for growth and advancement will motivate people to achieve high productivity.[10] McGregor's Theory Y holds—the individual will rise to the challenge of his capabilities.[11]

Principle 11: The Leadership Principle. People will follow those who represent a means of satisfying their own personal goals. Success will come to those who ensure that personal goals are compatible with those of the organization.

Principle 12: The Communications Principle. Productivity is a function of the communications burden. As the burden increases, productivity decreases. In other words, the less communication required, the higher the productivity.

We would all like to have an organization full of talented, self-motivated individuals. Things would get done with little or no management interference. Unfortunately, this is not the real world. Managers, like coaches, must motivate average people with acceptable skills to perform to their fullest. There is no simple formula for doing this. It is usually done by trial and error. My experience indicates that software people seem motivated by challenging work, a competitive environment, recognition, and the opportunity to grow professionally. A manager must adapt his management style to create rewards to re-enforce these motivators. Participative leadership has the best long-run chance for success, especially if it creates a dynamic environment in which people are excited about what they are doing.

Communication must be efficient, and, in general, written. Direction memos that define what is to be done, by whom, and when can be used effectively to communicate action plans for implementation. Meetings should be avoided unless they are economically justified. After-hours colloquia can be used profitably to communicate technical information to those who are interested.

Controlling: closing the loop

Planning and control are inseparable activities. Unplanned actions cannot be controlled because control involves keeping events on course by correcting deviations to plans. Plans furnish the standards for control. Controls should be diagnostic, therapeutic, accurate, timely, understandable, and economical. They should call attention to significant deviations and should suggest alternative means of correcting the difficulty. They should be imposed throughout the software development life cycle. This leads us to the three principles of control:

Principle 13: The Significance Principle. Controls should be implemented to alert managers promptly to significant deviations from plans.

Principle 14: The Measurement Principle. Effective control requires that we measure progress against objective, accurate, and meaningful standards.

Principle 15: The Exception Principle. The efficient manager will concentrate his control efforts on exceptions.

The failure to plan properly has caused many software projects to be uncontrolled. The more detailed and realistic the plan, the better the control.

Technical and personnel audits are useful control devices that are not widely used by the software industry. Technical audits are conducted by independent and objective teams to determine whether or not progress is as reported. Simply having a project team prepare for a technical audit early in the development is a useful exercise. Personnel audits are conducted by management to assess whether or not personnel development goals are being fulfilled. These audits help individuals ascertain where they need to improve to function more effectively in the achievement of their goals.

Classical techniques can be employed to improve control. PERT and GANT charting, milestone scheduling, and program budgeting are all useful tools.[12]

Matrix management gives rise to special control problems. In matrix management, a project organization manages the development and a line organization manages the people. The two organizations conflict with one another throughout the course of the development. Project managers must control people who do not report to them. They must ensure that these people get their job done on time. Project managers can improve their control by treating their relationships with the line as subcontracts. They should stimulate competition between line organizations and should always have two sources available to do a job. Several companies have their internal software organization compete with outside firms for work. If it makes sense financially, they get the job done internally. Project managers should insist on written progress reports and reviews. Line managers should insist on direction memos and authorization agreements that clearly define the work to be done and the schedule for it.

The technological revolution

We have stated that the software industry is very dynamic. Technical advances are causing it to change rapidly.[13] A manager must harness this change and put it to work, carefully assessing the risks associated with this change. A manager must not be conservative in the extreme. This gives rise to two more management principles:

Principle 16: The Technology Risk Principle. Technology should be used only when the risk associated with it is acceptable.

Principle 17: The Improvement Principle. The manager who insists on doing things the way they have always been done will fail. New approaches must be used to meet new challenges. Your competition will not allow you to remain conservative in the extreme.

I firmly believe that technology transfer is the primary means we have to combat the software problems the industry has been experiencing.

Conclusion

This paper serves as the overture to those that follow. It describes seventeen principles that can be applied by managers to plan, control, organize, staff, and direct their software activities and personnel more effectively.

I believe that the application of these principles and those contained in the readings will help managers avoid adhering to the last principle:[14]

Principle 18: The Peter Principle of Software Management. Managers rise to their level of incompetence and then are transferred to head a software development project.

References

1. Dennis W. Fife, *Computer Software Management: A Primer for Project Management and Quality Control*, US Department of Commerce, National Bureau of Standards, NBS Special Publication 500-11, July 1977.

2. Personal conversations with many corporate executives in banking; insurance and aerospace industries.

3. General Accounting Office, *Problems Found With Government Acquisition and Use of Computers from November 1965 to December 1976*, Report to the Congress, FGMSD-77-14, Mar. 15, 1977.

4. National Academy of Sciences, *Operational Software Management and Development for US Air Force Computer Systems*, 1977.

5. Frederick P. Brooks, *The Mythical Man-Month; Essays in Software Engineering*, Addison-Wesley, 1975.

6. George A. Steiner, *Top Management Planning*, The MacMillian Company, NY, 1969.

7. Harold Koontz and Cyril O'Donnell, *Principles of Management: An Analysis of Managerial Functions*, McGraw-Hill, NY, 1972.

8. Peter F. Drucker, *Management: Tasks, Responsibilities, Practices*, Harper and Row, NY, 1974.

9. B. S. Barry and J. J. Naughton, *Chief Programmer Team Operations Description*, RADC-TR-74-300, Vol. X, 1975.

10. F. Hertzberg, B. Mausner and B. B. Snyderman, *The Motivation of Work*, John Wiley & Sons, NY, 1959.

11. Douglas McGregor, *The Human Side of Enterprise*, McGraw-Hill, NY, 1960.

12. Bertram N. Abramson and Robert D. Kennedy, *Managing Small Projects*, TRW Report TRW-SS-69-02, Jan. 1969.

13. Barry W. Boehm, *Software Engineering*, TRW Report TRW-SS-76-08, Oct. 1976.

14. Donald J. Reifer, *Scientific Principles of Software Engineering*, Aerospace Corporation White Paper, 1975.

Cyrus F. Gibson and Richard L. Nolan

Managing the four stages of EDP growth

Running a new business is a different task
from running a middle-aged one or an old one;
the same is true of the EDP department

In all that has been said about the computer in business, there are few clues as to how the EDP department ought to grow or what management ought to be doing about the department at each stage of its growth. Here is a convenient categorization for placing the life crises of the EDP department in perspective, for developing the management techniques necessary or useful at various points, and for managing the human issues involved. These human issues, as a matter of fact, complicate the problems of growth at least as much as the hardware and software questions, which have been so well massaged in the literature; the authors show how these issues change shape as a company moves through the four stages of development. This article will be particularly helpful to the new

business that is about to buy its first computer. For the company in the throes of later-stage development, it offers a framework useful for identifying issues and evaluating and controlling the growth of EDP.

Mr. Gibson is assistant professor of business administration at the Harvard Business School, where he teaches in the organizational behavior area. He has done research and consulted extensively on problems of computer-resource management within organizations. Mr. Nolan is associate professor of business administration at the Harvard Business School and the author or coauthor of several recent HBR articles on information management. The work on which the following article is based was funded in part by the Division of Research of the school.

From the viewpoint of the executive vice president, "The EDP manager always waffles around when he has to explain his budget." From the viewpoint of the EDP manager, "The executive vice president never seems to understand why this department needs a lot of money."

The reason for this kind of impasse is clear enough: EDP, as corporations use it today, is so complex that controlling it, or even understanding it, is almost too difficult for words. However, through our work with a number of companies, we have reached certain conclusions about how EDP departments grow and how they should fit into the company's organization. These conclu-

sions offer a framework for communication for both the EDP manager and the senior managers to whom he reports.

There are four distinct stages in the growth of all EDP facilities, each with its distinctive applications, its rewards and its traumata, and its managerial problems. By breaking the evolution of the EDP department into four easy stages, it is possible to sort out the affairs of the department, if not into four neat, sequential packages, at least into four relatively small, sequential cans of worms.

The basis for this framework of stages is the recent discovery that the EDP budget for a num-

Exhibit I. Growth of applications

Stage 1 Cost-reduction accounting applications	**Stage 2** Proliferation of applications in all functional areas	**Stage 3** Moratorium on new applications; emphasis on control	**Stage 4** Data-base applications
Payroll	Cash flow	Purchasing control	Simulation models
Accounts receivable	General ledger	Scheduling	Financial planning models
Accounts payable	Budgeting		On-line personnel query system
Billing	Capital budgeting		On-line customer query system
	Forecasting		On-line source data entry (e.g., cost collection, order entry)
	Personnel inventory		
	Order processing		
	Sales		
	Inventory control		

ber of companies, when plotted over time from initial investment to mature operation, forms an S-shaped curve.[1] This is the curve that appears in the exhibits accompanying this article. The turnings of this curve correspond to the main events—often crises—in the life of the EDP function that signal important shifts in the way the computer resource is used and managed. There are three such turnings, and, consequently, four stages.

In the companies we know, there are remarkable similarities in the problems which arise and the management techniques applied to solve them at a given stage, despite variations among industries and companies, and despite ways in which EDP installations are used. Moreover, associated with each stage is a distinctive, informal organizational process. Each of these seems to play an important role in giving rise to the issues which need to be resolved if the stage is to be passed without a crisis and if the growth of the resource is to be managed to yield maximum benefit to the company.

Our purpose here is to describe the four stages in turn, listing the key characteristics of each

1. Richard L. Nolan, "Managing the Computer Resource: A Stage Hypothesis," *Communications of the ACM*, July 1973, p. 399.

and explaining the underlying organizational forces at work in each.

In the space of an article we can touch only on the main problems of EDP management at the different stages. Hence the view we present is bound to be somewhat simplified. Caution is advisable in another respect, too: history has not yet come to an end, and we are sure that the S-curve we describe and the stages it seems to follow do not represent the whole story. At the end of the S-curve of contemporary experience there will doubtless be more S-curves, as new EDP technologies emerge, and as companies become more ambitious in their use of EDP techniques and more sophisticated in systems analysis. However, we hope that the dynamics of later cost escalations will be clearer after the reader has finished with our description—clearer, and perhaps even predictable and controllable.

Four stages of growth

Three types of growth must be dealt with as an EDP department matures:

○ A growth in computer applications—see *Exhibit I.*

Exhibit II. Growth of personnel specialization

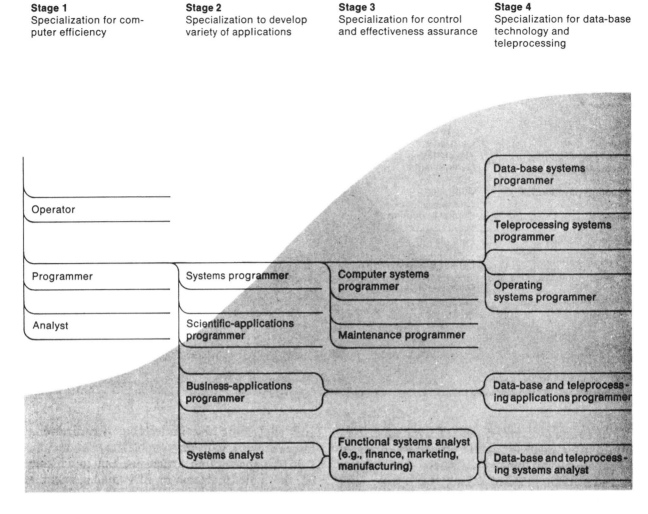

Stage 1	Stage 2	Stage 3	Stage 4
Specialization for computer efficiency	Specialization to develop variety of applications	Specialization for control and effectiveness assurance	Specialization for data-base technology and teleprocessing

○ A growth in the specialization of EDP personnel—see *Exhibit II*.

○ A growth in formal management techniques and organization—see *Exhibit III*.

The S-curve that overlies these three kinds of growth breaks conveniently into four segments, which represent the four stages of EDP growth: initiation, expansion, formalization, and maturity. Most notable are the proliferation of applications in Stage 2 (as reflected in *Exhibit I*) that causes the budget to increase exponentially, and the proliferation of controls in Stage 3 designed to curb this increase (as reflected in *Exhibit III*).

This sequence of stages is a useful framework for placing a company's current problems vis-à-vis EDP in perspective and helping its management understand the problems it will face as it moves forward. It is especially helpful for discussing ways to smooth out the chaotic conditions of change that have caused so many de-

railments in Stages 2 and 3. Even in our work with small companies, we have found the framework helpful—in obviating crises before they arise and in suggesting the kinds of planning that will induce smooth growth.

Thus one virtue of this framework is that it lays out for the company as a whole the nature of its task at each stage—whether it is a new company planning to buy its first computer, or a company in the throes of developing advanced applications, or a company with a steady, mature EDP facility.

Stage 1: Initiation

When the first computer is implanted in the organization, the move is normally justified in terms of cost savings. Rarely, at this point, does senior management assess the long-term impact of the computer on personnel, or on the organiza-

Exhibit III. Management techniques customarily applied in each of the four stages

	Stage 1 Lax management	Stage 2 Sales-oriented management	Stage 3 Control-oriented management	Stage 4 Resource-oriented planning and control
Organization	EDP is organized under the department of first-applications justification; it is generally a small department.	The EDP manager is moved up in the organization; systems analysts and programmers are assigned to work in the various functional areas.	EDP moves out of the functional area of first applications; a steering committee is set up; control is exerted through centralization; maintenance programming and systems programming become dominant activities.	EDP is set up as a separate functional area, the EDP manager taking on a higher-level position; some systems analysts and sometimes programmers are decentralized to user areas; high specialization appears in computer configuration and operation; systems design and programming take on a consulting role.
	Controls notably lacking; priorities assigned by FIFO; no chargeout.	Lax controls, intended to engender applications development; few standards, informal project control.	Proliferation of controls to contain a runaway budget; formal priority setting; budget justification. Programming controls: documentation, standards. Project management initiated; management reporting system introduced: project plan, project performance, customer service, personnel resources, equipment resources, budget performance. Chargeout introduced; postsystem audits. Quality control policies for computer system, systems design, programming, operations.	Refinement of management control system – elimination of ineffective control techniques and further development of others; introduction of data-base policies and standards; focus on pricing of computer services for engendering effective use of the computer.
	Loose budget	Loose budget	Strong budgetary planning for hardware facilities and new applications.	Multiple 3-5 year plans for hardware, facilities, personnel, and new applications.

tion, or on its strategy. Thus management can easily ignore a couple of crucial issues.

The location question

In Stage 1, the priority management issue is to fix departmental responsibility for the computer:

▽ Initially it makes economic sense to locate the computer in the department where it is first applied—very frequently, in accounting—and to hold that department responsible for a smooth introduction and a sound control of costs and benefits. The costs and benefits can be clearly stated and rigidly controlled under this approach —and they usually are.

△ However, the department where the computer will first be used—accounting, say—may not be the best location for the EDP facility later on. The later and more complex applications, such as inventory control and simulation modeling, should ideally be located in an autonomous department of computer services or management information systems which reports through a high-level manager.

But granted this longer perspective, management may decide on a less rigorous application of payback criteria for judging the performance of the initial application. Costs for "future development" may not be scrutinized too closely at this stage, and budgets may expand very early under this arrangement.

Many companies resolve this issue in obvious fashion. Management simply locates the facility within the department of first application for an initial period; then, when its viability has been proved and other applications develop, management creates the autonomous EDP unit.

In practice, however, this seemingly simple resolution conceals a serious trap. The department that controls the resource becomes strongly protective of it, often because a manager or a group within it wants to build up power and influence. When the time comes for computing to assume a broader role, real conflict arises—conflict that can be costly in terms of management turnover and in terms of lingering hostilities that inhibit the provision of computer services and applications across functional areas.

Fear of the computer

Another priority issue is to minimize the disruption that results when high technology is injected into an organization. Job-displacement anxieties appear; some people become concerned over doing old jobs in new ways; and others fear a loss of personal identity with their work. These fears may lead to open employee resistance. While reactions of this kind may occur at any of the stages, they can be particularly destructive in Stage 1, where the very survival of the EDP concept is at stake.

In plain fact some of these fears are probably justified. For example, some employees (although usually relatively few) may indeed lose their jobs when the computer is first installed.

On the other hand, the concerns that develop from rumor or false information are usually overblown, and they are readily transformed and generalized into negative sentiments and attitudes toward management, as well as the computer itself. The wise course for management is to spike rumors with the most honest information it has, however the chips may fall. Such

openness will at worst localize fears and resistances that must be dealt with sooner or later anyway.

Unless management is willing to recognize the seriousness of this anxiety, it risks a more generalized reaction in the form of unresponsive and uncreative work behavior, a broader and higher level of uncertainty and anxiety, and even sabotage, as a surprising number of cases have demonstrated.

Management can make no bigger mistake than to falsely reassure all concerned that the computer will not change their work or that it will mean no less work for everyone. Such comfort blankets lead to credibility gaps that are notoriously hard to close.

Thus the key to managing this process of initiation to the computer is to accept the fact that people's perceptions of reality and their views of the situation are what have to be understood and dealt with, rather than some "objective" reality.[2] These perceptions will be diverse; management cannot assume that all organizational members are equally enthusiastic about introducing efficiency and reducing costs. Where you stand depends on where you sit and on who you are. In communicating its intention to introduce EDP, management should remember this and tailor its communications accordingly.

There will be variations from one situation and company to another in the manner and detail in which management releases information about future location and about the impact of the computer. Depending on circumstance, management directives may best be communicated downward by an outsider, by a department head, or by the new EDP manager. In settings where employees are rarely informed of management planning, it may even be wise to explain to the echelons why they are being given the explanation; again, in settings where the echelons have participated in planning, a formal presentation may be less effective than open group discussion.[3]

Stage 2: Expansion

The excess computing capacity usually acquired when a company first initiates an EDP facility, combined with the lure of broader and more advanced applications, triggers a period of rapid expansion. The EDP area "takes off" into new projects that, when listed, often seem to have been selected at random. As *Exhibits I-III* show,

2. For a related argument, see James G. March and Herbert A. Simon, *Organizations* (New York, John Wiley, 1958), Chapter 6.

3. For further discussion of this point, see Paul R. Lawrence, "How to Deal With Resistance to Change," HBR January-February 1969, p. 4.

Stage 2 represents a steady and steep rise in expenditures for hardware, software, and personnel. It is a period of contagious, unplanned growth, characterized by growing responsibilities for the EDP director, loose (usually decentralized) organization of the EDP facility, and few explicit means of setting project priorities or crystallizing plans.

It is a period, further, in which the chaotic effects of rapid development are moderated (if they are moderated at all) only by the quality and judgment of the personnel directly involved in the process. While top management may be sensitive to some of the ill effects of the computer, it tends to be attracted to and carried along with the mystique of EDP as well.

This stage often ends in crisis when top management becomes aware of the explosive growth of the activity, and its budget, and decides to rationalize and coordinate the entire organization's EDP effort. The dynamic force of expansion makes this a fairly difficult thing to do, however.

Dynamics of early success

Once Stage 1 has passed, and the management and personnel of the computer area have justified and assured their permanent place in the organization, a new psychological atmosphere appears as the users from other departments (the customers) grow in number and begin to interact with the technical EDP staff. Although some users stick to economic value in judging the utility of computer applications to their particular problems and functions, other users develop a fascination with the computer and its applications as a symbol of progressive management techniques or as a status symbol for a department or individual. This fascination breeds an enthusiasm not moderated by judgment.

For their part, the technically oriented systems analysts tend to overgeneralize from the successes they have achieved with transaction-oriented computer-based systems (e.g., order processing, payroll, accounts receivable) in Stage 2. They often feel that "now we can do anything"—in other words, that they have mastered problems of communication with users, that their expertise is solid, and that they are ready to select and deal with projects primarily on the basis of their technical and professional interest. In this heady atmosphere, criteria of economic justification and effective project implementation take a back seat.

When the users' exploding demands meet the technicians' euphoric urge to supply, in the absence of management constraint, exponential budget growth results. Overoptimism and overconfidence lead to cost overruns. And once this sharp growth has begun, rationales created in the mood of reinforced enthusiasm are used to justify the installation of additional capacity; this in turn provides the need for larger numbers of personnel and for more rationales for applying the now expanded resource to whatever new projects seem attractive to the crowd. So the spiral begins.

The spiral is fed by the fact that as the resource increases in size and ambition, it must have more specialists.[4] Indeed, even without this capacity expansion, the continuing pace of technological development in the computer industry creates a constant need for new specialist talent, especially in Stage 2 and beyond. This "technological imperative" is a driving force that has caused the growth of numerous and quite diverse professional groups of computer personnel in the industrial environment. (The reader might find it helpful to review *Exhibit II* at this point.)

Many of these personnel come into the company with a primarily professional orientation, rather than an understanding of or sympathy for the long-term needs of an organization. Like the EDP specialists already employed by the company, these people will be far more interested in tackling technically challenging problems than in worrying about computer payback. If they are allowed to pursue their interests at will, the projects potentially most valuable from the company's viewpoint may never be worked on. Moreover, the chores of program maintenance and data-base development may be neglected, sowing the seeds of costly future problems.[5]

All these factors together lead to the evolution of an informal structure among computer personnel and between computer personnel and users. The lack of clear management guidelines for project priorities, for example, often results in sympathetic wheeling and dealing between EDP systems analysts and the user groups with a preference for those projects which offer the greatest professional challenge. Without specific directives for project developments or new hardware acquisition, too, computer personnel develop expectations of a loose work environment.

4. John Dearden, "MIS Is a Mirage," HBR January-February 1972, p. 90.

5. Richard L. Nolan, "Computer Data Bases: The Future Is Now," HBR September-October 1973, p. 98.

Some of the users, at the other end of the string, are easily enmeshed in impractical, pie-in-the-sky projects.

For short periods such an environment may be highly motivating for some, but, as we need hardly point out again, the other side of the coin is a rapidly growing budget—and a number of vocal and dissatisfied users.

In view of these informal dynamics and structures, what can management do to make this period one of controlled growth? How can control be introduced that will head off the impending crisis and dramatic cutbacks characteristic of such situations but at the same time not choke off experimentation with the resource and not turn off the motivation of specialists?

Here it is useful to compare the lists of management techniques shown for Stages 2 and 3 in *Exhibit III*. For the most part, the problems that arise toward the end of Stage 2 can be greatly alleviated by introducing right at the start of Stage 2 the techniques that companies ordinarily use in Stage 3.[6] Before carrying out this step, however, attention should be given to two other important strategies: acquiring necessary middle-management skills and improving the company's procedures for hiring computer personnel.

Acquiring managers

The main key to successful management in this stage is acquiring or developing middle managers for EDP who recognize the need for priorities and criteria in project selection and who have strong administrative skills: the ability to prepare plans and stick to budgets, the ability to seek out significant projects from users who may not be demanding attention, and, generally, the ability to manage projects.

Finding such managers more often than not means going outside the company, especially since most potential middle managers among systems analysts are usually caught up in the computer growth spiral. However, where it is possible, selection from within, particularly from the ranks of systems analysts, can serve the important function of indicating that career paths exist to management ranks. This can show computer technicians and technical experts that there are career rewards for those who balance organizational needs with professional interests.

6. For an approach to introducing these steps in either Stage 2 or Stage 3, see F. Warren McFarlan, "Management Audit of the EDP Department," HBR May-June 1973, p. 131.

Once those at the general-management level have determined that the time has come to institute such "human controls," the EDP manager must be brought to recognize the need for them (if, indeed, he does not recognize that need already) and the fact that he has the countenance and support of top management.

For his part, the EDP manager himself must resist the tempting pressures to see his resource grow faster than is reasonable. He has a delicate and important selling job to do in communicating this to other department managers who want his services. Once he is shored up with competent subordinate managers he will be free to carry out this role.

Finally, in addition to applying administrative controls, management needs to assess continually the climate of the informal forces at work and plan growth with that assessment in mind. The formal organization of middle managers in the EDP department makes such planning, and its implementation, viable.

Acquiring diverse personnel

Senior management must also recognize the increasing specialization of personnel within the computer department:

☐ At one extreme are the highly skilled and creative professionals, such as computer systems programmers. Their motivation and interest are oriented to the technology with which they work; they have relatively little interest in organizational rewards. Their satisfaction and best performance may be assured by isolating them organizationally, to some degree.

☐ At the other extreme are the analysts who work closely with functional departments of the company. These people may be expert in particular fields relevant to only a few industries or companies, performing tasks that require close interaction with both users and programmers. Their interests and value to the company can coincide when they perceive that career-path opportunities into general management are open to them.

☐ There are also the operators with important but relatively low-level skills and training, with some capabilities for organizational advancement, and with relatively little direct interdependence with others.

To organize and control these diverse specialists requires decisions based on one basic trade-off: *balancing professional advancement of special-*

ists against the need for organizational performance.

To cater to specialist professionals, for example, a company might isolate them in a separate department, imposing few organizational checks and gearing quality control to individual judgment or peer review. Such an arrangement might motivate a systems analyst to become the world's best systems analyst.

Emphasis on organizational values, in contrast, suggests that the company locate and control the specialists in such a way as to increase the chances that short-run goals will actually be achieved on schedule. This strategy risks obsolescence or turnover among specialists, but it successfully conveys the important message that some specialists' skills can advance a management career.

However, in the early stages management is well advised to avoid the issue entirely: the highly sophisticated professional should not be hired until his expertise is clearly required. Moreover, at the time of hiring, the specialist's expectations for freedom and professional development should be explicitly discussed in the context of organizational structure and controls (these controls include those administered by the middle level of EDP management), as part of the "psychological contract." [7]

Such discussion can go a long way toward avoiding misunderstanding during the period of rapid growth of computer applications. In effect, making clear the terms of the psychological contract is an example of the management of expectations. In this instance, it is one of the means that can be employed to introduce the organization, controls, and planning procedures that are needed to head off the crisis atmosphere of Stage 3.

Stage 3: Formalization

Let us assume that Stages 1 and 2 have run their bumpy courses without too much direct attention from top management. More likely than not, top management becomes aware of the runaway computer budget suddenly, and it begins a crash effort to find out what is going on. Its typical question at this point is, "How can we be sure that we can afford this EDP effort?"

Top management frequently concludes that the only way to get control of the resource is through drastic measures, even if this means replacing many systems analysts and other valuable technical personnel who will choose to leave rather than work under the stringent controls that are imposed during the stage. Firing the old EDP manager is by no means an unusual step. [8]

From the perspective of computer personnel who have lived through the periods of initial acceptance and growth, but who have not developed a sense of the fit of the computer resource within company functions and objectives, the changes top management introduces at this time may seem radical indeed. Often what was a decentralized function and facility is rather suddenly centralized for better control. Often informal planning suddenly gives way to formal planning, perhaps arbitrarily. This stage frequently includes the first formalization of management reporting systems for computer operation, a new chargeout system, and the establishment of elaborate and cumbrous quality-control measures (again, see *Exhibit III*).

In short, action taken to deal with the crisis often goes beyond what is needed, and the pendulum may swing too far. In response, some computer personnel may leave. What may be worse, most will "hunker down"—withdrawing from innovative applications work, attending to short-term goals, and following the new control systems and plans to the letter. All of this can occur at the expense of full resource utilization in the long run.

In addition, there is a parallel development that dovetails with the budget crisis to reinforce the overcontrol syndrome. Studies of computer usage show that the machines are first applied to projects that reduce general and administrative expenses—typically, replacement of clerical personnel in such tasks as accounting. Next come projects that reduce cost of goods, such as inventory control systems. The crisis atmosphere of Stage 3 roughly coincides with completion of these first two types of applications.

At this juncture the applications that have real potential for increasing revenues and profits and facilitating managerial decision making are still untouched. Financial-planning models and on-line customer service systems are two examples of such applications.

As senior management ponders the problems of Stage 3, it tends to associate the applications of the earlier stages with preexisting manu-

7. Harry Levinson et al., *Men, Management and Mental Health* (Cambridge, Harvard University Press, 1962).

8. See Richard L. Nolan, "Plight of the EDP Manager," HBR May-June 1973, p. 143.

al systems and straightforward cost-justification and control. In contrast, it finds projected applications for revenue-producing and decision-making projects hard to envision and define. The natural tendency is to assume that these projects will call for a faster, higher spiral of risk and cost. Thus senior management tends to introduce inappropriately strong controls that are designed, consciously or unconsciously, to put a stop to growth. This clearly may be too strong a reaction for the company's good.

Three sound steps

In general, three control steps that are appropriate and not unduly restrictive are available for most large EDP facilities in Stage 3. First, certain of the more established and less complex operations and hardware can be centralized. Second, the increasing impacts of computer applications can be flagged and defined for the top by introducing overseer and resource-allocation mechanisms at the general-management level. Third, some parts of the systems analysis function can be decentralized and other parts centralized, depending on where the systems work can best be done (we shall say more about this shortly).[9] Of course, this final step requires that the decentralized systems work be coordinated through a formal integrative mechanism.

But the real problem in Stage 3 is not what steps to take; it is how to take them. Management here is introducing change into a web of informal relationships and expectations. *How the changes are managed is as important as what the changes should be*, but more difficult to define.

That is, although there are few formal controls in the first two stages, the *informal* social structures and norms that have grown up by Stage 3 are very much a reality to the personnel involved. While it may appear that systems are replacing no systems, this will not be true:

◇ Lacking guidelines for project selection, systems analysts will have projected their own sets of priorities, either individually, as a group within the company, or as members of their profession.

◇ They will have created criteria and standards, although these will not ordinarily have

been written down or otherwise articulated for higher levels of management.

◇ Without project management guidelines, systems analysts and users will have developed their own rules and procedures for dealing with each other.

On the whole, the stronger these informal controls and structures are (and the weaker the formal controls and structures are, the stronger they will be), the more resistant the personnel will be to change and the more chaotic and traumatic the introduction of formal systems will be.

In managing changes as pervasive as these there is probably nothing worse than doing the job halfway. Doing nothing at all is disaster, of course; but management action that is undertaken on a crash basis—without enough attention to execution and second- and third-order consequences—will sharpen, not resolve, the crisis.

For example, management cannot afford to be either squeamish or precipitous in making personnel changes. Trying to introduce needed formalization of controls with the same personnel and the same organizational structure more often than not encourages conflict and the reinforcement of resistance rather than a resolution of the crisis; by refusing to fire or to enforce layoffs, senior management may simply prolong the crisis, create further dissension, and further demoralize personnel. On the other hand, management must be sure that it retains the experienced personnel who have the potential to function well in the mature stages of the operation—it may not always be obvious who these people are or what their future roles will be.

Thus, although the crisis of Stage 3 calls for action, it first calls for analysis and planning—planning that sets forth clear and explicit objectives for exploitation of the computer resource vis-à-vis the user departments.[10] Such a plan, once it is developed and understood, can turn anarchy back into evolution, while at the same time avoiding the kind of overkill control that results in underutilization and underrealization of the potential of the resource. Here are our suggestions for general plan direction.

1. Reposition the established components of the resource.

Whether or not EDP has been carefully managed in the past, most companies need to centralize some parts and decentralize other parts of the computer resource at about this point.

9. See the section which discusses the McKinsey study on effective users, in F. Warren McFarlan, "Problems in Planning the Information System," HBR March-April 1971, p. 78.

10. For mechanisms for improving the interface between EDP and users, see John Dearden and Richard L. Nolan, "How to Control the Computer Resource," HBR November-December 1973, p. 68.

The issue arises here because the company reaches a turning point in the way it uses the resource. As the EDP function evolves from the early cost-reduction applications of initiation and early growth toward projects aimed at improving operations, revenues, and the quality of unprogrammed and strategic decisions, the influence of the computer will begin to move up and spread out through the organization. The function may truly be called "MIS" instead of "EDP" from this stage forward.

We have already discussed the need for middle managers' involvement in this stage or an earlier stage. The internal structure they represent reinforces the desirability of making the MIS department autonomous and having it report to a senior level of management. At this point, also, it becomes imperative to reexamine and make explicit the rationales for existing applications that have proved beneficial and to routinize them, so that expensive specialist skills can be turned to new applications.

The pressures of new applications ventures, maturing management, specialist personnel, and increasing routine make centralization of the company's core hardware resources just about mandatory at this stage. Too, the centralization eases the tasks of maintenance of data and programs, data-base development, and some of the applications that will be coming up in Stage 4.

The very creation of a central "MIS division," however, creates additional problems.

2. Provide for top-management direction.

While centralization goes a long way toward placing the longer lead times, the greater complexity, and the higher development costs of new applications in perspective, it does not automatically help senior management to control the direction the resource takes.

Effective control derives from understanding, and some device is needed to educate senior management so that it can track and evaluate the department's progress sensibly. The device must also let the resource know what senior management's policies are and what is expected of it operationally and strategically.

This communications device becomes vital in Stage 3 because the resource has grown to a size and a power whereby its applications can affect the strategy and structure of the company as a whole. In a company where a working data base can be used to back up the corporate planning process, for example, corporate planning assumes a somewhat different shape from what it does

in a company that has no such data base available. This is clearly a point at which a person at the vice-presidential level (or even the presidential level) must accept responsibility for directing the evolution of the resource.

An active, high-level steering committee is one such device.[11] It provides a means for setting project priorities. It not only brings together those who should be concerned with overall management and planning for the company; it also provides a vehicle for confronting and resolving the political problems that inevitably arise with the computer's more direct impact on managers' roles, organizational structure, and resource allocation in Stage 3.

For, from a behavioral perspective, political issues dominate at this time as never before. Managers throughout the company now see that the applications coming through the pipeline may affect their own roles directly. In the past it was their subordinates who were most affected, and it was largely their own decision to approve or not approve a project; but now a given application may be supported from above and may impinge on their established patterns of work, their decision making, and even their ideas about what it is they do for a living.

Moreover, the prospect of applications that hint at long-term changes in organizational structures and formal departmental roles raises concern within both formal and informal groups of managers—concern about the impacts these changes will have on the strengths of their positions relative to other groups.

Such political issues can only be debated fruitfully before top management, and an expert, informed steering committee provides a convenient forum for this debate.

For his part, as a member of this committee as well as the head of his own department, the MIS manager should expect to assume a stronger role in general management councils. He should not, of course, expect to be exclusively responsible for setting priorities among projects that would benefit different groups, or for implementing significant changes completely under his own initiative.

3. Reorganize the systems analysis function.

Centralization, and tight guidelines and arbitration from a steering committee, however, can create a distance between the resource and its customers throughout the company. As Stage 3

11. F. Warren McFarlan, "Problems in Planning the Information System," HBR March-April 1971, p. 75.

draws to a close, the company will be planning its most important, most ambitious MIS applications to date. This is hardly a point at which to divorce the users from the resource by erecting an impenetrable divisional barrier. Complete centralization of the systems analysis function would constitute such a barrier.

In fact, gearing up for this new era of applications and controlling their impacts requires that the company revise the Stage 3 concept, staffing, and organization of the systems analysis function. The concept should change from systems analysts as developers of *products for* users to systems analysts as developers of *processes affecting* users. The distinction between product and process means, among other things, that the new applications should rarely be considered bounded projects; they will require continual modification as they are integrated into user decision making.

Therefore, systems analysts themselves will necessarily become more and more a constant element in the functioning of the users' areas. As a corollary, they will act as communications conduits between the users, on the one hand, and the computer resource and its programmers, on the other.

Organizationally, this suggests that some systems analysts should be decentralized to user locations while others are retained at the core to build a research and testing facility for the company and its planners. Thus the problem boils down to a trade-off between centralization and decentralization of systems analysts.

These, then, are our best suggestions for minimizing the strains of Stage 3: centralize certain components of the resource, install a steering committee or some equivalent thereof, and spread enough of the systems analysts through the company to ensure that users' needs are met adequately. For the company wise enough to employ these suggestions at the outset of Stage 2, the trauma of Stage 3 may be almost entirely avoidable.

Stage 4: Maturity

When the dust has settled over the changes of Stage 3, the computer resource will have reached maturity in the organization, and it will have the potential to return continuing economic benefits. The applications listed for Stage 4 in *Exhibit I* suggest how very significant the con-

tributions of the resource can be, if only they can be achieved.

The manager's dilemma

At this point the MIS manager has broken into the ranks of senior management, having risen to the level of vice president or equivalent thereof. In some instances he may even enjoy more than proportional support from the president for his view of his own function within the company. He faces this integrative dilemma:

▽ On the one hand, he is under pressure to maintain a steady work environment within his own unit. His line managers and specialists are now familiar with relatively formal structure and procedures; they are presumably satisfied with their career prospects, either within their professions or within the company. Thus they may well constitute a force resisting dramatic change, reorganization, or innovation. Similarly, at this point, senior management and the users probably have a general grasp of the existing technology and existing applications of the resource, and they are reluctant to see major changes.

△ On the other hand, the MIS manager, if he is doing his job well, will be heavily involved in planning for the future. He will be aware that computer technology and modes of application and organization are continuing to change.

Thus, if he chooses to maintain stability, he knowingly runs the risk that his resource will become outdated and inefficient. If he chooses to keep up with technology, he knowingly runs the risk that he will lose the integrative fabric that makes his function applicable to the user groups and the company as a whole.

The MIS manager must strike a balance between protecting an organizational entity and keeping that entity up to date in its technical environment. He has power and credibility, but he sees that these can be threatened either by too little change or by too much change.

There are no hard and fast rules for resolving this trade-off. The key, however, lies in the quality of communications between the MIS manager and top management, and between the MIS department and users.

Communications with the boss

By definition, the mature Stage 4 function is one which is being applied to the key tasks of the organization. This may well mean that most of the funding for MIS development is devoted to applications touching directly on critical business operations. This is the case of a large petrochemical firm with which we are familiar, where new applications focus on synthetic-fiber production activities.

But whether applications are for line operations or for management decision making, the computer manager in Stage 4 is, perhaps for the first time, in a position to communicate with top management in terms of meaningful, detailed plans.[12]

Because of the nature of his dilemma, he is bound to come under fire from the users—either for allowing parts of his department to obsolesce, in the name of stability, or for introducing change, in the name of progress and the state of the art. His relationship and communications with the top must be sound enough to allow him to weather the inevitable storms—given, of course, that the balance he strikes between stability and change is indeed reasonable in broad outline.

The experience of many suggests that the MIS manager and senior management think in terms of a three-year contract for the position, with explicit recognition that there will be organizational pressures to push out the MIS manager.

With long-term support from the top founded in such a basis, the MIS manager is in a position to legislate policies internally that will exploit the computer as fully as possible.

For his part, the senior line manager to whom a mature EDP department reports can little afford not to know the language of the computer personnel—at least to the extent necessary to evaluate project proposals.

Relations with users

In Stage 4, the MIS manager must also move to strengthen the bridges that have developed between the users and computer personnel. Assuming that it is well managed internally, the computer resource still has a continuing extensive interdependence with departments it serves.

The first difficulty here is that the users are many and the MIS manager only one. He cannot hope for identical relationships with all departments.

Secondly, users naturally tend to co-opt computer personnel into their organizational spheres. If this occurs to any significant extent, user parochialisms will erode the potential for the computer unit to act as an agent for innovation and change.

However, the bridges can be strengthened and the innovative capability of the unit can be increased simultaneously through a policy of "buffering" the different subunits from user influence. Specifically, performance standards and short-term control devices should be formalized for the more routine tasks (such as all machine operations and some programming) and the MIS personnel involved with these should be removed from frequent interaction with the users. A system of project management, too, serves much the same function.

Finally, the systems analysis function at the core should by this time have taken on the character of an influential research unit, controlled primarily through checks on the progress of its projects. These projects will probably not be within the direct purview of the user groups; in a mature department, they are usually focused on long-term applications not likely to be demanded spontaneously by user groups or by the systems analysts decentralized into those groups (e.g., corporate inventory control). The weight of this core group of analysts can be used to counterbalance undue user influence.

For example, when a user needs a new application, the core group might rough it out and approve the final, detailed design; but the final, detailed design itself should be the work of the systems analysts located in the user department. The decentralized analysts will be most familiar with the user's needs and best able to produce a working system for him; for their part, the systems analysts at the core can ensure that the system that is finally designed will mesh efficiently with the company's MIS efforts as a whole, to whatever extent this is possible.

The picture of EDP-user relationships that emerges here is one of considerable complexity and subtlety. Correspondingly, integrating this more specialized and internally differentiated EDP resource into the company as a whole becomes more difficult.[13] This integration requires that the MIS manager take steps to achieve common understanding of his objectives, not only with senior management but with all other functional managers at the vice-presidential level as well. The steering committee will be important as never before, not only as a committee for determining project priorities, but also as a

---

12. Ibid.

13. Paul R. Lawrence and Jay W. Lorsch, *Organization and Environment* (Boston, Division of Research, Harvard Business School, 1967).

sounding board for new techniques, policies, and changes within the MIS department itself.

Beyond Stage 4

Currently some large companies have reached the tail end of the S-shaped EDP budget curve: their departments are mature, in the sense defined by the exhibits. But has EDP evolution really come to an end for these companies? What can they expect in the future?

In retrospect, the curve seems to have been primarily driven by developments in hardware technology in the second- and third-generation computer systems. One thing certain is that computer technology advancements are continuing at an unrelenting pace. More S-shaped curves are inevitable.

Now, however, the advancements seem to be taking place more in software than in hardware; and at present the breakthrough most likely to start off another S-shaped EDP budget curve is the development of data-base technology. This development is providing a way to make the data collected and retained by the organization a companywide resource; and scores of middle management applications, such as computer modeling, appear to be on the way.

In the blush of enthusiasm for this newest advancement in computer technology, however, it is important to remember the painful lessons of the past. To efficiently exploit the newest technology, it must be managed. It must be reconciled with the capacity of the organization to assimilate new ways of doing business better. It is our belief that the forces underlying the crises and problems of the four stages we have described will also underlie future S-curves, such as one created by the emerging data-base technology. Consequently, management may be able to anticipate the problems and resolve them before they begin. A sign of success would be a dampening of the S-curve, with budgets rising more smoothly as future needs demand continuing investments and increasing budgets.

"Science is nothing but trained and organized common sense, differing from the latter only as a veteran may differ from a raw recruit: and its methods differ from those of common sense only as far as the guardsman's cut and thrust differ from the manner in which a savage wields his club."

Thomas Henry Huxley, 1825-1895
Collected Essays

SOFTWARE VISIBILITY
AND
THE PROGRAM MANAGER

by

Alan J. Driscoll, LtCol, USAF

Software and the Program Manager—What is software in the terms of a Program Manager? How can he manage software development in his program? The virtual explosion in the use of computer resources in modern weapon systems emphasizes the need for an understanding of computer software. Attempts to use inadequate software, lax software control, and the problems associated with software misuse, have been addressed repeatedly in current literature and speeches.

Software visibility is explained here by an Air Force author who tells how software problems affect costs, schedules, and performance; how to combat these problems; and, why software is of urgent importance to Program Managers.

PART I

INTRODUCTION

THE SITUATION

Software has meaning to a Program Manager only in terms of how it relates to his total program. Software, like hardware, is important in terms of cost, schedule, and performance, therefore it must be given the same type of management attention that is given hardware. Lack of this type of management attention has been all too evident. The result has been that problems in the early developmental phases—problems such as inadequate requirements definition and improper integration of hardware and software requirements have been aggravated—then magnified in later phases—by other problems such

as inadequate staffing and the inability to measure software development progress.

Affirmative action such as putting software at a high level in the Work Breakdown Structure and including software in the Systems Requirements Analysis (SRA) can alleviate many pervasive problems. None of the many actions required to avoid the problems can be accomplished without early, long-term planning.

To those professionally concerned with systems acquisition it is not surprising that there is a rising level of interest in software on the part of the government. This is especially true of the Department of Defense (DOD). The interest is due in part to the extremely high cost of software—regarded by many persons as being "merely" data. The key for any Program Manager in obtaining suitable software is to elevate software—remove it from the category of "data" and plan for its development on a level of importance with hardware.

Reprinted from *Defense Systems Management Review*, Volume 1, Number 2, Spring 1977.

SOFTWARE IMPORTANCE

For most weapon system development programs that incorporate both hardware and software, the computer software is a critical component relative to the overall operation of the system. (Mangold,[1] p 13). There are two reasons why the Program Manager should be concerned with the software of his system. First, software performance is critical to the success of his program. Second, his software will receive high-level attention. The need for an error-free computer program is obvious in the case of the guidance and control flight software for a missile such as the Minuteman Intercontinental Ballistic Missile (ICBM). Here a minor software error can cause inflight failure of a vehicle costing millions of dollars. An undetected flaw can seriously degrade the operational missile force. Although an error may not cause such spectacular results in many systems, schedule slips, rework, and degraded performance can escalate cost in a comparable manner.

The Need to Know

What does the Program Manager need to know and be concerned about regarding the software in his weapon system? Essentially, he needs to know the same basic things that he is required to know about his hardware. The basics are:

● Does the software meet performance requirements?
  ● Is the software within cost?
  ● Is the software on schedule?

In the "DOD Weapon Systems Software Management" study report prepared by Johns Hopkins University, it is stated that a lack of software visibility, when compared with that of hardware, contributed to the fact that software was not well managed.[2] The report also said that visibility could be increased by putting software on a par with hardware (Johns Hopkins,[2] p 2–4) and addressed ways of accomplishing this equality.

System Responsibility

This article is limited to software associated with embedded computer systems although some of the material presented may be applicable to general automatic data processing (ADP) systems. The research conducted was directed to systems that are under the purview of the Air Force 800 series regulations. Study was centered on the management of software from the viewpoint of a Program Manager who has responsibility for both hardware and software—the total system. *

Research and Governing Documents

Research for this article was conducted in three separate but related investigations. 1) The results of a search of current literature on problems that Program Managers encounter in software development, and potential solutions to those problems, are presented in Part II. 2) A review of applicable DOD Policy, Directives, and Regulations, is presented in Part III. In Part IV a summary and observations are presented.

SOFTWARE COSTS

Since the advent of the digital computer, the ratio of software costs to hardware (the computer and related peripheral equipment) costs have undergone enormous increase. This phenomenon is represented in Figure 1.

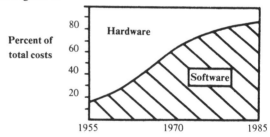

Figure 1.   Hardware/Software Trends
From *"Defense Management Journal,"*
Vol II(4):   24 (1975).

Similar charts have appeared in many publications and are commonly accepted as the conceptualization of increasing software costs. To Program Managers this situation raises the question: How can I get control of system software? How can I place emphasis upon software from where I stand?

---

* In this article software development activity is discussed only to the point when a completed computer program is ready for operational use. The operational, maintenance, and modification aspects of software are not discussed in any detail.

Relevance

The relevance of increasing software costs to Program Manager actions becomes clear when consideration is given the high number of weapon systems that contain computer systems. In an *Aviation Week* Conference Report, Jacques Gansler, Deputy Assistant Secretary of Defense for Materiel Acquisition, said that a Pentagon study "identified 115 different defense systems that employ "embedded computers" of which approximately one-half are now in service and the other half are under development." (Aviation Week,[3] p 43). Gansler is also quoted as saying "According to our estimate, the Pentagon is spending more than $3 billion annually for software for defense systems." (Aviation Week,[3] p 41). He went on to state that 68 percent of the amount is spent during system development and 32 percent is spent for operating and maintenance costs. Another estimator of software costs states that "Current annual expenditures for embedded computer systems exceed $2 billion, with more than 70 percent of this amount dedicated to software."[4]

This amount of money is obviously not a trivial sum, yet cost is only one facet of the software picture. The other side of the story is unsatisfactory software performance, or, more simply, its unreliability. Barry C. DeRoze, Directorate for Weapons Support Systems Acquisition, Office of the Assistant Secretary of Defense (Installations and Logistics), has said:

> "Although hardware reliability has improved substantially, the corresponding gains in system reliability have not been realized. This apparent contradiction arises because software unreliability— the failure of software to satisfy the stated operational requirements—has become the "tall-pole in the tent" in determining the reliability and operational readiness of systems." (DeRoze,[4] p 3).

Further indication of the high-level interest in software is expressed in the statements made by the Director of Defense Research and Engineering to the 94th Congress, Second Session, 1976:

> "The urgent need for reducing the costs of computer software was described in last year's Posture Statement. A DOD Directive resulting from a comprehensive study is currently being coordinated that will require the use of improved procedures in software acquisition. A DOD Software Management Steering Committee has been formally established to: (1) review DOD software technology programs, (2) recommend needed areas of research and emphasis, and (3) plan a balanced and coordinated software program."[5]

Management Visibility

Numerous studies have been made to ascertain how to improve the management of software. One of the foremost themes noted is the need for "management visibility" of software. For example, one of the four subelements of the main objective of the DOD Weapon Systems Software Management Program is "to promote management visibility."[6]

This then leads us back to the purpose of this article: To determine and report just what "software visibility" means to the Program Manager.

PART II
Software Management Ideas

THE PROCESS

To talk about software cost, schedule, and performance without covering the various steps in the software development process is almost impossible. It is difficult to separate cost, schedule, and performance, and it is very difficult to determine what the Program Manager should do to obtain visibility for each of these separate, yet closely related, factors. Here, the software development process is discussed along with the relation of cost, schedule, and performance visibility to each phase in the development process.

Definitions

The software development process has been defined by many people in many different ways. These steps range from the seven steps expressed by Eldon R. Mangold (Mangold,[1] p 2–8) to the three steps of Boyd Etheredge (Etheredge,[7] p 21).

Steps in the Process

The steps in the software development process as defined by Mangold:

1. System requirements
2. Software requirements
3. Preliminary design
4. Detailed design
5. Code and debug
6. Test and preoperations
7. Operation and maintenance

The steps in software development process as defined by Etheredge:

1. Analysis and design
2. Implementation and test
3. Delivery and maintenance

In writings about the cost of developing large-scale software programs, R. W. Wolverton discusses what he calls the 40–20–40 rule. (Wolverton, p 13). The rule was developed empirically and says that the total resources (cost) for software development will be split 40 percent for analysis and design, 20 percent for coding and debugging, and 40 percent for checkout and test. I have used a slight variation of these three phases that I label:

- *Analysis and Design.* This step includes the first four steps of Mangold's process.
- *Implementation.* This is the code and debug step of Mangold and Wolverton.
- *Verification.* A step essentially the same as the checkout and test step of Wolverton.

Various tools and ideas suggested by writers in government and industry as linking cost, schedule, and performance visibility throughout software development are examined here.

ANALYSIS AND DESIGN

Analysis and design begins with a definition of system requirements and progresses through the development process to software allocation to achieve complete design. The latter is a critical step that will affect the total development cycle. The criticality of establishing system requirements and software requirements is stressed by Winston W. Royce.

"...In our judgment the single most important cause of poor management of software projects is the inability to successfully accomplish these first two phases of requirements analysis." (Royce, p 1–13)

Royce goes on to say that without requirements analysis the *first* step in software development is design. This, of course, is a prelude to disaster. In actuality there are probably no projects where design is done without someone *thinking* they have defined the requirements. The real question then is: How do you know or ensure that the requirements have been defined in a proper manner? One step is to get the user involved. The ultimate requirements are his. Again quoting (Royce, p 1–21):

"...The user of the software must be capable of injecting his expertise into the software product..."

and

"...A complete, detailed, accurate set of performance and implementation requirements which has been fully coordinated with the user is the first step in ensuring compliance with operational requirements."

The Program Manager must ensure that his software people are involved in the total system engineering process, and interface directly with the user. Software requirements must be considered from the beginning by the user and developer in relation to all other system requirements. The Program Manager should have this in mind as the program progresses from a Required Operational Capability through the system specification to the computer program specifications. He should insist on the participation of the user in all design reviews.

Requirements must be defined early and with specificity. In the case of requirements that cannot be defined at the start, a schedule for such definition should be established and the software planned in accordance with the schedule. Too, the Program Manager should plan the development schedule to accommodate changing requirements. He should remember that software is affected by nearly every change in the weapon system design. (Bartlett,[10] p 6).

The latter statement suggests another point: the integration of hardware and software requirements. One aspect of this is the software/computer relationship. Obviously, the computer can have a big effect on the software, but the reverse effect may be even greater. The use of higher order languages is being promoted for development of defense software although the use of a higher order language is sometimes less efficient in terms of the required memory capacity and the speed of the computer. (Aviation Week,[3] p 41). The issue here for the Program Manager is to ensure that his systems engineering people plan for the fact that perhaps a larger, faster machine is required if the software cost, schedule, or performance (or all three) are not to be adversely affected. One recommendation of the DOD Weapon Systems Software Management Study, conducted by Johns Hopkins University, was to require that computer systems be sized to provide for uncertainties and requirement growth. As stated (Johns Hopkins,[2] p 6–22):

"...It is a basic feature of software that it can accommodate change provided it is not limited by hardware capacity or speed. Accordingly, an important part of software systems engineering is the judicious and controlled provision of growth capability."

Aside from the software-computer relationship, there is the larger relation of software to total system requirements. In *Government Executive*, August 1975, General Phillips, the Commander of the Air Force Systems Command was quoted as saying:

"We have come to the conclusion that we must engineer software in much the same way we engineer hardware...What all this boils down to is a full systems engineering approach to software development."

The process of applying system engineering to a requirements definition is often referred to as Systems Requirements Analysis. The effective use of Systems Requirements Analysis, particularly as it relates to software, is an area to be pursued by the Program Manager. (Bartlett,[10] p 14).

The effects of an adequate or inadequate requirements analysis or definition ripple through all phases of software development, including design. Changes in requirements cause changes in design and these in turn usually cause schedule changes. (Software changes continue throughout a project for a number of reasons including: requirements changes, hardware deficiency accommodation and new or modified interfaces. (TRW,[11] p 1–2)). Changes in schedule will, at a minimum, increase costs, and may preclude the meeting of all performance requirements. Ideally, every step should be completed prior to starting the next. According to Eldon R. Mangold:

"From a management standpoint, it is essential that the successive steps in the development process be restricted until the preliminary design is completed." (Mangold,[1] p 2–13).

In some programs, schedules have been so tight that coding was begun before an adequate analysis of program design could be performed. (TRW,[11] p 5–24). Again, the Program Manager must exert every effort to protect the program against the cost and schedule impacts of changes. Two areas where the Program Manager can accomplish this are, first, in planning and secondly, in configuration management.

"The planning of a computer program development is probably the source of fifty to seventy-five percent of all development problems. Planning does not have to be bad to lead to problems; but it must be exceptionally good to avoid them." (Bartlett,[10] p 10).

The above quote serves to emphasize the importance of planning. Planning pervades the entire development process. Substantive, early planning can assist in the avoidance of problems by providing schedule flexibility, and adequate computer size.

The application of configuration control to software is not new, but deserves top management attention because of its importance during build up of the architecture and logic as well as later. One of the problems with software management in the past has been that software was treated simply as data, not as a deliverable contract line item and thus did not get the same visibility as did hardware. The Johns Hopkins study recommended that major computer software involved in weapon systems development be designated, during full scale development, as configuration items and deliverables to include:

1) operational software;
2) development support software, and
3) test and integration software. (Johns Hopkins,[2] pp 2–5, 2–11).

The Air Force has taken steps to implement this recommendation.

Formal configuration management of software begins with the approval of the development specification that occurs about the time of preliminary design review. The preliminary design review also provides the first clear look at the software design and reflects the matching of the requirements to the design. Although the Program Manager cannot be expected to attend every design review in his program, he should stress the importance of these reviews to his software manager.

IMPLEMENTATION

Implementation is the step during which the design is converted to program code and debugged (or tested) to eliminate any errors that may exist (there will be errors). The analysis and design phase, although not easy to track, has some visible means of measuring progress that are similar to those for hardware (written requirements, flow charts, an analysis and design specification, etc.). The implementation phase poses different problems; it is difficult to find an appropriate way of determining status. Quoting (Johns Hopkins,[2] p 2–6):

"The abstract nature of software makes it difficult to measure progress and, hence, makes it even more necessary to formalize the steps in design, implementation, and test. The lack of such definition leads to difficulties in interface management and to the late discovery of inadequate requirements or design errors, with resulting slippages in schedules and increases in cost."

Problems

There are two basic problems involved here. One, it is the inclination of programmers to do the interesting work at the expense of dull work (documentation). Visible signs of programming progress are almost totally lacking. Another set of difficulties arises from the nature of the product. There are virtually no objective standards or measures by which to evaluate the progress of computer program development. (Wolverton,[*] p 1). Because of this situation we have what is known as the 90 percent syndrome. (Aviation Week,[3] p 42). This is expressed in Golub's Law #12 that says:

"...projects progress quickly until they are 90 percent complete, and then they remain 90 percent complete forever." (Grooby,[12] p 252).[*]

The Program Manager has several means at his disposal for tracking cost and schedule in any project. Among these are the Cost Performance Report (CPR) and, for smaller programs, the Cost/Schedule Status Report (C/SSR).[**] In the past these means have not been satisfactory for obtaining software visibility primarily because software was treated as "data" and/or was so low on the Work Breakdown Structure (WBS), if there at all, that it was never seen.

Milestones

The recommendation has been made that software be put in the WBS at a level equivalent to a hardware subsystem. (Borklund,[13] p 31, Johns Hopkins,[2] p 2–4). This would increase the visibility and understanding of software.

The question arises: "Is the CPR or C/SSR type information on software meaningful, even when available?" The CPR or C/SSR information will indicate whether the contractor is spending money at the rate he projected, but perhaps nothing about what actual progress has been achieved. If some set of measurable milestones is not established, progress

---

* This is one of "Golub's Laws of Computerdom," some humerous, but all too true expressions of what can go wrong in computer/software development.
** Discussed in detail in AFR 800–6 and AFSC Pamphlet 173–3.

will be measured in terms of time or dollars expended, that is, if 100 hours are estimated for a task and 100 hours have been expended then the task is complete.(Kreder [11] p 55). The estimating of cost and schedule for software (coding in particular) has been inaccurate and emphasizes the need for discrete milestones to evaluate progress. A series of design reviews (system, preliminary, critical) is at least a partial answer. In the Johns Hopkins report milestones are discussed and reference is made to MIL-STD-490, MIL-STD-483, and AFR 800–14, Vol II, noting that milestones are indicated in these documents but the work to be accomplished and the products that are to be delivered are not defined. The Johns Hopkins report did not reference MIL-STD-1521, a Standard that does define work and deliverables for design review and audits.

One approach to measurement has been proposed that I call the "all or nothing" system. In this system the project is broken into discrete tasks (for example, the coding of a module, component checkout, etc.) but attempts are not made to estimate or measure progress within the tasks. For any given task, progress is reported as either 0 percent (from start to almost finished) or 100 percent, the point at which the task is physically complete. This approach takes away the guesswork and eliminates the "90 percent syndrome." The Program Manager should be very careful about how much faith he places in the reports he receives (e.g., the CPR and C/SSR reports are only as valid as the estimates that go into them; and estimates for software have been notoriously inaccurate.)

VERIFICATION

Verification is the third of three phases that make up the software development process. Design is established in Phase One. Phase Two is the Implementation Phase where software is coded to satisfy the requirements, and Phase Three, the Verification Phase, determines whether or not Phase Two was successful in translating the requirements and design into a computer program that satisfies the operational needs of the user. Verification can take many forms, from a manual review of code to operational flight testing. One author describes verification as three interrelated functions. First is Code Verification, the process of determining whether the actual code is implemented in compliance with the computer program specifications. The second function is Validation, the process of testing the coded program against the specified design and performance criteria. The third function is Certification, where the testing process is extended to an operational (either real or simulated) environment. (Reifer, [15] p 22). Regardless of how the verification phase is defined, it is imperative that all requirements be tested against some measurable criteria. A requirement for which a feasible test does not exist or for which a test has not defined should not be allowed. (Bartlett, [10] p 6). The task for the customer (and therefore the Program Manager) is to ensure that all requirements can be tested.

Test Plans

To ensure that all requirements can be tested, consideration of the testing methods and criteria must be accomplished during requirements definition. The Program Manager must ensure software visibility in this process and emphasize its importance to his software people. The Program Manager will not be able to get directly involved at the lower levels of detail, but he can influence attention to software through insistence on thorough planning. Software test plans must be written to the same level of detail as the requirements in the development specifications. The test plans should require that each performance requirement of each computer program configuration end item be verified in some appropriate manner. Acceptance criteria should be specified. (Richards, [16] p 68).

Independent Verification

The discussion of software verification to this point has been restricted to that done by the developing contractor. An adjunct to verification by the developing contractor is the use of an independent verification contractor—an excellent means of providing software visibility for the Program Office and the Program Manager. (TRW, [11] p 5–9). This practice originated with a requirement for the independent check of software to insure nuclear safety and is becoming widespread. The practice, known as Independent Validation and Verification (IV&V), has been expanded to include software performance as well as nuclear safety criteria. When used properly, the IV&V contractor can provide the Program Manager comprehensive knowledge of all phases of software development. Because of having to verify that requirements have been met, the IV&V contractor is in an excellent position to provide feedback as to the testability of the requirements and the design at early design reviews.

GENERAL

Some additional means for obtaining software visibility, that apply throughout the development process, follow.

Methods of Contracting

The method of contracting employed to obtain software can have an effect on the ability of the Program Manager to obtain visibility. These methods of contracting include:

- Selection of a single contractor to develop a total system with the software treated as one of the contractor's several tasks, or
- Selection of one or more contractors to develop the software and another contractor to develop the hardware.

There are other variations of course, and there are advantages and pitfalls in all of them. N. E. Bolen, writing in "An Air Force Guide to Contracting for Software Acquisition," addressed the subject as follows:

"...The single system contract has the advantage of making one organization responsible for system performance."

"However, there is danger that the software development effort will not receive proper management attention and resources within the contractor's organization. (Bolen,[17] p 7).

Under the cited circumstances, the Program Manager must take deliberate action to ensure software visibility in development. Bolen went on to say:

"...Dividing the system acquisition into separate contracts so that one contractor is responsible for software alone provides the potential for better Air Force visibility of the contractor's progress;..."

Only the potential for increased visibility is provided by a separate software contract and the practice is not without potential problems. Among these could be a hardware/software integration problem that could place a considerable burden on the Program Manager's organization and staff.

Staffing

One of the problem areas in software acquisition identified by the Johns Hopkins report was the technical staffing of the Program Manager's organization. The report cited a lack of personnel experience in system engineering and software development as contributing to:

- Lack of policy guidance and planning, and
- Inadequate cost and schedule monitoring.

The Program Manager should get the best staff possible.

Aside from the number and quality of personnel on the staff, organization of the staff can also make a difference. The ways of organizing vary widely from vertical, or aggregate, through matrix. Also there are different forms of project approaches. Stephen P. Kieder, in an article entitled, "Why Projects Fail," discussed (what he called) the "Utilization Philosophy":

"...A most fundamental problem which affects many large companies is one which demands maximizing the utilization of personnel, as opposed to a project-oriented approach." (Kieder,[18] p 55).

Kieder explained that he was talking about the reassignment of people whenever there is a lull in the work and the continuity problems that occur when later these people return to a former job or are replaced by another person. In Kieder's words:

"...This is a disastrous approach because while it assures that people are always assigned to a project and utilization is high, it places an emphasis upon effort, not results."

Although Kieder's comments were directed toward the use of programmers in a large company, there is a lesson to be learned in terms of using personnel in such a way as to maintain continuity throughout any project. Keider also emphasizes the need to have one man responsible for the entire software project and not fragment responsibilities to the point where no one person is accountable. (Kieder,[18] p 54).

PART III

Authority and Constraints

The high-level attention given to software in recent years has fostered regulations and manuals having the purpose of producing software that satisfies the constraints of cost, schedule, and performance. For USAF programs, these documents cover the span from Department of Defense Directives to Air Force Systems Command (AFSC) pamphlets.

DEPARTMENT OF DEFENSE
DIRECTIVES AND POLICY

DODD 5000.1,

"Major System Acquisitions"

Department of Defense Directive 5000.1 does not make specific reference to software. This directive establishes policy for the acquisition of major programs (major programs are defined in DODD 5000.1) and management principles applicable to all programs.[IX] This directive applies to software as well as to hardware.

DODD 5000.29, "Management of Computer Resources in Major Defense Systems"

This directive establishes policy for the management and control of computer resources during development, acquisition, deployment, and support of major Defense systems.[IX] The DODD 5000.29 applies to major programs as described in DODD 5000.1; in addition, the principles apply to the acquisition of Defense systems that are not in the major acquisition category.

The DODD 5000.29 is a relatively new document (26 April 1976) and the intent is that it will not be in existence long, but that its policies and principles will be assimilated as an integral part of the established process of acquiring major Defense systems.

The most significant part of DODD 5000.29 is Section V, Policy, that, in general, states that computer resources in Defense systems must be managed as elements or subsystems of major importance during all phases of the life cycle with particular emphasis on computer software.

To ensure the early consideration of computer resource (including software) requirements, DODD 5000.29 requires they be included in the DSARC II * Review. To accomplish this, DODD 5000.29 lists the following items to be implemented in the Concept Formulation and Program Validation Phases of development:

- Risk analyses
- Planning
- Preliminary design
- Security definition
- Interface control definition
- Integration methodology definition

The risk areas, and a plan for their resolution shall be included in the Decision Coordinating Paper.

Another statement of policy is that computer software will be specified and treated as a configuration item.

To identify acquisition and life cycle planning factors and guidelines, a computer resources plan will be developed prior to DSARC II and maintained throughout the life cycle. (The Air Force plan that meets this policy requirement is discussed under AFR 800–14, Vol II.)

In parallel with the policy of making software a configuration item is the requirement to specify unique software support items as deliverables with DOD acquiring rights to item design and/or use.

Of particular interest to the Program Manager is the requirement for milestone definition and specific criteria to measure the attainment of these milestones. This requirement, of course, fits with the requirement to consider software as elements or subsystems of major importance, and the necessity to deal with software as a configuration item.

---

* **Defense System Acquisition Review Council II.**

Another item of policy which could have a significant impact is:

"...DOD approved High Order Programming Languages (HOLs) will be used to develop Defense system software, unless it is demonstrated that none of the approved HOLs are cost effective or technically practical over the system life cycle." (DODD 5000.29[17] p 3).

The DODD 5000.29 has made into DOD policy many of the suggested solutions to software problems that were reviewed in Part II of this article. A continuation of this trend is foreseen.

AIR FORCE REGULATIONS

AFR 800–14, Vol I, "Management of Computer Resources in Systems"

This is an especially important document inasmuch as it is the first in the series of Air Force acquisition or management oriented regulations to specifically address software. The stated objective of AFR 800–14, Vol I, is to:

"...insure that computer resources in systems are planned, developed, acquired, employed, and supported to effectively, efficiently and economically accomplish Air Force assigned missions."

In Section B of Vol I, the Program Manager is given the responsibility to:

" Provide management and technical emphasis to computer equipment and computer program requirements identified in the Program Management Directive." (AFR 800–14,[19] p 3).

There are several parts of AFR 800–14 that are of particular interest to the Program Manager from a software viewpoint. Under the heading of Air Force Policy the regulation states:

"...Computer resources in systems are managed as elements or subsystems of major importance during all life cycle phases."

Although some programs had in effect done this for years, for most programs implementation of this

requirement represents a significant departure from previous practice. The policy has a ripple effect into all aspects of software development. Also under Air Force policy is a paragraph enumerating those items that "...Program Management Directives require and Program Management Plans provide for." (AFR 800–14, Vol I,[20]). Some of these items are:

a. Establishment of computer technical and managerial expertise responsive to the Program Office which is independent of the system prime or the computer program development contractor, and, is preferably, an organic capability of the Program Office.
b. The specification and allocation of system performance and interface requirements to be met by .... computer programs.
c. The identification of .... computer programs as Configuration Items.
d. Work Breakdown Structures (MIL-STD-881) designed to facilitate identification of computer resource costs.
e. Coverage of .... computer programs during the conduct of system design reviews, audits, and management assessments.

Each of the five items mention an area of concern from past software experience.

Item a can be interpreted as the charter for one very real way in which the Program Manager can provide for software visibility—through organization. The Program Manager should exercise the flexibility given him by AFR 800–2 to set up a Program Office organization having a specific focal point for management of the program software efforts. The need for this was noted by Kieder in his article, "Why Projects Fail." (Kieder,[11] p 54).

The provision of AFR 800–14 stated in Item b could be a fallout of the earlier stated policy of software being "...elements or subsystems of major importance." (AFR 800–14, Vol I,[20] p 1). Because the Program Manager cannot be expected to review all system and interface specifications it is important that the Program Management Plan provide for proper treatment of software in the systems engineering process. The importance of correct definition of software requirements in the systems engineering process is difficult to overemphasize.

AFR 800–14, Vol II, "Acquisition and Support Procedures for Computer Resources in Systems" (An Air Force Working Group will review implementation of these procedures.)

Procedures that apply when implementing the policies of AFR 800–14, Vol I, and other publications that pertain to the acquisition and support of computer resources, are consolidated in Vol II of AFR 800–14. Volume II restates applicable portions of related publications and must be used with those publications. (AFR 800–14, Vol II,²¹ p 1–1).

Planning. Planning is discussed in Vol II as it relates to several specific functions. There are three planning functions in particular that are software peculiar: The Computer Resources Integrated Support Plan (CRISP), the Computer Program Development Plan (CPDP), and the Computer Resource Working Group (CRWG).

The Computer Resources Integrated Support Plan identifies organizational relationships and responsibilities for the management and technical support of computer resources. This is a cradle-to-grave plan for computer resources that assigns responsiblity for all areas of software acquisition and support. As such, CRISP has great potential to aid or hinder the development of software within the constraints of cost, schedule, and performance and should receive the effective backing of the Program Manager.

The Computer Program Development Plan is the development plan for software. Preparation of this plan is the responsibility of the implementing command, but the plan may be (and usually is) prepared by the contractor. This is a complete, detailed, development plan and is to contain items of particular interest from a software visibility viewpoint. Among these items are the contractor's development schedule for each Computer Program Configuration Item (and the proposed milestone review points) and the procedure for monitoring and reporting the status of computer program development.

The Computer Resource Working Group has as its prime purpose the preparation of the CRISP. The CRWG is initially chaired by the Program Office and has representatives from the implementing and supporting commands. Because of its membership and its purpose, the CRWG can be very useful when integrating requirements and in getting the user involved.

Engineering Management. Engineering management as applied to computer resources is described in terms of the system engineering process. One objective of engineering management is "...that computer resources are managed as an integral part of the total system." (AFR 800–14, Vol II,²¹ p 4–1).

Although all reviews can aid in obtaining software visibility, one aspect of critical design reviews should allow them to provide additional visibility, i.e., "...the CDR may be performed in stages as the logical design of Computer Program Components or groups of components is completed." (AFR 800–14, Vol II,²¹ p 7–4).

Testing. Tests of computer programs will be conducted under the same general ground rules as system hardware. (The principles of AFR 800–14 apply to testing of computer resources.) (AFR 800–14, Vol II,²¹ p 5–1). Development Test and Evaluation is divided into Configuration Item test and system level test. Each Computer Program Configuration Item (CPCI) must be tested and established as a qualified item suitable for the system level test.

Configuration Management (CM). As specified in AFR 65–3, CM will be applied to each Computer Program Configuration Item throughout the system acquisition cycle. (AFR 800–14, Vol II,²¹ p 6–1). Volume II of AFR 800–14 is explicit in this requirement and requires that computer program configuration management not be fragmented from the overall system configuration management. Reiterated are the procedures for applying configuration management to any part of a system (i.e., software being no different from hardware). One software peculiar item is the use of a Computer Program Identification Number (CPIN) for each CPCI. The CPIN is assigned by Air Force Logistics Command.

The identification of computer programs as configuration items in recent years has alleviated one of the major software problems of the past, specifically the control of changes and maintenance of a known baseline. Software baselines are now established and changes are controlled through the Engineering

Change Proposal system. Because of the relative ease with which software can be changed there is a great tendency to use software to correct hardware/design errors and deficiencies that become apparent late in system development. This usage takes advantage of one of the inherent characteristics of software and is not necessarily wrong. There is, however, a danger of not recognizing the great impact minor changes can have on schedules and costs owing to the additional, and required, testing and verification.

Although the regulation states that configuration management will be applied to each CPCI, it does not provide any guidelines as to what computer programs should be Computer Program Configuration Items. In many instances certain items of support software built by the development contractor should be designated deliverables (and CPCI) in addition to the operational software. This support software may be either that required for support during the production/deployment phases, or software tools usable in the development of other operational software. The Program Manager should ensure that his staff is aware of his policy on support software and that, when appropriate, such software is designated as a Computer Program Configuration Item(s).

Documentation. Documentation is needed during development to track progress and provide information for management visibility and decision making. (AFR 800–14, Vol II,'' p 7–1). This statement emphasizes one of the more important aspects of software, i.e., the only way to see progress in software (or the end product) is through documentation. This is not true of data. Data management in general is handled through a data management office in accordance with AFR 310–1 and through the use of techniques such as deferred ordering, deferred requisitioning (described in AFR 310–1 and Armed Services Procurement Regulation ASPR, Section 7), and an accession list.

Volume II, AFR 800–14 lists five categories of documents usually prepared by the contractor and used for performance monitoring: Configuration management, engineering, test, operation, and support. Of particular interest are specifications (engineering documents), because they document requirements and the actual computer program as coded.

Computer program specifications are written in accordance with MIL-STD-490, MIL-STD-483, and MIL-S-83490. To quote from AFR 800–14, Volume II:

"Specifications provide the basis for documenting requirements, controlling the incremental development between major program milestones and providing visibility."

Contractual Requirements. Contractual requirements are discussed in the regulation but, while different means of including software in the contract for a prime contractor are described, mention is not made of the possibility of a separate contract(s) for software. The point is made that the Program Manager should ensure that instructions to those who bid provide for preliminary contractor plans that describe the computer program development concept.

Computer programs should be identified at Level Three in the project Work Breakdown Structure. This statement is of major significance to the Program Manager. In a major program particularly, such as an airplane or a missile system, placing software at Level Three * of the project WBS could pose some problems as well as provide some real benefits. On the benefits side:

"Identification of computer program configuration items at Level Three of the WBS will provide the visibility necessary to evaluate cost, schedule, and performance of contractor efforts." (AFR 800–14, Vol II,'' p 8–2).

Conversely, if there is a large amount of software, consisting of several computer programs associated with different hardware (and perhaps being developed by different contractors) placing all software at Level Three of the WBS might not be feasible nor desirable. It might be quite difficult to correlate the WBS and the specification tree with the actual manner of software procurement.

* **MIL-STD-881A, "Work Breakdown Structures for Defense Material Items," has a series of appendices that show a summary Work Breakdown Structure for several types of systems (e.g., aircraft, missile, electronics). The only systems for which software (computer programs) is listed at Level Three of the WBS is electronics systems. Software is not shown at all in the other system's WBS.**

In the regulation AFR 800–14, Vol II, software is discussed as a contract deliverable. The statement is made that "contract deliverables are specified as line items in the contract," and that "while computer programs and documentation must be listed on the DD 1423,* the DD 1423 should be identified as an exhibit or attachment depending on the required management emphasis." (AFR 800–14, Vol II," p 8–2). An AFSC supplement to the ASPR, Section 9–603, expands on this direction. This supplement also requires computer software/computer programs/computer data bases to be specified as line/subline items in the contract schedule. There is still a dual treatment of software as a line item and as "data". This is handled by requiring that delivery of computer software/computer program(s)/computer data base(s) documentation be specified on separate DD Forms 1423 — DD Forms 1423 separate from those that specify the actual cards, tapes, etc.

OTHER GOVERNING DOCUMENTS

AFSC Pamphlet 800–3, "A Guide for Program Management"

The general considerations involved in managing the acquisition of a system are described in AFSCP 800–3. The pamphlet is intended as a guide and does not specify inflexible procedure through which all program goals are achieved. (AFSCP 800–3," p 1–1). The acquisition process is traced through its different phases, and a general description of the principal functions involved in managing systems acquisition programs is given. The portions of the AFSC Pamphlet 800–3 that are of interest to the Program Manager from a software peculiar viewpoint follow.**

- A System Design Review should address the allocated requirements for computer programs and interfacing equipment. (AFSCP 800–3," p 8–5).

- In the discussion of Critical Design Reviews, AFSCP 800–3 states the purpose of a CDR for a CPCI is to establish the integrity of computer program design at the level of flow charts or computer program logical design prior to coding and testing. (AFSCP 800–3," p 8–5). This view of the CDR in relation to the software development process is an idealistic one. In practice, the exigencies of schedule and money will often force coding to start prior to CDR. In fact, some software managers consider the CDR as a logical event to separate coding from the start of validation/verification.

- Under the heading entitled, "Configuration Management," software is mentioned only to the extent of pointing out that the selection of Configuration Items below prime-item level is a management decision accomplished through the systems engineering process and that each computer program is identified and documented by one macro flow chart. (AFSCP 800–3," p 9–4).

- "Data Management is the only chapter that has a section devoted to software. This section of AFR 800–3 lists several things to be addressed in determining how to satisfy operational requirements.*

In Chapter 16 great emphasis is placed on the role of the Program Manager in acquisition of computer programs. I quote:

"Early identification of computer resources, and technical and management expertise within the Program Offices is needed to manage and engineer the acquisition of functional subsystems that incorporate computer programs. The Program Manager must provide the management expertise to focus attention on computer program development and integration across the total system." (AFSCP 800–3," p 16–8).

---

* Department of Defense Form, DD 1423.

** Chapter 8, "Engineering Management," mentions computer programs several times to emphasize differences between hardware and software and points out peculiarities of software in the systems engineering process.

---

* Section D, Chapter 16, is titled, "Acquisition and Support of Computer Programs." I feel this section has been placed in the wrong chapter and the AFSCP 800–3 should be revised, in accordance with the guidelines of AFR 800–14 and the ASPR, to show that computer program are *not* data.

PART IV
Summary and Observations

As software has become a large segment of weapon system development, the problems of software cost, schedule, and performance have become critical to the successful fielding of most weapon systems. The cost, schedule, and performance problems have pervaded all phases of software development and have resulted from some seemingly unsolvable problems and various sins of omission as well as commission. Among the more important difficulties have been: (1) poor requirements definition; (2) inadequate system engineering; (3) inability to track software development progress, particularly during the implementation and verification phases; (4) inadequate change and configuration control (hence changes drive costs and schedules beyond acceptable limits); (5) improper matching of test and verification with requirements; and (6) nonavailability of support software when needed, resulting in maintenance problems and higher maintenance costs.

Software does not have exclusive rights to these problems; hardware is often subject to the same problems. However, software has been prone to the greater suffering because of the failure on the part of personnel having cognizance to recognize the importance of software. There are ways to alleviate most of the problems. If the Program Manager is going to control software cost, schedule, and performance, he must recognize the potential for problems to occur and take preventative action. Significant steps the Program Manager can take include:

(1) Get the user involved early. Require an early statement of user requirements and meaningful user participation in design reviews.

(2) Insist on full incorporation of software into the system requirement analysis process. Software must be engineered as an integral part of the weapon system.

(3) Place software at a high level in the WBS and remove it from the category of "data".

(4) Make full use of planning aids such as the program management plan and the CRISP to ensure all members of the program management team know what is expected and required.

(5) Make support software a deliverable item and when applicable make it a configuration item. This is particularly appropriate when software is to be transferred to a support or using command.

(6) Organize the Program Office to provide adequate technical support for software. Assign responsibility and accountability for this support to someone other than the Program Manager who cannot be the integrator.

(7) Plan the total program budget to provide adequate funds to implement the total software development program.

One thing that is present in all aspects of what the Program Manager must do to obtain software is planning. There is an old saying in the Real Estate Business that tells the three most important things to consider when buying a house: location, location, and location. An analogous comment on software would be that the Program Manager who wants adequate software would do well to pay prime attention to planning, planning, and planning. Experience has shown that if the plan does not include software in the System Requirement Analysis, it will not be included; if you do not plan for the use of a High Order Language, there may not be enough computer memory to handle the software; if the plan does not provide for allocation of funds to support proper software development, funds will not be available for use.

A primary point is this: The Program Manager can do little to alleviate problems of inadequate software and lack of control late in the development effort. The proper steps must be implemented in the early stages to assure the availabiltiy of software at a later date. The extent to which a Program Manager has control of software is a direct function of how well he plans for software development.

Lt Col Alan J. Driscoll is a graduate of the DSMC Program Management Course 76-2. He holds a BS in Mechanical Engineering from Purdue, an MS in Engineering Administration from Southern Methodist University, and is a graduate of the Air Command and Staff College. He has served as: Missile Systems Evaluator, SAC HQ; Minuteman Performance and Software Manager, and Chief, Performance and Software Division, USAF Space and Missile Systems Organization. He is now a Systems Manager, HQ, US Air Force Systems Command. This article is based on an Individual Study Paper that earned designation as a *Commandant's Distinguished Study*.

REFERENCES

Cited References

1. Mangold, Eldon R., "Software Visibility and Management," *Proceedings, TRW Symposium on Reliable, Cost-Effective, Secure Software*, Mar 74.

2. "DOD Weapons Systems Software Management Study," Technical Report, AD-A022 160, Applied Physics Laboratory, Johns Hopkins University, Jun 75.

3. "Software Improvement Plan Pushed," *Aviation Week*, 5 Apr 76.

4. DeRoze, Barry C., "An Introspective Analysis of DOD Weapons System Software Management," *Defense Management Journal*, Oct 75.

5. Dept of Defense, DDR&E, Director's Statement (94th Congress, 2d Session), "Program of Research Development, Test and Evaluation, FY 77," Washington, DC, 1976.

6. DeRoze, Barry C., "Weapon Systems Software Management," address to Software Task Groups, Defense Science Board, 25 Jul 75.

7. MAJ Boyd Etheredge, USAF, "Computer Software Management From the Point of View of the Systems Manager," Air Command and Staff College, Research Study, AD 920559, Air University, Maxwell AFB, AL, May 74.

8. Wolverton, R. W., "The Cost of Developing Large Scale Software," TRW Software Series, TRW-SS-12–01, Redondo Beach, CA, Mar 72.

9. Royce, Winston W., "Software Requirements Analysis, Sizing Plus Costing," *Proceedings, TRW Symposium on Reliable, Cost-Effective, Secure Software*, Mar 74.

10. Bartlett, Jan C., "Software Validation Study," Logicon Incorporated, Mar 73.

11. "Investigation of Software Problems," Space Transportation System Software Concepts Development Study, Vol II, AD 902103L, TRW Systems Group, Redondo Beach, CA, 31 Jul 72.

12. Grooby, John A., "Maximizing Return on EDP Investments," *Data Management*, Sep 72.

13. Borklund, C. W., "Getting the User Into the System, *Government Executive*, (Aug 1975).

14.   Kieder, Stephen P., "Why Projects Fail," *Datamation,* Dec 74.

      Reifer, D. J., "A New Assurance Technology for Computer Software," The Aerospace Corporation, AD A020483, El Segundo, CA, 1 Sep 75.

16.   Richards, Russell F., "Computer Software: Testing Reliability Models and Quality Assurance," Naval Postgraduate School, AD-A001260, Monterey, CA, Jul 74.

17.   Bolen, N. E., "An Air Force Guide to Contracting for Software Acquisition," Mitre Corporation, AD-A020 444, Bedford, MA, Jan 76.

18.   Dept of Defense, Directive 5000.1, " Major System Acquisitions," 18 Jan 77.

19.   _____, Directive 5000.29, "Management of Computer Resources in Major Defense Systems," 26 Apr 76.

20.   _____, AFR 800–14, Vol I, "Management of Computer Resources in Systems," Hq USAF, Washington, DC, 12 Sep 75.

21.   _____, AFR 800–14, Vol II, "Acquisition and Support Procedures for Computer Resources in Systems," Hq USAF, Washington, DC, 26 Sep 75.

22.   _____, *A Guide for Program Management,* Air Force Systems Command Pamphlet AFSCP 800–3, 9 Apr 76.

Additional References

Bullen, Richard H., "Engineering of Quality Software Systems: Software First Concepts," Mitre Corporation, AD A007 768, Bedford, MA, Jan 75.

Dept of Air Force, AFR 800–2, "Program Management," Hq USAF, Washington, DC, 16 Mar 72.

_____, AFR 800–6, "Program Control – Financial," Hq USAF, Washington, DC, 14 Jul 72.

_____, *Cost Management for Small Projects,* Air Force Systems Command Pamphlet AFSCP 173–3, 1 Oct 75.

Dept of Defense, MIL-STD-480, "Configuration Control of Engineering Changes, Deviations and Waivers," Washington, DC, Oct 68.

_____, MIL-STD-483, "Configuration Management Practices for Systems, Equipment, Munitions and Computer Programs," Washington, DC, 1 Jul 71.

_____, MIL-STD-490, "Specification Practice," Washington, DC, 18 May 72.

_____, MIL-STD-881, "Work Breakdown Structures for Defense Material Items," 1 Nov 68.

_____, MIL-STD-1521 (USAF), "Military Standard: Technical Reviews and Audits for Systems, Equipment and Computer Programs," Washington, DC, 1 Sep 72.

LTC John A. Manley, USAF, "Embedded Computer Systems Software Reliability," *Defense Management Journal,* Oct 75.

Mitre Corporation, "DOD Weapon System Software Acquisition and Management Study," Vol I and Vol II, MTR 6908, Jun 75.

In contrast to Dr. Brooks' presentation,
this portrait of failure is for those
who learn best from looking at bad examples.

WHY PROJECTS FAIL

by Stephen P. Keider

ONE OF THE PRIMARY causes for the failure of data processing projects is that such projects are often not initially defined, and therefore may lack a beginning and an end. Once a project has begun, no one seems to know:

- how the project was started;
- what the staffing is, or was, at any one point in time;
- what activities have been performed;
- when the project will end;
- what the project will accomplish.

Essentially, because projects are rarely formally defined, they are rarely completed. Completion occurs usually upon the death—or resignation—of the user the project services, or when the system is due for conversion. Completion is also a prerequisite for success, but a project is considered successful only if completed within the original time or budget estimates, and by how well it satisfies the user's needs.

An unsuccessful project, however, can be identified during several phases of its life cycle; and I shall here try to point to those very indicators.

Logically, any project can be time-divided into five distinct phases:

a) Pre-initiation period (usually measured in weeks or months)
b) Initiation period (measured in weeks)
c) Project duration (in months or years)
d) Project termination period (in weeks or months)
e) Post-termination period (occurring several months after project termination)

In each of the above phases, errors of commission or omission can have major impact upon the success of the total project.

Pre-initiation period

1) No standards exist for estimating how long the project will take. That is, each project is treated as a new and novel system with some individual responsible for estimation. His estimate will be based upon his own understanding of the project and its tasks, and on how quickly *he* can accomplish the subtasks. Little use is made of a history file of similar projects and actual versus originally estimated times.

2) Estimation is not done by the probable project leader, but rather, by whoever happens to be available at estimating time.

3) The project is not adequately defined. The request for an estimate usually takes the form of "John, we're planning to redo the payroll system. What do you think it will require?" "Payroll" may mean a number of different things to different people. Does it involve labor distribution? personnel information? leave accounting? salary, hourly and executive payroll? Any of the above can measurably impact the estimate of the project.

4) Short lead times are allowed for estimates, with corresponding inaccuracy as a result.

5) Personnel availability for the project is unknown. Estimates are usually prepared irrespective of who will perform the work. That is, an estimate of 34 days may be made, but only very junior personnel may be available; this will inflate the actual time. Although the resulting price/performance ratio may be excellent, the success of the project is rated in terms of actual versus estimated time, and on that basis the project may be a failure.

6) Staff desires are unknown. A project may be very appealing to one staff member, but repugnant to another. In both cases the actual time will be affected. Consequently, the Systems Manager must understand staff desires and assign projects accordingly where possible.

Initiation of project

1) Little documentation is available for existing, similar, or interfacing systems to provide the project leader with a data base to build upon.

2) Project leader responsibility is undefined. The leader has no idea what is expected of him, in regard to the project or the personnel assigned to work on it. Should he recommend alternative solutions? Can he recommend terminating the project? Can he remove personnel from it? Can he recommend dismissal?

3) Paper flow is handled poorly (or is nonexistent). Documentation regarding responsibilities, acceptance criteria, system objectives, etc., is not developed. Rather, documentation is limited to the technical aspects of the project.

4) Knowledge of "tools" to perform the project more efficiently is lacking. Are there modules, or subroutines already available which can be used? Is there a test data generator available? What about system design or documentation aids?

5) Definition of the project is vague, misleading, or totally wrong.

6) The project, between the time of the original estimate and its initiation, has changed without a corresponding change in the estimate.

7) Little or no time is spent in planning the project. Rather, analysis design and/or coding is begun immediately upon the project approval. The project leader is not permitted the "luxury" of planning: how he will attack the project; what tasks will be done first, second or third; what approach he will use; or what similar projects he will investigate or review.

8) Problem avoidance is not understood or considered. Oddly

WHY PROJECTS FAIL

enough, all projects begin with the premise that everything will go smoothly. Items such as lack of test time due to year-end closing are not considered until after the problem has occurred. By then, the project has already lost several days, or it is too late to provide an alternate source.

9) Resource requirements are not scheduled for the project. Critical items, such as keypunch, test time, user manual typing, secretarial, and printing requirements become a problem, and are addressed only *after* they have affected the project.

10) The project team's activities are not clearly presented to the end user. Only too often, the result is a series of "I thought . . ." "I assumed . . ." "Isn't he . . . ?" comments.

11) Project completion elements are not defined. That is, the project leader is not aware of what constitutes completion of the project. What is the end product? What test/acceptance criteria will be used? Who must sign off on project turnover? What constitutes turnover?

Duration of the project

1) Posting or reporting of project information is not performed, resulting in the project leader being unaware of what the completion percentage is, and the user being unaware of the impact of changes upon the original system.

2) Project reviews are typically exercises in trivia. They constitute a "How's it going, Jack? Any problems? No? Good! See you next week." The weak systems manager does not ask probing, detailed questions. He does not require that his personnel anticipate problems, but is primarily concerned with identifying problems which his project leader already has recognized.

3) Change of personnel is one of the major reasons why projects fail. Personnel, including project leaders, are removed from the project, with no adjustments to the schedule for time lost due to the changes. Whenever a team member is added to a project, there is a learning curve which impairs his efficiency on the project. It may be a day, or a month, but unfortunately, people movement is considered to be transparent to the project completion.

4) Adherence to standards and specifications is either not defined or, if defined, not followed. More often than not, standards do exist, especially in larger installations. They address documentation techniques, labeling, file names, etc. However, once an initial indoctrination is provided for a programmer/analyst, follow-up is ignored. The most expedient solutions are followed, resulting in several steps (modules) in the same program sequence addressing the identical file with different mnemonics. It results for example, in sketchy operations documentation without consideration for restart procedures. Maintenance then becomes a major part of project development.

5) Resource requirements are not anticipated. The major offenders in this area are:

- Data entry. Inadequate time is permitted for turnaround of source code preparation and/or test file operation. Worse, verification may not be performed, which almost invariably adds at least one day to the program development cycle.

- Computer Test Time. The lack of adequate test time becomes extremely critical toward the end of a project, when only one or two programs are being finalized. If turnaround is overnight, each minor change to a program adds at least one full day to the duration.

- Design Level Reviews. Whereas most of the time these are considered in project planning, it is rare that anything longer than a minute is assumed for duration between submission of design specifications and approval.

6) "Brute Force" Approach. In this type of shop, everything is designed and implemented from scratch with no thought given to the use of past projects, tools, or work simplification methods available to shorten the development cycle.

7) Lack of a project manager. It sounds strange, but many projects flounder through to completion without a rudder. The "DP Manager" is normally the project leader and he provides as much attention as he can considering his other duties. In general, very few installations have one man accountable for an entire project, but rather fragment the responsibilities to the point where no one person is accountable.

8) Lack of a Project Log. A project log can be an invaluable tool in performing post-mortems. Further, in companies which charge-back to the user the cost of resources used, it can be the mainstay in justifying such charge-backs.

9) Lack of a project audit trail. Data audit trails are considered the key to the development of any financially

"This is the list of good little boys and girls from IBM, Eastman Kodak and Xerox families who, due to their fathers' promotions have been relocated since they wrote you your Christmas letters."

sound accounting system. Yet very few project managers concern themselves with maintenance of a project workbook to provide a similar audit trail for project development.

10)　　　Lack of a skills inventory. Many projects are pursued with the project manager completely unaware of the skills available to him within his own shop. A skills inventory of past accomplishments of each staff member simplifies the staffing of a project and ensures that experience is "recyclable."

11)　　　Lack of project milestones. Because project milestones are not determined at the onset of a project, percentage of completion is usually equated to percentage of hours expended. For example, a project for which 100 hours has been estimated is 60% complete when 60 hours have been expended; when 90% of the hours have been expended, it is 90% complete. This can likewise be extrapolated to 140% complete when 140 hours have been expended.

12)　　　Staff members are considered "universally expert" During the estimation stage, and again during implementation, staff members are considered to be equally competent analysts, designers, programmers, librarians, documentation specialists, etc. They are assigned any of these functions with little consideration given to their ability. Invariably, this results in project delay.

13)　　　Utilization Philosophy. A most fundamental problem which affects many large companies is one which demands maximizing the utilization of personnel, as opposed to a project-oriented approach. When a lull occurs in a particular project, staff members are reassigned, because it is anathema to have people not performing "useful" (that is, design or programming) work. Consequently, when the project restarts, the same people may not be available, or worse yet, are available part time. This is a disastrous approach, because while it assures that people are always assigned to a project and utilization is high, it places an emphasis upon effort, not results.

Termination of the project

In the first place, it is my opinion that projects never terminate. Rather, they become like Moses, condemned to wander till the end of their days without seeing the promised land. However, for those projects that do "terminate," the following are key deficiencies.

1)　　　History/statistics are not determined or not updated. For example, at project termination, the project leader should make some attempt to

determine performance in light of certain objectives, or measurable criteria: how many programs were written? how many lines of code generated? average lines of code per day? average source statements per programmer? cpu test time required per programmer? per program? All of the above can be invaluable tools in the estimating and evaluating of future projects. It becomes the first step in the development of a "cost/resource accounting system" for dp projects.

2)　　　Quality Control. Typically, when a project is completed, it is never evaluated for quality. The qc criteria is "does the program run?" There are no grades (i.e., A, B, C, D, F) of programs. They are either "As" or "Fs."

The manager may evaluate personnel based upon quantity of code, programs or documentation produced, but in fact he never even considers evaluation based upon the quality of coding techniques used.

3)　　　Knowledge gained is rarely transferable. Once a project is completed, it goes through a procedure similar to "de-Stalinization," wherein all vestiges of association with a project are forgotten lest one be stuck with program maintenance. Inadequate time is allowed at the conclusion of the project for staff members to "dump" the knowledge gained or even provide meaningful insight into techniques used.

4)　　　Personnel are not evaluated. There is an ideal time, and only one, to evaluate performance of an individual on a project, and that is immediately at the conclusion of a project. Yet, only too often, personnel evaluation is tied into employment anniversary dates. Between the time an individual has completed a project and his next appraisal, a year may have lapsed. During that year he has had the opportunity to perpetuate mistakes initially made 12 months ago.

5)　　　Lack of formal turnover. Typically, a project termination is first known by the appearance of a new report. More realistically, a formal presentation should take place addressing:
　　a) initial objectives of the project
　　b) performance against these objectives
　　c) review of the end product
　　d) designation of principal contact for maintenance, etc.

6)　　　Recommendations for enhancement are not documented. At the conclusion of a project (if not earlier) the project team is in an ideal position to recommend enhancements to the system. If these are not quantified immediately, they will be lost forever.

Post termination

The key ingredient here is the conducting of user satisfaction surveys six to nine months after the completion of a project. The survey should address:
　　a) results versus objective
　　b) integrity of data
　　c) freedom from bugs
　　d) quantification of changes required
　　e) usefulness of information (i.e., should the system be continued?)

Summary

As a result of reviewing the development of a number of major systems, the above faults exist more often than not. However, the key problems appear in failing to understand the characteristics of a project:
- It has a beginning.
- It has an end.
- It uses multiple, finite resources.
- It has an objective.
- Its success can be measured in terms of time or dollars.
- It requires a leader.
- It requires a staff.
- It must be planned.
- Performance against plan must be reviewed.
- It coexists with other projects but is distinct from them.
- It is measurable (quantifiable).
- It may be a bad project (from the standpoint of usefulness). If it is, it must be altered, or terminated.
- Internal and external forces will affect a project; they must be identified.
- A project is a group of sub-projects.
- No project is unique.

Unless full attention is paid to each of these aspects of a project, the history of project failure will be played out once again.　□

A vice president and senior consultant with Neoterics, Inc., a Cleveland consulting firm, Mr. Keider has specialized in operations and systems auditing with emphasis on project management. He held positions in systems engineering, education management, and systems management while with IBM, where he spent 12 years prior to joining Neoterics.

A project manager debunks some mistaken ideas about computer system project management.

MYTHS THAT MISS

by David M. Farbman

Gather 'round, my project management friends . . . the iconoclast has come to town with a bag of broken myths.

Opinion
Managing a computer system development project is like any business. A truly knowledgeable, competent administrator can apply generally accepted personnel, budgeting, and motivational techniques to manage a development effort. Should this fail, a chief programmer or consultant can provide technical advice and act as a translator.

Fact
An administrator who has not personally programmed, or personally specified, or personally designed, or personally tested a system has no firsthand knowledge of what his people are doing. He cannot respond to delays or user concerns. He is at the mercy of incompetent staff or external forces.

The best way for a nontechnician to manage technical people is to turn over the entire project—people, users and all—to a chief programmer. Then, the administrative details should be turned over to a good chief of staff. After that, the administrator can perform the more important tasks himself.

Opinion A
Once the agreed functionality has been documented and signed, the user can relax and let you build your system. Of course, you will send him a copy of the weekly project status report to keep him informed. You will also expect him to witness the acceptance test so that he will sign a memo to the effect that all is as agreed upon.

Opinion B
It is poor practice to mail the status report to your user. You should appoint one of your junior analysts to hand-carry it over, so he can answer any of the user's questions about the project and its status. The analyst can also bring a list of questions from your programmer to the user.

An administrator with no firsthand knowledge of what his people are doing.

ILLUSTRATIONS BY BRUCE CAYARD

You can drive consultants harder than someone who will be with you after the project has been completed.

Fact

The user is the most important member of the team. He should be in almost continuous contact with you and can therefore pick up his own copy of the status report. He will then use it to assist you with his supervisors.

Designers and programmers should make a habit of showing the user partial solutions, doing walkthroughs, discussing implications to the user of technical options, etc. This will reduce acceptance test time, ease customer conversion, reduce maintenance, etc., when the user installs *his* system.

Opinion

The user must tell you what he needs. You document it. He signs it. All changes to applications are indications of the user's failure to know what he wants.

Fact

Most users don't know what they want; they almost never know what they need. Your job is to observe the problems he describes, suggest alternative solutions, verbally describe (or even act out) some work flows, and only then fully document the selected proposed functionality.

Any changes to specifications are indications of your failure to get into his brain, to see with his eyes, to extract his requirements, and to propose solutions to his needs.

Opinion

The best (or only) way to develop moderate-to-complex systems is by the enforced use of a staged development methodology (or project life cycle). This will assure that you know where you are at all times and force you to finish/demonstrate/document/walkthrough and get approval for Stage N before starting Stage N+1.

Fact

Systems developed "by the book" will inevitably miss every milestone. The book will be used by compulsive types to cross t's and dot i's rather than to expedite the delivery. The delays between stages can total more calendar days than the project itself.

Once the user has agreed that the rough functionality and approach is definitely cost-effective and viable, there is no reason why the design/development team could not start work a few days behind the analysis team. Further, the technical writing, training, conversion, and acceptance test team can each (on a part-time basis) be a week or two behind the design/development. This is similar to a programmer coding a single module and getting it into unit test while he is coding other modules or integrating several of them. These are all highly parallel situations; they can be sequenced to optimize overlap.

Every team must recognize that its success depends on the successful programs of the preceding teams. All will succeed—or none. A down-line person who observes a potential design improvement can discuss the issue with the designer who just finished it.

Opinion

Give me 10 good analysts, programmer/analysts and programmers and I will build the best computer system in the company.

Fact

You and 10 good technical people will cost your company over $500,000 a year in salary, space, benefits, holidays, vacation, etc. This does not include necessary resources such as computer time, printout and paper, etc. To make matters worse, if you succeed, what will you do with these good people (who love challenges, impossible deadlines, etc.) after the project is finished—put them on maintenance?

You would be better off with fewer people plus several consultants or temporary people. These can be let go the day you discover that they cannot perform as expected or when the project is completed and turned over. You also can drive consultants harder than someone who will be with you after the project is completed.

Opinion

The biggest waste of time/money/skills is to get halfway through projects and then pull the plug.

Fact

The true waste occurs when the project has been totally completed, turned over to the users, and the users won't (or can't) use it because of technical, political, or even apparently irrational reasons.

Opinion A

Before you write one line of code or draw the design flow diagram, the users must sign the functional specifications (including throughput). They are told over and over that you will develop the system exactly to the specs. Any changes will cause a sequence of meetings, threats, and cost overruns.

Opinion B

Actually it would be best to tell the user that all changes to the specs will be implemented in Phase II so that you can complete your initial agreement.

Fact

Your user is the person who requests your services, assists you in your job, demonstrates your system to upper management, tells the world of your success (or lack of it), and, in effect, signs your paycheck.

An administrator at the mercy of external forces.

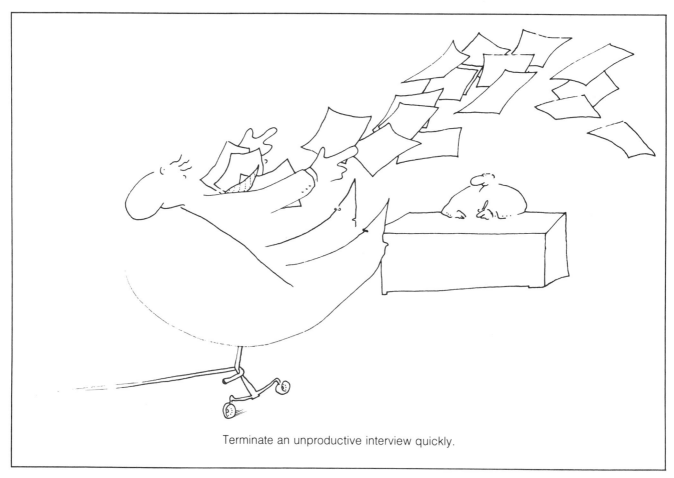

Terminate an unproductive interview quickly.

The best way to deal with functional changes is to separate them into two categories. The simple changes, such as report or screen layouts or modified computation, should be accepted without argument and documented back to the user to reflect understanding of the changes.

Complex changes, such as new files or completely new functionality or different/additional interfaces, must be thoroughly analyzed. They must be presented honestly, clearly, and calmly to the user with all options and all information about effects on cost and time for each option. No pressure should be applied. The user will then accept the heat for delays or overruns due to his corrected requirements.

Opinion
Preferred ways to estimate the probable length of a project are to:

1. Average the guesses of three of your analysts.

2. Use the IBM manual which allows 3.72 days per line of code per complexity factor (CF).

3. Ask a consultant.

Fact
The only way to estimate is to break down the total project, from absolute end to absolute end, into specific milestones with specific deliverables. Then, take each task and break it down to its basic components. Without buffers or allowance for problems, estimate the number of hours or days for each component. Make a list of all assumptions and constraints. Place the result on Gantt, Pert, and/or Milestone charts.

Opinion
Now that you have estimated correctly, add a 30% buffer to allow for those annoying contingencies that will delay your project. Make it 50% if what's-his-name is doing it.

Fact
Good programmers love challenges. After you have estimated correctly, cut the time by 50%. Give your staff a few days to relax before the impossible is started. Meanwhile, figure out a way. Line up your resources. Tell your management and user of your attempt—and good luck. If you miss your deadline, you still will be finished a lot sooner than if you were 30% later than your 30% buffered commitment.

Note: this procedure tends to "burn out" programmers, damage family life, and frazzle users. When it's over, be sure to properly reward those members of your team who will be expected to drive the next chal-

lenge. Don't reward those who failed to push or those whom you would like to demoralize.

Opinion
If you want a truly objective study of a project, or potential project, get a consultant. The more prestigious the company, the more thorough the study. When the effort starts, be open with the study team. Tell them your problems, doubts, and concerns. Also, describe some examples of solutions to the problem so that they can get a better picture of the scope of the desired product.

Fact
Ten out of ten studies, given the above, will run several weeks or months and will present you with a significant report on rag paper that you can take to your management. The study will restate, in four-syllable words, all your problems, doubts, and concerns. For an extra $10,000 they will throw in one of your originally described solutions.

To really get your money's worth, interview the consultants as if they were applying for a job in your problem area. Be extra rough during the interview; really make sure that the assigned people are absolutely qualified. It's O.K. to describe your problem as you see it today. Also, list the constraints. If, during the interview, the consultant fails to exhibit understanding and offer examples of viable solutions, end the interview. Do not waste further time. Do not be polite.

Opinion
The best way to interview technical people is to show them your area, tell them what you do, and explain what you expect from them. Observe such things as eye contact. Be sure that the person understands what is expected of him. Ask questions regarding goals, objectives, reasons for leaving, etc.

Fact
The best way to interview technical individuals is with the aid of your best technician. Ask highly specific closed questions in each area that may be required in the job. Ask, e.g.:
• What does a BCTR do?
• Why is four-wire bisynch not really considered fully duplexed?
• When would you use a Level 88?
• What are the sections of a functional specifications document?

Only after you have determined that the person has the skills you need should you bother to find out what he wants.

Opinion
Unfortunately, a good interview takes 60 to 80 minutes: 15 to 20 minutes for technical evaluation, 15 to 20 minutes for general evaluation, 15 to 20 minutes to talk about the company, and 15 to 20 minutes to wrap up, answer questions, and say goodbye.

Fact
A string of interviews by yourself, one of your project leaders, and your user that fails to lead to an offered and accepted job wastes everyone's time. If, during the initial technical evaluation, you determine that: the person could not do the job, cannot take pressure, does not know what he does not know, or the chemistry is bad because of quirks in your personality or his, terminate the interview. If you feel bad about this, have an associate call you away, and reschedule the interview to a future, indefinite time.

The above messages represent bits of hard-earned wisdom, gathered by an admitted iconoclast. It is hoped these bits will light the tunnel for the novice and alleviate the guilt the masters may feel for having practiced these rules all along.   ✳

DAVID M. FARBMAN

Mr. Farbman is a senior product manager with Citicorp. He is responsible for the design and development of a set of minicomputer-based packages to be provided to other banks. He has worked with IBM, Univac, Chase and other companies, and has taught computer science at the City University of New York.

Part II: Planning

"But since the affairs of men rest still uncertain, let us reason with the worst that may befall."

—Shakespeare, *Julius Caesar*

Planning is the most basic function of management. It is deciding in advance what to do, how to do it, when to do it, and who is to do it. It is setting objectives, breaking the work into tasks, establishing schedules and budgets, allocating resources, setting standards, and selecting future courses of action. It bridges the gap from where we are to where we want to be. Plans tend to be strategic when done by upper management and tactical when done by middle management and line supervision. The nine articles that follow focus attention on the key concepts, tools, and techniques associated with the management focus of planning.

The first two articles stress the need for planning and provide an approach for careful planning early in the project. Vaughan, in "Plan for Project Success," provides a three-step classical approach to creating a planning and control feedback system. Donelson, in "Project Planning and Control," provides a second approach based on completion of a six-part recipe and argues convincingly for the concept of producing a user's manual before the project plan is completed. Both authors stress the maxim, "those who fail to plan, plan to fail."

The next two articles by Maciariello discuss program management concepts, techniques, and tools. The first concentrates on setting verifiable objectives and developing plans to meet them. Work breakdown structures, network analysis, and technical performance planning are discussed as are other classical project management tools. The second article discusses budgeting, reporting, and controlling.

The next two articles provide a more detailed treatment of two of the subjects discussed by Maciariello. In "The Work Breakdown Structure in Software Project Management," Tausworthe discusses how the technique can be used effectively to help plan software projects. In "Using Graphic Management Tools," Reuter discusses the usage of break-even charts, learning curves, Gantt charts, PERT, and the line-balance chart.

The final three articles deal with the subject of software cost estimation. Brooks, in "The Mythical Man-Month," provides the views of an experienced manager about estimating the size and effort associated with software developments. Boehm, in "Software Engineering Economics," provides the reader with a summary of software cost estimating techniques and models and reviews progress in the field and discusses where current research is heading. Reifer, in "Poor Man's Guide to Estimating Software Costs," provides the reader with a simple and usable set of procedures for quickly developing a rough order of magnitude estimate of software costs. This article rounds out the discussion of planning with "how to" procedures for software estimating.

The success of any project depends upon many factors. Here are some steps you can take to overcome the problems involved.

By ANDERSON H. VAUGHAN

Plan for project success

■ Some users think of computers as black boxes. They believe that data is input and by some magic the black box produces perfect results. Other users are convinced that they are caught in a web of paper and technology, have no way to escape from the costs involved, and are a slave to a monster called EDP!

These views and others can develop when computers and people are mixed. One reason is that the technology involved has changed very rapidly in recent years. Another is that people change jobs. Also, a person's working environment changes with the changing needs of his business or organization.

What Happens in the Real World?

Many problems must be solved when people use computers. Problems come at least from:

1. Management
   - Not understanding their own problems.
   - Not making necessary policy decisions.
   - Issuing redirection before projects are completed.
   - Not including the Systems and Data Processing function in long range planning.
2. Vendors
   - Not adapting general software packages to fit an installation's needs.
   - Not providing sufficient training (for customers, their own personnel or both).
   - Not providing sufficient or timely field support.
   - Overselling their products.
   - Not understanding the needs and equip-

ment of other vendors.
   - Not stepping up to their responsibilities, then pointing at another vendor.
3. Users
   - Changing supervision in midproject.
   - Not changing supervision when it should be changed.
   - Asking for new systems because "it's the thing to do".
   - Asking for a change and then wanting it reversed some months later.
   - Neither controlling nor participating heavily in all phases of a project.
   - Not understanding what computers can do.
4. Systems and Data Processing
   - Not being management oriented.
   - Not understanding functional departments objectives and operating methods.
   - Not planning for the impact of negotiated contracts or new legislation.
   - Lack of a training program.
   - Lack of performance standards.
   - Lack of documentation.

What can you do about planning for project success? First, make every effort you can to find, hire and retain good people. They can make even a poorly planned project come out successfully through their own ingenuity and skill. Secondly, consider using the 3-step approach described below.

Step 1—Create a Long Range Plan. You need an organized approach. Start by identifying all modules of work or projects that you can. Ask the users in your company what they need. As they don't always know, you may need to advise them on what is available. Write down all that you know about each project. For example, give it a title, state the project goals, describe what it consists of and, if possible, estimate the man hours and hardware required to solve the problem.

Next, list all the projects in your priority sequence. Also show how they relate. Sometimes it is necessary to complete certain projects before others can be started. Others who review your priorities will need your insight on how selected projects fit together. Use numbering techniques, flowcharts with crisscrossing lines, cartoons or symbols to explain these relationships.

Now you're ready to discuss the projects identified. Review each project definition with the user involved. See if he agrees with the definition, determine the priorities *he* wants and obtain his estimate of the gross savings that will result from completing the project.

Next, conceive a plan or approach to meet the project objectives and solve the problems involved. If more than one solution or alternative is possible, describe what they are. Develop the solutions by using a sketch, simple narrative or flowchart. Then estimate the man hours and/or contribution required from the systems and programming group, the user and any vendors who are needed. These are " in the ball park" or "how big is the bread box" type estimates and are only as good as the project definition and your estimating skills will permit. *Do not schedule any projects yet or establish completion target dates.*

Once you have alternatives and estimates, go over the projects with users again. With different choices possible and an idea of the costs involved, many times the original project priorities will be changed to obtain savings from projects with the most payoff in the near or intermediate future. When this review is complete, integrate the pieces in the plan based on the relationships and priorities that have been agreed on.

Get management approval of the plan. If management reads the plan, thinks it's good and returns it, *you are in trouble!* However, if management participates in the development of the plan, changes priorities involved and establishes formal reviews to measure results, then you can expect management support and commitment of resources to the projects in the long range plan.

Step 2–Organize to Accomplish the Plan. Put together project teams consisting of systems analysts, programmers, users, management, consultants and auditors. A team may be devoted entirely to one large project. Or a team may be assigned all projects that affect a group of user departments. For example, one team may handle all administrative/financial projects, another marketing projects and another all production projects.

Why have project teams? There are several good reasons:

- Knowledge developed in team members is synergistic. What is learned on one project carries over to the next and makes it easier to get that next project done.
- Team members develop flexibility through exposure to most projects in the assigned area.
- New personnel can draw support from other members in the team.
- Competitive spirit between teams can result in improved project productivity.
- As project team activity includes the management of both projects and people, members develop supervisory capabilities.
- Project teams allow each member to make his own contribution, yet take advantage of the varying skills and preferences of each individual.

Lastly, the project team can be used to obtain project status, cover absences and perform maintenance type work.

Step 3–Establish a Project Management and Control System. The system that you use should fit your organization. If you adopt another company's system or some of their ideas, modify it for your group's terminology, control points and needs.

Subdivide a project into manageable pieces. Establish milestones as objectives so that results can be measured against something tangible. The number of phases in a project is arbitrary but again should fit your organization's need for control. Generally, project management systems use 4 to 6 phases. If you don't have a system now, consider using the following four-phase approach and modify it where you need to. The phases are: Phase 0—Assessment; Phase 1—Systems Concept; Phase 2—Detail Design; Phase 3—Implementation.

PHASE 0—ASSESSMENT

1. Develop general problem understanding.
2. Develop general solution.
3. Make gross estimates.
4. Plan personnel assignments.
5. Develop gross target dates.
6. Obtain departmental approvals.

Figure 1

PHASE 1—SYSTEMS CONCEPT
1. Define problem.
2. Determine objectives.
3. Develop policy.
4. Evaluate alternative solutions.
5. Specify exclusions and limitations.
6. Identify jeopardies.
7. Define interfaces.
8. Issue preliminary operations workload alert.
9. Prepare a Phase 1 Report.
10. Conduct design review.
11. Review Phase 1 Report with user.
12. Obtain user approval.

Figure 2

PHASE 2—DETAIL DESIGN
1. Perform detail investigation.
2. Develop detail systems flowchart.
3. Define rules, messages, logic and controls.
4. Publish operations workload alert.
5. Plan conversion methods.
6. Conduct departmental design review.
7. Prepare a Phase 2 Report.
8. Obtain user approval.

Figure 3

Phase Zero

Figure 1 shows the tasks to be performed in the assessment phase. The tasks requiring a general understanding of the problem, developing a solution and making estimates are about the same as those needed to make a long range plan. Use that material again.

Next, decide what people are available to support the project. Decide on which user people are required also, then select target dates for the milestones in the project. If the right people are not available this will affect the target dates.

Phase One

The tasks in this phase (see Figure 2) are critical to all subsequent effort. It is the planning phase. Establish policies or change them, determine the jeopardies if the project is not done and the risks involved if it is. Define what areas, subjects, physical locations, types of data and/or personnel, etc. will be included in the project and those that will not. Outline the plan of action to be followed throughout the project.

Write everything down. Prepare a report showing what is known and what is going to be done. If the project is big enough make a presentation to all functions involved to insure their understanding and approval. Include in the report:

a. A statement of the problem.
b. Alternatives and recommended solution.
c. Information flowcharts (not detailed flowcharts).
d. Volumes, sequences and frequencies.
e. Categories of data to be included or excluded.
f. Nonrecurring and recurring costs.
g. Gross and net savings.
h. Intangible benefits, advantages and *disadvantages*.
i. Personnel assignments including user support.

j. General project schedule.
k. Target date for Phase 2 completion.

The result of this phase should be an analysis of the technical, economic and *operational* feasibility of the project. Note that operational feasibility has been highlighted. In other words, is the solution not only technically possible and cost justifiable but *will it work* once it is installed?

Phase Two

This phase (see Figure 3) includes much of the systems work of the project. It is the architectural phase. It involves both analysis and synthesis.

Definitions established in this phase should include:

- Input/output formats
- Master file formats
- Accessing techniques
- Coding structures
- Edit rules
- Update rules
- Calculation rules
- Sort sequences
- Decision logic
- Controls required
- Recovery techniques
- Hardware required

If the project is big, a separate review with the user should be made to obtain his approval of the detail design. A Phase Two Report reflecting changes that have occurred since Phase One may also be required.

PHASE 3—IMPLEMENTATION
1. Develop programs.
2. Obtain forms, equipment and supplies.
3. Develop user instructions.
4. Educate user.
5. Test programs with unfriendly test data.
6. Perform systems test.
7. Set up or convert files.
8. Input new additional data.
9. Perform parallel tests.
10. Prepare and transmit documentation.
11. Start production.
12. Follow-up.
13. Publish closure letter.

Figure 4

If the project is small or medium sized, it is often possible to combine Phases One and Two to eliminate any unnecessary formality or paperwork.

Phase Three

The implementation phase (see Figure 4) covers the writing and testing of programs through the startup of the system and debugging. It is the building and occupancy phase. It includes most of the programming work of the project.

Note the activities that were necessary in prior phases before the first program is written. These prior activities are necessary to make programming effort both efficient and *effective*.

The user instructions referred to in Figure 4 should cover a description of the system, coding structures, inputs, outputs and error correction routines. Note that these instructions should be developed and published *before* users are trained to operate the system and that training should occur *before* the system is actually started.

Lastly, use the closure letter for more than stating the project is complete. It is a good place and time to give credit where credit is due, make recommendations for the furture or include a project critique.

Summary

There are many problems that must be solved when people decide to use computers in business. This is primarily caused by the nature of human beings, rapid technology change and the complexity of business today.

Due to these factors there is a strong need for good planning, management and control in achieving project success. This can be accomplished, however, by planning your work then working your plan. •**jsm**

Anderson H. Vaughan

Mr. Vaughan is Manager of Management Systems for the Firearms Division of Colt Industries of Hartford, Connecticut. Prior to joining Colt Firearms, he held positions with United Aircraft and Raytheon. He has twenty years of systems and data processing experience. A charter member and past President of ASM's Hartford Chapter, Mr. Vaughan has served as an ASM International Director, International Treasurer, and as ASM's representative to the American National Standards Institute. He has a B.S. degree from Ohio State University and a MBA from Boston University.

Project Planning and Control

by William S. Donelson

Reversing the usual process—by developing a user manual first rather than last—can ensure well-defined project objectives; a little math can determine what meeting those objectives will cost in time and money.

Management information system projects generally have two distinguishing characteristics: 1) they are late, and 2) there is usually a significant cost overrun. There may be other related problems such as improper definition, inadequate scope, poor design, poor programming, inadequate testing, cryptic documentation, and incomplete implementation. Attention to the two main characteristics should also shed some light on these.

There are, of course, many successful implementations of systems which have proven well worth their cost. The difference between the successful and unsuccessful systems may well lie in the manner in which the projects were managed. With better MIS project management tools, virtually all dp system implementations can be successful and cost effective.

Return on investment

If we look at a dp system as a purchased product (which it really is), what do we expect for our money? We might be tempted to say: profound problem definition, creative design, well-engineered execution, etc. But these items are conceptual attributes, not products. Just like any other purchase of goods and services, we are looking for a tangible product and effective service which performs as advertised and has a set of instructions telling us how to use it. We are buying a "bill of material" combination of product and service which may be defined as follows:

1. *A number of modules or programs* which permit data entry, detectable error identification and reentry, file maintenance, analysis, and reporting. These modules should work correctly.

2. *Implementation and operating tools,* including module linking "job control" decks, data base creation or conversion utilities, data backup and retention utilities, and job control decks for periodic operation.

3. *Instructions for use,* including a user manual with illustrated samples and step-by-step procedures for data preparation, error correction, and report utilization; and an operating manual for installation, data entry, and periodic operation.

4. *Technical documentation* for the systems analyst and programmer (and interested user) to aid in understanding the system.

5. *Training or educational service* to enable users, systems, programming and operations personnel to make optimum use of the system.

Summing up, when we buy a system we are buying programs, JCL, and documentation, and we expect some training services to enable us to implement and use them.

If we are purchasing a "package" from an outside vendor, we have in mind performance and economy requirements, and the price we can afford. Our task is matching the capability of various alternatives to our requirements at a given cost. We generally compromise in one or more areas, or we end up making modifications to meet our requirements.

If we are developing a package in-house (hopefully, because the capability cannot be purchased), the big difference is that we must state objectives and define requirements which must be converted into specifications. We then employ people with the technological capability to develop and deliver the product, hopefully in accordance with specification, at the proper due date, and at an agreed-upon price.

The goals are the same, for purchasing or developing systems, but there is an advantage in purchasing —the buyer gets to examine all the parts and then make his decision. In developing an in-house system, the parts won't be there to examine unless

some careful planning and carrying out is done. There's no magic to this; in fact, in-house development can be reduced to a six part recipe: producing a user manual, planning a framework for project control, estimating, scheduling, project control, and analysis of variance from estimates.

The user manual, it turns out, is very important to do first rather than last.

Part one: the user manual

The critical issues are stating objectives, defining and establishing specifications, and these are not trivial tasks! In virtually every area of enterprise, these items are conceived mentally and manifested on paper (text and drawings). For project oriented (as opposed to mass produced product) businesses, in only a few instances is it financially feasible to provide a tangible working prototype or model prior to development of the real thing. The finished product must be constructed from "paper" ideas and, all too often, both the quantity and quality of this "paper" is insufficient to determine the adequacy of design and to predict the success or failure of the outcome. In fact, too many systems definitions and specifications exist only orally and are not reduced to paper until after programming or implementation has started, if ever.

Would you buy a million dollar computer without reading its specifications and principles of operation manuals? The obvious answer is "no." Then why buy a dp system without demanding the same privileges? You don't have to.

To the user, the "system" is synonymous with the outputs (reports, crt screens, audio response, graphics, etc.) and inputs. The user should determine his reporting requirements and provide specifications with the aid of (not through delegation to) a systems an-

PLANNING

alyst, using concrete objectives as a guideline. The systems analyst must then determine the data base requirement to support this reporting capability, and the user should participate agressively in this data base definition activity. Finally, both the systems analyst and the user must determine the inputs, sources and timing of data needed to support the data base, and the reporting capability. The user must then be willing to bear the burden and expense of providing the input to gain the benefit of the output.

In many cases, the provider of the input resides in another department or division, and interdepartmental or interdivisional cooperation will be required to carry out the plan successfully. Keeping in mind that each functional area has its own objectives, incentives, and motivations which may conflict with those of other functional areas, this element of cooperation is a crucial matter.

As a result of having defined the outputs, data base and inputs (which are the "first cut" at requirements definition and specifications), we should be in a good position to construct a user manual with the following sections:

1. *Annotated sample reports* which are mocked up by writing proposed report formats on data entry sheets, keypunching, and listing the data with conventional dp utilities to produce realistic report facsimiles. (The keypunch approach is recommended over typing because changes are easier to make.) The annotation should cover the name, purpose, source, content, sequence, distribution, frequency and disposition of the report.

2. *Preliminary data base layouts* showing master file and detail record layouts and data base structure (list, hierarchy, network, sequential, etc.).

3. *Preliminary input layouts,* and procedures for entry including source of data, applicable edit rules and balancing procedures, error correction and reentry procedures with illustrated samples.

4. *Proposed coding structure tables* which identify and define the meaning of codes to be used by the user (customer type code, credit limit code, inventory ordering rule code, etc.). Even if the codes have not been defined at this point, there should be pages indicating that codes will be developed to represent data elements so that the users can clearly identify what will be required of them.

5. *A preliminary system flowchart* of input, processing and reporting modules and flows. This chart should depict interfaces to existing and planned systems and should be supported by a narrative explaining interface plans and anticipated problems, production schedule changes, etc.

6. *A system narrative* stating the requirements, scope, objectives, description, benefits, capability and limitations of the system (10 to 15 pages).

For a typical commercial system (receivables, materials requirements planning, general ledger), this manual will be about 100 pages and can be constructed fairly quickly if it is made a prerequisite to systems development (and this is a top management consideration). It may take 90 to 120 mandays to complete the user manual at a cost of $5,000-$15,000, but keep in mind that the whole project may cost $75,000-$150,000 or more and at the point this preliminary user manual is completed, no program specifications have been written, no programming has commenced, no computer test time has been consumed, no implementation has proceeded, and therefore, no costly mistakes have been made.

The manual must show on paper what the system will do, how it will work, who must support it and in what capacity, who will specifically benefit from it and how the total organization will benefit from it. Every participant in the system will have the opportunity to see what they are buying, to determine if the merchandise is good, and to propose (or insist upon) design modifications to better meet their requirements before they get locked into an inflexible system.

Part two: a framework

By identifying the object of planning, more than half the project planning battle is won. If a system is a set of programs, JCL, documentation (user reference material and procedures) and training, a project is nothing other than the framework in which the system is commissioned, defined, constructed and implemented. This framework is conceived and animated by people. Thus, the planning of a project is the planning of the framework within which the project will gain its identity, planning which addresses the following issues:

1. *Problem Definition.* Who wants the system (the user), why do they want the system (suspected problem), what do they want the system to do (scope), and how will the system benefit them (objectives).

2. *Project Organization.* Who will authorize the project (management), who will manage the project (project manager or steering committee), and who will participate in the project (project team consisting of users, MIS personnel and dp personnel).

3. *Problem Analysis.* What is the real problem and what is the cause? Can the problem be eliminated or mitigated, or do we have to construct a system to handle it? (A lot of "make work" systems could stop here because there is no real problem).

4. *System Definition.* The environment, inputs, data base, flows, rules and procedures which will solve the problem. This should manifest itself in the form of a user manual as defined earlier.

5. *System Review and Approval.* The formal process of reviewing the requirements and specifications against proposed capability to ensure a good match. The focal point is the user manual and the project turning point is here. The project can proceed with review and approval by all functional area mangers affected by the system and final authorization by top management; it can go back to any prior step for rework; or it can, as scrap, be terminated. If a positive decision is not made within a reasonable time, usually the project will continue into detail design and programming stages without approval and authorization until a cost, time, design, or some other obstacle is encountered. This may be the reason for a high project failure rate—the system never gets completed for lack of cooperation, or never gets implemented because of lack of consent by required contributors.

6. *Detail Design.* Program specifications relating to processing of inputs, maintenance of files and production of reports.

Module Class	STATEMENTS* PER MODULE		PROGRAMMING RATE (Statements per hour)		COMPUTER TEST HOURS PER MODULE
	Mean	Standard Deviation	Mean	Standard Deviation	
1. Data definition	62	52	16	N/A	.7
2. One-time utility	177	92	30	N/A	.7
3. Conversion utility	449	179	24	N/A	3.2
4. General utility	260	120	5	4.5	8.9
5. Data base interface "bridge"	450	150	10	1.8	8.1
6. Edits	1715	415	16	4.2	19.0
7. Updates	1278	528	20	7.8	11.3
8. Processing	1186	108	8	1.4	27.0
9. Major extracts	530	29	15	3.9	6.1
10. Minor extracts	186	76	7	3.0	4.6
11. Major reports	907	436	8	2.5	19.7
12. Minor reports	260	95	9	5.1	5.0
(N/A = Not Available)					

*does not include COPIED data definition statements.

Table 1. Programming and testing estimates for new applications developed in COBOL in a batch processing IBM 360/40 environment.

7. *Programming and Testing.* The conversion of the ideas on paper into the bill of deliverable products. Along with this should go a high degree of project management, project control, and revision of documentation.

8. *Training and Implementation.* The delivery of the product and performance of related services.

9. *Post-Implementation Review.* The *formal* process measuring how well the capabilities of the product and service matched the requirements, and the subsequent fine tuning of the system to accomplish a good match.

Project planning has only these two essential ingredients: a framework for conduct, and a user manual for manifestation. Without these, it is not possible to estimate, schedule and control the project and to analyze the deviation from the plan. Items 4 and 5 provide the proper background for project estimation, scheduling and control. Items 6, 7 and 8 are the proving ground for the estimation, scheduling and control and Item 9 provides the opportunity for analysis of variance from plan.

Part three: estimating

The preliminary user manual provides the focal point for project estimation. The quantifiable components for estimating are the numbers of each functional type of module or program which will be required to construct the system, and by this time we should have an accurate forecast of the number of each type due to the preliminary system flowchart in the manual. A typical commercial system has at least 12 categories of functional components:

1. *Data definition books.* File, record and transaction layouts which are stored in a library and *copied* into programs as required.

2. *One-time utilities.* Programs to create files, generate test data, simulate processing, and test called subroutines.

3. *Conversion utilities.* Programs to convert or reformat data files and transactions from existing systems to the new system format.

4. *General purpose utilities.* Modules to perform repeated functions which are used by different control modules (date conversions, table lookups, calculations, etc.).

5. *Data base interface utility.* Here I am advocating the use of a "bridge" between application programs and *most* data base management systems to provide a higher degree of data independence, to assure physical integrity of the data base (by auditing adds, deletes and updates), and to provide file content and utilization statistics. This bridge relates functional entry points (open, close, read, write, explode, implode, etc.) for application

modules to technique-oriented entry points and commands supplied by data base management packages (MRAN, CDIR, ADD-M, DELVD, GET UNIQUE, etc.).

6. *Edit modules.* Programs which assure the logical integrity of data entered into the system and which provide error listings or alerts. (One module per transaction type or family of transactions is assumed.)

7. *Update modules.* Programs which update the data base. (This function may be performed within the same module as the editing function, but it is, nevertheless, a separate function which produces audit trails or activity reports.)

8. *Processing modules.* Programs which do extensive calculations, analyses, and manipulations of data, resulting in possible additional file maintenance.

9. *Major data base extracts.* Programs which select data from the data base for subsequent (or simultaneous) analysis and reporting.

10. *Minor data base extracts.* Same as Item 9, but less complex.

11. *Major Reports.* Programs which report the results of major extracts and processing and which are complex in nature (multiple levels of control breaks and totals, sophisticated row and column formatting, and possibly further access to the data base.)

12. *Minor Reports.* Same as Item 11, but simple in structure.
(Note that the project manager who tightly controls the data definition books and data base interface utility will produce a well constructed system in terms of architecture and adaptability to change. Also, if the file maintenance function is strictly confined to file maintenance modules, there will be less latitude for the occurrence of difficult to locate system bugs.)

For typical commercial application systems, each class or type of module has a mean number of statements per module (and standard deviation), and also has a measurable programming rate in terms of mean and standard deviation of numbers of statements per hour. Computer test requirements are also a quantifiable by module type. Comprehensive study by the author has revealed the statistics in Table 1, based upon new applications development using COBOL in a batch processing IBM 360/40 environment. (For system modifications, as opposed to new systems development, other languages, on-line processing, or other hardware, different statistics will have to be compiled. These statistics will no doubt vary somewhat by installation due to differences in methods, standards, and personnel experience levels, and each installation should adjust these statistics to account for these differences. As explained later, the

analysis of variance technique will be instrumental in providing the basis for refinement of these statistics.)

System analysis and design hours are approximately 110% of programming hours for an entire project, assuming that this function has responsibility for project management, analysis, design, user manual preparation, program specification writing, program quality control, test results analysis, user training, system implementation (as opposed to program implementation and operations support, which is typically done by lead programmers), and post implementation review. COBOL programs may be keyed and verified at the rate of 125 statements per hour, assuming an average of 32 characters per statement (if more characters per statement are coded, the number of statements per module should decrease, and the total keystrokes per module class should remain fairly constant).

By determining the number of modules in each class, it becomes feasible to forecast systems analysis and design hours, programming hours, keypunch hours and computer test hours. Knowing the cost per hour of these resources (approximations are $20/hour for systems analysis and design, $15/hour for programming, $9/hour for keypunch and $50/hour for computer time— although computer chargeout rates can vary substantially), it is possible to estimate project costs as follows:

Total Cost =

$$\sum_{i=1}^{12} Mi \left[\left(\frac{(Si + ai\ \sigma si)\ (1.1\ Rs + Rp)}{(Pi + \beta i\ \sigma pi)} \right) + \left(\frac{(Si + ai\ \sigma si)\ Rk}{125} \right) + Ti\ Rc \right]$$

Where i = module class or type
    M = number of modules per class (from planner's estimate)
    S = mean number of statements per module per class (from Table 1)
    σS = standard deviation of S (from Table 1)
    a = selected multiple of σs (from planner's estimate)
    P = programming statements per hour (from Table 1)
    σP = standard deviation of P (from Table 1)
    β = selected multiple of σp (from planner's estimate)
    T = mean number of computer test hours per module per class (from Table 1)
    Rs = hourly charge for systems analysis and design
    Rp = hourly charge for programming
    Rk = hourly charge for keypunch
    Rc = hourly charge for computer test time

PLANNING

This cost algorithm and set of statistics address the costs of project development through implementation and post implementation review which accrue within the MIS/DP department.

(Note that this estimation technique is very much akin to building construction cost estimating, a primary tool of which is cost per square foot.)

The specific costs associated with user participation during development have been purposely omitted from the cost estimation algorithm for various reasons (the author believes this type of cost must be estimated on an incremental cost basis or on an opportunity cost basis). However, the total hours of user involvement are believed to be about 50 to 100% of total systems analysis and design hours, and can run even higher in some cases. Also, clerical effort required for one-time data conversion can be very substantial, but is rather easily estimated.

Part four: scheduling

Once a project estimate is established in terms of man-hours and dollars, we are in a position to establish a master project schedule. Analysis of prior projects has revealed the distribution of resource consumption over project duration (again, these statistics

	PROJECT PHASE				
Resource	Systems Analysis	Detail Design	Programming And Test	Training And Implementation	Post Implementation Review
Systems analysts	24%	26%	30%	13%	7%
Programmers	0%	16%	55%	24%	5%
Keypunch	0%	0%	90%	10%	0%
Computer	0%	0%	68%	30%	2%

Table 2. Estimated resource consumption over the life of a project (again using batch COBOL on an IBM 360/40).

may require some refinement by the reader in order to be applicable to their specific environment) shown in Table 2.

If each project phase is treated as a separate entity and the rule is made that subsequent phases cannot be initiated until the current phase is completed, then we can establish a master schedule for each phase. The estimated hours for each resource are multiplied by the percent of resource consumed in each phase, yielding resource hours per phase. A safe assumption is that a project participant can contribute a maximum of 123 productive hours per calendar month (2087 hours/year-80 hours holiday-80 hours sick leave-80 hours vacation ÷ 12 months/year x 0.8 productivity factor). If the project personnel are 100% allocated to the project, we can compute minimum elapsed months for each phase of systems analyst and programmer utilization as follows:

Required hours by resource by phase ÷
(# personnel allocated × 123).

We may also wish to establish a constraint on computer test time utilization in any one month based upon a reasonable limit per programmer (say, 20 hours/month) or based upon a total availability of x hours/month. This can be converted into minimum elapsed months per phase as follows:

Computer hours required in each phase ÷
(# programmers allocated to phase × 20)

or,

Computer hours required in each phase ÷ x.

In most cases, we can assume infinite capacity for keypunching because of the number of outside service bureaus available and the relatively minor cost of this resource (1-3% of project total).

We then take the largest elapsed months figure (systems analyst, programmer or computer) in each phase as one would establish a critical path with PERT analysis. The sum of the largest figures from each phase represents the minimum total project duration. Design review time (two to four weeks or longer) should be allowed between analysis and detail design, and several months should be allowed between implementation and post-implementation review to establish a system performance record (keep in mind, the system is operational at the end of implementation, but the project should continue until fine tuning of the system is completed).

In the elapsed time between implementation and post-implementation review, problems should be noted; however, attempts to correct minor problems should be discouraged and only major disruptive system, programming, and operational problems should be fixed immediately. In this manner, the level of program and system bugs builds up to a meaningful work load which is most efficiently handled at one time, the time being when 95% of all problems have been detected. This is usually three to four months after implementation, provided that the system operates on a minimum weekly basis. (Systems whose cycles are monthly or longer rarely achieve

bug-free status.) This technique of allowing minor bugs to accumulate minimizes the disruption caused by frequent changes, some of which cause additional problems.

From the project master schedule, it is possible to establish a detail schedule for each activity and each participant. In doing this, timing, sequence, and resource availability problems will appear which did not appear at the master or macro-schedule level, and the planner can make schedule adjustments to handle them. When the final detail schedule is summed back up to a macro level, the overall duration of the project may change ± 15% or more from the first iteration of the master schedule.

This top-to-bottom and bottom-back-to-top approach preserves the principle that the whole is equal to the sum of its parts, and we end up with detail schedules for each activity and each participant. This detail will be useful for project control.

Part five: project control

Project control implies and requires a controllable situation and a means of accountability to measure progress against the plan. If every person records hours worked against one project control number, the project is automatically out of control because there is no "individual" accountability. Therefore, a participant code or name must be assigned to every participant and a subproject code or name to every activity, so that actual progress against plan can be recorded at the micro level. In this manner, overall progress of the project can be measured, problem areas can be identified or predicted, and action can be taken in advance to prevent an out-of-control activity from resulting in disruption. To measure progress, however, to-date actual progress versus plan is not sufficient. If the plan calls for 100 hours to complete an activity, and 60 hours have been consumed to-date, we cannot assume that the activity is 60% complete. An independent estimate of percentage of completion of each activity by each participant is needed. With the "percent complete" known at the activity level, dividing actual hours to date (times 100) by percent complete yields a *projected actual*. If the summation of projected actuals adversely affects the project estimate and schedule for the current phase to an unrecoverable degree, alternative plans should be established and cleared with management. A revised schedule and budget generally results, being strangely characteristic of building construction and product development projects.

The estimation of percent completion at the detail activity level is a tenuous task, as the person who is

PLANNING

doing the detail work has a subconscious desire to report good news to the project administrator in order to appear to be where he is expected to be. Typically, dp personnel report 25% completion when they start an activity, 50% completion when they are really 25% complete, 75% completion when they are really 50% complete, and 95% complete for the remaining duration until they are really 100% complete. A well thought out antilogarithmic function combined with independent estimates of hours to complete lagging activities will smooth this reporting problem. For individual performers who consistently operate within expectations, detail progress review may not be necessary. These people know their capabilities and limitations, and will advise the project manager of anticipated problems. (They also are the type who will take work home and do it when necessary to prevent project disruption and avoid personal embarrassment, so one may never know they had a problem.) For inconsistent performers, a regularly scheduled progress review meeting should be held.

The percentage completion reporting method is not free of major pitfalls, however. In fact, the method is a highly subjective exercise. In the early stages of a project, it is difficult to distinguish between 5% completion and 10% completion, yet the resultant projection can vary 100% based on which number is chosen. Thus, for perhaps the first half of a project, this method is at best unreliable and may cause project control alarms to sound needlessly.

Project milestone reporting is perhaps a more suitable alternative. Using this method, each task or sub-project is divided into scheduled elementary steps (for example: flowcharting, coding, first compile, first unit test, first volume test, final test, etc.), and the completion of each step is reported on a master project schedule. If the master schedule is established using a PERT or critical path technique, it is possible to measure the overall impact on the master schedule caused by schedule variances of individual tasks. This places much more emphasis on getting tasks done on time and focuses attention on critical areas which are running behind schedule.

The ideal method of project control would be based on a marriage of the two techniques. If cumulative percent time distributions were established over all phases of each typical subproject, milestone reporting of each would automatically yield an associated percentage of completion, thereby giving a project manager both current status and an estimate to completion. There is much room for creativity and applied research in the discipline of project control.

Part six: analysis of variance

The purpose for analysis of variance from plan is to identify specific factors which caused project cost and schedule under- and overruns (mostly the latter), and to help us do a better job of estimating, scheduling and control of the next project. To illustrate the concept, let's take a specific example. The hours and cost estimation technique shows that programming cost is a function of four factors:

Number of programs $\times$ Statements
per program $\div$
Statement coding rate per hour $\times$
Hourly cost of programmers

The programming estimation technique employs two standards: statements per program and statement coding rate per hour. The numbers embodied in these standards may be questioned. However, these standards are a starting point, and positive decision rules can improve them to the point where they work for a particular environment, staff, language, and computer.

Let us make the following representations:

P = number of planned programs
ΔP = actual number of programs $- P$
S = standard statements per program
ΔS = actual statements per program $- S$
H = standard hours per coded statement (reciprocal of statements per hour)
ΔH = actual hours per statement $- H$
R = planned hourly cost
ΔR = actual hourly cost $- R$

Our initial cost plan is $P \times S \times H \times R$. The actual cost will be $(P + \Delta P) \times (S + \Delta S) \times (H + \Delta H) \times (R + \Delta R)$ which expands into 16 compound factors. We are interested in five of the compound factors, and we allocate the other 11 using standard cost accounting methods. The five factors of interest are:

A. The original plan: $P \times S \times H \times R$
B. Change due to ΔP: $\Delta P \times S \times H \times R$
C. Change due to ΔS: $P \times \Delta S \times H \times R$
D. Change due to ΔH: $P \times S \times \Delta H \times R$
E. Change due to ΔR: $P \times S \times H \times \Delta R$

We are now prepared to explain actual results which deviate from plan in a meaningful and analytical manner. If the number of programs changed, we should have known early in design phase, and, although our original master plan should never be changed, we can have a working plan which gets revised by upper management consent. If the hourly cost rates changed, we should have known about that in advance and called this to the attention of upper management. The only remaining elements to explain are C and D. If there was a significant variance either way (say, more than $\pm$ 10%) due to ΔS, an analysis should be made of the programs in question to explain the variance in terms of the manner in which the programs were written. If the programs are acceptable, and the relationship $-0.1 <$ (Item C $\div$ Item A) < 0.1 does not hold, a change in the "S" standard may be appropriate for future use. If the programs are not acceptable, project control administration or programming standards may have been inadequate. If there was more than $\pm$ 10% variance in the plan due to ΔH, a performance review should be held on an exception basis with those doing the work to explain the variance. If these people's performance is judged to be acceptable, and the relationship $-0.1 <$ (Item D $\div$ Item A) < 0.1 does not hold, a change in the "H" standard may be advisable. If the performance was judged to be substandard, project control administration may have been inadequate or personnel recruitment and development practices may be poor.

The analysis of variance and subsequent review provide an explanation for variance from plan and suggest areas for improvement in future projects.

Voila!

There is no substitute for managerial capability, good judgment and a conservative approach in planning, estimating, scheduling and controlling a project, but these quantitative methods can significantly reduce errors in estimating and scheduling MIS projects, and can lead to improved planning and control.   ✳

Mr. Donelson is corporate manager —MIS quality assurance for the Harris Corp., Cleveland. His 15 years in dp include previous service with Glidden, General Electric, and his own consulting practice.

■ Program Management is a managerial function which includes the responsibility for determining objectives, organizing, planning, scheduling, budgeting, directing, and controlling effort required to achieve the technical, cost, and schedule objectives of a complex engineering, manufacturing, or construction program in the private or public sector. A program manager has full responsibility for delivery of a product which meets technical specifications on a timely basis within the proposed cost. The program manager seldom has complete authority over the functional organizations producing the product. This rather questionable division of responsibility and authority is at the heart of both the strengths and

multiple programs, the traditional organization arrangement provides the economies of specialization in functional groups. Each group is provided with maximum incentive to excel in its respective field. On complex projects, however, this advantage must be weighed against the loss of coordination which results on the overall project because of the relatively weak guidance, direction, and integration given to each program. Continuous direction, problem solving, and integration are required for complex programs that are challenging the present state of the technical art. Such programs are characterized by great uncertainty in engineering and manufacturing.

Figure 2 shows the same organization with the

Making program management work

Part I

By DR. JOSEPH A. MACIARIELLO

the conflicts inherent in this form of organization structure.

In a traditional organization, the responsibility for program work is normally allocated to a company's general management unless the program is large enough to warrant a separate department or organization. The complexity, budget limitations, and urgent time requirements of many individual programs demand total management even though any one program may not warrant establishing a separate department or organization.

Figure 1 represents a typical traditional aerospace organization chart. All programs are managed by a general manager. Where programs are of a routine nature (pure or near pure production) and demand little individual scrutiny, the organization is adequate to manage multiple programs under the guidance of a senior manager. Priorities are established and conflicts are resolved by him.

In organizations concerned continuously with

Program-Management philosophy superimposed. This organization retains the advantage of functional excellence, an advantage which is disturbed if the functions report directly to the program managers, while providing overall management at the program level. In addition, the customer is provided with a single point of contact within the firm rather than having responsibility dispersed among functional groups.

Although a good deal of difficulty has been experienced in making the transition from function to program management, one general manager, George[8], attributes the success of the concept in his organization to 1) total management commitment and support, 2) equal organizational status accorded to program and functional managers and 3) a thorough educational campaign throughout the department.

Once so organized, the program manager is ready to begin to solve the complex problems of the program; problems that include advancing the state of the art and meeting extremely tight schedules within the constraints of tight budgets and stringent procurement regulations. Probably no other type of management is faced simultaneously with so many problems.

The program-management system must provide the framework within which competent program managers can pursue the customer's technical objectives within the time and cost constraints of the program. Yardsticks of measurement for objectives must be established which are in the customer and contractor's common interest; the process must provide for management by objectives and exception. Such a system is summarized by the closed-loop system diagram of Figure 3.

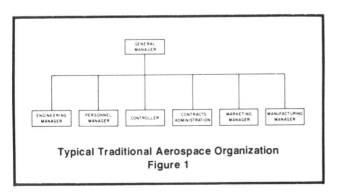

Typical Traditional Aerospace Organization
Figure 1

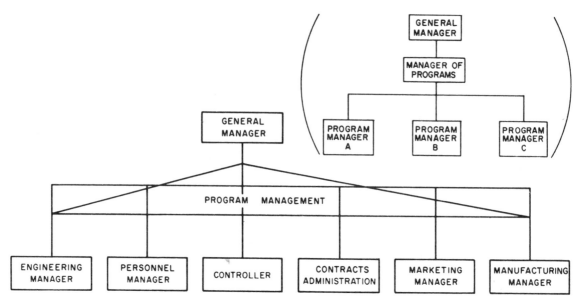

Typical Aerospace Organization Under Program Management
Figure 2

According to this figure, the system is initiated by determining and setting objectives. Objectives, of course, can be defined for the customer, the company, and the program. Objective setting for the program involves a two-step process: 1) determining, in a qualitative sense, just what the end items of the program are and 2) setting quantitative goals for each such end item and its subdivision.

The program-management system attempts to bring objective setting and management by objectives to life by establishing target values for each parameter and parameter subdivision. It provides the vehicle for defining program objectives and goes one step further by establishing target values for the technical, cost, and schedule parameters which allow the manager to manage by objectives and control by exception.

The second step of the system requires logical, consistent, coordinated plans to meet objectives. Network Analysis provides a basis for planning complex projects; it is a basic tool upon which this management system structure is built.

From the network plans, which depict total program requirements, detailed schedules are developed with the goal of validating these plans. From schedules which validate plans, realistic budgets are developed for each functional group based upon the work to be performed as identified by the network.

The schedule and the budget, once approved by the program manager, become the authorizing documents for the implementation of functional effort. The approval phase enables the program manager to exercise control over the expenditure of funds in functional groups and enables him to recover part of the authority lost by operating under this system.

The functional groups thus are similar to vendors whose service a program manager is purchasing but without a formal contract. By limiting the scope of the work covered by the budget and by performing this review function throughout the program, the program manager exercises control over program progress and expenditures. In essence he engages in short-term performance contracting.

The integrated program-management system provides an integrated cost, schedule, technical performance, cost effectiveness, and profit-control system which produces management information on an exception basis to provide the data required for control. Through the use of simulation, effects of proposed solutions to problems with many implications can be evaluated prior to implementation thus providing a laboratory for program management. Decisions made by the program manager, after simulation runs, instigate the recycling process. The decisions can alter objectives, plans or schedules in order to achieve control. The system is meant to function as an integrated whole.

Objective Setting

Cyert and March[2] list five classes of goals for an organization. The goals are for production, inventory, sales, market share, and profit. These goals are general enough to apply to most firms. Each program within the firm, however, requires goals or objectives that are derived from overall firm objectives. A program then assumes an atmosphere of a separate business entity whose goals are presumably congruent with those of the firm.

94

Long-run goals of the firm, however, often may be in basic conflict with the short-run profit objectives of on-going programs. The customer may identify his needs incorrectly; however, it is in the program manager's interest to give the customer what he wants in order to earn maximum incentive profit regardless of the long-run consequences to the customers. On the other hand, it may be to the long-run advantage of the firm to convince the customer that his program is ill conceived in relation to the objectives the customer professes to have.

For example, the federal automobile emission program was developed in response to political pressures and resulted in legislation reducing emissions of hydrocarbons and carbon monoxide. The automobile industry gave the customer just what is wanted. As Thimm[s] points out, "By relying on leaner mixtures and on higher combustion temperatures to reduce carbon monoxide and hydrocarbon, the automobile industry chose what then seemed the path of least resistance. . . . The automobile industry thus chose the easiest way to reduce carbon monoxide pollution though it *knew* that it had to lead either to a sharp increase in oxides of nitrogen pollution or to increased gasoline concentration and inferior performance or both."

The automobile emission program appears to have made matters worse for the public, possibly to the long-run detriment of the automobile industry since further political pressures may lead to smaller cars and less profitable automobiles, not to mention increased efforts to shift the public's transportation demand to other means besides the automobile. All this could have been prevented if sufficient analysis were done by any one of the big three automobile producers and presented systematically to the public. The short-run program response of the industry, however, is bound to lead to lower long-run profits.

This example illustrates the potential conflict be-

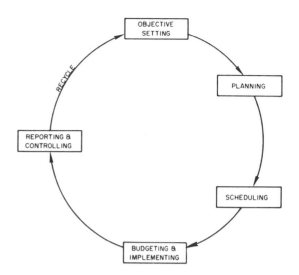

Program Management System Diagram
Figure 3

tween the strategic planning process of an organization and short-run profit goals of individual programs. A great emphasis in program control systems on short-run profit performance rather than long-run profit performance surely is a mistake. A balance between near term and long term performance is required of program managers if basic goal conflict and dysfunctional performance are to be avoided.

Once total program objectives are determined, given these potential resolvable conflicts, objectives are then set for each part of the program which then become the measurement yardsticks of the functional groups employed on a program. The program manager and functional supervisors can then manage by objectives if there exists an accurate and timely feedback mechanism to provide information regarding the status of these time, cost, technical performance, and profit objectives.

The program management system through the vehicle of the Work Breakdown Structure (WBS), provides the tool to determine and set program objectives. The work breakdown structure is a hierarchical division of program requirements that resembles an organization chart.

Figure 4 provides an example of a partial work breakdown structure drawn from the aviation industry with the total program depicted as level zero. The contractual deliverable end items (CEI) are Level 1 subdivisions of the WBS and the vehicle sub-systems and components are Levels 2-4. Notice that at Level 1 certain items (e.g., program management) are not truly CEI's but must be accounted for and controlled separately from deliverable end items and therefore are given level one status with *no* further subdivision on the WBS.

In a typical program, the WBS is established prior to drawing the detail plans. Once the WBS is de-

Dr. Joseph A. Maciariello

Dr. Maciariello is Assistant Professor of Administration and Management and co-director of the Program Management Institute at Union College, Schenectady, New York. He joined the Institute of Administration and Management at Union in 1967 and has been teaching graduate courses in Management Control and Information Systems, Managerial Economics, and Financial Management. Prior to his current position, Dr. Maciariello served as a management consultant with a New York consulting firm, and as a Senior Financial Control Administrator with the Space and Life Systems Department of United Aircraft's Hamilton Standard Division.

scribed, plans, schedules, and budgets are drawn utilizing the WBS. After so defining the program, the WBS is utilized to set cost, time, and technical performance objectives for each level of the WBS by establishing target values for each of these parameters.

Peter F. Drucker[3] states that the only principle of management that can harmonize the goals of the individual with the goals of the whole organization is management by objectives and self-control. The principle "motivates the manager to action, not because somebody tells him to do something or talks him into doing it, but because the objective needs of his task demand it." This principle is incorporated within the WBS technique and brings Drucker's theory of objective setting to life.

The WBS allows us to achieve these desired results by allowing us to:
1. specify in a clear and concise form the ingredients of the program,
2. provide the structure for identifying the responsibilities of each functional organization and identifying its effort with that of the whole,
3. provide a guide to manage by objectives by identifying performance targets at each WBS level and by facilitating the comparison of actual performance with target values,
4. provide the tool to motivate personnel since they now are given targets to accomplish knowing that their performance will be evaluated based upon their ability to meet these targets, and they
5. enable managers, both program and functional, to utilize the concept of self-control in moving toward the targets.

This last item is accomplished by providing the manager with feedback on actual progress for the particular WBS level for which he is responsible. He is given the opportunity to correct the problem prior to passing the information up the organization structure. The WBS does not produce all the information

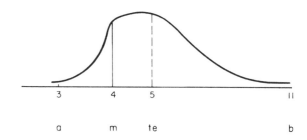

a = OPTIMISTIC TIME ESTIMATE

m = MOST LIKELY TIME ESTIMATE

b = PESSIMISTIC TIME ESTIMATE

te = ACTIVITY EXPECTED COMPLETION TIME

**Three Time Estimate of PERT
Figure 5**

for self-control, but by serving as the basis for detailed program planning, it establishes the framework for management by objectives and self-control.

Planning to Achieve Objectives

No other aspect of program management is so vital to success as planning. Because of the large number of interrelated tasks required for completion of any complex program, detailed planning is crucial. The added uncertainty that accompanies activities that are to be accomplished for the first time intensifies the need for detailed planning and provision for uncertainty.

There are two fundamental approaches used in the planning stages of the program-management system for making provision for uncertainty. The initial approach is carried out by the customer and is called the concept formulation phase. Concept formulation is defined as the preliminary technical and economic tests that provide the basis for a decision to embark upon a project.

The following prerequisites should be accomplished during concept formulation prior to authorizing engineering development:
1. The technology required to perform the development must be sufficiently at hand.
2. The performance goals must be defined.
3. The optimum technical approaches must be determined.
4. The benefit-cost ratio must be determined greater than one.
5. The cost-effectiveness of the program must be determined to be greater than other potential programs.
6. Schedule estimates must be acceptable.

Any programs that pass the concept formulation phase are ready to enter the development phase

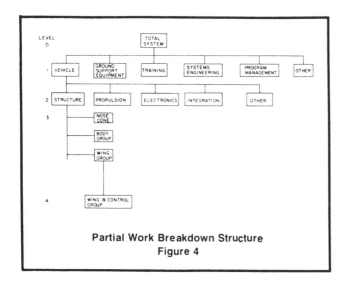

**Partial Work Breakdown Structure
Figure 4**

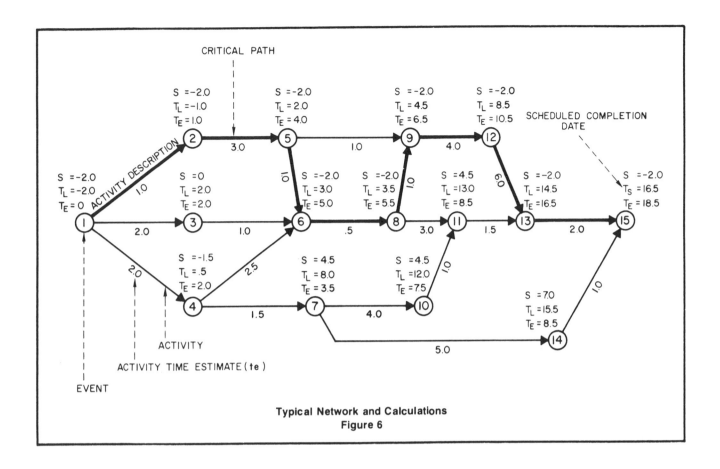

Typical Network and Calculations
Figure 6

where they also later can be rejected if they prove infeasible or uneconomic.

Concept formulation tends to erect a filter in an attempt to minimize the possibility that projects are accepted which are technologically infeasible or uneconomic. The information provided by concept formulation tends to reduce the uncertainty associated with project estimates.

The second approach to reduce the remaining uncertainty in program plans is provided by Network Analysis through the use of probability theory. Activities, which are tasks to be performed in order to achieve objectives, are identified on networks and time estimates are provided for each activity in the program. For activities whose time estimates are considered uncertain, three activity time estimates are provided and the beta distribution is used to determine the expected completion time of an activity. The well known formula for the computation of expected values is:

$$(1) \qquad te = \frac{a + 4m + b}{6}$$

where a is optimistic estimate for the activity if everything goes well, b is the pessimistic completion time if everything goes wrong, and m is the most likely completion time of the activity.

The three-time estimate is illustrated in Figure 5, assuming a beta distribution. Assuming a = 3, m = 4, and b = 11 in formula (1) for the expected comple-

tion time of an activity (te), the expected completion time is 5.

The expected completion time of 5 is the mean of the distribution and divides the area under the curve in half. The standard deviation for the beta distribution is estimated to be one-sixth of the range of the values and is given by:

$$(2) \qquad te = \frac{b - a}{6} = \frac{11 - 3}{6} = 1.3$$

The standard deviation for an event is determined by calculating the square root of the sum of the squares of the activity standard deviations on the longest path (T_E) to the particular event or:

$$(3) \qquad T_E = \sqrt{\Sigma (\gamma\, te)^2}$$

The probability of completing any activity on or before the scheduled completion date is then determined as follows:

$$(4) \qquad Z = \frac{T_S - T_E}{\gamma\, T_E}$$

where T_S is scheduled completion time in weeks from contract start and T_E is the expected completion time in weeks from contract start. The probability is then found by locating a Y value in a normal distribution table with Z. If Z is positive, Y is added to .5. Conversely, if Z is negative, Y is subtracted from .5. The resultant probability is the probability of completing a given event on schedule. If negative slack exists

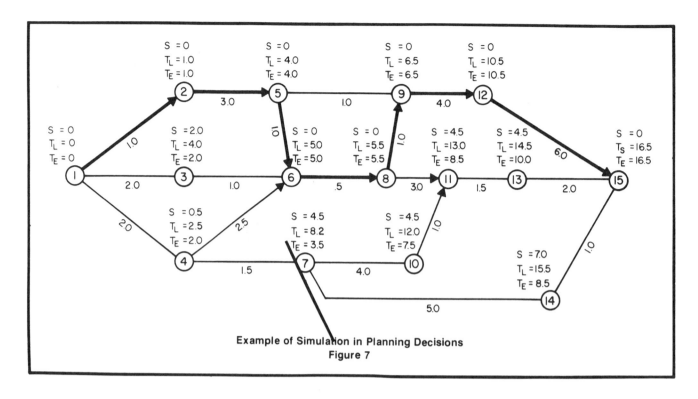

Example of Simulation in Planning Decisions
Figure 7

(i.e., $T_E > T_S$) Z will be negative and the probability of completing on schedule would be less than .5. If positive slack exists (i.e., $T_E < T_S$), the probability of completing the event on schedule would be greater than .5.

Although the initial goal of Network Analysis was to provide a probabilistic assessment of the uncertainty involved in completing a project on time, users soon found that the three-time estimate proved to be an administrative burden if provided for each activity. This led to almost exclusive use of the single time estimate (m) on the premise that the times provided were only estimates and one estimate would be just as useful as three.

The use of single time estimates rather than three-time estimates has not solved the problem, but rather has simply ignored it. Uncertainty, which in most cases is not provided for, continues to be the leading character in the drama.

When single-time estimates are provided for activities, the estimates are normally the "m" or most-likely value. The most likely or modal value is the one that occurs most frequently but it is certainly not the average, expected, or mean time. It is simply the value that is expected to occur most often. For many activities in complex programs, the "true" distribution of activity time values is probably positively skewed. Many things can go wrong for these activities and few things can go much better than anticipated by the most-likely estimate. All this suggests that when we have many such activities, some of the things that could go wrong, will! The most likely values, therefore, turn out to be *quite optimistic*.

This, however, is not the worst of it. Even when three estimates are provided for each activity there are reasons to expect that our calculations will remain optimistic. This second problem has been referred to by Moder and Phillips[6] as the merge-event bias problem and is taken up later.

Network Analysis

The tool which the program-management system provides to accomplish the detailed program planning to meet the objectives set forth in the Work Breakdown Structure is Network Analysis. By constructing a network for each of the lowest level items of the WBS, network plans for the entire program are developed.

Once a network is established for each of the lowest level items on the WBS, time estimates are provided for each activity and the entire program becomes an input to the computer program where expected completion dates (T_E) are calculated for each event along with required completion dates (T_L). By comparing expected with required and subtracting, slack (S) is determined for each event. The longest path in the network is termed the critical path, which is defined as the path with the greatest amount of negative slack (least algebraically) or the least amount of positive slack. Figure 6 is an example of the network. The calculations are normally performed by the computer program.

The network is a model of a program which can be experimented with like any other model to determine the effects of isolated changes on the whole system. This is important since the many interdependencies which exist in a program prevent one from determining quickly and accurately the effect of a single change on the whole network. The

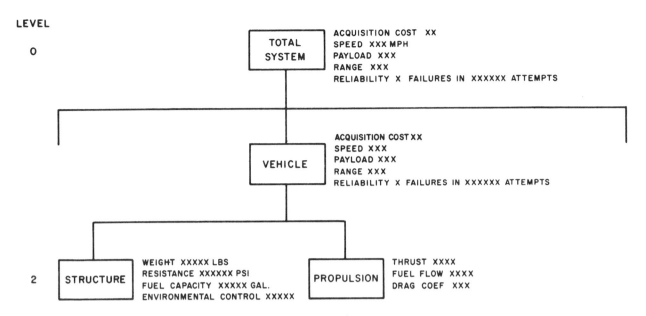

Simplified Work Breakdown Structure
Illustrating Technical Performance Planning
Figure 8

computer program provides a rapid means of determining the effects of changes being contemplated before the actual decisions are made.

Figure 6 illustrates a network on which the activities are performed both in series and in parallel. Some of the activities that are planned in series can be done in parallel, but the risk of rework increases since the reason for performing some activities in series is to gain the advantage of increased knowledge. Some of these operations may be performed without such knowledge which when available may necessitate rework.

Figure 7 shows the effect of removing the constraint placed up at the start of event 13 by activity 12 to 13 in Figure 6. By removing the constraint to event 13, 2.0 weeks are saved (T_E is reduced by 2.0 weeks) and the plan now meets the program objectives by removing the —2.0 weeks of slack. Simulation can be used in this manner in order to determine the effects of proposed changes upon the plan prior to altering the plan or the objectives.

The merge-event-bias problem creates consistently optimistic estimates of expected times at node events —events which have two or more activities merging into them. The bias comes about because all paths other than the most limiting path into a merge event are ignored in network calculations. Depending on the mean time and variances of the subcritical paths in relation to the critical path leading into a merge event there is a chance that a non-critical path will in fact become critical. This is illustrated by Holmes[8] in the following sample network where event 5 is the only merge event in the network and where three

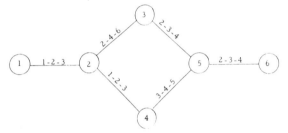

time estimates (in days) are provided for each activity. Of the two paths merging into event 5, path 2-3-5 is shown to be one day longer than path 2-4-5. By creating representative probability distributions for each activity and summing the probability distributions for each of these two paths we have:

Path 2-3-5 = T_1

Activity 2-3 = t_1		Activity 3-5 = t_2		Path 1 = T_1)	
t_1	$P(t_1)$	t_2	$P(t_2)$	T_1	$P(T_1)$
2	.2	2	.2	4	.04
4	.6	3	.6	5	.12
6	.2	4	.2	6	.16
				7	.36
				8	.16
				9	.12
				10	.04

Path 2-4-5 = T_2

Activity 2-4 = t_3		Activity 4-5 = t_4		Path 2 = T_2)	
t_3	$P(t_3)$	t_4	$P(t_4)$	T_2	$P(T_2)$
1	.2	3	.2	4	.04
2	.6	4	.6	5	.24
3	.2	5	.2	6	.44
				7	.24
				8	.04

These path probabilities give the subjective probability of completing each path at the indicated times.

The network technique normally leads us to choose the highest average value of the two paths merging at event 5. The highest average value is from path 2-3-5 and is 7 days. However, there is a small chance that path 2-4-5 may be finished in 8 days (i.e., if everything goes wrong on activities 2-4 and 4-5) and will be more limiting than path 2-3-5. It is this possibility that creates the additional optimistic bias in network calculations. If we were to compute a joint probability distribution (T) for both paths (T_1, T_2), the following distribution would result:

T	P(T)
4	.0016
5	.0432
6	.1856
7	.4224
8	.1872
9	.1200
10	.0400

This joint maximum distribution is one that is positively skewed (and therefore not normal) with an expected value not of 7 days (i.e., the average value of path 2-3-5) but rather of 7.3 days! The true expected value (T_E) to complete event 6 is not 12 days as calculated by the normal network technique but rather 12.3 days—resulting in an optimistic bias of 1/3 of a day.

The merge-event bias will only be significant when the two merge paths are of nearly the same duration. In order to allow for this optimistic bias in complex programs, it is necessary for program management to maintain a contingency or unallocated time period.

This completes our discussion of the planning of the time parameter. The final output of the planning process for the time parameter is an overall plan which meets (including the contingency) the time objectives of the project. If the first approximation fails to meet the time objectives of the project, then logical revisions to the networks or the objectives are required until a valid plan is produced. The use of the slack value applies also to scheduling considerations and will be taken up later when that topic is considered. We turn presently to technical performance planning.

Technical Performance Planning

The technical performance characteristics which the product should exhibit upon completion are translated into design parameters for each level of the WBS. Design parameter budgets are established for each level of the WBS in conjunction with the overall performance objectives of the total system. The design parameter budgets are monitored by each design group and are entered periodically into the computer program of the integrated system where they are compared with the desired parameter values. Figure 8 illustrates this technical performance planning where the WBS serves as the integrating vehicle. A key point to note is that an individual may be responsible for more than one WBS item, but only one individual is responsible for any one WBS item. This provides for clear cut delegation of responsibility and sets objectives which are used to manage.

There are a number of general steps that should be adhered to in technical performance planning which seem to apply to almost any complex program that involves a considerable amount of engineering development work. These steps are as follows:

1. Isolate analytically, through simulation, or from historical experience the technical parameters of the program to which overall program performance is most sensitive. The crucial parameters chosen = n must be measurable by direct observation or by tests.
2. Establish desired values for each such parameter at various stages of the life of the program.
3. Conduct tests or observations at periodic points in the program and compare anticipated final performance based upon actual progress with desired performance.
4. Simulate alternative courses of action which are designed to remove any variance between desired and anticipated performance.
5. Choose among alternative courses of action that (or those) which yields the most effective and efficient solution when consideration is also given to their impact on expenditures, schedules, and profit.

Experience indicates that two caveats should be observed in the technical performance planning process: 1) one should not clutter the system with many relatively unimportant parameters for tracking purposes and 2) timely testing is of the essence in programs where design progress is proceeding at a rapid pace.

References

1. Robert N. Anthony, *Management Accounting*, Fourth Edition, Homewood, Illinois, Richard D. Irwin, 1970.
2. R.M. Cyert and J.G. March, *A Behavioral Theory of the Firm*, Englewood Cliffs, N. J., Prentice-Hall, 1963.
3. Peter F. Drucker, *The Practice of Management*, New York, Harper and Row, 1954.
4. Jay W. Forrester, *Industrial Dynamics*, Cambridge, Mass. MIT Press, 1961.
5. Lockheed-Georgia Company, Sentinel System, Marietta, Georgia, Lockheed Training Department, 1965.
6. Joseph J. Moder and Cecil R. Phillips, *Project Management with CPM and PERT*, Second Edition, New York, Van Nostrand Reinhold Company, 1970.
7. Edward B. Roberts, *Dynamics of Research and Development*, New York, Harper and Row, 1963.
8. Program Management Institute (1st Annual), July 23-27, 1973. Institute of Administration and Management, Union College, Schenectady, N. Y. Selected papers.
   a. Warren Bruggeman, *Making Program Management Work*.
   b. Charles W. George, *Future Requirements for Managing Complex Programs*.
   c. Donald H. Holmes, *The Use of Subjective Probabilities in Program Management*.
   d. Joseph A. Maciariello, *The Program Management System: An Integrated View*.
   e. Alfred L. Thimm, *The Dynamics of Program Management*.
   f. David Wilemon, *Interpersonal Dynamics in the Management of Large Programs*.

Making program management work

Part II

By DR. JOSEPH A. MACIARIELLO

In this final part of the article, the author emphasizes how standard tools can be integrated with a few original ones to help manage complex programs.

Program plans determine what must be done, when it must be done, and who is to accomplish the work. It is the job of scheduling to determine how the work is going to be done within the sequential and total time constraints of the plans.

The goal of scheduling in the program-management system is to *continually* validate plans. Scheduling is the process of loading manpower to perform work on all programs in an optimum manner. In order to do this and trade-off manpower, functional management must have an indication as to performance against the plan for their function on each program. The networks provide this indicator through the slack calculations mentioned previously.

There are many considerations in scheduling that are not included within the planning function. Although the plans provide a feasible schedule for accomplishing the work, this schedule is not always practical when all constraints are considered. Scheduling considerations which are not a part of the pure planning process are:

1. Sufficient manpower to perform each activity in an optimal manner is assumed to be available when formulating plans. Scheduling recognizes the limited availability of manpower and the competition among programs for the same work force.

2. Common facilities are often required by multiple activities (e.g., test rigs). The scheduling process must resolve these conflicts.

3. Customer funding for the program is not always granted at a uniform rate which can affect the progress of work. Therefore, customer funding limitations enter into the scheduling function.
4. State work laws and regulations must be considered in scheduling when overtime is being utilized.
5. The nature of the incentive agreement negotiated between the contractor and customer with regard to the relative value to the customer of various deliverable end items becomes a factor in scheduling.

As mentioned in part 1, networks provide the basis for scheduling. Figure 9 illustrates a functional printout of one program that becomes the basis for scheduling when compared with printouts of identical functions for all programs. By comparing activities with positive and negative slack, the functional manager is able to emphasize those activities that are jeopardizing program plans by releasing manpower or facilities which would otherwise be used by other less critical activities or programs. By considering only negative slack activities for corrective action, he is able to manage by exception. He has on the printout the desired completion date (required date), the predicted completion date (expected date), and the variance (slack) which is an error term requiring the introduction of a decision to stabilize the system.

The program-management system allows for optimizing performance by providing slack values and a "Time Analysis." Time Analysis is accomplished by loading activities of the same function, showing positive and negative slack so as to provide a graphical look at the work to be performed and the latitude available for resource reallocation. This is illustrated in Figure 10 utilizing the functional printout presented in Figure 9 for the function called "drafting."

As shown in Figure 10, certain functional activities are on, ahead or behind schedule. By graphically displaying the activities within a function, scheduling decisions can be made based upon an analysis of slack (positive and negative).

The greatest delays caused by scheduling can be eliminated by incorporating a resource allocation option within a computer program which will permit the insertion of resources available and compare these with the resources required to eliminate negative slack conditions. Manpower is loaded and time analysis performed by building in an algorithm that identifies resources which can be substituted for one another and by utilizing slack to reallocate resources and minimize program duration. Time Analysis must be done on a total functional basis across program lines in order to optimize total functional performance and develop schedules which validate the plans of each program. One can logically accomplish this by combining all program oriented effort of the department or company for which one functional group is responsible in order to insure optimization of total functional performance while validating program plans.

It is important in program management to recognize that a plan must be constructed for the entire program and that scheduling can only be done on a short-term basis due to the five considerations mentioned previously. The portion of the plan that is scheduled is termed a "scheduled plan" and is entered into the computer system. Although distant activities cannot be scheduled, it is important to preserve a valid plan for distant work since the time estimates and interrelationships of the entire plan determine the time requirements (required dates) of the work which can be scheduled.

The recognition of scheduling as a separate function from planning is important in achieving true program control. If the plan alone is used as a schedule for performing the work, and if slack is used with no consideration for other activities and competing programs, the ability to optimize performance is restricted, and the value of the system lessened.

Budgeting

Budgeting is the task of planning expenditures but is based upon an approved schedule for the performance of the work. Since many complex programs in defense and non-defense fields have incurred large cost overruns, it is necessary that the management system emphasize cost control rather than mere product cost accumulation; the latter being a characteristic of traditional cost-accounting systems. Historical cost information is normally totally absent for new complex programs so cost standards are impossible to arrive at without planning the new program in detail.

Traditional budgeting techniques track cost as a function of time rather than as a function of work performed. A budget is established for a *period of time* and expenditures are compared to the budget for that period of time to determine performance. This procedure is fine for programs that are in the production phase. The procedure is defective for programs which require much development since performance against a budget for these projects depends upon the amount of work accomplished during the time period and its quality. Unlike routine manufacturing programs, progress and technical performance for complex projects cannot be taken for granted.

Traditional budgeting systems are used to:

PRECEDING/SUCCEEDING EVENT NUMBERS	ACTIVITY	TIME ESTIMATE	START DATE	EXPECTED COMPLETION DATE	REQUIRED COMPLETION DATE	SLACK
001-002	PREPARE DETAIL DRAWINGS-101	2.0	01/01/68	01/15/68	01/29/68	2.0
011-012	PREPARE DETAIL DRAWINGS-105	4.0	01/15/68	02/15/68	02/15/68	0.0
021-022	PREPARE DETAIL DRAWINGS-208	3.0	02/01/68	02/22/68	02/15/68	-1.0
031-032	PREPARE DETAIL DRAWINGS-304	1.5	02/01/68	02/11/68	02/04/68	-1.0
051-052	PREPARE DETAIL DRAWINGS-508	2.5	02/15/68	03/03/68	03/01/68	-0.4

Simplified Functional PERT Printout
Figure 9

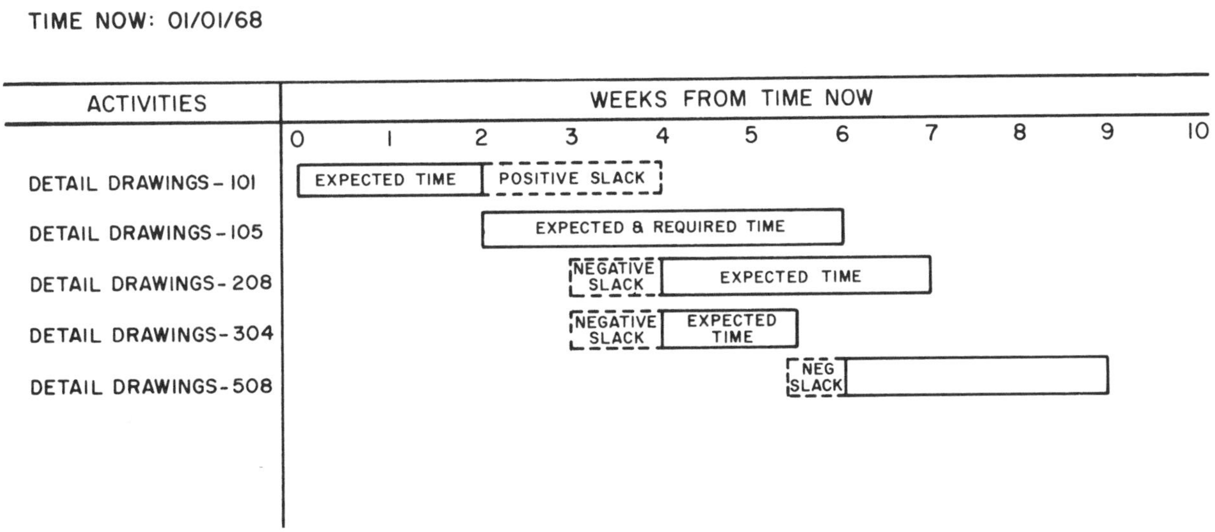

TIME NOW: 01/01/68

Time Analysis Chart for Functional Scheduling
Figure 10

1. Communicate and coordinate the objectives and plans of the subdivisions of an organization,
2. Commit operating management to agreed upon budgets for conducting their operation, and
3. Compare actual performance with standard in order to take *future* corrective action.

By concentrating on the financial variable alone, the traditional techniques have the very critical weakness of not considering quality and timeliness of the product being produced; characteristics that are critical to new programs.

The WBS and network are utilized by the program management system in budgeting. The WBS, once developed, is coded to facilitate the summarization of cost vertically to arrive at the cost of end items and the total program; and horizontally to summarize costs for a particular function. Budgeted costs are then compared with actual costs to determine over or under expenditure to date and that projected at project completion. Figure 11 illustrates the planning of expenditures at each level of the WBS.

In order to prepare the budget, a number of steps are required. These steps are:

1. The project is defined by the WBS, the lowest level of which is the work package level.
2. These work packages, which are the respon-

sibility of first line supervisors, are represented on the network as one or more activities required to complete a meaningful task.

3. Cost estimates are provided for each work package; the costs are estimated on the basis of manhours and other resources required to perform the activities comprising the task.

4. As schedules are developed for each work package, unnecessary manpower costs or premium material payments are eliminated by smoothing resources through the allocation of slack activities to periods when the skills are not required by critical activities.

Budgets are established, by function, for each work package of the project during the *planning stage*. However, only those work packages whose activities have been scheduled are authorized by the program manager for performance. This is necessary since *scheduling is required* in order to make budgets firm. This control of the authorization of work at periodic intervals throughout project life is the focal point of control for the program manager. In addition, he must insure that a reserve fund is maintained for unforeseen problems. He does this by withholding a management reserve from each work package authorization and thus establishes stringent, challenging (but not impossible) budgets for functional performance while attempting always to maintain a reserve to be used for contingencies.

The activity performance and dollar expenditure targets as well as a schedule for each work package are then issued with the statement of work. These targets are utilized by the responsible individual for monitoring work package progress and detecting problems. Figure 12 illustrates the authorizing document. It brings the objectives, plans, and schedules down to the lowest level for control. By this detailed planning, the program-management system emphasizes management by objectives from the program manager down to the line supervisor responsible for execution.

The first-line supervisor participates in cost estimating and these estimates, once approved by the program manager, serve as yardsticks for internal measurement and control. Labor and overhead rates are entered into the computer program and are segregated by functional skills and year. This allows the computer program to accept hours and material dollars for estimates, thus reducing the administrative burden of preparing budgets manually. The program simply proceeds to summarize budgets at each level of the WBS to establish targets or cost objectives.

One crucial aspect of the budgeting process for control purposes is that it should emphasize controllable costs. Program management can hardly be expected to be responsible for allocated overhead costs that vary as the volume of the firm varies. It should only be asked to absorb costs that are derived from a standard overhead rate developed on the basis of long-run normal - volume data. For purposes of control, however, the system ought to emphasize only that part of overhead that is traceable to the program and not that which is allocated from other departments, although standard overhead costs allocated from other departments ought to be included when evaluating program profitability.

Reporting and Controlling

The purpose of any management report is to point out the error term, which is defined as the difference between the desired parameter value and the actual value exhibited by the system. A report in itself controls nothing and is an expensive exercise unless feedback control is the result. The program - management system does not manage, but rather provides the framework for management. The entire system has been designed to facilitate the operating decision - making process and does not make any decisions itself. The managerial decision is a requirement to close the loop.

The program-management system facilitates decision - making by translating technical, cost, and schedule *objectives* into plans, schedules, and budgets. These objectives become the desired program values against which actual and projected results are compared. These results may also be integrated to produce a measure of cost effectiveness (discussed below) and expected profit at completion.

The reporting system should provide exception information tailored to each level of management and integrated to show the results of *interacting parameter performance*. The cost and technical position should be evaluated at each level of the WBS to produce a measure of cost effectiveness which is compared with an objective. Cost effectiveness should then be integrated with schedule position to arrive at the expected profit, given the negotiated incentive structure.

Exceptions are noted by WBS item in all reports, and detailed information can be made available on an exception basis for program problem areas. The program manager progresses from the general problem area to the specific problem.

Reporting requirements differ with each level of management. As the organizational level of management becomes lower, the detail required for the manager's intelligent evaluation and decision increases. At the lowest level of management, maximum detail on every work package and activity is

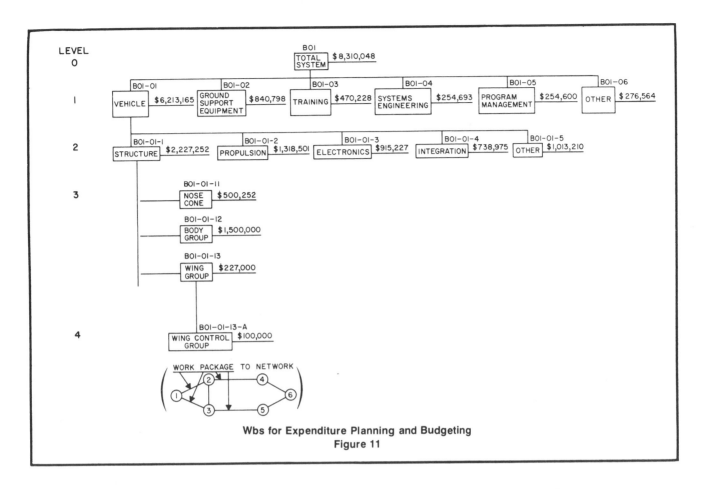

Wbs for Expenditure Planning and Budgeting
Figure 11

required in order to appraise performance against its detailed goals. An integrated program management system provides the tool for control by exception for each level of management.

The degree to which control is important to the contractor becomes readily apparent by a look at the contract he negotiated with the customer. If a fixed price contract is negotiated with the customer, under and over cost targets will be absorbed or obtained by the contractor. The program - management system should as well as possible quantitatively evaluate the effects of program changes on cost - effectiveness and expected profits. System cost effectiveness reflects the combined status of the technical and cost parameters and is combined with schedule status to arrive at incentive profit. System cost effectiveness should indicate the various levels of utility the customer enjoys with various possible technical performance and cost outcomes. It is a measure that recognizes that the ideal is rarely possible in the real world and that we often must be satisfied with one of many sub-optimal levels of technical performance and cost. Cost - effectiveness levels must be negotiated between the customer and the contractor. These levels recognize that there are trade-offs between cost and performance and that a higher level of performance at a higher cost may be more desirable

than a lower level at a reduced cost.

There is a summary reporting vehicle which the system may produce for reporting status to program management. The report presents, by WBS item, schedule performance, present and projected costs, and technical performance. System cost effectiveness and profit are calculated, compared with the objective and the variance is computed. The report is of WBS level 1 only. Lower levels of management receive lower WBS information, fashioned to its needs for control.

The program manager receives his report periodically and notes deviations in any parameter. He first checks the effects of program status on profit and if adverse, he investigates system cost effectiveness. If the system cost effectiveness target is not being attained, he can attribute the degradation in profit expectation to either cost or performance. If system cost effectiveness is not the cause of poor profit projection, then the schedule parameter is investigated. The parameters deviating from the objectives are isolated by this report and are associated with a WBS level end item. The program manager then calls for the related WBS items and continues to probe in this exception manner until he isolates the component where the difficulty is located. Once the component and the parameters which are deviating from objec-

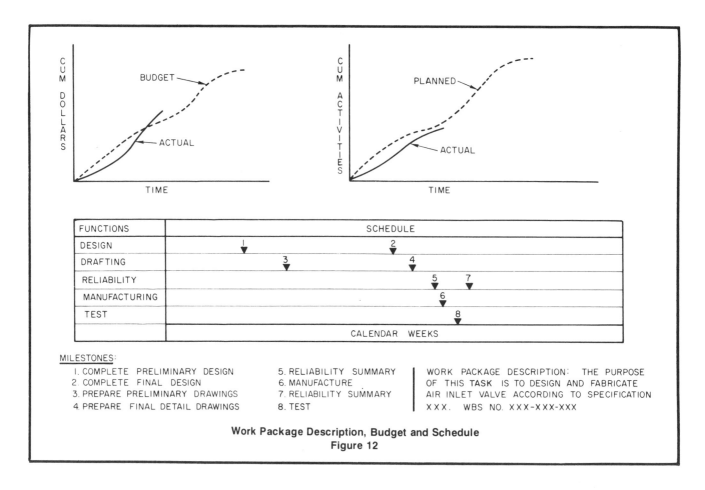

MILESTONES:

1. COMPLETE PRELIMINARY DESIGN
2. COMPLETE FINAL DESIGN
3. PREPARE PRELIMINARY DRAWINGS
4. PREPARE FINAL DETAIL DRAWINGS

5. RELIABILITY SUMMARY
6. MANUFACTURE
7. RELIABILITY SUMMARY
8. TEST

WORK PACKAGE DESCRIPTION: THE PURPOSE OF THIS TASK IS TO DESIGN AND FABRICATE AIR INLET VALVE ACCORDING TO SPECIFICATION XXX. WBS NO. XXX-XXX-XXX

Work Package Description, Budget and Schedule
Figure 12

tive are identified, the program manager proceeds to find solutions.

Alternate solutions are proposed and their impact upon profit is ascertained through simulation. The alternative that maximizes system cost effectiveness and schedule will maximize profits and is the logical decision. When the decision is implemented, the recycle phase is initiated and may result in the alteration of objectives, plans, schedules, or budgets. This cycle continues throughout the life of the program.

With an incentive contract built into the program management system through customer negotiations, the results which maximize profits must bring maximum satisfaction to the customer. The overall objectives of the company and the customer are mutually achieved through the maximization of profits. Goal congruence is therefore facilitated by the program-management system.

Information provided by the reporting system permits information feedback to be used for control. There is no requirement for all this information to be presented to program management, as a matter of fact, the minimum amount of output necessary for control should be presented to each level of management. *The most perfect control system is one that absorbs the maximum amount of information and exhibits externally the least amount of information that is consistent with management requirements.* The program-management system absorbs schedule, cost, and technical information periodically from all areas of the program and presents only what is required to stabilize the system and achieve program objectives.

A Diagnosis

The following method of analysis will be that of System Dynamics described by Forrester[4]. The system is initiated with objectives, plans, and schedules that determine the required program resources. Program resources affect the production rate but in a nonlinear manner. Since engineering development involves creative engineering, an increase in the labor force does not necessarily produce a corresponding increase in productivity. The productivity rate is influenced by (among many other things) engineering motivation which cannot be quantified although its effect does significantly influence program progress.

Motivating personnel on a program and resolving conflicts are still very much an art and as such they have not been addressed by this integrated procedure. Motivation is a managerial function that cannot be systemized and computerized. There are factors, however, which seem to influence the level of enthusiasm and therefore the rate of productivity on programs. These factors include the status·of a program, the future business prospect of the firm, and the value which higher levels of management place on a particular program.

A program with a history of problems tends to perpetuate an attitude of indifference which contributes to additional problems. The future business prospects of a firm determine the opportunities that will be made available to existing members and influence the morale level of the firm which in turn influences the rate of progress. The attitude top management adopts toward a particular program influences the desires of talented personnel to be associated with the program and therefore contributes to the rate of progress.

There are a number of lessons that emerge from the experiences of program managers on the Apollo Program which have been recorded for us by Wilemon[8]. Among his empirical findings were that:

1) The lower punishment and reward authority of program managers over functional groups supporting the program, the greater the potential for human conflict.
2) The less specific cost, time, and technical performance objectives were understood, the greater the likelihood of dysfunctional conflict.
3) The greater the confusion over roles of participants of a program, the greater the likelihood of conflict.
4) The greater the degree to which functional people believe their roles have been usurped by the program manager, the greater the potential for conflict.

Points two and three are resolved directly by the objecting setting and planning process described earlier in this paper. Points one and four must be handled by the incentive structure of the organization and are likely to be far more difficult to resolve, especially point four.

Reporting Delays

A delay in recognizing real program progress exists within this system and is a function of the detail to which schedules are established. The more detail schedules contain, the sooner progress or problems will be noted since the "guideposts" for measurement will have shorter time intervals, but there still will be a delay between the real event and its reporting. When program progress is reported by the functional groups, bias and noise result since functional supervision is measured by its rate of progress and will tend to be optimistic in its reporting of true progress unless activities are explicitly defined and the analyst who receives the information verifies its accuracy.

One method the program-management system utilizes to accomplish this is through the use of a dictionary of standard activities, and descriptions of what must be accomplished to consider an activity complete. This dictionary serves to better indentify completed activities and improves communications within the program group while establishing the basis for a historical file of time and cost data, which is useful for estimating future jobs. The rate of reporting progress varies, depending upon the nature of the program, the degree of criticality, the importance of the program, and customer requirements. Progress reporting is seldom done more frequently than biweekly.

Data on program progress is obtained from functional groups and must be processed in order to assess status, thus creating processing delays. In addition, program progress must be analyzed after receiving the output reports, thus creating additional delays.

Technical progress from the program reporting phase enters the cost-effectiveness module for cost - effectiveness calculation with cumulative expenditures. The program resources at their respective rates comprise the rate of program expenditures; they become an addition to past expenditures and are used with future predictions to report expenditures at completion. Expenditures are a result of program resource application and their reporting is delayed by the accumulation and processing cycle.

The above discussion illustrates that an over - expenditure on a program is simply a delayed symptom of program problems and not the cause. It illustrates the secondary role which should be accorded monetary data in any control system for managing complex programs. The traditional action taken when a program is in financial difficulty is to quickly reduce the direct manpower assigned to the program in an attempt to reduce program expenditures. The integrated system points up the fallacy of this decision since once cost effectiveness is calculated and merged with schedule progress, expected profit at program completion may be reduced since the schedule effect of such a decision may outweigh the cost saving and result in a lower rather than higher expected profit. This is treated more fully below.

Cost effectiveness is a calculation of the technical efficiency of the product at the projected cost. The cost system projects the cost at completion (C) by the following formula:

$$C = \frac{a}{v} \times B$$

where a = Actual cost to date
       v = Value of work performed to date
       B = Budget Cost at completion.

The preceding calculation is made at each of the lowest WBS items and v is determined by accumulating the budgeted costs of work completed to date. The significance of the calculation of cost at completion is that when compared with the budget (B) an over or under expenditure is predicted *prior* to the completion of work since this calculation is made at periodic intervals throughout program duration. With traditional budgeting techniques, an over or under expenditure can be determined only after the task is complete or the budget exceeded. Clearly, for management action, information after the fact is not very worthwhile, although quite characteristic of the kind of information provided by budgeting systems.

Another major difficulty with traditional budgeting techniques is that *cost* is an isolated parameter which is used alone to determine the "health" of the program. As pointed out earlier, monetary information is really a symptom of program status and doesn't depict causes of over or under - expenditure. Secondly, no comparison is made in traditional systems between expenditures and projected technical performance of the product. For example, an under expenditure position on a program does not mean the program is healthy unless the projected technical performance of the product equals or exceeds objectives. An over expenditure of funds that results in operating economies in the product may, in terms of cost effectiveness, be desirable.

The cost-effectiveness calculation and its effect upon profit is determined by comparing it with desired cost effectiveness and computing a variance, although there is a delay in the calculation of the variance which is the lag from the time funds are expended and progress reported unless the calculation is made and reported.

The cost-effectiveness calculation becomes a part of the rate-of-profit calculation along with schedule progress information from the progress report. The incentive contract provisions which are negotiated by the contractor with the customer set forth the incentives on each one of the three parameters as well as the technical guarantees which become minimum constraints. The rate of profit, projected to program completion, is computed by integrating schedule progress and cost effectiveness with the incentive contract provisions.

The rate of profit is then used to determine the profit value of the program at completion assuming that the plan for completion becomes reality. This profit value is compared with the desired or target profit at completion and if an error term results, it initiates a recycle which can result in revisions to objectives, plans, or schedules in order to achieve the desired profit at completion. Prior to incorporating any change, revisions are simulated and predicted results evaluated. The decisions to be simulated are arrived at first by noting the variance projected in profit and then by determining its cause. The cause may be in cost effectiveness or it may be in schedule. Once found alternative courses of action are simulated to determine their effect upon profit prior to selecting the desired action.

The interaction of variables described in this section illustrates the importance of treating the program as an integrated system; it warns against piecemeal solutions that treat symptoms rather than basic problems.

Conclusion

Here we have described an integrated system for managing complex programs. The details of the computer programs are included in the material referenced, especially within Moder and Phillips[6]. The emphasis throughout has been on providing a description of how many rather standard tools along with a few original ones integrate to form the nucleus of a system that should be useful for the management of many complex programs. The system, while fairly general, must be modified to meet special individual program characteristics.   ●jsm

References

1. Robert N. Anthony, *Management Accounting,* Fourth Edition, Homewood, Illinois, Richard D. Irwin, 1970.
2. R.M. Cyert and J.G. March, *A Behavioral Theory of the Firm,* Englewood Cliffs, N. J., Prentice-Hall, 1963.
3. Peter F. Drucker, *The Practice of Management,* New York, Harper and Row, 1954.
4. Jay W. Forrester, *Industrial Dynamics,* Cambridge, Mass. MIT Press, 1961.
5. Lockheed-Georgia Company, Sentinel System, Marietta, Georgia, Lockheed Training Department, 1965.
6. Joseph J. Moder and Cecil R. Phillips, *Project Management with CPM and PERT,* Second Edition, New York, Van Nostrand Reinhold Company, 1970.
7. Edward B. Roberts, *Dynamics of Research and Development,* New York, Harper and Row, 1963.
8. Program Management Institute (1st Annual), July 23-27, 1973. Institute of Administration and Management, Union College, Schenectady, N. Y. Selected papers.
   a. Warren Bruggeman, *Making Program Management Work.*
   b. Charles W. George, *Future Requirements for Managing Complex Programs.*
   c. Donald H. Holmes, *The Use of Subjective Probabilities in Program Management.*
   d. Joseph A. Maciariello, *The Program Management System: An Integrated View.*
   e. Alfred L. Thimm, *The Dynamics of Program Management.*
   f. David Wilemon, *Interpersonal Dynamics in the Management of Large Programs.*

The Work Breakdown Structure in Software Project Management*

Robert C. Tausworthe

Jet Propulsion Laboratory

Reprinted with permission from *The Journal of Systems and Software*, *1*, pages 181-186. Copyright © 1980 by Elsevier/ North Holland, Inc.

The work breakdown structure (WBS) is a vehicle for breaking an engineering project down into subproject, tasks, subtasks, work packages, and so on. It is an important planning tool which links objectives with resources and activities in a logical framework. It becomes an important status monitor during the actual implementation as the completions of subtasks are measured against the project plan. Whereas the WBS has been widely used in many other engineering applications, it has seemingly only rarely been formally applied to software projects, for various reasons. Recent successes with software project WBSs, however, have clearly indicated that the technique can be applied and have shown the benefits of such a tool in management of these projects.

This paper advocates and summarizes the use of the WBS in software implementation projects. It also identifies some of the problems people have had generating software WBSs, and the need for standard checklists of items to be included.

INTRODUCTION

If one were to be given the task of writing a program, such as that structurally illustrated in Figure 1, in which the target language instruction set was not intended to be executed by some dumb computer, but, instead, by intelligent human beings, then one might be thought to have an easier job than colleagues who write their programs for machines. However, a little reflection will show that this job is much more difficult

for a number of reasons, among which are ambiguities in the English language and a multitude of human factors [1]. However, such a program, often named the PLAN (Figure 2), is an essential part of almost every industrial project slated for success.

One of the difficulties in writing this program is the supplying of enough detail so as to be executable without allowing ambiguity. Another is getting the right controls into the program so that the programees perform as stated in the PLAN. Still another is making the PLAN complete, with all contingencies covered and a proper response to each supplied. One final problem of note here is making the plan bug-free, or reliable, so that once execution starts, if everything proceeds according to the PLAN, there is no need to deviate.

Programmers well-schooled in modern techniques [2] would approach the writing of this PLAN in a structured way, using top–down design methodology, modular development, stepwise refinement, hierarchic layering of detail, structurally sound constructions, and semantically definite documentation. Such an approach would tend to bring a measure of organization to the PLAN, understandability to its documentation, and reliability to its execution. If created in this way, the resulting format of the PLAN work tasks would have the attributes of what is known in the engineering industry as a "work breakdown structure" [3], structurally illustrated in Figure 3.

The work breakdown structure (WBS) is an enumeration of all work activities in hierarchic refinements of detail, which organizes work to be done into short, manageable tasks with quantifiable inputs, outputs, schedules, and assigned responsibilities. It may be used for project budgeting of time and resources down to the individual task level, and, later, as a basis for progress reporting relative to meaningful management milestones. A software management plan based

---

*The work reported in this paper was carried out at the Jet Propulsion Laboratory of the California Institute of Technology under contract NAS 7-100, sponsored by the National Aeronautics and Space Administration.

Address correspondence to Robert C. Tausworthe, Jet Propulsion Laboratory, 4800 Oak Grove Drive, Pasadena, California 91103.

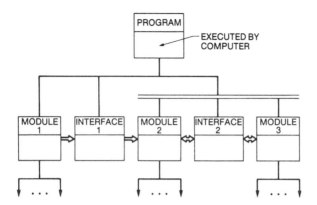

Figure 1. The modular hierarchy of a program.

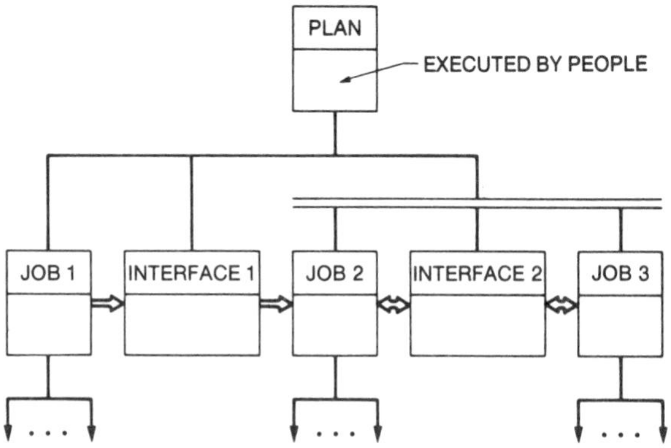

Figure 3. The work breakdown structure (WBS).

on a WBS contains the necessary tools to estimate costs and schedules accurately and to provide visibility and control during production.

Such a plan may be structured to evaluate technical accomplishments on the basis of task and activity progress. Schedules and PERT/CPM [4] networks may be built upon technical activities in terms of task milestones (i.e., accomplishments, outputs, and other quantifiable work elements). Projected versus actual task progress can be reviewed by technical audit and by progress reviews on a regular (say, monthly or biweekly) basis. Formal project design reviews are major checkpoints in this measurement system.

But knowing modern programming theory does little good if one does not also have the programming experience to which to apply it. Similarly, the knowledge of what a WBS is, what its goals are, what its benefits are, and what its structure is supposed to be like, does not necessarily instruct one in how to apply that knowledge toward developing a WBS for a particular project.

In the following sections of this paper, I shall review some of the characteristics and benefits of the

Figure 2. The PLAN is a people program.

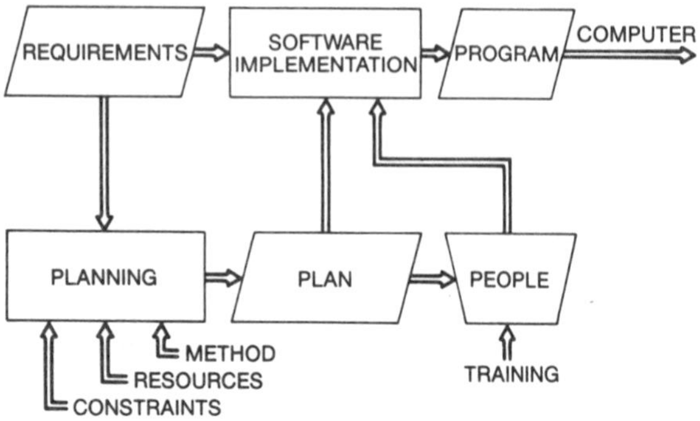

WBS and discuss how these can be developed and applied in software implementation projects. This material will be oriented principally toward new-software production tasks, although many of the concepts will be applicable also to continuing maintenance and operations tasks.

THE WORK BREAKDOWN STRUCTURE

The goals assumed here for generating the WBS are to identify work tasks, needed resources, implementation constraints, and so on, to that level of detail which yields the accuracy stipulated in the original PLAN, and to provide the means for early calibration of this accuracy and corrective replanning, if required, during the actual implementation.

How refined should this WBS be? Let me answer this question by showing how the WBS and schedule projection accuracy are interrelated.

If a project has identified a certain number of equal-effort "unit" milestones to be achieved during the course of implementation, then the mere number of such milestones achieved by a certain date is an indicator of the progress toward that goal. A graph of accumulated milestones as a function of time, sometimes called a "rate chart," permits certain predictions to be made about the future completion date rather handily and with quantifiable accuracy, especially if the milestones are chosen properly. Figure 4 shows a rate chart of a hypothetical software project.

Let it be supposed that it is known a priori, as a result of generating the WBS, that a project will be completed after M milestones have been met. These milestones correspond to all the tasks that have to be accomplished, and can be accomplished once and for all (i.e., some later activity does not reopen an already completed task; if one does, it can be accommodated by making M larger to include all such milestones as

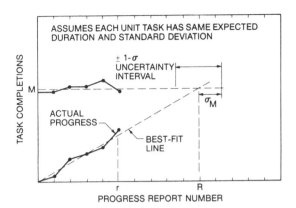

Figure 4. Conceptual progress rate chart.

separate events). The number M, of course, may not be precisely known from the first, and any uncertainty in M is certainly going to affect the accuracy of estimated completion date. Such uncertainties can be factored in as secondary effects later, when needed for refinement of accuracy.

Now, let it be further supposed that it has been possible to refine the overall task into these M milestones in such a way that each task is believed to require about the same amount of effort and duration to accomplish (Figure 5). Viewed at regular intervals (e.g., biweekly or monthly). a plot of the cumulative numbers of milestones reported as having been completed should rise linearly [5] until project completion.

More quantitatively, let m be the average number of tasks actually completed during each reporting period, and let σ be the standard deviation of the actual number of milestones completed each reporting period about this mean value (the values of m and σ are presumed to be constant over the project duration). The value of m is a reflection of the team average pro-

Figure 5. The unit task.

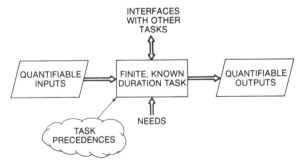

- SIZED FOR A SINGLE INDIVIDUAL

- NO FURTHER BREAKDOWN INTO SUBTASKS

ductivity and σ is a measure of the ability to estimate their production rate. Both attest to team effectiveness: first, in their ability to produce and, second, in their ability to create a work plan that adequately accounts for their time.

By design, the mean behavior of the milestone completion status is linear, a straight line from the origin with slope m. The project should require M/m reporting periods to complete, which time, of course, should not depend on whether a WBS was made (I am discounting, in this discussion, whether WBS generation increases or decreases productivity). Thus, M/m should be a constant value, relatively speaking. If M is made large, tasks are smaller and shorter, so proportionately more of them are completed each reporting period. The project schedule will, in fact, assume some productivity or mean accomplishment rate, but an actual performance value will generally be unknown until progress can be monitored for some period of time.

However, although the numbers M and σ may not affect team productivity, they do directly influence the effectiveness with which a project can monitor its progress and predict its future accomplishments. Generation of a WBS, of course, gives (or estimates) the parameter M. Monitoring the completion of milestones provides estimates for m and σ. From these, projections of the end date and calculations for the accuracy of this prediction can be made. Based on such information, the project can then divert or reallocate resources to take corrective action, should progress not be deemed suitable.

In this simplified model, a least-square-error straight-line fit through the cumulative milestone progress over the first r reports (of an expected $R = M/m$ reports) at regular ΔT intervals will predict the time required to reach the final milestone. It will also provide an estimate of m and σ. The normalized predicted completion date may be expected to deviate from the projected value (as a one-sigma event) by no more than [5]

$$\sigma_M \leq 1.48\, \sigma_1\, (R/rM)^{1/2}$$

within first-order effects. The value $\sigma_1 = \sigma/m^{1/2}$ represents the normalized standard deviation of an individual task milestone (it is limited to values of less than unity in the underlying model), and σ_M represents the deviation in time to reach milestone M.

The bound permits the specification of WBS characteristics that enable accurate early predictions of future progress. High overall accuracy depends on a combination of low σ_1 and large M. One may compensate for inaccurate appraisals of productivity only by generating a very detailed WBS.

As an example, suppose that a 10% end-date prediction accuracy is required (i.e., $\sigma_M = 0.1$) by the end of the first quarter ($r/R = 0.25$) of a project. Then, as shown in Figure 6, the trade-off figure is $M/\sigma_1^2 = 876$. Hence, if the WBS is highly uncertain ($\sigma_1 = 1$), that WBS should contain 876 unit milestones. If the project is confident that it can hold more closely to its average productivity (and has most contingencies provided for) with $\sigma_1 = 0.5$, then it needs only about 220 milestones. A 1-person-year project with biweekly reporting, one milestone per report (26 milestones in all), must demonstrate a $\sigma_1 = 0.17$ level of task prediction accuracy.

It is therefore both necessary and important to generate a detailed WBS rather carefully and to monitor milestone achievements relative to this WBS very faithfully, if accuracy in predicting the future progress of a project is of great importance.

REASONABLE SCHEDULE ACCURACY

A project engineer on a 2-year, 10-person task may perhaps be able to manage as many as 876 subtasks, each formally assigned and reported on. That amounts to about one subtask completion per week from each of the other nine workers; but the generation of the descriptions for the 876 tasks will require considerable effort. Moreover, it is unlikely that such a detailed plan would have a σ as large as one week; if the project engineer is able to break the work accurately into 876 week-long subtasks, task deviations can probably be estimated to well within a week.

The ability of the project engineer (or planning staff) to generate a clear and accurate WBS will determine the level to which the WBS must be taken. Greater accuracy of the work breakdown definition produces greater understanding and clarity of the actions necessary to complete task objectives. If the work is understood, readily identified, and achievable as discerned, the confidence of reaching the objectives is high. Thus, the further the subtask descriptions become refined, the better the estimator is able to assess the individual subtask durations and uncertainties. Refinement ceases when the appropriate M/σ_1^2 is reached.

Practically speaking, a work plan with tasks shorter than 1 week in duration will usually require too much planning and management overhead to be worthwhile. On the other hand, a work plan with tasks longer than 1 or 2 weeks will probably suffer from a large σ_1. Thus, a breakdown into 1- or 2-week subtasks is probably the most reasonable target for planning purposes.

A work year consists of about 47 actual weeks of work (excluding vacation, holidays, sick leave, etc.). Therefore, a project of w workers can reasonably accommodate only about $47w/d$ tasks per year (including management tasks) each of duration d weeks; spread over y years, the total number of milestones can reach $M = 47wy/d$, so that the practical accuracy limit one may reasonably expect at the one-quarter point in a project ($r/R = 0.25$) is about

$$\sigma_M \leq 0.432\sigma_1(d/wy)^{1/2}.$$

Note that accuracy is related to the total person-year effort in a project, other things being equal. A 3-person-year project completing 1 task per person-week can expect to have $\sigma_M \leq 0.216\sigma_1$. With a $\sigma_1 = 0.4$ (±2 days per weekly task), the end-date estimation accuracy is within 10%.

GENERATING THE WBS

There is no mystery about making a WBS. People do it all the time, although they seldom call the result a WBS. Most of the things we do, in fact, are probably first organized in our heads, and for small undertakings, most of the time that works out well. For more complex undertakings, especially those involving other people, it becomes necessary to plan, organize, document, and review more formally.

The general algorithm for generating a WBS is even fairly simple to state. It goes something like this:

1. Start with the project statement of work, and put this TASK on top of the "working stack."
2. Consider the TASK at the top of the working stack. Define technical performance objectives, end-item objectives, reliability and quality objectives, schedule constraints, and other factors, as appropriate; inputs and materials required for starting the task; accomplishments and outputs that signal the completion of the task; known prec-

Figure 6. WBS unit milestones and variance ratio.

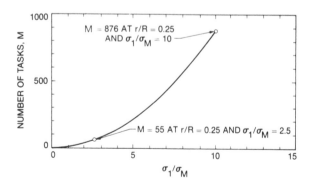

edent tasks or milestones; known interfacing tasks; and resources required, if known. Determine whether this task can be accomplished within the duration (or cost) accuracy goal.

3. If the goal is achieved, skip to the next step; otherwise, partition the current TASK into a small number of comprehensive component subtasks. Include interfacing tasks and tasks whose output is a decision regarding substructuring of other subtasks. Mark the current TASK as a "milestone," pull its description off the working stack, push it onto the "finished stack," and push each of the subtask descriptions onto the working stack.

4. Repeat from step 2 until the working stack is empty.

5. Sequence through all items from the "finished" stack and accumulate durations (costs) into the proper milestones.

The steps in this algorithm are not always simple to perform and cannot always be done correctly the first time or without sometimes referring to items already put into the "finished" list. The process is one of creation and thus requires judgment, experience, identification of alternatives, trade-offs, decisions, and iteration. This last is required since, as the project statement of work is refined, eventually the implementation of the program itself appears as one of the subtasks to be refined. When this subtask is detailed into component parts, the work descriptions begin to follow the influences of the program architecture, organizational matters, chronological constraints, work locations, and "whatever makes sense."

Therefore, the formation of the WBS, the detailed planning, and the architectural design activity are all mutually supportive. The architecture indicates how to structure the tasks, and the WBS goals tell when the architectural phase of activity has proceeded far enough. Scheduling makes use of the WBS as a tool and in turn influences the WBS generation by resolving resource conflicts.

There are many subtasks in a software project, however, that are not connected with the architecture directly, such as requirements analysis, project administration and management, and preparations for demonstration and delivery. The structure of these subtasks, being independent of the program architecture, can be made fairly standard within a given organization for all software productions. However, since there is no automatic or closed-loop means to guarantee that all the planning factors needed in the WBS actually get put into it, a standard WBS checklist can be a significant boon to proper software project planning, to decrease the likelihood of something "dropping through the cracks."

STANDARD WBS CHECKLIST

Previous experience [6] at the Jet Propulsion Laboratory with WBS methodology has permitted moderately large software implementation projects to detect schedule maladies and to control project completions within about 6% of originally scheduled dates and costs. The WBSs were formed by individuals with extensive software experience, overseen by an expert manager. None of the software individuals had ever made a WBS before, and the manager had never tried one on a software project. Together, with much travail, they assembled ad hoc items into a workable system.

A candidate standard WBS outline and checklist is currently being assembled and evaluated within the Deep Space Network (DSN) at the Jet Propulsion Laboratory. This standard WBS checklist includes many factors gained from previous successes and contains items to avert some of the identified shortcomings. Table 1 shows the upper-level structure of this WBS checklist. Detailed task descriptions are also in the process of documentation and evaluation. A short application guidebook is planned, to instruct cognizant individuals in the method, approach, and practice.

Such a checklist and guidebook, together with useful automated WBS entry, update, processing, and report generation aids, impose standards on software projects that are intended to facilitate the project management activity and make it more effective. Initial scheduling and downstream rescheduling of subtasks are aided by a WBS data base that contains precedence relationships, durations, costs, resource requirements, resource availability, and similar constraints on each subtask. PERT and critical-path methods (CPM) are applied directly to the WBS database, resulting in a preliminary schedule. Alterations of this schedule are then effected by editing the WBS via additional constraints recorded into the data base. Actual production progress is measured by marking milestone completions. These are then plotted into a rate chart and all significant milestones are projected to a best-estimate completion date.

PROBLEMS

The WBS is a well-known, effective project engineering tool. It has not been applied to software projects as often as to hardware and construction, probably because the planning and architectural design tasks in software have not always been sufficiently integrated as to be mutually supportive for several reasons: all of the management, support, and miscellaneous tasks were seldom fully identifiable and de-

Table 1. SOFTWARE IMPLEMENTATION PROJECT: Outline of Detailed Work Breakdown Structure

1. ANALYZE SOFTWARE REQUIREMENTS
   1.1 Understand functional and software requirements
   1.2 Identify missing, vague, ambiguous, and conflicting requirements
   1.3 Clarify stated requirements
   1.4 Verify that stated requirements fulfill requestor's goals
   1.5 Assess technology for supplying required software
   1.6 Propose alternate requirements or capability
   1.7 Document revised requirements
2. DEVELOP SOFTWARE ARCHITECTURE
   2.1 Determine architectural approach
   2.2 Develop external functional architecture
   2.3 Develop software internal architecture
   2.4 Assess architected solution vs. requirements
   2.5 Revise architecture and/or renegotiate requirements
   2.6 Document architecture and/or changed requirements
3. DEVELOP EXTERNAL FUNCTIONAL SPECIFICATION
   3.1 Define functional specification standards and conventions
   3.2 Formalize external environment and interface specifications
   3.3 Refine, formalize, and document the architected external operational view of the software
   3.4 Define functional acceptance tests
   3.5 Verify compliance of the external view with requirements
4. PRODUCE AND DELIVER SOFTWARE ITEMS
   4.1 Define programming, test and verification, QA, and documentation standards and conventions
   4.2 Formalize internal environment and interface specifications
   4.3 Obtain support tools
   4.4 Refine and formalize the internal design
   4.5 Define testing specifications to demonstrate required performance
   4.6 Define QA specifications
   4.7 Code and check the program
   4.8 Demonstrate acceptability and deliver software
5. PREPARE FOR SOFTWARE SUSTAINING AND OPERATIONS
   5.1 Train cognizant sustaining and maintenance personnel
   5.2 Train cognizant operations personnel
   5.3 Deliver sustaining tools and materials
   5.4 Deliver all software and data deliverables to operations
   5.5 Install the software and data into its operational environment
   5.6 Prepare consulting agreement between implementation and operations
6. PERFORM PROJECT MANAGEMENT FUNCTIONS
   6.1 Define project goals and objectives
   6.2 Scope and plan the project
   6.3 Administrate the implementation
   6.4 Evaluate performance and product
   6.5 Terminate the project

tailable during the planning phase; because separation of work into manageable packets quite often requires design decisions properly a part of the detailed design phase; because a basis for estimating subtask durations, costs, and other constraints has not existed or been known; and because software managers have not been trained in WBS methodology. Modern software engineering studies of phenomenology and methodology are beginning to close the gaps, however.

The existence of useful tools and methods does not ensure their acceptance; nor does their acceptance ensure project success. Plans and controls are essential project aids but unfortunately do not guarantee success either. The WBS is a planning, monitor, and control tool whose potential for successful application within a software project has been demonstrated. However, further research and demonstrations are necessary before a WBS-oriented software planning and control methodology and system are as well integrated into the software industry as structured programming has only recently become. Fortunately, many organizations and individuals are sensitive enough to the software management crisis of past years that headway is being made [7].

Happily, the solutions will almost certainly not be unique, but will range over limits that accommodate management and programming styles, organizational structures, levels of skill, areas of expertise, cost and end-date constraints, and human and technical factors.

REFERENCES

1. I. Avots, Why Does Project Management Fail? *California Management Review* XII (1), 77–82, Fall 1969.
2. Robert C. Tausworthe, *Standardized Development of Computer Software,* Prentice-Hall, Englewood Cliffs, N.J., 1977.
3. V. G. Hajek, *Management of Engineering Projects,* McGraw-Hill, New York, 1977.
4. DoD and NASA Guide, PERT/COST, Office of The Secretary of Defense and NASA, Washington, D.C., June, 1962.
5. Robert C. Tausworthe, Stochastic Models for Software Project Management, Deep Space Network Progress Report No. 42–37, Jet Propulsion Laboratory, Pasadena, California, February 1977, pp. 118–126.
6. M. McKenzie and A. P. Irvine, Evaluation of the DSN Software Methodology, Deep Space Network Progress Report No. 42–46, Jet Propulsion Laboratory, Pasadena, California, August, 1978.
7. M. M. Lehman et. al., *Software Phenomenology,* working papers of The Software Life Cycle Management Workshop, U.S. Army Institute for Research in Management Information and Computer Science, Atlanta, Georgia, August 1977.

Author presents use of the break-even chart, the learning curve, the Gantt chart, PERT and the line balance chart.

DR. VINCENT G. REUTER

Reprinted with permission from *Journal of Systems Management*, Volume 30, Number 4, April 1979, pages 6-17. Copyright © 1979 by The Association for Systems Management.

Using Graphic Management Tools

■ In recent years, the development of computers and quantitative techniques provides an aura of mystique about management methods. Managers are often awed and confused by these techniques and consequently search for more readily understood and adaptable management tools. Fortunately, several basic *graphic* management tools exist that are useful toward the more effective management of the firm's operations. However, a major question is whether or not management is availing itself of the opportunity to use such graphic approaches. Answers concerning the utilization of five such tools form a basic portion of this article.

Utilization Study and Methodology

This article accomplishes three purposes: (1) to present briefly the basic concept of five different graphic management tools; (2) to present applications and benefits of each tool; and (3) to present data concerning the utilization of each such tool. The study for the latter purpose relies on primary data developed by the author. Secondary data concerning utilization of the graphic management tools was scarce and was limited to only one of the five tools—PERT.

Based upon the need for improved productivity and reduced cost, the author conducted a major research study to determine the extent to which firms in five states—Arizona, California, Illinois, New York, and Pennsylvania were using selected management tools and techniques. This article extracts pertinent information concerning the utilization status of the following selected graphic management tools or techniques: (1) the breakeven chart, (2) the learning curve, (3) the Gantt chart, (4) PERT, and (5) the Line of Balance chart.

Firms were selected on a stratified sample basis from five states. One thousand questionnaires were addressed to the top executives for each firm; 228 responses (22.8%) were received. For each line item listing a specific management tool or technique in the study, the questionnaire respondents were requested to check one of the following responses: (1) never heard of it, (2) know about, never used, (3) small experimental use, (4) occasional use, (5) continuing and routine use, (6) used, later rejected, (7) do not know situation, and (8) no response.

In Table 1, those responding "never heard of it," "know about, never used," "do not know situation," and "no response," were grouped as *nonusers* of the specific item. Firms responding with "occasional use," or "continuing and routine use," were considered definite *users*.

Break-Even Charts

The break-even chart, which originated approximately 70 years ago, is a graphic management tool that depicts the relationship of fixed and variable costs to sales volume. The horizontal axis shows the

DR. VINCENT G. REUTER

Dr. Reuter is Professor of Management at Arizona State University. He holds B.S.C., M.A., and Ph.D. degrees from the University of Iowa. Prior to entering university teaching, Dr. Reuter held managerial positions at Curtiss-Wright, Republic Aviation, and Minneapolis-Honeywell, and he has been an industrial engineer with two management consulting firms. He is the author of over 30 publications.

units of production or sales for each unit time. The vertical axis is scaled in dollars. Fixed costs do not generally change with changes in volume, and they are plotted first as a horizontal line. Sine variable costs increase proportionately with production volume increases, this line slopes upward from the intersection of the fixed costs with the vertical axis. A third line is used to plot the sales revenue over the range of sales volume, and this line slopes upward starting at zero. Figure I shows that fixed costs remain at $300,000 regardless of the volume produced. The break-even point is reached at roughly 15,000 units of production with total fixed and variable costs of approximately $700,000. It is important to realize that our best estimate of the break-even "point" is actually a good-sized area on the chart and the point itself is within the area. Profitability or loss can be measured on the left-hand scale as the vertical distance between the revenue line and the total cost line for any given volume level. With a production volume of 20,000 units sold for each year, the profit projection shown in Figure I is approximately $100,000 ($975,000 − $875,000).

Figure II shows that by superimposing two or more break-even charts, comparative evaluations of alternative approaches may be conducted as an aid to decision making.

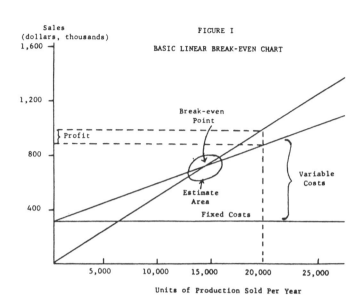

Sales (dollars, thousands)

FIGURE I

BASIC LINEAR BREAK-EVEN CHART

Units of Production Sold Per Year

TABLE I

UTILIZATION OF SELECTED GRAPHIC MANAGEMENT TOOLS
By Percentages*, N = 228**

Management Tool	Nonusers		Users			
	Know About, Never Used	Miscellaneous*	Occasional Use	Continuing and Routine Use	Small Experimental Use	Rejections
1. Break-even chart	22.4	6.5	25.0	36.0	10.1	0.0
2. Learning curve	22.4	14.9	22.8	32.5	7.0	0.4
3. Gantt charts	18.4	29.7	22.4	22.4	5.3	1.8
4. PERT, CPM (Network analysis)	32.5	13.1	28.5	12.7	11.0	2.2
5. Line of balance	26.3	48.7	11.4	8.3	3.5	1.8

*Row total equals 100 percent including total for miscellaneous unlisted status categories of: (1) "Never heard of it," (2) "Don't know situation," and (3) "No response."

**Firms surveyed in the states of Arizona (63), California (51), Illinois (33), New York (44), and Pennsylvania (37) = Total of 228 firms.

Source: Vincent G. Reuter - "Utilization of Selected Management Tools and Techniques," (unpublished research study, Arizona State University, Tempe, Arizona).

Applications of the break-even chart are helpful toward making decisions concerning: (1) Output and profit goals; (2) Pricing policy; (3) Selection of products, product line, and promotional effort; (4) Make or buy; (5) Equipment selection and replacement.

From Table I, it may be seen that 25.0 percent of the firms reported occasional use and 36.0 percent reported continuing and routine use for a total of 61.0 percent firms considered to be users of the break-even chart. An additional 10.1 percent reported small experimental use. Non-users of 28.9 percent included 22.4 percent who knew about but did not utilize the break-even concept. Apparently, the using firms were satisfied with their applications of the break-even charts because no firm reported rejecting the tool once adopted. Table II indicates that all size firms utilize the break-even chart fairly uniformly with only slightly higher usage as the firm size increases.

The Learning Curve

The learning curve is a representation of the commonsense observation that the unit cost of a new product decreases as more units of the product are made. The manufacturer, through the repetitive production process, learns how to make the product at lower cost. In 1936, it was found that the unit time will be reduced at a decreasing rate that follows a specific and predictable pattern such as a *negative exponential function*.[1]

Early studies on the learning-curve effect in both aircraft production and shipbuilding gave rise to an 80 percent learning curve for those industries.[2] This means that every time the production quantity dou-

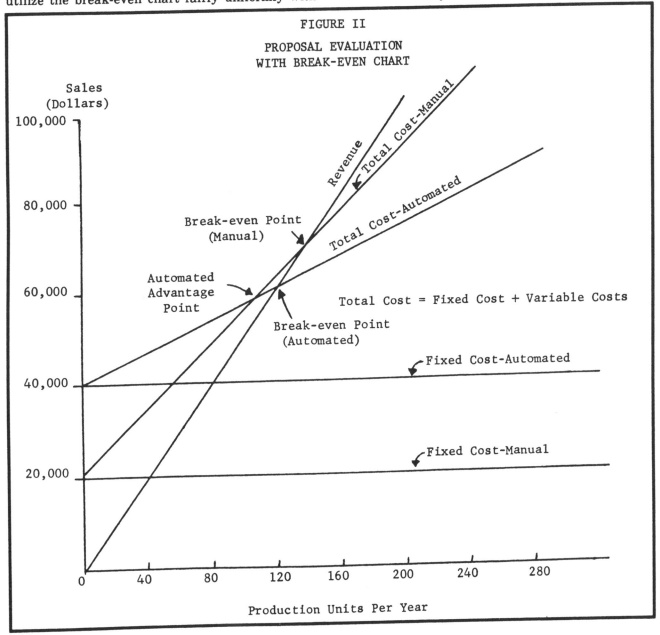

FIGURE II

PROPOSAL EVALUATION
WITH BREAK-EVEN CHART

Total Cost = Fixed Cost + Variable Costs

TABLE II

UTILIZATION OF SELECTED GRAPHIC MANAGEMENT TOOLS BY EMPLOYEE FIRM SIZE
By Percentages, N=228

(1)	(2)	(3)	(4)	(5)	(6)	(7)
		Not		Utilization Percentage by Firm Size**		
Item Number	Management Tool	Knowledge-able*	Up to 250	250-499	500-up	All Firms
Graphic approaches to planning and control:						
1 Break-even chart		6.6	54.3	61.1	63.3	61.0
2 Learning curve		14.9	41.3	42.6	65.6	55.3
3 Gantt charts		29.8	10.9	29.7	63.2	44.8
4 PERT, CPM (Network analysis)		13.1	19.6	20.4	57.8	41.2
5 Line of balance		48.7	8.6	14.9	25.8	19.7
Number of firms			46	54	128	228

*Sum of miscellaneous categories from Table I, i.e., "Never heard of it," "Do not know situation," and "No response."

**Sum of user categories from Table I, i.e., "Occasional use as needed," and "Continuing, routine use."

States surveyed included Arizona, California, Illinois, New York, and Pennsylvania.

Source: Vincent G. Reuter, "Utilization of Selected Management Tools and Techniques." (Unpublished research study, Arizona State University, Tempe, Arizona.)

bles, the cumulative average labor hours will be 80 percent of that for the previous quantity.[3] All industries or all types of work do not necessarily use the same learning curve. For example, the shipbuilding study cited provided a range between 74 to 90 percent.[4]

Studies made in the aircraft, electronics, and small electromechanical subassembly fields indicate that learning rates of 75 to 95 percent are typical.[5] In theory, learning curves can vary from the upper limit of 100 percent which implies no learning, and the lower limit of 50 percent which implies learning at an impossible rate (0 time required to produce the doubled quantity).[6] However, in practice, the percentage usually ranges from 60 percent, representing very great improvement, to 100 percent, representing no improvement at all.[7] Furthermore, different types of labor provide different percentages of learning within any given firm. For example, machine or fabrication type labor has a lower learning rate, approximating the 90 to 95 percent range, because the speed of the job is more dependent upon the capability of the equipment than the skill of the operator. The operator's learning in this situation is largely confined to improvement of setup and maintenance times. On the other hand, assembly or manual type operations generate the most rapid improvement and will have learning curves in the 65 to 85 percent range. Because of these differences, a learning curve should be developed for each category of labor.

To provide a ready means for projecting future effects, it is desirable to plot the learning curve on graph paper. When drawn on arithmetical graph paper (Figure III), the curve forms a hyperbolic curve and is of little value for predictions. However, by plotting the data on logarithmetic graph paper (Figure IV), the learning curve takes the form of a straight line that readily permits extrapolation into the future.

The learning curve discussed to this point is called the Cumulative Average Curve which represents the average number of direct labor hours required to produce all the units up to a given lot size. By taking the complement of the slope of this line $(1 - .32 = .68$ for an 80 percent curve), a unit curve may be constructed parallel to the original curve expressing the number of direct labor hours to produce a particular unit. For example, from Figure IV we find the cumulative average hours per unit for the first 16 units is equal to approximately 40 hours and the time required for production of the sixteenth unit is approximately 27 hours, (i.e., 68 percent of that for the cumulative average direct labor hours).

The learning curve projects learning or improvement on the part of the worker plus progress in management and engineering. The operator learns through experience and develops increased dexterity and skills, thereby avoiding errors, and improving quality. Managers and engineers also aid in facilitating faster production through streamlining of work and materials flow; improvement of tooling, processes, and materials; and enhanced product designs and production methods. Because of this broader concept whereby costs are reduced with increased volume for many reasons beyond the learning process involved with direct labor, the phenomenon has also been called many names besides the learning curve, such as: time-reduction curve, experience curve, progress curve, improvement curve, performance curve, and efficiency curve. However, because of its primary importance and through the custom of many years, the term learning curve has prevailed as the generic name for the concept.

The learning curve has many applications—costing; price negotiations; make or buy decisions; budgeting; output schedules; work force size; facilities and equipment requirements; progress payments; cash flow and capital expenditures; performance rating; and procurement scheduling.

The need for the learning curve in making accurate predictions is particularly acute for new-product-evaluation decisions since the quality of these decisions determines the long-run profitability of the firm. Many companies have built successful marketing and production strategies based on the learning curve; increasing a firm's product volume and market share will also bring cost advantages over the competition by means of the learning curve phenomenon.

Realizing that under the learning curve concept the labor and other costs will come down with increased volume, firms cut their prices in order to entice more customers and thereby produce the self-fulfilling prophecy of reduced costs. For example, the electronics industry charts future semi-conductor

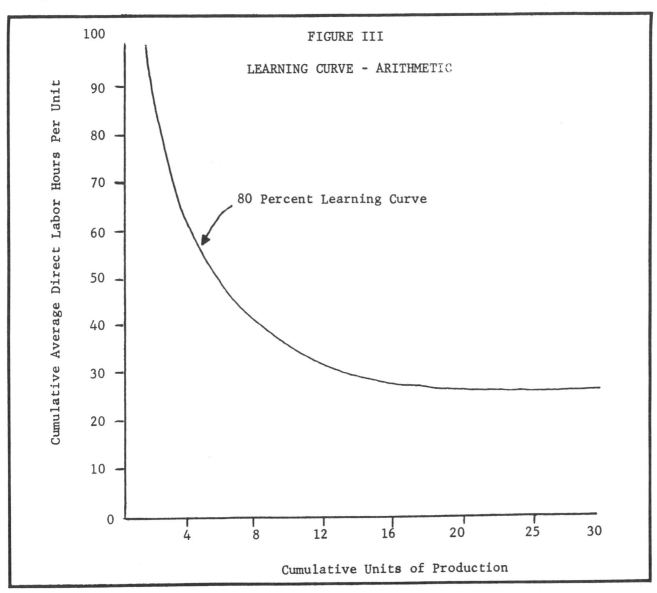

FIGURE III

LEARNING CURVE - ARITHMETIC

80 Percent Learning Curve

Cumulative Average Direct Labor Hours Per Unit

Cumulative Units of Production

prices based largely on a 73 percent learning curve found to prevail in that industry. The consequent dizzying pace of price cutting from $2,000 to $10 in just over five years for digital watches is accelerating the shakeout of producers in that market so that there are only three major firms left in that business.[8]

A prime example of a learning curve application is in forecasting output. For instance, if the size of the labor force is kept constant, the declining trend of labor hours per unit resulting from learning will produce a rising trend of deliveries while utilizing the same resources.

Table I shows the learning curve has slightly fewer users than the break-even chart—22.8 percent occasional use and 32.5 percent routine use for a total of 55.3 percent users for the learning curve. Experimental usage with the learning curve was also smaller at 7.0 percent. The percentage of nonusers for the learning curve at a total of 37.3 percent was greater than for the break-even curve because of the increase in the miscellaneous nonuser category. The rejection rate was low, indicating apparent satisfaction with the learning curve once adopted.

Table II indicates that usage is approximately equal at 42 percent for firms below 500 employees;

however, the usage rate for the learning curve jumps markedly to 65.6 percent for firms with more than 500 employees.

Gantt Charts

The basic concept of the Gantt charts was developed by Henry L. Gantt during World War I. The earliest Gantt charts were comprised of a series of activity bars plotted against a time scale. Each bar represented the beginning, duration, and end of time for a particular segment of the total job to be done. Today, many modified versions of the Gantt chart are used for planning and scheduling and then recording progress against these schedules. The latter function is accomplished by indicating within each time bar interval the percentage of that activity that is completed at any given point in time.

The Gantt chart may be adapted to any type of process and may control different types of resources—men, equipment, or activity against a time scale. There are three basic types of Gantt charts: (1) Project Planning Chart, (2) Load Chart, and (3) Reserved Time Planning Chart.

The Project Planning Chart is a predecessor of the PERT chart and is used to map out the detailed steps

FIGURE IV

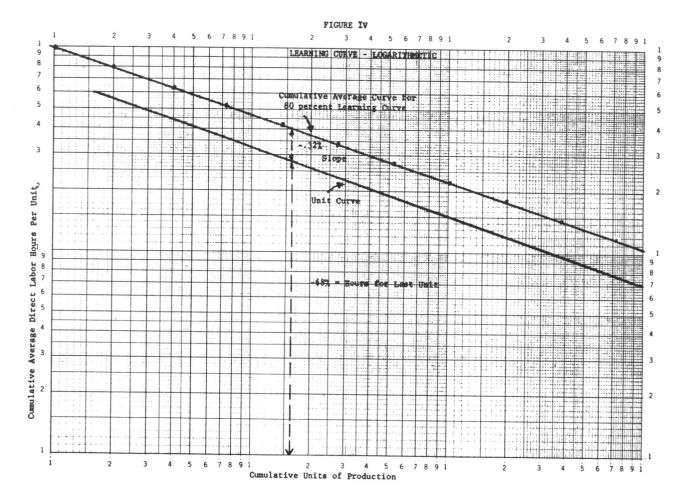

overtime, multishift operations, or subcontracting, (3) whether to accept or reject orders, and (4) where and how to make priority assignments on future orders.[9] In slack periods, the Gantt Load Chart is helpful in making decisions concerning: (1) idle capacity available for contract work, (2) types of work needed to keep men and machines utilized, and (3) when and how much to reduce the work force.[10]

The Gantt Reserved Time Planning Chart (not shown) gives each machine schedule in greater detail than the Load Chart. It shows at a glance the status of specific orders. Again, only critical or bottleneck resources would be charted.

Gantt charts are relatively inexpensive to construct and can be easily and effectively utilized for planning and scheduling purposes. They can be readily reproduced to serve as illustrations in executive reports. Disadvantages of Gantt charts include: (1) they do not show the interdependencies of the various activities involved, and (2) keeping the charts current is a problem. Fortunately, there are mechanical Gantt charts in use that employ colored string, pegs, and cards to improve and simplify the replanning problem.

Table I points out that the occasional and routine usage for the Gantt charts is equal for a total of 44.8 percent users. The experimental usage was only 5.3 percent. The total nonuser category concerning the Gantt charts included only 18.4 percent of those who knew about but never used the tool. For such a basic and long existing concept, a surprisingly large percentage of firms, 29.7 percent, were apparently unfamiliar with the Gantt chart. The low rejection rate once again appears to indicate satisfaction with the technique.

Table II shows the Gantt chart to have the pattern of increasing utilization with increasing size of the firm—only 10.9 percent utilization for firms up to 250 employees, 29.7 percent for firms with 250-499 employees, and 63.2 percent for firms with over 500 employees. Apparently, the larger firms have greater need to plan, schedule, and control critical and bottleneck operations.

PERT

PERT (Program Evaluation Review Technique) evolved from Gantt charts in 1958 at approximately the same time as CPM (Critical Path Method) as a management tool to handle the larger and more complex projects. As developed initially, PERT was applicable where there was no established system for completing a complex program and therefore there was no basis for estimating the time required to complete each task within the program. A probabalistic

FIGURE VI

GANTT LOAD CHART

Milling Machine Department

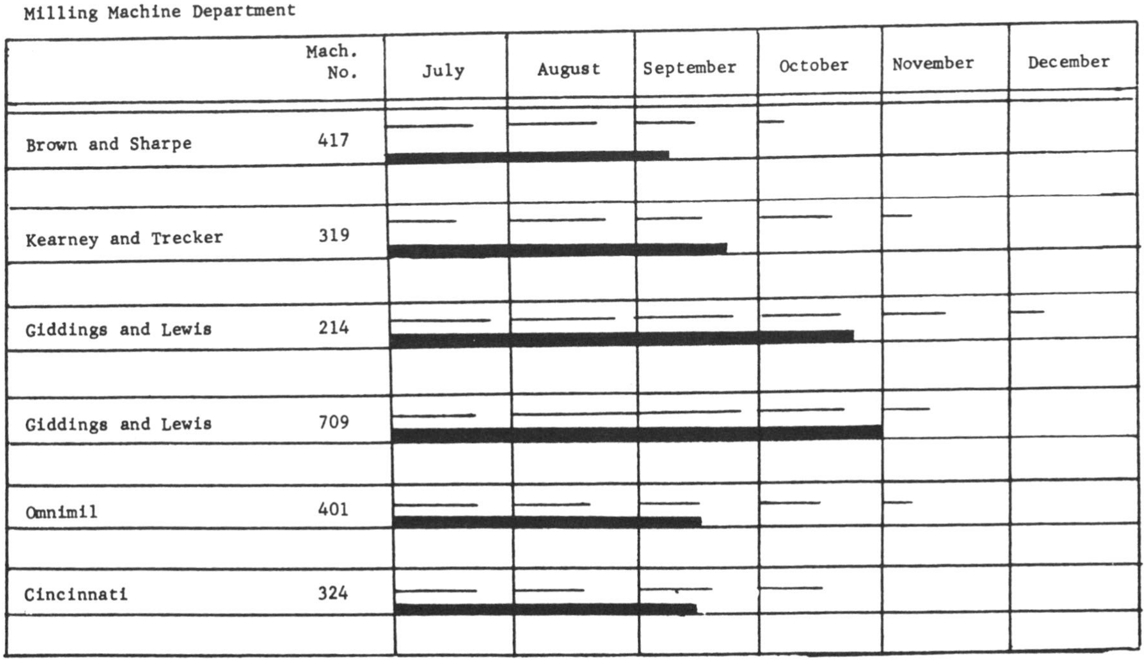

	Mach. No.	July	August	September	October	November	December
Brown and Sharpe	417						
Kearney and Trecker	319						
Giddings and Lewis	214						
Giddings and Lewis	709						
Omnimil	401						
Cincinnati	324						

Light lines show percent of each month that machines have scheduled work. Heavy lines show cumulative load.

Adapted from Elwood S. Buffa, Modern Production Management, 4th edition (New York: John Wiley and Sons, 1973), pp. 578-9.

to accomplish target objectives. Figure V shows a typical project planning chart. By looking at the week ending September 25, the current status of various activities may be noted. For example, materials procurement and parts fabrication for parts 2 and 5 are behind schedule; part 3 is on schedule; and parts 1 and 4 are ahead of schedule.

The Load Chart is useful during peak or heavy load periods. A specimen is shown in Figure VI. It uses light lines to indicate the percent of each time period for which specific departments, machines, or men have work scheduled. Heavy continuous lines are used to show the cumulative load for each individual resource item. Such a chart will not be maintained for all resources but only for critical or bottleneck machines.

Load Charts may be useful during peak load periods to make decisions concerning: (1) when and where additional capacity is required through the addition of men or equipment, (2) whether to use

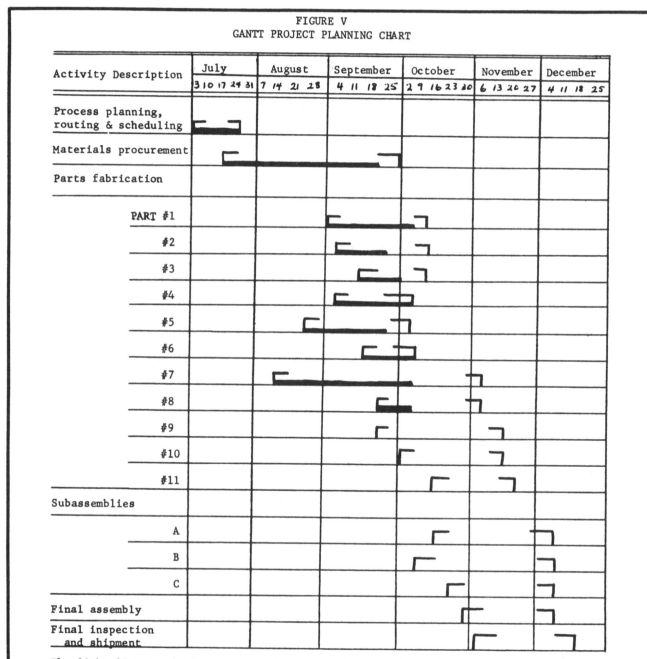

FIGURE V
GANTT PROJECT PLANNING CHART

The light line at the bottom of each activity bracket shows the percentage completion for each activity of any given point in time.
Adapted from Elwood S. Buffa, Modern Production Management, 4th Edition (New York: John Wiley & Sons, 1973), p. 576.

approach was developed using three different estimated time values in order to derive a single time expected (t_e) value for each factor. CPM, on the other hand, was usually applied to projects wherein the individual tasks had been done before and where it vas therefore possible to predict performance times airly accurately. In 1962, a second generation of PERT was developed called PERT/Cost which identifies the alternative trade-off decisions in terms of cost as well as time. It requires the development of budget and cost accounts that parallel the definition of tasks (activities) contained in the network. The aim was to complete a complex program on time within specified budgeting limits. Today, PERT and CPM have evolved in actual practice to the point that they are very similar; in addition, PERT is the most widely known and most frequently used version of the network models; consequently, discussion will be confined to PERT only.

Figure VII, while greatly oversimplified, shows a basic PERT network. In practice, preparing a PERT network is a very complex task and must be done by people who know the job best. The first step is to list all the *activities* involved toward completion of the project. After defining the project in terms of necessary activities and events, the next step is to construct the network by arranging them in a precedence relationship by asking: What must precede each activity or event? What must normally follow it? What can be done concurrently with it? These activities are shown on the PERT network as arrows connecting two circles. The circles represent *events* which mark beginning or completion of an activity.

The third step is to develop a time estimate (T_e) for each activity on the network. The fourth step is to calculate the earliest expected completion date (T_E) for each event in the network. Notice from Figure VII that the T_E for event number six is equal to seventeen days because that is the sum of the *longest* path to that point. The project total is equal to thirty-three days and represents the total of the heavy dark line, which is the longest path through the network. This dark line, representing the longest time chain, is commonly called the *critical path* in that it determines the minimum time for completion of the project.

The fifth step is to focus attention upon time and cost reduction on the critical path either to ensure meeting the established completion date or to explore the possibility of reducing the established time. Resources may be shifted as warranted to optimize and expedite the attainment of objectives. The network also shows how far noncritical activities can slip behind schedule before they become critical.

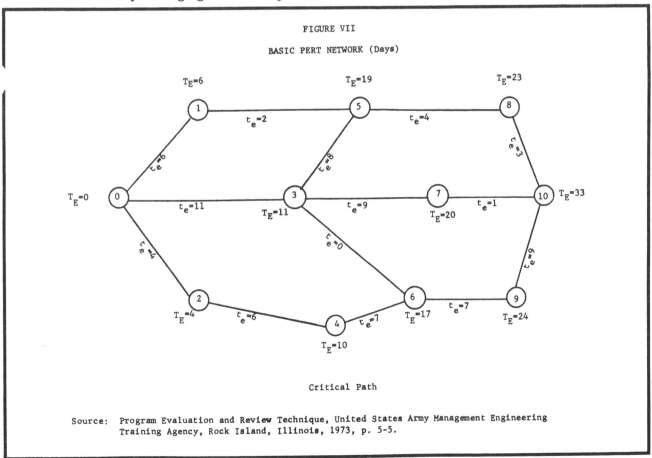

FIGURE VII

BASIC PERT NETWORK (Days)

Critical Path

Source: Program Evaluation and Review Technique, United States Army Management Engineering
          Training Agency, Rock Island, Illinois, 1973, p. 5-5.

PERT has many applications—it may be used in the introduction of new equipment, maintenance operations, introduction of new products, advertising programs, mergers or acquisitions, starting a new Broadway play, etc. The cost of implementing PERT is usually estimated at less than 1 percent, with cost and time benefits ranging from 2 percent to 10 percent of the project cost. One source is more liberal and states that, "Network analysis can commonly be expected to reduce the time taken by a project by at least 10 percent and to improve the utilization of resources by at least 5 percent...."[11]

Although not all-inclusive, some advantages and disadvantages concerning the utilization of PERT are as follows:

Advantages of PERT

1. Forces planning to help avoid omissions and duplications.
2. Shows interrelationship in work flow.
3. Provides insights into improved utilization of needed resources.
4. Spotlights critical elements in time for corrective action.
5. Permits alternative simulations.
6. Provides progress checkpoints and performance yardsticks for control
7. Can be readily adapted to the computer.
8. Aids communication and understanding.
9. Provides time and cost savings.

Disadvantages of PERT

1. Reluctance of managers to use; may prefer simpler Gantt charts.
2. Poor time estimates.
3. Pessimistic time bias; built in "fudge factors."
4. Cost and time of implementation.

According to Table I, PERT usage is primarily for occasional use with 28.5 percent responses compared to only 12.7 percent for continuing and routine use. The total reported usage is 41.2 percent which conforms very closely to the 44 percent rate found in an earlier study.[12] Experimental usage at 11.0 percent is greater than for any of the five graphic tools surveyed. The rejection rate is also the largest reported for the five graphic tools, but is still relatively low at 2.2 percent. With total nonusers of 45.6 percent, a surprisingly large number of firms, 32.5 percent, report that they know about but have never used either PERT or a network analysis approach.

Table II also shows only 13.1 percent of all firms surveyed were not knowledgeable about PERT. Once again, the firms with over 500 employees utilized the technique to a greater degree than the smaller firms—57.8 percent versus approximately 20 percent.

Line of Balance

Line of Balance (LOB) is essentially a charting technique whereby the actual progress of components and subassemblies is monitored and compared to scheduled cumulative delivery date requirements by charting that is based on the lead times ahead of final assembly. It is most appropriate for assembly operations involving a number of distinct key components. It employs the exception principle to point out where management must concentrate its attention in order to get the project back on schedule.

The Line of Balance technique is comprised of the following four elements or phases listed in the sequence in which each is normally developed when conducting a Line of Balance study of a production process.

1. **Objective Chart**—The planned cumulative delivery schedule compared to actual deliveries.
2. **Program Chart**—The production plans with the sequence and lead time required for each activity.
3. **Program Progress Chart**—The current status of performance for each key point.
4. **Line of Balance**—Comparison of program progress to objective.

The objective of a production process, where the end item is being produced under contract, is the required delivery schedule. The delivery information used and needed in an LOB analysis is of two kinds—planned and actual. The planned delivery schedule shows the expected and contractual cumulative delivery requirement. The actual delivery curve shows the deliveries actually made by the producer to the time of the analysis.

The objective chart shows both the planned and acutal cumulative delivery dates, which are plotted on the same chart so as to match performance against the planned objectives. This is normally shown as Part A of Figure VIII. For simplicity, Figure VIII shows a straight schedule delivery curve; in reality, it would curve upward because of the learning curve effect.

The program chart depicts the producer's planned process of production. This plan is derived in terms of the planned key operations or assembly points, and their lead time relationships to final completion. These operational points are steps in the manufacturing cycle, the completion of which can be used to monitor intermediate progress of production toward its ultimate goal. Charting the programs is the result of detailed study done collectively by plant management, the process engineering staff, and other members of a team responsible for conducting the Line of Balance analysis. Guides useful for constructing the program chart include shop drawings, bills of materials, process charts, machine loading charts, assembly line layouts, and shop orders.

The program chart is developed from three aspects:
1. The determination of operations to be performed.
2. The determination of the sequence of operations.
3. The determination of processing and assembly lead time.

Having determined items 1, 2, and 3 above, the program chart is constructed by using a time scale in units commensurate with the overall lead time as shown in Part B of Figure VIII.

The program progress chart depicts actual program progress in terms of quantities of materials, parts, and subassemblies which have passed through the individual check points or control points of the program plan, including those contained in end items already completed. On the program progress chart, the same quantity scale is used for the vertical axis as was used for the objective delivery chart. The horizontal axis corresponds, by duplication of numbers, to the numbered control points depicted in the program chart. The program progress chart is essentially a graphic presentation of a physical inventory taken at the various control points. Notice that this is not strictly a numerical count, for if two units of the same subassembly are required at the final assembly step, the inventory count at that point would be the total number of subassemblies divided by two. The progress chart must be updated each time a study is made.

Striking the Line of Balance for a specific date may be accomplished upon completion of the three foregoing charts. The data must be analyzed from a larger perspective to show the quantities required at each control point to support the delivery schedule. The procedure for striking the Line of Balance is as follows:

a. Place the three charts on one piece of paper. The progress chart is placed to the right of the objective chart, and the program plan is placed below the progress chart as in Figure VIII.
b. Plot the balance quantity (inventory) for each respective control point on the progress chart.
c. Starting with the study date on the horizontal

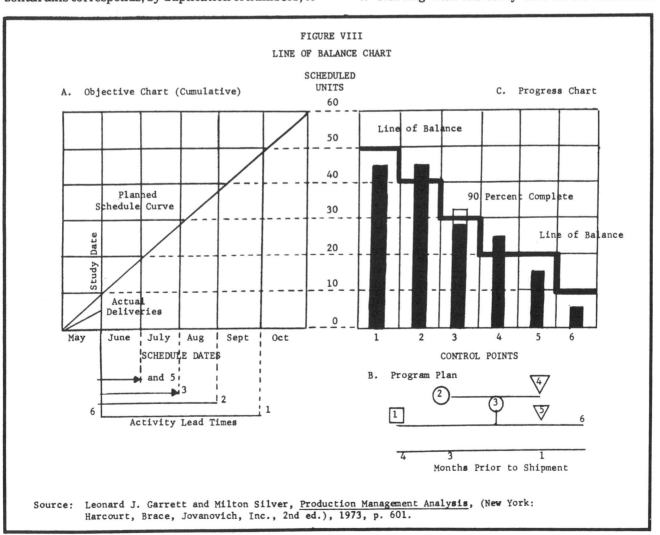

FIGURE VIII
LINE OF BALANCE CHART

Source: Leonard J. Garrett and Milton Silver, Production Management Analysis, (New York: Harcourt, Brace, Jovanovich, Inc., 2nd ed.), 1973, p. 601.

axis of the objective chart, mark off, to the right, the time (working days, weeks, or usually months, as appropriate) in lead time for each control point. This lead time information is obtained from the program chart.

d. Project a vertical line from each point on the horizontal axis to the planned cumulative delivery schedule. At the point of intersection, project a horizontal line to the corresponding bar on the progress chart. This is the balance quantity for each bar.

e. Join the balance quantities to form one staircase line across the face of the progress chart. The Line of Balance shows those activities which are on or ahead of schedule and those items which are behind schedule. A program that was exactly on schedule would result in a Line of Balance which would intersect the top of every bar on the progress chart. Essentially, the Line of Balance measures where the project *is* with respect to where it *should be*. Looking at Figure VIII, activities 2 and 4 are ahead of schedule, whereas activities 1, 3, 5, and 6 are behind schedule. Obviously, corrective action must be taken to accelerate deliveries for those activities which are behind schedule.

In order to keep people from getting unduly upset about items that are behind schedule, some firms show the number of parts started and nearly completed by an outline bar superimposed above the solid bar that shows the number of units actually completed on the progress chart as with activity 3 in Figure VIII.

The LOB chart will become rather complicated if more than fifty key check points are to be monitored. This may be overcome by using subsidiary charts to follow the main chart. The completion date of the subsidiary charts would be the date on which the subproject must be ready to plug into the overall plan.

Table I shows the majority of firms are nonusers of the Line of Balance concept. In fact, of the total nonuser percentage of 75.0 percent, 48.7 percent are in the miscellaneous category and apparently even unaware of the Line of Balance concept. Only 11.4 percent of the firms reported occasional use and 8.3 percent continuing and routine use of the Line of Balance. Experimental usage was low at only 3.5 percent—the lowest of the five graphic management tools surveyed. Rejections at 1.8 percent were low but relatively larger than for the other graphic tools.

Table II indicates that the Line of Balance chart has the greatest percentage of non-knowledgeable firms at 48.7 percent versus 29.8 percent for Gantt charts, the next highest. Usage of 19.7 percent when considering all firms surveyed is less than half of any other graphic management tool surveyed. Again, the larger firms have the greatest utilization at 25.8 percent versus 14.9 percent for firms with 250-499 employees, and only 8.6 percent for firms with less than 250 employees.

Summary

Based upon a research survey of 228 firms in five states, several generalizations are apparent from the survey findings: (1) the graphic management tools utilized by a majority of all firms included the break-even chart and the learning curve; (2) a sizable majority of firms (74.0 percent) reported not using the Line of Balance chart; (3) there is a relatively low rate of experimental use for all the specific tools; (4) there are very few rejections once the tool is utilized; and (5) in every instance there was a discernable pattern showing that the larger firms make heavier use of the graphic management tools.

Except for the low usage with the Line of Balance chart, the high use of all the other four graphic management tools is encouraging. The low rate of experimental use indicates that the rate of change is very slow; however, once the graphic management tools are accepted, users are apparently well satisfied with their use because very few are subsequently rejected.

The graphic management tools discussed in this article are relatively basic. Their greater utilization could be helpful toward the improved planning, scheduling, and controlling of a firm's activities.[13]

•jsm

REFERENCES

1. The relationship may be expressed mathematically as $Y = aN^{-b}$ where Y = the accumulated average time per unit, N = number of units produced, a = time required to produce the first unit, and $-b$ = the negative exponent associated with the learning rate.
2. S. A. Billion, "Industrial Learning Curves and Forecasting," *Management International Review,* #6, 1966, p. 68.
3. The discussion and figures contained herein are based on the cumulative average-hours learning curve phenomenon. Learning curves can also be plotted in terms of actual labor hours per last unit produced. However, a majority of firms find the approach used here as most applicable to their processes.
4. S. A. Billion, *op. cit.,* p. 68.
5. Lamar Lee, Jr. and Donald W. Dobler, *Purchasing and Materials Management,* (New York: McGraw Hill, Inc., 1971), p. 145.
6. *Ibid.*
7. Richard A. Johnson, William T. Newell, and Roger C. Vergin, *Operations Management,* (Boston: Houghton Mifflin Company, 1972), p. 394.
8. "The Great Digital Watch Shake-out," *Business Week,* May 2, 1977, p. 78.
9. Leonard J. Garrett and Milton Silver, *Production Management Analysis,* (New York: Harcourt, Brace, Jovanovich, Inc., 2nd ed., 1973), p. 557.
10. *Ibid.*
11. P. G. Moore, *Basic Operational Research* (London: Sir Isaac Pitman & Sons, Ltd., 1968), p. 32.
12. Peter Schoderbek, "A Study of the Application of PERT," *Academy of Management Journal,* (September, 1965), p. 199.
13. The author expresses his thanks to the Research Grants Committee of Arizona State University for partial funding of the research.

THE MYTHICAL MAN-MONTH

HOW DOES A PROJECT GET TO BE A YEAR LATE? . . . . . . ONE DAY AT A TIME.

By Frederick P. Brooks, Jr.

Dr. Brooks was part of the management team charged with developing the hardware for the IBM 360 system. In 1964 he became the manager of the Operating System/360 project; this trial by fire convinced him that managing a large software project is more like managing any other large undertaking than programmers believe and less like it than professional managers expect.

About his OS/360 project, he says: "Managing OS/360 development was a very educational experience, albeit a very frustrating one. The team, including F. M. Trapnell who succeeded me as manager, has much to be proud of. The system contains many excellences in design and execution, and it has been successful in achieving widespread use. Certain ideas, most noticeably device-independent input/output and external library management, were technical innovations now widely copied. It is now quite reliable, reasonably efficient, and very versatile.

The effort cannot be called wholly successful, however. Any OS/360 user is quickly aware of how much better it should be. The flaws in design and execution pervade especially the control program, as distinguished from language compilers. Most of the flaws date from the 1964-1965 design period and hence must be laid to my charge. Furthermore, the product was late, it took more memory than planned, the costs were several times the estimate, and it did not perform very well until several releases after the first."

Analyzing the OS/360 experiences for management and technical lessons, Dr. Brooks put his thoughts into book form. Addison-Wesley Publishing Company (Reading, Mass.) will offer "The Mythical Man-Month: Essays on Software Engineering", from which this article is taken, sometime next month.

NO SCENE FROM PREHISTORY is quite so vivid as that of the mortal struggles of great beasts in the tar pits. In the mind's eye one sees dinosaurs, mammoths, and saber-toothed tigers struggling against the grip of the tar. The fiercer the struggle, the more entangling the tar, and no beast is so strong or so skillful but that he ultimately sinks.

Large-system programming has over the past decade been such a tar pit, and many great and powerful beasts have thrashed violently in it. Most have emerged with running systems—few have met goals, schedules, and budgets. Large and small, massive or wiry, team after team has become entangled in the tar. No one thing seems to cause the difficulty—any particular paw can be pulled away. But the accumulation of simultaneous and interacting factors brings slower and slower motion. Everyone seems to have been surprised by the stickiness of the problem, and it is hard to discern the nature of it. But we must try to understand it if we are to solve it.

More software projects have gone awry for lack of calendar time than for all other causes combined. Why is this case of disaster so common?

First, our techniques of estimating are poorly developed. More seriously, they reflect an unvoiced assumption which is quite untrue, i.e., that all will go well.

Second, our estimating techniques fallaciously confuse effort with progress, hiding the assumption that men and months are interchangeable.

Third, because we are uncertain of our estimates, software managers often lack the courteous stubbornness required to make people wait for a good product.

Fourth, schedule progress is poorly monitored. Techniques proven and routine in other engineering disciplines are considered radical innovations in software engineering.

Fifth, when schedule slippage is recognized, the natural (and traditional) response is to add manpower. Like dousing a fire with gasoline, this makes matters worse, much worse. More fire requires more gasoline and thus begins a regenerative cycle which ends in disaster.

Schedule monitoring will be covered later. Let us now consider other aspects of the problem in more detail.

Optimism

All programmers are optimists. Perhaps this modern sorcery especially attracts those who believe in happy endings and fairy godmothers. Perhaps the hundreds of nitty frustrations drive away all but those who habitually focus on the end goal. Perhaps it is merely that computers are young, programmers are younger, and the young are always optimists. But however the selection process works, the result is indisputable: "This time it will surely run," or "I just found the last bug."

So the first false assumption that underlies the scheduling of systems programming is that *all will go well*, i.e., that *each task will take only as long as it "ought" to take*.

The pervasiveness of optimism among programmers deserves more than a flip analysis. Dorothy Sayers, in her excellent book, *The Mind of the*

THE MYTHICAL MAN-MONTH

Maker, divides creative activity into three stages: the idea, the implementation, and the interaction. A book, then, or a computer, or a program comes into existence first as an ideal construct, built outside time and space but complete in the mind of the author. It is realized in time and space by pen, ink, and paper, or by wire, silicon, and ferrite. The creation is complete when someone reads the book, uses the computer or runs the program, thereby interacting with the mind of the maker.

This description, which Miss Sayers uses to illuminate not only human creative activity but also the Christian doctrine of the Trinity, will help us in our present task. For the human makers of things, the incompletenesses and inconsistencies of our ideas become clear only during implementation. Thus it is that writing, experimentation, "working out" are essential disciplines for the theoretician.

In many creative activities the medium of execution is intractable. Lumber splits; paints smear; electrical circuits ring. These physical limitations of the medium constrain the ideas that may be expressed, and they also create unexpected difficulties in the implementation.

Implementation, then, takes time and sweat both because of the physical media and because of the inadequacies of the underlying ideas. We tend to blame the physical media for most of our implementation difficulties; for the media are not "ours" in the way the ideas are, and our pride colors our judgment.

Computer programming, however, creates with an exceedingly tractable medium. The programmer builds from pure thought-stuff: concepts and very flexible representations thereof. Because the medium is tractable, we expect few difficulties in implementation; hence our pervasive optimism. Because our ideas are faulty, we have bugs; hence our optimism is unjustified.

In a single task, the assumption that all will go well has a probabilistic effect on the schedule. It might indeed go as planned, for there is a probability distribution for the delay that will be encountered, and "no delay" has a finite probability. A large programming effort, however, consists of many tasks, some chained end-to-end. The probability that each will go well becomes vanishingly small.

The mythical man-month

The second fallacious thought mode is expressed in the very unit of effort used in estimating and scheduling: the man-month. Cost does indeed vary as the product of the number of men and the number of months. Progress does not. *Hence the man-month as a unit for measuring the size of a job is a dangerous and deceptive myth.* It implies that men and months are interchangeable.

Men and months are interchangeable commodities only when a task can be partitioned among many workers *with no communication among them* (Fig. 1). This is true of reaping wheat or picking cotton; it is not even approximately true of systems programming.

When a task cannot be partitioned

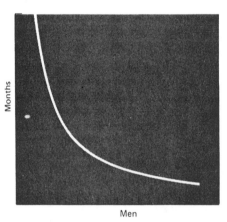

Fig. 1. The term "man-month" implies that if one man takes 10 months to do a job, 10 men can do it in one month. This may be true of picking cotton.

because of sequential constraints, the application of more effort has no effect on the schedule. The bearing of a child takes nine months, no matter how many women are assigned. Many software tasks have this characteristic because of the sequential nature of debugging.

In tasks that can be partitioned but which require communication among the subtasks, the effort of communication must be added to the amount of work to be done. Therefore the best that can be done is somewhat poorer than an even trade of men for months (Fig. 2).

The added burden of communication is made up of two parts, training and intercommunication. Each worker must be trained in the technology, the goals of the effort, the overall strategy, and the plan of work. This training cannot be partitioned, so this part of the added effort varies linearly with the number of workers.

V. S. Vyssotsky of Bell Telephone Laboratories estimates that a large project can sustain a manpower build-up of 30% per year. More than that strains and even inhibits the evolution of the essential informal structure and its communication pathways. F. J.

Corbató of MIT points out that a long project must anticipate a turnover of 20% per year, and new people must be both technically trained and integrated into the formal structure.

Intercommunication is worse. If each part of the task must be separately coordinated with each other part, the effort increases as $n(n-1)/2$. Three workers require three times as much pairwise intercommunication as two; four require six times as much as two. If, moreover, there need to be conferences among three, four, etc., workers to resolve things jointly, matters get worse yet. The added effort of communicating may fully counteract the division of the original task and bring us back to the situation of Fig. 3.

Since software construction is inherently a systems effort—an exercise in complex interrelationships—communication effort is great, and it quickly

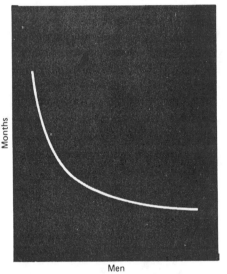

Fig. 2. Even on tasks that can be nicely partitioned among people, the additional communication required adds to the total work, increasing the schedule.

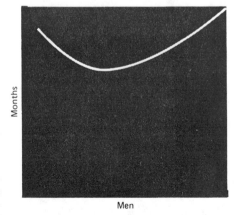

Fig. 3. Since software construction is complex, the communications overhead is great. Adding more men can lengthen, rather than shorten, the schedule.

dominates the decrease in individual task time brought about by partitioning. Adding more men then lengthens, not shortens, the schedule.

Systems test

No parts of the schedule are so thoroughly affected by sequential constraints as component debugging and system test. Furthermore, the time required depends on the number and subtlety of the errors encountered. Theoretically this number should be zero. Because of optimism, we usually expect the number of bugs to be smaller than it turns out to be. Therefore testing is usually the most mis-scheduled part of programming.

For some years I have been successfully using the following rule of thumb for scheduling a software task:

⅓ planning

⅙ coding

¼ component test and early system test

¼ system test, all components in hand.

This differs from conventional scheduling in several important ways:

1. The fraction devoted to planning is larger than normal. Even so, it is barely enough to produce a de-

of the schedule.

In examining conventionally scheduled projects, I have found that few allowed one-half of the projected schedule for testing, but that most did indeed spend half of the actual schedule for that purpose. Many of these were on schedule until and except in system testing.

Failure to allow enough time for system test, in particular, is peculiarly disastrous. Since the delay comes at the end of the schedule, no one is aware of schedule trouble until almost the delivery date. Bad news, late and without warning, is unsettling to customers and to managers.

Furthermore, delay at this point has unusually severe financial, as well as psychological, repercussions. The project is fully staffed, and cost-per-day is maximum. More seriously, the software is to support other business effort (shipping of computers, operation of new facilities, etc.) and the secondary costs of delaying these are very high, for it is almost time for software shipment. Indeed, these secondary costs may far outweigh all others. It is therefore very important to allow enough system test time in the original schedule.

two choices—wait or eat it raw. Software customers have had the same choices.

The cook has another choice; he can turn up the heat. The result is often an omelette nothing can save—burned in one part, raw in another.

Now I do not think software managers have less inherent courage and firmness than chefs, nor than other engineering managers. But false scheduling to match the patron's desired date is much more common in our discipline than elsewhere in engineering. It is very difficult to make a vigorous, plausible, and job-risking defense of an estimate that is derived by no quantitative method, supported by little data, and certified chiefly by the hunches of the managers.

Clearly two solutions are needed. We need to develop and publicize productivity figures, bug-incidence figures, estimating rules, and so on. The whole profession can only profit from sharing such data.

Until estimating is on a sounder basis, individual managers will need to stiffen their backbones, and defend their estimates with the assurance that their poor hunches are better than wish-derived estimates.

Regenerative disaster

What does one do when an essential software project is behind schedule? Add manpower, naturally. As Figs. 1 through 3 suggest, this may or may not help.

Let us consider an example. Suppose a task is estimated at 12 man-months and assigned to three men for four months, and that there are measurable mileposts A, B, C, D, which are scheduled to fall at the end of each month.

Now suppose the first milepost is not reached until two months have elapsed. What are the alternatives facing the manager?

1. Assume that the task must be done on time. Assume that only the first part of the task was misestimated. Then 9 man-months of effort remain, and two months, so 4½ men will be needed. Add 2 men to the 3 assigned.

2. Assume that the task must be done on time. Assume that the whole estimate was uniformly low. Then 18 man-months of effort remain, and two months, so 9 men will be needed. Add 6 men to the 3 assigned.

3. Reschedule. In this case, I like the advice given by an experienced hardware engineer, "Take no small slips." That is, allow enough time in the new schedule to ensure that the work can be carefully and

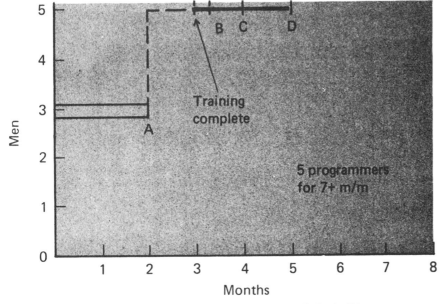

Fig. 4. Adding manpower to a project which is late may not help. In this case, suppose three men on a 12 man-month project were a month late. If it takes one of the three an extra month to train two new men, the project will be just as late as if no one was added.

tailed and solid specification, and not enough to include research or exploration of totally new techniques.

2. The *half* of the schedule devoted to debugging of completed code is much larger than normal.

3. The part that is easy to estimate, i.e., coding, is given only one-sixth

Gutless estimating

Observe that for the programmer, as for the chef, the urgency of the patron may govern the scheduled completion of the task, but it cannot govern the actual completion. An omelette, promised in ten minutes, may appear to be progressing nicely. But when it has not set in ten minutes, the customer has thoroughly done, and that rescheduling will not have to be done again.

4. Trim the task. In practice this tends to happen anyway, once the team observes schedule slippage. Where the secondary costs of delay are very high, this is the only feasible action. The manager's only alternatives are to trim it formally and carefully, to reschedule, or to watch the task get silently trimmed by hasty design and incomplete testing.

In the first two cases, insisting that the unaltered task be completed in four months is disastrous. Consider the regenerative effects, for example, for the first alternative (Fig. 4 preceding page). The two new men, however competent and however quickly recruited, will require training in the task by one of the experienced men. If this takes a month, *3 man-months will have been devoted to work not in the original estimate.* Furthermore, the task, originally partitioned three ways, must be repartitioned into five parts, hence some work already done will be lost and system testing must be lengthened. So at the end of the third month, substantially more than 7 man-months of effort remain, and 5 trained people and one month are available. As Fig. 4 suggests, the product is just as late as if no one had been added.

To hope to get done in four months, considering only training time and not repartitioning and extra systems test, would require adding 4 men, not 2, at the end of the second month. To cover repartitioning and system test effects, one would have to add still other men. Now, however, one has at least a 7-man team, not a 3-man one; thus such aspects as team organization and task division are different in kind, not merely in degree.

Notice that by the end of the third month things look very black. The March 1 milestone has not been reached in spite of all the managerial effort. The temptation is very strong to repeat the cycle, adding yet more manpower. Therein lies madness.

The foregoing assumed that only the first milestone was misestimated. If on March 1 one makes the conservative assumption that the whole schedule was optimistic one wants to add 6 men just to the original task. Calculation of the training, repartitioning, system testing effects is left as an exercise for the reader. Without a doubt, the regenerative disaster will yield a poorer product later, than would rescheduling with the original three men, unaugmented.

Oversimplifying outrageously, we state Brooks' Law:

> Adding manpower to a late software project makes it later.

This then is the demythologizing of the man-month. The number of months of a project depends upon its sequential constraints. The maximum number of men depends upon the number of independent subtasks. From these two quantities one can derive schedules using fewer men and more months. (The only risk is product obsolescence.) One cannot, however, get workable schedules using more men and fewer months. More software projects have gone awry for lack of calendar time than for all other causes combined.

Calling the shot

How long will a system programming job take? How much effort will be required? How does one estimate?

I have earlier suggested ratios that seem to apply to planning time, coding, component test, and system test. First, one must say that one does *not* estimate the entire task by estimating the coding portion only and then applying the ratios. The coding is only one-sixth or so of the problem, and errors in its estimate or in the ratios could lead to ridiculous results.

Second, one must say that data for building isolated small programs are not applicable to programming systems products. For a program averaging about 3,200 words, for example, Sackman, Erikson, and Grant report an average code-plus-debug time of about 178 hours for a single programmer, a figure which would extrapolate to give an annual productivity of 35,800 statements per year. A program half that size took less than one-fourth as long, and extrapolated productivity is almost 80,000 statements per year.[1]. Planning, documentation, testing, system integration, and training times must be added. The linear extrapolation of such spring figures is meaningless. Extrapolation of times for the hundred-yard dash shows that a man can run a mile in under three minutes.

Before dismissing them, however, let us note that these numbers, although not for strictly comparable problems, suggest that effort goes as a power of size *even* when no communication is involved except that of a man with his memories.

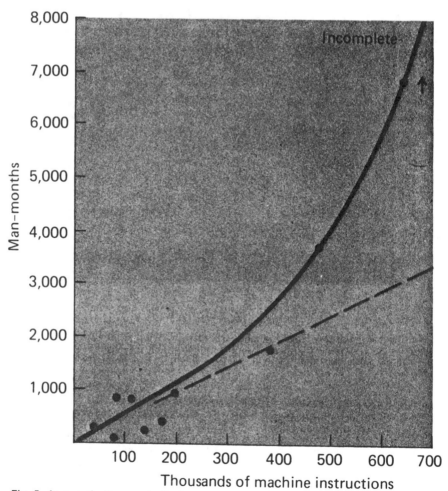

Fig. 5. As a project's complexity increases, the number of man-months required to complete it goes up exponentially.

Fig. 5 tells the sad story. It illustrates results reported from a study done by Nanus and Farr[2] at System Development Corp. This shows an exponent of 1.5; that is,

effort = (constant)×(number of instructions)[1.5]

Another SDC study reported by Weinwurm[3] also shows an exponent near 1.5.

A few studies on programmer productivity have been made, and several estimating techniques have been proposed. Morin has prepared a survey of the published data.[4] Here I shall give only a few items that seem especially illuminating.

Portman's data

Charles Portman, manager of ICL's Software Div., Computer Equipment Organization (Northwest) at Manchester, offers another useful personal insight.

He found his programming teams missing schedules by about one-half—each job was taking approximately twice as long as estimated. The estimates were very careful, done by experienced teams estimating man-hours for several hundred subtasks on a PERT chart. When the slippage pattern appeared, he asked them to keep careful daily logs of time usage. These showed that the estimating error could be entirely accounted for by the fact that his teams were only realizing 50% of the working week as actual programming and debugging time. Machine downtime, higher-priority short unrelated jobs, meetings, paperwork, company business, sickness, personal time, etc. accounted for the rest. In short, the estimates made an unrealistic assumption about the number of technical work hours per man-year. My own experience quite confirms his conclusion.

An unpublished 1964 study by E. F. Bardain shows programmers realizing only 27% productive time.[5]

	Prog. units	Number of programmers	Years	Man-years	Program words	Words/ man-yr.
Operational	50	83	4	101	52,000	515
Maintenance	36	60	4	81	51,000	630
Compiler	13	9	2¼	17	38,000	2230
Translator (Data assembler)	15	13	2½	11	25,000	2270

Table 1. Data from Bell Labs indicates productivity differences between complex problems (the first two are basically control programs with many modules) and less complex ones. No one is certain how much of the difference is due to complexity, how much to the number of people involved.

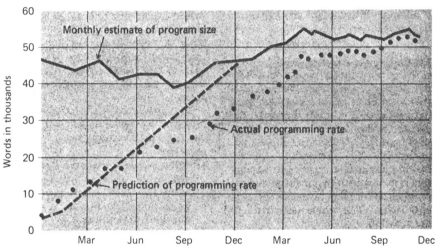

Fig. 6. Bell Labs' experience in predicting programming effort on one project.

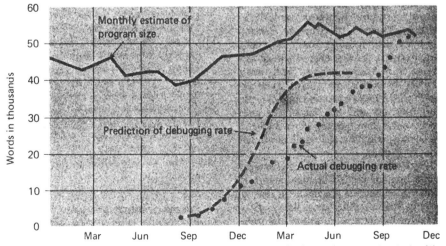

Fig. 7. Bell's predictions for debugging rates on a single project, contrasted with actual figures.

Aron's data

Joel Aron, manager of Systems Technology at IBM in Gaithersburg, Maryland, has studied programmer productivity when working on nine large systems (briefly, *large* means more than 25 programmers and 30,-000 deliverable instructions). He divides such systems according to interactions among programmers (and system parts) and finds productivities as follows:

Very few interactions	10,000 instructions per man-year
Some interactions	5,000
Many interactions	1,500

The man-years do not include support and system test activities, only design and programming. When these figures are diluted by a factor of two to cover system test, they closely match Harr's data.

Harr's data

John Harr, manager of programming for the Bell Telephone Laboratories' Electronic Switching System, reported his and others' experience in a paper at the 1969 Spring Joint Computer Conference.[6] These data are shown in Table 1 and Figs. 6 and 7 .

Of these, Fig. 6 is the most detailed and the most useful. The first two jobs are basically control programs; the second two are basically language translators. Productivity is stated in terms of debugged words per man-year. This includes programming, component test, and system test. It is not clear how much of the planning effort, or effort in machine support, writing, and the like, is included.

The productivities likewise fall into two classifications: those for control programs are about 600 words per man-year; those for translators are about 2,200 words per man-year. Note that all four programs are of similar size—the variation is in size of the work groups, length of time, and number of modules. Which is cause and which is effect? Did the control programs require more people because they were more complicated? Or did they require more modules and more man-months because they were assigned more people? Did they take longer because of the greater complexity, or because more people were assigned? One can't be sure. The control programs were surely more complex. These uncertainties aside, the numbers describe the real productivities achieved on a large system, using present-day programming techniques. As such they are a real contribution.

Figs. 6 and 7 show some interesting data on programming and debugging rates as compared to predicted rates.

OS/360 data

IBM OS/360 experience, while not available in the detail of Harr's data, confirms it. Productivities in range of 600-800 debugged instructions per man-year were experienced by control program groups. Productivities in the 2,000-3,000 debugged instructions per man-year were achieved by language translator groups. These include planning done by the group, coding component test, system test, and some support activities. They are comparable to Harr's data, so far as I can tell.

Aron's data, Harr's data, and the OS/360 data all confirm striking differences in productivity related to the complexity and difficulty of the task itself. My guideline in the morass of estimating complexity is that compilers are three times as bad as normal batch application programs, and operating systems are three times as bad as compilers.

Corbató's data

Both Harr's data and OS/360 data are for assembly language programming. Little data seem to have been published on system programming productivity using higher-level languages. Corbató of MIT's Project MAC reports, however, a mean productivity of 1,200 lines of debugged PL/I statements per man-year on the MULTICS system (between 1 and 2 million words)[7]

This number is very exciting. Like the other projects, MULTICS includes control programs and language transla-

tors. Like the others, it is producing a system programming product, tested and documented. The data seem to be comparable in terms of kind of effort included. And the productivity number is a good average between the control program and translator productivities of other projects.

But Corbató's number is *lines* per man-year, not *words!* Each statement in his system corresponds to about three-to-five words of handwritten code! This suggests two important conclusions:

- Productivity seems constant in terms of elementary statements, a conclusion that is reasonable in terms of the thought a statement requires and the errors it may include.
- Programming productivity may be increased as much as five times when a suitable high-level language is used. To back up these conclusions, W. M. Taliaffero also reports a constant productivity of 2,400 statements/year in Assembler, FORTRAN, and COBOL.[8] E. A. Nelson has shown a 3-to-1 productivity improvement for high-level language, although his standard deviations are wide.[9]

Hatching a catastrophe

When one hears of disastrous schedule slippage in a project, he imagines that a series of major calamities must have befallen it. Usually, however, the disaster is due to termites, not tornadoes; and the schedule has slipped imperceptibly but inexorably. Indeed, major calamities are easier to handle; one responds with major force, radical reorganization, the invention of new approaches. The whole team rises to the occasion.

But the day-by-day slippage is harder to recognize, harder to prevent, harder to make up. Yesterday a key man was sick, and a meeting couldn't be held. Today the machines are all down, because lightning struck the building's power transformer. Tomorrow the disc routines won't start testing, because the first disc is a week late from the factory. Snow, jury duty, family problems, emergency meetings with customers, executive audits—the list goes on and on. Each one only postpones some activity by a half-day or a day. And the schedule slips, one day at a time.

How does one control a big project on a tight schedule? The first step is to *have* a schedule. Each of a list of events, called milestones, has a date. Picking the dates is an estimating problem, discussed already and crucially dependent on experience.

For picking the milestones there is

only one relevant rule. Milestones must be concrete, specific, measurable events, defined with knife-edge sharpness. Coding, for a counterexample, is "90% finished" for half of the total coding time. Debugging is "99% complete" most of the time. "Planning complete" is an event one can proclaim almost at will.[10]

Concrete milestones, on the other hand, are 100% events. "Specifications signed by architects and implementers," "source coding 100% complete, keypunched, entered into disc library," "debugged version passes all test cases." These concrete milestones demark the vague phases of planning, coding, debugging.

It is more important that milestones be sharp-edged and unambiguous than that they be easily verifiable by the boss. Rarely will a man lie about mile-

> None love
> the bearer of bad news.
> *Sophocles*

stone progress, *if* the milestone is so sharp that he can't deceive himself. But if the milestone is fuzzy, the boss often understands a different report from that which the man gives. To supplement Sophocles, no one enjoys bearing bad news, either, so it gets softened without any real intent to deceive.

Two interesting studies of estimating behavior by government contractors on large-scale development projects show that:

1. Estimates of the length of an activity made and revised carefully every two weeks before the activity starts do not significantly change as the start time draws near, no matter how wrong they ultimately turn out to be.
2. *During* the activity, *over*estimates of duration come steadily down as the activity proceeds.
3. *Underestimates* do not change significantly during the activity until about three weeks before the scheduled completion.[11]

Sharp milestones are in fact a service to the team, and one they can properly expect from a manager. The fuzzy milestone is the harder burden to live with. It is in fact a millstone that grinds down morale, for it deceives one about lost time until it is irremediable. And chronic schedule slippage is a morale-killer.

"The other piece is late"

A schedule slips a day; so what? Who gets excited about a one-day slip? We can make it up later. And the other piece ours fits into is late anyway.

A baseball manager recognizes a nonphysical talent, *hustle*, as an essential gift of great players and great teams. It is the characteristic of running faster than necessary, moving sooner than necessary, trying harder than necessary. It is essential for great programming teams, too. Hustle provides the cushion, the reserve capacity, that enables a team to cope with routine mishaps, to anticipate and forfend minor calamities. The calculated response, the measured effort, are the wet blankets that dampen hustle. As we have seen, one *must* get excited about a one-day slip. Such are the elements of catastrophe.

But not all one-day slips are equally disastrous. So some calculation of response is necessary, though hustle be dampened. How does one tell which slips matter? There is no substitute for a PERT chart or a critical-path schedule. Such a network shows who waits for what. It shows who is on the critical path, where any slip moves the end date. It also shows how much an activity can slip before it moves into the critical path.

The PERT technique, strictly speaking, is an elaboration of critical-path scheduling in which one estimates three times for every event, times corresponding to different probabilities of meeting the estimated dates. I do not find this refinement to be worth the extra effort, but for brevity I will call any critical path network a PERT chart.

The preparation of a PERT chart is the most valuable part of its use. Laying out the network, identifying the dependencies, and estimating the legs all force a great deal of very specific planning very early in a project. The first chart is always terrible, and one invents and invents in making the second one.

As the project proceeds, the PERT chart provides the answer to the demoralizing excuse, "The other piece is late anyhow." It shows how hustle is needed to keep one's own part off the critical path, and it suggests ways to make up the lost time in the other part.

Under the rug

When a first-line manager sees his small team slipping behind, he is rarely inclined to run to the boss with this woe. The team might be able to make it up, or he should be able to invent or reorganize to solve the problem. Then why worry the boss with it? So far, so good. Solving such problems is exactly what the first-line manager is there for. And the boss does have enough real worries demanding his action that he doesn't seek others. So all the dirt gets swept under the rug.

But every boss needs two kinds of information, exceptions for action and a status picture for education.[12] For that purpose he needs to know the status of all his teams. Getting a true picture of that status is hard.

The first-line manager's interests and those of the boss have an inherent conflict here. The first-line manager fears that if he reports his problem, the boss will act on it. Then his action will preempt the manager's function, diminish his authority, foul up his other plans. So as long as the manager thinks he can solve it alone, he doesn't tell the boss.

Two rug-lifting techniques are open to the boss. Both must be used. The first is to reduce the role conflict and inspire sharing of status. The other is to yank the rug back.

Reducing the role conflict

The boss must first distinguish between action information and status information. He must discipline himself *not* to act on problems his managers can solve, and *never* to act on problems when he is explicitly reviewing status. I once knew a boss who invariably picked up the phone to give orders before the end of the first para-

SYSTEM/360 SUMMARY STATUS REPORT
OS/360 LANGUAGE PROCESSORS + SERVICE PROGRAMS
AS OF FEBRUARY 01.1965

A=APPROVAL
C=COMPLETED

*=REVISED PLANNED DATE
NE=NOT ESTABLISHED

PROJECT	LOCATION	COMMITMNT ANNOUNCE RELEASE	OBJECTIVE AVAILABLE APPROVED	SPECS AVAILABLE APPROVED	SRL AVAILABLE APPROVED	ALPHA TEST ENTRY EXIT	COMP TEST START COMPLETE	SYS TEST START COMPLETE	BULLETIN AVAILABLE APPROVED	BETA TEST ENTRY EXIT
OPERATING SYSTEM										
12K DESIGN LEVEL (E)										
ASSEMBLY	SAN JOSE	04/--/4 C 12/31/5	10/28/4 C	10/13/4 C 01/11/5	11/13/4 C 11/18/4 A	01/15/5 C 02/22/5				09/01/5 11/30/5
FORTRAN	POK	04/--/4 C 12/31/5	10/28/4 C	10/21/4 C 01/22/5	12/17/4 C 12/19/4 A	01/15/5 C 02/22/5				09/01/5 11/30/5
COBOL	ENDICOTT	04/--/4 C 12/31/5	10/28/4 C	10/15/4 C 01/20/5 A	11/17/4 C 12/08/4 A	01/15/5 C 02/22/5				09/01/5 11/30/5
RPG	SAN JOSE	04/--/4 C 12/31/5	10/28/4 C	09/30/4 C 01/05/5 A	12/02/4 C 01/18/5 A	01/15/5 C 02/22/5				09/01/5 11/30/5
UTILITIES	TIME/LIFE	04/--/4 C 12/31/5	06/24/4 C		11/20/4 C 11/30/4 A					09/01/5 11/30/5
SORT 1	POK	04/--/4 C 12/31/5	10/28/4 C	10/19/4 C 01/11/5	11/12/4 C 11/30/4 A	01/15/5 C 03/22/5				09/01/5 11/30/5
SORT 2	POK	04/--/4 C 06/30/6	10/28/4 C	10/19/4 C 01/11/5	11/12/4 C 11/30/4 A	01/15/5 C 03/22/5				03/01/6 05/30/6
44K DESIGN LEVEL (F)										
ASSEMBLY	SAN JOSE	04/--/4 C 12/31/5	10/28/4 C	10/13/4 C 01/11/5	11/13/4 C 11/18/4 A	02/15/5 03/22/5				09/01/5 11/30/5
COBOL	TIME/LIFE	04/--/4 C 06/30/6	10/28/4 C	10/15/4 C 01/20/5 A	11/17/4 C 12/08/4 A	02/15/5 03/22/5				03/01/6 05/30/6
NPL	HURSLEY	04/--/4 C 03/31/6	10/28/4 C							
2250	KINGSTON	03/30/4 C 03/31/6	11/05/4 C	12/08/4 C 01/04/5	01/12/5 C 01/29/5	01/04/5 C 01/29/5				01/03/6 NE
2280	KINGSTON	06/30/4 C 09/30/6	11/05/4 C			04/01/5 04/30/5				01/28/6 NE
200K DESIGN LEVEL (H)										
ASSEMBLY	TIME/LIFE		10/28/4 C							
FORTRAN	POK	04/--/4 C 06/30/6	10/28/4 C	10/16/4 C 01/11/5	11/11/4 C 12/10/4 A	02/15/5 03/22/5				03/01/6 05/30/6
NPL	HURSLEY	04/--/4 C 03/31/7	10/28/4 C			07/--/5				01/--/7
NPL H	POK	04/--/4 C	03/30/4 C			02/01/5 04/01/5				10/15/5 12/15/5

Fig. 8. A report showing milestones and status is a key document in project control. This one shows some problems in OS development: specifications approval is late on some items (those without "A"); documentation (SRL) approval is overdue on another; and one (2250 support) is late coming out of alpha test.

THE MYTHICAL MAN-MONTH

graph in a status report. That response is guaranteed to squelch full disclosure.

Conversely, when the manager knows his boss will accept status reports without panic or preemption, he comes to give honest appraisals.

This whole process is helped if the boss labels meetings, reviews, conferences, as *status-review* meetings versus *problem-action* meetings, and controls himself accordingly. Obviously one may call a problem-action meeting as a consequence of a status meeting, if he believes a problem is out of hand. But at least everybody knows what the score is, and the boss thinks twice before grabbing the ball.

Yanking the rug off

Nevertheless, it is necessary to have review techniques by which the true status is made known, whether cooperatively or not. The PERT chart with its frequent sharp milestones is the basis for such review. On a large project one may want to review some part of it each week, making the rounds once a month or so.

A report showing milestones and actual completions is the key document. Fig. 8 (preceding page), shows an excerpt from such a report. This report shows some troubles. Specifications approval is overdue on several components. Manual (SRL) approval is overdue on another, and one is late getting out of the first state (ALPHA) of the independently conducted product test. So such a report serves as an agenda for the meeting of 1 February. Everyone knows the questions, and the component manager should be prepared to explain why it's late, when it will be finished, what steps he's taking, and what help, if any, he needs from the boss or collateral groups.

V. Vyssotsky of Bell Telephone Laboratories adds the following observation:

I have found it handy to carry both "scheduled" and "estimated" dates in the milestone report. The scheduled dates are the property of the project manager and represent a consistent work plan for the project as a whole, and one which is a priori a reasonable plan. The estimated dates are the property of the lowest level manager who has cognizance over the piece of work in question, and represents his best judgment as to when it will actually happen, given the resources he has available and when he received (or has commitments for delivery of) his prerequisite inputs. The project manager has to keep his fingers off the estimated dates, and put the emphasis on getting accurate, unbiased estimates rather

than palatable optimistic estimates or self-protective conservative ones. Once this is clearly established in everyone's mind, the project manager can see quite a ways into the future where he is going to be in trouble if he doesn't do something.

The preparation of the PERT chart is a function of the boss and the managers reporting to him. Its updating, revision, and reporting requires the attention of a small (one-to-three-man) staff group which serves as an extension of the boss. Such a "Plans and Controls" team is invaluable for a large project. It has no authority except to ask all the line managers when they will have set or changed milestones, and whether milestones have been met. Since the Plans and Controls group handles all the paperwork, the burden on the line managers is reduced to the essentials—making the decisions.

We had a skilled, enthusiastic, and diplomatic Plans and Controls group on the os/360 project, run by A. M. Pietrasanta, who devoted considerable inventive talent to devising effective but unobtrusive control methods. As a result, I found his group to be widely respected and more than tolerated. For a group whose role is inherently that of an irritant, this is quite an accomplishment.

The investment of a modest amount of skilled effort in a Plans and Controls function is very rewarding. It makes far more difference in project accomplishment than if these people worked directly on building the product programs. For the Plans and Controls group is the watchdog who renders the imperceptible delays visible and who points up the critical elements. It is the early warning system against losing a year, one day at a time.

Epilogue

The tar pit of software engineering will continue to be sticky for a long time to come. One can expect the human race to continue attempting systems just within or just beyond our reach; and software systems are perhaps the most intricate and complex of man's handiworks. The management of this complex craft will demand our best use of new languages and systems, our best adaptation of proven engineering management methods, liberal doses of common sense, and a God-given humility to recognize our fallibility and limitations.

References

1. Sackman, H., W. J. Erikson, and E. E. Grant, "Exploratory Experimentation Studies Comparing Online and Offline Programming Performance," *Communications of the ACM*, 11 (1968), 3-11.

2. Nanus, B., and L. Farr, "Some Cost Contributors to Large-Scale Programs," *AFIPS Proceedings, SJCC*, 25 (1964), 239-248.

3. Weinwurm, G. F., *Research in the Management of Computer Programming.* Report SP-2059, 1965, System Development Corp., Santa Monica.

4. Morin, L. H., *Estimation of Resources for Computer Programming Projects*, M. S. thesis, Univ. of North Carolina, Chapel Hill, 1974.

5. Quoted by D. B. Mayer and A. W. Stalnaker, "Selection and Evaluation of Computer Personnel," *Proceedings 23 ACM Conference*, 1968, 661.

6. Paper given at a panel session and not included in the *AFIPS Proceedings*.

7. Corbató, F. J., *Sensitive Issues in the Design of Multi-Use Systems.* Lecture at the opening of the Honeywell EDP Technology Center, 1968.

8. Taliaffero, W. M., "Modularity the Key to System Growth Potential," *Software*, 1 (1971), 245-257.

9. Nelson, E. A., *Management Handbook for the Estimation of Computer Programming Costs.* Report TM-3225, System Development Corp., Santa Monica, pp. 66-67.

10. Reynolds, C. H., "What's Wrong with Computer Programming Management?" in *On the Management of Computer Programming.* Ed. G. F. Weinwurm. Philadelphia: Auerbach, 1971, pp. 35-42.

11. King, W. R., and T. A. Wilson, "Subjective Time Estimates in Critical Path Planning—a Preliminary Analysis," *Management Sciences*, 13 (1967), 307-320, and sequel, W. R. King, D. M. Witterrongel, and K. D. Hezel, "On the Analysis of Critical Path Time Estimating Behavior," *Management Sciences*, 14 (1967), 79-84.

12. Brooks, F. P., and K. E. Iverson, *Automatic Data Processing, System/360 Edition.* New York: Wiley, 1969, pp. 428-430. □

Dr. Brooks is presently a professor at the Univ. of North Carolina at Chapel Hill, and chairman of the computer science department there. He is best known as "the father of the IBM System/360," having served as project manager for the hardware development and as manager of the Operating System/360 project during its design phase. Earlier he was an architect of the IBM Stretch and Harvest computers.

At Chapel Hill he has participated in establishing and guiding the Triangle Universities Computation Center and the North Carolina Educational Computing Service. He is the author of two editions of "Automatic Data Processing" and "The Mythical Man-Month: Essays on Software Engineering" (Addison-Wesley), from which this excerpt is taken.

Software Engineering Economics

BARRY W. BOEHM

Abstract—**This paper summarizes the current state of the art and recent trends in software engineering economics. It provides an overview of economic analysis techniques and their applicability to software engineering and management. It surveys the field of software cost estimation, including the major estimation techniques available, the state of the art in algorithmic cost models, and the outstanding research issues in software cost estimation.**

Index Terms—**Computer programming costs, cost models, management decision aids, software cost estimation, software economics, software engineering, software management.**

I. INTRODUCTION

Definitions

The dictionary defines "economics" as "a social science concerned chiefly with description and analysis of the production, distribution, and consumption of goods and services." Here is another definition of economics which I think is more helpful in explaining how economics relates to software engineering.

Economics is the study of how people make decisions in resource-limited situations.

This definition of economics fits the major branches of classical economics very well.

Macroeconomics is the study of how people make decisions in resource-limited situations on a national or global scale. It deals with the effects of decisions that national leaders make on such issues as tax rates, interest rates, foreign and trade policy.

Microeconomics is the study of how people make decisions in resource-limited situations on a more personal scale. It deals with the decisions that individuals and organizations make on such issues as how much insurance to buy, which word processor to buy, or what prices to charge for their products or services.

Economics and Software Engineering Management

If we look at the discipline of software engineering, we see that the microeconomics branch of economics deals more with the types of decisions we need to make as software engineers or managers.

Clearly, we deal with limited resources. There is never enough time or money to cover all the good features we would like to put into our software products. And even in these days of cheap hardware and virtual memory, our more significant software products must always operate within a world of limited computer power and main memory. If you have been in the software engineering field for any length of time, I am sure

you can think of a number of decision situations in which you had to determine some key software product feature as a function of some limiting critical resource.

Throughout the software life cycle,[1] there are many decision situations involving limited resources in which software engineering economics techniques provide useful assistance. To provide a feel for the nature of these economic decision issues, an example is given below for each of the major phases in the software life cycle.

- *Feasibility Phase:* How much should we invest in information system analyses (user questionnaires and interviews, current-system analysis, workload characterizations, simulations, scenarios, prototypes) in order that we converge on an appropriate definition and concept of operation for the system we plan to implement?

- *Plans and Requirements Phase:* How rigorously should we specify requirements? How much should we invest in requirements validation activities (automated completeness, consistency, and traceability checks, analytic models, simulations, prototypes) before proceeding to design and develop a software system?

- *Product Design Phase:* Should we organize the software to make it possible to use a complex piece of existing software which generally but not completely meets our requirements?

- *Programming Phase:* Given a choice between three data storage and retrieval schemes which are primarily execution time-efficient, storage-efficient, and easy-to-modify, respectively; which of these should we choose to implement?

- *Integration and Test Phase:* How much testing and formal verification should we perform on a product before releasing it to users?

- *Maintenance Phase:* Given an extensive list of suggested product improvements, which ones should we implement first?

- *Phaseout:* Given an aging, hard-to-modify software product, should we replace it with a new product, restructure it, or leave it alone?

Outline of This Paper

The economics field has evolved a number of techniques (cost-benefit analysis, present value analysis, risk analysis, etc.)

---

[1] Economic principles underlie the overall structure of the software life cycle, and its primary refinements of prototyping, incremental development, and advancemanship. The primary economic driver of the life-cycle structure is the significantly increasing cost of making a software change or fixing a software problem, as a function of the phase in which the change or fix is made. See [11, ch. 4].

Manuscript received April 26, 1983; revised June 28, 1983.

The author is with the Software Information Systems Division, TRW Defense Systems Group, Redondo Beach, CA 90278.

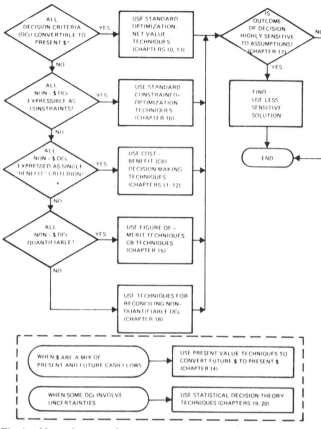

MASTER KEY
TO SOFTWARE ENGINEERING ECONOMICS
DECISION ANALYSIS TECHNIQUES

Fig. 1. Master key to software engineering economics decision analysis
techniques.

for dealing with decision issues such as the ones above. Section
II of this paper provides an overview of these techniques and
their applicability to software engineering.

One critical problem which underlies all applications of
economic techniques to software engineering is the problem of
estimating software costs. Section III contains three major
sections which summarize this field:

   III-A: Major Software Cost Estimation Techniques

   III-B: Algorithmic Models for Software Cost Estimation

   III-C: Outstanding Research Issues in Software Cost Estimation.

Section IV concludes by summarizing the major benefits of
software engineering economics, and commenting on the
major challenges awaiting the field.

II. Software Engineering Economics Analysis
Techniques

Overview of Relevant Techniques

The microeconomics field provides a number of techniques
for dealing with software life-cycle decision issues such as the
ones given in the previous section. Fig. 1 presents an overall
master key to these techniques and when to use them.[2]

---

[2] The chapter numbers in Fig. 1 refer to the chapters in [11], in
which those techniques are discussed in further detail.

As indicated in Fig. 1, standard optimization techniques
can be used when we can find a single quantity such as dollars
(or pounds, yen, cruzeiros, etc.) to serve as a "universal sol-
vent" into which all of our decision variables can be converted.
Or, if the nondollar objectives can be expressed as constraints
(system availability must be at least 98 percent; throughput
must be at least 150 transactions per second), then standard
constrained optimization techniques can be used. And if cash
flows occur at different times, then present-value techniques
can be used to normalize them to a common point in time.

More frequently, some of the resulting benefits from the
software system are not expressible in dollars. In such situations, one alternative solution will not necessarily dominate
another solution.

An example situation is shown in Fig. 2, which compares
the cost and benefits (here, in terms of throughput in transactions per second) of two alternative approaches to developing an operating system for a transaction processing system.

- *Option A:* Accept an available operating system. This
  will require only $80K in software costs, but will
  achieve a peak performance of 120 transactions per
  second, using five $10K minicomputer processors, be-
  cause of a high multiprocessor overhead factor.
- *Option B:* Build a new operating system. This system
  would be more efficient and would support a higher
  peak throughput, but would require $180K in soft-
  ware costs.

The cost-versus-performance curve for these two options
are shown in Fig. 2. Here, neither option dominates the
other, and various cost-benefit decision-making techniques
(maximum profit margin, cost/benefit ratio, return on investments, etc.) must be used to choose between Options
A and B.

In general, software engineering decision problems are
even more complex than Fig. 2, as Options A and B will
have several important criteria on which they differ (e.g.,
robustness, ease of tuning, ease of change, functional
capability). If these criteria are quantifiable, then some type
of figure of merit can be defined to support a comparative
analysis of the preferability of one option over another. If
some of the criteria are unquantifiable (user goodwill, programmer morale, etc.), then some techniques for comparing
unquantifiable criteria need to be used. As indicated in Fig. 1,
techniques for each of these situations are available, and
discussed in [11].

Analyzing Risk, Uncertainty, and the Value of Information

In software engineering, our decision issues are generally
even more complex than those discussed above. This is because the outcome of many of our options cannot be determined in advance. For example, building an operating system with a significantly lower multiprocessor overhead may
be achievable, but on the other hand, it may not. In such circumstances, we are faced with a problem of *decision making
under uncertainty,* with a considerable *risk* of an undesired
outcome.

136

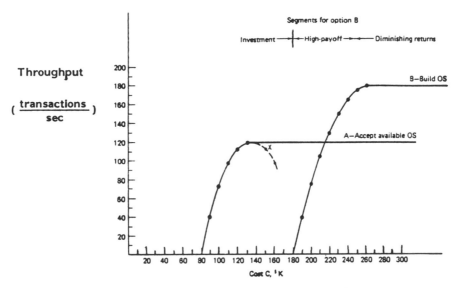

Fig. 2. Cost-effectiveness comparison, transaction processing system options.

The main economic analysis techniques available to support us in resolving such problems are the following.

1) Techniques for decision making under complete uncertainty, such as the maximax rule, the maximin rule, and the Laplace rule [38]. These techniques are generally inadequate for practical software engineering decisions.

2) Expected-value techniques, in which we estimate the probabilities of occurrence of each outcome (successful or unsuccessful development of the new operating system) and complete the expected payoff of each option:

$$EV = Prob(success) * Payoff(successful\ OS)$$
$$+ Prob(failure) * Payoff(unsuccessful\ OS).$$

These techniques are better than decision making under complete uncertainty, but they still involve a great deal of risk if the Prob(failure) is considerably higher than our estimate of it.

3) Techniques in which we reduce uncertainty by *buying information.* For example, *prototyping* is a way of buying information to reduce our uncertainty about the likely success or failure of a multiprocessor operating system; by developing a rapid prototype of its high-risk elements, we can get a clearer picture of our likelihood of successfully developing the full operating system.

In general, prototyping and other options for buying information[3] are most valuable aids for software engineering decisions. However, they always raise the following question: "how much information-buying is enough?"

In principle, this question can be answered via statistical decision theory techniques involving the use of Bayes' Law, which allows us to calculate the expected payoff from a software project as a function of our level of investment in a prototype

or other information-buying option. (Some examples of the use of Bayes' Law to estimate the appropriate level of investment in a prototype are given in [11, ch. 20].)

In practice, the use of Bayes' Law involves the estimation of a number of conditional probabilities which are not easy to estimate accurately. However, the Bayes' Law approach can be translated into a number of *value-of-information guidelines*, or conditions under which it makes good sense to decide on investing in more information before committing ourselves to a particular course of action.

Condition 1: There exist attractive alternatives whose payoff varies greatly, depending on some critical states of nature. If not, we can commit ourselves to one of the attractive alternatives with no risk of significant loss.

Condition 2: The critical states of nature have an appreciable probability of occurring. If not, we can again commit ourselves without major risk. For situations with extremely high variations in payoff, the appreciable probability level is lower than in situations with smaller variations in payoff.

Condition 3: The investigations have a high probability of accurately identifying the occurrence of the critical states of nature. If not, the investigations will not do much to reduce our risk of loss due to making the wrong decision.

Condition 4: The required cost and schedule of the investigations do not overly curtail their net value. It does us little good to obtain results which cost more than they can save us, or which arrive too late to help us make a decision.

Condition 5: There exist significant side benefits derived from performing the investigations. Again, we may be able to justify an investigation solely on the basis of its value in training, team-building, customer relations, or design validation.

Some Pitfalls Avoided by Using the Value-of-Information Approach

The guideline conditions provided by the value-of-information approach provide us with a perspective which helps us avoid some serious software engineering pitfalls. The pitfalls

---

[3] Other examples of options for buying information to support software engineering decisions include feasibility studies, user surveys, simulation, testing, and mathematical program verification techniques.

below are expressed in terms of some frequently expressed but faulty pieces of software engineering advice.

Pitfall 1: Always use a simulation to investigate the feasibility of complex realtime software. Simulations are often extremely valuable in such situations. However, there have been a good many simulations developed which were largely an expensive waste of effort, frequently under conditions that would have been picked up by the guidelines above. Some have been relatively useless because, once they were built, nobody could tell whether a given set of inputs was realistic or not (picked up by Condition 3). Some have been taken so long to develop that they produced their first results the week after the proposal was sent out, or after the key design review was completed (picked up by Condition 4).

Pitfall 2: Always build the software twice. The guidelines indicate that the prototype (or build-it-twice) approach is often valuable, but not in all situations. Some prototypes have been built of software whose aspects were all straightforward and familiar, in which case nothing much was learned by building them (picked up by Conditions 1 and 2).

Pitfall 3: Build the software purely top-down. When interpreted too literally, the top-down approach does not concern itself with the design of low level modules until the higher levels have been fully developed. If an adverse state of nature makes such a low level module (automatically forecast sales volume, automatically discriminate one type of aircraft from another) impossible to develop, the subsequent redesign will generally require the expensive rework of much of the higher level design and code. Conditions 1 and 2 warn us to temper our top-down approach with a thorough top-to-bottom software risk analysis during the requirements and product design phases.

Pitfall 4: Every piece of code should be proved correct. Correctness proving is still an expensive way to get information on the fault-freedom of software, although it strongly satisfies Condition 3 by giving a very high assurance of a program's correctness. Conditions 1 and 2 recommend that proof techniques be used in situations where the operational cost of a software fault is very large, that is, loss of life, compromised national security, major financial losses. But if the operational cost of a software fault is small, the added information on fault-freedom provided by the proof will not be worth the investment (Condition 4).

Pitfall 5: Nominal-case testing is sufficient. This pitfall is just the opposite of Pitfall 4. If the operational cost of potential software faults is large, it is highly imprudent not to perform off-nominal testing.

Summary: The Economic Value of Information

Let us step back a bit from these guidelines and pitfalls. Put simply, we are saying that, as software engineers:

"It is often worth paying for information because it helps us make better decisions."

If we look at the statement in a broader context, we can see that it is the primary reason why the software engineering field exists. It is what practically all of our software customers say when they decide to acquire one of our products: that it is worth paying for a management information system, a weather forecasting system, an air traffic control system, an inventory control system, etc., because it helps them make better decisions.

Usually, software engineers are *producers* of management information to be consumed by other people, but during the software life cycle we must also be *consumers* of management information to support our own decisions. As we come to appreciate the factors which make it attractive for us to pay for processed information which helps *us* make better decisions as software engineers, we will get a better appreciation for what our customers and users are looking for in the information processing systems we develop for *them*.

III. SOFTWARE COST ESTIMATION

Introduction

All of the software engineering economics decision analysis techniques discussed above are only as good as the input data we can provide for them. For software decisions, the most critical and difficult of these inputs to provide are estimates of the cost of a proposed software project. In this section, we will summarize:

1) the major software cost estimation techniques available, and their relative strengths and difficulties;

2) algorithmic models for software cost estimation;

3) outstanding research issues in software cost estimation.

A. Major Software Cost Estimation Techniques

Table I summarizes the relative strengths and difficulties of the major software cost estimation methods in use today.

1) *Algorithmic Models:* These methods provide one or more algorithms which produce a software cost estimate as a function of a number of variables which are considered to be the major cost drivers.

2) *Expert Judgment:* This method involves consulting one or more experts, perhaps with the aid of an expert-consensus mechanism such as the Delphi technique.

3) *Analogy:* This method involves reasoning by analogy with one or more completed projects to relate their actual costs to an estimate of the cost of a similar new project.

4) *Parkinson:* A Parkinson principle ("work expands to fill the available volume") is invoked to equate the cost estimate to the available resources.

5) *Price-to-Win:* Here, the cost estimate is equated to the price believed necessary to win the job (or the schedule believed necessary to be first in the market with a new product, etc.).

6) *Top-Down:* An overall cost estimate for the project is derived from global properties of the software product. The total cost is then split up among the various components.

7) *Bottom-Up:* Each component of the software job is separately estimated, and the results aggregated to produce an estimate for the overall job.

The main conclusions that we can draw from Table I are the following.

• None of the alternatives is better than the others from all aspects.

• The Parkinson and price-to-win methods are unacceptable and do not produce satisfactory cost estimates.

TABLE I
STRENGTHS AND WEAKNESSES OF SOFTWARE
COST-ESTIMATION METHODS

Method	Strengths	Weaknesses
Algorithmic model	• Objective, repeatable, analyzable formula • Efficient, good for sensitivity analysis • Objectively calibrated to experience	• Subjective inputs • Assessment of exceptional circumstances • Calibrated to past, not future
Expert judgment	• Assessment of representativeness, interactions, exceptional circumstances	• No better than participants • Biases, incomplete recall
Analogy	• Based on representative experience	• Representativeness of experience
Parkinson Price to win	• Correlates with some experience • Often gets the contract	• Reinforces poor practice • Generally produces large overruns
Top-down	• System level focus • Efficient	• Less detailed basis • Less stable
Bottom-up	• More detailed basis • More stable • Fosters individual commitment	• May overlook system level costs • Requires more effort

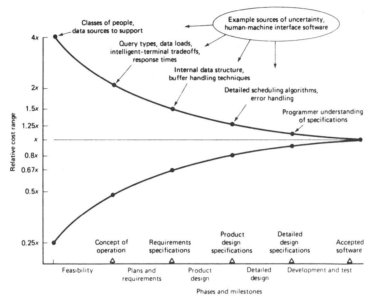

Fig. 3.   Software cost estimation accuracy versus phase.

• The strengths and weaknesses of the other techniques are complementary (particularly the algorithmic models versus expert judgment and top-down versus bottom-up).

• Thus, in practice, we should use combinations of the above techniques, compare their results, and iterate on them where they differ.

Fundamental Limitations of Software Cost Estimation Techniques

Whatever the strengths of a software cost estimation technique, there is really no way we can expect the technique to compensate for our lack of definition or understanding of the software job to be done. Until a software specification is fully defined, it actually represents a range of software products, and a corresponding range of software development costs.

This fundamental limitation of software cost estimation technology is illustrated in Fig. 3, which shows the accuracy within which software cost estimates can be made, as a function of the software life-cycle phase (the horizontal axis), or of the level of knowledge we have of what the software is intended to do. This level of uncertainty is illustrated in Fig. 3

with respect to a human–machine interface component of the software.

When we first begin to evaluate alternative concepts for a new software application, the relative range of our software cost estimates is roughly a factor of four on either the high or low side.[4] This range stems from the wide range of uncertainty we have at this time about the actual nature of the product. For the human–machine interface component, for example, we do not know at this time what classes of people (clerks, computer specialists, middle managers, etc.) or what classes of data (raw or pre-edited, numerical or text, digital or analog) the system will have to support. Until we pin down such uncertainties, a factor of four in either direction is not surprising as a range of estimates.

The above uncertainties are indeed pinned down once we complete the feasibility phase and settle on a particular concept of operation. At this stage, the range of our estimates diminishes to a factor of two in either direction. This range is

---

[4] These ranges have been determined subjectively, and are intended to represent 80 percent confidence limits, that is, "within a factor of four on either side, 80 percent of the time."

reasonable because we still have not pinned down such issues as the specific types of user query to be supported, or the specific functions to be performed within the microprocessor in the intelligent terminal. These issues will be resolved by the time we have developed a software requirements specification, at which point, we will be able to estimate the software costs within a factor of 1.5 in either direction.

By the time we complete and validate a product design specification, we will have resolved such issues as the internal data structure of the software product and the specific techniques for handling the buffers between the terminal microprocessor and the central processors on one side, and between the microprocessor and the display driver on the other. At this point, our software estimate should be accurate to within a factor of 1.25, the discrepancies being caused by some remaining sources of uncertainty such as the specific algorithms to be used for task scheduling, error handling, abort processing, and the like. These will be resolved by the end of the detailed design phase, but there will still be a residual uncertainty about 10 percent based on how well the programmers really understand the specifications to which they are to code. (This factor also includes such consideration as personnel turnover uncertainties during the development and test phases.)

B. Algorithmic Models for Software Cost Estimation

Algorithmic Cost Models: Early Development

Since the earliest days of the software field, people have been trying to develop algorithmic models to estimate software costs. The earliest attempts were simple rules of thumb, such as:

• on a large project, each software performer will provide an average of one checked-out instruction per man-hour (or roughly 150 instructions per man-month);

• each software maintenance person can maintain four boxes of cards (a box of cards held 2000 cards, or roughly 2000 instructions in those days of few comment cards).

Somewhat later, some projects began collecting quantitative data on the effort involved in developing a software product, and its distribution across the software life cycle. One of the earliest of these analyses was documented in 1956 in [8]. It indicated that, for very large operational software products on the order of 100 000 delivered source instructions (100 KDSI), that the overall productivity was more like 64 DSI/man-month, that another 100 KDSI of support-software would be required; that about 15 000 pages of documentation would be produced and 3000 hours of computer time consumed; and that the distribution of effort would be as follows:

Program Specs:	10 percent
Coding Specs:	30 percent
Coding:	10 percent
Parameter Testing:	20 percent
Assembly Testing:	30 percent

with an additional 30 percent required to produce operational specs for the system. Unfortunately, such data did not become well known, and many subsequent software projects went through a painful process of rediscovering them.

During the late 1950's and early 1960's, relatively little progress was made in software cost estimation, while the frequency and magnitude of software cost overruns was becoming critical to many large systems employing computers. In 1964, the U.S. Air Force contracted with System Development Corporation for a landmark project in the software cost estimation field. This project collected 104 attributes of 169 software projects and treated them to extensive statistical analysis. One result was the 1965 SDC cost model [41] which was the best possible statistical 13-parameter linear estimation model for the sample data:

$$MM = -33.63$$
$$+9.15 \text{ (Lack of Requirements) } (0\text{-}2)$$
$$+10.73 \text{ (Stability of Design) } (0\text{-}3)$$
$$+0.51 \text{ (Percent Math Instructions)}$$
$$+0.46 \text{ (Percent Storage/Retrieval Instructions)}$$
$$+0.40 \text{ (Number of Subprograms)}$$
$$+7.28 \text{ (Programming Language) } (0\text{-}1)$$
$$-21.45 \text{ (Business Application) } (0\text{-}1)$$
$$+13.53 \text{ (Stand-Alone Program) } (0.1)$$
$$+12.35 \text{ (First Program on Computer) } (0\text{-}1)$$
$$+58.82 \text{ (Concurrent Hardware Development) } (0\text{-}1)$$
$$+30.61 \text{ (Random Access Device Used) } (0\text{-}1)$$
$$+29.55 \text{ (Difference Host, Target Hardware) } (0\text{-}1)$$
$$+0.54 \text{ (Number of Personnel Trips)}$$
$$-25.20 \text{ (Developed by Military Organization) } (0\text{-}1).$$

The numbers in parentheses refer to ratings to be made by the estimator.

When applied to its database of 169 projects, this model produced a mean estimate of 40 MM and a standard deviation of 62 MM; not a very accurate predictor. Further, the application of the model is counterintuitive; a project with all zero ratings is estimated at minus 33 MM; changing language from a higher order language to assembly language adds 7 MM, independent of project size. The most conclusive result from the SDC study was that there were too many nonlinear aspects of software development for a linear cost-estimation model to work very well.

Still, the SDC effort provided a valuable base of information and insight for cost estimation and future models. Its cumulative distribution of productivity for 169 projects was a valuable aid for producing or checking cost estimates. The estimation rules of thumb for various phases and activities have been very helpful, and the data have been a major foundation for some subsequent cost models.

In the late 1960's and early 1970's, a number of cost models were developed which worked reasonably well for a certain restricted range of projects to which they were calibrated. Some of the more notable examples of such models are those described in [3], [54], [57].

The essence of the TRW Wolverton model [57] is shown in Fig. 4, which shows a number of curves of software cost per object instruction as a function of relative degree of difficulty

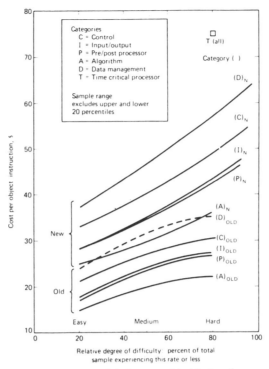

Fig. 4. TRW Wolverton model: Cost per object instruction versus relative degree of difficulty.

(0 to 100), novelty of the application (new or old), and type of project. The best use of the model involves breaking the software into components and estimating their cost individually. This, a 1000 object-instruction module of new data management software of medium (50 percent) difficulty would be costed at $46/instruction, or $46 000.

This model is well-calibrated to a class of near-real-time government command and control projects, but is less accurate for some other classes of projects. In addition, the model provides a good breakdown of project effort by phase and activity.

In the late 1970's, several software cost estimation models were developed which established a significant advance in the state of the art. These included the Putnam SLIM Model [44], the Doty Model [27], the RCA PRICE S model [22], the COCOMO model [11], the IBM-FSD model [53], the Boeing model [9], and a series of models developed by GRC [15]. A summary of these models, and the earlier SDC and Wolverton models, is shown in Table II, in terms of the size, program, computer, personnel, and project attributes used by each model to determine software costs. The first four of these models are discussed below.

The Putnam SLIM Model [44], [45]

The Putnam SLIM Model is a commercially available (from Quantitative Software Management, Inc.) software product based on Putnam's analysis of the software life cycle in terms of the Rayleigh distribution of project personnel level versus time. The basic effort macro-estimation model used in SLIM is

$$S_s = C_k K^{1/3} t_d^{4/3}$$

where

S_s = number of delivered source instructions
K = life-cycle effort in man-years
t_d = development time in years
C_k = a "technology constant."

Values of C_k typically range between 610 and 57 314. The current version of SLIM allows one to calibrate C_k to past projects or to past projects or to estimate it as a function of a project's use of modern programming practices, hardware constraints, personnel experience, interactive development, and other factors. The required development effort, DE, is estimated as roughly 40 percent of the life-cycle effort for large systems. For smaller systems, the percentage varies as a function of system size.

The SLIM model includes a number of useful extensions to estimate such quantities as manpower distribution, cash flow, major-milestone schedules, reliability levels, computer time, and documentation costs.

The most controversial aspect of the SLIM model is its tradeoff relationship between development effort K and between development time t_d. For a software product of a given size, the SLIM software equation above gives

$$K = \frac{\text{constant}}{t_d^4}.$$

For example, this relationship says that one can cut the cost of a software project in half, simply by increasing its development time by 19 percent (e.g., from 10 months to 12 months). Fig. 5 shows how the SLIM tradeoff relationship com-

TABLE II
FACTORS USED IN VARIOUS COST MODELS

GROUP	FACTOR	SDC, 1965	TRW, 1972	PUTNAM, SLIM	DOTY	RCA, PRICE S	IBM	BOEING, 1977	GRC, 1979	COCOMO	SOFCOST	DSN	JENSEN
SIZE ATTRIBUTES	SOURCE INSTRUCTIONS			X	X		X	X		X	X	X	X
	OBJECT INSTRUCTIONS	X	X		X	X							
	NUMBER OF ROUTINES	X				X					X		
	NUMBER OF DATA ITEMS						X			X	X		
	NUMBER OF OUTPUT FORMATS								X			X	
	DOCUMENTATION				X		X				X		X
	NUMBER OF PERSONNEL			X			X	X			X		X
PROGRAM ATTRIBUTES	TYPE	X	X	X	X	X	X	X		X			
	COMPLEXITY		X	X		X	X			X	X		
	LANGUAGE	X		X					X	X	X	X	X
	REUSE			X		X		X	X	X	X		X
	REQUIRED RELIABILITY			X		X				X	X		X
	DISPLAY REQUIREMENTS				X					X	X		X
COMPUTER ATTRIBUTES	TIME CONSTRAINT		X	X	X	X	X	X	X	X	X	X	X
	STORAGE CONSTRAINT		X	X	X	X	X		X	X	X	X	X
	HARDWARE CONFIGURATION	X				X							
	CONCURRENT HARDWARE DEVELOPMENT	X			X	X	X			X	X	X	X
	INTERFACING EQUIPMENT, S/W										X	X	
PERSONNEL ATTRIBUTES	PERSONNEL CAPABILITY			X		X	X			X	X	X	X
	PERSONNEL CONTINUITY						X				X		
	HARDWARE EXPERIENCE	X		X	X	X	X		X	X	X	X	X
	APPLICATIONS EXPERIENCE		X	X		X	X	X	X	X	X	X	X
	LANGUAGE EXPERIENCE			X		X	X		X	X	X	X	X
PROJECT ATTRIBUTES	TOOLS AND TECHNIQUES			X		X	X	X		X	X	X	X
	CUSTOMER INTERFACE	X					X				X	X	
	REQUIREMENTS DEFINITION	X				X	X				X	X	X
	REQUIREMENTS VOLATILITY	X			X	X	X		X	X	X	X	X
	SCHEDULE			X		X					X	X	X
	SECURITY						X				X	X	
	COMPUTER ACCESS			X	X		X	X		X	X	X	X
	TRAVEL/REHOSTING/MULTI-SITE	X			X	X					X	X	X
	SUPPORT SOFTWARE MATURITY									X		X	
CALIBRATION FACTOR				X		X				X			
EFFORT EQUATION	$MM_{NOM} = C(DSI)^X$, $X =$		1.0		1.047		0.91	1.0		1.05 - 1.2		1.0	1.2
SCHEDULE EQUATION	$t_D = C(MM)^X$, $X =$						0.35			0.32 - 0.38		0.356	0.333

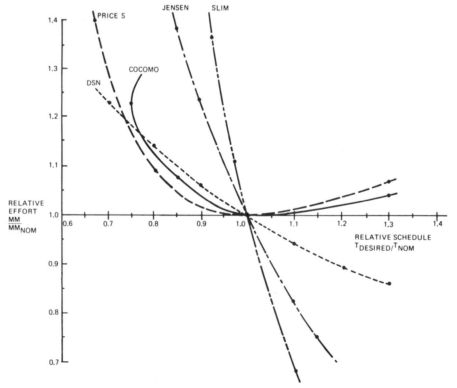

Fig. 5.   Comparative effort-schedule tradeoff relationships.

TABLE III
DOTY MODEL FOR SMALL PROGRAMS*

$$MM = 2.060 \, I^{1.047} \prod_{j=1}^{j=14} f_j$$

Factor	f_j	Yes	No
Special display	f_1	1.11	1.00
Detailed definition of operational requirements	f_2	1.00	1.11
Change to operational requirements	f_3	1.05	1.00
Real-time operation	f_4	1.33	1.00
CPU memory constraint	f_5	1.43	1.00
CPU time constraint	f_6	1.33	1.00
First software developed on CPU	f_7	1.92	1.00
Concurrent development of ADP hardware	f_8	1.82	1.00
Timeshare versus batch processing, in development	f_9	0.83	1.00
Developer using computer at another facility	f_{10}	1.43	1.00
Development at operational site	f_{11}	1.39	1.00
Development computer different than target computer	f_{12}	1.25	1.00
Development at more than one site	f_{13}	1.25	1.00
Programmer access to computer	f_{14}	Limited Unlimited	1.00 0.90

* Less than 10,000 source instructions

pares with those of other models; see [11, ch. 27] for further discussion of this issue.

On balance, the SLIM approach has provided a number of useful insights into software cost estimation, such as the Rayleigh-curve distribution for one-shot software efforts, the explicit treatment of estimation risk and uncertainty, and the cube-root relationship defining the minimum development time achievable for a project requiring a given amount of effort.

The Doty Model [27]

This model is the result of an extensive data analysis activity, including many of the data points from the SDC sample. A number of models of similar form were developed for different application areas. As an example, the model for general application is

$$MM = 5.288 \, (\text{KDSI})^{1.047}, \qquad \text{for KDSI} \geqslant 10$$

$$MM = 2.060 \, (\text{KDSI})^{1.047} \left(\prod_{j=1}^{14} f_j \right), \qquad \text{for KDSI} < 10.$$

The effort multipliers f_i are shown in Table III. This model has a much more appropriate functional form than the SDC model, but it has some problems with stability, as it exhibits a discontinuity at KDSI = 10, and produces widely varying estimates via the f factors (answering "yes" to "first software developed on CPU" adds 92 percent to the estimated cost).

The RCA PRICE S Model [22]

PRICE S is a commercially available (from RCA, Inc.) macro cost-estimation model developed primarily for embedded system applications. It has improved steadily with experience; earlier versions with a widely varying subjective complexity factor have been replaced by versions in which a number of computer, personnel, and project attributes are used to modulate the complexity rating.

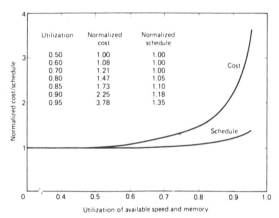

Utilization	Normalized cost	Normalized schedule
0.50	1.00	1.00
0.60	1.08	1.00
0.70	1.21	1.00
0.80	1.47	1.05
0.85	1.73	1.10
0.90	2.25	1.18
0.95	3.78	1.35

Fig. 6. RCA PRICE S model: Effect of hardware constraints.

PRICE S has extended a number of cost-estimating relationships developed in the early 1970's such as the hardware constraint function shown in Fig. 6 [10]. It was primarily developed to handle military software projects, but now also includes rating levels to cover business applications.

PRICE S also provides a wide range of useful outputs on gross phase and activity distributions analyses, and monthly project cost-schedule-expected progress forecasts. Price S uses a two-parameter beta distribution rather than a Rayleigh curve to calculate development effort distribution versus calendar time.

PRICE S has recently added a software life-cycle support cost estimation capability called PRICE SL [34]. It involves the definition of three categories of support activities.

• *Growth:* The estimator specifies the amount of code to be added to the product. PRICE SL then uses its standard techniques to estimate the resulting life-cycle-effort distribution.

• *Enhancement:* PRICE SL estimates the fraction of the existing product which will be modified (the estimator may provide his own fraction), and uses its standard techniques to estimate the resulting life-cycle effort distribution.

- *Maintenance:* The estimator provides a parameter indicating the quality level of the developed code. PRICE SL uses this to estimate the effort required to eliminate remaining errors.

The COnstructive COst MOdel (COCOMO) [11]

The primary motivation for the COCOMO model has been to help people understand the cost consequences of the decisions they will make in commissioning, developing, and supporting a software product. Besides providing a software cost estimation capability, COCOMO therefore provides a great deal of material which explains exactly what costs the model is estimating, and why it comes up with the estimates it does. Further, it provides capabilities for sensitivity analysis and tradeoff analysis of many of the common software engineering decision issues.

COCOMO is actually a hierarchy of three increasingly detailed models which range from a single macro-estimation scaling model as a function of product size to a micro-estimation model with a three-level work breakdown structure and a set of phase-sensitive multipliers for each cost driver attribute. To provide a reasonably concise example of a current state of the art cost estimation model, the intermediate level of COCOMO is described below.

Intermediate COCOMO estimates the cost of a proposed software product in the following way.

1) A nominal development effort is estimated as a function of the product's size in delivered source instructions in thousands (KDSI) and the project's development mode.

2) A set of effort multipliers are determined from the product's ratings on a set of 15 cost driver attributes.

3) The estimated development effort is obtained by multiplying the nominal effort estimate by all of the product's effort multipliers.

4) Additional factors can be used to determine dollar costs, development schedules, phase and activity distributions, computer costs, annual maintenance costs, and other elements from the development effort estimate.

Step 1–Nominal Effort Estimation: First, Table IV is used to determine the project's development mode. Organic-mode projects typically come from stable, familiar, forgiving, relatively unconstrained environments, and were found in the COCOMO data analysis of 63 projects have a different scaling equation from the more ambitious, unfamiliar, unforgiving, tightly constrained embedded mode. The resulting scaling equations for each mode are given in Table V; these are used to determine the nominal development effort for the project in man-months as a function of the project's size in KDSI and the project's development mode.

For example, suppose we are estimating the cost to develop the microprocessor-based communications processing software for a highly ambitious new electronic funds transfer network with high reliability, performance, development schedule, and interface requirements. From Table IV, we determine that these characteristics best fit the profile of an embedded-mode project.

We next estimate the size of the product as 10 000 delivered

TABLE IV
COCOMO SOFTWARE DEVELOPMENT MODES

Feature	Mode		
	Organic	Semidetached	Embedded
Organizational understanding of product objectives	Thorough	Considerable	General
Experience in working with related software systems	Extensive	Considerable	Moderate
Need for software conformance with pre-established requirements	Basic	Considerable	Full
Need for software conformance with external interface specifications	Basic	Considerable	Full
Concurrent development of associated new hardware and operational procedures	Some	Moderate	Extensive
Need for innovative data processing architectures, algorithms	Minimal	Some	Considerable
Premium on early completion	Low	Medium	High
Product size range	<50 KDSI	<300 KDSI	All sizes
Examples	Batch data reduction Scientific models Business models Familiar OS, compiler Simple inventory, production control	Most transaction processing systems New OS, DBMS Ambitious inventory, production control Simple command-control	Large, complex transaction processing systems Ambitious, very large OS Avionics Ambitious command-control

TABLE V
COCOMO NOMINAL EFFORT AND SCHEDULE EQUATIONS

DEVELOPMENT MODE	NOMINAL EFFORT	SCHEDULE
Organic	$(MM)_{NOM} = 3.2(KDSI)^{1.05}$	$TDEV = 2.5(MM_{DEV})^{0.38}$
Semidetached	$(MM)_{NOM} = 3.0(KDSI)^{1.12}$	$TDEV = 2.5(MM_{DEV})^{0.35}$
Embedded	$(MM)_{NOM} = 2.8(KDSI)^{1.20}$	$TDEV = 2.5(MM_{DEV})^{0.32}$

(KDSI = thousands of delivered source instructions)

source instructions, or 10 KDSI. From Table V, we then determine that the nominal development effort for this Embedded-mode project is

$$2.8(10)^{1.20} = 44 \text{ man-months (MM)}.$$

Step 2–Determine Effort Multipliers: Each of the 15 cost driver attributes in COCOMO has a rating scale and a set of effort multipliers which indicate by how much the nominal effort estimate must be multiplied to account for the project's having to work at its rating level for the attribute.

These cost driver attributes and their corresponding effort multipliers are shown in Table VI. The summary rating scales for each cost driver attribute are shown in Table VII, except for the complexity rating scale which is shown in Table VIII (expanded rating scales for the other attributes are provided in [11]).

The results of applying these tables to our microprocessor communications software example are shown in Table IX. The effect of a software fault in the electronic fund transfer system could be a serious financial loss; therefore, the project's RELY rating from Table VII is High. Then, from Table VI, the effort multiplier for achieving a High level of required reliability is 1.15, or 15 percent more effort than it would take to develop the software to a nominal level of required reliability.

TABLE VI
INTERMEDIATE COCOMO SOFTWARE DEVELOPMENT EFFORT MULTIPLIERS

Cost Drivers	Ratings					
	Very Low	Low	Nominal	High	Very High	Extra High
Product Attributes						
RELY Required software reliability	.75	.88	1.00	1.15	1.40	
DATA Data base size		.94	1.00	1.08	1.16	
CPLX Product complexity	.70	.85	1.00	1.15	1.30	1.65
Computer Attributes						
TIME Execution time constraint			1.00	1.11	1.30	1.66
STOR Main storage constraint			1.00	1.06	1.21	1.56
VIRT Virtual machine volatility*		.87	1.00	1.15	1.30	
TURN Computer turnaround time		.87	1.00	1.07	1.15	
Personnel Attributes						
ACAP Analyst capability	1.46	1.19	1.00	86	.71	
AEXP Applications experience	1.29	1.13	1.00	91	.82	
PCAP Programmer capability	1.42	1.17	1.00	86	.70	
VEXP Virtual machine experience*	1.21	1.10	1.00	.90		
LEXP Programming language experience	1.14	1.07	1.00	95		
Project Attributes						
MODP Use of modern programming practices	1.24	1.10	1.00	91	82	
TOOL Use of software tools	1.24	1.10	1.00	.91	.83	
SCED Required development schedule	1.23	1.08	1.00	1.04	1.10	

* For a given software product, the underlying virtual machine is the complex of hardware and software (OS, DBMS, etc.) it calls on to accomplish its tasks

TABLE VII
COCOMO SOFTWARE COST DRIVER RATINGS

Cost Driver	Ratings					
	Very Low	Low	Nominal	High	Very High	Extra High
Product attributes						
RELY	Effect: slight inconvenience	Low, easily recoverable losses	Moderate, recoverable losses	High financial loss	Risk to human life	
DATA		$\frac{DB\ bytes}{Prog.\ DSI} < 10$	$10 \leq \frac{D}{P} < 100$	$100 \leq \frac{D}{P} < 1000$	$\frac{D}{P} \geq 1000$	
CPLX	See Table 8					
Computer attributes						
TIME			≤ 50% use of available execution time	70%	85%	95%
STOR			≤ 50% use of available storage	70%	85%	95%
VIRT		Major change every 12 months Minor: 1 month	Major: 6 months Minor: 2 weeks	Major: 2 months Minor: 1 week	Major: 2 weeks Minor: 2 days	
TURN		Interactive	Average turnaround <4 hours	4–12 hours	>12 hours	
Personnel attributes						
ACAP	15th percentile*	35th percentile	55th percentile	75th percentile	90th percentile	
AEXP	≤4 months experience	1 year	3 years	6 years	12 years	
PCAP	15th percentile*	35th percentile	55th percentile	75th percentile	90th percentile	
VEXP	≤1 month experience	4 months	1 year	3 years		
LEXP	≤1 month experience	4 months	1 year	3 years		
Project attributes						
MODP	No use	Beginning use	Some use	General use	Routine use	
TOOL	Basic microprocessor tools	Basic mini tools	Basic midi/maxi tools	Strong maxi programming, test tools	Add requirements, design, management, documentation tools	
SCED	75% of nominal	85%	100%	130%	160%	

* Team rating criteria: analysis (programming) ability, efficiency, ability to communicate and cooperate

TABLE VIII
COCOMO MODULE COMPLEXITY RATINGS VERSUS TYPE OF
MODULE

Rating	Control Operations	Computational Operations	Device-dependent Operations	Data Management Operations
Very low	Straightline code with a few non-nested SP[α] operators: DOs, CASEs, IFTHENELSEs. Simple predicates	Evaluation of simple expressions: e.g., A = B + C * (D − E)	Simple read, write statements with simple formats	Simple arrays in main memory
Low	Straightforward nesting of SP operators. Mostly simple predicates	Evaluation of moderate-level expressions, e.g., D = SQRT (B**2−4.*A*C)	No cognizance needed of particular processor or I/O device characteristics. I/O done at GET/PUT level. No cognizance of overlap	Single file subsetting with no data structure changes, no edits, no intermediate files
Nominal	Mostly simple nesting. Some inter-module control. Decision tables	Use of standard math and statistical routines. Basic matrix/vector operations	I/O processing includes device selection, status checking and error processing	Multi-file input and single file output. Simple structural changes, simple edits
High	Highly nested SP operators with many compound predicates. Queue and stack control. Considerable intermodule control.	Basic numerical analysis: multivariate interpolation, ordinary differential equations. Basic truncation, roundoff concerns	Operations at physical I/O level (physical storage address translations; seeks, reads, etc). Optimized I/O overlap	Special purpose subroutines activated by data stream contents. Complex data restructuring at record level
Very high	Reentrant and recursive coding. Fixed-priority interrupt handling	Difficult but structured N.A.: near-singular matrix equations, partial differential equations	Routines for interrupt diagnosis, servicing, masking. Communication line handling	A generalized, parameter-driven file structuring routine. File building, command processing, search optimization
Extra high	Multiple resource scheduling with dynamically changing priorities. Microcode-level control	Difficult and unstructured N.A.: highly accurate analysis of noisy, stochastic data	Device timing-dependent coding, micro-programmed operations	Highly coupled, dynamic relational structures. Natural language data management

[α] SP = structured programming

TABLE IX
COCOMO COST DRIVER RATINGS: MICROPROCESSOR
COMMUNICATIONS SOFTWARE

Cost Driver	Situation	Rating	Effort Multiplier
RELY	Serious financial consequences of software faults	High	1.15
DATA	20,000 bytes	Low	0.94
CPLX	Communications processing	Very High	1.30
TIME	Will use 70% of available time	High	1.11
STOR	45K of 64K store (70%)	High	1.06
VIRT	Based on commercial microprocessor hardware	Nominal	1.00
TURN	Two-hour average turnaround time	Nominal	1.00
ACAP	Good senior analysts	High	0.86
AEXP	Three years	Nominal	1.00
PCAP	Good senior programmers	High	0.86
VEXP	Six months	Low	1.10
LEXP	Twelve months	Nominal	1.00
MODP	Most techniques in use over one year	High	0.91
TOOL	At basic minicomputer tool level	Low	1.10
SCED	Nine months	Nominal	1.00
Effort adjustment factor (product of effort multipliers)			1.35

The effort multipliers for the other cost driver attributes are obtained similarly, except for the Complexity attribute, which is obtained via Table VIII. Here, we first determine that communications processing is best classified under device-dependent operations (column 3 in Table VIII). From this column, we determine that communication line handling typically has a complexity rating of Very High; from Table VI, then, we determine that its corresponding effort multiplier is 1.30.

Step 3–Estimate Development Effort: We then compute the estimated development effort for the microprocessor communications software as the nominal development effort (44 MM) times the product of the effort multipliers for the 15 cost driver attributes in Table IX (1.35, in Table IX). The resulting estimated effort for the project is then

$$(44 \text{ MM}) (1.35) = 59 \text{ MM}.$$

Step 4–Estimate Related Project Factors: COCOMO has additional cost estimating relationships for computing the resulting dollar cost of the project and for the breakdown of cost and effort by life-cycle phase (requirements, design, etc.) and by type of project activity (programming, test planning, management, etc.). Further relationships support the estimation of the project's schedule and its phase distribution. For example, the recommended development schedule can be obtained from the estimated development man-months via the embedded-mode schedule equation in Table V:

$$T_{\text{DEV}} = 2.5(59)^{0.32} = 9 \text{ months.}$$

As mentioned above, COCOMO also supports the most common types of sensitivity analysis and tradeoff analysis involved in scoping a software project. For example, from Tables VI and VII, we can see that providing the software developers with an interactive computer access capability (Low turnaround time) reduces the TURN effort multiplier from 1.00 to 0.87, and thus reduces the estimated project effort from 59 MM to

$$(59 \text{ MM}) (0.87) = 51 \text{ MM.}$$

The COCOMO model has been validated with respect to a sample of 63 projects representing a wide variety of business, scientific, systems, real-time, and support software projects. For this sample, Intermediate COCOMO estimates come within 20 percent of the actuals about 68 percent of the time (see Fig. 7). Since the residuals roughly follow a normal distribution, this is equivalent to a standard deviation of roughly 20 percent of the project actuals. This level of accuracy is representative of the current state of the art in software cost models. One can do somewhat better with the aid of a calibration coefficient (also a COCOMO option), or within a limited applications context, but it is difficult to improve significantly on this level of accuracy while the accuracy of software data collection remains in the "±20 percent" range.

A Pascal version of COCOMO is available for a nominal distribution charge from the Wang Institute, under the name WI-COMO [18].

Recent Software Cost Estimation Models

Most of the recent software cost estimation models tend to follow the Doty and COCOMO models in having a nominal

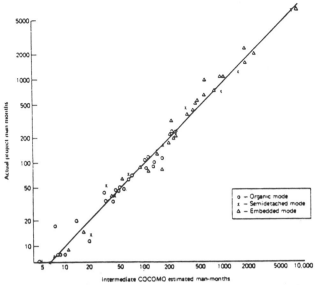

Fig. 7. Intermediate COCOMO estimates versus project actuals.

scaling equation of the form $MM_{\text{NOM}} = c(\text{KDSI})^x$ and a set of multiplicative effort adjustment factors determined by a number of cost driver attribute ratings. Some of them use the Rayleigh curve approach to estimate distribution across the software life-cycle, but most use a more conservative effort/schedule tradeoff relation than the SLIM model. These aspects have been summarized for the various models in Table II and Fig. 5.

The Bailey-Basili meta-model [4] derived the scaling equation

$$MM_{\text{NOM}} = 3.5 + 0.73 (\text{KDSI})^{1.16}$$

and used two additional cost driver attributes (methodology level and complexity) to model the development effort of 18 projects in the NASA-Goddard Software Engineering Laboratory to within a standard deviation of 15 percent. Its accuracy for other project situations has not been determined.

The Grumman SOFCOST Model [19] uses a similar but unpublished nominal effort scaling equation, modified by 30 multiplicative cost driver variables rated on a scale of 0 to 10. Table II includes a summary of these variables.

The Tausworthe Deep Space Network (DSN) model [50] uses a linear scaling equation ($MM_{\text{NOM}} = a(\text{KDSI})^{1.0}$) and a similar set of cost driver attributes, also summarized in Table II. It also has a well-considered approach for determining the equivalent KDSI involved in adapting existing software within a new product. It uses the Rayleigh curve to determine the phase distribution of effort, but uses a considerably more conservative version of the SLIM effort-schedule tradeoff relationship (see Fig. 5).

The Jensen model [30], [31] is a commercially available model with a similar nominal scaling equation, and a set of cost driver attributes very similar to the Doty and COCOMO models (but with different effort multiplier ranges); see Table II. Some of the multiplier ranges in the Jensen model vary as functions of other factors; e.g., increasing access to computer resources widens the multiplier ranges on such cost drivers as personnel capability and use of software tools. It uses the Rayleigh curve for effort distribution, and a somewhat more conservative effort-schedule tradeoff relation than SLIM (see Fig. 5). As with the other commercial models, the Jensen model produces a number of useful outputs on resource expenditure rates, probability distributions on costs and schedules, etc.

C. Outstanding Research Issues in Software Cost Estimation

Although a good deal of progress has been made in software cost estimation, a great deal remains to be done. This section updates the state-of-the-art review published in [11], and summarizes the outstanding issues needing further research:

1) Software size estimation;
2) Software size and complexity metrics;
3) Software cost driver attributes and their effects;
4) Software cost model analysis and refinement;
5) Quantitative models of software project dynamics;
6) Quantitative models of software life-cycle evolution;
7) Software data collection.

1) Software Size Estimation: The biggest difficulty in using today's algorithmic software cost models is the problem of providing sound sizing estimates. Virtually every model requires an estimate of the number of source or object instructions to be developed, and this is an extremely difficult quantity to determine in advance. It would be most useful to have some formula for determining the size of a software product in terms of quantities known early in the software life cycle, such as the number and/or size of the files, input formats, reports, displays, requirements specification elements, or design specification elements.

Some useful steps in this direction are the function-point approach in [2] and the sizing estimation model of [29], both of which have given reasonably good results for small-to-medium sized business programs within a single data processing organization. Another more general approach is given by DeMarco in [17]. It has the advantage of basing its sizing estimates on the properties of specifications developed in conformance with DeMarco's paradigm models for software specifications and designs: number of functional primitives, data elements, input elements, output elements, states, transitions between states, relations, modules, data tokens, control tokens, etc. To date, however, there has been relatively little calibration of the formulas to project data. A recent IBM study [14] shows some correlation between the number of variables defined in a state-machine design representation and the product size in source instructions.

Although some useful results can be obtained on the software sizing problem, one should not expect too much. A wide range of functionality can be implemented beneath any given specification element or I/O element, leading to a wide range of sizes (recall the uncertainty ranges of this nature in Fig. 3). For example, two experiments, involving the use of several teams developing a software program to the same overall functional specification, yielded size ranges of factors of 3 to 5 between programs (see Table X).

The primary implication of this situation for practical software sizing and cost estimation is that *there is no royal road to software sizing.* This is no magic formula that will provide an easy and accurate substitute for the process of thinking through and fully understanding the nature of the software product to be developed. There are still a number of useful

TABLE X
SIZE RANGES OF SOFTWARE PRODUCTS PERFORMING SAME FUNCTION

Experiment	Product	No. of Teams	Size Range (source-instr.)
Weinberg & Schulman [55]	Simultaneous linear equations	6	33-165
Boehm, Gray, & Seewaldt [13]	Interactive cost model	7	1514-4606

things that one can do to improve the situation, including the following.

• Use techniques which explicitly recognize the ranges of variability in software sizing. The PERT estimation technique [56] is a good example.

• Understand the primary sources of bias in software sizing estimates. See [11, ch. 21].

• Develop and use a corporate memory on the nature and size of previous software products.

2) Software Size and Complexity Metrics: Delivered source instructions (DSI) can be faulted for being too low-level a metric for use in early sizing estimation. On the other hand, DSI can also be faulted for being too high-level a metric for precise software cost estimation. Various complexity metrics have been formulated to more accurately capture the relative information content of a program's instructions, such as the Halstead Software Science metrics [24], or to capture the relative control complexity of a program, such as the metrics formulated by McCabe in [39]. A number of variations of these metrics have been developed; a good recent survey of them is given in [26].

However, these metrics have yet to exhibit any practical superiority to DSI as a predictor of the relative effort required to develop software. Most recent studies [48], [32] show a reasonable correlation between these complexity metrics and development effort, but no better a correlation than that between DSI and development effort.

Further, the recent [25] analysis of the software science results indicates that many of the published software science "successes" were not as successful as they were previously considered. It indicates that much of the apparent agreement between software science formulas and project data was due to factors overlooked in the data analysis: inconsistent definitions and interpretations of software science quantities, unrealistic or inconsistent assumptions about the nature of the projects analyzed, overinterpretation of the significance of statistical measures such as the correlation coefficient, and lack of investigation of alternative explanations for the data. The software science use of psychological concepts such as the Stroud number have also been seriously questioned in [16].

The overall strengths and difficulties of software science are summarized in [47]. Despite the difficulties, some of the software science metrics have been useful in such areas as identifying error-prone modules. In general, there is a strong intuitive argument that more definitive complexity metrics will eventually serve as better bases for definitive software cost estimation than will DSI. Thus, the area continues to be an attractive one for further research.

3) Software Cost Driver Attributes and Their Effects: Most of the software cost models discussed above contain a selection of cost driver attributes and a set of coefficients, functions, or tables representing the effect of the attribute on software cost (see Table II). Chapters 24–28 of [11] contain summaries of the research to date on about 20 of the most significant cost driver attributes, plus statements of nearly 100 outstanding research issues in the area.

Since the publication of [11] in 1981, a few new results have appeared. Lawrence [35] provides an analysis of 278 business data processing programs which indicate a fairly uniform development rate in procedure lines of code per hour, some significant effects on programming rate due to batch turnaround time and level of experience, and relatively little effect due to use of interactive operation and modern programming practices (due, perhaps, to the relatively repetitive nature of the software jobs sampled). Okada and Azuma [42] analyzed 30 CAD/CAM programs and found some significant effects due to type of software, complexity, personnel skill level, and requirements volatility.

4) Software Cost Model Analysis and Refinement: The most useful comparative analysis of software cost models to date is the Thibodeau [52] study performed for the U.S. Air Force. This study compared the results of several models (the Wolverton, Doty, PRICE S, and SLIM models discussed earlier, plus models from the Boeing, SDC, Tecolote, and Aerospace corporations) with respect to 45 project data points from three sources.

Some generally useful comparative results were obtained, but the results were not definitive, as models were evaluated with respect to larger and smaller subsets of the data. Not too surprisingly, the best results were generally obtained using models with calibration coefficients against data sets with few points. In general, the study concluded that the models with calibration coefficients achieved better results, but that none of the models evaluated were sufficiently accurate to be used as a definitive Air Force software cost estimation model.

Some further comparative analyses are currently being conducted by various organizations, using the database of 63 software projects in [11], but to date none of these have been published.

In general, such evaluations play a useful role in model refinement. As certain models are found to be inaccurate in certain situations, efforts are made to determine the causes, and to refine the model to eliminate the sources of inaccuracy.

Relatively less activity has been devoted to the formulation, evaluation, and refinement of models to cover the effects of more advanced methods of software development (prototyping, incremental development, use of application generators, etc.) or to estimate other software-related life-cycle costs (conversion, maintenance, installation, training, etc.). An exception is the excellent work on software conversion cost estimation performed by the Federal Conversion Support Center [28]. An extensive model to estimate avionics software support costs using a weighted-multiplier technique has recently been developed [49]. Also, some initial experimental results have been obtained on the quantitative impact of prototyping in [13] and on the impact of very high level nonprocedural languages in [58]. In both studies, projects using prototyping and VHLL's were completed with significantly less effort.

5) Quantitative Models of Software Project Dynamics: Current software cost estimation models are limited in their ability to represent the internal dynamics of a software project, and to estimate how the project's phase distribution of effort and schedule will be affected by environmental or project management factors. For example, it would be valuable to have a model which would accurately predict the effort and schedule distribution effects of investing in more thorough design verification, of pursuing an incremental development strategy, of varying the staffing rate or experience mix, of reducing module size, etc.

Some current models assume a universal effort distribution, such as the Rayleigh curve [44] or the activity distributions in [57], which are assumed to hold for any type of project situation. Somewhat more realistic, but still limited are models with phase-sensitive effort multipliers such as PRICE S [22] and Detailed COCOMO [11].

Recently, some more realistic models of software project dynamics have begun to appear, although to date none of them have been calibrated to software project data. The Phister phase-by-phase model in [43] estimates the effort and schedule required to design, code, and test a software product as a function of such variables as the staffing level during each phase, the size of the average module to be developed, and such factors as interpersonal communications overhead rates and error detection rates. The Abdel Hamid–Madnick model [1], based on Forrester's System Dynamics world-view, estimates the time distribution of effort, schedule, and residual defects as a function of such factors as staffing rates, experience mix, training rates, personnel turnover, defect introduction rates, and initial estimation errors. Tausworthe [51] derives and calibrates alternative versions of the SLIM effort-schedule tradeoff relationship, using an intercommunication-overhead model of project dynamics. Some other recent models of software project dynamics are the Mitre SWAP model and the Duclos [21] total software life-cycle model.

6) Quantitative Models of Software Life-Cycle Evolution: Although most of the software effort is devoted to the software maintenance (or life-cycle support) phase, only a few significant results have been obtained to date in formulating quantitative models of the software life-cycle evolution process. Some basic studies by Belady and Lehman analyzed data on several projects and derived a set of fairly general "laws of program evolution" [7], [37]. For example, the first of these laws states:

"A program that is used and that as an implementation of its specification reflects some other reality, undergoes continual change or becomes progressively less useful. The change or decay process continues until it is judged more cost effective to replace the system with a re-created version."

Some general quantitative support for these laws was obtained in several studies during the 1970's, and in more recent studies such as [33]. However, efforts to refine these general laws into a set of testable hypotheses have met with mixed results. For example, the Lawrence [36] statistical analysis of the Belady-Lahman data showed that the data supported an even stronger form of the first law ("systems grow in size over their useful life"); that one of the laws could not be formulated precisely enough to be tested by the data; and that the other three laws did not lead to hypotheses that were supported by the data.

However, it is likely that variant hypotheses can be found that are supported by the data (for example, the operating system data supports some of the hypotheses better than does the applications data). Further research is needed to clarify this important area.

7) Software Data Collection: A fundamental limitation to significant progress in software cost estimation is the lack of unambiguous, widely-used standard definitions for software data. For example, if an organization reports its "software development man-months," do these include the effort devoted to requirements analysis, to training, to secretaries, to quality assurance, to technical writers, to uncompensated overtime? Depending on one's interpretations, one can easily cause variations of over 20 percent (and often over a factor of 2) in the meaning of reported "software development man-months" between organizations (and similarly for "delivered instructions," "complexity," "storage constraint," etc.) Given such uncertainties in the ground data, it is not surprising that software cost estimation models cannot do much better than "within 20 percent of the actuals, 70 percent of the time."

Some progress towards clear software data definitions has been made. The IBM FSD database used in [53] was carefully collected using thorough data definitions, but the detailed data and definitions are not generally available. The NASA-Goddard Software Engineering Laboratory database [5], [6], [40] and the COCOMO database [11] provide both clear data definitions and an associated project database which are available for general use (and reasonably compatible). The recent Mitre SARE report [59] provides a good set of data definitions.

But there is still no commitment across organizations to establish and use a set of clear and uniform software data definitions. Until this happens, our progress in developing more precise software cost estimation methods will be severely limited.

IV. Software Engineering Economics Benefits and Challenges

This final section summarizes the benefits to software engineering and software management provided by a software engineering economics perspective in general and by software cost estimation technology in particular. It concludes with some observations on the major challenges awaiting the field.

Benefits of a Software Engineering Economics Perspective

The major benefit of an economic perspective on software engineering is that it provides a balanced view of candidate software engineering solutions, and an evaluation framework which takes account not only of the programming aspects of a situation, but also of the human problems of providing the best possible information processing service within a resource-limited environment. Thus, for example, the software engineering economics approach does not say, "we should use these structured structures because they are mathematically elegant" or "because they run like the wind" or "because they are part of the structured revolution." Instead, it says "we should use these structured structures because they provide people with more benefits in relation to their costs than do other approaches." And besides the framework, of course, it also provides the techniques which help us to arrive at this conclusion.

Benefits of Software Cost Estimation Technology

The major benefit of a good software cost estimation model is that it provides a clear and consistent universe of discourse within which to address a good many of the software engineering issues which arise throughout the software life cycle. It can help people get together to discuss such issues as the following.

• Which and how many features should we put into the software product?

• Which features should we put in first?

• How much hardware should we acquire to support the software product's development, operation, and maintenance?

• How much money and how much calendar time should we allow for software development?

• How much of the product should we adapt from existing software?

• How much should we invest in tools and training?

Further, a well-defined software cost estimation model can help avoid the frequent misinterpretations, underestimates, overexpectations, and outright buy-ins which still plague the software field. In a good cost-estimation model, there is no way of reducing the estimated software cost without changing some objectively verifiable property of the software project. This does not make it impossible to create an unachievable buy-in, but it significantly raises the threshold of credibility.

A related benefit of software cost estimation technology is that it provides a powerful set of insights on how a software organization can improve its productivity. Many of a software cost model's cost-driver attributes are management controllables: use of software tools and modern programming practices, personnel capability and experience, available computer speed, memory, and turnaround time, software reuse. The cost model helps us determine how to adjust these management controllables to increase productivity, and further provides an estimate of how much of a productivity increase we are likely to achieve with a given level of investment. For more information on this topic, see [11, ch. 33], [12] and the recent plan for the U.S. Department of Defense Software Initiative [20].

Finally, software cost estimation technology provides an absolutely essential foundation for software project planning and control. Unless a software project has clear definitions of its key milestones and realistic estimates of the time and money it will take to achieve them, there is no way that a project manager can tell whether his project is under control or not. A good set of cost and schedule estimates can provide realistic data for the PERT charts, work breakdown structures, manpower schedules, earned value increments, etc., necessary to establish management visibility and control.

Note that this opportunity to improve management visibility and control requires a complementary management commitment to define and control the reporting of data on software progress and expenditures. The resulting data are therefore worth collecting simply for their management value in comparing plans versus achievements, but they can serve another valuable function as well: they provide a continuing stream of calibration data for evolving a more accurate and refined software cost estimation models.

Software Engineering Economics Challenges

The opportunity to improve software project management decision making through improved software cost estimation, planning, data collection, and control brings us back full-circle to the original objectives of software engineering economics: to provide a better quantitative understanding of how software people make decisions in resource-limited situations.

The more clearly we as software engineers can understand the quantitative and economic aspects of our decision situations, the more quickly we can progress from a pure seat-of-the-pants approach on software decisions to a more rational approach which puts all of the human and economic decision variables into clear perspective. Once these decision situations are more clearly illuminated, we can then study them in more detail to address the deeper challenge: achieving a quantitative understanding of how people work together in the software engineering process.

Given the rather scattered and imprecise data currently available in the software engineering field, it is remarkable how much progress has been made on the software cost estimation problem so far. But, there is not much further we can go until better data becomes available. The software field cannot hope to have its Kepler or its Newton until it has had its army of Tycho Brahes, carefully preparing the well-defined observational data from which a deeper set of scientific insights may be derived.

REFERENCES

[1] T. K. Abdel-Hamid and S. E. Madnick, ''A model of software project management dynamics,'' in *Proc. IEEE COMPSAC 82*, Nov. 1982, pp. 539–554.
[2] A. J. Albrecht, ''Measuring Application Development Productivity,'' in *SHARE-GUIDE*, 1979, pp. 83–92.
[3] J. D. Aron, ''Estimating resources for large programming systems.'' NATO Sci. Committee, Rome, Italy, Oct. 1969.
[4] J. J. Bailey and V. R. Basili, ''A meta-model for software development resource expenditures,'' in *Proc. 5th Int. Conf. Software Eng.*, IEEE/ACM/NBS, Mar. 1981, pp. 107–116.
[5] V. R. Basili, ''Tutorial on models and metrics for software and engineering,'' IEEE Cat. EHO-167-7, Oct. 1980.
[6] V. R. Basili and D. M. Weiss, ''A methodology for collecting valid software engineering data,'' Univ. Maryland Technol. Rep. TR-1235, Dec. 1982.
[7] L. A. Belady and M. M. Lehman, ''Characteristics of large systems,'' in *Research Directions in Software Technology*, P. Wegner, Ed. Cambridge, MA: MIT Press, 1979.
[8] H. D. Benington, ''Production of large computer programs,'' in *Proc. ONR Symp. Advanced Programming Methods for Digital Computers*, June 1956, pp. 15–27.
[9] R. K. D. Black, R. P. Curnow, R. Katz, and M. D. Gray, ''BCS software production data,'' Boeing Comput. Services, Inc., Final Tech. Rep., RADC-TR-77-116, NTIS AD-A039852, Mar. 1977.
[10] B. W. Boehm, ''Software and its impact: A quantitative assessment,'' *Datamation*, pp. 48–59, May 1973.
[11] ——, *Software Engineering Economics*. Englewood Cliffs, NJ: Prentice-Hall, 1981.
[12] B. W. Boehm, J. F. Elwell, A. B. Pyster, E. D. Stuckle, and R. D. Williams, ''The TRW software productivity system,'' in *Proc. IEEE 6th Int. Conf. Software Eng.*, Sept. 1982.

[13] B. W. Boehm, T. E. Gray, and T. Seewaldt, ''Prototyping vs. specifying: A multi-project experiment,'' *IEEE Trans. Software Eng.*, to be published.
[14] R. N. Britcher and J. E. Gaffney, ''Estimates of software size from state machine designs,'' in *Proc. NASA-Goddard Software Eng. Workshop*, Dec. 1982.
[15] W. M. Carriere and R. Thibodeau, ''Development of a logistics software cost estimating technique for foreign military sales,'' General Res. Corp., Rep. CR-3-839, June 1979.
[16] N. S. Coulter, ''Software science and cognitive psychology,'' *IEEE Trans. Software Eng.*, pp. 166–171, Mar. 1983.
[17] T. DeMarco, *Controlling Software Projects*. New York: Yourdon, 1982.
[18] M. Demshki, D. Ligett, B. Linn, G. McCluskey, and R. Miller, ''Wang Institute cost model (WICOMO) tool user's manual,'' Wang Inst. Graduate Studies, Tyngsboro, MA, June 1982.
[19] H. F. Dircks, ''SOFCOST: Grumman's software cost eliminating model,'' in *IEEE NAECON 1981*, May 1981.
[20] L. E. Druffel, ''Strategy for DoD software initiative,'' RADC/DACS, Griffiss AFB, NY, Oct. 1982.
[21] L. C. Duclos, ''Simulation model for the life-cycle of a software product: A quality assurance approach,'' Ph.D. dissertation, Dep. Industrial and Syst. Eng., Univ. Southern California, Dec. 1982.
[22] F. R. Freiman and R. D. Park, ''PRICE software model—Version 3: An overview,'' in *Proc. IEEE-PINY Workshop on Quantitative Software Models*, IEEE Cat. TH0067-9, Oct. 1979, pp. 32–41.
[23] R. Goldberg and H. Lorin, *The Economics of Information Processing*. New York: Wiley, 1982.
[24] M. H. Halstead, *Elements of Software Science*. New York: Elsevier, 1977.
[25] P. G. Hamer and G. D. Frewin, ''M. H. Halstead's software science—A critical examination,'' in *Proc. IEEE 6th Int. Conf. Software Eng.*, Sept. 1982, pp. 197–205.
[26] W. Harrison, K. Magel, R. Kluczney, and A. DeKock, ''Applying software complexity metrics to program maintenance,'' *Computer*, pp. 65–79, Sept. 1982.
[27] J. R. Herd, J. N. Postak, W. E. Russell, and K. R. Stewart, ''Software cost estimation study—Study results,'' Doty Associates, Inc., Rockville, MD, Final Tech. Rep. RADC-TR-77-220, vol. 1 (of two), June 1977.
[28] C. Houtz and T. Buschbach, ''Review and analysis of conversion cost-estimating techniques,'' GSA Federal Conversion Support Center, Falls Church, VA, Rep. GSA/FCSC-81/001, Mar. 1981.
[29] M. Itakura and A. Takayanagi, '' A model for estimating program size and its evaluation,'' in *Proc. IEEE 6th Software Eng.*, Sept. 1982, pp. 104–109.
[30] R. W. Jensen, ''An improved macrolevel software development resource estimation model,'' in *Proc. 5th ISPA Conf.*, Apr. 1983, pp. 88–92.
[31] R. W. Jensen and S. Lucas, ''Sensitivity analysis of the Jensen software model,'' in *Proc. 5th ISPA Conf.*, Apr. 1983, pp. 384–389.
[32] B. A. Kitchenham, ''Measures of programming complexity,'' *ICL Tech. J.*, pp. 298–316, May 1981.
[33] ——, ''Systems evolution dynamics of VME/B,'' *ICL Tech. J.*, pp. 43–57, May 1982.
[34] W. W. Kuhn, ''A software lifecycle case study using the PRICE model,'' in *Proc. IEEE NAECON*, May 1982.
[35] M. J. Lawrence, ''Programming methodology, organizational environment, and programming productivity,'' *J. Syst. Software*, pp. 257–270, Sept. 1981.
[36] ——, ''An examination of evolution dynamics,'' in *Proc. IEEE 6th Int. Conf. Software Eng.*, Sept. 1982, pp. 188–196.
[37] M. M. Lehman, ''Programs, life cycles, and laws of software evolution,'' *Proc. IEEE*, pp. 1060–1076, Sept. 1980.
[38] R. D. Luce and H. Raiffa, *Games and Decisions*. New York: Wiley, 1957.
[39] T. J. McCabe, ''A complexity measure,'' *IEEE Trans. Software Eng.*, pp. 308–320, Dec. 1976.
[40] F. E. McGarry, ''Measuring software development technology: What have we learned in six years,'' in *Proc. NASA-Goddard Software Eng. Workshop*, Dec. 1982.
[41] E. A. Nelson, ''Management handbook for the estimation of computer programming costs,'' Syst. Develop. Corp., AD-A648750, Oct. 31, 1966.
[42] M. Okada and M. Azuma, ''Software development estimation study—A model from CAD/CAM system development experiences,'' in *Proc. IEEE COMPSAC 82*, Nov. 1982, pp. 555–564.

[43] M. Phister, Jr., "A model of the software development process," *J. Syst. Software*, pp. 237–256, Sept. 1981.

[44] L. H. Putnam, "A general empirical solution to the macro software sizing and estimating problem," *IEEE Trans. Software Eng.*, pp. 345–361, July 1978.

[45] L. H. Putnam and A. Fitzsimmons, "Estimating software costs," *Datamation,* pp. 189–198, Sept. 1979; continued in *Datamation,* pp. 171–178, Oct. 1979 and pp. 137–140, Nov. 1979.

[46] L.H. Putnam, "The real economics of software development," in *The Economics of Information Processing,* R. Goldberg and H. Lorin.   New York: Wiley, 1982.

[47] V. Y. Shen, S. D. Conte, and H. E. Dunsmore, "Software science revisited: A critical analysis of the theory and its empirical support," *IEEE Trans. Software Eng.*, pp. 155–165, Mar. 1983.

[48] T. Sunohara, A. Takano, K. Uehara, and T. Ohkawa, "Program complexity measure for software development management," in *Proc. IEEE 5th Int. Conf. Software Eng.*, Mar. 1981, pp. 100–106.

[49] SYSCON Corp., "Avionics software support cost model," USAF Avionics Lab., AFWAL-TR-1173, Feb. 1, 1983.

[50] R. C. Tausworthe, "Deep space network software cost estimation model," Jet Propulsion Lab., Pasadena, CA, 1981.

[51] ——, "Staffing implications of software productivity models," in *Proc. 7th Annu. Software Eng. Workshop,* NASA/Goddard, Greenbelt, MD, Dec. 1982.

[52] R. Thibodeau, "An evaluation of software cost estimating models," General Res. Corp., Rep. T10-2670, Apr. 1981.

[53] C. E. Walston and C. P. Felix, "A method of programming measurement and estimation," *IBM Syst. J.*, vol. 16, no. 1, pp. 54–73, 1977.

[54] G. F. Weinwurm, Ed., *On the Management of Computer Programming.*   New York: Auerbach, 1970.

[55] G. M. Weinberg and E. L. Schulman, "Goals and performance in computer programming," *Human Factors,* vol. 16, no. 1, pp. 70–77, 1974.

[56] J. D. Wiest and F. K. Levy, *A Management Guide to PERT/CPM.* Englewood Cliffs, NJ: Prentice-Hall, 1977.

[57] R. W. Wolverton, "The cost of developing large-scale software," *IEEE Trans. Comput.*, pp. 615–636, June 1974.

[58] E. Harel and E. R. McLean, "The effects of using a nonprocedural computer language on programmer productivity," UCLA Inform. Sci. Working Paper 3-83, Nov. 1982.

[59] R. L. Dumas, "Final report: Software acquisition resource expenditure (SARE) data collection methodology," MITRE Corp., MTR 9031, Sept. 1983.

Barry W. Boehm received the B.A. degree in mathematics from Harvard University, Cambridge, MA, in 1957 and the M.A. and Ph.D. degrees from the University of California, Los Angeles, in 1961 and 1964, respectively.

From 1978 to 1979 he was a Visiting Professor of Computer Science at the University of Southern California. He is currently a Visiting Professor at the University of California, Los Angeles, and Chief Engineer of TRW's Software Information Systems Division. He was previously Head of the Information Sciences Department at The Rand Corporation, and Director of the 1971 Air Force CCIP-85 study. His responsibilities at TRW include direction of TRW's internal software R&D program, of contract software technology projects, of the TRW software development policy and standards program, of the TRW Software Cost Methodology Program, and the TRW Software Productivity Program. His most recent book is *Software Engineering Economics*, by Prentice-Hall.

Dr. Boehm is a member of the IEEE Computer Society and the Association for Computing Machinery, and an Associate Fellow of the American Institute of Aeronautics and Astronautics.

A Poor Man's Guide To Estimating Software Costs

November 1, 1985

Prepared By:
Donald J. Reifer

Prepared For:
Texas Instruments, Inc.
Lewisville, Texas 75067
Purchase Order #W1853969

Acknowledgement

The author acknowledges that he built on the work of J.D. Aron[1] to produce this guide. He also acknowledges the valuable inputs given by D. D. Galorath of RCI and P. Moore and J. Moseley of Texas Instruments during the guide's preparation.

Purpose

The purpose of this guide is to provide the reader with a simple and usable set of procedures for estimating the cost of a software project. While many detailed estimating models exist, few of these can be used quickly by the average software engineer to derive a rough order of magnitude estimate of software cost. Yet the crude estimates of costs are needed immediately especially around the time that budgets are being prepared. This guide remedies this prob-

lem by arming the reader with a procedure that allows him/her to develop a cost estimate within approximately thirty minutes.

Scope

The estimating procedure contained within this guide is applicable to medium to large scale software projects (over 10,000 lines and 10 people). It is generic in nature and can be used to estimate costs for most types of software applications.

The guide should be used with caution because its lack of detail results in estimates that tend to be imprecise. Yet, often we only have the time and energy to produce such a simple estimate. Therefore, we believe the guide will serve a useful purpose within the software community.

Estimating Procedure

The nine step procedure illustrated below should be followed to develop a cost estimate for your software project. Each step is explained in depth in subsequent sections of this report:

[1]J.D. Aron, "Estimating Resources for Large Programming Systems," *Software Engineering: Concepts and Techniques*, Litton Educational Publishing, Inc., 1976.

Step	Task
1	Define The Work Elements
2	Determine Software Size
3	Assess Difficulty
4	Define Risk And Its Impact
5	Estimate Personnel Resources
6	Adjust Estimate
7	Extrapolate Estimate
8	Schedule Estimate
9	Reiterate

Step 1:   Define the Work Elements

Many projects get into trouble because they fail to estimate all the work software people must complete in order for the team to be successful. Many questions including those that follow must be answered before an estimate can be developed:

- What activities are to be included within the scope of this estimate and what are others going to cover in their estimates?

- What programs are to be included within this estimate and what aren't (e.g., hardware built-in test, etc.)?

- What are the documentation requirements?

- What are the operational support requirements?

- How volatile are the operational and performance requirements (if they exist)?

- Do I understand enough about the nature of the job to come up with a rough order of magnitude estimate?

- Do I need help and where do I get it?

We can't answer any of these questions for you in this guide. Rather, we can provide you with a structure so that you won't forget something during your frenzied analysis of the situation. Let's look at two areas where structure can help.

A Top-Level Software Work Breakdown Structure

The following list of functional activities represents a shopping list of the tasks software organizations are usually asked to do. Each takes time and effort and each contributes to the scope of your estimate. Review this list to determine what your estimate will and will not encompass. Then, use this information in Step 7 when you extrapolate your estimate.

Software Work Breakdown Structure

1.0 Software
- 1.1 Software Systems Engineering
  - 1.1.1 Support To Systems Engineering
  - 1.1.2 Support To Hardware Engineering
  - 1.1.3 Software Engineering Trade Studies
  - 1.1.4 Requirements Analysis (System)
  - 1.1.5 Requirements Synthesis (Software)
  - 1.1.6 Equations Analysis
  - 1.1.7 Interface Analysis
  - 1.1.8 Support to System Test
- 1.2 Software Development
  - 1.2.1 Deliverable Software
    - 1.2.1.1 Requirements Analysis
    - 1.2.1.2 Architectural Design
    - 1.2.1.3 Procedural Design
    - 1.2.1.4 Code
    - 1.2.1.5 Unit Test
    - 1.2.1.6 Software Integration Test
    - 1.2.1.7 Technical Reviews
    - 1.2.1.8 Technical Training
  - 1.2.2 Non-Deliverable Software
  - 1.2.3 Purchased Software
    - 1.2.3.1 Capabilities Analysis & Specifications
    - 1.2.3.2 Package Evaluation
    - 1.2.3.3 Package Acquisition
    - 1.2.3.4 Package Installation, Demonstration & Training
  - 1.2.4 Development Facilities & Tools
- 1.3 Software Test & Evaluation
  - 1.3.1 Software Development Test & Evaluation
  - 1.3.2 End-Product Acceptance Test
  - 1.3.3 Test Bed & Tool Support
  - 1.3.4 Test Data Management
  - 1.3.5 Test Reviews
- 1.4 Management
  - 1.4.1 Project Management
  - 1.4.2 Administrative Support

[For those interested, this work breakdown structure is fully explained in RCI-TR-013.]

Assessing Relative Effort

The next thing you must do is determine how much effort to allocate for inherited software. The following chart illustrates how to deal with legacy (existing software that is to be reused). Many people assume existing software comes for free. That is rarely the case. Even the best of existing programs has to be integrated and tested as a system and that takes time and effort.

	New Software	Modified Existing Software	Converted Software
Analysis & Design	40%	15%	5%
Code	20%	10%	5%
Test & Evaluation	40%	40%	30%
Relative Effort	100%	65%	40%

The selection of the appropriate column in Table 1 is a function of the degree of reuse or legacy. Reading the chart, we see that modified existing software takes 65% of the effort involved in developing new software. Converted software takes 40% of the effort involved in developing new software. The entries in the corresponding rows identify why this is the case. Coding modified software takes half the effort of coding a similar new software package.

Armed with your assessment of the work and software involved, move on to Step 2. In Steps 2 to 5, you will learn how to develop a quick and dirty estimate. In Steps 6 and 7, you will adjust estimates to deal with technical and risk factors and extrapolate resulting estimates to cover all the work involved. In Step 8, you will schedule the effort and in Step 9, reiterate.

Step 2: Determine Software Size

Use one of the following three approaches to estimate the size of your software:

(1) *Engineering Judgement (Least Precise)*
$$S = f * (\text{size of similar packages})$$
where S = expected size (executable assembly lines)

f = fudge factor determined by experience and politics

(2) Average Size Approach[1]
$$S = n * (\text{average unit size})$$
where S = expected size (executable assembly lines)

n = number of units

[1]Must sketch out a rough architectural design

(3) *Statistical Approach (Most Precise)*

$$S = \frac{a + 4m + b}{6} \qquad d = \frac{(b - a)}{6}$$

where S = expected size (executable assembly lines)

d = standard deviation

a = minimum possible size

m = most likely size

b = maximum possible size

Realize that sizing a software system in executable assembly lines is an imprecise thing. Lines can represent memory locations or high level language statements. Be sure that you define what you mean by the term statement or else everyone including yourself will get confused. Note that when we use the word "line" in this guide, we refer to executable assembly instructions exclusive of commentary and data declaratives.

To use the statistical approach, take your initial estimate and assume it to be the minimum possible size (a). Next, take the size of your main memory (if reasonable) and use it as your maximum possible size (b). Lastly, use your judgment to estimate where in between these two you will wind up (most likely size or m). Be reasonable, not optimistic when you select these numbers.

Step 3: Assess Difficulty

Use Table 2 to rate the relative difficulty of your software:

Step 4: Define Risk and Its Impact

Many factors can influence software costs. The trick is to define those to which the estimate is sensitive and then quantify their cost impact.

The following matrix (Table 3) can be used to identify risk and how it impacts your cost estimate. Some typical risk factors are illustrated to show how their impact on cost can be quantified.

Step 5: Estimate Personnel Resources

The preliminaries are now done. You should have the following items at your disposal:

- The work elements to be included within the scope of your estimate (Step 1)
- A table defining how you will handle reused or inherited software (Step 1)
- A software size estimate (Step 2)
- A software difficulty assessment (Step 3)
- A table quantifying the impact of identified risk factors (Step 4)

Using the table on the following page, it is an easy matter to select an average cost per executable assembly lines and multiply it by the system size to obtain a base cost for software development.

$$\boxed{\text{Cost} = \text{Size} * \text{Dollars/Line}}$$

The selection of a row in the table is a function of your difficulty rating. The selection of column depends on the proposed schedule. The reason there are multiple columns is that software cost does not vary proportionately with schedule.

If you have reused software, the estimating algorithm is modified as follows:

$$\boxed{\begin{array}{c}\text{Cost} = \text{Size (New)} * \$/\text{Line} + \text{Size (Reused)} * \$/\text{Line} * \\ \text{(Relative Effort Factor)}\end{array}}$$

Realize that cost per instruction represents the burdened cost exclusive of fee when used within this guide (Table 4).

Realize that cost per executable assembly line represents the burdened cost exclusive of fee when used within this guide. As an example, if you had eighteen months to develop a medium difficulty software package which consisted of 10,000 new and 5,000 converted executable assembly line, the equation would be used as follows:

Cost = (10,000) * ($40) + (5,000) * ($40) * (0.40)

Cost = $400,000 + $80,000

Cost = $480,000

Table 2

Difficulty Category	Characteristics	Examples
Easy	• Few interactions with other system elements • Simple algorithms • Have previous experience in application • Data-driven architecture	• Payroll Systems • Report Generation Systems • Hardware Diagnostics
Medium	• Some interactions with other system elements • Suitable algorithms exist • Have previous experience in application • New machine or language	• Numerical Analysis Systems • Production Control Systems • Management Information Systems
Hard	• Many interactions with other system elements • Algorithms are new • Requirements are volatile • Limited past experience in application • Message-driven architecture	• On-line Systems • Real-Time Software • Systems Software • Message Switching Systems

157

Table 3: Risk Matrix

Risk Item	Risk Reduction Approach	Cost Impact
Late delivery of hardware	Acquire time on another system	Computer time costs
New operating system	Benchmark early and perform acceptance testing before use	Manpower to prepare benchmark and perform acceptance test
Feasibility of software requirements	Feasibility analysis and simulation	Manpower and computer time to conduct analysis
Staffing up	Start recruiting and training early	Recruiting and training costs
Feasibility of software design	Peer reviews	Added effort to prepare for and conduct design walkthroughs
Lack of management visibility	Require use of detailed work packaging and weekly reporting	Added effort to prepare inputs to variance analysis system
Configuration integrity of software products	Use a formal change control system revolving around a program library	Purchase price of library software plus costs of administering the formal system
Lack of a test discipline	Use an independent test group and get them involved early	Costs of establishing and using test group

158

Table 4: Base Cost Table

Difficulty \ Duration	Less Than 1 Year	1–2 Years	2–3 Years	Over 3 Years
Easy	$40	$30	$25	$40
Medium	$50	$40	$35	$50
Hard	$75	$50	$45	$65
Units	$/Line	$/Line	$/Line	$/Line

As another example, if you had at most one year to develop a hard software package which consisted of 10,000 to 20,000 new executable assembly lines, the equation would be used as follows:

Cost = (10,000) * ($75) to (20,000) * ($75)

Cost = $750,000 to $1,500,000

Now that you have your base development cost, move on to Step 6. Don't forget that cost is defined as burdened cost exclusive of fee when used in this guide. Also realize that this base cost only encompasses the software development work tasks. The estimate will have to be extrapolated to handle other work related activities software people will accomplish like support to system engineering and systems test.

Step 6: Adjust Estimate

Now that we have our base cost for software development, we can adjust it up or down for various technical and risk factors. Take your base cost estimate and adjust it as follows for the following four factors:

1. *Language Adjustment*

   If you selected a high level programming language like FORTRAN or PASCAL, congratulations. Take your estimate and reduce it by 50% when your size counts represent executable assembly lines:

$$Cost_1 = \frac{Cost}{2}$$

2. *Capacity Adjustment*

   If you are computer size or time limited, you have problems and we have to penalize you. The problem here is that it takes a great deal of effort to squeeze the software into the limited machine resources. Take your new cost and multiply it by a factor of 3 for those lines requiring special attention (over 75% usage):

$$Cost_2 = \frac{LSA}{LT} (Cost_1) * 3 + Cost_1$$

where LSA = Lines Requiring Special Attention
LT = Total Lines Of Executable Assembly Code

3. *Methodology Adjustment*

   Congratulations, you are entitled to a bonus if you are going to use modern software methods which include, as a minimum, structured programming, peer reviews and a modern design method like structured design or a tool like a design language. Take your adjusted cost and reduce it by a factor of 1.5.

$$Cost_3 = \frac{Cost_2}{1.5}$$

4. *Risk Adjustment*

   Now, take the adjusted cost and add to it the dollar cost you estimated for risk in Step 4. You now have your adjusted cost estimate for software development (WBS elements 1.2 and 1.3):

$$Adjusted\ Cost\ (C) = Cost_3 + \$Risk$$

This step should be used to make any additional adjustments you feel are necessary to deal with personnel, environmental or management issues.

Continuing with our first example, the costs were $480,000. Let us assume that the dollar risk of development is $100,000. Let's adjust as follows:

Table 5

WBS Reference	Cost Item	Nominal Cost	Amount
1.2–1.3	Software Development and Test	C	
1.1.1–1.1.7	Software Systems Engineering	(0.05 to 0.1) * C	
1.1.8	System Test and Evaluation	(0.30 to 1.0) * C	
1.4	Management	(0.10 to 0.3) * C	
1.5	Product Assurance	(0.06 to 0.1) * C	
1.6	Operations and Support[1]	C	
	External Documentation[2]	(0.25 to 0.5) * C	
	Total	(1.76 to 3.0) * C	

Adjustment Factor	Adjusted cost
• Language (we are using FORTRAN)	$240,000
• Capacity (we have no constraints)	$240,000
• Methodology (we are going to use all the best techniques)	$160,000
• Risk (unfortunately, we have a lot of risk)	$260,000

Again, these cost figures represent burdened costs exclusive of fee.

Step 7: Extrapolate Estimate

The next step extends the adjusted estimate we derived in Step 6 to cover all those work elements we identified other than software development. The cost of these work elements can often exceed the cost of the software development. As mentioned early in this guide, estimators often forget to include some work elements in their forecasts. Later on in the project, they have to suffer the consequences. To help you avoid making this mistake, Table 5 can be used along with the assumptions you made relative to your Work Breakdown Structure in Step 1 to develop an estimate of these additional costs.

The extrapolated estimate can increase the cost to 3.0 times that of your adjusted cost estimate (C). Again, these costs represent burdened cost exclusive of fee.

1 Operations and support represents the cost of maintaining a software system after it is given to the user. The average life of a large system is typically 10 years, while small systems last at most 2 years. The annual recurring cost can be fixed by dividing C by its expected life.

2 External documentation refers to the cost of repackaging documentation to meet customer requirements. If applicable, such costs should be shown by new WBS entry designated 1.2.1.9.

Step 8: Schedule Effort

Now comes the point in time when you have to try to put all the pieces of the puzzle together. Based upon your original schedule, you now have to allocate time to each of your work elements and determine person-loading. You should have the following items at your disposal:

- The work elements you included within your estimate (Step 1)
- A table quantifying risk (Step 4)
- Resource estimates for each work element (Steps 6 and 7)

We suggest that you attack the scheduling problem from both ends. First, start at the beginning and create an activity network that shows the interrelationships between individual tasks. Then, start with the end date and work backward using the same activity network to see if everything jells. Don't worry if it doesn't at first. It almost never does. Determine the critical path through your schedule next using PERT (Program Evaluation & Review Techniques). Adjust it as necessary to compensate for the risk you've identified in Step 4. Finally, smooth out the initial resource loading by leveling your non-critical path activities. An automated project management tool helps especially if there are a large number of tasks.

Step 9: Reiterate

Undoubtedly, inconsistencies and holes will appear as you schedule the individual work elements and determine resource-loading. As a result, you will have to reiterate the estimate several times to straighten these things out. Just as you finish, your boss will come in and ask the following questions:

- Can we do it in half the time?
- Can we do it for half the money?
- Can we do more for the same money?

Be prepared to rework your estimate almost instantaneously. Remember, when it comes to estimating, Murphy was an optimist.

Good luck!

Quick and Dirty Rules of Thumb

When all else fails, use the following rules of thumb to develop a quick and dirty estimate for your software project:

- Programmer Productivity (Including Comments)
  - HOL Lines/Person-Month - 85 to 165
  - Assembly Lines/Person-Month - 100 to 500
- Cost Per Executable Assembly Line Of Code
  - Range - $12 to $200
  - Average - $50
- Allocation Of Effort (As %)
  - Analysis & Design - 40%
  - Code   - 20%
  - Test & Evaluation - 40%
- Allocation Of Time (As %)
  - Analysis & Design - 45%
  - Code   - 25%
  - Test & Evaluation - 30%
- Other Costs (As % Development Cost)
  - Project Management - 7 to 10%
  - Acquisition Management - 10 to 20%
  - Software Systems Engineering - 3 to 10%
  - Configuration Management - 3 to 5%
  - Quality Assurance - 5 to 10%
  - Documentation (External) - 25 to 50%
  - System Test Support - 30 to 100%
  - Independent V&V - 12 to 35%
- Cost of Maintenance (As % Development Cost)
  - First Year - 15 to 20%
  - Second Year - 12 to 18%
  - Third Year - 10 to 12%
- Hardware Usage Per Deliverable Link Of Code
  - PPU Time In Minutes - 0.8 min/line
  - CPU Time In Minutes - 0.1 min/line
  - Core Resident Time   - 1.6 min/line
  - Quantity Of Jobs   - 0.2 job/line
  - Lines Of Printout   - 1300 lines/line

Remember, costs represent burdened cost exclusive of fee.

Validating an Estimate

Use any or all of the following approaches to validate a software cost estimate:

1. Have two different organizations generate independent estimates. Then, compare them and try to resolve the differences.

2. Have two different people from your organization, each using a different method, generate an estimate. Have them meet to resolve the differences and reach a consensus estimate.

3. Ask how the estimate compares with your previous experience (assumes you have a lessons learned data base for your organization) in the following areas:
   - Cost per instruction?
   - Size versus function?
   - Technology versus cost?

4. If all else fails,   compare your experience with the following data base of experience (Table 6):

Table 6

Type of Software	Average Cost* Per Instruction**	Cost Range Per Instruction**
Avionics Or Flight Software	$200	$150 - 350
Real-Time Command & Control Software	$ 75	$ 12 - 200
Systems Software	$ 65	$ 35 - 150
Scientific Software	$ 50	$ 15 - 150
Business Applications Software	$ 35	$ 10 - 80

*Cost is defined as burdened cost exclusive of fee

**Instruction is defined as an executable assembly line exclusive of comments and data declarations.

Annotated Bibliography

There are literally hundreds of papers, reports and articles on the subject of software cost estimating and modeling. The following four sections, in our opinion, are the most informative from a poor man's point of view:

1. Barry W. Boehm, *Software Engineering Economics*, Prentice-Hall, 1981.

   A very thorough treatment of the factors which impact the cost of a software development. Lots of examples are included as is a detailed procedure for deriving a cost estimate and assuring its fidelity with reality.

2. Marsha Finfer and Russell Mish, *Software Acquisition Management Guidebook: Cost Estimation and Measurement*, ESD-TR-78-140, March 1978.

   This excellent survey discusses the role of various parametric models in developing estimates for software used within various command, control and communications systems.

3. Daniel D. Galorath and Donald J. Reifer, *Final Report, Analysis of the State-of-the-Art Of Parametric Software Cost Modeling*, RCI-TR-016, 8 August 1980.

   This report summarizes the state-of-the-art of parametric software cost modeling. It evaluates nine of the most popular cost models and discusses both their advantages and disadvantages from a user vantage point.

4. Lawrence H. Putnam, *Tutorial Software Cost Estimation and Life-Cycle Control: Getting the Software Numbers*, IEEE Computer Society, IEEE Catalog Number 165-1, 1980.

   This tutorial volume concentrates on the use of the statistical approach for estimating software costs. Full of facts and figures. Some interesting articles included in this volume.

Part III: Organizing

"We trained hard . . . but it seemed that everytime we were beginning to form into teams we would be reorganized . . . I was to learn later in life that we tend to meet any new situation by reorganizing; and a wonderful method it can be for creating the illusion of progress while producing confusion, inefficiency and demoralization."

—Petronius Arbiter, 210 B.C.

For most managers, the term "organization" implies a formalized structure of roles or positions within which they must operate to get their jobs done. To arrive at this structure, a firm must define management's span of control and authority responsibility, staff-project-line, and departmental relationships. Most middle managers don't have much say over the way a firm elects to organize itself. Instead, their influence is directed toward establishing lateral and hierarchical communications and teamwork within the operational units that they control. All of these topics are addressed in the five papers that follow.

The first three articles discuss options and criteria used to determine what type of organization is best for software activity. Milutinovich and Kanter, in "Organizing the MIS Department," discuss centralization versus decentralization and the impact of selecting either on a hypothetical company. In "Principles of Organization Planning," Stevens explains why and how organization planning is accomplished and how it can be used to fulfill business strategies and cope with operational problems. In "Organizing for Successful Software Development," Daly identifies several structures and the factors governing choice and then discusses the effect of organization on productivity.

The next article discusses the issues associated with the concept of matrix management. Harden and Gretsch, in "Operating Dynamics of Matrix Management," describe the interrelationships and conflicts that typically exist between the functional and the project organizations and discuss how effectiveness can be improved when conflicts inherent in matrix management are managed.

The final article discusses the use of team organizations. Mantei, in "The Effect of Programming Team Structures on Programming Tasks," analyzes and evaluates the concepts of a chief programer team and an egoless team. Recommendations are offered for putting team approaches into practice and for furthering research in the area of team selection and structuring.

Organizing the MIS department

By DR. JUGOSLAV MILUTINOVICH and
HOWARD A. KANTER

■ Many companies, especially conglomerates, are not realizing an adequate rate of return on their data processing investment. Although a reorganization may be needed, a comparison of the advantages and disadvantages of centralization vs. decentralization should be made before any changes, additions, or modifications are incorporated.

Any approach should be consistent with a company's overall management philosophy. The MIS manager who runs counter to the rest of his company will face a difficult challenge.[1] Above all, the new set up should best utilize existing assets to deliver the highest level of services at the lowest possible cost.

Advocates of decentralization offer the following major arguments:

1. Familiarity with local problems. The solution of complex problems within complex environments requires familiarity with this environment.

2. Rapid response to local processing needs. Rapid turn-around is easier at the local level, especially if intracorporate communications are limited. Communication facilities can be increased but costs must be weighed against benefits.

3. Profit and loss responsibility. The computer can be a major profit or loss factor and often the local manager is in the best position to decide what is best for the facility he manages.

4. Sacrifice of individual needs. There is a tendency when using a centralized system to lose sight of users' needs and consider just the overall organization's objectives.

The Other Side

Advocates for centralization counter with:

1. Company-wide consolidation of operating results. Plant data is required at the corporate level; therefore, systems, including design, coding schemes and data representation, must be compatible. This compatibility is achieved by centralized control and direction of hardware/software.

2. Economies of scale—hardware. When several computers are replaced by one large computer, economies of scale can be measured approximately according to Grosch's Law, which states that the ratio of the power of two computers is approximately equal to the ratio of their costs squared. The result is the achievement of economies of scale in hardware.

3. Economies of scale—people. Grosch's Law seems to apply here, too. A survey of 2,000 companies showed that the number of employees per dollar of

Dr. Jugoslav S. Milutinovich

Dr. Milutinovich is Assistant Professor of Management at Temple University. He has done considerable research in the areas of individual and organizational behavior and operations and general management. Professor Milutinovich holds a doctorate in management and statistics from New York University. He is a frequent author. Dr. Milutinovich also is a consultant to government and business.

Howard A. Kanter

Mr. Kanter is on the Management Advisory Services staff of Price Waterhouse & Co., Chicago office. He was previously Director of MIS for the Walworth Company in Philadelphia. Mr. Kanter is a graduate of Roosevelt University and has done postgraduate work at Temple and Roosevelt Universities. He is a member of ASM, ACM, and DPMA, and presently serves on the Board of Directors of the DPMA Chicago Chapter. He holds a CDP from that organization.

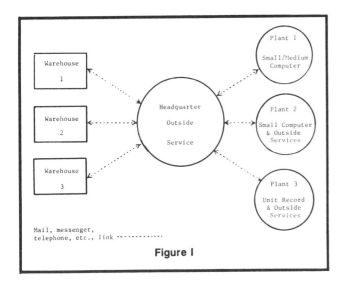

Mail, messenger,
telephone, etc., link ············

Figure 1

equipment rental declines as the size of the installation increases. At the same time, the average wages paid to corporate personnel increase as the size of the installation increases. The cost to the installation is a declining function of size. Economies of scale exist if either the average cost of larger installations is lower or if the quality (producing acceptable programs in reasonable lengths of time) is improved at the same cost.[2] It can be more difficult in a small installation to produce quality work due to personnel problems. A small number of people forced to perform a large number of functions and tasks usually do not have time to develop a high degree of specialization. This situation can result in a poorer quality.

4. Shortage of qualified personnel. Larger, centralized operations can be more attractive than smaller units since some data processing personnel will have more allegiance to technology than to a company. They will, therefore, want to work where the latest technology is being used. In addition, a centralized organization means fewer individual staff members; hence, the affect of turnover will be less.

5. Ease of control. It is easier for corporate executives to control individual operations when reporting systems are uniform. Analogous systems within operating divisions, especially where similar products are manufactured, are, in part, redundant and an impediment to control.

6. Ease of growth. There is the ability to meet unexpected or rapid expansion of a single user's requirements with a relatively small expansion in the aggregate data processing resources.

Model Company

Top management and the Director of MIS considered the advantages and disadvantages of the old decentralized MIS as well as a centralized one before moving to restructure the MIS function in our *model* company. Assume this company is a metal processing concern consisting of a headquarters location, three manufacturing facilities and three warehouses, all widely dispersed. Each plant produces similar products. Prior to centralization, orders were taken for standard products through warehouses and for special products through both plants and warehouses. Financial statements were prepared on a plant basis and were consolidated at headquarters.

The data processing facilities diagrammed in Figure 1 contain a small-medium computer at Plant 1, a small computer and the use of outside services at Plant 2, and unit record equipment plus the extensive use of outside services at Plant 3. There is no automated equipment at the warehouses and considerable use of outside services at the headquarters level.

A relatively short study disclosed the following major difficulties in the decentralized MIS system.

1. Computer equipment was unbalanced. Plant 1 was over capacity; Plants 2 and 3 were under.
2. Each plant claimed unique requirements, but really the subsystems were analogous; therefore, redundancy, higher costs, and failure to meet corporate information requirements prevailed throughout subsystems development.
3. The company's systems capabilities were fragmented and would have been too costly to rebuild on an adequate, individual-location basis. Furthermore, the increased capacity desired could not have been justified at this level.
4. There was a lack of control over data processing costs, expenditures and standards of performance.

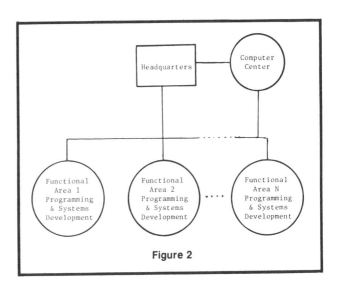

Figure 2

5. Corporate-wide MIS systems development was not planned.
6. A unified front could not be presented to a computer vendor.
7. Hardware planning, systems development and the use of outside services did not follow corporate needs.

To efficiently use the computer at a low cost for a wide variety of problems, a centralized MIS was approved by top management.

Choosing Alternatives

Before choosing the specific form of centralized organization, various alternative forms were considered by the Director of MIS and top management to determine which form would be most beneficial.

1. Centralized hardware with decentralized system development and programming. This form of centralization provides for hardware economies of scale and allows local systems development for local systems needs. Its disadvantages include the fragmentation of systems and programming resources, the difficulty in providing for a common data base, the potential difficulty inherent in crossing divisional lines, and nonstandardized systems and program development. This form of centralization is presented in Figure 2.

2. Centralized hardware and programming with decentralized systems development. This form, presented in Figure 3, provides for hardware economies of scale, and provides for a consolidated programming resource. The same difficulties exist here except for the consolidation of the programming resources.

3. Centralized systems and programming with decentralized hardware. This form of centralization, shown in Figure 4, eliminates the fragmentation of systems and programming resources and allows for standardization of system and program development.

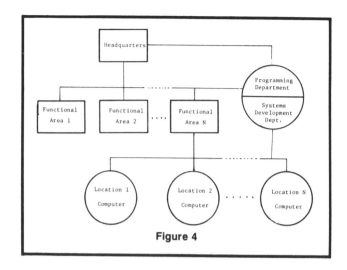

Figure 4

Its main disadvantage is the fractionalization of the corporate hardware which leads to a loss in economies of scale. However, headquarters has some control and can insure that the hardware used by all decentralized subsystems is compatible.

4. Centralized hardware, systems, and programming with directly linked satellite installations. This organizational form, presented in Figure 5, has almost all of the advantages of centralization. By providing some satellite control over access to the central computer and a small satellite support staff, most of the advantages of decentralization may also be achieved. The satellite installation may report to the headquarters manager or to the manager of the satellite location.

5. Centralized hardware, systems, and programming with autonomous satellite installations. This organizational pattern, see Figure 6, is an alternative form of the centralized organization with satellites (see #4), allowing autonomous control over satellite computer operations by the satellite manager. This form of centralization is best for organizations with profit centers in which the manager is directly responsible for profit and loss. Although he is still totally dependent on centralized hardware, systems, and programming, he can exercise some administrative control over the inputs and outputs used and the cost of computer resources. It is also possible for a satellite to have its own system and programming staff for limited maintenance and modification of the satellite's system. There is a danger the autonomous manager gradually may attempt to expand his computer facilities to the point where the satellite's facilities will become a decentralized computer center.

After careful consideration of the advantages and disadvantages of the different forms of centralization, top management decided to adopt Alternative #5 since, in our model company, plants and

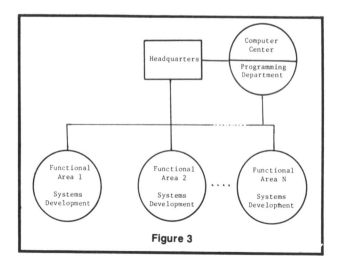

Figure 3

warehouses are profit centers and each manager is directly responsible to management for profit and loss.

The reorganization of the MIS function into a centralized MIS system was to be carried through three phases. During Phase I of centralization (Figure 7), only Plant 1 would be on-line with the new headquarters computer. During this phase, a special emphasis was placed on overcoming the resistance to change by employees in the decentralized MIS subsystems. If successful, Phase I would lead to Phase II, linking all plants and warehouses with the upgraded headquarters computer center. Phase III would establish the total centralized MIS and management would have timely access to all pertinent business information.

Accomplishments

Here is what the centralization of the MIS activity during Phase I considered and accomplished:

There were certain characteristics that the central computing site configuration needed, most important of which was the ability to execute a number of multiple programs. This ability was required because of the proposed modest increase in the scale of the central processing unit (CPU). Furthermore, to achieve simultaneous data communications to and from the remote station and to support the multiprogramming system, adequate main storage and sufficient I/O resources would be required.

The operating system chosen was selected to meet the following requirements:

a. Minimum use of main storage.
b. Ability to support a multiprogramming system.
c. Contain a spooling mechanism for maximum operational efficiency.
d. Support source program and procedure libraries for backup in order to minimize

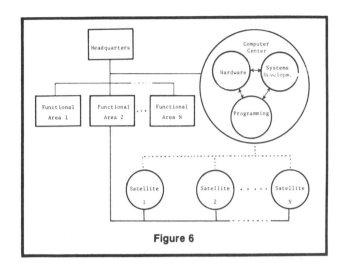

Figure 6

transmission requirements and decrease the effects of operational error.

Standards and procedures were adopted. They allowed that only a logically defined machine (subset of a physical machine) be used in systems design and subsequent programming. Close adherence to these rules eliminated endless scheduling problems and increased efficiency. Furthermore, definition and installation of programming standards were necessary to help prevent future problems. Procedures, construction of programs, and data management were standardized for efficiency.

The central site staff was to be a small group of highly competent and flexible individuals who were free to travel. The MIS Director was to be either a member of the executive committee or he was to report directly to an executive. This central group was to have the following specific functions:

a. New systems analysis and design.
b. Data processing standards.
c. Documentation standards
d. Project control
e. Hardware and software evaluation and selection and
f. Technical support to remote users.

Remote Organizational Units

There were two basic alternatives in hardware selection, on-line Remote Job Entry (RJE) and off-line data collection and dissemination. Use of inside or outside time-sharing services was not considered here but could prove useful.

The decision was made to use a nonintelligent RJE alternative. This was based on cost, central-site supportability, competency of local and remote technical staff and local applications that were not appropriate for central processing.

Remote organizational units used software de-

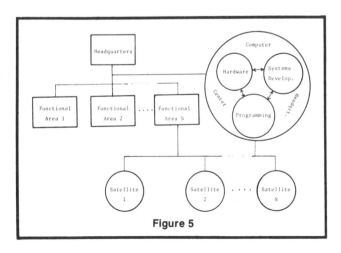

Figure 5

veloped by a central computer-support group. Software had to satisfy the needs of each remote organizational unit and be of standard form. Where it was necessary, special software programs were developed to correct specific problems of certain organizational units. The standards that applied to the central computer organization also applied to the remote organization.

The remote site staff was to consist of a department manager (ideally on the location's decision-making staff) and as many technical support personnel as could be economically justified. However, there had to be at least one system-trained person in addition to the manager to provide management with support in the identification and solution of problems and maintenance of the local subsystem. It was important that the remote unit management would have "its own" personnel dedicated to solving local problems.

The remote staff was free to modify and implement systems that did not have a corporate impact, e.g., a payroll rate change. However, even such changes had to be communicated to the central site person responsible for documentation, program backup and protection. Systems development of a more complex nature, not easily handled by the remote staff, caused a request for assistance from the corporate systems group. The existence of a highly qualified remote staff was imperative because they were in day-to-day interface with the problems and staffs at both the local and headquarters level.

Implementation Phase I

The first phase of the centralization effort, the installation of a computer at the headquarters, nonintelligent remote job entry terminals (RJE) at Plant 1, and a complete corporate technical staff, was planned according to the previous guidelines. However, execution of the plan was considerably disrupted by the resistance to change by staff members at Plant 1. This problem was not fully anticipated by management as it was assumed that staff would welcome positive changes. However, staff members in Plant 1 opposed the change on several grounds. Although they had more powerful resources available through the remote job entry terminals, not having the "flashing lights" present was of major concern to them and to some of the remote users. The staff felt that its power, status and control were diminished with the introduction of RJE terminals. Another reason for the resistance was economic. This was as important as the other reasons. Finally, the staff felt that informal group structure was threatened.

The result was a high absence rate, tardiness, longer computer downtime, poor work performance, slowdown and conflict with the headquarters staff.

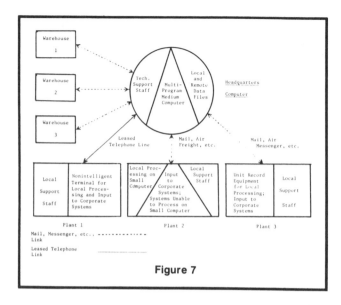

Figure 7

Speedy implementation of Phase I was not achieved. To make the situation worse, staff from Plants 2 and 3 supported the staff of Plant 1 because they were sure of being next in line for reorganization during Phase II. Management had to take another look at the problem. It found:

1. Staff members were not informed about proposed changes in their subsystems.
2. Department managers and staff were not asked for their opinion about the new system changes.
3. Staff members were not asked to participate in the planning.
4. Top management made no assurances regarding planned staff changes; therefore, staff felt insecure about their positions.
5. Staff members felt that the change was too sudden and too great.

Management decided to systematically initiate changes by giving more information to employees about the changes and by asking staff members for opinions and suggestions. Finally, management considered individual and group needs and aspirations. Although management recognized its mistakes, it was six months before the revised Phase I system conversion, testing, scheduling and training could begin.

The initial cutover to the central computer was made. The entire technical staff was on standby to handle those problems which, despite detailed planning, occurred. In two months there was reluctant acceptance by the users in Plant 1. At the end of six months of operation, the system was functioning smoothly, and achieving all major objectives.

As a result of the successful first phase, there were some major benefits to the corporation. Voluminous print jobs were reduced to manageable volume. This was necessitated by the terminal's relatively low print speed, which forced a realistic review of all reports. All corporate use of outside services was eliminated with significant savings plus internal control over the systems. Three shifts of computer processing at Plant 1 were provided while only two shifts of operation at the remote location were required. This operated by using the first shift for testing and data input from the plant; the second shift processed the data at the central site while the terminal was unmanned; the third shift transmitted the results of the second shift processing.

Functional units in the plant (Inventory Control, Accounting, etc.) were charged back for their computer use. This resulted in an identified charge to the appropriate using department rather than a buried charge to administration. In addition, users were careful and certain of requests for additional reports.

The plant manager had the lowest possible fixed cost equipment installed. Because of his P/L responsibility, he could cut expenses by not requesting various reports or by reducing their frequency. If he had his own high fixed cost computer installation, this option would not have been available. Input of Plant 1 data required for corporate operations was removed from the vagaries of the postal service and placed on a timely, reliable basis.

Implementation Phase II

Based on the success achieved in the initial phase of centralization, intelligent RJE terminals are planned for all plants. Warehouses will be linked to the central computer system through data entry/receiving terminal devices. During Phase II, all subsystems will be linked with the headquarter's computer center via a data communication network. Phase II is the extension of Phase I to all subsystems within the company, whereby each will have a direct link with the headquarter's computer center. This is a simple updating of the total system in which further extension of benefits accrued through Phase I will be achieved.

During the second phase of implementation, resistance to change of staff will be minimized by taking into account experiences from Phase I; staff members from all remote organizational units will participate actively in the planning process of this phase. Guidelines presented for Phase I will be extended to all subsystems.

Implementation Phase III

Phase III is planned as a total MIS and will give access to pertinent current information about almost

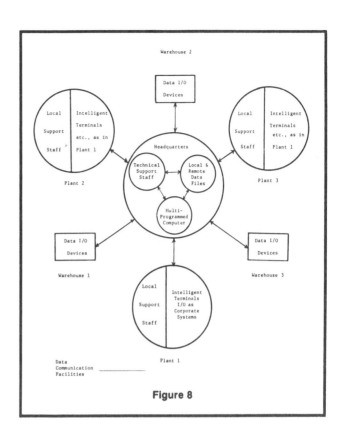

Figure 8

any aspect of business operation to all levels of management. In order to achieve the desired efficiency and objectives, the new MIS would be updated with a larger multiprogrammed computer. The final stage after full implementation should decrease the inventory of spare parts and improve the inventory control process, decrease the in-process stock with fewer stockouts, improve customer service and scheduling, improve equipment utilization, improve flow of material and information, improve clerical efficiency, assure timely and accurate records and eliminate or simplify certain clerical jobs. The new centralized total MIS will give management access to timely information for the decision-making process at all levels and in all geographically dispersed operating units (the main objective of centralization).

While centralization is not a technique that can be used universally, it can be a major step toward the goal of presenting on a timely basis, from geographically dispersed operating units, information for top management to plan, control and organize the business. This, combined with improved facilities for the operating units, justified the effort required to centralize. ●jsm

References
1. Glaser, G.: The Centralization vs. Decentralization Issue: Arguments, Alternatives and Guidelines. *Data Base,* 1970, Vol. 2, No. 3.
2. Solomon, M. B.: Economics of Scale and Computer Personnel. *Datamation,* 1970, Vol. 16, No. 3, p. 107.

Principles of Organization Planning

BY ROBERT I. STEVENS

■ Organization planning has the following basic functions:

- Make detailed in-depth studies of the management organizational structure of headquarters departments, groups, and units and recommend appropriate changes including regrouping of companies or parts of companies, realigning functions and consolidating or dividing functions or units into larger or smaller entitites. This is accomplished for purposes of management control or cost considerations or to provide greater visibility and management attention.
- Define missions of departments, groups, units, functions, etc.
- Review or prepare position descriptions of key management positions in the applicable study.
- Give guidance to various subsidiaries and units that have their own organization planning activities either full time or on a part time basis.

In addition, organization projects are conducted to facilitate accomplishment of an operational change such as installing a new or revised method or system, introduction of a new product, an expanded market, etc., in which functional considerations must be evaluated in addition to the usual organization factors.

Basically, organization studies evaluate the current organization structure and staffing taking into consideration planned growth and profit or functional objectives. As necessary, the business mission of an operating unit or function is revised or clarified so that specific organizational responsibility is defined. Close interrelationship is maintained with the required functional areas or line units necessary to get pertinent facts to arrive at a conclusion.

Part of each manager's job is to organize his area of responsibility. In a small company, organization planning is accomplished by each manager for his function and by the President for overall company considerations. In larger companies, the managers

and President have less time to devote to such activity and this function is assigned to a specialized staff member as a part-time or full-time function with top management getting involved only in broad policy and approval actions.

As you can see, organization planning does not consist of merely plotting an organization chart after a review of the span of control and a few other basic fundamentals, but rather is a detailed study noting business strategies and operational problems plus systems, business planning, manpower planning and market considerations.

Rules of Organization Planning

The first rule of organization planning is to "define the business mission." Without an understanding of the business mission there can be no meaningful organization structure, definition of functions, position descriptions, position specifications, work flow or work measurement that can be objectively and mean-

ROBERT I. STEVENS

Robert I. Stevens is Director-Organization Administration with International Telephone and Telegraph, Inc. at its world headquarters in New York City. He holds a Certificate in Business Administration from Union College, Cranford, New Jersey; a B.A. in Economics from Rutgers University, and has completed all graduate work except his thesis toward an M.A. in Economics at New York University. Mr. Stevens is a past president of the New York Chapter, Association for Systems Management. He has earned the ASM Merit, Achievement and Distinguished Service Awards and twice has been named as "Outstanding Member" by the New York Chapter.

ingfully related to each other. This principle holds whether we are reviewing the corporate structure, a functional department, company, section, etc. This leads us to "what is a business mission?"—and why it gives perspective and meaning to functions, descriptions, specifications, work flow and measurement.

Basically, a business mission is the responsibility assignment of a section, department, division, company, group or corporation defined in specific terms. The same approach applies to both organizing or reorganizing an area. With an existing area, the planner should be sure to check that the business mission has not changed over the past several years and to make certain that the unit manager and his supervisors concur with the mission definition. He should then proceed to structure an organization based on that mission to what he believes it "ought to be." Then he can compare his concept with the existing structure, note the differences and determine what trade-offs should be made, what effects they will have, what their impact will be on headcount, manpower utilization, work capacity and cost. On the basis of that analysis, he should be prepared to make organization recommendations and to defend them. After agreement, he will prepare position descriptions of key functions.

In either case, the restructuring of a new organization or the revision of an existing organization, the planner starts from the same place—the business mission—because organizations are designed to "do" and that which must be done must first be defined before we can organize to "do it."

In working with corporate departments, major groups, divisions or subsidiaries, the concept and approach are the same even regardless of the mission or the managerial plane involved. For example, the Comptroller's department may be responsible for developing and implementing methods to account for and control the company's revenues, expenses, assets, liabilities and stockholders' equity. A detailed analysis of the organization planning for a Billing Section is shown in the case history.

Conclusion

In developing an organization plan, recommendations should be prepared based on the writer's honest convictions and not be tailored to agree with the desires of top management or to suit political situations. However, once the recommendations are presented, a pragmatic approach should be adopted so that timing, personalities, skill levels, etc., are considered in arriving at recommendations acceptable to management. A "half a loaf" is better than nothing and a "half a loaf" today and a "half a loaf" next year equals total acceptance.

Organization projects are received from various sources; by request from top management, functional departments or groups, or may be initiated by the director responsible for organization planning in response to a need that he has identified.

Recommendations should receive a definite "approval" by management. Unless a clear cut "green light" is received, full support from the area being reviewed may not be forthcoming and implementation can be challenged at any time with resulting chaos, loss of momentum and possible loss of the project's efforts.

In some situations the installation of an organization tailored to meet a system will require additional personnel. However, in other instances the amount of activity and thus the number of people can be reduced.

Once approval is obtained, it is important that action be taken to assist in the implementation of the approved recommendations. If a new or revised system is included in the approved recommendations, this should be checked from time to time to see that it is installed properly and that no "bugs" develop causing a breakdown.   •jsm

CASE HISTORY

The Billing Section of an Accounts Receivable Department within a Comptroller's department might have the following business mission:

"In accordance with pre-scheduled billing dates, prepares and mails statements to customers for purchases made between the first and last day of customers' individual billing months. Ensures that customers who have balances beyond sixty days of their billing date receive a reminder in their following bill, and that the Credit department is provided with a list of such customers for follow-up. Ensures that bad credit risks, bad debtors and inac-

tive customers are removed from active sales files as appropriate. Provides timely, economical and efficient billing to the customer. Offers prompt, courteous and accurate responses to customer inquiries regarding their accounts."

The Billing Section's mission or assignment can be described as a number of interrelated activities.

Having defined the Billing Section's assignment it is important that it be reviewed with the manager of the Billing Section, his supervisor and other applicable managers to ensure that all affected areas agree. If they do not agree, the differences must be pinpointed and resolved. Without such agreement as to the section's mission there can be no possibility of planning an effective and economical organization structure.

Once the mission definition is accepted, the organization planner must research the vital facts and statistics of the business that have a direct relationship to the Billing Section. Included will be such items as:

- Procedure of accumulation and segregation of individual customer's transactions.
- Procedure of preparing cumulative statements for individual customers.
- Procedure of including duplicate slips bearing customer's signature for each transaction or group of transactions with cumulative statement of individual customers.
- Volume in dollars of credit sales made per month.
- Volume of transactions per month in credit sales.
- Total number of approved credit customers of the business.
- Average frequency of use per month of credit by customer.
- Sequence and flow of credit transaction information from sales person to Billing Section.

There may be other information the organization planner will want but with the above data now at his disposal, he can begin his task of planning and staffing a structure to fulfill a defined business mission.

It is almost certain that the Billing Section will have a manager. It will be his job to plan, organize, direct and control the activity and people for which he is responsible in such a manner as to carry out the business mission efficiently and economically. Similarly, because of the nature of his section's mission, the manager will have to interrelate with other section and department heads such as sales and credit to ensure that the flow of information both to and from his section is timely and accurate. He or she will also have to be customer-relations conscious. He must be able to balance the workload within his department to take care of seasonal peaks, imbalances in numbers of customers per billing period and so on, either by shifting of his available work force, use of part-time help, temporary help, etc.

An understanding of the mission and the business statistics as to number of credit customers and frequency of use of credit will give the planner an idea of how many bills must be rendered per month. If the billing dates are selected on the basis of the first letter of the customer's surname, he will have an idea of the number of bills which must be rendered each day. Together with knowledge of the work flow from sales clerk to billing, this will provide the planner

with the sequence of tasks to be performed and will permit establishment of means and methods of dividing the work activity; e.g., filing clerks, cumulative statement clerks and cumulative statement audit clerks. The volume of the work will permit the planner to apply work measurement and in turn will enable him to begin defining staffing needs in each category of work to be performed. Similarly, both the numbers of categories of work and the defined levels of staffing in each category will enable the organization planner to determine the type and number of supervisors required for the billing activity. From this information he should be able to write the supervisors' position descriptions and job specifications. The job specifications can be used by the Personnel department to define the job grade and job salary range.

The filing clerks, cumulative statement clerks and cumulative statement audit clerks positions mentioned above must also be described and job specifications written, for supervisory requirements will depend on the number and the nature of these clerical positions.

Based on the Billing Section's mission statement, the section might have an Account Maintenance supervisor responsible for ensuring that newly approved credit customers are phased into the billing cycle and inactive accounts that have been dormant for a pre-set period are phased out. Volume of activity and the work that must be performed will determine whether one or more people are required. And again, the position or positions must be described.

The volume of total business and the number of monthly inquiries from customers will determine whether a full-time customer relations and service function is needed. If the function is needed then the question must be answered as to whether it is strictly a telephone service, a customer correspondence activity, or both. Again, the work must be described and measured and on that basis both position descriptions and staffing can be determined.

If the organization work revealed a need for every position mentioned the Billing Section's organization chart would look like Figure 1.

This case history may have omitted various functions of billing, credit and accounts receivable of other Billing Sections. This emphasizes a major point that one can't organize what one doesn't understand. Thus, in addition to a clear and concise mission statement concurred in by the unit manager and his supervisors and a knowledge of the vital statistics of the business that have a direct bearing on the unit being organized, the organization planner must also understand the nature, flow sequence and volume of the work to be performed. Without these elements he cannot organize effectively. ●jsm

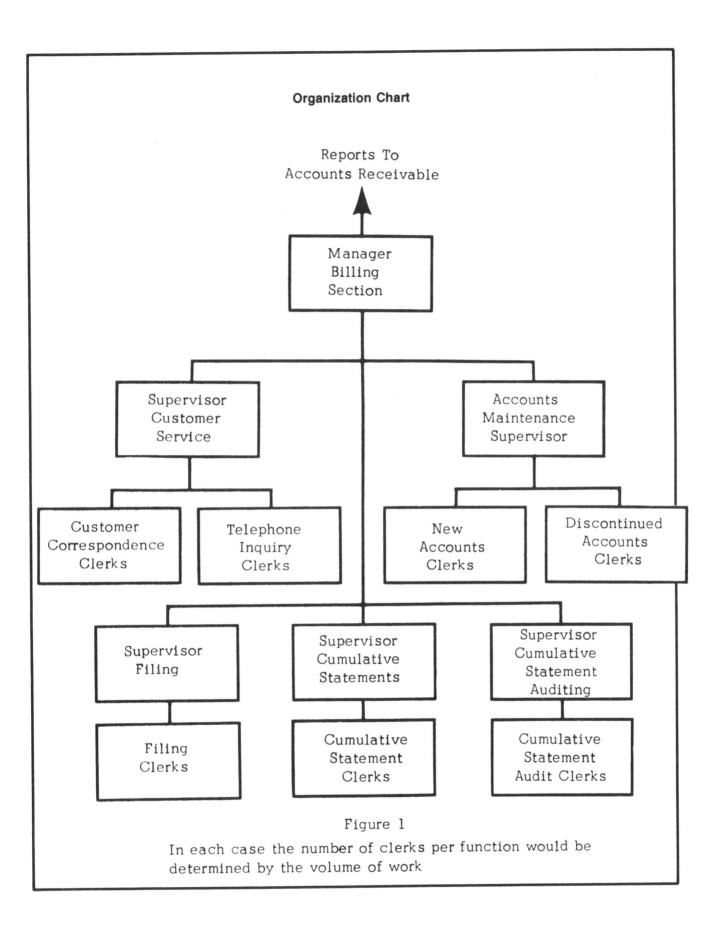

Organization Chart

Reports To
Accounts Receivable

Manager
Billing
Section

Supervisor
Customer
Service

Accounts
Maintenance
Supervisor

Customer
Correspondence
Clerks

Telephone
Inquiry
Clerks

New
Accounts
Clerks

Discontinued
Accounts
Clerks

Supervisor
Filing

Supervisor
Cumulative
Statements

Supervisor
Cumulative
Statement
Auditing

Filing
Clerks

Cumulative
Statement
Clerks

Cumulative
Statement
Audit Clerks

Figure 1

In each case the number of clerks per function would be
determined by the volume of work

Software managers who succeed in establishing effective organizations will enjoy development rates 1,200% better than managers who fail.

ORGANIZING FOR SUCCESSFUL SOFTWARE DEVELOPMENT

by Edmund B. Daly

Software development requires competent technologists, competent managers and an effective organization structure. The synergistic effect of these three elements differentiates successful development organizations from those forced to operate in a chaotic environment. A good organization structure is meaningless without a well-defined design methodology and without effective management practices. The organization structure brings together technologists and management, but the structure must work within the culture of the organization.

An organization can be described by the way it handles information flow, or by its hierarchical structure—the way it looks on an organization chart. In either case, one must first consider an organization as a group of managers and technologists and then attempt to decompose these personnel in a manner best fitting the projects to be developed. *Organization structures must be dynamic and must be modified to accommodate the project (or work activity) environment.*

An interesting analogy can be established between concepts employed in organizational decomposition and concepts employed in software decomposition. In fact, if one employs the same decomposition rules for both the job to be performed and the people who are to perform the job, a very effective organizational decomposition can be achieved. The common decomposition rules are:

Software: Each software segment should be small so that it can be easily understood (20 source lines).
Organization: Each software team should be small so that it can be effectively controlled (Chief Programmer Group).

Software: Each software segment should be loosely coupled from other software segments.
Organization: Each software team should be assigned a unit of work which allows for minimal coupling among software teams.

Software: Each software segment should enjoy high cohesion (performs one function).
Organization: Each software team should be assigned a work unit that is highly cohesive. (One team should not design diagnostic software and supporting software, such as compilers.)

Software: The scope of effect of a software segment should be a subset of scope of control.
Organization: Software teams should be grouped together (reporting to one manager) in such a manner so that the decisions made within the manager group have minimal effect on the work of other managerial groups.

Software: As software is decomposed into a hierarchy of segments, higher level segments perform decision-making and lower level segments do the actual work.
Organization: In an organization structure the managerial hierarchy performs decision-making (more abstract and longer range decisions at higher levels of management) and the lower organization levels perform the actual work.

Software: Pathological connections should be avoided, or if not, at least fully documented. A pathological connection is a communication link not following the hierarchical software structure.

Organization: Pathological connections should be avoided among programmers in an organizational structure.

Fig. 1 illustrates the similarity between a software hierarchy and an organizational hierarchy when one applies the same rules to the decomposition of both work and people. This hierarchy is a basic entity in GTE's software development methodology.

The correlation depicted in Fig. 1 shows that interfaces between modules within a subprogram are controlled by the chief programmer, who is assigned the responsibility for developing one or more subprograms. Interfaces between subprograms within a class are controlled by the first line manager (or an appointee), who is responsible for the development of a software class. Note that in a matrix organization structure (which will be described in detail later), the technical coordination among subprograms will be performed by the project manager.

Let us assume the new development organization is required to develop two projects: Project A and Project B. Each project has three major functions to perform: real-time software development (operating systems), support software development (compilers), and hardware development (computers).

Fig. 2 shows six separate organizational entities, one entity for each technology for each project. The lower levels of the hierarchies shown in Fig. 1 can be viewed as existing within each box in Fig. 2. Now the manner in which we combine these separate organizations will give us a project organization structure (Fig. 3), a functional organization structure (Fig. 4), or a matrix organization structure (Fig. 5).

FACTORS IN SELECTING STRUCTURES A combination of both matrix and project structures (where small project teams are created within the environment of a larger matrix superstructure) is the most advanta-

The matrix organization has the capability of exhibiting concern both for people and for projects.

geous for organizations responsible for developing both large and small projects. In most practical situations, the organizational structure selected is dependent on the following factors:

1. *Size of each software development.* Number of programmers/ engineers whose output must be combined to make up one working system.

2. *Number of projects.* Few larger projects (above 30 people) or many small projects (under 10 people).

3. *Scope of development.* Types of work activity being performed at any one time. Are all programmers involved in active development? Are some involved in planning for new projects, some involved in new design, and some involved in software maintenance?

4. *Environment.* A laboratory organization structure must recognize and be able to cope with the corporate culture and structure in which it exists. There is no such entity as a "project organization" in a development environment when the project organization controls only 30% of the resources needed to complete the project and the external environment is functionally structured and controls the remaining 70%.

5. *Physical limitations.* Is the project being developed in one location or in many locations, possibly in different countries?

6. *Organizational culture.* What style of manager exists within the organization? And more importantly, what organization structure does the organization's chief officer feel comfortable with?

Project Organization. This structure can be most effectively employed when an organization has many small projects to develop and when each project is developed at one location. The project structure requires that at least 70% of the resources needed to bring a project to completion is under the direct control of one line manager. This one person performs both the functions of project manager (technical) and line manager (administrative).

The advantages of the project organization are:

- Project and administrative decisions are made at the lowest possible organizational level thus allowing quicker decisions and better project control.
- Since full authority for the project is under the control of one person, interfaces are minimized and project responsibility is strictly defined (in case something goes wrong).
- This structure tends to mold system generalists and management personnel who are not assigned to functional specialties.

- Motivation is high during the active development period—programmers tend to identify with the project.

The disadvantages are:

- Projects must be kept small.
- Higher level management often loses track of project progress since their immediate involvement is not required.
- Economics of scale for critical resources can not be achieved. It is difficult to assign one "compiler" expert to three different projects. At least the project structure does not help cope with this problem.
- Training is costly since experts in all phases of development are required on each project. As an example, if one system software load must be generated for a given project, a member of the project organization must be trained in the techniques of generating a load. He may only utilize this training for a few weeks.
- Movement of programmers, especially good ones, from one project to another is difficult.
- Attrition is low during the active project development but often becomes excessive when the project is completed. Either programmers feel a loss of identity or alternative positions on other projects are not attractive.
- Probably the most serious flaw in this structure is that it inhibits both commonality among projects and generation of good software development standards and methodologies.

Functional Organization. This, the oldest form of organizational structure, is seldom used in medium to large development organizations. The concepts associated with a functional organizational structure are important only in so far as they serve as a base behind the more complex matrix structure. The basic problem is that all decisions that cross functional boundaries are made by one individual—the administrative and technical head of the functional organization. Very few managers are able to deal effectively with this much authority and often bottlenecks result, such as schedule slippages, project overruns, and poor quality. Also, the superhuman manager on top of the functional organization often gets bogged down in today's problems, leaving the organization's future to chance.

The advantages of a functional organization are:

- For a strong manager (hopefully free from megalomania) this organization sets a stage for very tight, centralized control.
- Since all the people associated with one specialty are centralized under a func-

tional manager (e.g., one functional manager controls all real-time software development for all projects), commonality among projects can be effectively controlled. Also, selected personnel can be set aside to establish standards and advanced development methodologies, and ensure that industry-wide technological advancements are effectively included in the functional manager's internal operation.

- People establish affinity to a profession or to an organization rather than to a project, thus eliminating the attrition many development organizations face when the project technologists are assigned to nears completion.
- Adapts effectively to the long-range aspects—acquiring advanced technologies, and training and retaining personnel. This structure is capable of concentrating on the individual rather than the project.

The disadvantages of this form of organization are:

- Resolution of interface problems are made by one manager for all projects.
- Limits the creation of system generalists since all technologists are assigned to one functional specialization.
- Exhibits poor project control in terms of meeting development costs, schedules, and quality.

Matrix Organization. The project structure and the functional structure attempt to optimize one organizational constraint. Project structures tend to force an organization to concentrate on *short-term project goals* such as schedule, cost, and project quality. Functional structures tend to force concentration on *long-term goals* such as commonality among projects, technological advancement, improved standards of operation, and critical skills economics of scale.

The matrix operation is a complex organizational structure that attempts to optimize two or more organizational constraints simultaneously. Some matrix structures have been grown in an attempt to optimize multiple organizational constraints. Dow Corning, for example, has instituted a four-dimensional structure aimed at simultaneously optimizing project, function, territory, and strategy. Simple matrix structures are two-dimensional (Fig. 6). Here we see a structure that attempts the advantages of the two simpler structures, project and functional. The project side of the matrix concentrates on short term project objectives. The functional side of the matrix concentrates on longer term organizational objectives.

Probably the major disadvantage

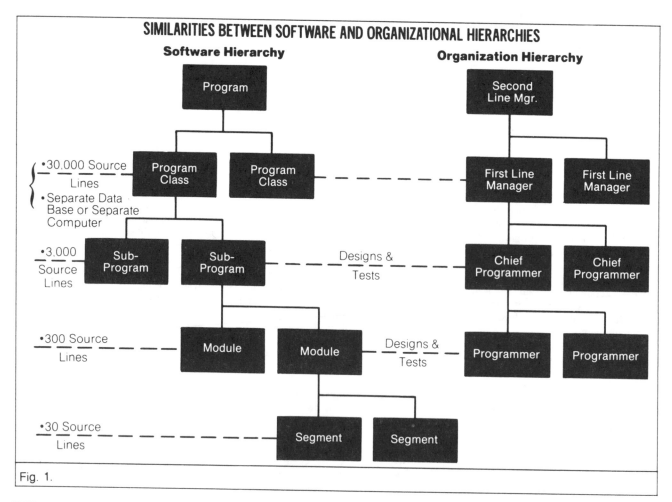

SIMILARITIES BETWEEN SOFTWARE AND ORGANIZATIONAL HIERARCHIES

Software Hierarchy — Organization Hierarchy

Program

•30,000 Source Lines
•Separate Data Base or Separate Computer

Program Class — Program Class ----- First Line Manager — First Line Manager

Second Line Mgr.

•3,000 Source Lines

Sub-Program — Sub-Program ----- Designs & Tests ----- Chief Programmer — Chief Programmer

•300 Source Lines

Module — Module ----- Designs & Tests ----- Programmer — Programmer

•30 Source Lines

Segment — Segment

Fig. 1.

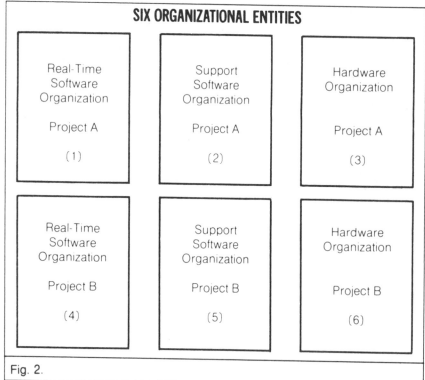

SIX ORGANIZATIONAL ENTITIES

| Real-Time Software Organization Project A (1) | Support Software Organization Project A (2) | Hardware Organization Project A (3) |
| Real-Time Software Organization Project B (4) | Support Software Organization Project B (5) | Hardware Organization Project B (6) |

Fig. 2.

Fig. 1 shows that there is a similarity between the software and organization hierarchies when the same rules are applied to the decomposition of work and people. The lower levels of the hierarchies in Fig. 1 can be viewed as existing within each box in Fig. 2.

to a matrix operation is that there is no single person responsible for the success of each project; the responsibility is truly shared between the functional line managers and the project managers. In the matrix philosophy, the functional manager decides *how* to do the job. He supplies all resources for development to take place. The project manager decides *what* to do. He controls the dollars. Dollars are allocated to the functional manager as part of a contractual agreement to perform work.

I have found that not all managers can work effectively in a matrix organization; many managers do not like the division of project responsibility. Unlike project organizations, the matrix does not have, and cannot tolerate, either a bureaucratic manager (must follow the rules) nor an autocratic manager (must

DECEMBER 1979

do it my way).

In the face of conflict, the method of management operation in a matrix structure is for the project side and functional side to:
- Trust each other.
- Put all the facts on the table.
- Agree to a resolution. If this cannot be accomplished, both sides should compromise. As a last resort (admitting defeat) the problem should be brought to the "boss" who presides over both sides.

An often discussed disadvantage of the matrix is that it is a "two-boss system," meaning that a certain number of people in the organization have two bosses. However, I believe that if authority is properly defined and projects properly planned, the "two-boss" problem can be beneficial rather than detrimental.

MATRIX PROJECT PLANNING

If a development group decides to implement a matrix organization, top management must first define, in detail, the responsibility and authority of both the functional and project sides of the matrix. This is often done. What is overlooked in many situations is projects must be planned differently in a matrix environment. The matrix is a very powerful structure. Unlike either a project or functional structure, the matrix has an inherent capability to properly control "single project" development taking place in diversely located facilities or multiple companies. In a matrix environment, all work is effectively subcontracted rather then passed down through multiple levels of management.

For software design to take place properly within a matrix structure, one must ensure that project planning allows for subcontracting. To ensure this, the project group (usually expanded by temporary assignment of funtional chief programmers and group leaders) will decompose the total project (using work breakdown structure techniques if necessary) into small subprojects. In software, a small project would be one subprogram (3,000 source lines). Each subproject is then fully defined by the project group prior to subcontracting. The resulting package is called a "cost account," and it is this package which will be subcontracted to the functional software development line organization.

Sitting on the functional side of the fence, the functional manager sees his responsibility as one of developing many small projects (cost accounts). The functional software group will be contracting for these cost accounts with many different project groups. The important con-

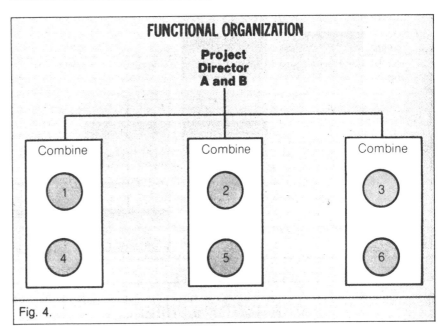

PROJECT ORGANIZATION

Project A Director

Project B Director

1 2 3 4 5 6

Fig. 3.

FUNCTIONAL ORGANIZATION

Project Director A and B

Combine 1 4

Combine 2 5

Combine 3 6

Fig. 4.

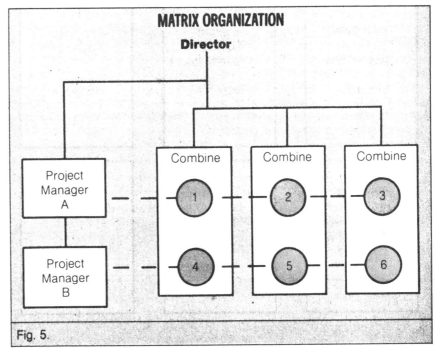

MATRIX ORGANIZATION

Director

Project Manager A

Project Manager B

Combine 1 4

Combine 2 5

Combine 3 6

Fig. 5.

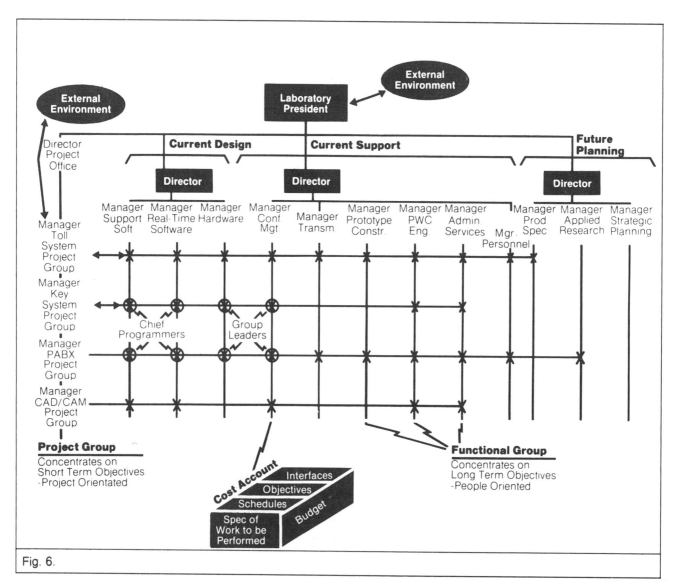

Fig. 6.

cept is that each cost account must be fully defined by the responsible project group prior to subcontracting so that it looks like an independent small project to the functional line group and so that the interfaces between these cost accounts can be monitored and controlled by the project group as active development takes place.

The major advantages of the matrix organization structure are:
- The matrix structure enjoys the intrinsic capability to optimize two or more organizational objectives simultaneously: project, functional, geographical strategic objectives.
- The functional dimension of the matrix structure allows for project commonality, advancement in technology and standards, sharing of critical resources among projects. Simultaneously, the project dimension allows for string

schedule, quality and cost control.
- The matrix structure enables technologists to be matured in either a technological speciality via the functional dimension or as system generalists via the project dimension.
- Due to the power of the matrix structure, it allows for effective coordination and control of large software development performed in diversely located organizations.

Disadvantages are:
- The matrix is a complex structure and as such requires mature management capable of working without excessive autocratic or bureaucratic tendencies. For this reason, matrix organizations must be introduced gradually rather than installed.
- Functional and project authority is divided in the matrix structure. This requires that approximately 15% of the

development staff (the chief programmers) must work for two bosses. Often this two boss system imposes conflicting demands on Chief Programmers.
- A matrix structure requires more formal project planning and control techniques than does a project structure. This is due to the "subcontracting" philosophy utilized in matrix organizations.
- Small developments and some medium-sized developments cannot be effectively managed utilizing the matrix due to overhead costs and division of responsibility. Thus, in most development environments utilizing the matrix, a Project organization philosophy should be employed as a substructure. As a general rule, those projects requiring less than 10 programmers should not be placed into a matrix unless there is excessive commonality with other projects being

Software management's objective: an environment in which high quality software can be developed with minimal resources.

developed or maintained within the organization.

The Management Grid. A popular tool for measuring management style is based on a concept developed by R. R. Blake and J. S. Mouton. This tool is referred to as the management grid. The grid, shown in Fig. 7, represents a two-dimensional analysis of managerial behavior: concern for production and concern for people. A manager who demonstrates extensive concern for people will score high on the vertical axis. A manager who demonstrates extensive concern for production will score high on the horizontal scale. An ideal manager will exhibit behavior characteristics which place him high on both scales, thereby approaching 9.9 on the managerial grid. I have found that the management grid applies to management styles exhibited by organizations as well as by individual managers.

By applying the management grid to organization theory we can see that the characteristics of a project structure tend to force the management style exhibited by the total organization into the lower right-hand quadrant of the grid since this structure stresses project objectives. On the other hand, a functional organization structure tends to force the exhibited management style into the top left-hand quadrant since this structure stresses people rather than projects.

The matrix organization, properly implemented, can now be shown to have a very powerful advantage over either of the two simpler structures (project or functional) since it has the capability of exhibiting concern for people via its functional dimension and concern for projects via its project dimension.

It is extremely rare to find an organization where all the managers fall in the 9.9 quadrant of the management grid. It is, however, easier to find managers who exhibit personality characteristics which place them in the 1.9 quadrant. It is also not too difficult to find managers who fall within the 9.1 quadrant.

By placing the 9.1 type managers in the project side of the matrix structure and the 1.9 type managers in the functional side, a synergistic effect occurs whereby the organization, as a whole, can be seen as exhibiting 9.9 quadrant management.

ORGANIZATION AND SOFTWARE PRODUCTIVITY

We have looked at various heuristics that can be used to decompose a software organization into manageable parts, and have shown that these parts can then be put together in one of three basic struc-

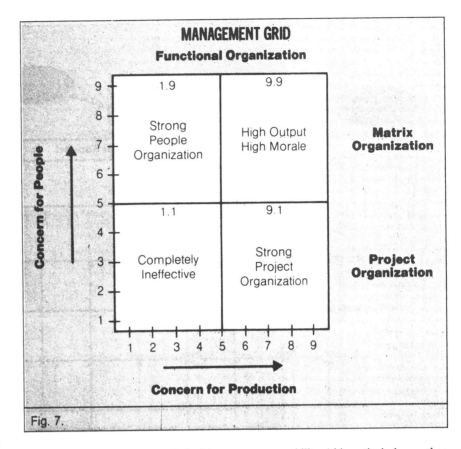

MANAGEMENT GRID
Functional Organization

Fig. 7.

tures: functional, project or matrix. Now let us analyze a third facet, organizational efficiency. Organizational efficiency is the intrinsic ability of an organization to generate quality software in minimal time with minimal resources. Once the efficiency of an organization has been determined, we can begin to solve a problem that plagues all software management: how to accurately estimate software development effort.

Software development rates are normally measured in "executable source lines generated per programmer hour." The major factors which influence software development rates are the complexity of the software being designed (see Table 1 for a condensed complexity model which has been shown to be effective for our developments); the capability of the programming staff hired to perform the development; the activities required to generate and support commercial software (Table 2); and the efficiency of the organization within which the development is performed.

Experience we have gained in GTE has indicated that the effort required to develop a commerical software package (measured in executable source lines developed per hour) can vary by 6 to 1 depending on the software complexity (see Table 1); by 2 to 1 depending on program-

mer capability (this ratio is lower than that experienced by other organizations, because all programmers must follow a well-defined methodology for software development and, more importantly, the talented programmers have been assigned the more complex software tasks); by 12 to 1 depending on the management and technological methodologies utilized within the organization structure.

Although a significant amount of literature is available describing software complexity models and the effect of programmer capability on software productivity, too little attention has been given to the effects that an organization (along with its engrained methodologies) has on software development rates.

Organizations affect software productivity in three ways: first, the structure used to organize programmers; second, the systems used to plan and control the software development; and third, the management/technical methodologies employed.

Organizations manage these factors with different levels of effectiveness. The most effective organizations can develop high quality commercial software at rates approaching 12 to 1 better than organizations that do not contain the necessary talent to properly manage software development activities.

Based on this dichotomy of management styles, we can segregate software development organizations into one of three categories: dated software organizations, modern software organizations, and state-of-art software organizations.

Dated Software Organization. We have found that development groups using dated organizational techniques have a low software productivity rate. These organizations do not employ composite design techniques nor do they follow a rigid methodology for software implementation. If documentation standards exist at all, they are poor, not formally defined, and poorly planned. Attrition is usually high and the feeling of software professionalism is not a significant aspect of the programming environment. The first four systems in Table 3 illustrate development rates of systems utilizing these concepts.

Modern Software Organization. As a software development organization matures, it establishes stricter controls over the development process. These organizations have enjoyed an improvement in software development rates of 300% over organizations using ineffective techniques for the same type of software listed above. System E in Table 3 illustrates the development rate of a large software system utilizing these more advanced design and management techniques.

Some of the techniques employed by these more efficient organizations:

1. Organizational structures are optimized around the projects being developed. Project structure and matrix structure are both used.

2. Organization hierarchy includes both chief programmers and feature chiefs, as well as a thoroughly documented and enforced design methodology.

3. Standard techniques are employed for decomposing software into functional entities. Techniques employed are transaction analysis, transform analysis, pseudo code, Jackson technique.

4. Strict software documentation standards are established and rigorously enforced. These standards are established to meet the following objectives: documentation is completely computer generated; documentation is a direct output of the design process and is the entity which undergoes design and code reviews; documentation defines software function, inputs and outputs; documentation is structured and accompanied by a hierarchy chart.

COMPLEXITY MODEL

Raw Software Design Hours (RDH) equals the product of (E) which represents organizational efficiency; (B) which represents program specific variables and (N) which represents number of executable instructions.

Thus $RDH = E \cdot B \cdot N$

The complexity model is employed to estimate the variable (B) where B is the product of B_1 times $B_2 \ldots B_9$.

B_1 =	.8	If the project development is aided by a set of interactive support tools. Else B_1 = 1.0.
B_2 =	.95	If the program is developed by one programmer.
=	1.15	If the program is developed by more than 15 programmers.
B_3 =	1.0	If the number of independent module inputs and output items is less than five.
=	1.1	If greater than five.
=	1.2	If greater than 10.
B_4 =	1.25	If this module has been specified as real-time critical.
B_5 =	1.5	If the module contains a very complex algorithm or has a significant hardware interface.
=	1.0	If the module is purely data manipulative.
B_6 =	1.2	If the module algorithm is not similar to previous work.
=	1.0	If the algorithm is similar.
B_7 =	1.5	If the module is modified from an existing module and only new or changed instructions are included in the instruction count.
=	1.0	Is a new module.
B_8 =	1.25	If the module has been specified as memory size critical.
B_9 =	1.1	If batch is employed and turnaround is greater than four hours.

Table 1.

SUPPORT REQUIREMENTS

$$S = \frac{\text{Raw Software Design Hours (RDH)}^*}{\text{Total development hours up to one year after turnover to customer}^{**}}$$

Based on 3,000,000 Hours of Historical Statistics		
Software Design Hours —Project Size—	Value of "S"	Type of Design
400,000 Hours	1.9	New design—no existing base
100,000 Hours	2.0	
20,000 Hours	1.7	
200,000 Hours	2.1	Modified design using existing base
20,000 Hours	2.2	
50,000 Hours	1.5	Design maintenance after first year
10,000 Hours	1.9	

*Includes only software design hours required to decompose predefined subprograms into modules and segments, code, unit test, string test, integration test and all design documentation.

**Includes configuration management, supervision, laboratory support, evaluation, general project support, field support and design maintenance to one year after turnover to customer plus software design hours and planning hours leading to high level design.

Table 2.

DEVELOPMENT STATISTICS

System	Commercially Available to Customer	Size of Program (New Instructions)	Development Rate Instructions Per Hour
A	1972	160,000	.33*
B	1973	117,000	.43
C	1974	111,000	.53*
D	1977	220,000	.52*
E	1979	131,000	1.2*

*Executable object

Table 3.

5. Design walkthroughs are held at each level of software decomposition. Preestablished review formats are employed with standard reports generated. Reviews are formally scheduled to ensure programmer time is made available. Only commercial documentation is reviewed at these meetings. Adherence to design standards, documentation standards, and quality, inter cost account interfaces are ensured by these reviews.

6. Walkthroughs are conducted for each feature prior to system testing. During feature review the customer's requirement specification is validated against evaluation test plans and the software functional designs.

7. Structured code is employed, embodied within a medium high level compiler such as PASCAL. Code reviews and code walkthroughs are conducted following a predefined process. The chief programmer and at least one peer programmer read each module of code.

8. Strong management planning and control systems are employed. These systems help plan and control software quality, time, and cost. An ideal system combines PERT networks and the concepts of C/SCSC (a cost/schedule control system developed by the U. S. Department of Defense).

9. All major software interfaces and data structures are defined before detail design begins. Data structures and software interfaces form a contract which is monitored and controlled throughout design and testing.

10. Management attempts to hire and retain the correct mix of software personnel: 30% with more than six years' experience, 40% with between three and six years' experience, and 30% with college degrees and less than three years' experience.

State-of-Art Software Organization. Organizations which are at the state of art in software development should enjoy productivity of from 200% to 400% over modern software organizations. The higher percentage prevails in larger, very complex software developments. These organizations employ all the techniques described above and in addition utilize advanced concepts of a "software factory." This concept is a consolidated set of powerful development tools which allow software managers and programmers to perform the innovative aspects of software development and automate most of the more rudimentary tasks. Projects which have used this consolidated set of supporting tools have experienced significant improvement in developing rates.

The types of tools which have been shown to be most promising in improving development efficiency are described below:

1. A program which accepts rough software documentation as input and performs the following four processes: checks that all data variables have been defined and inserts a definition of each data element into the software documentation package; formats documentation according to predefined standards; generates data base maps and flow charts from data declarations and structured code; generates hierarchy chart from raw software documentation.

2. A requirement language processor and a design language processor. These processors allow the support system to understand constraints in both the system requirements documentation and the commercial software design documentation. This process allows for cross-correlation between the system specification and the design documentation and also allows for check of completeness.

3. A software library concept which allows for effective storage and subsequent retrieval of functional software modules. This process allows for extensive reuse of software modules both within a given development as well as allowing for the reuse of functional modules among different developments.

4. Utilization of an ultrahigh-level programming language. This language allows for automatic code generation from a source language that describes operational processes.

5. Other less important tools, which include a design integrity analyzer, a software interface processor, a functional test plan generator, and various configuration control, design maintenance, and project management processors.

The objective of software management is to establish an environment in which high quality software can be developed using minimal resources. To achieve this objective, we must not only consider the organizational structure but also the control systems and management/technical methodologies employed within the organizational structure. Those software managers who suceed in establishing an effective organization will enjoy software development rates 1,200% better than those managers who fail.   ✳

EDMUND B. DALY

Mr. Daly was recently appointed executive director-electronic switching of GTE Automatic Electric Laboratories, where during the past 10 years he has held the positions of assistant to the executive director, director-Advanced Development Laboratory, and director-EAX Operations Laboratory. He holds a BSEE and MSEE from the University of Illinois, Urbana, and a BA and MBA from the University of Chicago.

Reprinted from *NAECON '77 Record*, 1977. Copyright © 1977
by The Institute of Electrical and Electronics Engineers, Inc.

OPERATING DYNAMICS OF MATRIX MANAGEMENT

W. R. Harden, W. R. Gretsch

Westinghouse Electric Corporation
Baltimore, Maryland

ABSTRACT

Major weapon systems contractors have required a unique and dynamic organization structure
in order to cope with the myriad of problems that
arise in the performance of the goals of the contract. The matrix or project form of organization structure has been utilized for many years.

In theory, the project/functional management
matrix interlaces the organization to bind it together and promote coordination. Desired goals
of the project structure are to satisfy the customer in terms of a program that meets its cost
objectives, schedule requirements, and performance needs. Functional management must assemble
the necessary resources of talent and facilities
to successfully perform the job and to achieve
for the project structure it's desired goals.
The fact that DOD contractor has a variety of contracts in various phases of completion results in
both benefits and pitfalls: Synergism and efficiency results in better achievement of goals, and
internal competition for resources results in potential fragmentation and dissipation. The interactions between multiple programs and functional
management can result in conflicts within the organization.

INTRODUCTION

Operating dynamics determine the success or
failure of projects, and, therefore, of the organization undertaking them. Unfortunately, we have
been schooled to think about the organization of
people as a process of building lasting relationships into a stable, defined, optimized, efficient structure. This is secure, dependable, and
predictable. However, the nature of the things
we need to accomplish has changed -- and so have
we all, ourselves. In our advanced technological
environment projects can be so large and demand
such an extraordinary amount of resources that the
conventional ways of accomplishing them no longer
work. We simply don't have the resources, or the
time anymore to survive if we base our actions on
"steady, state conditions", to borrow a term from
the engineers. The Matrix approach to management
has the potential to handle the vast complexity,
flexibility and responsiveness of management that
must occur in order to get a project completed and
for a contractor to remain competitive in his market place.

Many times the customer also lives in a dynamic, changing environment, that he also attempts to deal with by having a matrix organization.
In the past it has been possible to strive towards a single point contact between the two matrices -- customer and contractor. This only
works when the situation can be stabilized -- and
this desire has brought many endeavors to ruin --
with the two matrices trying valiantly to cope,
while being anchored at the pivot. The problem
to be solved changes, the goal changes, the capabilities change, the environment is different,
the people grow or change in capabilities, the
technical or operational base evolves differently
and we are stuck. The quartet of program and
functional organizations at customer and contractor goes into gyration about the pivot of an obsolete perception and hence, the interaction
causes dynamic oscillations to occur. And this is
largely caused by the belief that we must stabilize the situation to deal with it. Ah -- if we
only had some tools to deal with the dynamics . .
. . . But, we do -- a whole body of knowledge
about feedback control systems and their dynamic
behavior, that enables us to predict outcomes,
correct them calm down their oscillations, prevent their saturation, improve their response
time, readjust their outputs, operate within safe
limits, and correct for internal problems. It
will be the purpose of this paper to briefly review this topic and to attempt to put into perspective the benefits that can truly occur.

FUNCTIONAL ORGANIZATION

In considering the dynamics that occur between the various branches of a matrix organization it is logical to review the roles that the
two key groups play. Functional management is
traditionally thought of being the vertical aspects of an organization. This traditional view
results from the normal bureaucratic or pyramid
image that is associated with functional management. The format of functional management follows
the path of worker-supervisor-manager and so on
up to top management. It is the simplest form of
management structure to evolve and even in informal groups the vertical hierarchy of structure
exists.

The typical functional organization seeks to
maintain the classical principles of organization
structure. "Unity of command" is illustrated as
a key point. No worker shall have more than one
superior! Classical theory teaches that report-

ing to two or more superiors often results in confusion, loss of productivity, conflict and poor morale. The basic problem with "unity of command" is that if pushed to its extreme, it requires that all instructions -- indeed all influence of any kind must flow through one superior to his subordinates.

Secondly, "span of control" states that there is a limit to the number of subordinates that should report to one superior. Some theorists have pointed out that as the number of people reporting to a superior increases arithmetically, the number of possible interrelationships among them and with the superior increases geometrically, rapidly reaching a point at which the structure becomes too complex for management by a single individual. Obviously if this principle is followed, the number of managerial tiers in the organization increases substantially.

Functional organizations emerge out of technical specializations and the need to pool workers of common occupational activities into a cooperative effort. Thus, engineers are placed into engineering organizations, financial people in finance departments, etc. The area of technical specialization acts as the fertile ground for technical growth towards a career.

The functional management is charged with providing an adequately trained staff that is responsive to the changing technology that drives the business. Maintaining the level of staff along with high technical excellence is required to compete in business. To achieve this they must provide an environment that cultivates the growth of skill of their people. This environment can extend from the formal sending of employees to company sponsored technical courses to counseling directions towards advanced academic degrees to that of specific job assignments. When the role of functional management as applied to technical growth is coupled to the guidance and direction of individual career growth, one main role of the functonal manager is established. He is to handle all the necessary facets of an employee's career to help insure a proper and logical career growth.

A second aspect of the charter of functional management is the accomplishment of the work. In this role, the functional manager has control of the resources that are necessary to perform his specialized duties. His resources are those of material, space, money, equipment and personnel. He is responsible for accomplishing the assigned area of specialized work within the allocated costs and schedule constraints. In addition, he must balance and manage the technical aspects that govern the technical performance of the job. This balancing of cost, schedule, and performance is the major role of the functional manager. As will be shown in the following sections as soon as several programs appear, the balancing act between cost, schedule and performance becomes tenuous.

Functional management also is to provide the interpretation and development of policy and to be prepared to fully execute it. Its guidance in

these matters is key to a smoothly operating functional group.

Consequently, the job of functional management is quite complex. In a dynamic environment, the type which exists in a DOD contractor organization, the functional manager is simultaneously juggling the roles of policy interpreter, developer, and implementer, cost-schedule and performance judge and policeman -- and maintainer of technical excellence. When one interlaces the program organization on top of the functional organization, a dynamic life style can emerge. In order to see this energetic organization develop, let's review the role of program management.

PROGRAM MANAGEMENT

In the complex environment of customer/contractor interactions the corresponding Program Managers are usually thought of as the focal point in the interaction. The contractor program manager like that of his customer counterpart bears the full responsibility. It is through this focal point that the direction and success or failure of the program occurs, in a static environment. Simply stated the program manager makes it happen as long as he controls the total situation.

In industry, the program manager has been selected because he can usually cut across all function lines and bring together the diverse resources required to make the program happen. In the contractor's own shop, the program manager acts as the unifying agent in that his goals are customer oriented not internally oriented. In cutting across the traditional structure he usually employs an authority based on the power of stature and position. Hence, one of the inherent difficulties he must overcome is the power base from which he must operate. Since he is typically a leader of an ad hoc group his administrative authority is low. Since the use of power is one of the least effective ways to sustain good results -- his personality, persuasiveness, and competance are essential.

By no means should one misconstrue that the program manager is in a weak position. Since the program manager is typically the general manager's representative to the customer, he also has the close confidence of the general manager. Obviously the program manager through this close link with the general manager can bring significant pressure to the functional organization. Hence while the program manager usually has minimum administrative authority he does have significant persuasive authority which causes the job to get done. However, he better not draw on this too often.

The program manager must gather resources from the various functional groups. Consequently, he must be skillful and knowledgeable when he deals with such diverse groups as engineering, reliability, quality control, production, contracts etc. When there is a single program, there is little problem for the program manager to gather the resources. Add multiple programs with the same functional resources and one can easily see some of the beginning seeds for "dynamic" operation.

In general, the primary goal of the program manager is to insure that his program constantly maintains his cost, schedule, and performance. It sounds simplistic, but keeping this triad together is probably the most difficult task the program manager has. When this occurs, his customer is happy. But seldom does this happen without deliberate, conscious effort. Since cost, schedule, and performance are the key goals of the program manager, competition for the resources required to achieve these goals rapidly breeds another dimension to the dynamic operation of a matrix organized company. Competition for resources will be shown to be a key contributor to the dynamic operation of a matrix organization, as will be the need to dispose of the resources when not needed.

MATRIX ORGANIZATION

The traditional matrix organization is composed of the program organization overlaid horizontally over the vertical functional management structure. This approach to organizational structure is usually employed when it is desired to produce large projects within desired cost, schedule, and performance standards. The main advantages of the matrix organization are the following:

"1. The project in the organization is emphasized by designating one key individual as the focal point for all matters pertaining to it.

2. Utilization of manpower can be flexible because a reservoir of specialists is maintained in functional organizations.

3. Specialized knowledge is available to all programs on an equal basis; knowledge and experience can be transferred from one project to another.

4. Project people have a functional home when they are no longer needed on a given project.

5. Responsiveness to project needs and customer desires is generally faster because lines of communication are established and decision points are centralized.

6. Management consistency between projects can be maintained through the deliberate conflict operating in the project-functional environment.

7. A better balance between schedule, cost, and performance can be obtained through the built-in checks and balances (the deliberate conflict) and the continuous negotiations carried on between the project and the functional organizations.

8. Interfunctional competition tends to be minimized by the intervention of the project manager." (1)

Of course, there are some disadvantages to a matrix organization. The balance of power between the functional and the project organizations must be watched so that neither one erodes the other. The balance between schedule, cost, and performance must also be continually monitored so that neither group favors cost or time or technical performance. When multiple programs are in a matrix organization, the competition between programs for resources stimulates the dynamic life of the company because of the multi-faceted interaction that must occur between the programs and functional management.

DYNAMICS

As has been postulated, the dynamics of a matrix organization occur primarily because of the presence of several programs along with the functional organization in a changing environment. Competition for resources exists in two forms. First, the programs need the committed technical help to fulfill the contractual obligations, and secondly, the function groups are looking to the programs to employ their manpower. The interactions that can occur can be illustrated in Figure 1. This multitude of interconnections causes significant communication problems. As an example, consider the case where two programs need the services of a key technical person. In that case, the general manager usually has to settle the differences between the programs. Who wins?

Consider the life cycle of a given program as shown in Figure 2.

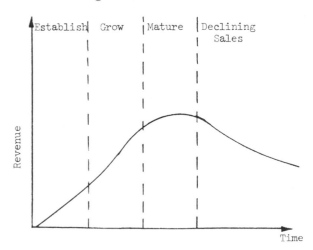

FIGURE 2: PROGRAM PHASES

Several programs are shifted in time phase and overlapped as shown in Figure 3 and point X is considered the time of the conflict either program C or program B would have the best chance of obtaining the services of the individuals. Depending upon the type of technical skill required, program B would have a better reason to obtain the skilled people it needs since it is in the growth phase. Program A should relinquish the skills required since it is in a declining sales phase. However, it probably is entrenched, and would resist.

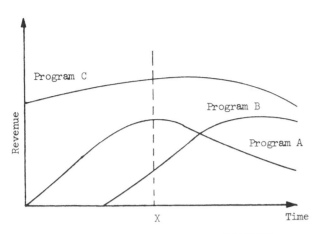

FIGURE 3: PHASES OF MULTIPLE PROGRAMS

Without the intervention of functional management, the resolution to the question of a skilled person's availability results in a compromise. Compromise has usually been referred to as a result of a "lose-lose" situation. Lose-lose methods are based on the philosophy that a "half a loaf" is better than none. In the above situation, the compomise would result in the entrenched program getting the more skilled person. A better decision process for this situation is a concensus process (win-win) where all concerned meet to come to a decision which is the best overall. In an open meeting like this, convened by functional management, vested interests tend to be overshadowed by the greater common good -- due to the understanding of the total picture that is jointly developed. This is not an adversary process in which there is negotiation and "horse-trading". To reach a concensus all the interested parties work on a situation based upon understanding of each other's needs -- and in the end try to agree that the best overall decision has been reached even though it may not completely satisfy any one individual. In the example cited, the manager of the entrenched program would probably agree that it would be best overall of the growing program got the critical skills, and he would go away trying to successfully implement the solution and sell it to his own people.

CONFLICT

One of the best ways to deal with conflict is to recognize it as a legitimate process that can be helpful -- if worked with properly. This requires the right atmosphere -- which must be created and supported by the matrix. One way is to deliberately assign a task leader whose job description is to operate at the matrix intersection and lead the task -- taking direction from both functional and program management. This straightforward approach makes sure that the problems are faced and dealt with. The task leader derives his authority and responsibility from both sources -- but has to satisfy both too. This "linking pin" position is effective at each corresponding level of program and functional

hierarchies. The success of this approach is dependent upon the individual, and the support he gets. His job is to work out the conflicts for the overall good. With this direct approach conflict ceases to be as threatening and can be dealt with creatively.

FEEDBACK CONTROL SYSTEM

In the matrix management system the program management provides direction as to what effort will be accomplished, when it will be performed, and how much is budgeted, as seen in Figure 1. Functional managers provide direction, who will perform certain tasks, how they will be accomplished, and how well they are to be accomplished. Jointly, they decide where the work will be accomplished. This can be diagrammed as in Figure 4.

This figure illustrates the application of classical feedback theory on the matrix organization. Feedback has long been the core of all management decisions and the nature of the feedback can certainly influence the behavior of the management responses to the feedback.

If one were to review the engineering aspects of a feedback control systems such key parameters as time delay, linearity, gain, stability, bandwidth and noise all come to mind. These terms always influence the output regardless of the nature of the input. Consequently, if this model is applied to the matrix organization certain combinations of the parameters influence the operations of the organization.

The ideal case is stability where all inputs are handled in a linear continuous manner. If the task leader is able to maintain his role and influence the feedback, he can always cause a reaction that has no perturbations upon the control system. Obviously, the management control system must take a significant measure of the output in order to get a proper sample of the information. Any non-linearity or limiting features in the feedback components can cause a disruption of the control system.

Each manager views the sampled information through his own filter, which is determined by his past experiences, hang-ups, and vested interests. Also each manager is limited by his charter, his overall resources, and his capabilities. With the program manager and functional manager both looking at the sampled results and operating on it, the chance of getting a more accurate feedback correction is improved. However, where the managers responses overlap, there is the chance of local oscillation and system instability. This instability will continue until a solution (hopefully in a win-win situation) is resolved. Additionally, if the information out or the management control system is different from either the program manager or functional manager, or if it has different delay, instability can again set it. This can provide wild oscillations in the organization which must quickly be brought under control possibly by a third party.

The task leaders role is quite complex because he has been assigned personnel usually on an ad hoc basis which may not necessarily be totally acceptable (as happened to Program B). His role now is to keep this mixture of skills moving in such a manner that the job is completed in terms of cost, schedule, and performance. Any differences in responsiveness of his assigned personnel can again cause delays which could cause organization instability.

By utilizing the feedback control system analogy an insight into the dynamics of an organization can be seen. The simplistic control system of Figure 4 really contains many sub-loops with many different influences. These sub-loops can contribute an added dimension to the stability or lack of to the organization. Certainly one can think of many combinations that create unique senarios in their own organizations.

SUMMARY

Functional management and program management must function together in a closed loop feedback system. A dynamic organization usually results because of the sheer immensity of the problem of complete and accurate information all phased in a timely manner. Any shift in the information content or accuracy causes transients in the organization. Since the feedback is quick, fast responses can be generated. The matrix organization has long been shown to have a fast reaction to problems. This speed also causes a dynamic exhilarating organization experience.

REFERENCES

1. David I. Cleland and William R. King, "Systems Analysis and Project Management", McGraw-Hill, New York.

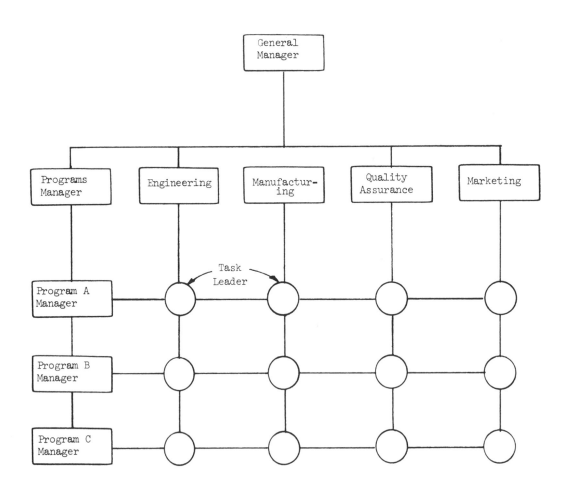

FIGURE 1: MATRIX ORGANIZATION

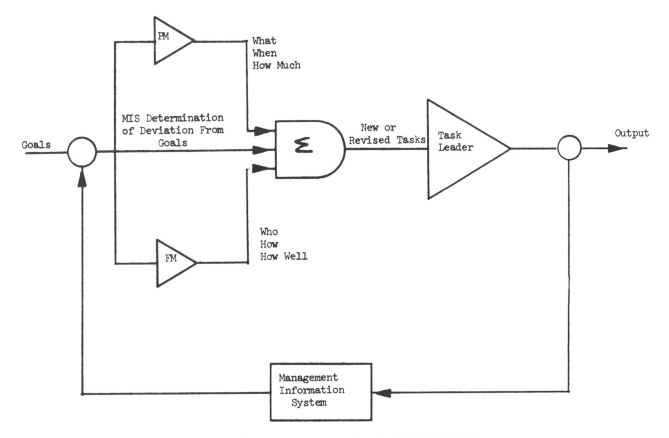

FIGURE 4: MATRIX ORGANIZATION FEEDBACK SYSTEM

"The Effect of Programming Team Structures on Programming Tasks" by M. Mantei from *Communications of the ACM*, Volume 24, Number 3, March 1981, pages 106-113. Copyright 1981, Association for Computing Machinery, Inc., reprinted by permission.

The Effect of Programming Team Structures on Programming Tasks

Marilyn Mantei
The University of Michigan

1. Introduction

Two philosophies for organizing programming teams have achieved a moderate amount of popularity, if not utilization, in the data processing field. These are the egoless programming team proposed by Weinberg [28] and the chief programmer team proposed by Mills [18] and implemented by Baker [1]. In Weinberg's structure, the decision-making authority is diffused throughout project membership; in Baker's team, it belongs to the chief programmer. Communication exchanges are decentralized in Weinberg's team and centralized in the chief programmer organization. Neither structure is totally

SUMMARY: The literature recognizes two group structures for managing programming projects: Baker's chief programmer team and Weinberg's egoless team. Although each structure's success in project management can be demonstrated, this success is clearly dependent on the type of programming task undertaken. Here, for the purposes of comparison, a third project organization which lies between the other two in its communication patterns and dissemination of decision-making authority is presented. Recommendations are given for selecting one of the three team organizations depending on the task to be performed.

Key words and phrases: chief programmer team, project management, software engineering, group dynamics, programming team structures
CR Categories: 3.50, 4.6
Author's address: M. Mantei, Graduate School of Business Administration, The University of Michigan, Ann Arbor, MI 48109.
© 1981 ACM 0001-0782/81/0300–0106 75¢.

decentralized, democratic, centralized, or autocratic, but both Weinberg and Baker present arguments on why their methods will lead to superior project performance. Baker's project succeeds with a specific, difficult, and highly structured task. Weinberg's recommendations have no specific task in mind.

Research conducted in small group dynamics [7, 23, 27] suggests that a decision to use either team structure is not clear-cut and that there are strong task dependencies associated with each group's performance. The next two sections an-

alyze Weinberg and Baker's organizations. In Section 4, a third, commonly encountered team organization is presented for the purposes of comparison. The fifth section conducts this comparison, recommending which of the three structures should be selected for a given property of a programming task.

2. An Analysis of Weinberg's Team Structure

Weinberg is a promoter of the egoless programming concept. His teams are groups of ten or fewer

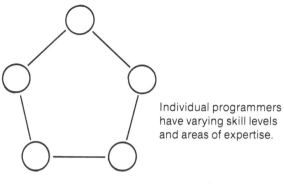

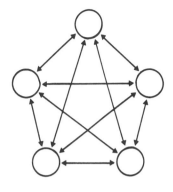

Individual programmers have varying skill levels and areas of expertise.

(a) Management Structure

(b) Communication Channels

Fig. 1. Egoless Team Structure. Authority is dispersed and communication linkages decentralized.

programmers who exchange their code with other team members for error examination. In addition to code exchanges, goals are set by group consensus. Group leadership is a rotating function, becoming the responsibility of the individual with the abilities that are currently needed. Figure 1(a) illustrates the basic management structure of an egoless team; Figure 1(b) shows the communication exchanges that occur within this structure. The team proposed by Weinberg is acknowledged to be mythical in light of today's organization practices, but Weinberg feels that it is the appropriate organization for the best qualitative and quantitative code generation. Using the factors of amount of code produced, of time to produce code, and of error freeness to gauge programming performance, some task-related problems occur with Weinberg's team structure.

Bavelas [3] and Leavitt [14], in their experiments on centralized and decentralized group problem-solving behavior, found that decentralized groups take more time and generate twice as many communications as centralized groups. This suggests that a Weinberg group would function well in long-term continuing projects without time constraints (such as program maintenance). It would not, however, adequately perform a rush programming project.

A second weakness of Wein-berg's proposal is the *risky shift phenomena* [5]. Groups engage in riskier behavior than individuals, both because of the dispersion of failure and the high value associated with risk taking in Western culture. In the case of a group programming team, decisions to attempt riskier solutions to a software problem or to establish high risk deadlines would be more easily made. In a software project with a tight deadline or a crucial customer, a group decision might cause the project to fail.

The democratic team structure works best when the problem is difficult. When the problem is simple, performance is better in an autocratic highly structured group [12]. Ironically, democratic groups attempt to become more autocratic as task difficulty increases. In the decentralized group, the additional communication which aided in solving the difficult problem is superfluous; it interferes with the simple problem solution. Tasks such as report generation and payroll programming fall into the category of simple tasks—for these, a Weinberg group is least efficient.

The decentralized group is lauded for its open communication channels. They allow the dissemination of programming information to all participants via informal channels. By virtue of code exchanges and open communication, Weinberg concludes that the product will be superior. March and Simon [16] point out that hierarchical structures are built to limit the flow of information, because of the human mind's limited processing capabilities. In the decentralized groups, as investigated by Bavelas, although twice as many communications were exchanged as in centralized groups, the groups often failed to finish their task. Similarly, individuals within a nonstructured programming group may be unable to organize project information effectively and many suffer from information overload. The structure and limited flow associated with hierarchical control may be assets to information assimilation.

Decentralized groups exhibit greater conformity than centralized groups [11]; they enforce a uniformity of behavior and punish deviations from the norm [20]. This is good if it results in quality documentation and coding practices, but it may hurt experimental software development or the production of novel ideas.

Despite the pressure to conform and an apparent lack of information organization, decentralized groups exhibit the greatest job satisfaction [23]. For long projects hurt by high turnover rates, job satisfaction is a major concern. Job satisfaction is also important for healthy relationships with the public or a customer— if indeed this is a necessary element of the programming project.

In summary, Weinberg's decentralized democratic group does not perform well in tasks with time constraints, simple solutions, large information exchange requirements, or unusual approaches. A difficult task of considerable duration which demands personal interaction with the customer is optimal for a Weinberg team.

3. An Analysis of Baker's Team Structure

Baker describes the use of a highly structured programming team to develop a complex on-line information retrieval system for the New York Times Data Bank; the team is a three-person unit. It consists of a *chief programmer*, who manages a *senior level programmer* and a *program librarian*. Additional programmers and analysts are added to the team on a temporary basis to meet specific project needs. Figure 2(a) illustrates the structure of the chief programmer team; the communication channels are shown in Figure 2(b).

The chief programmer manages all technical aspects of the project, reporting horizontally to a project manager who performs the administrative work. Program design and assignment are initiated at the top level of the team. Communication occurs

through a programming library system, which contains up-to-date information on all code developed. The program librarian maintains the library and performs clerical support for the project. Rigid program standards are upheld by the chief programmer.

The Baker team is a centralized autocratic structure in which problem solutions and goal decisions are made at the top level. The task which the team undertakes is well-defined, but large and complex. Definite time constraints exist. Baker concludes that this compact highly structured team led to the successful completion of the project and that it has general applicability.

Several weaknesses exist in Baker's argument. Shaw [21] finds that a centralized communication network is more vulnerable to saturation at the top level. Information from all lower modes in this structure flows upward to the parent mode. Baker's team was intentionally small and worked with a highly structured system for managing project information; both these factors were critical to the success of the project. A third, equally important factor was the team leader's ability to handle project communication. This ability is closely related to the leader's software expertise. A less experienced leader or a more complex problem might have changed the project's success, even with staffing constraints and information management. Yourdon [29] points out that

the effective chief programmer is a rare individual and indicates that most so-called chief programmer teams are headed by someone who is unlikely to adequately handle the communication complexity.

Centralized groups exhibit low morale [3]; this, in turn, leads to dissatisfaction and poor group cohesiveness. Members of highly cohesive groups communicate with each other to a greater extent than members of groups with low cohesion [15]. With a clearly defined problem that is split into distinct modules, this lack of communication will have little impact, but an ill-defined problem with many interfaces would suffer in a chief programmer team environment. The two software modules (the interface systems) on this project which might have served as indicators of this communication condition are, as a matter of fact, developed as a joint effort between the chief programmer and another team member.

Communication in a status hierarchy tends to be directed upward; its content is more positive than that of any communication directed downward [27]. In a tricky, difficult programming task, this favorable one-way flow of communication denies the group leader access to a better solution or, at least, an indication of problems in the current solution. Decentralized groups generate more and better solutions to problems than individuals working alone [25]—such as a chief programmer. The major basis for the success

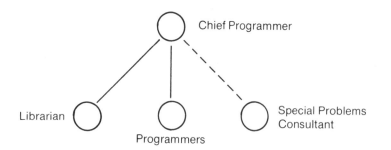

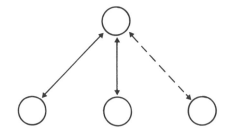

(a) Management Structure   (b) Communication Channels

Fig. 2. Chief Programmer Team Structure. Authority is vested in the chief programmer and communication is centralized to this individual.

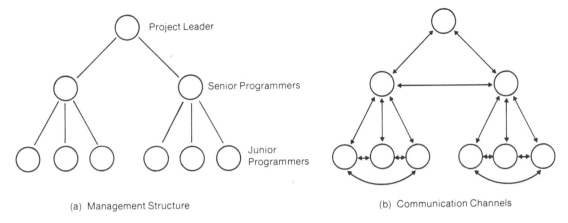

Project Leader

Senior Programmers

Junior
Programmers

(a) Management Structure

(b) Communication Channels

Fig. 3. Controlled Decentralized Team Structure. Authority is vested in the project leader and senior programmers, but communication at each level of the management hierarchy is decentralized.

of the New York Times Data Bank project was the team's ability to meet the delivery date. A centralized structure completes tasks more quickly than any decentralized form of control [14], but perhaps a more creative solution might have resulted from a different approach. Proponents of good software management stress concern for the software life cycle [8, 9, 13]. This implies that consideration be given not only to project completion schedules but to the software's usability, cost to the customer, and modifiability.

In summary, communication exists to a much lesser degree in centralized groups and is directed toward the manager. Both difficult tasks requiring multiple inputs for solution and unstructured tasks requiring substantial cooperation fare poorly in this kind of communication environment. Group morale and, thus, goal motivation are low in such a hierarchical structure. A simple, well-structured programming task with rigid completion deadlines and little individual interface with the client is perfect for the chief programmer team.

4. An Analysis of a Controlled Decentralized Team Structure

In practice, programming team structures vary considerably. Most take on some form of organization

that draws from both Weinberg's egoless team and Baker's chief programmer team. A third, frequently used organization which we will call the controlled decentralized (CD) team is described in this section.

The controlled decentralized team has a project leader who governs a group of senior programmers. Each senior programmer, in turn, manages a group of junior programmers. Figure 3(a) illustrates the organization of this group; Figure 3(b) indicates the flow of communication that takes place in this type of group structure.

Metzger [17] describes this organization as a reasonable management approach. He makes two recommendations: First, he suggests that intermediate levels of management are preferable to requiring all senior programmers to report to the project leader and, second, he recommends that the programming groups be partitioned not according to code module assigned, but in terms of the type of role played in the project, e.g., test, maintenance, etc. Shneiderman [24] lists this structure as the most probable type of project organization. Like Yourdon [29], he suggests that the individual subgroups in the project participate in structured walkthroughs and code exchanges in the manner of Weinberg's egoless teams.

The CD team possesses control over the goal selection and decision-making aspects of the Baker team and the decentralized communication aspects of the Weinberg team. Setting project goals and dividing work among the groups are the tasks of the project leader. More detailed control over the project's functions is assigned to the senior programmers. Within each programming subgroup, the organization is decentralized. Problem solving is a group activity as is checking for code errors. Each group leader serves as the sole recipient or gatekeeper of project information for the subgroup and acts as a liaison with the leaders of the other groups. The communication and control problems of the egoless and chief programmer teams do not disappear in a CD structure but occur in the subgroups of the controlled decentralized team that correspond to the Weinberg and Baker teams: Thus, the properties of the subtask allocated to any of the subgroups interact, in a similar fashion, with the subgroup structure.

The decentralized subgroups of the CD team work poorly with highly structured or simple tasks. Group solutions are best directed at difficult problems. Much of the creative and difficult part of programming is planning the design and partitioning the work. In the CD structure this work is completed by the project leader. The senior programmers then take on their portion of the task and develop a group solution. Ironically, when the task is most difficult, the team structure is least effective. A poll of programming managers and academics indicated that the area they believed needed the most attention in software engineering was the planning and design stage [26], the work carried out by the CD team project leader.

With small problems, the CD team is unnecessary since its very structure presumes the existence of a larger project. As Brooks [6] points out, even though adding individuals to a project increases the communication problems and, thus, the effectiveness of the project's members, it is still necessary to have large teams for those programming tasks which are so large they could not be accomplished in a reasonable length of time by a few programmers.

Although control over projects is exercised from above, the group problem-solving approach at lower levels will take longer, and projects will be more likely to fall behind in meeting deadlines. The structure of the CD team would tend to centralize the egoless programming subgroups. Because of the senior programmer's gatekeeper role, he or she would emerge as an informal leader in group sessions. This, in turn, would lower individual satisfaction with the project and generate the ensuing problems of a high job turnover rate and group socialization difficulties. Because of this strong tendency toward centralization, shorter projects are best for the CD structure.

A controlled decentralized team is an effective error-purge mechanism. The code walkthroughs and group input at the code generation level will filter out many errors. Code generated in this fashion is more reliable than code coming from a chief programmer team operation.

Programming tasks that are not easily subdivided suffer in a CD team. Note in Figure 3(b) that communication between groups occurs at the senior programmer level. Projects requiring micro-decision communication about code interfaces cannot expect this communication to be conveyed effectively through a liaison person functioning at a macro level in the project.

In summary, the controlled decentralized team will work best for large projects which are reasonably straightforward and short-lived. Such teams can be expected to produce highly reliable code but not necessarily on time or in a friendly manner. They are ill-suited for long-term researchlike projects.

Team Structure and Programming Task Relationships

This section describes seven salient properties of programming tasks and compares the performance of each team structure discussed in relationship to these task properties. The relevant properties are:

(1) *Difficulty.* The program required to solve the problem can be complex, consisting of many decision points and data interfaces, or it may be a simple decision tree. Distributed processing systems and projects with severe core or rapid response time constraints fall into the *difficult* category. Much of the scientific programming would come under the *simple* category heading.

(2) *Size.* Programs may range from ten to hundreds of thousands of lines of code for any given project.

(3) *Duration.* The lifetime of the programming team varies. Maintenance teams have a long lifetime; one-shot project teams have a short lifetime.

(4) *Modularity.* If a task can be completely compartmentalized into subtasks, it is highly modular. Most programming problems can be split into subtasks, but the amount of communication required between the subtasks determines their modularity rating. A tape system for payroll reports is a highly modular task.

A data management system for the same purpose has a low degree of modularity.

(5) *Reliability.* Some tasks such as patient monitoring systems have severe failure penalties, while other tasks, such as natural language processing experiments, need not be as reliable, although working programs are always desirable. The reliability measure depends on the social, financial, and psychological requirements of the task.

(6) *Time.* How much time is required for task completion? Is the time adequate or is there time pressure? The penalty for not meeting a deadline strongly affects this measure.

(7) *Sociability.* Some programming tasks require considerable communication with the user or with other technical personnel, such as engineers or mathematicians, while other tasks involve interaction with the team alone. Computer center consulting groups that develop user aids have higher sociability requirements than groups programming their own set of software tools.

Throughout this paper, the labels egoless programming team and chief programmer team have prevailed. For the purposes of comparison, these terms have been changed to names reflecting the decision-making authority and communication structure of the teams. The three teams are:

1. Democratic Decentralized (DD). This group is like Weinberg's proposed team; it has no leaders, but appoints task coordinators for short durations. Decisions on problem solutions and goal direction are made by group consensus. Communication among members is horizontal.

2. Controlled Decentralized (CD). The CD group has a leader who coordinates tasks. Secondary management positions exist below that of the leader. Problem solving remains a group activity but partitioning the problem among groups is a task of the leader. Communication is decentralized in the subgroups and centralized along the control hierarchy.

Table I. Recommended Team Structures for Programming Task Features.

Group Structures	Programming Task Characteristics													
	Difficulty		Size		Duration		Modularity		Reliability		Time Required		Sociability	
	High	Low	Large	Small	Short	Long	High	Low	High	Low	Strict	Lax	High	Low
Democratic Decentralized	X			X	X		X		X			X	X	
Controlled Decentralized		X	X		X			X	X					X
Controlled Centralized		X	X		X			X		X	X			X

3. *Controlled Centralized* (*CC*). This group is like Baker's team. Both problem solving and goal directions are generated by the team leader. Communication is vertical along the path of control.

The expected interaction of each of these team structures with the factors governing program tasks can be drawn from experimental research on small group dynamics. To assess performance quality, team structures are assumed to be evaluated on the quality of generated code and the time in which the code generation was completed.

Table I lists recommended group structures for each task variable. Under the category *task difficulty*, simple problems are best performed by a centralized structure which completes tasks faster. Decentralization works best for difficult problems. Groups are found to generate more and better solutions than individuals. Unfortunately, the CD team is centralized precisely where the problem is difficult. The DD team is the best solution for difficult problems. For simpler programming tasks, a CC or CD structure is recommended.

As programming tasks increase in size, the amount of cooperation required among group members increases. Group performance is negatively correlated with the cooperation requirements of a task. As tasks become *very large*, the DD group is no longer viable because of its cooperation requirements. CC and CD groups can be effectively regrouped into smaller structures to handle the task. When the task size requires a smaller number of programmers, the DD group performs better because of its high level of communication. For *very small* tasks, the CC group is best because it does not require the additional communication of democratic groups; but then, a group is unnecessary. An individual will do.

The duration of the task interacts with group morale. Short tasks may not require high group morale, whereas long tasks will suffer from high personnel turnover if morale is low. DD groups have high morale and high job satisfaction. This should be the preferred group structure for ongoing tasks. The CC and CD groups are effective for short-term tasks.

If task modularity is low, the DD group performs best because of its higher volume of communication. Cooperative (read DD) groups have higher orderliness scores than competitive (read CC) groups [10]. This orderliness is essential for maintaining the interfaces of a low modularity task. Nondirective leadership has been found to be most effective when a task has a high multiplicity of solutions. Directive leadership is best for tasks with low multiplicity solution choices [22]. A DD group can be characterized as having nondirective leadership, CC and CD groups as having directive leadership. High modularity tasks have a low multiplicity of solutions, and thus the CD and CC groups can be expected to exhibit the best performance given such tasks.

CC and CD groups perform well when confronted with high reliability requirement problems. Decentralized groups have been found to make less errors and produce better solutions to problems. A CC group is more error-prone and probably should never be used for projects in which relatively simple errors can result in disaster.

A decentralized group takes longer to complete a problem than a centralized group. If tasks have severe time constraints, a CC team is best. When time is not crucial, the low motivation of CC groups can interfere with task completion. Therefore, the more democratic groups are preferred, with the DD structure being the best choice.

If a task requires high sociability, the DD team structure is best. Groups learn faster than individuals (such as the team leaders of CC groups). Therefore, a DD group would understand a user's interface problem in a shorter period of time. DD groups are higher in social interaction and morale than CD or CC groups. These traits will enhance their social relationships with the task contacts.

6. Conclusion

Many programming task features interact with each other, e.g., a large project is often a difficult one. Group structures that are effective for one aspect of a task may be totally wrong for another. In selecting a team structure, it is important to use a decision-making algorithm to prioritize, weight, or combine the crucial task variables.

Little experimental work on programming team and task interaction has been carried out. Basili and Reiter [2] found relationships between the size of a programming group and several software metrics. They also

COMPUTING
PRACTICES

found cost differential behavior arising from the software development approach taken, with structured techniques being notably cheaper. Only one programming task was performed by the experimental groups. Weinberg's suggestions on group organization are anecdotal and Baker's conclusions are confounded by the team personnel and the programming methods selected.

Most of the research on group problem-solving behavior was conducted in a laboratory setting with students and tasks of short duration. A problem exists in trying to apply these conclusions to the external work environment. In particular, programming tasks generally involve an entirely different time span than laboratory experiments. Becker [4] scathingly criticizes these "cage" experiments. Rogers [19] suggests substituting network analysis field work to understand the effects of group structures.

None of these task/structure recommendations have been tested in a software development environment. Despite all these shortcomings, the application of a body of research on group dynamics to the organization of personnel on a programming project is a step forward from the hit-and-miss guessing that is the current state of the art.

References

1. Baker, F.T. Chief programmer team management of production programming. *IBM Syst. J. 1* (1972), 57–73. Baker presents a case history of a program project management organization, the chief programmer team. This compact management strategy coupled with top-down program development methods achieves above average success in terms of productivity and error-free code.

2. Basili, V.R., and Reiter, R.W., Jr. The investigation of human factors in software development. *Comptr. 12*, 12 (Dec. 1979), 21-38. This paper examines the impact of a programming team's size and program development approach, disciplined or ad hoc, on the software product. The disciplined method resulted in major savings in development efficiency and smaller groups built larger code modules.

3. Bavelas, A. Communication patterns in task-oriented groups. *J. Acoustical Soc. America 22* (1950), 725–730. Bavelas describes an experiment in which the communication structures of a circle, wheel, and chain were imposed on small groups by the physical arrangement of cubicles and message slots. Each structure was then measured for its problem-solving efficiency.

4. Becker, H. Vitalizing sociological theory. *Amer. Sociological Rev. 19* (1954), 377–388. Becker refers to the small group laboratory studies as "cage studies" and recommends their use by sociological theorists only for an awareness of such studies' limiting conditions.

5. Bem, D.J., Wallace, M.A., and Kogen, N. Group decision making under risk of adversive consequences. *J. Personality and Social Psychol. 1* (1965), 453–460. This paper demonstrates, in a context of adversive consequences (loss of money, induced nausea, etc.), that unanimous group decisions concerning matters of risk shift toward greater risk-taking than individual decisions. Moreover, the authors provide evidence that the underlying process for the risky shift is a diffusion of the responsibility among group members.

6. Brooks, F.P., Jr. *The Mythical Man-Month: Essays on Software Engineering.* Addison-Wesley, Reading, Mass., 1975. This work is a lyrical, enjoyable, and sage discussion of the problems and pitfalls that beset a mammoth software project—developing the IBM 360 operating system.

7. Cartwright, D., and Zander, D., Eds. *Group Dynamics: Research and Theory.* 3rd edition, Harper and Row, N.Y., 1968. This serves as an excellent compendium of the spurt of group dynamics research activity in the late 1950s which laid the groundwork for what we know about group behavior today.

8. Cave, W.C., and Salisbury, A.B. Controlling the software life cycle—The project management task. *IEEE Trans. Soft. Engr. SE-4*, 4 (July 1978), 326–334. This paper describes project management methods for controlling the life cycle of large software systems distributed to multiple users. It emphasizes responding to user satisfaction and user requirements and suggests methods to establish and maintain control in an extended dynamic environment.

9. De Roze, B.C., and Nyman, T.H. The software life cycle—A management and technological challenge in the department of defense. *IEEE Trans. Soft. Engr. SE-4*, 4 (July 1978), 309–318. De Roze and Nyman describe the software life cycle management policy and practices that have been established by the Department of Defense for improving the software development process.

10. Deutsch, M. The effects of cooperation and competition upon group process. *Human Relations 2* (1949), 129–152, 199–231. Deutsch describes an experiment which establishes two forms of group relationships, cooperative and competitive. Besides better communication, increased orderliness and higher productivity result when the cooperative group relationship exists.

11. Goldberg, S.C. Influence and leadership as a function of group structure. *J. Abnormal and Social Psychol. 51* (1955), 119–122. The experiment described in this paper compares

group influence on group members in three organization structures: a star, a fork, and a chain. Individuals holding central positions were influenced less than other group members.

12. Guetzkow, H., and Simon, H.A. The impact of certain communication nets upon organization and performance in task-oriented groups. *Mgmt. Sci. 1* (1955), 233–250. The authors establish three communication structures: all-channel, wheel, and circle; they then examine their effect on solving a relatively simple communication problem. The restrictions of the wheel organization aided the solution process, whereas those of the circle hindered it. The lack of restrictions in the all-channel case also hurt the solution process.

13. Jensen, R.W., and Tonies, C.C., Eds. *Software Engineering.* Prentice–Hall, Englewood Cliffs, N.J., 1979. Here, several breakdowns of what constitutes a software life cycle are presented. The authors indicate that if the customer-use phase is included in this breakdown, the time spent on the code development constitutes a relatively small portion of the project.

14. Leavitt, H.J. Some effects of certain communication patterns on group performance. *J. Abnormal and Social Psychol. 46* (1951), 38–50. Leavitt compares problem-solving effectiveness in both wheel and circle communication structures. The wheel structure was faster but the circle structure accounted for fewer errors.

15. Lott, A.J., and Lott, B.E. Group cohesiveness, communication level, and conformity. *J. Abnormal and Social Psychol. 62* (1961), 408–412. This paper describes an experiment in which groups were scored on cohesiveness and then tallied for the amount of communication generated in a discussion session. Highly cohesive groups communicated more.

16. March, J.G., and Simon, H.A. *Organizations.* Wiley, New York, 1958. March and Simon focus on the members of formal organizations as rational men. From this, they point out that the basic features of organizational structure and function derive from characteristics of the human problem-solving process and rational choice.

17. Metzger, P.W. *Managing a Programming Project.* Prentice-Hall, Englewood Cliffs, N.J., 1973. Metzger suggests a project organization constrained in terms of the types of tasks that are undertaken in the development of a software system. He goes on to describe how these tasks should be managed via this hierarchical arrangement.

18. Mills, H.D. Chief programmer teams: Principles and procedures. IBM Rep. FSC 71-5108, IBM Fed. Syst. Div., Gaithersburg, Md., 1971. Mills suggests that the large team approach to programming projects could eventually be replaced by smaller, tightly organized and functionally specialized teams led by a chief programmer.

19. Rogers, E.M., and Agarwala-Rogers, R. *Communication in Organizations.* Free Press, N.Y., 1976. The basic research on group structures in small group network communication is summarized and critiqued in a thoroughly readable manner.

20. Schachter, S. Deviation, rejection and communication. *J. Abnormal and Social Psy-*

chol. 46 (1951), 190–207. This article describes an experiment in which three group members were paid to respectively 1) deviate from, 2) follow, and 3) change over to the group position taken on an issue. Groups with high cohesiveness scores produced greater rejection only of the deviant individual.

21. Shaw, M.E. Some effects of unequal distribution of information upon group performance in various communication nets. *J. Abnormal and Social Psychol. 49* (1954), 547–553. In this paper, the amount of independence and, thus, individual satisfaction are examined in various group structures. Low centralization in groups led to member satisfaction.

22. Shaw, M.E., and Blum, J.M. Effects of leadership styles upon performance as a function of task structure. *J. Personality and Social Psychol. 3* (1966), 238–242. Shaw and Blum describe an experiment in which they manipulated the leadership of two groups to be nondirective or directive. Given three tasks of varying solution multiplicity, directive leadership performed best with low multiplicity tasks.

23. Shaw, M.E. *Group Dynamics: The Psychology of Small Group Behavior.* McGraw-Hill, N.Y., 1971.

24. Shneiderman, B. *Software Psychology.* Winthrop, Cambridge, Mass., 1980. Shneiderman discusses the good and bad points of the Weinberg and Baker teams and a third conventional team. He notes that an egoless team may be difficult to maintain and a competent chief programmer hard to find, concluding that the currently existing conventional organization has strong chances for successful projects—especially with a competent manager.

25. Taylor, D.W., and Faust, W.L. Twenty questions: Efficiency of problem solving as a function of the size of the group. *J. Experimental Psychol. 44* (1952), 360–363. Taylor compares individual problem-solving to group problem-solving in a game of 20 questions. Even after several days of practice, groups of two and four individuals asked less questions to discover an answer than sole participants.

26. Thayer, R.H., Pyster, A., and Wood, R.C. The challenge of software engineering project management. *Comptr. 13,* 8 (Aug. 1980), 51–59. The three authors report on a survey of software project management experts who were asked to indicate the most important issues facing software engineering. The structure of programming projects was rated as unimportant; planning received the highest ratings.

27. Thibaut, J.W., and Kelley, H.H. *The Social Psychology of Groups.* Wiley, N.Y., 1959. The second section of this book presents a general theory for group formation and group dynamics—in particular, the status systems within groups, conformity requirements, group goal setting behaviors, and the roles played by individuals within the group. In all, not light reading for the nonsociologist.

28. Weinberg, G. *The Psychology of Computer Programming.* Van Nostrand Reinhold, N.Y., 1971. Weinberg provides homilies, advice, and some wisdom about the psychological considerations of the programming process. It is here that he suggests the egoless approach to programming and discusses its potential advantages—Weinberg is short on supportive research, but the book is fun to read.

29. Yourdon, E. *Managing the Structured Technique.* Prentice-Hall, Englewood Cliffs, N.J., 1976. Yourdon discusses the chief programmer team and Weinberg's egoless debugging techniques in a complete scenario for project management. He labels the chief programmer team impractical because of the dearth of true chief programmers.

Part IV: Staffing

"My good people are my most precious resource."

—*Donald J. Reifer*

Staffing means recruiting the right people, developing their capabilities, and then retaining them. It is not a function that can be delegated solely to the personnel department. Good people are essential to a company's success, and it is management's responsibility to identify, train, and motivate these people so that they try their hardest and do their best on the job. The nine articles that follow were selected to shed light on these points.

In his article, "Skills Matrixing," Jahnig describes how Chase Manhattan Bank coped with its human resources problems and how it developed several tools for use in creating definitive career paths based on specific job skills within its matrix organization. These tools reportedly have reduced employee turnover drastically.

Bowen and Hall, in "Career Planning for Employee Development: A Primer for Managers," view the theory of career planning and describe and evaluate career planning approaches. They provide the reader with an understanding of the concepts needed to establish meaningful career paths within a data processing organization.

Hiring programing personnel is the subject of the next two articles. Swanson and Devore, in "A Structured Approach to Hiring," describe the procedures used by Kansas State University for screening, interviewing, and selecting programers. Siegel, in "Investing in New Employees," describes practices employed by the United States Fidelity & Guaranty Co. for selecting and training programer trainees. This article provides some keen insights into the problems inherent in selection.

Training inexperienced programers is always a trying and costly venture. In "Training Programmers under Simulated 'Live' Conditions," Dolan discusses the approach used by Western Electric to train programmers to produce complicated, real-time software electronic switching applications.

The next two articles discuss management development. DiBeradinis, in "Approach to Management Development," describes the advantages and limitations of three training and instructional approaches. Gellerman, in "Developing Managers without Management Development," discusses how small companies can develop their managers without investing time and money in large training programs.

Grove, in "Employee Appraisal: When You're the Judge," describes a measurement system that is useful in evaluating the technical performance and managerial potential of programming personnel. Although mostly qualitative in nature, the approach does look at many of the dimensions that constitute acceptable job behavior.

In the last article, "Turning around Turnover," Acker discusses an approach that can be used to combat turnover. Retaining critical staff resources today is a major problem facing most software managers. Help in this area is indeed useful.

Skills Matrixing

by Frederick F. Jahnig

Put 1,100 data processing people into the same department and personnel management problems multiply. Are matrixes the answer?

At the Chase Manhattan Bank, in the early '70s, the lack of effective personnel management techniques in data processing was causing serious and expensive operational problems. These included high employee turnover, low productivity, rapidly escalating project costs, delays in developing new automated systems, and a general feeling of inefficiency.

Chase is the country's third largest bank, and its data processing resources are very large. The bank operates three computer centers stuffed with a variety of machines including an IBM 370/168, two 158s, one 360/65MP, one Burroughs B7700, a B6700, four B3500s, four Univac Spectra 70/45s, half a dozen Digital Equip. Corp. PDP-11s, and a few others. Its data processing staff—*not* including data entry personnel—has 1,100 people. Of these, 550 are "professionals"—programmers and analysts and their managers.

Personnel problems involving 1,100 people are big problems, and Chase had them. In addition to a turnover rate of 35-38% per year and all the other problems mentioned, we were having difficulties maintaining our technology at the state of the art. Skills development had slowed, and in spite of the number of people available, we lacked the capabilities to do some of the things the company needed.

Our professionals were confused. They were unhappy, and many of them were taking their talents elsewhere.

These problems have largely been solved during the last two years, but the solutions were not easy to implement.

The solutions involved restructuring the entire organization and developing a new set of personnel development techniques and tools.

Matrix management

Our first step was to alter the shape of our organization to put it into a form which would help us emphasize personnel development. We added to our line organization, which was a vertical project-oriented structure, another management layer, making it a specialized kind of matrix (see Fig. 1).

The result is that each dp employee has two managers: his line manager who gives him his specific work assignments, and his manpower or pool

MATRIX DATA PROCESSING ORGANIZATION STRUCTURE

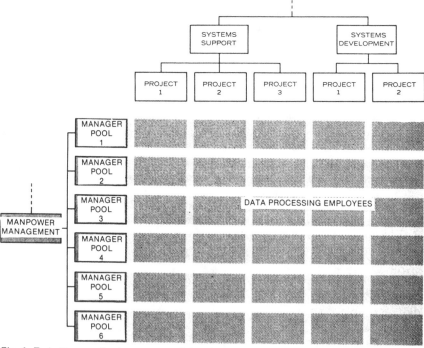

Fig. 1. To better emphasize personnel development, Chase Manhattan Bank organized its programmers, analysts and other professionals into a matrix structure. Project managers worry only about projects. Manpower managers worry about personnel problems. Each manpower manager has only people with similar titles reporting to him; even systems analysts and senior systems analysts are separated.

manager who is responsible for his training and career development.

Each employee belongs to one of six pools or staff units, depending on his skills. For example, one pool contains mostly systems analysts. Senior systems analysts belong in another pool. Among other advantages derived from this pooling is that a pool manager is capable of maintaining the integrity of a position classification across department or project lines. There are many other advantages, too.

Conceptually this was a fine way to develop and manage the manpower resource, but converting to this organization also forced us to redo all our manpower management processes. That, too, proved beneficial. Among other things, it led us to develop five related management tools: a career ladder, a set of position descriptions, a skills glossary, a training catalog, and the "skills matrix" which helps make the other four useful.

An outside consulting firm was engaged to assist in evaluating our problems. With its help we soon turned up a significant gap between the skills inventory of our staff and the skills needed to get the job done. The gap was found by simply comparing each employee's skills with the job responsibilities assigned him. To make sure the job responsibilities assigned were appropriate, we examined department procedures and standards, conducted interviews and circulated questionnaires. It's always a surprise to see how differently managers and staff see themselves, their functions, and their responsibilities—and how far off target everyone can be about their job assignment.

Once the job responsibilities had been defined, we determined what position titles we wished to associate with each set of responsibilities. This led us to invent several new job titles, including "technical specialist" and "systems specialist" and three more that have to do with systems engineering. It led us to discard a few positions also, like "systems analyst trainee," a slot which previously required no programming training!

Career ladders & job descriptions

Given the set of positions we wanted, we worked with the consultants to create our first tool, a "career ladder." (See Fig. 2 for a portion of the career ladder). This tool shows which way is up in our dp hierarchy. It displays clear, distinct career path guideposts which tell our staff where they are, where they are headed, how far it is to their destination, and what

skills are needed to get there. It outlines interpath mobility and shows all available career routes open to each member of our dp organization.

The career ladder provides both management and staff with a positive overview of organizational relationships. It also can be made more sophisticated to show paths into the dp group and out of the group into other sections of the company. However, exposure, training, and education must be ready for those who choose to leave the dp group, particularly in the realm of management development; we have not yet developed these.

The second tool created is a set of position descriptions, which basically attach words to the position slots we created. Each position has a pre-

determined acceptable level of skills broken down into nine subsets: hardware, languages, system software, technical skills, project skills, interface, applications, business and industry, and supervisory.

Skills glossary & training catalog

Our third tool is a detailed "skills glossary," a dictionary that defines the data processing skills required across our installation. (Fig. 3 is an example of the breakdown of one skill, programming in COBOL.) The glossary lists four levels of proficiency: conceptual knowledge, familiarity, good working knowledge, and comprehensive knowledge.

The glossary is updated on a

CAREER LADDER

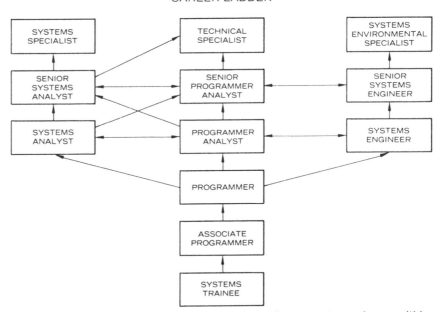

Fig. 2. The career ladder shows the job path alternatives open to employees within the dp department. It does not yet reflect branches into and out of the department.

SKILLS GLOSSARY
IBM COBOL

Level 1—CONCEPTUAL KNOWLEDGE

Knowledge of structure of COBOL program, various divisions, syntax conventions, major verbs. Has coded and debugged at least one minor program.

Level 2—FAMILIARITY

Has coded and tested five or more nontrivial programs or modules using major COBOL verbs and logic branches.

Level 3—GOOD WORKING KNOWLEDGE

Has used sequential and random access methods, printer options subscripting and debugging aids such as TRACE, memory dumps, looping options.

Level 4—COMPREHENSIVE KNOWLEDGE

Has used indexing, SORT verb with input/output procedures, modular programming techniques. Is knowledgeable concerning various trade-offs between logical equivalent coding schemes. Knows COBOL interface techniques.

Fig. 3. Four-level skills "definitions" are contained in the skills glossary which is used to build position descriptions.

TRAINING CATALOG

1. COURSE TITLE——Introduction to Programming

    NUMBER ——S03

    DESCRIPTION ——This course will introduce the basics of data processing. Topics of instruction will include the history of EDP, components of a third generation data processing system, data recording concepts, numbering systems, systems phases and applications and the concepts of programming and the operating system. The mode of instruction is to be both lecture and self study. The course will be graded.

2. COURSE TITLE——ANS COBOL Coding

    NUMBER ——I 02

    DESCRIPTION ——This course will cover the structure of COBOL program divisions, syntax conventions, major verbs, subscripting and I/O options for sequential access. Intensive workshop sessions are included, with compiles and executions being submitted. Emphasis will be placed upon the IBM compiler options. The mode of instruction is to be lecture. This is a graded course.

3. COURSE TITLE——ANS COBOL Programming Efficiencies

    NUMBER ——I 03

    DESCRIPTION ——This course will provide an analysis of ANS COBOL coding emphasizing the efficient use of the programming language. Specific verbs will be covered with reference to generated instructions. The following will also be included: report writing, sort features, segmentation, debugging, and linkage conventions. Workshops will be set up to use techniques learned. The mode of instruction is to be lecture. This is a graded course.

4. COURSE TITLE——Advanced Programming Techniques

    NUMBER ——I 10

    DESCRIPTION ——This course will provide detailed discussions on resource allocation processes of multiprogramming environments, multiprogramming techniques, dynamic module loading and execution and the tradeoffs of using various program segmentation techniques.

Fig. 4. Courses in the training catalog relate directly to the four proficiency levels defined in the skills glossary.

Fig. 5. The skills matrix ties all the other tools together. It is possible to look up, for any position classification, the skills proficiencies required and even the courses available for developing those skills.

periodic basis and distributed to the entire staff. Originally the list contained 50 skills, but several have been added, including skills involving minicomputers, data bases, and data communications.

There is a direct fallout for targeted dp education from the glossary, and that is the fourth tool, the training catalog. The catalog explains how needed skills can be acquired. It lists the course material required to advance from one level to the next in the skills glossary. Fig. 4 illustrates the portion of the catalog related to IBM COBOL programming.

The four tools, the career ladder, position descriptions, skills glossary, and training catalog, had to be interrelated to be effective, and therefore the fifth tool, the skills matrix, was developed.

The integrated skills matrix

The matrix is a master cross reference and skills profile for each position. It defines each position and describes its required skill levels. It provides a skills hierarchy where the upper range of one job interlocks with the minimum entry level into the next higher position in the sequence, and thereby provides a clear understanding of the skills needed to progress from one position to the next in a chosen career path. (Fig. 5.)

The matrix has three dimensions. It contains: (1) the glossary's 50-plus skills broken down into the four proficiency levels; (2) the training catalog's course titles; and (3) the job classifications of the set of position descriptions. At the point where the three dimensions meet, it shows the appropriate skill requirement for each position and the related course material for acquiring that level of proficiency of that skill.

Once the matrix was completed, tool building was over. The tools were put into operation. People were trained and oriented. The implementation program and schedule is too detailed to show here, but it worked—partly, we think, because the employees participated directly with management in the skills evaluation process.

When the implementation was completed, in 1972, Chase had a new, stronger management structure and the tools to support it.

The results

Overall, we have a system of managing human resources that provides control and enables employees to realize their own career goals. It motivates employees through their own ambition, channels their energy into productivity by satisfying their career goals, and displays the bank's commitment to their development in a visible, tangible, and objective form.

Employee turnover has decreased drastically and is now running at something near 10%. While we recognize that economic conditions influenced this, we have been able to retain significant numbers of qualified people and are no longer losing them to other companies.

We started with a huge staff but still limited capabilities. Nearly half of those employees are no longer with us, though we still have an equally large number. The present staff is more capable and can handle the jobs assigned us.

Our few years with the skills matrix have shown that it is a viable tool. However, there are still some areas that need to be addressed. One of them is the quantum jump from the highest technical proficiency level into management. We have recognized the importance of the technical specialist who does not wish to become a manager, and made a position for him. But we have not yet smoothed the transition for those who wish to manage.

Another deficiency results from the manner in which the tools were made. Since the core of the matrix is concerned with technical dp skills, it does not address the skills needed in other parts of banking. Thus career pathing from dp into those areas is limited. The reverse problem of bringing people into dp from other areas of the bank is even more difficult. We are now addressing both these deficiencies by adding management and banking skills to our program.

In spite of its current inadequacies, we believe our approach to human resources management is a success, and that we have taken an effective first step. ✼

Since joining Chase Manhattan Bank in 1960, Mr. Jahnig has held the positions of personnel representative, systems analyst, personnel officer, assistant treasurer, and second vice president. He is now group executive of manpower management for data processing and vice president.

Donald D. Bowen
Douglas T. Hall

Career Planning
for Employee Development

A Primer for Managers

© 1977 by the Regents of the University of California, Reprinted from
CALIFORNIA MANAGEMENT REVIEW, Volume XX, Number 2, pp.
23-35 by permission of the Regents.

We are beginning to see substantial evidence that people do rather poorly at managing their careers, even those with advanced professional degrees.[1] Seventy-three percent of the graduates from MIT's master's program change jobs within the first five years of employment; another study involving several firms reports a figure of 50 percent for employees with master's degrees.[2] And executives are not immune. Faced with career crises, many cope poorly. Others who are more successful, however, seem to be better planners. They are described as decisive, with clear goals and a strong sense of identity.[3]

We suspect that there would be immense savings in both organizational productivity and personal stress if employees planned their careers more effectively. We propose to review briefly some behavioral science research and theory bearing upon the subject of career planning. The second half of the discussion describes alternative career planning techniques and evaluates each in terms of the requirements and criteria developed from the research and theory.

Current Career Planning and Personnel Practices

Many current personnel practices seem to hinder rather than help employees make sound career decisions. Unrealistically optimistic recruiting pitches are the norm, despite some evidence to indicate that turnover and training costs can be reduced by providing new employees with a balanced picture of the job.[4] The first year of many management training programs is devoted to job rotation or similar make-work activities at the very time when the new employee most needs a challenging assignment to test his or her capabilities. Moreover, subsequent career progress in management may be much more likely for management trainees who are given a challenging position in their first job.[5]

Many large firms currently engage in manpower planning, including the charting of career paths for their managerial and professional employees. The employees involved, however, are usually not permitted to contribute to this process. Their careers are planned by higher-level executives (perhaps acting as "sponsors") and specialists in the personnel department. And performance appraisals often do not provide the employee with a clear picture of where he or she stands in the organization's plans. While most companies claim to provide periodic performance appraisals, lower-level employees often report that they are seldom, if ever, reviewed. Even where there is a systematic performance appraisal system in effect, upper management is frequently exempted from the review procedure. Hence, performance appraisal systems are likely to leave a feedback gap at both higher and lower levels of the organization.[6]

Performance appraisal and manpower planning, even when performed effectively, are only partial answers, at best. Epstein[7] argues persuasively that the paternalism of these programs runs counter to both the values of today's managers and the needs of the organization for more flexible employees. The organization, in manpower planning, usually assumes responsibility for making the decisions and the judgments affecting the employee. (Ironically, in such a system the executives deciding subordinates' futures may not even plan their *own!*) As we shall demonstrate, there is considerable research and theory to indicate that goal setting has its most constructive influence on the motivation and behavior of the employee only in those situations wherein people set their own objectives.

Identity, Subidentities, and the Whole Person

One important characteristic of the fully functioning person is what Erikson calls *identity:* a sense of "wholeness," the primary developmental task of late adolescence. The young person who successfully acquires a sense of identity sees a unity "... between that which he conceives himself to be and that which he perceives others to see in him and to expect of him." Vocational choice is a large element in developing an identity: "In general it is the inability to settle on an occupational identity which disturbs young people."[8] Failure to achieve a sense of

Donald D. Bowen is Associate Professor of Management at the University of Tulsa. His research and consulting interests are in motivation, careers, women and minorities, and organization development. In addition to various journal articles, he is co-author of *Experiences in Management and Organizational Behavior.*

Douglas T. Hall is Earl Dean Howard Professor of Organizational Behavior and Chairman of the Department of Organizational Behavior at Northwestern University. His research and consulting activities deal with career development and pathing women's careers, the impact of management structure and policies on career success, and dual career families. His publications include *Careers in Organizations.*

identity leaves the person in a state of *identity confusion.*

The person with a clear sense of identity has: (1) clear goals; (2) which are not in conflict with each other; (3) a sense of continuity between his past experiences, present, and future; and (4) a plan for achieving his or her future goals.

A secure sense of identity is clearly necessary to effective functioning in adulthood. But there are forces we all experience which constantly threaten to disturb or fragment our sense of unity and wholeness. As adults we are called to move from role to role, normally playing our roles in sequential fashion, but occasionally acting in more than one role simultaneously. We all acquire several roles: father, mother, plant manager, lodge member, church member, and so forth. Each of these roles engages only one portion of our identity (a subidentity) as we perform in the role.

The notion of subidentity is helpful in studying careers. When the individual is able to integrate all of his or her subidentities, an overall sense of identity is developed. Failing to integrate one's major subidentities leads to fragmentation and alienation from oneself.

Effective adaptation to role demands is one requirement for maintaining an integrated identity. We would also propose, however, that an individual must experience *psychological success* in dealing with life's tasks, including adapting to role demands.

Psychological Success

We normally think of success in terms of achieving the rewards that are socially defined as the marks of success: prestige, position, money, fame, power, security, and so forth. But we all know of instances wherein people have achieved these rewards and remained unhappy. Success, as we see it, requires a subjective sense of having achieved the rewards that a person values and thereby enhancing his or her self-esteem in the process. This notion of *psychological success* was initially developed by Lewin and subsequently elaborated by Argyris.[10] Lewin conducted a number of studies in which people were asked to set targets or goals for themselves. Lewin then looked at how people's subsequent

Figure 1. Model of Career Growth Through Psychological Success

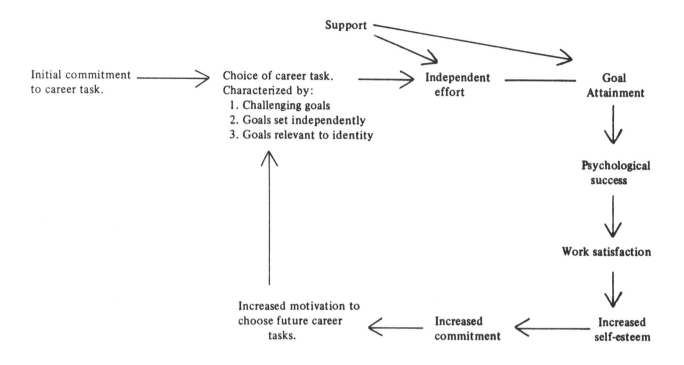

From D. T. Hall, "Potential for Career Growth," *Personnel Journal* (March 1971), 1971.

goals and self-esteem were affected after they had either succeeded or failed in achieving their original targets. When people were successful, they tended to set even more challenging goals on the next task and they experienced greater self-esteem. After failure, the responses depended upon the level of self-esteem. If a person was initially high in self-esteem, they would persist, rather than lowering their goals after the failure. Persons lower in self-esteem lowered their aspirations as one might expect. Indeed, for persons low in initial self-esteem, even success did not lead to setting more ambitious goals; these individuals would often quit while they were ahead—as if they could not believe that they could ever succeed again, or could not accept the current success which contradicted their sense of unworthiness.

The results of several studies related to the psychological success process can be portrayed graphically in a model of career growth.[11] The major steps are as follows:

1. Initial commitment to career task leads to

2. Choice of a career task involving challenging but feasible goals, where the goals are set by the person involved and are relevant to his or her self-concept (identity). This, in turn, leads to

3. High independent effort, especially in a supportive climate, and thus to

4. A greater likelihood of goal attainment (which is likely to attract more support from superiors and others in the organization).

5. With achievement of one's goals comes psychological success and job satisfaction, leading to

6. Increased self-esteem, particularly in the form of an increased sense of one's competence (new or more clearly articulated subidentities). This generates

7. Increased commitment and involvement, and thus an increased probability of

8. Motivation to choose even more challenging career tasks in the future.

These relationships are portrayed in Figure 1.

Implications for Career Progress

If the theory developed thus far is valid, two central propositions about career development follow.

1. Developing and maintaining a positive, well-integrated sense of identity determines an individual's capacity to deal with challenging, changing, ambiguous, and perhaps conflicting role demands facing an adult in our society. *For the working adult, the sequential and expanding work roles of the occupational career become a major source of subidentity elaboration, necessitating on-going and increasing effectiveness in identity integration.*

2. Since initial commitment to the career task determines the level of goals a person sets, and since these goals should be relevant to one's identity, *it is vitally important* that the individual have a clear idea of his or her needs at the time the goals are set. In other words, one's goals can only sustain the intense independent effort necessary for achievement of these aims to the extent that the goals are consistent with and based upon central needs and values in one's life.

Implications for Career Planning

Our discussion of psychological success led us to the conclusion that setting one's own goals and objectives is a prerequisite to experiencing psychological success. Moreover, we noted that the goals set must be relevant to the central needs and potentialities, the identity of the individual. The capacity to set meaningful goals thus becomes dependent upon one's sense of identity. Acquiring a unified sense of identity is a dynamic, rather than a static process. With each new role acquired in life, one can avoid identity diffusion or role confusion only to the extent that one can develop or expand one's subidentities in a manner both consistent with the demands of the role and congruent with the core identity. Successful career planning and development must be a process which accompanies each job change or role transition, beginning before the new role is undertaken to assure establishment of objectives and goals, and continuing through the adaptation period to facilitate the integration of the emerging subidentity.

Alternatives for Career Planning

What are the alternatives available for the better management of employee careers? Management wants the benefits of a management group which is self-directed, self-controlled, responsible, and proactive. The employees gain from the personal development resulting from more effective career planning as well as in terms of the material and psychic rewards associated with career advancement and progress.

There are several types of programs or activities which management can sponsor or provide to foster these aims. In this section, we will review several career planning activities and comment upon each in terms of practical or procedural considerations, and in terms of the probable effect of each in terms of our theory of identity integration and psychological success. These career planning alternatives are outlined in the Appendix.

Individual activities. "Individual activities" include any type of effort the individual employee undertakes without assistance from others such as company officials or external counselors. The typical "self-help" program, of course, is simply the personal planning of career objectives, perhaps in collaboration with one's family or friends. Bolles' book, *What Color is Your Parachute?*,[12] provides an excellent guide for self-help activities. The employer may encourage such activity, but this type of career planning really depends entirely upon the individual employee's ability and willingness to develop his or her own plans. For the employee with extraordinary capacity for self-direction and adequate access to information on occupational and job market possibilities, individual exploration meets some of the important requirements for achieving psychological success: the individual chooses his or her own goals and the means for achieving these goals. Moreover, there is usually little out-of-pocket cost to the individual or the employer.

The potential shortcomings of this strategy are several. Most people do not have a wide knowledge of the employment opportunities available to them. Equally important, at least, is the difficulty the employee is likely to encounter in obtaining a systematic self-assessment and development of the necessary self-awareness for effective planning. Family and friends may be helpful as a psychological support group to help the employee through a career crisis, but they usually lack the expertise and will probably be as blind as the employee to the need for systematic periodic routine planning when there is no crisis.

Counselor-client activities. There are two major variants of this type of activity: the testing approach, the clinical approach, and a third which combines these two approaches. All of these activities involve an individual client-professional counselor relationship. The counselor may be an employee of the organization or an independent professional specializing in the field. Many larger firms are employing in-house counselors in increasing numbers to assist employees.[13]

In the *testing approach,* the guidance or vocational counselor's primary function is to administer psychometric tests such as aptitude, vocational interest, or personality tests in order to feed the results back to the client. The external counselor will probably also provide information on employment possibilities and job-hunting skills. The testing and feedback may provide employees with valuable information for planning their careers, particularly in cases where the employee feels totally incapable of identifying his or her own career interests. There are a number of potential shortcomings to this form of career guidance, however, some of which apply more to the internal counselor than the external professional.

1. Individual counseling tends to be expensive and its cost-effectiveness may be less than for strategies that work with groups of employees.

2. If the service is crisis-oriented, the employee will tend to use it only as a support activity during a period of traumatic transitions. This short-term goal-setting process is contrary to the long-term goal-setting process we advocate.

3. In many organizations, people may be stigmatized if other employees know about their having sought the advice of the "company shrink."

4. Individual counseling sessions do not contribute to organizational development. Internal group workshops, on the other hand, help employees develop norms of openness, sharing, and trust which can carry over to improvement of day-to-day interactions in the organization.[14]

5. Rather than focusing on helping the employee to develop skills in identifying his or her own needs and capabilities, the test-oriented counselor acts as an "expert" in providing information on the person's suitability for certain types of occupations. If the information thus provided does not square with the employee's self-image, it will often be ignored or distorted.[15]

6. The counselor who is a full-time employee of the organization may occasionally experience an ethical bind akin to that of the company physician—whose interests come first? The employee's? Or the organization's?

7. In contrast to group approaches to career counseling, the individual counseling situation does not provide a built-in mechanism for validation of feedback. The client has no ready means for checking the counselor's perceptions or test results with others who can see him or her behaving in the same situation from which the counselor draws his inferences.

8. In the testing approach, interpersonal feedback on how the person interacts with others is likely to be minimal, since the emphasis is on internal traits or aptitudes.

In the *clinical* variant of the counseling approach, the counselor relies on the interpersonal client-counselor interviewing process as a source for developing the data sought by the client to assist in career planning. Tests may be used as an adjunct to the process, but the primary mechanism is the quasi-psychotherapeutic interview. Clinical counseling may be the "treatment of choice" in situations of severe maladaptation or acute crisis. Many clinical counselors use nondirective interviewing, a process where the counselor avoids giving advice or directions, but rather, helps employees explore their own needs and values in order to set their own goals. In the nondirective relationship, the primary emphasis on self-exploration precludes the counselor taking a more directive role such as might be necessary to suggest alternative employment opportunities or provide information on the job market. (There may be a few nondirective counselors who can play both roles, but we tend to doubt whether most could, or would, be interested in attempting to combine two such incompatible functions.)

The limitations to the clinical version of counseling are similar to those already listed for the testing approach.

Independent professional psychological consultants are most likely to combine the testing and clinical approaches into a package service for clients. Naturally, this is a relatively expensive professional service (although perhaps not in terms of the benefits to the client). The combined approach provides some internal basis for checking the information received: the client may be able to compare the counselor's perceptions with his or her test results, assuming that the counselor does not feel compelled to "see" the client in a manner consistent with the test results. Professional consultant firms may escape the incompatibility of the tester and counselor roles by having different people perform the two tasks.

The liabilities of the combined testing-clinical approach, again, are similar to those previously listed for the testing approach.

Boss as counselor or coach. Most organizations have formal performance appraisal systems, but as already noted, they tend to have certain chronic deficiencies. Personnel at the top and the bottom of the organization may not receive the intended benefits. More importantly, perhaps, the traditional performance appraisal is poorly designed to help employees correct deficiencies and plan their careers.[16] The superior is required to play both judge and helper simultaneously, and the subordinate is too defensive to "hear" constructive feedback. Research at General Electric indicated that, in fact, little change in behavior occurred as a result of this type of appraisal.

More informally, the boss might attempt to act as a "coach" for the subordinate. Where mutual trust is high and the subordinate does not feel intimidated by the superior's power, this might be an effective format for career planning. Coaching requires an unusually patient and dedicated boss, however, and one with both exceptional interpersonal skills and the determination to provide systematic coaching even when day-to-day business problems demand his or her attention elsewhere. Supervisory training programs have been developed in several companies to improve supervisors' skills in counseling and coaching. The primary advantage of the boss as coach or counselor is that the boss should have considerable knowledge of how the subordinate actually behaves on the job over long periods of time.

Management by objectives (MBO) is popular as an alternative to traditional performance appraisal in a growing number of organizations. MBO attempts to overcome many of the shortcomings of traditional performance appraisals by casting the superior in a helping role while the subordinate sets his or her own performance objectives and takes the lead in evaluating progress toward achieving these objectives. Some theorists recommend including goals for personal development as well as goals for organizational performance in setting of objectives. Others observe that this is seldom done, or if it is, it may constitute an invasion of privacy except when the personal goal component is purely voluntary.[17]

Our view is that MBO and career planning may complement each other in *some* organizations. However, most organizations are likely to find that MBO, alone, is an inadequate vehicle for career planning: MBO (and performance appraisal) works on a fairly short time perspective, while career planning is a long-range proposition. Moreover, most superiors are not adequately trained in providing the permissive, supportive atmosphere necessary for concentrated contemplation of life objectives, and the employee does not have the benefit of working in the group setting needed to verify feedback received. From the employee's perspective, it is not likely that either the traditional or MBO appraisal, or coaching, will provide information on career opportunities outside of the employing organization.

Group activities. Under the heading of group activities, we will discuss assessment centers and two types of life planning workshops. The common element in all of these techniques is that they all involve a group milieu; they all deal with counselees as a group to some extent, rather than leaving them to their own devices or approaching the career planning task in a dyadic counselor-client relationship. A fourth type of activity, the crisis-oriented workshop, will also be discussed, because it shares some of the characteristics of potentially productive career planning activities. Strictly speaking, however, the crisis workshop is not a career planning activity, because it is focused on resolving a single career crisis rather than providing periodic routine assessment of career progress and objectives.

Assessment centers, operated by the firm, as at AT&T, or provided by consulting firms, are presently very popular as aids to management in identifying promotion potential of managerial employees. Since most assessment centers provide for giving feedback to candidates (if they want it) at the end of the assessment, it would appear that the assessment center would facilitate career planning. The assessment center uses both paper and pencil and situational tests to develop a great deal of information about the candidate very quickly. Multiple judges or observers provide input into the assessment which can be provided to the employee. There is some evidence that the assessments in assessment centers are more valid than those provided by individual evaluators as in counselor-client relationships. The cost per employee (usually borne by the employer) is relatively modest.[18]

We suspect, however, that the assessment center, as frequently used, can be a poor medium for career planning. Given the lack of research on these issues, our conclusions reflect expectations based upon our theory, rather than conclusions drawn from empirical evidence.

The assessment center is a stressful experience for the participants,[19] which is unlikely to be conducive to receptiveness to constructive negative feedback. And, as all parties are perfectly aware, the assessment center's primary objective is to further the organization's interest in identifying high potential candidates for management. To the extent that the center serves the needs of the individual candidate, this latter function remains purely secondary. The activities of the center are designed to provide the employer with insight about the candidate's potential, rather than to help the participant understand him- or herself better.

Since attendance is frequently required,[20] most centers do not begin with participants voluntarily seeking opportunities to set objectives for themselves. The entire strategy is designed to help the organization fulfill its goals, which may or may not lead to meaningful outcomes for the participants. The involuntary character of the experience would, we predict, raise employees' defenses and discourage them from using the situation for productive career planning.

Finally, the assessment center is normally a one-shot treatment, rather than an experience repeated periodically as we hypothesize must be done to update and reconfirm career plans. However, a few firms appear to be moving toward periodic reassessment, a change which would enhance the value of the center in career planning. Moreover, there is probably considerable variation between programs, with some

more dedicated to providing feedback in a non-threatening, supportive atmosphere, which could also expand the center's usefulness in career planning.

There are a number of *group strategies for career planning,* generally known as "life planning" or "career planning" workshops which appear particularly promising as techniques for achieving the critical objectives we have identified for effective career planning. These group activities can provide a number of advantages not available in most of the approaches described previously. The idea for career planning workshops originated with pioneers in the T-group movement, particularly Herb Shepard, who foresaw the potential for using features of the T-group to increase career planning effectiveness.

The basic features of the group which contribute to more effective career planning deserve attention.

1. *Sources of information:* The leader and other participants can provide information on alternative solutions to career problems, job opportunities, or other new ideas which might not come to light without the additive resources of the group.

2. *Shared concerns:* Most people, unless given the opportunity to explore this issue in a group, assume that their own concerns and problems are unique and therefore all the more unresolvable. In the group, they find that others share a great many of their concerns, worries, and aspirations, decreasing the individual's sense of isolation and generating a realization that, since others *do* understand their problems, they will have the capability of providing relevant support and information for career planning.

3. *Shared responsibility for helping:* The group develops a norm that participants *should* help each other, emotionally and by supplying needed information. Thus, the group becomes a source of support for each participant, and, as our model would predict (see Figure 1), support leads to increased independent effort toward goal attainment.

4. *Development of social skills:* The group provides a secure experimental situation in which individuals can experiment with, rehearse, and learn new social skills, such as job interviewing, selling one's ideas, and getting along with a difficult boss.

5. *Modelling:* One of the important ways we learn new behavior is to imitate other people who behave in a way we would like to develop. The workshop leader and other participants may serve as important models for each other, and the workshop situation provides an environment where the individual may experiment with new behavior.

6. *Motivational impact:* The group setting provides not only the interpersonal feedback necessary to identity development, but also acts as a powerful *stimulant* for participants to deal constructively with fundamental issues. Experiences of confirmation or disconfirmation have a deep impact on the participant's self esteem and motivation to grow. Personal goals developed in the group are likely to be both challenging and realistic, and research indicates that commitment to achieving these goals will be higher.[21]

There are, of course, some drawbacks to the workshop approach to career planning. Some of both the advantages and limitations to the technique depend largely upon whether the workshop is an in-plant or company-sponsored activity just for the employees of that organization. The alternative is to conduct the workshop with participants from different organizations. This raises questions of the cost of the program and who pays for it. For the company, the cost per participant for sizable numbers of employees would be modest, perhaps comparable to the cost of an assessment center and less than for individual counseling. If individuals personally bear the cost, the outlay may represent a sizable dent in the household budget.

Crisis-oriented workshops. Before concluding, we would like to describe one other related type of workshop: the crisis-oriented workshop. Although not designed as a periodic or routine career planning experience, the format of these workshops generally follows the design of the career planning workshops already described.

Occasional accounts of workshops employing group-based organization development techniques to help individuals at a time of a career crisis may be found in the literature. One program was designed to help demoted sales managers adapt to their new assignments; another was aimed at assisting laid-off employees.[22] Generally the techniques and objectives of these

workshops are consistent with the requirements we see as necessary for productive career planning. They are, however, designed to deal with a single, unique situation, and therefore tend to concentrate on the short-term issues without provision for periodic reassessment and long-term objectives. Working through the potentially disabling anxieties of the participants to enable them to begin coping effectively is a major objective and requires a highly skilled leader with the patience and willingness to deal with these issues. For most firms, this will require obtaining external professional assistance.

The crisis-oriented workshop would seem to have little payoff to the organization if the affected employees are slated for termination. The motivation to sponsor such an activity must come from a management with unusually humanistic values and social consciousness. Over the long run, perhaps, and here no one can say for sure, there may be real benefits to the organization in terms of community image and morale among the employees who remain with the organization.

Issues in Career Planning

Managers who must decide whether the organization should allocate resources to a career planning workshop must weigh a number of important considerations.

1. Is the organization willing to sponsor an activity that might lead some employees to decide to leave the organization? (This might not be all bad in terms of the long-term savings in future frustrations and personnel problems not presently foreseen.)

2. If the organization sponsors career planning, to what extent can the organization integrate related activities such as performance appraisal and manpower planning to achieve a synergistic effect? Failure to take some action in this area would seem to increase the likelihood of a greater divergence between individual and organizational goals.

3. How frequently should career planning be made available? There is no research evidence to help the manager with this decision. Crisis situations such as demotions or early retirement programs clearly can be alleviated by development of a special workshop for this purpose. For

regular review of career plans, however, an interval of every two years seems intuitively appropriate.[23]

4. If the program is to be held in-house, should the participant groups be organized around intact working groups, or should they bring together persons from various parts of the organization? If intact groups are used, progress on the career planning activity may be delayed while the group works through interpersonal differences among members. On the other hand, if the organization is involved in organization development efforts, the career planning workshop can be a valuable adjunct to team-building activities. Organizing the groups by bringing together strangers from within the organization or sending employees to an external program should facilitate getting to the primary issues of career planning more quickly.

5. Should the internal program provide information to participants on job opportunities in other organizations? If the answer is affirmative, the organization may have to take special measures to assure that this information is systematically collected and disseminated. External programs which bring participants together from a number of organizations have some built-in capability in this regard.

6. The internal program has greater potential for building ongoing support groups as long as participants live in the same geographical area. This ongoing feature is more difficult to provide in an external program.

7. Should the organization build its own capability to provide the career planning workshop leadership, or should it rely on external consultants? The external consultant is probably less threatening and more credible to participants than an internal leader. A major concern which may also arise for an internal program, but especially where the leader is an employee of the organization, involves the issues of voluntariness and confidentiality. *Violation of either of these groundrules will most certainly destroy the usefulness of the program completely.*

8. Who should attend? If career planning is not provided to all employees, the organization may not tap potentially valuable resources at the operating level. Budget constraints and consideration of potential payoffs may dictate making the program available only to managerial and professional employees, however.

Deciding to provide a career planning workshop to employees would appear to have the potential for substantial payoffs to the employer in improving the productivity of employees. At the same time, undertaking such a program should only be done after management has given careful thought to the types of issues just raised. A one-shot, canned program approach can create serious difficulties later if management has not thought through these issues carefully.

Summing Up

Effectiveness in career planning depends, as we have seen, upon the individual's capacity to develop self-awareness and a strongly integrated core identity. Over time, this sense of identity is constantly challenged by demands of the job and other life roles. The proactive, independent person develops goals and objectives which lead to solution of these problems and increased personal effectiveness. Most people probably react more passively and less effectively.

In reviewing the possible approaches to career planning, we felt that there were distinct advantages to the organization which actively supports career planning on a regular periodic basis. Comparing the do-it-yourself approach, various forms of counseling or coaching strategies, and the use of career planning workshops, we feel some confidence in recommending that management seriously consider the workshops. The argument favoring the workshops rests primarily on the capacity of these types of programs to provide the support, feedback, modelling, and opportunity to experiment, conditions which are critical to a person's development. It is also important, though, that management insists upon research to *evaluate* any kind of career intervention attempted. Organizations that decide to take the lead in experimenting with this rather new technique may gain a considerable competitive edge in learning how to use their people more effectively and profitably by releasing the potential available when each employee becomes a more effective manager of his or her own career.

Acknowledgments: We are indebted to James A. Wilson and Larry E. Mainstone for their insightful comments on earlier drafts of this article.

REFERENCES

1. See D. Super, *The Psychology of Careers* (New York: Harper & Row, 1957) and S. B. Sarason, E. K. Sarason, and P. Cowden, "Aging and the Nature of Work," *American Psychologist* (Vol. 30, No. 5, 1975).

2. See E. H. Schein, "How Graduates Scare Bosses," *Careers Today* (Vol. 1, No. 1, 1968) and J. S. Livingston, "The Troubled Transition: Why College and University Graduates Have Difficulty Developing Careers in Business," *Journal of College Placement* (April-May 1970).

3. See E. E. Jennings, *The Executive in Crisis* (New York: McGraw-Hill, 1965); W. E. Henry, "Psychodynamics of the Executive Role," *American Journal of Sociology* (Vol. 54, No. 4, 1969); P. C. Cummin, "TAT Correlates of Executive Performance," *Journal of Applied Psychology* (Vol. 51, No. 1, 1967); and J. P. Campbell, M. D. Dunnette, E. E. Lawler, & K. E. Weick, *Managerial Behavior, Performance and Effectiveness* (New York: McGraw-Hill, 1970).

4. See L.I.A.M.A. *Recruitment, Selection, Training, and Supervision in Life Insurance* (Hartford: Life Insurance Agency Management Association, 1966) and J. P. Wanous, "Effects of Realistic Job Preview on Job Acceptance, Job Attitudes, and Job Survival," *Journal of Applied Psychology* (Vol. 58, No. 3, 1973).

5. See D. E. Berlew & D. T. Hall, "The Socialization of Managers: Effects of Expectations on Performance," *Administrative Science Quarterly* (Vol. 11, No. 3, 1966) and D. T. Hall and E. E. Lawler, "Unused Potential in Research and Development Organizations," *Research Management* (Vol. 12, No. 5, 1969).

6. See Hall and Lawler, op. cit., and Campbell et al., op. cit.

7. "Career Management Programs," *Personnel Journal* (Vol. 53, No. 3, 1974).

8. Erik Erikson, *Identity: Youth and Crisis* (New York: W. W. Norton, 1968), pp. 87; 132.

9. The term *subidentity* was introduced by Daniel Miller in "The Study of Social Relationships: Situation, Identity, and Social Interaction," in S. Koch (ed.), *Psychology: A Study of a Science* (New York: McGraw-Hill, 1973). For applications of the concept to the study of careers, see D. T. Hall, "A Model of Coping with Role Conflict: The Role Behavior of College Educated Women," *Administrative Science Quarterly* (Vol. 17, No. 4, 1972).

10. See K. Lewin, T. Dembo, L. Festinger, & P. Sears, "Levels of Aspiration" in J. McV. Hunt (ed.), *Personality and the Behavior Disorders* (New York: Ronald Press, 1944) and C. Argyris, *Integrating the Individual and the Organization* (New York: Wiley, 1964).

11. For further discussion of the development of the model, see D. T. Hall, "Potential for Career Growth," *Personnel Journal* (Vol. 34, No. 3, 1971) and D. T. Hall & F. S. Hall, "The Relationship Between Goals, Success, Self-Image and Involvement Under Different Organization Climates," *Journal of Vocational Behavior* (1977, in press).

12. C. Bolles, *What Color is Your Parachute?* (Berkeley, Calif.: Ten Speed Press, 1972).

13. See W. F. Glueck, *Personnel: A Diagnostic Approach* (Dallas: Business Publications, 1974).

14. See R. T. Golembiewski, *Renewing Organizations: The Laboratory Approach to Planned Change* (Itasca, Ill.: Peacock, 1972).

15. See J. P. Siegel, "The Subject Evaluates the Test: Knowledge of Results and the Self-Concept," *Proceedings,* 77th Annual Convention, American Psychological Association, 1969.

16. See D. McGregor, "An Uneasy Look at Performance Appraisal," *Harvard Business Review* (Vol. 35, No. 3, 1957) and H. H. Meyer, E. Kay, and J. R. P. French, Jr., "Split Roles in Performance Appraisal," *Harvard Business Review* (Vol. 43, No. 1, 1965).

17. See H. L. Tosi, J. R. Rizzo, and S. J. Carroll, "Setting Goals in Management by Objectives," *California Management Review* (Summer 1970) and H. Levinson, "Management by Whose Objectives?" *Harvard Business Review* (Vol. 48, No. 4, 1970).

18. The A. T. & T. program is described in D. W. Bray, R. J. Campbell, and D. L. Grant, *Formative Years in Business: A Long-term AT&T Study of Management Lives* (New York: Wiley, 1974). The popularity of the assessment center is documented by Campbell et al., op. cit., and Glueck, op. cit. The provisions for feedback are described in W. C. Byham, "The Assessment Center as an Aid in Management Development," *Training and Development Journal* (December 1971), and research on the effectiveness of assessment centers is summarized in A. Howard, "An Assessment of Assessment Centers," *Academy of Management Journal* (Vol. 17, No. 1, 1974).

19. See Byham, op. cit., and Howard, op. cit.

20. See Byham, op. cit.

21. See K. Lewin, "Group Decision and Social Change," in G. E. Swanson, T. M. Newcomb, and F. L. Hartley (eds.), *Readings in Social Psychology*, rev. ed. (New York: Holt, 1952).

22. For descriptions of applications, see Golembiewski, op. cit., and G. F. J. Lehner, "From Job Loss to Career Innovation," in W. W. Burke (ed.), *Contemporary Organization Development: Conceptual Orientations and Interventions* (Washington, D.C.: National Institute for Applied Behavioral Science, 1972).

23. See E. F. Huse, *Organization Development and Change* (St. Paul: West Publishing, 1975).

24. See J. K. Fordyce and R. Weil, *Managing with People* (Reading, Mass.: Addison-Wesley, 1971).

Appendix. Characteristics of Various Career Planning Activities and Probable Contribution to Career Success

Activity	Potential Advantages	Potential Shortcomings	Probable Impact on Psychological Success and Identity Integration
Individual Activities			
1. Personal planning with possible aid of self-help materials.	a. For persons with strong motivation and adequate sources of information, may be adequate for goal setting. b. Cost is minimal	a. Most people need interpersonal feedback to develop a complete and accurate self-evaluation. b. No built-in mechanism for checking completeness of information on occupational opportunities or for correcting distorted views of self. c. No opportunity to explore new occupational possibilities.	Considerable potential contribution because individual sets own goals. Actual contribution likely to be minimized, however, because the activity lacks mechanisms for exploration of new potentials, interpersonal feedback, and social support to maintain motivation.
Counselor-Client Activities			
2. Testing Approach: Guidance counselor administers vocational interest and aptitude tests and feeds data back to client—may also provide information on occupations, job market, and job-hunting techniques.	Test results and information supplied may be of considerable value for client.	a. Usually expensive. b. Client has no way of testing validity of counselor's views or test results. c. Interpersonal feedback likely to be minimal.	Since people do not readily accept disconfirming data in situations where there is no opportunity to validate the information, contribution may be relatively limited.
3. Counselor Approach: Emphasis on interpersonal exploration of client's needs with counsellor.	Skillful counselor may provide valuable input for self-assessment.	a. No mechanism for checking validity of counselor's perceptions. b. Most helpful in exploring personal needs; minimal stress on occupational information. c. Usually expensive.	Potentially helpful, subject to the limitations that client must experience insights produced as valid and must check validity with other persons outside of the counseling situation.
4. Combination Testing and Clinical Approach	a. Combines benefits of both Testing and Counseling Approaches b. Checking test results against perceptions of counselor provides some mechanism for "validating" information.	a. Potentially very expensive. b. Most counsellors are not equally proficient in both approaches. c. Counselor may experience a need to see client in a manner consistent with test results.	Essentially the same as for #3.
Boss as Counselor or Coach			
5. Superior regularly or periodically assesses subordinate's performance and provides feedback and suggestions for improving performance and/or career opportunities.	a. Superior may have an excellent opportunity to observe subordinate's behavior in a number of work activities.	a. The superior's power can be highly threatening, causing subordinate to be defensive, cautious, and closed to feedback.	a. If done as a part of performance appraisal, depends on format. Traditional performance appraisal unlikely to be productive. MBO with substantial self-evaluation by subordinate may be helpful, since subordinate sets own goals, etc., and takes lead in assessment.

Activity	Potential Advantages	Potential Shortcomings	Probable Impact on Psychological Success and Identity Integration
	b. Superior knows career opportunities within the organization. c. Superior can provide assignments to expand subordinate's capabilities.	b. Superior's first loyalty is likely to be seen as to the interests of the organization, not subordinate. c. Not likely to integrate nonwork aspects of subordinate's life with career issues.	b. If done as informal coaching, can be very effective to the extent that superior provides relatively nondirective assistance which maximizes subordinate's freedom to choose.

Group Activities

6. **Assessment Center:** usually conducted by or sponsored by employer. Employee is tested by a number of pencil and paper tests and is presented with situational tests and interviews where performance is observed and evaluated. Evaluators are often other managers trained in the technique. Psychologists design Center and interpret test results.	a. Substantial amounts of data can be developed quickly.
	
	b. Multiple judges on panel and results of several tests provide variety of perspectives for candidate.
	
	c. Moderate cost—usually borne by employer.
	
	d. Some evidence for more valid predictions than available through Counselor-Client Approaches.
		a. High threat situation:
		  1. Employee likely to feel "on the spot" and anxious about results—not an optimal situation for feedback.
		  2. Center serves interests of employer first, which may be incompatible with interests of employee.
		
		b. Primary emphasis is not on setting of personal goals.
		
		c. Data generated primarily applicable to career with employing organization, only.
		
		d. Interpersonal feedback frequently not a prime or major objective.
		
		e. Does not provide information on other job possibilities especially outside of employing organization.
			a. Likely to be minimized to the extent that employee:
			  – cannot really choose not to attend.
			  – Is not involved in design of activities.
			  – Is threatened by long-term career implications of evalution.
			  – Receives minimal or threatening feedback.
			
			b. No explicit provision for goal-setting.
			
			c. No support group for planning or dealing with career crises.

Activity	Potential Advantages	Potential Shortcomings	Probable Impact on Psychological Success and Identity Integration
7. Life Planning Workshop: Conducted within Organization. A set of semistructural experiences are presented which encourage participants to assess their values, situation, etc., to set goals, and to develop greater self-awareness through interpersonal interaction with other participants.	a. No cost to participant. b. Encourages personal goal setting. c. Wide exploration of self and needs encouraged. Copious interpersonal feedback generated. d. Supportive environment. e. Development of "supportive groups" and opportunities to assess and develop job-relevant skills possible. f. Other participants are frequently valuable sources of information on career alternatives. g. Goals developed and development needs can be integrated into parallel organizational programs. h. Can be a part of an organization development effort.	a. Normally do not provide occupational information, especially for careers outside of the organization. b. Employers leery of processes which may encourage employees to leave organization. c. Provision for periodic follow-up probably necessary to maximize value to most participants. d. Participants may not be encouraged to explore changing jobs or careers.	a. Specifically designed to provide identity integration and psychological success through personal goal-setting and enhanced self-awareness. b. If conducted within organization benefits may be somewhat limited by need for program to serve employer's needs and by reluctance of employees to open up in groups of colleagues. c. Only design which explicitly requires small group design to maximize feedback and opportunity to validate data.
8. Life Planning Workshop: Conducted outside of organization.	a. Same as b through g, above. b. Low threat situation. c. Potential for developing job-hunting skills possible.	a. Moderate cost to participants unless underwritten by employer. b. Normally do not provide occupational information on job markets, nature of jobs, etc. c. See b and c, above.	a. See a and c, above.

A highly organized and precise procedure for hiring programmers provides the maximum in objectivity, efficiency, speed, and hopefully success

A STRUCTURED APPROACH TO HIRING

by Trevor J. Swanson and John J. Devore

The need to hire two Programmer II's (a classified position defined by the State of Kansas) for the Kansas State Univ. computing center resulted in the adoption of a very structured approach to fill the positions. It was hoped a structured approach would elicit the greatest amount of information to base a decision upon and, thus, lead to a more objective decision.

Pressure to make an objective and reliable choice of candidates to fill the positions came primarily from two sources. There was a wealth of well-qualified people to choose from and affirmative action guidelines had to be strictly followed. Further, because the need for help was critical, we hoped to find, interview, evaluate, and hire in the space of two weeks. Names of candidates for Programmer II positions at KSU are supplied by the state of Kansas in the form of a list of five eligible candidates per position. The state determines eligibility by candidates' scores on a test similar to IBM's Programming Aptitude Test (PAT). Those familiar with PAT know that this method of evaluating programmers, or programming potential, ranks right beside divination in its reliability. So we needed information more significant than the PAT score about each person on the list of eligible candidates.

The general rule-of-thumb for meeting affirmative action guidelines is that a minority candidate is hired if all else

between two candidates appears equal. Obviously, technical and experiential equality is a difficult condition to judge in an objective manner, and objective judgments are not only hard to justify but frequently less than exceptional in quality. Trying to make this judgment in an objective manner resulted in the inclusion of technical, structured questions in the actual interview process.

It may be useful to define our concept of structured hiring before dealing with the individual steps in detail. By "structured" we mean highly organized. There was an overall organization to the procedure: creating position descriptions, scheduling the interviews, specific steps in the actual interview, a post interview process, an evaluation, and a specific format for notifi-

"Not only do we have a great retirement plan, but also our employees age more quickly."

cation of candidates. Since time was short, we planned to complete the process within a week and a half (and we almost succeeded). There was also a structured approach to the actual interviews which had specific preliminary steps, a particular format for the physical setting, and an organized recording of information about candidates. Further, the interview questions were common for all interviewees and structured according to information sought.

Creating position descriptions was the first step in the overall procedure (see box for a description of one of the two positions). As far as possible, the descriptions reflected the true nature of the work to be performed. Thus, the most carefully contrived part of the description was that dealing with job duties. The exercise of creating the description had the additional advantage of compelling both a thorough examination of the nature of the work presently constituting the duties for the Programmer II, and also a careful look at what future work should be.

The second, and major, part of the process was to conduct the actual interviews. An hour and a half was allowed for each candidate. This generally broke down to 15 minutes of preparatory work, an hour of questioning, and a 15-minute individual post-interview analysis. All of the candidates were interviewed through a two-day period.

During the 15 minutes spent in pre-interview planning, each candidate, located in another office, was asked to fill out or update a very brief employment form. The pre-interview time can be varied for each candidate depending upon the length of time it was anticipated he/she would need to complete the form. The candidate was also given the detailed position descriptions to study prior to being questioned.

Two interviewers and a recorder (secretary) were present during the interview. An attempt was made to have all concerned sit *around* a desk so that the questioning would seem less like an inquisition. A tape recording of each interview was also made to facilitate the interviewers' occasional reconstruction of questions and answers. (Only one tape was reviewed. One candidate failed to adequately answer a technical question, and the recording was used to determine if the question was clearly stated by the interviewers. It had been.) Each candidate was asked at the outset of the interview if the recording would be a bother. Although currently an act of ill repute on the national scene, none of the candidates objected to being taped. Each

---

Name of Interviewee: _____
Interviewer: _____
Date: _____

Interviewer

1. What courses have you taken in computer science? Describe the kind of computer science work and the breadth of the total academic work.
2. What paid work experience do you have? What kind of interaction with people did you have in these work experiences? Responsibility? Authority?
3. What kind of service have you provided to others—community or other service in high school or college? Leadership positions held?
4. Do you have ideas about the form that continued professional development should take? Do you have specific plans to continue your formal education?
5. Have you made a technical presentation to more than 20 persons? What experience have you had writing?
6. How do you go about creating internal documentation for a source program? Describe the user documentation and the technical program documentation necessary for a program or system.
7. Have you had experience doing consulting work? Please describe this experience. Have you had experience doing programming work, significant programming projects in the classroom, or any computer-related experience for which pay was gained?
8. If you were given the task of copying one tape to another, how would you do it? What is the extent of your use of library programs?
9. What operating system language experience, experience with file systems, tape, or disc have you had?
10. What do you do when you begin to debug your output?
11. If a wrong result is obtained from a program without any diagnostic errors, what advice would you give to proceed?
12. Describe the debugging aids of various languages you know.
13. When would you advise a rerun without changing the program?
14. Under what conditions would you advise getting an object deck as opposed to a load module?
15. What are the relative merits of modular code as opposed to in-line coding?

In which positions are you interested?

Perform appropriate set(s) of questions

Information services applicants only

1. What is your statistical experience? Course work? What is: a dependent variable; an independent variable; an observation?
2. An individual who has data with missing values is in need of advice. What advice would you give him?
3. What experience do you have in numerical analysis? Course work?
4. What sources of applications software do you know of?
5. What do you know about program library organization schemes (manual and machine oriented)?
6. What is your experience with program, subroutines, and procedure libraries?
7. What experience do you have with CAI, CMI and other uses of the computer for instructional purposes?

General questions

16. What is the basic principle of structured programming?
17. What is the basic principle of top-down coding?
18. Indicate the structure of a large general-purpose third generation computer.
19. Indicate the purpose of a paging algorithm.
20. What is a virtual machine?
21. What do you think you can contribute to the computing center?

Interview Questions.

interviewer would ask three or four logically interconnected questions in a row, although either would interrupt at any time in order to ask the candidate to enlarge upon a particular question.

Upon encountering questions which pertained strictly to one or the other position, the candidate was allowed to express his/her inclination to apply for both positions, or one of the two. At this time, the candidates were also asked if they had further questions about either of the two positions or duties thereof. Since the managers of the involved sections were doing the interviewing, they individually asked the questions pertaining to their positions.

The questions were of two major kinds: general questions eliciting background and career plans, and technical questions. Of the general questions, there were a certain number of the mom and apple pie variety:

"What do you think you can contribute to the Kansas State Univ. computing center?"

"Will you be involved in community service activities of any kind as a permanent resident of this area?"

"How does this job fit into your overall career plans?"

This kind of question was generally asked toward the end of the interview.

Candidates were asked general information questions at the beginning of the interview. Some of these questions were:

"What courses have you taken in computer science?"

"What degrees do you now hold?"

"What is your overall grade point average for these degrees?"

"What paid programming experience do you have?"

This kind of question was asked at the beginning to allow the candidate to become familiar with the situation while answering direct, obvious questions which had just been encountered on the employment form; i.e., these questions were designed to relax the candidate while he/she adjusted to the interview process and the interviewers.

Technical questions, both "situational" and "informational," were also asked. An example of a situational question for the information services position was:

"Given the situation that a graduate student approaches you, indicating that his advisor has sent him over to have the computer analyze his data, what steps would you take to handle the situation?"

Another was:

"How would you handle a situation where a user asked your opinion of the best library routine to handle a particular analysis? Assume you are aware of the routines available in your library and several available across the country."

One technical information question took the form of asking the candidate to write a short deck listing program. This was prefaced by the questions:

"What programming languages are you familiar with? In what special languages or systems are you proficient? Examples: ECAP, minicomputers, COGO, EISPACK."

The interviewer then requested:

"In the language you feel most comfortable using, write a complete program to read records from the card

---

Programmer II
Information Services
Full time, permanent
Shift: 8 a.m.-12 Noon, 1 p.m.-5 p.m.
Starting date—December 15-January 1

Percentage of time | **Duties**

40-50% **Program Set-up, Execution, and Verification:** Performs the necessary programming, scheduling, and verification of computing activities for center users primarily using library routines. Involves working with packaged statistical systems such as Statistical Package for the Social Sciences (SPSS) and the BMD series.

25-30% **User Interaction:** Assists the manager of information services in the interaction with computing center users concerning the availability, selection, and recommendation of library routines. In specific areas of expertise, independent interaction with users will be performed. Provide assistance with technical problems concerning the use of library programs. Special emphasis is given to statistical and mathematical analysis and test scoring and grade book analysis. Other useful knowledge includes computer aided instruction course preparation, numerical analysis, and mapping.

10-15% **System Evaluation and Recommendation:** Participates in the evaluation of the computing center's needs for library program modification and acquisition. Performs detailed technical and financial analyses necessary for support of recommendations concerning library programs. Perceptive to user problems which cause difficulties because of library documentation facilities, procedures, or administrative practice.

10-15% **Development and Maintenance of the Machine-readable Libraries:** In particular, development of analytical tools to measure library use and effectiveness, testing of library programs, correcting or updating library routines, providing user aids in the form of keyword indices, and providing other retrieval aids.

5-10% **Technical Writing:** Participation in the preparation and editing of the Users Guide and the Newsletter, user oriented descriptions of library routines and user guidelines to technical procedures, and program logic documentation.

Programmer II position description.

| | Tech-nical | Commu-nication ability | Experience | | Course work | Degrees | GPA | Apparent attitude | Maturity | Documen-tation experience | Recom-menda-tions | Career plans | List deck program |
			kind	depth									
Ms. Gamine													
Mr. Blatherskite													
Ms. Seraphic													
Mr. Galoot													
Mr. Ambsace													
Ms. Brandex													

Fig. 1. Candidate/quality grid.

reader and print those records on a printer."

Both interviewers had room on their pre-typed list of questions to briefly note answers given by the candidate.

Immediately after each interview, a brief evaluation was made while particular answers were still fresh in our minds. To facilitate this process a grid sheet (Fig. 1, page 59) was used with a score of 1 (low) to 5 (high) given for each candidate/quality. Although the qualities were discussed by the interviewers, each had a grid sheet in which to record an independent judgment. If it had been subsequently discovered that a wide gap existed in the scores given by the two interviewers, the tapes could have been used to arbitrate differences.

After all the actual interviews had been conducted, the most subjective part of the hiring process had to be accomplished; one candidate had to be selected for each position. Obviously the numbers on the grid sheet could not simply be added, as this would be analogous to adding apples, oranges, and elephants; the result would be meaningless. A suitable formula with proper weighting for different candidate qualities could be derived, but this is not only a questionable process in dealing with humans but also one that is probably unnecessary.

Selection was easily narrowed to two or three candidates for each position on the basis of interview answers and technical background considerations. Candidates were finally selected by eliminating equivalent qualities from consideration and carefully analyzing the available information on the remaining qualities of each candidate. This selection process was formalized by having the manager of each section involved send a justification for his selection, in the form of a memo, to the associate director of the computing center.

After the selected candidates were offered and had accepted the positions via telephone, others were notified that they had not been selected. This was done by phone so that they could consider other opportunities at the earliest possible time. In addition, formal letters of notification were mailed soon after the phone calls.

Several random observations about this structured hiring process might be made. First, there was a surprising degree of agreement between the interviewers regarding the relative qualities of individual candidates. Second, we learned that the questions should be even more structured than they were. For instance, it was rather devastating for candidates to be asked for definitions of an "independent variable" and a "dependent variable" after they had revealed no knowledge of statistics. Lower level questions should be skipped if the preceding level question reveals no knowledge of a subject. Merely outlining the questions with appropriate indentions would be a considerable help in alleviating this problem.

The structured approach to hiring enabled us to swiftly, reasonably objectively, and successfully fill vacancies where the need was critical. We are now in the process of hiring a Computer Operator Trainee and a Programmer I using the same procedure. Further, the administrative data processing dept. on campus has adopted the procedure in order to hire four Programmer I's. The final success of this structured approach to hiring will be revealed by the success of selected candidates in their respective positions. Only time will tell whether the choices were wise, but the reaction of those involved, including applicants, indicates that the success of the method will exceed our initial expectations. □

Dr. Swanson is manager of information services at the Kansas State Univ. computing center, and is an instructor of computer science there. Previously with the Univ. of California at Irvine, he has a PhD from Southern Illinois Univ.

Mr. Devore is manager of programming services at the Kansas State Univ. computing center. He has been in the computer field since 1968, and his past experience includes systems programming and user consulting.

Investing in New Employees

by Charles Siegel

There is more to hiring than just finding someone likeable, and more to training programmers than just teaching how to code.

What do a 47 year old librarian, a 30 year old clergyman, a 29 year old clerk, a 27 year old Math Ph.D. and a 22 year old college graduate have in common? They were all participants in United States Fidelity & Guaranty Company's entry-level programmer/analyst training program, a program that enabled the firm to expand its staff nearly threefold in less than three years without the usual problems of high attrition and delayed productivity.

USF&G is a large multi-line insurance company headquartered in Baltimore. Its premium sales are just under $1 billion, and its subsidiary, Fidelity & Guaranty Life, has just under $3 billion in insurance policies in force. The company serves its nationwide clientele through 61 branch offices, but has centralized its data processing in its home office. Branches communicate with the dp center's IBM 370/158 and 145 through intelligent terminals.

When the company decided in 1971 to automate many of its policy-writing and policy maintenance functions, and to build an on-line system for its life insurance subsidiary, the application development staff had 32 persons, too few to do the job required. Now the staff has 109. In making the transition from 32 to 109 persons, 79 inexperienced trainees were hired and put through a new kind of training program. Though not all 79 are still with the company, the majority of them are. Further, those new hires became productive employees in a relatively short period. Both facts, the high employee retention and fast productivity, can be attributed to the success of that training program.

It was apparent from the beginning of the expansion that much of the hiring would have to be of trainees, for two reasons. First, we could not find enough experienced persons looking for jobs at the time. Second, USF&G's past experience indicated that the job longevity of most experienced personnel was not high. With few exceptions, experienced people tend to leave one installation for the same reasons they left the one before. (The exceptions are people who have been forced to move to Baltimore, usually because their spouses were moved there, or very bright individuals stuck in shops where seniority rules. In any case, there were not enough of these two groups to meet USF&G's demands for people.)

Actually, the firm's experience with retaining trainees had also been bleak. Trainees had previously been hired one at a time and trained using courses available from outside vendors. That method was ineffective. Trainees were not able to become productive quickly enough, and often left before ever becoming productive. USF&G has been able to alter that picture, however, by paying careful attention to all three phases of the process of adding employees to the staff: selection, training, and placement.

Selection

In the past, USF&G used the IBM Programmer Aptitude Test (PAT) as a screening device, considering for employment any applicants who passed. A later analysis of the performance of these people showed that the candidates who did poorly on the test did poorly as programmers, but that the candidates who did well on the test might do well as programmers or poorly. USF&G has since established the PAT as an initial screening device only and requires candidates to score an "A" on it. The PAT is given to any candidate who requests it. Employees of the corporation are given identical consideration as non-employees and must meet all of the requirements, including the "A" grade. No further testing is used.

All those candidates who score an "A" are scheduled for an interview, which is the most important part of the selection process. There are at least four people present with the applicant at the interview; two of the five user division managers, the data processing education coordinator, and the training class coordinator. At times, the systems and programming manager also sits in. The two division managers are rotated so that all five interview an equal number of candidates and so all division managers interview with all others.

The interview is scheduled for an hour, in which time the interviewers attempt to determine something about the candidate's job longevity, verbal facility, personality, curiosity, maturity, judgment, drive, motivation, growth potential and community orientation. The greatest importance is placed on growth potential, motivation, drive, and longevity. To measure these qualities, the interviewers have access to the candidates' school records dating back to high school. Course content and grades play an important part in determining these four traits. For example, if a candidate does poorly in one major but well in another, this *may* show lack of drive. Did he do poorly because he did not like the material and wasn't willing to work hard enough? Summer employment during college is considered a plus. Nonsocial or nonathletic extracurricular activity are also found to be traits of a good employee.

The tone of the interview changes from stress at the beginning to a friendly around-the-table discussion at the end. (Although some feel that stress interviewing is poor, it has been successful at USF&G.) At the conclusion of the interview, the interviewers discuss the candidate and individually write a critique of him.

Weekly, the eight-person interview team meets for selecting candidates. All decisions on whether to make an offer must be unanimous. In the earlier selection sessions, the candidates are split into three groups. Those to whom we will make offers, those we will not make offers to, and those with whom we will conduct further interviews. At the last session, the final offers are made and an ordered waiting list of five names is constructed.

That is how USF&G selects, but there is a significant question of whom to

NEW EMPLOYEES

select. There isn't any magic formula. In the first class we held, we made what we now consider a mistake by hiring 10 young men right out of college. (See Table 1.) Five of them left within 12 months.

In our second class, we tried to hire the 15 brightest people we could find. We accepted one applicant with only an A.A. degree but with a grade point average of 4.0. All the rest had higher degrees, including some M.A.'s, M.S.'s, and Ph.D.'s. The average undergraduate grade point average, of the candidates who received a bachelor's degree, was 3.43. There was no question that the goal of hiring the brightest people we could find was achieved. The performance of this class has since justified its promise. We then became concerned that there might be too many chiefs and no indians. In the next class, we opted for less talented people. Although we did not hire 15 indians, the class definitely was not as talented as its predecessor. We now feel that hiring less qualified people was a mistake. *You should hire the best qualified people even if you end up with all chiefs!* The chief will write better code quicker, will become productive earlier, and, even if he quits to become a chief in someone else's shop, he will leave lasting work.

The USF&G training program has clearly shown that the best candidate for a successful career in programming is a college graduate who has spent several years in another discipline and decides on a career change. These trainees have shown a clear perseverance and bring a maturity to the shop that is not found in candidates who have had no prior work experience. Our worst results have been with men right out of college who never worked before. Women out of college show better longevity than their male counterparts, especially those with math or science majors. And a considerable success has been achieved by people switching from the teaching professions, especially high school science teachers. It is impossible to select on these guidelines, of course, because there are always exceptions like excellent programmers who were men just out of college.

We have hired high school graduates through Ph.D.'s. We make no distinction between the education level once they are hired. All candidates start at the same salary with no exception. Our experience has shown that those with advanced degrees progress faster than those with bachelor's degrees, and those with bachelor's degrees progress faster than those with high school diplomas. However, again there are ex-

ceptions. If proper care is taken, a high school graduate can have excellent success.

Training

At the time we begin interviewing candidates for the training class, we also interview application development personnel who volunteer to work on the "faculty." USF&G is fortunate in having several ex-high school and college teachers who have enabled us to bring professional teaching, with excellent knowledge of data processing, to the classroom. Some members of our faculty have participated in more than one of the classes even though they are not relieved of their regular duties to teach.

There are four application development people on the faculty for each class. Though some of them have had prior teaching experience, all are required to attend teachers' training seminars put on by the corporate education department. This includes their being videotaped while teaching.

Two people serve especially important roles in the training. One is the data processing education coordinator, a senior level dp person whose fulltime job is to assure adequate professional education for the class in all aspects of data processing, not just application development.

The other is the class coordinator, a middle level application development staff member. Very critical to the success of the program, it is he (or she in our case) who sets the tone for the

class. She acts as supervisor, assigns lab problems, checks code written by students, keeps records, and administers tests. She has a strong voice in the final placement of trainees and files a full critique of each.

The nature of the position of class coordinator makes it necessary to relieve that person of regular duties for five months (for testing, interviewing, teaching, and followup). This puts the person "behind" other programmers who do not interrupt their careers, but the added experience of supervising 15 people proves valuable later, and the coordinators do recover from their absence.

We believe it is important that on the first hour of the first day the class become involved in programming, therefore the class members clear new hire paperwork during the week before the class starts. When the students enter the classroom, they have all the necessary manuals, pads and other tools of their trade. They are introduced to the faculty and begin immediately to learn data processing fundamentals.

The class day is split into nine periods. Each period on each day is preplanned, so the class knows what subject will be covered on what day.

In the nine-week course, the trainees learn data processing fundamentals, introduction to system 370, os/vs concepts, os/vs JCL, os/vs dump reading, documenting procedures, os/vs utilities and sort merge, linkage editor, advanced JCL, and a USF&G subset of

Candidates Screened for Training Classes					
	June 1972	June 1973	January 1974	July 1974	December 1974
Took PAT	77	150	108	178	187
Passed PAT	48	87	67	127	88
Interviewed	42	82	65	111	78
Offers	21	17	17	21	17
Total hired	15	16	15	17	16
Men hired	10	8	8	8	6
Women hired	5	8	7	9	10

Table 1. The Programmer Aptitude Test is the first step in USF&G's screening. Candidates must score an "A." During the course of the five classes, the proportion of men to women hired has been nearly reversed. (The numbers for the January '74 class are smaller because the class was announced late.)

Employees Retained After Training								
	Start		Left Within 12 Months		Left Within 18 Months		Still Employed	
	M	F	M	F	M	F	M	F
June 1972	10	5	5	0	6	1	4	3
June 1973	8	8	0	0	0	0	6	8
January 1974	8	7	0	0	2	0	6	7
July 1974	8	9	1	1	1	1	7	8
December 1974	6	10	1	0	0	0	5	10

Table 2. For the first class, twice as many men were hired as women. Most of these were fresh college graduates, and half left within one year. The firm learned from the experience. Most of the employees hired for the next class are still with the company now, more than two years later.

COBOL. The trainees learn that they can only use the GO TO statement to exit from a performed paragraph, that no numbers can appear in the procedure division and other things associated with a full structured concept of programming. Their first program is structured, and all code they write is structured because they know no other way. The trainees are also put into teams and are encouraged to work together on their projects.

The curriculum includes labs, lectures, and business courses, given in a mix to prevent boredom. Toward the end of the nine weeks, lab courses predominate.

In addition to data processing training, the trainees are given insurance courses and must pass a basic insurance exam to graduate from the program. It is unfortunate that data processors often consider themselves technicians in their discipline instead of bankers, manufacturers or whatever they are employed at. This leads to data processors having great data processing loyalty and little or no industry loyalty. To overcome this, in addition to the insurance program, we bring department heads from user departments to the class to explain to the trainees what the user's function is in the corporation. In addition to making the trainee feel a part of the enterprise, it gives the user manager an early introduction to the data processing personnel who will be dealing with him in the future. This has been a very rewarding aspect of the training program.

Placement

At the beginning of the last week of the class, the five division managers meet to put in their requests for the trainees. These requests are not for a particular individual, but for the type of person they need. Since the trainees have had a very successful history, there are usually more requests than trainees, and disputes are arbitrated by the systems and programming manager.

Before the class graduates, the systems and programming manager meets with the class coordinator and the faculty to assign the trainees to their groups. A strong attempt is made to match the trainees' strengths and weaknesses with the future supervisor's strengths and weaknesses. Care is also taken to break up training class cliques if any exist.

The next morning, the students are told of their assignments and spend the rest of the morning with their new supervisors. This gives them the continuity they need to go from the highly charged and organized training state to the sometimes chaotic real world at-mosphere. When they reach their permanent desk the Monday after the class, there will be an assignment waiting for them.

The results—it pays off

Not everyone that the course touches automatically turns into a super programmer. The selection process has been good enough, however, that only two trainees were encouraged to try something else. (One of them went into another field; the other went to another company.) Of those who complete the course, there are also mixed degrees of success. Although we attempt to teach programming—by having the students produce several iterations of their program designs on scratch sheets before even translating them to COBOL—only about the top third of the class will mature into top "programmers;" we must also admit that many of the bottom third will be "coders." Almost all of them become productive employees within three months of completing the class, however.

As a junior programmer, he will be assigned to work with a more experienced programmer, perhaps in a team. Frequently the senior person serves as a resource to the new programmer in helping to better structure his code.

The only problem we have encountered is one of the trainee having to do maintenance on a non-structured program. We have succeeded in turning this to our advantage because it is usually easier for the new programmer to rewrite the code in question then attempt to do maintenance on it. In this way we are reducing the cost of future maintenance and have already seen a noticeable reduction in present maintenance costs.

The result of this training program has been the development of a well-trained staff that shows excellent potential for good longevity with USF&G (see Table 2). In the first class, the five men who left within 12 months were all just out of college and had never worked before. All of those five went to work "next door" for more money. Of the other people who were trainees and left, with one exception, all left USF&G either to move out of town or because they decided the data processing business did not fit them. The two 1973 trainees who left moved out of town and obtained positions in the business which were normally reserved for people with twice their experience.

There are also some fringe benefits to the training program. There is an *esprit de corps* among the class that continues long after their training program ends. It manifests itself in anniversary lunches and such and, more important to the corporation, in the passing of knowledge from group to group. As in all large installations, it is difficult to keep all programmers informed even with informal newsletters and formal updates to standards manuals. The class groups, with their informal system of information exchange, see to it that new techniques developed in one area quickly spread through the shop.

The cost of this program is relatively high, due partly to the amount of time spent interviewing prospective candidates. We spend roughly 1,000 hours interviewing candidates for each class, and another 1,000 hours in instruction. Computer costs for the class run about $4,500. Therefore the cost of selecting students and teaching the course is roughly $29,500, or about $2,000 per trainee. Trainee salaries for the period are $1,400, making the total investment in each employee $3,400.

The cost of hiring through headhunters, for comparison, is not much lower. We used headhunters for about two years. Not only were the employees supplied usually of low quality, but they stayed less than two years on the average. Headhunter fees averaged $2,000. Employment costs ran approximately $500 more, and relocation expenses sometimes added $1,000 more. We feel training is cheaper than using headhunters, especially considering that the trained employees already know our programming techniques and even a little about USF&G's way of doing business.

We now have reached the staff size necessary for our workload. With our low turnover rate, we do not know when we will need another class. But our success has been good enough that we plan to further lower our recruitment of experienced people, and to conduct classes of inexperienced people instead when we need more staff. It pays. ❋

Mr. Siegel is systems and programming manager at United States Fidelity and Guaranty Company, where his previous responsibility was as project manager in the development of a full life insurance policy-writing, daily maintenance and valuation system. He is also active in SHARE.

TRAINING PROGRAMMERS UNDER SIMULATED "LIVE" CONDITIONS

Mr. E. R. Dolan
Western Electric
Lisle, Illinois

Dept. 7233

This paper discusses a unique training process
designed to bring inexperienced programmers on
board a technical project quickly and effectively. The nature of the project is
described along with the inadequacies that
surfaced with previous training techniques.
The major portion of the paper is devoted to
a step by step description of the training
method. Included are the inputs, outputs,
software tools, and specifications required
to complete the procedure. Finally, the
overall benefit that has resulted from
programmers completing this training is
summarized.

Customers from a number of suburban and rural
telephone offices are serviced by Western
Electric Electronic Software Systems called
No. 2(2B) ESS. There are currently 570
such offices in service. Part of the
software used to run the No. 2 ESS machine
is generated by a Translation Data Table
Generation (TDTG) System. The function of
the No. 2 TDTG is to construct the initial
data structures used by the call processing
programs (generic program) and to subsequently
grow the office at periodic intervals.

TDTG programs build the telephone office data
base (i.e., translations) by processing input
supplied by telephone company engineers.
Input and translations data produced are
derived from definitions, rules, and output
table layouts produced by Bell Laboratories.
The output is structured into a variety of
variable sized data tables. These data
tables are combined into one file (functional
listing) for purposes of hardcopy review.
The functional listing can be thought of as a
snapshot of all the data within an ESS machine
at the time the TDTG system ran. This data
is represented in octal format with each word
containing 8 digits. The output layout of
a data table could be illustrated as such.

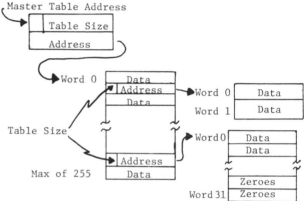

The link list structure of the TDTG output
illustrated here would correspond to one
translator (one or two program modules). A
Translator will usually contain the code for
at least one feature or group of related features.
As stated, the link list configuration to be
built by the system software will be based
upon the input supplied (features requested)
by the Telephone Company.

The software of the TDTG system consists of
approximately 210 PL/1 and 55 Assembler
programs, plus a number of data base files.
The system utilizes very advanced coding
techniques along with a variety of "home brewed"
data base access methods and macros, and is regarded as quite complex and difficult to learn.
Thus, when an experienced project member with over
2 years experience leaves, it is necessary to
bring someone new into the team and have them
contributing as soon as possible. If a new
member can be expedited up the learning curve,
overload conditions and/or schedule slippages
can be minimized.

Although the need for faster contribution has
been recognized for some time, the previous training methods did not really address this problem.
New hires were typically given a week-long

Reprinted from *COMPSAC '80, Proceedings*, November 1980,
pages 242-246. Copyright © 1980 by The Institute of Electrical and Electronics Engineers, Inc.

introductory course into telephony and ESS, and then exposed to several PL/1 modules after a few weeks. There was very little documentation for the new member to work with and he/she rarely worked on entire programs. Generally, the amount of code written was limited to a few lines to correct a small problem. As a result, the new member did not get a good overview of the entire system, was limited in the experience they obtained, and could not contribute on difficult problems. The time span required for this method took from four to six months. Some period of time was inefficiently employed during and after the training period. The process of watching video-tapes, attending lectures, supplemented with coding problems, did not prepare new hires adequately. They were not always able to work independently and progress would be retarded during heavy periods of concentrated development activity.

Inadequacies with the training procedures became accentuated during the early part of 1978. At that time, the No. 2 TDTG group was finishing a major effort on modules to support new features developed by Bell Labs. It was learned in the spring of that year that two members of TDTG would be lost to the team by July. Replacements for these two openings were to be filled by college graduates.

The long learning curve was unacceptable in this situation. What was needed was a new training method that would cover a wide variety of topics in a short period of time and let the inexperienced people get their hands on actual engineering specifications and corresponding code to familiarize themselves with TDTG. The approach decided upon was a progressive one. The initial training would introduce the basics required for each module, while subsequent training would build on the complexity of previously completed code. This would reinforce prior procedures and allow for the continuous learning of newer ones. The "building block" technique does, however, require some "formal" education at the start. The first few days would consist of learning to work with the documents and tools required. These include the translations data layout documents, the translations input definitions (Translation Guide), engineering specifications, trouble reports (description of change to be made to a module), TSØ, UNIX, and JCL. Generally, a week-long introductory course covering telecommunications and ESS was found to give adequate background for someone to start this new training program.

The first two weeks of the training are intended to provide a fairly good introduction to TDTG and ESS. System procedures and practices are defined in a "No. 2 ESS TDTG Documentation" book. The trainee will use this often as a review and reference manual. It contains numerous examples of coding techniques, descriptions of complex translators, module interfaces, and definitions of terms. This documentation has proven invaluable in enabling the trainee to work and learn on their own.

After obtaining a general view of scope and objectives of the TDTG system (software), the trainee is given a relatively simple module to look at. This program is written in PL/1 with approximately 100 lines of code. The general function of a small module like this is to support a retrofit from one generic to another, usually no more involved than building some words differently or adding some new words. The Programmers Application (PA) book will give the structural layout of these old and new translations.

With the aforementioned documents and initial training modules, the trainee can review and study some of the basic methods used by TDTG. This includes features of PL/1 used (preprocessor variables, base pointers, arrays, etc.) and TDTG methods (Macros, input forms, isolating bits with wordmasks, etc.). A person with Computer Science background usually has little problem in working with the PL/1 and TDTG methods. Someone with this experience (but with a strong math background) usually has to spend 1-2 weeks learning PL/1 and then can learn the features without much loss in time. The first module provides the focal point where the trainee really becomes involved with the PA and TG. They can look at the layout of every data word in a picture format, and determine how specific input items (as defined in the TG) are used to build the translation data table. Generally, an experienced member of the team sits with the trainee and is able to answer questions concerning the module and support documents.

When the trainee is deemed ready, seven program specs are provided to work on. These are the specifications originally written for the actual programs. The specs define the inputs, outputs, and the process to be used in building the translation data tables. The first module studied is used as a guide in coding for these specs. Modules written by the trainee are copies of actual programs and are linked out under dummy-names, to be used later in testing. Each of the specifications gradually become more difficult, with a greater number of involved procedures required with each succeeding module.

The specifications for the first and last

learning modules follow.

Program Specification
For Module
ROFOPxxD

1. The function of this module is to retrofit the No. 2 ESS EF-1 generic version of the Office Options table to the EF-2 generic version. The ESS 2500-1 form will be required input to the growth module to complete the retrofit. See Translations Guide, Division 4.

2. Input - the old ØFFØPO (Office Options) translator (EF-1, one word).

3. Output - the updated ØFFØPO (Office Options) translator (EF-2, one word).

4. Process:

   4.1 Read the old Office Options data. Copy the old (EF-1) data to new data table (EF-2) except for the following:

      4.1.1 If the old data table has bit positions 1 and 2 equal to one, set bit position 1 in the new table equal to one. Otherwise, set new position one equal to zero.

      4.1.2 Set new bit position 2 = 0.

      4.1.3 Set new bit position 12 = 0.

      4.1.4 Set new bit position 20 equal to old bit position 13 and zero old positions 13 and 14.

   4.2 Write out the new Office Options data table in the EF-2 generic format.

Program Sepcification
For Module
RTSCDxxD

1. The purpose of this module is to convert the No. 2 ESS EF-1 generic TSCDAT (Trunk Scanner Cross Reference Table) translator to the EF-2 generic format.

2. Input - the EF-1 TSCDAT translator, 12 words long.

3. Output - the EF-2 TSCDAT translator, 32 words long.

4. Process:

   4.1 Read the old TSCDAT table.

   4.2 Move the Master Trunk Scanner Number (MTSN) field from bits 10-13 to bits 16-20. The field will be set to all ones for an unequipped MTSN, and extended by one bit.

   4.3 Move the Universal Trunk Scanner Number (UTSN) field from bits 6-9 to bits 7-11. The field is extended by one bit and is to be all ones for an unequipped UTSN.

   4.4 The DS field is to be moved from bit 19 to bit 14.

   4.5 The Equipment Number (EQPT NO.) field will be extended on the left by one bit. It will therefore occupy bits 2-6 of the new data table, compared to bit 2-5 in the old format. For unequipped trunk scanners, the field is to be set to all ones, rather than all zeros.

   4.6 The SE, FE, and M fields remain unchanged.

   4.7 Extend the size of the TSCDAT table from 12 words to 32 words.

   4.8 Write out the new TSCDAT data table.

It can be seen by looking at these specs how their difficulty increases. The first exercise involves the setting of certain bits, while the last ones completely reconstruct a translator's data structure. These training modules require detailed work with the PAs and TG and brings out certain interrelationships between the data table. Throughout these modules, the trainee is gradually exposed to a greater perspective of the overall system and basic procedures are continually reviewed.

After each module is compiled, the entire TDTG team participates in a structured walk-through of the code. The trainee explains the function of the module and the other programmers offer suggestions and comments to improve the code and/or make sure it conforms to standards and procedures used by other TDTG modules. For example, many times the specification, PA, and/or the TG is interpreted incorrectly causing the code to be wrong. A walk-through enables the trainee to see how the mistakes occur and to avoid them in the future. Inconsistencies found are generally typical of normal day to day oversights, and the trainee is made aware of them before being exposed to actual production code.

Following the walk-through on each practice module, testing is done. The trainee learns how to relate the code, PA, and functional listing to each other. This is where the trainee sees the actual results of the code. Based on the functional listing and the data structure layout in the PA, the trainee can see if the data was built correctly. The message file (warning or error messages) and program store (ESS memory) map will also give clues as to possible input translations errors and incomplete or conflicting data tables. Each test executes the programs based on test data the trainee has created, using the TG and input forms.

Through this testing process, the trainee learns how to establish a specific test environment through "data base overwrites" and input data preparation. Testing also provides the opportunity to gain experience with work files (Q-files) and core dumps. Methods for going through common core dumps are described in the No. 2 Documentation book. This gives a step by step procedure which enables the trainee to debug programs almost entirely on their own while obtaining a much clearer view of the entire system. If errors are found, the process of recompiling and testing occurs.

Previously, there was very little structure to the training procedure. The steps and amount of learning varied with the types of problems occurring and the level of knowledge shared by co-workers. It could be depicted as in the figure below.

Now formality exists through a definite structure, with the ability to measure the trainee's pace and initial productivity. See the following diagram which illustrates the new process.

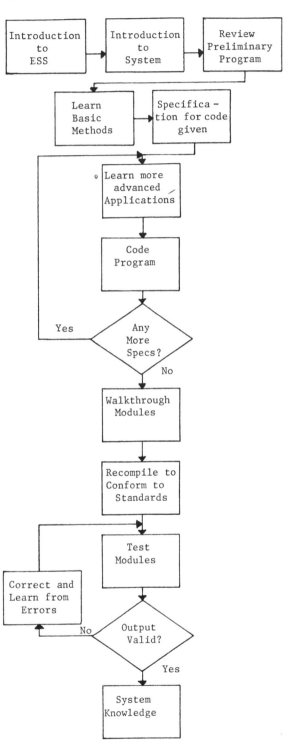

It has been observed that newer people learn more when they are doing the work themselves. Other differences that were brought out with the new method include:

*New hire is more independent and thus more apt to become familiar with other aspects of the system.

*The length of time for the training is shortened considerably.

*More "real" code is written, enabling more tools to be implemented.

*Subjects covered are broader in scope.

*More interesting topics are explored and learned.

Other team members are not required to spend as much time with the trainee, leaving time for their work.

Similar environments could use this training method with these generalized steps as guidelines:
1. Give basic introduction to system - this includes having documentation at hand to be used as a manual and reference.

2. Have some (5-7) practice modules (copies of actual programs in production) that can be written in a short time. They should be relatively easy, and somewhat similar in function, but become gradually more involved. Specifications describing inputs, process, and outputs should also be available.

3. Give one module to the new hire as a guide in writing the practice programs. It should be comparable to the practice modules in the degree of difficulty.

4. After reviewing the reference program, the new hire can write the code for the practice modules at a comfortable pace.

5. Walkthroughs of the code are made after all programs are written to obtain co-worker input. Programs without certain required conventions or standards should be changed.

6. Tests using these modules are run to execute the code and verify that the load module is correct.

7. Errors found during testing are corrected and tests are rerun.

Four new TDTG members (three with and one without computer science background) have gone through this training program, completing it in 1½ to 2 months as compared to the 4 to 6 months experienced previously. In that short 2 month period, however, the new TDTG member has covered a wider range of topics and information. They have become more familiar with a greater variety of skills and tools, and are capable of providing productive work much sooner than prior methods of training would have allowed. For example, two new hires were writing entire programs within six months of their starting dates. This was not possible before the training program. Future time can be used to sharpen the skills needed for trouble shooting and/or design.

In summary, these training modules augmented by the No. 2 ESS TDTG documentation provide the opportunity for new team members to write code for actual programs using the documents and tools they will need every day. It is unique in fact that the programmer can actually design, write, and test what can be considered real code and evaluate output produced in the same environment they will eventually work in.

Acknowledgement:

Credit for the development and initiation of this training process goes to Don Keeley, Linda Malik, and Mary Sheehan. These three members of TDTG are directly responsible for the overall benefit of this procedure.

Article takes a critical look at three popular approaches in training and instructional development; the job-task analysis approach, the self-actualization approach, and the systematic contingency approach.

Reprinted with permission from *Journal of Systems Management.* August 1977. Copyright © 1977 by The Association for Systems Management.

Approach to Management Development

BY DR. JAMES PETER DiBERADINIS

■ Administrators in general and personnel managers in particular have grappled with the problem of designing training programs which are both relevant to the participant and effective in increasing employee productivity, but they have not achieved much success.

One corporate executive put it aptly:

"We need to divest ourselves of the 'medicine show' label and throw away the snake oil that is supposed to cure all training ailments. The new emphasis for the modern day training or organizational development departments should be a focus on assessing training needs and de-emphasize the 'whistles' and the show-and-tell and after-the-fact aspects of training that have plagued us in the past. Only then can we feel confident we are providing relevant training programs that will, in the long run, show favorable payback to the organization."

The next ten years will increase the challenge to both public and private enterprise to deal with rapid change and growth that all aspects of our society are realizing.

Public and private organizations as closed systems with fixed structures, goals, functions and boundaries, are dead. The futuristically oriented manager is coming to see his business organization as an open dynamic system, dependent upon planned and frequent interaction within the multi-dimensional environment.

Personnel and training directors must have proven tools at their disposal to monitor and assess the organization's internal and external needs. The usefulness of the training director will depend upon open-system approaches to training.

When there are no systematic analyses to assess the instructional needs or a frame of reference to plan and evaluate effectiveness of training techniques, a cycle of training fads will result.

The Job-Task Analysis Approach

The most apparent underlying assumptions of the job-task approach are that the manager(s) are being trained because (1) he is not doing his job effectively, (2) the efficiency level of the manager and/or of the unit is suffering, and/or (3) the manager's position has either been enlarged or changed. The basic principles of training design consist of identifying the task components that make up the desired performance and incorporating these components into a program for total performance. The job-task analysis approach can be further classified as a unidimensional approach. However, the unidimensional approach, gives rise to profound problem issues. First, it limits training directors to a prescriptive model, which is not based on analyzing the whole person. Secondly, it inhibits an open-dynamic approach to training and learning. If the assessment of the task becomes the only criterion for formulating and designing training programs, the total human/environmental system has been overlooked and its attributes excluded from the analysis.

The organization, individual perception and motivation, and internal and external environmental forces are all salient factors which, if incorporated into any training design will increase success.

DR. JAMES PETER DiBERARDINIS
Dr. DiBerardinis is Assistant Professor of Speech Communication at Montana State University in Bozeman. He has also been a social scientist at the Westinghouse Learning Corporation.

Self-Actualization Approach

Programs that focus upon the behavioral awareness and personal growth of the participants have been recent entries into the field of management training and development. Some of the better known approaches of this type are the T-Group, the Management Grid, and Kepner-Tregoe. Although these approaches differ widely in their operational techniques, their philosophical thrust centers around behavioral change through self-actualization. Of the three approaches, there is little doubt that T-Groups have become the most popular training device.

While T-Group training seems to produce observable changes in behavior, the utility of these changes on individual performance in their organizational roles remains to be demonstrated. More research has been conducted on T-Group training than any other single human development technique, however, the problems of observation and measurement are considerably more difficult in T-Group research than in most other areas.

The goals of the T-Group method are to increase self-awareness, increase sensitivity, increase awareness of group processes, heighten capacity to take action in problem situations and increase ability to learn how to learn. These goals, are said to be transferred to the actual organizational environment in the form of greater job "satisfaction" on the part of the individual, and increased productivity for the organization. These benefits have yet to be validated.

Research, reveals both theoretical and practical inadequacies in the functioning and effectiveness of T-Group training. First, theoretically, the T-Group accomplishes its goals by creating an atmosphere of tension and anxiety, while at the same time maintaining an environment of permissiveness, openness and "psychological safety." This atmosphere in turn encourages the individual to use frank, accurate and relevant feedback to change undesirable interpersonal behaviors. The problem here is that tension and anxiety, and "psychological safety" are incompatible, mutually exclusive conditions, and it is still an open question as to whether an anxious state is in fact the most suitable condition for learning.

On the practical level, T-Group training suffers many difficulties which severely constrain the effects of the method. T-Groups usually meet in an isolated environment, which is atypical of the institutional or organizational setting. Second, the strategies chosen to deal with group and interpersonal conflict have very little resemblance to the strategies employed by their own organizations. Third, there is little evidence of a long-term transferability of training outcomes to the job setting. Fourth, "laboratory culture" encourages an attitude on the part of the participants that T-Group training is a game and can be easily discarded when found dysfunctional. Finally, due to the nature of its free-form, most evaluative efforts have been "ex post facto" in nature, therefore, they have no predictive utility. The redeeming characteristics of a T-Group approach have not surfaced in the literature.

Systematic Contingency Approach

Well-conceived training programs are designed to achieve goals that meet the needs of both the organization and the individual. Proficiency and personal growth should be the aim of all training efforts. There is always the temptation to begin training without a thorough analysis of these needs. Unfortunately, many programs are doomed to failure because some training directors are more interested in conducting the training programs than in assessing the needs of the individual participant and the organization, while other programs fail because their instructional design is too narrow to reflect the organizational objectives. The contention here is that most training directors, when developing instructional programs, infrequently consider the uniqueness of the situation or the changing environment in which it exists. Without such considerations, they heighten the chances of making inappropriate decisions. Therefore, the "chance" of making a right decision is only a chance.

One of the consequences of adapting to a systematic contingency concept is a rejection of simplistic, universal approaches in training development. Rather than searching for a single remedial approach to all training problems, there should be a tendency to examine the functions of the organization in relation to the needs of the trainee, and the pressures facing him. Consideration of the internal and external environmental forces on the trainee and his managerial position leads to the development of a systematic contingency approach.

Identification of points of conflict and interaction between the organizational and the individual allows for the development of training objectives, criteria for evaluation and systematic program planning. The following are suggestions for determining the interacting factors:

1) Place a high degree of effort in selecting the factors that appear to have the most effect on the individual and the organization. Such factors as task performance, organizational structure (management style), external environmental characteristics, etc., will usually have great bearing on individual and organizational performance.

2) Carefully examine the interaction of these factors, so as to determine points of conflict and tension. For example, if the managerial style employed by an individual(s) is not in harmony with the overall organizational philosophy and structure, the instructional design should include intervention techniques to deal with this conflict.

3) Such diagnostic assessment makes it possible to specify learning objectives for the training program. The objectives provide direction and input for the program design, and in turn, establish the criterion measures that will be used to evaluate the effectiveness of the training program and the transferability of the learning.

By successfully diagnosing such factors as the nature of the task, the organizational structure, the internal and external environmental forces, and other pertinent factors, the management developer will be more able to design a training program which is satisfying to the participant, relevant to his/her work environment and productive for the sponsoring organization.   •jsm

References
1. Richard Morano. "Determining Organizational Training Needs." *Personnel Psychology,* 1973. 26, p. 487.

Developing Managers Without Management Development

Saul W. Gellerman

"Development," as used here, is the learning that occurs independently of instruction. It is primarily the result of experience. Whether it carries the individual very far beyond what he was taught depends partly on his learning capacity, but more importantly on the quality of his experience and on whether he is encouraged to learn from it. In the present review I also want to point out that:

• *Whether an organization succeeds in assuring its supply of competent managers depends far more on how it runs its business than on the sophistication, or even the use, of formal training programs.*

• *Four specific aspects of the organization's management of itself are the keys to both the quality and quantity of its future talent supply. These are: organization structure, job design, career planning, and control systems.*

• *Formal management training programs are neither necessary nor sufficient for this purpose, although they can significantly strengthen the organization that uses these four tools effectively.*

• *The process of developing subordinates can be anxiety-provoking for executives, and this, rather than the inherent difficulty of the process, is the principle obstacle to its wider use.* **S.W.G.**

Management is essentially a set of skills involving the application of certain principles. The principles can be taught to or inferred by the individual, but their application can only be learned. I can teach you the principles of swimming, but you will not learn to swim until you get into the water and find your own way of using those principles. Similarly, management principles can be taught, but the only way of learning to use them is by trying to manage.

Large organizations have obvious advantages over smaller ones with respect to formal "management development" programs. They have larger training budgets, can more easily spare managerial time for course attendance, and are usually more sophisticated in selecting both potential managers and course materials. However, smaller organizations have no disadvantage with regard to structuring themselves so that development is likely to occur. Thus there is no reason why a company that cannot afford large-scale investments in *training* its managers need despair of *developing* them.

This article sets forth a general strategy for encouraging the development of managers. It is based on certain principles which must be understood if it is to be used effectively. Accordingly, the principles are stated first:

Principle 1: Fighting human nature is a losing game

The conditions under which development is likely to occur are known and it is largely futile to expect much development to occur in the absence of those conditions. Basically, this means that the work that managers are assigned to must be instructive in itself, and that their superiors must be charged with exploiting the instructional potentialities that present themselves in the normal course of that work. On the other hand, formal instruction of the classroom variety—even when competent and pertinent—provides little incremental skill when there is no immediate opportunity to practice what is taught.

Principle 2: Development occurs as the response to a challenge

Our attention is naturally drawn to our own attempts to

Dr. Gellerman, president of Saul Gellerman/Consulting, Inc., is a diplomate of the American Board of Professional Psychology. His article is in extension of his presentation last fall before the Securities Industry Association.

Reprinted with permission from *The Conference Board Record*, Volume X, Number 7, July 1973. Copyright © 1973 by Conference Board.

cope with a problem, and the lessons in those attempts impress themselves naturally upon our memories. In the absence of problems demanding solution our attention ordinarily wanders, and the results of those wanderings seldom add much to our store of knowledge. As a rule we learn only when we have to; that is, when a satisfactory response to the situation in which we find ourselves is not already within our repertoire.

This principle has two important implications:

Very little development can be expected simply because people desire it. Therefore attempts to develop managers by selecting people with a strong personal drive to expand their managerial skills, or by encouraging such a desire with inspirational messages, are likely to have limited success at best.

Very little development can be expected to occur on a convenient schedule. Most promotions are timed to meet the organization's needs rather than the individual's growth rate. As a result, many promotions occur after the individual has passed his peak of readiness. Similarly, the principles taught in training courses are most likely to be applied if opportunities to do so occur shortly after they are taught. But courses are usually scheduled at the convenience of the training department and managers are released for training at the convenience of their superiors. Thus the relationship between the timing of training and opportunities to practice it is usually random.

Principle 3: Development is more like farming than manufacturing

In manufacturing we assume that most of the variables affecting the result we wish to achieve are, or can be put, under our control. In agriculture we assume that few of these variables are, or can be, under our control. In manufacturing our strategy is to design a system with all the appropriate controls we need. In agriculture it is to influence those few variables we can control as much as we can in hopes that nature will be reasonably cooperative with all the other variables. Thus the plant manager can, for example, control temperature and humidity if he needs to, but the farmer can only pray for the right amount of rain.

The organization that wants to develop its managerial talent is in fact much closer to the farmer's situation and is better served by his strategies. Its objectives, therefore, are simply to create conditions in which good men are likely to grow naturally, and then hope that they will. This is a disappointing formula for those who perpetually hope to get results by "doing something"; but surely there is a lesson for us in the fact that so many of the "somethings" we have done to develop managers have turned out to be fads.

The manufacturing approach to developing managers is characterized by four emphases which can be summarized alliteratively: *select* them, *school* them, *slot* them in the right jobs, and *show* them your appreciation with appropriate rewards. The assumption is that the right kind of talent, when exposed to this treatment, will develop; and, of course, sometimes it does. But the yield of this "4-S" approach is limited when it is not adequately reinforced by opportunities to learn from experience.

What follows is a description of an essentially "agricultural" approach: creating conditions in which learning from experience is likely to occur. It is not offered as an alternative to the manufacturing approach where that is in use, but rather as a vital supplement. The agricultural approach can stand by itself, where necessary, in organizations where size or budgetary limitations preclude sophisticated selection and schooling methods. The basic idea is to so construct the organization that it becomes, in effect, a talent farm.

Organization structure

The number and content of jobs, the number of levels of decision-making authority, and the division of projects into assigned responsibilities—in brief, organization structure—is inevitably an expression of management's assumptions about how the talent available to it is best utilized. Once embedded in that structure, those assumptions tend to become self-fulfilling prophecies. Both job performance and personal development are limited to the confines of the experiences provided within the structure, and this evidence is taken as confirmation of the wisdom inherent in its design. Therefore, changes in organization structure are hard to induce because they generate their own (sometimes spurious) appearance of inevitability.

With respect to development, organization structure can be confining or liberating. The confining effect is usually unintentional and unrecognized, because structure is seldom designed with developmental consequences in mind. But if the organization pursues development as a serious goal, its structure should be designed to be liberating: to encourage experiences from which useful learning can be derived.

The ideal structure for developmental purposes is a small, self-contained unit requiring little or no external support, which has an undivided responsibility for the attainment of some major organizational purpose. The more the unit to which the individual is attached conforms to this "task force" form, the more likely is he to encounter experiences from which he can learn; unfortunately, the obverse is not only true but more common. Functional organization—that is, centralizing work of a given type in specialized departments regardless of which major project that work applies to—may have certain advantages, but development is not one of them.

The task force is in effect a miniature version of the

larger organization of which it is a part. But its internal communication lines are much shorter, permitting faster response and easier checking to be sure that messages are understood. The small task force develops managerial generalists because it can afford no specialists. Lacking depth in any given function, they more than compensate for that by showing through direct, everyday experience how actions taken in one part of the organization enhance or inhibit actions taken in other parts. The parochial regard of each function for its own work, to the comparative disregard of the organization's larger purposes—so common and so damaging in large, functionally specialized organizations—hardly has a chance to develop in a task force.

Service in such a task force provides the manager with what is in effect a one-man organization development program. He learns—or rather, can learn—that most essential of leadership skills: the fine art of making other people effective. By contrast, his colleagues in a larger unit are more likely to encounter the wall of misunderstanding and sheer ignorance that functional organization builds between an organization's components. He is far less likely to develop the view that other components are unwise or unnecessary or both: a view that would not serve him well should he ever be elevated to top management levels.

Another advantage of the smaller unit is that everyone is near the top, which virtually eliminates the problem of unrecognized talent. The two major obstacles to talent recognition in a large organization—visibility and sponsorship—are obviated. The ability of the organization to identify its more promising managers early in their careers is maximized. An added plus is that job performance is likely to loom larger than personal attractiveness in winning such attention, since individual contributions are more readily identified in a task force than in a larger organization.

Task force organization is more feasible than it may at first appear. Many profit (or cost) centers are essentially moves in this direction, as are product management groups. Dependence on central staffs for scarce or expensive specialists can be minimized through the matrix organization approach, which in this case would have two or more task forces sharing the services of such specialists. The old shibboleth that no one can work effectively under more than one boss has been effectively punctured by demonstrations that task force leaders who talk to and trust each other can share otherwise prohibitively expensive specialists.

In fact, the principle limit on the feasibility of task force organization is management's readiness to depart from tradition. By breaking the large pyramidal organization into what is in effect a loosely linked network of small pyramids, even organizations of substantial size can become hothouses of managerial development at little or no sacrifice of operating efficiency.

Job design

We ordinarily think that the job of a job is to get the work that is assigned to it done, and we therefore design jobs with solely operational objectives in mind. But jobs have another job, which is the development of their incumbents. The proportion of managerial jobs whose primary function is development should increase at every level of authority and should reach 100% no lower than the level immediately below the chief executive.

A job stimulates development when some of its responsibilities have *not* been mastered. This is why the prescription of many executives for the development of their subordinates for the coming year—"more seasoning in his present position"—can easily be a fallacy. It is also why investigative, trouble-shooting, consulting, or teaching assignments can be among the most significant developmental experiences in a man's career.

Jobs contribute to the development of their incumbents under certain conditions, and it is to the advantage of the organization to create those conditions:

First, the individual has not yet mastered the job, and he knows this.

Second, mastery of the job is within his capabilities, and he has enough optimism to at least hope that this may be true.

Third, achieving that mastery is more likely to lead to new learning opportunities than to long spells of practicing what was long since mastered, and the individual knows this, too.

This reasoning runs contrary to conventional wisdom in two respects: one is the problem of what to do about managerial *mistakes,* and the other concerns the desirability of developing *experts*.

One of the tacit principles underlying the design of most jobs is the avoidance of errors. This is done both by excluding responsibilities that even approach the limits of the incumbent's abilities, and by a system of checks through which superiors review—and presumably detect any errors in—a subordinate's work. Obviously, to design jobs so that they are not mastered is to court errors.

In practice, however, errors may go undetected for months or even forever, simply because thorough checks of a manager's work are seldom feasible. Also, the evaluation of many managerial decisions (especially when their consequences may take months or years to unfold) is necessarily subjective. Whether it is an error or a farsighted coup may depend, in other words, on who does the evaluating and on when he does it. In sum, errors are not necessarily easy or even desirable to avoid.

A case can even be made in favor of errors. Nothing is quite so instructive, chastening or memorable as the error from which one is encouraged to learn, rather than to hide. The consequences of most errors are less than catastrophic—unless they are made dangerous to careers, in which case they are likely to accumulate insidiously with other hidden errors.

What happens to executive control when jobs are designed to be at least partially unmastered, and errors are the basis for instruction rather than punishment? Obviously, it changes; but it certainly isn't dismantled. The fine line between putting the organization in jeopardy and precluding the development of the manager is approached less timidly than it usually is. Some risks are costlier when not taken.

A good analogy for defining how much control is "enough" comes from skiing. To ski in control means to be able to stop if necessary. To manage in "enough" control means to know enough of what a subordinate is doing to be able to prevent truly catastrophic errors. The rest are the subordinate's problem—and his opportunity to learn. In evaluating the subordinate's performance, the superior is more concerned by any recurrent errors than with the number that occur once. Indeed, an absence of errors in an unmastered job is cause for alarm: the subordinate may be sticking too timidly to the rulebook to learn anything but the rules.

The desirability of experts is a hardy old fallacy that is likely to linger on, more because it satisfies emotional needs than because of major benefits to the organization. An "expert," if there is such a thing, is someone who knows his job too well to make an error, and he presumably acquires his expertise through long service in the same job. In other words, he first masters his job and then overlearns it, ad infinitum, until he can do his work flawlessly without even thinking about it.

That, of course, is the fallacy. Long service in an essentially unchanged job is likely to lead to thoughtlessness, blindness to new developments and resistance to change. In the absence of the necessity to learn, most people just stop learning. This doesn't mean that we must rush someone off to a new job the moment he masters his old one. Even if that were feasible, we can safely reap the rewards of our training investment for a while—but not indefinitely.

The emotional needs that experts satisfy are those of the executives whose policies create them, not those of the experts: first, a bogus sense of security, as if one were really surrounded by infallible lieutenants; second, an easy rationalization for keeping a man where he is when it would be inconvenient or risky to move him.

Finally, that entire class of jobs that has too long been misnamed "trainee" should be overhauled and, in many cases, abolished. Many management trainee jobs have actually been little more than holding pens for overqualified coolies. They are given routine chores because no one knows quite what to do with them, and because it is presumed that "learning the business from the ground up" will do them no harm. But the experience of being a coolie prepares one for nothing grander than being an older coolie.

For someone with management potential, orientation to the basics of an enterprise can and should be accomplished briskly. The only real management trainee—in the sense of someone who is learning to manage—is someone in a managerial job.

Career planning

While it is obviously fatuous to attempt to plan anyone's career very far into the future, it is equally fatuous not to do so for the forseeable future. In the case of managers, this usually extends into the three-to-five year range. Somewhere within that period it will probably be desirable to introduce some major modification into the manager's job, because within that period he will probably master his present job and return an ample dividend on the organization's training investment.

It is also obvious that most of those modifications cannot be promotions, in the sense of giving the manager authority over more assets and/or people than he previously had. Fortunately, development can proceed without promotion. (Although not without reward: pay and status indicators should signal the successful closing of a career phase and entry into a new one.) The modification can be the addition of a new responsibility, the replacement of old responsibilities or even a complete change of responsibilities.

The aim is always to confront the manager with a new learning opportunity. In a larger sense the aim is to convert the management team to a learning group and to convert the managerial career into a license or mandate to learn. Responsibilities are deliberately shifted among jobs or sought in hitherto untried activities. This kind of ferment occurs willy-nilly in a rapidly growing company and actually helps to accelerate its growth: a beneficent circular relationship develops between organizational and individual growth. But even in static or slowly growing firms the process of redistributing responsibilities can be deliberately *managed* to encourage the blossoming of careers.

Sometimes the main reason for denying a developmental opportunity to a promising manager is that it is already "taken" by someone else who is performing adequately and has no immediate prospects of promotion. This raises the delicate, and therefore seldom-faced, question of whether the organization "owes" a managerial job to anyone, and if so whether first-come-first-served is the most appropriate principle to apply. The problem is especially acute in closely held or family owned companies, in which the roles of ownership and management are often commingled.

If the organization is committed to ensuring its supply of managers by developing them internally, it must regard managerial jobs as learning opportunities; and in that sense it cannot "owe" them to anyone. No cut-and-dried formulas are possible here, but there clearly will be occasions when a manager whose performance has been adequate will be asked to relinquish his responsibilities to someone who can benefit from the learning opportunity inherent in that job. Such changes are made immeasurably easier if the organization has established (or if necessary, decreed) a policy of "tours of duty" for middle and top level jobs.

This concept is already well-established for overseas management assignees and for military officers. Relief from the assignment marks the end of the incumbent's expected contribution to it and the completion of what he undertook to do: there are no implications of failure. The concept has much to recommend it. But its implications for top management must be faced squarely: a tour of duty system is viable only in a reasonably fluid organization in which managers relieved from one job are accommodated in vacancies created by relieving still other managers. Insistence by top executives on retaining their own assignments indefinitely retards the flow of reassigned managers below them and can even render the entire system ineffective. The tour of duty concept may, in other words, make inevitable the confrontation between the long-range interests of the organization as a whole and the individual interest of its leaders.

Development is not easily bought.

Control systems

In a traditional organization the control function of a superior is to make sure that his subordinates are doing their jobs as it was planned that they should be done. This responsibility is not abandoned when the organization accepts the responsibility for enhancing the development of its managers; but the emphasis upon it is brought into balance, with an emphasis on seeing to it that subordinates are learning from their jobs.

In practice this means that the subordinate's decisions are discussed, rather than prescribed or proscribed; and that while the superior will offer advice upon request, he is more likely to be alarmed than flattered by an excess of requests. Both the superior and the subordinate managers have new roles to learn if the latter is to grow into something more than a carbon copy of the former.

Learning new roles is never easy, but it is easier when

the individual sees more clear-cut advantage for himself if he does learn from it. For this reason it must be noted that superiors are not only more likely to find their new roles more difficult to learn—because there is less personal advantage in it for them than there is for their subordinates—but that the reluctance of superiors to adapt themselves to a coaching/controlling role will inevitably inhibit the development of many subordinates.

The process of conversion from controlling roles to coaching/controlling roles is subtle, delicate, and too easily frustrated by undersupport or sabotage. Paradoxically, the process itself needs to be controlled if it is to be effective; and the key to that control is the tour of duty system. A manager who cannot be relieved when his tour is completed because an adequate replacement is not available has clearly failed to develop his subordinates. The same is true of managers to whom presumably developable subordinates are assigned, but who persistently fail to provide adequately developed replacements to other departments.

Such failures raise serious doubts about fitness for top-level positions, since similar failures there can choke the entire development system. Further, whatever financial rewards are used should surely be more liberal for those managers whose subordinates are judged by *subsequent* superiors to be well-prepared than those whose subordinates are judged otherwise. A system of appropriate retroactive rewards should not be beyond our ingenuity. The main function of a reward is to emphasize what the organization considers important; and when development is rewarded only by lip service, the clear implication to most managers is that development isn't really important.

In the long run an organization is better served by leaders who have learned to cope with anxiety than those who have merely learned how to avoid it. Anxiety is inherent in the development process for superior and subordinate alike. The superior consciously risks the errors of his subordinate, while the subordinate shoulders full accountability for decisions that are at least partially new to him. Anxiety, like old-fashioned medicines, is unlikely to be enjoyable, but it can be beneficial. It is seldom disabling. If it is, it should be read as a clear signal that the individual is ill-equipped (at least for the present) to participate in his own or anyone else's development.

Management style

Some organizations attract, hold and develop capable managers without being overly concerned with courses, seminars, audio-visual materials, and the like. Whether by design or luck, they have managed to create an environment in which good men can grow.

In itself this is no reason for curtailing formal management development programs. But the ultimate yield from our investment in those programs depends much less on their content than on what the company's own style of management permits its managers to practice. To shop around for the ''right'' course or the ''right'' consultant is futile if what is taught cannot be effectively applied to, and reinforced on, the job.

In the end, life itself is our most potent teacher. If it is so organized as to be constrained, repetitive and safe, it will teach us to ignore opportunities and shun the unknown.

If it is so organized as to be challenging and risky, life will teach us to adapt to change and to evaluate the potential payoff in risk. The way in which an organization manages itself today is, willy-nilly, the classroom in which its next generation of managers acquire both the vision and the blindspots with which they will meet the future.

EMPLOYEE APPRAISAL:

WHEN YOU'RE THE JUDGE

At review time, you are the sole judge of your subordinates' work. But you must not only assess their performance, you must also motivate them to improve.

by Andrew S. Grove

Why are performance reviews a vital part of the management system of most organizations? And why do we review the performance of our subordinates? I posed both questions to a group of middle managers and got the following responses:

• To assess the subordinate's work
• To improve performance
• To reward performance
• To motivate subordinates
• To provide feedback
• To provide discipline
• To provide direction
• To justify raises
• To reinforce the company culture.

Next, I asked the group to imagine themselves as supervisors giving a review to a subordinate, and asked what their feelings were. Some of the answers: pride, anger, anxiety, discomfort, guilt, empathy/concern, embarrassment, frustration.

Finally, I asked the group to think back to some of the performance reviews they had received and asked what, if anything, was wrong with them. Their answers were quick and many:

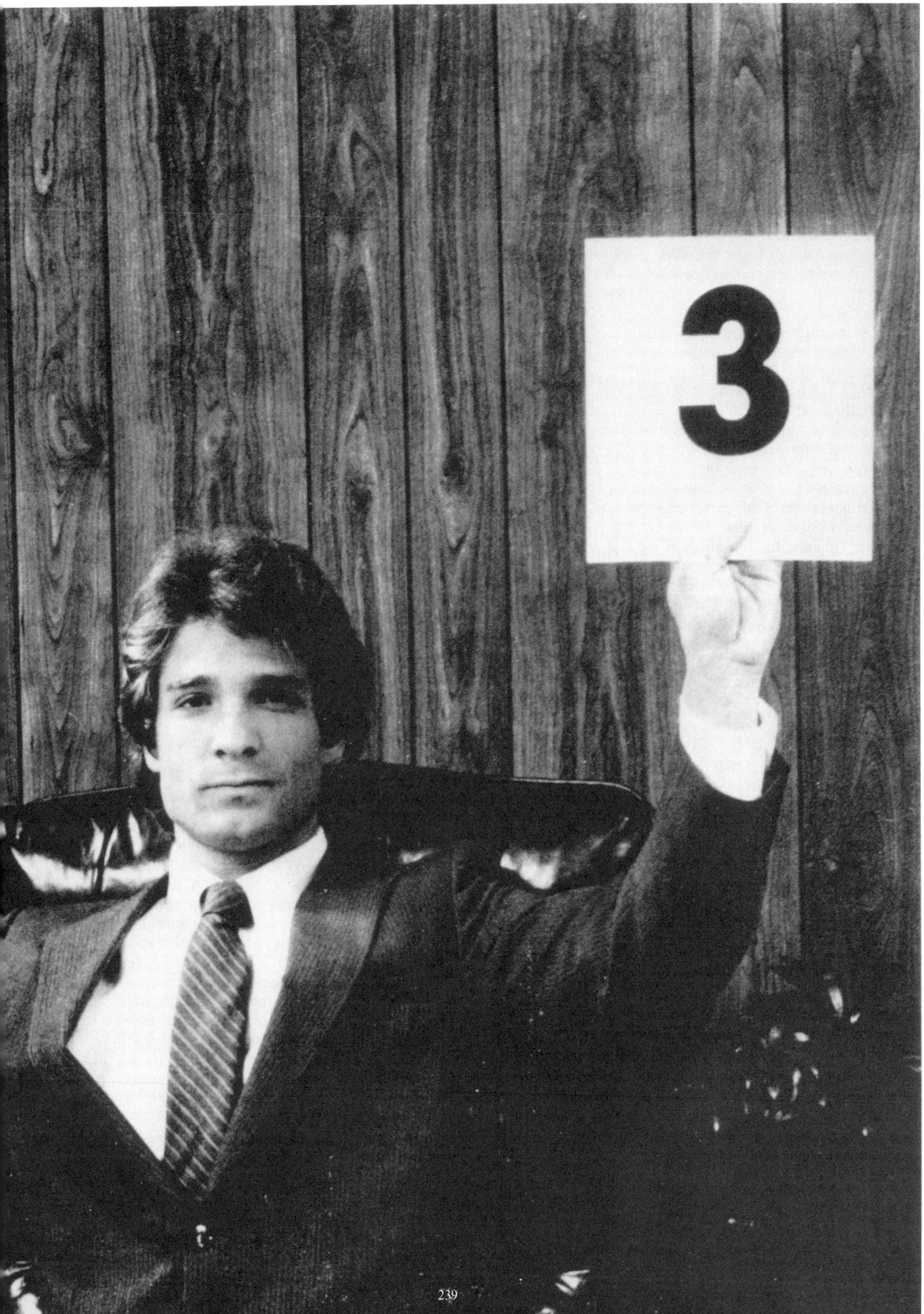
3

Employee Appraisal

- Review comments too general
- Mixed messages (inconsistent with rating or dollar raise)
- No indication of how to improve
- Negatives avoided
- Supervisor didn't know my work
- Only recent performance considered
- Surprises.

This should tell you that conducting performance reviews is a very complicated and difficult business, and that we managers don't do an especially good job at it.

The fact is that giving such reviews is the *single most important form of task-relevant feedback* supervisors can provide. It is how we assess our subordinates' level of performance and how we deliver that assessment to them individually. It is also how we allocate the rewards—promotions, dollars, stock options, or whatever we may use. The review will influence a subordinate's performance—positively or negatively—for a long time, and that makes the appraisal one of

---

"Most jobs involve activities that are not reflected by output in the period covered by the review."

---

the manager's highest-leverage activities. In short, the review is an extremely powerful mechanism, and it is little wonder that opinions and feelings about it are strong.

But what is its fundamental purpose? Though all the responses given to my questions are correct, there is one that is more important than any of the others: *to improve the subordinate's performance*.

The review is usually dedicated to two factors: first, the *skill level* of the subordinate, to determine what skills are missing and to find ways to remedy that lack; and second, to intensify the subordinate's *motivation* in order to get him or her on a higher performance curve for the same skill level.

The review process also represents the most formal type of institutionalized leadership. It is the only time a manager is mandated to act as judge and jury: We managers are required by the organization that employs us to make a judgment regarding a worker and then to deliver that judgment to him, face to face.

A supervisor's responsibility here is obviously very significant. What preparation have we had to do the job properly? About the only experience I can think of is that, as subordinates, we've been on the receiving end. But, in general, our society values avoiding confrontation. Even the word "argument" is frowned upon, something I learned many years ago when I first came to this country from Hungary.

In Hungarian, the word "argument" is frequently used to describe a difference of opinion. When I began to learn English and used the word "argument," I would be corrected. People would say, "Oh no, you don't mean 'argument,' you mean 'debate,'" or "You mean 'discussion.'"

Among friends and peers you are not supposed to discuss politics, religion, or anything that might possibly produce a difference of opinion and a conflict. Football scores, gardening, and the weather are okay. But we are taught that well-mannered individuals skirt potentially emotional issues. The point is that delivering a good performance review is really a unique act, given both our cultural background and our professional training.

Don't think for a moment that performance reviews should be confined to large organizations. They should be part of managerial practice in organizations of any size and kind. If performance matters in your operation, performance reviews are absolutely necessary.

Two aspects of the review—assessing performance and delivering the assessment—are equally difficult. Let's look at each in a little more detail.

Assessing performance

Assessing the performance of professional employees objectively is very difficult because there is no cut-and-dried way to measure and characterize a professional's work completely. Most jobs involve activities that are not reflected by output in the period covered by the review. Yet we have to give such activities appropriate weight as we assess a person's performance. Anybody who supervises professionals, therefore, walks a tightrope: He or she must be objective, but must not be afraid of using judgment, even though a judgment is, by definition, subjective.

To make an assessment less difficult, a supervisor should decide what it is he or she expects from a subordinate and then attempt to judge whether the subordinate performed to expectations. The biggest problem with most reviews is that we don't usually define what it is we want from our subordinates, and, as noted, if we don't know what we want, we are surely not going to get it.

Let's consider the concept of the managerial "black box." With this concept, we can characterize performance by *output measures* and *internal measures*. The first represent the output of the black box, and include such tangibles as completing designs, meeting sales quotas, or increasing the yield in a production process—factors we can, and should, plot on charts. The internal measures take into account activities that go on inside the black box: Whatever is being done to create output for the period under review as well as that which sets the stage for the output of future periods. Are we reaching our current processing goals in such a way that two months from now we are likely to face a group of disgruntled data-center employees? Are we positioning and developing people in the organization in such a way that our business can handle its tasks in the future? Are we doing all the things that add up to a well-run department?

There is no strict formula by which

Employee Appraisal

we can compare the relative significance of output measures and internal measures. In a given situation, the proper weighting could be 50/50, 90/10, or 10/90, and could even shift from one month to the next. But at least we should know which variables are being traded off.

Another kind of trade-off has to be considered: weighing long-term-oriented against short-term-oriented performance. A programmer needs to complete a project on a strict schedule to meet some vital organizational requirement. He or she may also be working on a design method that will make it easier for others to design similar programs in the future. The professional obviously needs both activities evaluated and reviewed. But which is more significant?

A way to help weigh questions like this is the idea of "present value," used in finance: How much will the future-oriented activity pay back over time? And how much is that worth today?

There is also a time factor to consider. The subordinate's output during the review period may have all, some, or nothing to do with his or her activities during the same period. Accordingly, the supervisor should look at the time offset between the activity of the subordinate and the output that results from that activity.

This is one lesson I learned the hard way. The organization of one of the managers reporting to me had had a superb year. All output measures were excellent: Sales increased, profit margins were good, the products worked—you could hardly even think of giving anything but a superior review to the person in charge. Yet I had some misgivings. Turnover in his group was higher than it should have been, and his people were grumbling too much. There were other such straws in the wind, but who could give credence to elusive signs when tangible, measurable performance was so outstanding? So the manager got a very positive review.

The next year, his organization took a nose dive. Sales flattened, profits declined, product development was delayed, and the turmoil among his subordinates deepened. As I prepared the next review of this manager, I struggled to sort out what had happened. Did the manager's performance deteriorate as suddenly as his organization's output measures indicated? What was going on? I concluded that the manager's performance was improving in the second year, even as things seemed to go to hell. The problem was that his performance had not been good a year earlier. The output indicators merely represented work done years ago—the light from distant stars, as it were—which was still holding up. The time offset between the manager's work and the output of his organization was just about a year.

Greatly embarrassed, I regretfully concluded that the superior rating I had given him was totally wrong. Trusting the internal measures, I should have had the judgment and courage to give the manager a much lower rating than I did in spite of the excellent output indicators, which did not reflect the year under review.

The time offset between activity and output can also work the other way around. In the early years of Intel, I was called upon to review the performance of a subordinate who was setting up a production facility from scratch. It had not manufactured anything as yet, but, of course, the review could not wait for tangible output. I had had no prior experience supervising someone who did not have a record of concrete output. I gave my subordinate credit for doing well, even though output remained uncertain. As managers, we are really called upon to *judge* performance, not just to see and record it when it's in plain sight.

Finally, as you review managers, should you be judging their performance or the performance of the group under their supervision? You should be doing both.

Ultimately, you are after the performance of the group, but the manager is there to *add value* in some way. You need to determine what that is, so you must ask yourself: Is the manager doing anything with his group? Is he hiring new employees? Is he training the people he has, and doing other things that are likely to raise the output of the team in the future? The most difficult issues in determining a professional's performance will be based on asking questions and making judgments of this sort.

One big pitfall to avoid is the "potential trap." At all times you should force yourself to assess performance, not potential. By "potential" I mean form rather than substance.

I was once asked to approve the performance review of a general manager whose supervisor rated him highly for the year. The manager was responsible for a business unit that lost money, missed its revenue forecast month after month, slipped engineering schedules, and in general showed poor output and internal measures over the year. I could not approve the review. Subsequently, his supervisor said, "But he is an outstanding general manager. He is knowledgeable and handles himself well. It's his organization that did not do well, not the manager himself!"

This explanation cut no ice with me because *the performance rating of a manager cannot be higher than the one we would accord to his organization!* It is very important to assess actual performance, not appearances; real output, not good form. Had the manager been given a high rating, Intel would have signaled to all at the company that to do well, you must "act" like a good manager—talk like one and emulate one—but you don't need to perform like one.

A decision to promote is often linked, as it should be, to the performance review. We must recognize that no action communicates our manager values to an organization more clearly and loudly than whom we promote. By elevating someone we are, in effect, creating role models for others in our organization.

There is an old saying that when we promote our best sales representative, we ruin a good sales rep and get a bad manager. But if we think about it, we have no other choice. When we promote our best, we are saying to our subordinates that performance is what counts.

It is hard enough to assess our subordinates' performance, but we must also try to *improve* it. No matter how well a subordinate has done, we can always suggest ways to improve, something about which a manager need not feel embarrassed. Blessed with 20/20 hindsight, we can compare what the subordinate did against what he or she might have done, and the variance can tell both of us how to do things better.

There are three L's to keep in mind when delivering a review: level, listen, and leave yourself out.

You must level with your subordinate—the credibility and integrity of the entire system depend on your being totally frank. And don't be surprised to find that praising someone in a straightforward fashion can be just as hard as criticizing without embarrassment.

> "Giving reviews is the single most important form of task-relevant feedback supervisors can provide."

The word "listen" has special meaning here. The aim of communication is to transmit thoughts from the brain of person A to the brain of person B. Thoughts in the head of A are first converted into words, which are enunciated and, via sound waves, reach the ear of B; as nerve impulses they travel to B's brain, where they are transformed back into thoughts and presumably kept.

Should person A use a tape recorder to confirm the words used in the review? The answer is an emphatic "No!" Words themselves are nothing but a means; getting the

right thought communicated is the end. Perhaps B has become so emotional he can't understand something that would be perfectly clear to anyone else. Perhaps B has become so preoccupied trying to formulate answers that she can't really listen

and get A's message. Perhaps B has tuned out and as a defense is thinking of going fishing. All of these possibilities can and do occur, and all the more so when A's message is laden with conflict.

How, then, can you be sure you are really being heard? What techniques can you employ? Is it enough to have your subordinate paraphrase your words? I don't think so. What you must do is employ *all* of your sensory capabilities. To make sure you're being heard, you should *watch* the person you are talking to. Remember, the more complex the issue, the more

Performance-appraisal sample

NAME ___John Doe___ **JOB TITLE** ___Materials Support Supervisor___
REVIEW PERIOD _____ 2/82 _____ **TO** _____ 8/82 _____

Description of job assignment:
Responsible for managing the production-planning process and the manufacturing-specifications process, including maintenance and development.

Accomplishments during this review period:
The production-planning process was significantly changed this year [Output measure: good]. Sites were well coordinated and all administrative activities were done efficiently.

Evaluation (Areas of strengths, areas for improvements):
John transferred to Materials Support in early February. The production-planning process was having some difficulties at the time. John got up to speed very quickly and was able to take over the job from his predecessor very effectively.

In the manufacturing-specifications area, John's efforts have been far less successful. He puts extra effort into his work, but the results have not been satisfactory. I think the problem has two causes:

1. John has a hard time defining clear, concise, and specific goals. An example of this is the difficulty he has in setting good objectives and getting key results [Internal measure: lacking; activity vs. output]. Another example is the mushy conclusion of the manufacturing-specification system review in March. We still don't have a clear definitive statement of where the spec system is heading and how it's going to get there. Without specific goals, one can very easily fall into the trap of "working on" something without reaching the objective.

2. John seems easily satisfied that having a meeting on a subject constitutes progress. This happened in the area of training associated with manufacturing specs [Note: statement supported by example]. John should spend more effort prior to each meeting defining what specific

prone communication is to being lost.

Does your subordinate give appropriate responses to what you are saying? If his or her responses—verbal and nonverbal—do not completely assure you that what you've said has gotten through, it is *your responsibility* to keep at it until you are satisfied that you have been heard and understood.

This is what I mean by *listening*: employing your entire arsenal of sensory capabilities to make certain your points are being properly interpreted by your subordinate's brain. All the intelligence and good faith used to prepare your review will produce nothing unless this occurs. Your tool, to say it again, is total listening.

All of us have had professors who lectured by looking at the blackboard, mumbling to it, and carefully avoiding eye contact with the class.

The reason? Knowing their presentations were murky and incomprehensible, these teachers tried to avoid confirming visually what they already knew. Don't imitate your worst professors while delivering performance reviews. Listen with all your might to make sure your subordinate is receiving your message, and don't stop delivering it until you are satisfied you got through.

The third L is "leave yourself out." It is very important to understand that the performance review is about and for your subordinate. So your own insecurities, anxieties, guilt, or whatever should be kept out of it. The subordinate's problems are the issue, not the supervisor's, and it is the subordinate's day in court.

Anyone called upon to assess the performance of another person is likely to have strong emotions before and during the review, just as actors have stage fright. You should work to control these emotions so that they don't affect your task, though they will well up no matter how many reviews you've given.

"On the one hand ... on the other"

Most reviews probably fall into the "On the one hand ... on the other" category, containing both positive and negative assessments. (See pages 242 and 243 for a sample appraisal.) Common problems of this type of review include superficiality, cliches, and laundry lists of unrelated observations. All of these will leave your subordinate bewildered and will hardly improve future performance, the review's basic purpose.

The key to successfully delivering this type of review is to recognize that your subordinate, like most people, has only a *finite capacity* to deal with facts, issues, and suggestions. You may know seven truths about an employee's performance, but if that employee has the capacity to absorb only four, you will, at best, waste your breath on the other three. At worst, you will have left your subordinate with a case of sensory overload; he or she will go away without getting anything out of the review.

results he wants to accomplish.

John's prior finance background has really helped in a variety of work areas. For example, John voluntarily helped the purchasing group sort out some of its finance problems—an effort above and beyond the call of duty. [Compliments need examples, too!]

John would like to be promoted to the next management level. This will not happen at this time, but I am satisfied that his capabilities will allow him to be promoted eventually. Before that happens, however, John must be able to take complex projects, like the manufacturing-spec system, and show results. This requires a clear and concise breakdown of problems, identification of goals, and establishment of the way to achieve those goals. [Attempt to show how to improve performance.] John, for the most part, will have to achieve this on his own. While I will help when needed, John has to be the primary driver. Only when he shows that he is capable of independent work along these lines can he be promoted.

In summary, John is capable of doing his current job. I realize that John has had difficulty in changing from a finance to a manufacturing environment. I will continue to try to help him—particularly in setting goals and defining ways of accomplishing his tasks. John's performance in Materials Support is rated as "meets requirements"—a rating he should definitely be able to improve.

RATING: ☐ Does not meet requirements
☑ Meets requirements
☐ Exceeds requirements
☐ Superior

*Immediate supervisor: _CAV_	**Date:**	**8/10/82**
*Approving supervisor: _JHF_	**Date:**	**8/15/82**
**Matrix manager: _Arne_	**Date:**	**8/10/82**
Personnel Administrator: _Sam_	**Date:**	**8/18/82**
***Employee: _John Doe_	**Date:**	**8/22/82**

*Two levels of management plus personnel required for checks and balances.
**Review was prepared jointly with head of the Material Manager's Council: an example of dual reporting.
***Employee signature shows that he has been given the review; does not necessarily mean that he agrees with it.

Employee Appraisal

The purpose of the review is not to cleanse *your* system of all the truths you may have observed, but to improve *your subordinate's* performance. So here, less may very well be more.

How can you target a few key points? First, consider as many aspects of your subordinate's performance as possible. You should scan progress reports, performance against quarterly objectives, and one-

on-one meeting notes. Then sit down with a blank piece of paper, and as you consider your subordinate's performance, write everything down. Do *not* edit in your head. Include *everything*, knowing that doing so doesn't commit you to do *anything*. Factors major, minor, and trivial can be included in any order. When you have run out of items, you can put away all your supporting documentation.

Now, from your worksheet, look for relationships between the various items listed. You will probably begin to notice that certain items are different manifestations of the same phenomenon, and that there may be some indications *why* a certain strength or weakness exists. When you find such relationships, you can start calling them "messages" for the subordinate. At this point, your worksheet might look something like the one illustrated.

Again, from your worksheet, begin to draw conclusions and specific examples to support them. Once your list of messages has been compiled, ask yourself if your subordinate will be able to *remember* all of the messages you have chosen to deliver. If not, you must delete the less important ones. Remember, what you couldn't include in this review, you can probably take up in the next one.

If you have discharged your supervisory responsibilities adequately throughout the year, holding regular one-on-one meetings and providing guidance when needed, there should never be any surprises at a performance review, right? Wrong. Using the worksheet, you sometimes come up with a message that startles you. You're faced with either delivering the message or not. But since the purpose of the review is to improve your subordinate's performance, you must deliver it. Preferably, a review will not contain any surprises, but if you uncover one, swallow hard and bring it up.

With a little soul-searching, you may come to realize that you have a major performance problem on your

---

Performance-appraisal worksheet sample

Positives

Planning process much better! (Quick start)

Good report to Materials Council

Helped on purchasing cost-analysis project

Negatives

Spec process: zero!

Debating society meetings—all mushy

Poor kick-off for spec training

Confused on computer use

Doesn't listen to peers

Messages

1. Good results on planning system (analytical/financial background useful).

2. Hard time setting clear, crisp goals—satisfied with activities instead of driving results!

3. Computer knowledge (No—let's just concentrate on No. 2).

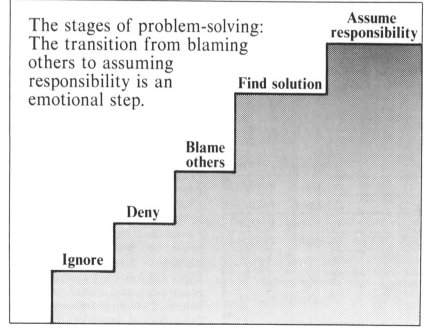

The stages of problem-solving: The transition from blaming others to assuming responsibility is an emotional step.

Assume responsibility

Find solution

Blame others

Deny

Ignore

---

hands. You have a subordinate who, unless turned around, could be fired. To deal with the problem, you and your subordinate will likely go through stages commonly experienced in problem-solving of all kinds and particularly in conflict resolution. (See the illustration on page 244 .) You'll find these occurring definitely during and possibly after the "blast" review, which is basically an exercise of resolving conflict about a big performance problem.

A poor performer has a strong tendency to *ignore* the problem. Because this is so, a manager needs facts and examples to demonstrate the reality. Progress of some sort is made when the subordinate *actively denies* the existence of a problem rather than ignoring it passively, as before. Evidence can overcome resistance here as well, and we enter the third stage, when the subordinate admits that there is a problem, but maintains it is "not *my* problem." Instead, he or she will *blame others*, a standard defense mechanism. Using this defense, the poor performer can continue to avoid the responsibility and burden of remedying the situation.

These three steps usually follow one another in fairly rapid succession. But matters tend to get stuck at the blame-others stage. If your subordinate does have a problem, there's no way of resolving it if he or she continues to blame others. The poor performer has to take the biggest step, namely, *assuming responsibility*. The poor performer has to say not only that there is a problem but, "If it is my problem, I have to do something about it. If I have to do something, it is likely to be unpleasant and will definitely mean a lot of work on my part." Once responsibility is assumed, however, *finding the solution* is relatively easy. This is because the move from blaming others to assuming responsibility constitutes an emotional step, while the move from assuming responsibility to finding the solution is an intellectual one. The first is harder to do.

It is the reviewer's job to get the

subordinate to move through all of the stages to that of assuming responsibility, though finding the solution should be a shared task. The supervisor should keep track of what stage matters are at. If the supervisor wants to go on to find the solution when the subordinate is still denying or blaming others, nothing can happen. Knowing where you are will help you both move through the stages *together*.

In the end, there are three possible outcomes. One, the subordinate

---

"It is very important to assess actual performance, not appearance; real output, not good form."

---

accepts your assessment and your recommended cure, and commits to taking it. Two, the poor performer disagrees completely with your assessment, but still accepts your cure. Three, the employee disagrees with your assessment and does *not* commit to do what you've recommended. As the supervisor, which of these should you consider *acceptable* resolutions to the problem?

I feel very strongly that any outcome that includes a *commitment* to action is acceptable. Complex issues do not lend themselves easily to universal agreement. If your subordinate is committed to changing the situation, you have to assume he or she is sincere. It is certainly more desirable

for you and your subordinate to agree about the problem and the solution, because that will make you feel that the employee will enthusiastically work toward remedying it. So, up to a point, you should try to get your subordinate to agree with you. But even if you can't, accept a commitment to change and go on.

Don't confuse emotional comfort with operational need. To make things work, you do not need people to side with you; you only need them to commit themselves to a course of action that has been decided upon. There seems to be something not quite nice about expecting people to walk down a path they'd rather not be on. But on the job, we are after a person's performance, not our psychological comfort.

I learned the distinction between the two during one of the first reviews I had to give. I was trying very hard to persuade my subordinate to see things my way. He simply would not go along with me and finally said to me, "Andy, you will never convince me, but why do you insist on wanting to convince me? I've already said I will do what you say." I shut up, embarrassed, not knowing why. It took me a long time before I realized I was embarrassed because my insistence had a lot to do with making me feel better and little to do with running a business.

If it becomes clear that you are not going to get your subordinate past the blame-others stage, you will have to assume the formal role of the supervisor, endowed with position power, and say, "This is what I, as your boss, am instructing you to do. I understand that you do not see it my way. You may be right or I may be right. But I am not only empowered, I am required by the organization for which we both work to give you instructions, and this is what I want you to do." Then proceed to secure your subordinate's *commitment* to the course of action you want and thereafter monitor his or her *performance* against that commitment.

Recently, one of my subordinates wrote a review that I considered

Employee Appraisal

superficial—lacking analysis and depth. After some discussion, my subordinate agreed with my assessment, but he considered the issue not important enough, as he put it, to spend time rewriting the review. After more spirited discussions, we still were deadlocked. Finally, I took a deep breath and said to him, "Look, I understand that you don't consider it worth your time to do it. But I *want* you to do it." Then I added, "I guess there is a basic difference between us. The integrity of the performance-review system is just more important to me than it is to you. That is why I have to insist." He looked back at me and, after a moment, simply said, "Okay." He thought I was out in left field and resented the fact that I made him spend time on something he thought was unimportant, but he committed himself to redo the review, and, in fact, did it well. His subordinate ended up getting the reworked, much more thorough and

> "When we promote our best, we are telling our subordinates that performance is what counts."

thoughtful review, and the fact that his review was rewritten without the agreement of *my* subordinate made no difference to him.

Reviewing the ace

After trying to establish the principles of performance appraisal with a group of about 20 middle managers, I asked them to take a review they had once received and to analyze it according to our new criteria. The results were not what I expected, but I did learn from them.

This group consisted of achievers, and their ratings were mostly very high. The reviews were exceptionally well written, much better than the average. However, in content, they tended to be retrospective assessments, analyses of what the sub-

ordinate had done in the course of the prior year. Even though their key purpose was to improve the subordinate's future performance, a majority of the reviews made little or no attempt to define what the subordinate needed to do to improve performance or even to maintain the current level.

It seems that, for achievers, the supervisor's effort goes into determining and justifying the judgment of the superior performance, while giving little attention to how they could do even better. But for poor performers, the supervisor tends to concentrate heavily on ways they can improve performance, providing detailed and elaborate "corrective-action programs," step-by-step affairs meant to ensure that these marginal employees can pull themselves up to meet minimum requirements.

I think we have our priorities reversed. Shouldn't we spend more time trying to improve the performance of our stars? After all, these people account for a disproportionately large share of the work in any organization. Put another way, concentrating on the stars is a high-leverage activity: If they get better, the impact on group output is very great indeed.

We all have a hard time saying things that are critical, whether we're talking to a superior employee or a marginal one. We must keep in mind, however, that no matter how stellar a person's performance level is, there is *always* room for improvement. Don't hesitate to use the 20/20 hindsight

provided by the review to show anyone, even an ace, how he or she might have done better.

Other Practices

Is it a good idea to ask the subordinate to prepare some kind of self-review before the supervisor's review? Let me answer the question this way: Your own review is obviously important to you, and you really want to know how your supervisor assesses your year's work. If you prepare a review and give it to your supervisor, who simply changes the format, retypes it, gives you a superior rating, and then hands it back to you, how will you feel? Probably cheated. If you have to tell your supervisor about your accomplishments, he or she obviously doesn't pay much attention to what you are doing. Reviewing the performance of subordinates is a formal act of leadership. If supervisors permit themselves to be prompted in one

> "Performance reviews should be part of managerial practice in organizations of any size and kind."

way or another, their leadership and their capacity for it will begin to appear false. The integrity of the supervisors' judgment here must be preserved. They must commit themselves through an up-front judgment of their subordinates' performance if the health and vitality of the review process are to be maintained.

What about asking your subordinate to evaluate *your* performance as a supervisor? This might be a good idea. But you should make it clear that it's your job to assess your staff's performance, while their assessment of you has only advisory status. The point is, they are not your leader; you are theirs. And under no circumstances should you pretend that you and your subordinates are

Employee Appraisal

equal during performance reviews.

Should you deliver the written review before, during, or after the face-to-face discussion?

What happens if you have the review first and then give your subordinate what you've written later? Upon reading it, the subordinate may find a phrase not "heard" earlier and blow up over it.

What about delivering the written review *during* the discussion? One manager told me that he gives the subordinate a copy of the review with instructions to read the first several paragraphs, which they then discuss. Grouping the paragraphs, supervisor and subordinate work their way through the appraisal. I can see a problem with this. How can a supervisor ask subordinates to stop at paragraph three when they are so eager to read the rest of what they've got? Another manager told me that he reads the written review to his sub-

ordinate to try to control the session. But here, too, the subordinate is left eager to know what comes next and might not pay attention to what is really being said. Also, when subordinates are given a written review during the discussion, they won't have the time to think about what it says and are likely to walk away muttering, "I should have said this in response, and I should have said that." For a good meeting of minds, your subordinates should have time to work out their reactions to what's in the review.

In my experience, it's best to give subordinates the written review sometime *before* the face-to-face discussion. They can then read the whole document privately and digest it. They can react or overreact and then look at the "messages" again. By the time the two of you get together, the subordinate you're reviewing will be much better prepared.

Preparing and delivering a performance assessment is one of the hardest tasks you'll have to perform as a manager. The best way to learn how to do one is to think critically

---

"The review process represents the most formal type of institutionalized leadership."

---

about the reviews you yourself have received. If you've been lucky, the tradition of good performance reviews has been handed down from supervisor to subordinate, which has helped to maintain the integrity of the system in your company. Nevertheless, people constantly need to be prodded into doing a good job of reviewing. Each year, I read something like 100 evaluations, all of those written by my own subordinates and a random selection from throughout Intel. I comment on them and send them back for rewrites or with a complimentary note. I do this with as much noise and visibility as I can, because I want to reiterate and reaffirm the significance the system has and should have for every Intel employee. Anything less would not be appropriate for the most important kind of task-relevant feedback we can give our subordinates. □

Andrew S. Grove is president and a founder of Intel Corp. This is the second and last article Computer Decisions *has excerpted and adapted from his book* High Output Management. *(The first, on meetings, appeared in the January issue.) Copyright© 1983 by Andrew S. Grove; reprinted by permission of Random House Inc.*

Turning around turnover

by Stanley R. Acker, Ph. D.

Controlling turnover is no simple assignment with easy solutions, such as increasing salary.

After understanding the dynamics of turnover and diagnosing the situation specific to an employee within a department, the problems can be effectively attacked with both traditional solutions— salary, fringe benefits—as well as less costly, yet viable untraditional answers.

In spite of the business cycle, excessive turnover continues to be a key problem faced by computer management.

But before trying to control it, it is necessary to define turnover as the voluntary separation of any employee whom the organization would have preferred not to lose. Thus, separations from payroll due to retirement, layoff, being fired, etc., are not included. Nor are instances of resignation in which the employee leaves just one jump ahead of the pink slip.

Turnover is not limited to resignations.

Transfers to other components of the company also are included. Loss of a valued individual to another department can be just as devastating as loss to another company. When such transfers have a negative impact, they must be considered as turnover by the losing component.

The sheer cost of turnover alone should attract the attention of the manager. While it is difficult to isolate such costs accurately, estimates are generally quite high.

In an informal survey (conducted by the author), the average cost of recruiting plus relocation ranged from as low as $3,000 per hire to over $8,000. Training costs are harder to pinpoint, but most managers attribute a major portion of the salary for the first three months to orientation and break-in. The range for the total cost of recruiting, relocating and training seems to be on the order of $6,000 to $10,000 or more per hire.

Mid-project resignation

More difficult to estimate is the impact on the output of a department when someone resigns in the middle of a project, leading to an opening which goes unfilled for several months, thus forcing the rest of the staff to work excessive overtime. The overtime issue can lead to

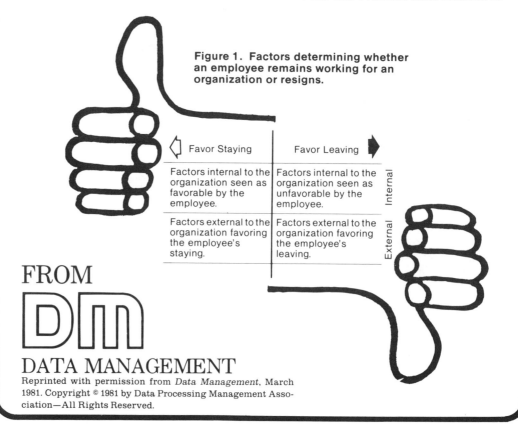

Figure 1. Factors determining whether an employee remains working for an organization or resigns.

Favor Staying	Favor Leaving	
Factors internal to the organization seen as favorable by the employee.	Factors internal to the organization seen as unfavorable by the employee.	Internal
Factors external to the organization favoring the employee's staying.	Factors external to the organization favoring the employee's leaving.	External

FROM

DM
DATA MANAGEMENT

other resignations, causing turnover to feed on itself.

The dynamics of turnover

Before attempting to control turnover, each manager should understand some of its dynamics.

Most attempts to identify turnover causes have not been rewarding. Reliance is typically placed on the exit interview to provide data. There are drawbacks to this approach. Employees are known to be careful about what they say in the exit interview, not wanting to leave a bad impression. They know that they may need a reference from the organization in the future. Frequently, some socially acceptable reason will be given for the decision, and it usually contains at least an element of truth. "My spouse needs a drier climate." "I wanted a chance to work with distributed processing." "My parents are getting older and I need to live nearer to them." And so on.

When it is all put together, there are no apparent common threads. There does not seem to be anything there which the organization could "fix." Despite considerable effort, no one is any closer to understanding the turnover than before.

Turnover reasons to describe

The problem with this approach is that it is too simplistic. Turnover is a form of behavior and the causes of behavior can never be explained in simple terms. Whether an individual elects to remain with an organization or to resign should be thought of in terms of a complex field of four kinds of forces. Figure 1 shows their interrelationship.

Some forces are under the control of the company. These are depicted in the top half of Figure 1. Others are external to the organization. These are represented by the bottom half of the diagram. In the upper left are those internal factors which are seen by the employee in a favorable light and exert a positive force in the decision-making process. These may include such things as:

- I like my boss.
- There is challenge and variety in my job.

- I work for a highly successful organization.
- I expect to be promoted in the near future.
- I have a lot of freedom in scheduling my working hours.

Internal factors which have a negative impact are in the upper right. Examples of these might include:

- I can't get on the computer to run my tests without a long wait, or else I have to run on batch.
- I have to work too much overtime near the end of a project just because someone else fell behind schedule in the earlier phases.
- There is a slow response time at the terminals.
- I do not have a private office.
- Good work doesn't get enough recognition.

External factors which favor the employee's staying are represented on the lower left of the diagram. Examples of these might include:

- We like our house and would hate to move.
- Our kids like this school system more than any they have been in before.
- I don't like to go through adjusting to new situations.

External factors which favor the employee's leaving are represented in the lower right hand box of the diagram. Examples of these might be:

- I am getting calls every week about jobs which would be immediate promotions.
- I have always wanted to live in _____ and I know I could get a job there.
- I could work with the latest equipment at another company.
- Taxes here are oppressive.

At each moment in time, all of these forces are in resolution, producing a decision to stay or leave. Where the predominance of force is solidly on the left side of the diagram, that decision is infrequently reviewed. As the two sides approach equilibrium, the decision may be reviewed almost daily. In the latter instance, it may not take much in the

way of an event or change to shift the balance to the right, leading to a resignation. When a minor incident apparently stimulates a resignation, it seems incomprehensible to the manager because he or she does not see or know about *all* of the factors which the employee considered in arriving at the decision. By the same token, exit interview data often reveals only the precipitating factor and fails to uncover all of the contributing factors.

One complication in understanding turnover is that not everyone values the same things. For example, the location of the job is of paramount importance for some people;

Turnover directly relates to an employee's personal value system.

---

for others, it makes little difference. Such variance adds complexity; but fortunately it does not reduce the usefulness of the concept as a basis for developing turnover-control strategies.

Diagnosing the situation

Diagnosis of the situation is fundamental.

The objective is to identify the factors which the people in the computer organization place in the four boxes. This must be done systematically and on a comprehensive basis.

In approaching diagnosis, it is generally safe to assume that employees place high value on working in an organization where things go well. A smoothly-working organization produces fewer frustrations for the employee than one which has a low level of efficiency. People like to be able to take pride in the organization of which they are a part. Employees do not like to be associated with a loser. Nor do they enjoy working where there is constant friction and uncertainty. Thus, a basic premise of diagnosis is that anything which is seen as interfering with the effectiveness of the organization is likely to contribute to turnover.

The challenge is to find ways to obtain the needed information. It must be remembered that one of the boxes (upper right) contains information which probably reflects negatively on the organization, and another (lower right) which could make the company appear deficient by comparison with other companies. Consequently, employees could withhold important information if they feared that providing it would lead to some form of retribution.

Selecting an appropriate strategy is extremely important.

In doing so, the situation in the organization will have to be carefully considered. In a very open, ideal organization, good results might be obtained by having employees attend group meetings where they are asked to identify factors they consider important in the turnover equation. This would have the drawback that it would be difficult to determine whether the employees were really being candid. If they were to withhold just one very important piece of information, it could affect the obtained results very substantially.

Serious consideration should be given to an employee survey to develop diagnostic information.

This is one of the oldest tools available in the field of employee communications, and, if properly handled, can produce excellent results. A key advantage is that it provides complete anonymity for respondents. While there are sound books on survey methodology, such as Nadler's,[2] this option is hardly for the amateur. Professional assistance is strongly recommended.

Another method of diagnosis is use of a trusted third party to develop the necessary information through confidential interviews of employees.

This has the advantage of allowing problems and situations to be described and explained in detail. A possible disadvantage is that its success depends on the ability of the interviewer. It is possible for the interviewer to bias the results by the way the questions are asked or by inaccurately recording what has been said in reply. When carried out by someone with the proper skills,

however, excellent results can be achieved.

No matter which approach to diagnosis is used, the major emphasis of this phase must be on the identification of those factors which are under the control of the organization. While there should be awareness of the external factors, the internal ones deserve the most attention.

Most organizations will be able to identify factors which are significant impediments to effectiveness. Here are some examples taken from actual situations:

- In a terminal environment, a shortage of terminals forces programmers to do more desk checking than they would prefer.
- The overall reputation of the MIS and/or DP department with users is rather low because of disputes over priorities; this poor reputation detracts from the pride of accomplishment of the software people who are doing work of very high quality.
- Constant friction between computer operations and systems analysis is upsetting to everyone.
- Excessive overtime is necessary and programmers are talking about organizing a union.

Problem solving

Once the situation has been diagnosed, problem-solving can begin.

This may be carried out by the management team or by a special task force. The objective, of course, is to find ways to eliminate negative factors; enhance existing positive

---

Raising salaries sometimes is a "quick fix" to a deep seated personnel problem in the DP center.

---

factors; create additional positive factors; and to convert, where possible, negatives into positives. Appropriate problem-solving techniques, such as those described by Schein[3] and Kaufman,[1] are employed to ensure that optimum solutions are reached.

It will be discovered that some of the internal factors are not subject to control by the management of the computer group. Policies set by the corporation might be an example. Whatever is fixed or given in the situation, if it has a negative impact, the strategy must be to develop positives of sufficient strength to serve as an offset. Whatever is done which shifts the balance of forces in favor of staying will reduce turnover. It is not necessary to eliminate all negatives or to solve all problems.

Salary rates are an example. Whenever turnover is discussed, someone usually takes the position that the only way to reduce it is to raise salaries. This may or may not be an appropriate action. Compensation is a factor which is weighed by employees along with all other factors; it does not, in most instances, outweigh everything else. There is undoubtedly some correlation between salary scales and turnover, but empirical observation says it is not as high as many might believe.

Raising salary schedules could be a way of providing a "quick fix," but it may not be the most lasting or the most economical.

Usually a more productive way of looking at the situation is to ask what can be changed or improved which will encourage people to stay in spite of salaries which are no more than "competitive." It may turn out that a change in rates makes sense, but that should not be done without a complete look at the total situation. If, for whatever reasons, the organization elects to raise salaries in lieu of making changes which would lead to improvement in effectiveness, it will usually be electing a much more costly approach, and certainly one which does not leave the organization any stronger.

Follow-up

Regardless of what emerges from the problem-solving phase, it is necessary to provide for systematic follow-up to ensure that planned solutions are properly implemented and maintained. Careful records of turnover should be kept and trends examined regularly to see if the changes and improvements have had an impact.

In any dynamic situation, as old problems are solved, new ones emerge to replace them. Recognizing this, the wise manager will not wait until negative factors begin to creep back into the situation before recycling turnover control efforts. For some organizations, the use of organizational diagnosis and related problem-solving has become a continuous process. It can and should become a way of life in any organization which values good management.

The most critical step in controlling turnover is to recognize that control is possible. Some managers will not want to make such an admission because doing so would obligate them to take steps to solve the problem. And that would mean more demands on their time and require more effort than they feel able to put forth. For those who do accept this challenge, however, lasting results can be achieved which are not only economically sound but gratifying to the entire organization as well. Control of turnover is a concept which deserves careful thought by every DP manager. ∎

About the author

Dr. Acker is president of Acker Associates, a Stamford, CT, based consultant firm specializing in human resources management.—Ed.

References
1. *Kaufman, Roger.* Identifying and Solving Problems: A System Approach. *University Associates, La Jolla, CA, 1976.*
2. *Nadler, David A.* Feedback and Organization Development: Using Data-Based Methods. *Addison-Wesley, Reading, MA, 1977.*
3. *Schein, Edgar H.* Process Consultation: Its Role in Organization Development. *Addison-Wesley, Reading, MA, 1969.*

Part V: Directing

"To resolve to make your meaning plain, even at the cost of some trouble to yourself, is more important than any other single thing."

—*Ernest Gowers*

Directing is the interpersonal aspect of managing. It requires telling people what to do and monitoring them to ensure that they do it. To direct subordinates effectively, a manager is concerned with motivation, communication, and leadership. The nine articles that follow were selected to provide readers with a review of the concepts of participative management and experiences associated with them.

Stevens and Krochmal discuss how managers can motivate their subordinates to achieve greater productivity. Their article, "Engineering Motivators and Demotivators," relates motivation to job satisfaction and, consequently, technical performance.

The next three articles deal with leadership and leadership style. In "Leadership is Crucial," Kimmerly discusses how the management functions of direction and control interrelate. He advocates balance so that the control system employed is not preceived as a threat by the workers to be motivated. In "Leadership Effectiveness of Program Management," Thamhain and Wilemon discuss how leadership style affects performance in various project-oriented work environments. In "Grid Management" the concept of management style is discussed and a self-assessment procedure is provided to allow the reader to determine a style by using the concept of management grid.

Raudsepp, in "Are You Getting Through to Your Staff?" discusses the all important topic of communications. Techniques for reducing misunderstandings are described in a way that make them useful for the practicing manager.

French and Hollmann, in "Management by Objectives: The Team Approach," provide a simple explanation of the concept of management by objectives and show how it can be used to complement various leadership styles. They argue successfully that the MBO concept is fully compatible with participative, team-leadership styles. This result has some interesting ramifications if applied to egoless and chief programer teams (see *Tutorial on Structured Programming: Integrated Practices* by V.R. Basili, and F.T. Baker, IEEE Computer Society, 1981, for details on the team approaches).

In "Delegate Your Way to Success," Raudsepp discusses the all important topic of delegation. In addition to providing a self-assessment procedure, the article identifies ways of making delegation easier for all concerned.

The last two articles are parodies on management styles. Adizes, in "Mismanagement Styles," describes four roles of management that enable him to construct a typology of organization incompetence in accordance with the Peter Principle. Watt, in "The Advanced Manager," uses the negative to describe what a manager should and should not do if he/she wants to be effective.

253

IEEE 1977 National Aerospace and Electronics Conference

THE PRACTICING ENGINEER-MANAGER

ENGINEERING MOTIVATORS AND DEMOTIVATORS

HOWARD P. STEVENS
SSS Consulting Inc.

JEROME J. KROCHMAL*

By understanding the relative strength of various motives it is possible to identify key motivational stimuli effective with Engineers. They exhibit a high degree of task or "achievement" motivation, little relationship, and almost no influence or "power" motivation.

Both positive and negative stimuli can be identified to maximize the motivation and potential satisfaction for typical engineers. Managers who understand both the motive and the stimuli may often be able to better "direct" the individual and predict or influence the outcome of situations that engineers are involved in.

Practicing Engineers are unusual people. They tend to differ dramatically from others they usually work with. They are not like managers and administrators, or even accountants or personnel specialists (others who also have specific knowledge). To understand the engineer, to have a "feel" for what may make him go, it is helpful to look at least briefly at motivation itself.

Research over the past decade (by McClelland and others**) has identified three major variables that seem to account for a large part of the work motivation in an individual. These three motives which can now also be measured with some degree of confidence, are being used to identify individuals who tend to both enjoy and succeed in different work areas and careers. For each vocation, engineering, managing, sales, there is a consistency, a definite pattern or profile of motives that is characteristic of individuals who prosper in that field.

Three Basic Work Motives

In our research we have defined a motive in the simple sense as a press or drive toward a specific kind of goal (reward or pay-off). The key motives center around (1) performing and becoming skillful at tasks, (2) meeting and forming relationships with people (popularity), and (3) influencing or directing people or events (impact). In people, motivation is commonly seen as the amount of satisfaction or positive feeling they have about reaching a given goal. The "Motivation" they feel before the goal is reached is an anticipation of that satisfaction.

	TASK	*RELATIONSHIP*	*INFLUENCE*
OBJECTIVE	THINGS	PEOPLE	ACTIVITY/PROCESS
DESIRE	TO BE USEFUL AND SKILLFUL OR TO ACCOMPLISH	TO BE POPULAR	TO BE IMPORTANT AND HAVE IMPACT
FEELING I GET (THE PAY)	ACHIEVEMENT	AFFILIATION OR ACCEPTANCE	POWER

* A.F. Wright Aeronautical Lab.
**David C. McClelland, "Achievement Motivation Can Be Developed," *Harvard Business Review*, Nov.-Dec., 1965.

Working to Get Things Done

Task Motivation is most similar to the desire to be useful and practical or to accomplish something. It is typically "thing" oriented or directed toward making, building, changing, or creating. The feeling associated with task motivation is the sense of accomplishment or achievement. An individual who exhibits a high degree of Task (or Achievement) Motivation can usually be described with specific characteristics:

Task Characteristics

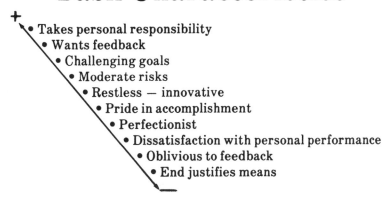

+
- Takes personal responsibility
- Wants feedback
- Challenging goals
- Moderate risks
- Restless — innovative
- Pride in accomplishment
- Perfectionist
- Dissatisfaction with personal performance
- Oblivious to feedback
- End justifies means
–

Working for Friendship

Relationship motivation is an interest in people, the desire to be popular, and the desire to establish and maintain personal relationships with others. The feeling associated with relationship motivation is one of acceptance or camaraderie with others. An individual with strong motivation for relationships can usually be identified with these specific characteristics:

Relationship Characteristics

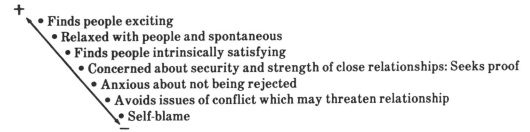

+
- Finds people exciting
- Relaxed with people and spontaneous
- Finds people intrinsically satisfying
- Concerned about security and strength of close relationships: Seeks proof
- Anxious about not being rejected
- Avoids issues of conflict which may threaten relationship
- Self-blame
–

Working for the General Good or for Personal Recognition

Influence motivation centers its concern around activity or processes. The desire is to have impact on people and events, and in that sense to be important or significant in the activities and accomplishments of others.

The feeling one gets is in the sense of importance. A high influence motivation frequently suggests the following typical characteristics:

Influence Characteristics

+
- Having impact for the sake of others
- Joins organizations/organized sports — apt to become officers
- Concern for group goals
- Prestige supplies
- Gives group feeling of competence
- Enjoys personal dominance
- Survival of the fittest
- Accepts win/lose situations as a natural part of life
- Aggressive impulses: heavy drinking, gambling, speeding, physical fights

255

MOTIVATION —
HOW STRONG AND HOW LONG LASTING

The Effect of "Sticks and Carrots"

Everyone recognizes that motivation can vary in intensity. We can be extremely excited and enthusiastic about a particular project, theme, or idea at one time, and then lose interest or even become negative to it at another. On occasion, it may even be cyclical where we can gain interest, lose interest, and then gain it again.

Research has demonstrated that these three basic motives may be stimulated in two ways. In a simpler sense, motivation can be positive, that is, toward some desirable outcome or goal, or it can be negative. Negative motivation is directed toward escaping from, or preventing, some undesirable outcome.

MOTIVATION VALENCE

Whether a motivation is positive or negative greatly controls its strength and duration. In general, positive motivations (toward something desirable) tend to be self-sustaining. The more a person has the opportunity to reach his goals, the more likely he is to want to reach more goals. Negative motivation, on the other hand, tends to decrease if it is satisfied. The more one escapes negative results or outcomes, the less likely he is to be motivated to do anything else.

The strength of a felt negative motivation is directly related to the proximity of the negative stimulus, and increases rapidly at close proximity (in either time or physical space) to the impending negative "goal" as in Figure 1.

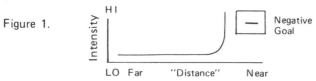

Figure 1.

Positive motivation is not as sensitive to proximity and increases gradually and rather consistently as the positive goal is approached. It can be almost as intense at a great distance as when the goal is near.

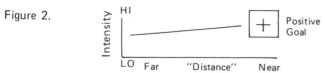

Figure 2.

In practical terms, a negative motive is not stimulated as intensely at a great distance (in either time or physical space) and many negative aspects may not even be perceived at a distance. A positively task motivated person thus may not even think much about the possibility of failure of a project two years down the road, or have very strong feelings if he does think about it. Yet the same person may become intensely concerned about a much smaller and less significant "problem" that is coming up this afernoon.

Motivation, of course, is usually not that simple. Most "goals" in life have both negative and positive motivating valences to them. This helps to explain why the honor of an invitation to present a paper at an exclusive high-powered conference of experts may be exciting six months away, while the actual writing, correcting, and editing, etc. may seem a huge burden one week before the deadline.

To the high achiever, the positive aspects of interested experts, unique work, positive feedback on the accomplishments to be reported are all positive motivators; and, six months before, they are all that are perceived (or felt). The negative aspects, of writing, English grammar, corrections — all more mundane, routine, and therefore potentially frustrating factors, are usually not perceived or considered until time (proximity) demands they be done. In some cases even the person himself doesn't seem to understand why he gets himself "trapped" at the last moment to rush around trying to get those elements completed and "out of the way." He doesn't realize that the negative motivation aspects do not "press" until they are proximate.

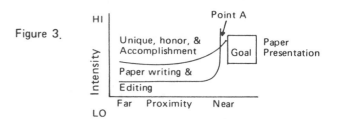

Figure 3.

In Figure 3, Point A is the point where the motivation appears to switch from being positive (an honor and pleasure) to being negative (an obligation and a burden) — from "I want to do it" to "I wish I didn't have to" (Goal Avoidance).

The same variation can work in reverse as well, which explains why a negative factor that is postponed for six months may cease to have any impact at all.

Time and physical space are fairly easy to measure and with some practice it is possible to predict the motivational effect a given "stimulus" may have on an individual, an engineer for example. Psychological space or distance is harder to estimate.

PSYCHOLOGICAL SPACE
Two Factors That Affect Motivation

Internal Motivation and External Stimuli

In order to stimulate a motive, it must be present in the individual. The greater the motive, the less stimulation is necessary, and vice-versa. Thus, an individual who has a high task motive needs only a hint of a positive stimulus; a "unique challenge," for example, to turn him on.

If he has a high negative task motive, then only a hint that things are going wrong is enough to trigger him.

An individual with a low positive task motive and a high negative task motive may need to be stimulated and re-stimulated and guaranteed that things won't fail to even raise an interest. Likewise, an individual with a low negative task motive and a high positive task motive may need to believe that the roof has already caved in to even slow him down.

In simple terms, whether an individual is more stimulated by the chance for achievement or the fear of failure will determine how he reacts. The positive motive is more likely to last, by itself, with little outside stimulation (or manipulation by others); the negative motive is liable to remain more dormant without stimulation from the outside.

If an engineer has a positive task motive, an opportunity for challenge may be all that is necessary. If he has a high negative motive, however, a stimulus will have to be pretty visible and close at hand to get him to act. But that, of course, is why we need managers. If every task an engineer was expected to perform could be loaded with positive motive stimuli and totally free of negative stimuli, most engineers and most everyone else would do admirably without much direction. Most tasks and most organization goals have both elements, however. The successful manager learns how to step out of the way of positive opportunities or maximizes these stimuli. He lets the internal motivation develop on its own. Likewise, he manipulates negative factors to be the maximum constructive stimuli. He may, for example, tell the engineer that the deadline is two weeks earlier, to bring the negative stimulus closer to the engineer and thus more "stimulating." He realizes that the engineer may work just as hard to overcome negatives as he will to gain positives. It just takes more "negative stimulation" if he has a low internal negative motive, or "more" positive stimulation if he has a low positive motive.

A word of caution: The clever engineer may "work" to overcome or avoid the negative goals in ways that differ from our expectation. He may, for example, get someone else to write the paper rather than settling down himself to "get it over with." As a result, it is often easier to reassign duties than it is to stimulate a low negative motive or low positive motive. In fact, it is a maxim that it is easier to *select* the individual to *fit* the situation than it is to change the individual's behavior very much in a situation that does not naturally stimulate his motives.

Based on McClelland's work, McBer and Company has been continuously researching and graphing typical profiles for a variety of career professions. While a given individual may be an exception, of course, the evidence does suggest that typical profiles clearly distinguish practical engineers from upper level managers, staff personnel, entrepreneurs (those who start their own businesses), etc. The profiles represent a measure of both positive and negative aspects of a motive combined.

ENGINEERS ARE TASK MOTIVATED

The motive profile plotted in Figure 4 (see next page) suggests practical engineers (as opposed to engineering managers, etc.) have very high task motivation, very little affiliation or relationship motivation, and almost no influence motivation. Incidentally, they were more similar to salesmen than most other career fields, which may explain why many engineering students end up in engineering sales.

Task Motivation in General and Engineers in Particular

Typical engineers who exhibit a high degree of task motivation have a tendency to take, and even demand, a high degree of control over their own activities. They need feedback and continually seek to know if they are progressing, what's happening, and how they are doing. In fact, this trait is so characteristic that we typically expect to see them with reports, charts, stats, or whatever sources of information will keep them in touch with what's going on. They like moderate (not extreme) risks and challenging goals. Routine bores typical engineers, and they get restless and often look for something new and unique if things are progressing too smoothly or too routinely. They do take a great deal of pride in their own accomplishments and set high goals, sometimes to excess. When they are frustrated and become negatively motivated, they may be severely critical of their own performance and can be greatly dissatisfied with their personal performance, even when others may say that it was good enough. As a result, they are sometimes seen as too perfectionistic — unwilling to let something go until *they've* decided it's ready, no matter how much someone else needs it. They may set their sights on a goal with such vigor that they are oblivious to anything else. When concentrating, they may not even hear others talking. Because of this they sometimes appear to be independent and insensitive.

In general, they are impressed with excellence and the unique and are continually looking for an easier or a different way to accomplish things. They also frequently have a difficult time accepting or understanding others who do not seem to be equally internally task motivated, for example, politicians, social workers, personnel people, and most "paper pushers" (administrators). They often have a hard time doing nothing, and would rather be active even if it's only busy work if there is little else to do. For that reason they always seem to have a variety of projects unfinished. It would seem to be some kind

Figure 4.

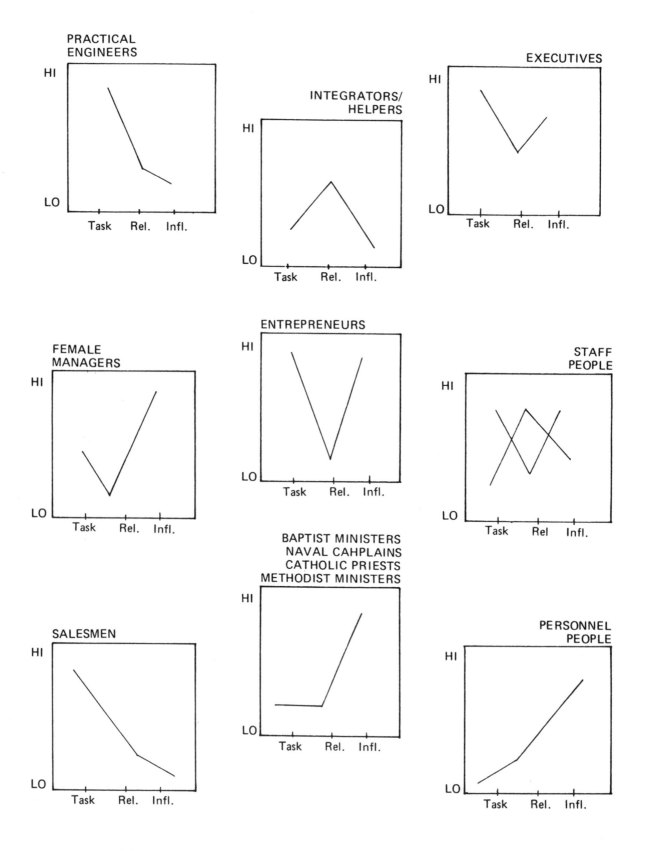

258

of back-up security so that they'll make sure they will always have something to do.

Probably the trait that is most typically bothersome to other individuals is their insensitivity to other motives or values. Sometimes their goal (their own task motive) becomes so important that almost any method of reaching it is considered as a possibility — "the end justifies the means." People who have a high relationship or influence need are often horrified by this attitude.

By way of comparison, it may be worthwhile to look at two other sets of characteristics, relationship and influence motivation, to give us a clearer understanding of what practical engineers are not.

The Need to Be Popular

Relationship motivation centers around the need to like and be liked by others. These people might be called "Very Friendly Types." Friendly Types, who exhibit a high degree of relationship motivation, typically find people stimulating and are almost always relaxed and spontaneous in dealing with people. They come across, therefore, as very natural and comfortable in almost any social situation. (Very seldom are practical engineers natural and comfortable in *any* social situation.) Friendly Types continually seek contact with people and find people intrinsically satisfying. As a result, they tend to gravitate towards social situations and even establish working conditions that allow them ample social and interpersonal contact. Not only do they like to meet new people, they particularly enjoy establishing new relationships as well as maintaining old ones.

In some cases, when they feel unsure of themselves and motivation is negative, they become concerned about their relationships and work to protect them. As this develops, they frequently seek proof or reassurance of their relationships, sometimes on a rather continual or repetitive basis. Friendly Types can become very anxious about being rejected, and when the anxiety is severe enough, they may even avoid any situation where there is a possibility of being rejected. Typically, they tend to avoid issues of conflict in an interpersonal situation, particularly if these conflicts are seen as things that may hurt someone. They will seldom pursue or debate arguments in a situation that seems even in the slightest way to threaten the relationship. (Engineers typically are more than willing to pursue a debate or argument regardless of who it's with.)

Because of the Friendly Types' concern for maintaining relationships, they have a tendency to be very apologetic, and this may appear as a tendency for self-blame. (Practical engineers, on the other hand, sometimes have a greater difficulty in apologizing and admitting that they are wrong than almost anything else that they might do.) It is important for Friendly Types to please others and maintain activities and attitudes that are pleasing to others; as a result, they frequently find themselves in the middle and are seen as the ones to turn to for smoothing things out or acting as an arbitrator or go-between of two conflicting sides. (The practical engineer, on the other hand, is more likely to be one of the conflicting sides, and almost never the go-between.)

Engineers can have some sympathy for people who are relationship motivated, particularly if they are stereotyped in that role, such as "women," mothers, secretaries, etc. They do have little real *understanding*, however, and have to be continually reminded that people do have feelings and get offended, etc. Many engineers (if they did not have good secretaries) would even forget their own wives' birthdays, regardless of how much trouble they got into for forgetting them the year before. Interestingly, many engineers think they are pretty friendly people, and so they may appear until you discover their "Friends" are other people who have similar goals or habits and they are really interested in what these others are doing. Such "relationships" are really satisfying the need to learn more, and keep up with interesting activities in a pleasant way.

The Need to Be Influential

Those who exhibit a high degree of influence motivation (such as managers), whom we will call "Influencers," seem to enjoy having impact, having their influence felt, frequently for the sake of others. They enjoy getting things done, doing favors and they generally impress others with a willingness to join in to get things done. They are inclined to be joiners in general, whether it be in organized sports, clubs, or other kinds of organizations, and it is typical of them to eventually become officers of these organizations.

When all is going well, they have a definite concern for group goals and can frequently put group needs ahead of personal needs. As a result, they may sometimes be seen as willing to sacrifice for the general good of the group or sacrifice quality for the sake of acceptance. (Engineers, on the other hand, if they believe that something is right, will seldom sacrifice their standards just so that more people will like it.) Influence people get a kick out of prestigious supplies, such as spacious houses, expensive cars, or well-appointed offices. They usually enjoy looking good, dressing appropriately, and being at their best. Sometimes they are thought of as meticulous, as a result. When they work with a group, they often tend to "pump up" the group, increasing the spirit or atmosphere, making various members of the group *feel* more competent.

When influencers are less comfortable with themselves and their motivation turns negative, they have a tendency towards dominance, and domination is the impression they give. When the chips are down, they can become hard and strong fighters who firmly believe in the survival of the fittest; but they are willing to accept losing situations as a natural part of life. They are not bothered by the fact of having to have a winner and a loser, and they enjoy the competition. They deal particularly well with political or complex social situations as a result. In some instances Influencers can be severely frustrated, which may lead to a tendency toward drinking, gambling, speeding, and other aggressive impulses. This is a result of a frustrated motive opportunity, however, rather than just an aspect of the motivation itself.

Engineers have a very difficult time understanding why people with influence motivation are so concerned about social pressure or political aspects, or whether or not the majority of people will think something is right. Engineers are often grated by the need to positively influence other people, the need for public relations, etc. While they can intellectually accept such efforts as necessary, they still think of them as an unfortunate waste of time.

In looking at these different motives and valences, and focusing in on the task motivation of the engineer, our research has identified several types of "turn-ons," as well as "turn-offs," for engineers.

Positives or "Turn-Ons"	Negatives or "Turn-Offs"
Moving forward on project when *he* feels it is appropriate, having & maintaining control	Waiting for politics, paperwork, etc. or things he can't control
Being able to measure his own progress	Not knowing how he's doing, or how his work is progressing
Having to keep in close touch only with project progress (that affects him)	Having to keep up with things that don't directly concern him; e.g., administrative meetings
Communication that is brief and to the point, practical and somewhat pragmatic	Policy statements, personnel forms, regulations and any long-worded "legaleze"
Practical work	Having to remember feelings, birthdays, and social events
Personal goals, in specific project goals	Group concerns and organizational goals

In summary, the research suggests that we may look at a practical engineer as a specialized individual who needs to be treated in a certain way. Consider the following tips to live effectively, or more agreeably, with the practical engineer:

Try to screen him from politics and things done just for appearance, as much as possible. Agree to the desired specific results from a project and give him his own head as much as possible in getting there. Have an assistant or someone do his "social work" for him, or, at least, with judicious reminders make it as easy as possible. Emphasize the uniqueness or unusualness of projects he is to work on; don't ask him to manage or motivate others who aren't proteges. Give him feedback as often as possible on how he's doing. Accept that he is liable to be opinionated and too outspoken for his own good. Realize and help others to realize that he often offends others without the slightest realization that he has. Keep personnel people and others with high influence and no achievement motivation as far away from him as possible. Remember that he can't accept doing things the traditional way and the proper way if he thinks there is a quicker and easier way. Give him full credit for anything he does, but remember he is more interested in stimulating goals and greater responsibility than your gold medal. Don't make him stand up for his awards too much; he'll belittle them, particularly if they are not awards from others in his field. He does like praise like anyone else, but hates to admit it. Make believe he's a genius that the world doesn't understand *Treat him like that and he's just liable to perform like one.* And if he's really turned on, put him in a fireproof room; he'd never get out because he'd never *hear* the alarm!

As a final thought, a minister we knew once summed up the engineer by saying, "He isn't that interested in *getting* to heaven, he wants to build one here!"

No dp group can perform up to its potential without the right mix of controls. Directives are useful, but . . .

LEADERSHIP IS CRUCIAL

by William C. Kimmerly

Regardless of how well an organization defines objectives, develops strategies, and implements plans, its eventual level of success will depend significantly on the quality and effectiveness of its management control function. This is especially true for the dp organization, which is particularly vulnerable to events and conditions that can complicate the control process.

Organizations exist so that the different tasks needed to accomplish common objectives can be coordinated, and the actions of individuals engaged in carrying out these tasks can be more effectively managed. In the absence of effective controls, people may work toward individual rather than common goals. The full meaning of the concept of control can, however, be somewhat elusive. In one sense, the term suggests the use of quantitative methods to measure the extent to which actual results correspond to expected results, followed by corrective action to redress unfavorable variances. In another sense, control relates to a condition or state of being, within which the overall efforts and direction of an organization remain effectively focused on a common purpose. In other words, there is a sense of overall control. In the first sense, the emphasis is on measurement and comparison; in the second sense, the emphasis is on maintaining an effective level of overall guidance, and suggests reasonable success in leading people to accept this guidance.

I will define control in terms of two distinguishing characteristics. The first relates to the degree of formality associated with the implementation and monitoring of a control measure; the second relates to the extent to which a control measure is required to exist.

Certain control measures are formally stated and rigidly enforced—rules against accessing an organization's sensitive databases without proper authorization, for example. Other controls exist in a very informal sense and receive little or no formal enforcement—e.g., an organizational dress code. Formal controls will be assumed to be either quantitative in nature or grounded in accepted rules or conventions. Informal controls will be assumed to be more qualitative in nature and based upon the individual employee's sense of purpose, commitment, or responsibility.

The second key distinguishing characteristic is the extent to which a control measure is required to be in place. Certain controls are simply an implicit result of formal organization—the requirement to follow Equal Employment Opportunity regulations, for example. Others are largely discretionary, their implementation depending upon the judgment of an accountable manager—e.g., the decision to implement a standard project management system. Given this basis of distinction, there are four general categories of control: implicit formal controls, implicit informal controls, discretionary formal controls, and discretionary informal controls. These distinctions are important because different management approaches and different considerations are often necessary for the effective implementation of each.

Clearly, managers cannot be involved in every decision an employee makes, or monitor every action taken by every employee. The best that can be done is to develop a control framework that leads to the right decisions being made and the right actions being taken most of the time.

Moreover, all decisions and all actions do not have the same degree of importance. The manager must be able to weigh the potential adverse consequences of formal controls in a given area—like employee resentment and lower morale—against the potential adverse consequences of inadequate controls. Common sense usually suffices here, but sometimes the issues will be extremely complex and the correct approach not so obvious. This is particularly true for the dp organization and its complex control environment. Therefore, a systematic approach is needed.

VALUABLE, LIMITED RESOURCES A key point underlying much of the following discussion is the fact that the time, attention, and influence of a manager are valuable but limited resources. All managers have a number of control objectives for their organizations, but some objectives are much more important than others. The successful manager will not want to waste influence on low-priority objectives. Instead, he or she will ensure that controls relating to these low-priority areas are enforced in ways that do not require continuing, visible management time and involvement.

Typically, the kinds of controls that can be approached in this way fall into either the implicit control category (formal or informal) or the discretionary formal control category. This means that the highest return on the investment of a manager's time and influence will be in the area of discretionary informal controls. This is the area that makes it possible to establish the kinds of normative behavior patterns that move the organization toward its keystone objectives.

Implicit formal controls. As indicated above, certain control requirements arise simply as an inherent consequence of formal organization. Because many of these requirements are grounded in legal or other formal considerations, the control measures themselves must be approached in a formal way. For example, Equal Employment Opportunity regulations control the actions of individuals involved in hiring, training, promotion, and related personnel actions. This is a control measure backed by the force of federal law; manage-

Formal procedures can ensure compliance without visible senior management involvement.

ment has no choice but to implement it in a formal way to ensure the required level of compliance.

Such control requirements do not usually need the ongoing, in-depth attention of the senior manager. This is not to say that the manager will regard these requirements as unimportant. Rather, formal procedures can ensure compliance without visible senior management involvement.

Depending upon the priorities of a particular manager, implicit controls can also be the basis for a discretionary form of control. For example, a manager might feel strongly about the EEO issue and seek to establish an aggressive program and a heightened level of sensitivity to related issues. This will necessitate a more sophisticated and more encompassing form of control than formal regulations might require. Maintaining such a level of control *does* require the visible, ongoing attention and influence of the senior manager.

Implicit informal controls. There are implicit controls that permit an informal approach to the definition of specific control measures and compliance requirements. Rules that relate to hours of work are one example. Typically, employees are not completely free to determine where and when they will carry out their assigned tasks, but aside from requirements imposed by wage and hour laws or union contracts (which are actually implicit formal controls), this can be, and often is, an area of relative informality.

Implicit informal controls are obviously an important part of the orderly functioning of an organization. As with implicit formal controls, however, the effective manager will tend to devote little time to enforcing them unless a problem exists. Most management attention is focused on these controls during their definition and implementation.

FAMILIAR CONTROL CATEGORY

Discretionary formal controls. This is probably the most familiar category of controls. The distinguishing feature of discretionary formal controls is the fact that once the decision has been made to implement them, they require formal compliance if they are to be effective. For example, the particular mix of budgets, standards, policies, regulations, and procedures implemented by a manager reflects his or her discretion as to which organizational and individual activities are to be controlled.

A few years ago, the term structured was very popular in many dp organizations (and is still popular in some). The term was applied to a collection of proce-

dures designed to control in a very precise way the actions of individuals engaged in specific activities—systems analysis, systems design, program development, or program coding, for example. These controls were discretionary in that they did not have to be in place in order for the dp organization to carry out its mission effectively; the manager could implement them or not depending upon his or her perception of their worth.

The controls were formal in that once implemented they were highly visible and served to limit the actions and decisions of individuals engaged in a given activity. Thus, structured requirements were unmistakable, unequivocal controls, optional in their adoption but not in their operation.

Because of the impact discretionary formal controls can have on an organization, the effective manager will want to examine their consequences carefully before authorizing them. To help in this examination, the manager will first want to separate the overall control requirements of the organization into key individual control areas.

Just as the concept of control in its broad, generic sense is too vague to serve as a framework for analytical discussion, control as an all-encompassing organizational requirement is too imprecise to serve as a basis for the development of discretionary formal controls. Control areas must first be defined that correspond to each of the key functions the organization must perform. In the dp environment, specific control areas might include software development, capacity management, data resource management, and so on. Each of these must have a central management focus in order to systematically influence behavior toward the key management objectives for that area.

Once control areas are defined and discretionary formal controls are developed or proposed, the relationships among control measures for each control area must be examined to ensure that conflicts are minimized and their collective impact is acceptable. Unless this kind of analysis is performed on a continuing basis, a well-integrated set of discretionary formal controls will be difficult to develop and maintain.

While each dp organization is unique in certain respects, most will want to have discretionary formal controls in place in key areas such as software development (project management and documentation standards or guidelines), data resource management (database modification procedures and data naming conven-

tions), capacity planning and performance measurement (uptime, response time, or throughput standards), and computer security (access controls and usage restrictions). There will undoubtedly be other areas where discretionary formal controls will be required; the appropriate mix will depend upon the specific organization.

Thus, there are two important things to remember in determining the appropriate mix of discretionary formal controls. The first is that the right mix depends upon a careful analysis of the key components of the overall control requirements of a particular organization. This includes a continuing examination of how well the various controls fit with each other and how well they collectively support the overall mission of the organization. Second, the dp manager will want these controls to be well understood and followed without requiring much in the way of his or her continuing involvement.

EFFECTIVE USE OF CONTROLS

Discretionary informal controls. The existence of a basic framework of implicit controls and discretionary formal controls provides an organization with enough cohesiveness among task definitions and operating procedures to function in a mechanistic manner. In order for the organization to represent more than a bureaucratic shell, however, senior management must give it substance, vitality, and strategic direction through the effective use of discretionary informal controls.

Perhaps the most important thing a dp manager can do here is to establish an effective level of normative control for the dp staff. The eventual success of the organization will depend upon the extent to which the dp staff is able to internalize the highest objectives of the manager—in effect, to make these objectives their own. For this process to take place, there must be a control environment that continuously and systematically encourages each employee to select from among the available range of actions those which are most supportive of these keystone objectives.

While this process might at first appear to be manipulative, it really is not; it is, in fact, the essence of leadership. Yet it is also more than leadership. It is leadership grounded in a full awareness of the linkages that exist among the various functions of management (such as control and leadership) and the relationships that exist between employee motivation and key environmental and cultural considerations.

Achieving this level of control is more difficult in a dp shop than in other

If the organization is to represent more than a bureaucratic shell, senior management must give it substance, vitality, and strategic direction.

organizations. In addition to the fact that the technological ground is moving continuously beneath the feet of the dp manager, the typical makeup of the staff presents additional problems. Unlike most engineering or accounting organizations, for example, which tend to have relatively homogeneous mixtures of skills and training experience represented on their staffs, the dp organization typically contains a wide variety of skills, backgrounds, educational levels, and levels of competence. This mixture of capabilities and interests can generally be divided into two groups, each having its own unique set of interests, loyalties, and motivational (hence control) considerations. I will refer to the first group as technicians, the second as generalists.

The technicians will often be computer science graduates, although not necessarily so. Members of this group are characterized by their strong orientation toward the very technical aspects of the dp discipline. The professional loyalties of this group are typically directed outward toward the numerous societies, associations, and user groups that form the touchstone of professional status and identification for this relatively young discipline. As a result, in the absence of the mitigating influence of an effective control function, this group will tend to focus narrowly on matters of technical interest and ignore larger issues, overarching missions, and, in particular, the practical needs of local users.

The generalist group will usually be made up of a varied collection of skills and backgrounds. I have observed, for example, an eight-person applications programming section that included the following college majors: music, psychology, mathematics, physics, history, accounting, biology, and education. Such mixtures are common. While the skill level of this group will vary much more dramatically than that of the technical group, the best of the generalists will often be as good as or better than any in the technical group. The major control difficulty associated with this group is, of course, its diversity of interests and motivational considerations.

MANAGER FACES DILEMMA Thus, the manager is faced with a dilemma in attempting to establish an effective framework of informal discretionary controls. On the one hand, he must establish a framework of normative controls that can guide the organization as a whole; on the other hand, each distinct group has its own set of interests and loyalties that must be effectively channeled.

Assume, for example, that a key control objective of the dp manager is the development of a service-oriented organization that recognizes first-rate user support as the highest performance objective. This means that individuals must be controlled in the sense that their actions and

decisions systematically and continuously reflect the influence of this objective. Simple lip service to this objective by the dp manager will not cause this to happen. The dp manager must demonstrate visibly through continuing actions his genuine interest in this key objective. The question that arises is this: what actions can the manager take that will influence technicians toward this objective without unduly diluting their technical abilities, and at the same time cause the diverse interests of the generalists to cohere around this central objective?

One approach is to systematically identify and publicize each significant accomplishment that demonstrates both the effective use of technology and a deep understanding of user needs. Such accomplishments might include innovations in making systems both cost-effective and extremely easy to use, the development of systems that provide especially useful information for end users, or the development of dp solutions that lead to significant improvements in productivity or otherwise help the organization in an especially significant way.

The key is to concentrate on those accomplishments that require a blend of abilities, those that technicians could not accomplish without an appreciation for and understanding of user requirements, and that generalists could not accomplish without the required degree of technical competence. An effective framework of normative controls requires that the members of each group work to maintain a reasonable balance in their skills or perspectives. Technicians must be constantly alert to the need to relate technology to practical needs, while generalists must realize that without the required technical skills they cannot develop effective solutions for user problems that they might otherwise understand very well.

Specific manifestations of concern and interest on the part of the dp manager can take many forms. For example, a program of formal awards—plaques, pins, bonuses, and other immediate, tangible forms of recognition might help in certain environments. An even stronger stimulus, however, will be the perceived pattern of skills and accomplishments that lead to special recognition or perhaps eventually to promotions.

Unfortunately, in many dp environments it is the rule rather than the exception that achievements of a highly technical nature get singled out for praise, and even lead ultimately to promotions to management positions, while the ability to balance technology and user requirements receives

"Your money comes in to your account automatically and is paid out automatically. At the moment, I'm sorry to say, it's out."

Immediate, tangible forms of recognition might help in certain environments.

much less attention and very little praise. As a result, many of these organizations eventually find themselves in serious trouble because their staffs, which over time contain an increasing number of technicians in supervisory positions, are continuously preoccupied with the unfocused, unorchestrated pursuit of technological achievements, while failing to maintain a balanced perspective relative to the real needs of users. Because of the resulting inefficiencies and lack of focus, this condition often leads to a continuing demand for more employees when the real need is for better management control and direction.

MUST BELIEVE DEEPLY Nonetheless, even a sound approach to the development of role models will not result in an effective level of normative control unless the manager believes deeply in his key objectives and demonstrates this belief on a continuing basis. This belief can be demonstrated by the kinds of questions routinely asked, the meetings attended, the kinds of reports requested, and so on. By doing this, the dp manager will perpetuate a process that leads eventually to a kind of osmotic permeation of his key objectives.

The importance of an enlightened approach to discretionary informal controls in general, and normative controls in particular, extends far beyond the dp organization. For American industry, success in regaining some of its lost vitality and leadership will depend upon the ability to develop well thought out and enlightened objectives upon which to build a framework of discretionary informal controls. But as with the dp organization, the key to real progress is the development and continuation of an organizational environment characterized by genuinely shared objectives and a common sense of purpose based upon high standards and ideals. Superficial enthusiasm, erratic support, or attempts to achieve these objectives through formal controls alone (such as the simple issuance of quality assurance directives) will not work. Each manager, if he is to be successful, will have to work extremely hard at exercising the very highest calling of management, the requirement to lead through example and personal involvement and, in so doing, to establish a level of normative control that eventually becomes self-sustaining.

Because of rapidly changing dp technology and the diverse mixture of skills that make up the typical dp staff, the dp organization presents a more difficult control challenge than many other organizations. The effective dp manager will therefore have to be particularly adept at developing and maintaining a balanced control framework, giving particular attention to a careful partitioning of the organization's overall control requirements, the development of a consistent set of discretionary formal controls, and the effective use of discretionary informal controls. ◉

William C. Kimmerly has over 17 years experience in dp planning and management. His special interests include information resource management and dp strategic planning. He's presently associated with Martin Marietta Energy Systems Inc. in a dp planning and administration capacity.

Reprinted from *IEEE Transactions on Engineering Management*, Volume EM-24, Number 3, August 1977. Copyright © 1977 by The Institute of Electrical and Electronics Engineers, Inc.

Leadership Effectiveness in Program Management

HANS J. THAMHAIN, MEMBER, IEEE, AND DAVID L. WILEMON

Abstract—The paper reports the results of an exploratory field study designed to investigate the effectiveness of leadership styles in various project-oriented work environments.

The study concludes that the effectiveness of project managers depends primarily on their leadership style and work environment. A leader-oriented management approach appears most effective in a poor work environment, while in a good organizational climate a team-oriented style seems to be most effective.

The findings presented should help the professional project manager to understand the complex interrelationships among position power, leadership style, and organizational variables. Through this understanding he may be able to identify the leadership style which optimizes project performance in his specific work.

INTRODUCTION

MANAGING projects is, without question, a difficult job. Not only does it require sophisticated tools and special organizational design considerations, but also a different breed of manager. Five areas that require special managerial skills [1] are often cited by project leaders as necessary conditions for project success

coping with a multidisciplinary project environment;
dealing with problems across functional lines;
building effective teams at various organizational levels;
handling conflicts effectively;
managing change.

Specifically, the project manager must be able to integrate various supporting disciplines in a continuously changing work environment. In his search for multidisciplinary problem resolution, he must often cross functional lines to deal with personnel over whom he has limited direct formal authority. Moreover, he has to build teams at various levels of the project organization. This requires an understanding of interpersonal dynamics to make sure that various specialists contribute to the end objective of the project. Thus the challenge is for the project manager to provide an environment conducive to the motivational needs of his team members. Equally important to successful project performance is the project manager's ability to deal effectively with the inevitable conflict situations. Taken together, the role of the project manager is a difficult one. His project success often depends significantly on his ability to deal effectively with human behavior in a multidisciplinary environment [2].

Several research studies have investigated managerial leadership styles in general management situations. Conclusions stress the situational nature of leadership effectiveness [3]. That is, leadership effectiveness appears to be a function of at least three sets of variables: leadership style, the situation, characterized by the task and organizational environment, and the characteristics of the followers. This paper explores project manager leadership and its situational effectiveness.

THE STUDY

Approximately 125 managers from a variety of project-oriented companies were asked to participate in the research. A usable sample of 68 project managers and 33 of their superiors was eventually obtained. A questionnaire was used as the principal data collection instrument. In addition, reviews of the study were conducted with a number of project managers to assist in the interpretation of the data.

It was felt that within the changing work environment of the project manager, the interaction between the project manager, his team, and the environmental context of the project needs to be examined before any conclusions on the effectiveness of a particular leadership style can be drawn. Therefore, the investigation was designed to collect data on three sets of variables

1) characteristics of project work environment;
2) characteristics of leadership style of project managers;
3) effectiveness rating of project managers.

The Work Environment

The study utilizes part of Rensis Likert's typology to characterize the project-organized environment [5]. Three modified sets of variables were identified

1) organizational climate:
    quality of communication;
    continuity of work;
    career growth;
2) task complexity:
    skill-level requirements;
    multidisciplinary nature;
    project size and duration;
3) position power of the project manager:
    degree of control over personnel;
    control over budgets, schedule, and performance;
    degree of P&L responsibility;
    resource sharing with functional organization.

In addition, a fourth set of variables was collected on the type of organizational structure. Project managers were asked to select from a set of 5 organization charts the one which

Manuscript received October 25, 1976; revised February 23, 1977. This paper was presented in part at the Project Management Institute Seminar/Symposium in Montreal, Que., Canada, October 1976.

H. J. Thamhain is with GTE Sylvania, Needham, MA 02194.

D. L. Wilemon is with the Marketing Management Department, School of Management, Syracuse University, Syracuse, NY 13210.

best represented their own organization, or to draw their own version. The charts represented: 1) matrix organization, 2) individual project organization, 3) internal functional project organization, 4) staff project organization, 5) projectized organization, and 6) own version drawn by project manager and later on classified during research evaluation.

The actual questions and scales used in the survey are described in the Methodological Appendix, Part I.

Project Manager Leadership

As previously stated, a project manager's ability to perform effectively may depend on his leadership style, the task complexity, the required technological sophistication, and the climate of the organization in which he functions. In analyzing project management leadership, it is particularly important to understand how tasks are accomplished. Contrary to functional management, influences, such as direct rewards and punishments, may be in the hands of supporting department managers. Further, the overall influence a project manager has may vary over the life of his project, since complexity, budgets, client demands, and functional interfaces change. Thus effective leadership relates the human, technical, and situational variables of a project in a complex manner.

For the current investigation, sixteen statements were designed to reflect the project managers' general orientation toward developing support. The framework of this investigation uses French and Raven's topology of interpersonal influences which had been modified by Gemmill, Thamhain, and Wilemon for various power style studies on project managers [6]

The actual questions and scales used in the survey are described in the Methodological Appendix, Part II. The items were designed to assess the project leaders' attitudes toward both formally derived influence sources and individually derived influences for gaining support. The formally derived influence sources are typified by authority, rewards, and punishments, while the individually derived influence sources are related to the intrinsic motivations of project team members. Examples are the project manager's attitude toward assisting contributors in their career development, matching team member interests and capabilities with task requirements, making efforts to provide a smooth transition from one project to the next job assignment, and establishing positive interpersonal relationships with team members.

To measure the leader's attitude, project managers were asked to indicate on a six-point scale (very important–important–somewhat helpful–I am indifferent about it–might do more harm than good–might be detrimental) how important each influence method is in gaining support from project personnel. For example, to measure the perceived importance of authority, three statements were used for scoring

the project manager should have formal authority;
the project manager should let his personnel know that he has this authority;
the organization should let the project personnel know who is in command.

Hence, an independent set of scores was obtained on the perceived importance of each influence base. This method allowed project managers to be ranked according to their perceived style.

Analysis of the data indicated that some project managers rely primarily on the formally derived organizational influence bases, while others prefer building their support by focusing on the needs and concerns of individual contributors. For the purpose of this study, we defined two leadership categories.

1) *Style I* is primarily a leader-centered approach to management; it is characterized by project managers who demonstrate a preference for organizationally derived influence sources such as authority, reward, and punishment.

2) *Style II* is primarily a team-centered management approach; it is characterized by project managers who focus on the needs of their team members in deriving the influences for their project support.

The actual statements used in the questionnaire and their classification is shown in the Methodological Appendix, Part II.

Effectiveness Rating of Project Managers

A measure of managerial effectiveness was obtained by contacting the superiors of the 68 project managers investigated. Each superior was asked to rate the project manager relative to his peers on overall project performance. A 0–100-percent scale was used. The specific statements used in the questionnaire are shown on the Methodological Appendix, Part III.

RESULTS

The results are presented in two parts. First, an analysis is performed on the sample of project managers regarding their shared control over personnel. Second, a correlation analysis between managerial leadership style and managerial effectiveness is presented to formulate some tentative conclusions about the most suitable leadership style for different project situations. All correlation figures were obtained by Kendall rank order correlation methods.

Shared Control Over Project Personnel

Project managers often interact with the various functional and staff departments in managing their programs. Depending on the type of project organization, the project manager has different degrees of control over resources. At the outset of this study it was expected that project managers in a matrix organization would share more resources and have less control over project budgets, schedules, and performance than in a projectized organization. We expected this because the matrix organization is more of an overlay on the functional organization than the projectized form which is relatively independent of other support groups. However, with the exception of profit and loss responsibility summarized in Fig. 1, the data in Figs. 2 and 3 show that project managers in matrix organizations perceive themselves with essentially the same amount of control over resources, budgets, schedules, and performance as their counterparts in projectized organizations.

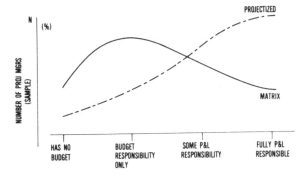

Fig. 1. Perceived P&L responsibility of project managers.

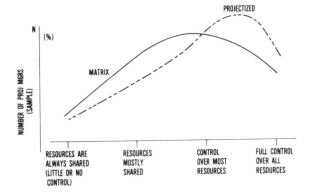

Fig. 2. Perceived resource sharing (follows approximately the same distribution for both matrix and projectized organizations).

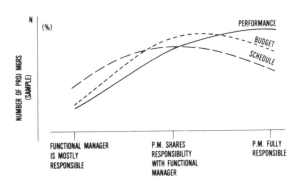

Fig. 3. Perceived control over projects.

This is a significant finding because it indicates that the position power of a project manager probably depends less on the particular organizational type with which he is associated than the organizational climate and the task structure.

Similar findings surfaced during analysis of shared control over project personnel. Project personnel often serve two masters, the project manager and the functional manager. The more a project organization leans toward a functional structure, the more control is vested with the functional manager. Therefore, project managers in a matrix organization should experience less control over project personnel than in a projectized environment. The actual data shows, however, that project managers in matrix organizations experience almost the same degree of control over support department personnel as project managers in projectized organizations. Furthermore, the degree of control seems to be independent of project size. That is, the perceived control of project man-

WHO HAS CONTROL OVER ASSIGNED PERSONNEL REGARDING WORK DIRECTION?

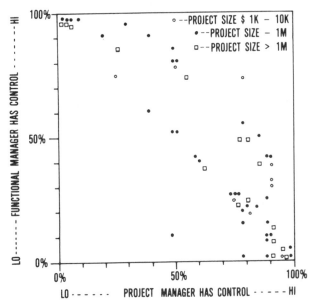

Fig. 4. Shared control over project personnel regarding work direction. (Control ranges from full sharing to no sharing regardless of project size.)

WHO HAS CONTROL OVER ASSIGNED PERSONNEL REGARDING REWARD AND PUNISHMENT?

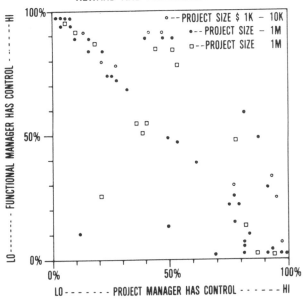

Fig. 5. Shared control over project personnel regarding reward and punishment. (Control ranges from no control to full control by the project manager regardless of project size.)

agers over their personnel varies from low to high regardless of the project size. Figs. 4 and 5 summarize these shared control characteristics for both "control over work assignments" and "control over reward and punishment."

Effectiveness of Managerial Styles

Figs. 6 and 7 show the type of leadership style which is most favorably associated with project managers' performance

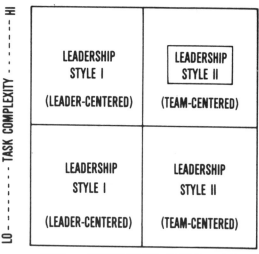

Fig. 6. Most effective leadership style of project managers considering organizational climate and task complexity.

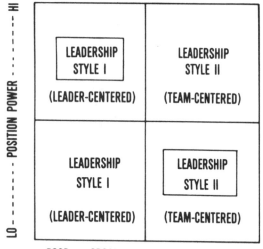

Fig. 7. Most effective leadership style of project managers considering organizational climate and position power.

under different environmental conditions. Kendall Tau partial correlation techniques were used to obtain the correlation figures based on the perceived project management leadership style and the effectiveness rating provided by their superiors.

The statistical correlation between project management performance and the managerial style indicated in each of the quadrants is in the range of $\tau = 0.20$ to $\tau = 0.33$ with an average confidence level of $p \geqslant 90$ percent. A *framed* style indicates a particularly strong association between leadership style and performance of $\tau \geqslant 0.35$ with $p \geqslant 95$ percent. The data suggest that leadership style I, the leader-centered approach, appears to be the most effective in a poor organizational climate while leadership style II, the team-centered approach, appears to be most effective in a good organizational climate.

More specifically, the quantitative data suggest that the poorer the organizational climate (as measured by the quality

of communication, the continuity of work, and the career growth) the more likely a project manager will succeed with leadership style I. That is, the more he relies on leader-centered approaches to project management, the more effective he may be perceived to be by his superior. Contrarily, the better the organizational climate and the more a project manager relies on leadership style II (team-centered), the more likely it is that he will receive a high performance rating from his immediate superior.

From the summaries provided in Figs. 6 and 7, it is interesting to note that the choice of an effective leadership style seems to depend primarily on the organizational climate with little influence from task complexity or position power. The strength of the association between style and climate is, however, substantially influenced by the task and position power. More precisely, the data indicate the following.

Leadership style I (leader-oriented) is more likely to be effective in a poor organization climate, particularly if associated with high position power.

Leadership style II (team-oriented) is more likely to be effective in a good organizational climate, particularly if associated with high task complexity and/or low position power.

It should be emphasized that project managers do not necessarily operate in extreme environments characterized by "very good" or "very poor" conditions. Therefore, the project management style needs to be adapted to the mix of the prevailing working conditions.

SUMMARY AND DISCUSSION

While project management has gained widespread recognition as an organizational concept, it is only recently that there has been much interest in the leadership requirements of the project leader. The early research which did focus on the leadership styles primarily concentrated on the influence modes used in gaining compliance from support personnel [7]. Moreover, little attention has been focused on possible differences in the effectiveness of leadership styles depending on various task complexities or organizational climates. This research has attempted to develop new insights into these relationships.

Based on the exploratory study, several conclusions can be tentatively formulated.

1) The effectiveness of the project manager depends on his leadership style and his work environment. As shown in Figs. 6 and 7, leadership style I, a leader-oriented management approach, appears most effective in a poor organizational environment where communications, work continuity, and career growth are inferior. However, in a good organizational climate, leadership style II, a team-oriented style, seems to be most effective.

2) Task complexity and the position power of the project manager does not appear to be an important determinant of the leadership style. While the effectiveness of a particular style may be influenced by the degree of position power and task complexity, the choice between style I and style II seems to depend only on the organizational climate.

The rationale for leadership style I effectiveness is tentatively formulated as follows. In a poor organizational "climate," the project managers may need to exert strong direction over their project personnel. In such cases, project personnel may follow the directives of the project manager because of: the authority he possesses, the rewards at his disposal, and to avoid the penalties he may use against them. In addition, in such a climate, the only "order" project participants "see" is that which comes from the directive style of the project leader. For some project team members, this may reduce the anxieties they experience while working in an environment characterized by low degrees of work continuity, poor communications, and limits on career growth opportunities.

On the other side, leadership style II appears to be more effective in a good organizational climate because project participants are not as threatened by individual and organizational concerns. They are more apt to be responsive not only to the project leader's willingness to develop individual relationships with them and their professional capabilities, but also to his efforts to maximize the functioning of the total team. This may typify the kind of environmental context within which the highest levels of team "integration" occur. Environments are not, however, always predictable. Rapid environmental change is not unusual in project management. Personnel, budgets, project scope, and client demands may trigger change within the project. Thus a project manager needs to be flexible in his leadership approach [8].

Several suggestions can be derived from this study which can increase the project manager's effectiveness. First, an audit of the host organization should be undertaken to identify the potential causes of a poor organizational climate. Second, a decision should be made whether the determinants of organizational climate can be changed. Third, if they can be altered or modified, a program to alleviate the conditions should be initiated.

Some of the elements of organizational climate, such as work continuity and career growth, are influenced by both organizational internal and external factors such as general economic conditions. Others, such as quality of communication, are under the control of the organization. Management can often influence these elements in spite of their partial external dependence. Specifically, management can do the following.

Top Management can help in building the organizational climate by performing effective long-range business planning and keeping people informed about the basic corporate objectives and business prospects. This may reduce the anxiety often created by an uncertain future and may help to increase the perception of the quality of organizational climate, particularly with regard to work continuity and career growth. Project start-up and phase-out practices are other important areas to be considered. Personal morale and motivation often decline toward the end of a program because employees fear termination or transfer to less desirable jobs. Top management can avoid problems by setting up an appropriate project organization which provides home office features and a system for phasing projects effectively. Such a system may include policies for transferring personnel between projects and interproject training programs.

Delineation of clearly defined decision channels and support of project managers in dealings with functional support departments may yet be other areas of top management involvement toward building a favorable organizational climate.

Project Managers must understand the interaction of organizational and behavioral elements in order to build an environment conducive to their team's motivational needs. The flow of communication seems to be one of the major factors which influences the quality of the organizational climate. Since the project manager must build multifunctional teams at various organizational layers, it is important that key decisions are properly communicated to all project-related personnel. By openly communicating the project objectives and those of its subtasks, unproductive conflict may be minimized. Regularly scheduled status review meetings can be an important vehicle for communicating project-related issues.

Effective planning early in the life cycle of a project is another action which will have a favorable impact on the organizational climate. This is particularly so because project managers have to integrate various disciplines across functional lines. Insufficient planning may eventually lead to interdepartmental conflict and discontinuities in the work flow.

Furthermore, the project manager can influence the work environment by his own actions. His concern for the project team members, his ability to integrate the personal goals and needs of project personnel with project goals, and his ability to create personal enthusiasm in the work itself can foster a climate which is high in motivation, work involvement, open communication, and subsequent project performance. We found, for instance, that work challenge is a catalyst which helps to integrate personal and project objectives. It is an influence source over which project managers have a great deal of control. Although the total work structure is normally fixed, individual assignments can be made to accommodate the interest and preferences of project personnel.

In summary, project managers must not only be able to adopt their leadership style to the prevailing work situation, but should also have the ability to develop an organizational climate conducive to the effective functioning of high performing project teams [9]. This requires the effort of a highly skilled project manager plus top management commitment.

METHODOLOGICAL APPENDIX

I. ASSESSMENT OF WORK ENVIRONMENT OF THE PROJECT MANAGER AND HIS ORGANIZATION

A questionnaire with 11 statements and one diagram was used to characterize the project-organized environment in three areas: 1) organizational climate, 2) task complexity, and 3) position power of the project manager. To minimize the potential bias introduced by social science jargons, the following statements and scales were developed to measure variables of the above sets. Project managers were asked, in detail, to indicate on a three- or four-point scale how accurate each statement described their work environment.

1. To Assess Organizational Climate

1.1) How good is *communication* across functional lines?
    a) Very good, as good as for vertical information flow.

b) Adequate, but not quite as good as vertical flow.

c) It is difficult to communicate across functional lines.

d) Very poor, there is no way of proper communication across functional lines.

1.2) How well is *work continuity* being provided from one project to the next?

    a) Very well, there is always a smooth transition from one job to the next; no hassles.

    b) Some slack time between jobs. Individual effort is often necessary to find a new assignment.

    c) It is always difficult to find a new assignment of personal satisfaction.

    d) Finding new assignments is individual responsibility. Phase outs are often accompanied by lay offs.

1.3) What is the potential *career growth* for member' of your project organization?

    a) Very good, the organization helps to develop individual careers and provides growth continuity throughout the various projects.

    b) Career growth depends largely on the opportunities that exist with a new project. Past performance influences advancement.

    c) Advancement opportunities exist mostly during the formation of a new project with little growth during the life cycle of the project.

    d) There is little advancement potential from project to project. None during the project life cycle.

2. To Assess Task Complexity

2.1) What *Skill Levels* do project team members need within your organization?

    a) Highly skilled professionals.

    b) Both highly skilled and semiskilled professionals.

    c) Semiskilled personnel.

    d) Unskilled project personnel.

2.2) What *Disciplinary Diversification* do project team members need within your organization?

    a) Most personnel deal with the same project discipline.

    b) Personnel work on similar project disciplines.

    c) Project teams are mostly multidisciplinary.

2.3) *How many task teams* are typically required to complete a project/program?

    a) 1; b) 5; c) 10; d) 20; e) 50; f) 100; or g) more.

2.4) What *size of projects/programs* are you responsible for?

    a) $1000; b) $10 000; c) $100 000;

    d) $1 000 000; e) $10 000 000; or f) $100 000 000.

2.5) What is the *Life Cycle* of a typical project or program?

    a) 1 week; b) 1 month; c) 6 months; d) 1 year; or e) 3 years.

3. To Assess Position Power of the Project Manager

3.1) Who has *Control Over Assigned Project Personnel?* (Please place "x" in each plane to indicate power sharing between project manager and functional managers.) (See Fig. 8.)

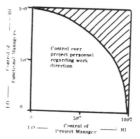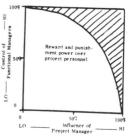

Fig. 8.

3.2) Please check the degree of the program/project manager's *accountability* regarding budget, schedule, and performance.

    a) PM is fully responsible for . . . budget . . . schedule . . . performance.

    b) PM shares responsibility with functional managers for . . . budget . . . schedule . . . performance.

    c) Responsibility rests mostly with functional managers for . . . budget . . . schedule . . . performance.

3.3) What degree of *P&L responsibility* does the program office have?

    a) Full P&L responsibility.

    b) Some P&L responsibility.

    c) Accountable for negotiated budget.

    d) Has no budget of its own.

3.4) To what degree do you, as project manager, have to *share resources* with functional departments or other programs?

    a) The project manager has full control over all facilities, personnel, and support functions.

    b) The project manager has control over most resources needed for program/project. Shares certain (maybe accounting, etc.).

    c) The project manager has only a few key functions reporting directly to him. Most personnel and facilities are shared with other projects.

    d) The project manager shares all facilities and personnel with other project managers.

II. ASSESSMENT OF PROJECT MANAGERS' ATTITUDES TOWARD SOURCE OF INFLUENCE OF GAINING SUPPORT

A questionnaire with sixteen statements was used to measure the general attitude of project managers toward developing support from functional support personnel. Project managers were asked to indicate on a six-point scale how important each statement is for gaining support from project personnel. The scale was graded as follows: 1) very important; 2) important; 3) somewhat helpful; 4) I am indifferent about it; 5) might be detrimental to gaining support.

Style I

The following statements describe organizationally derived influence sources, characteristic of a leader-centered approach to management, classified as style I.

1) The project manager should have formal authority.

2) The project manager should let his personnel know that he has this authority.

3) The organization should let the project personnel know who is in command.

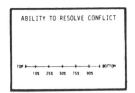

Fig. 9.

4) The project manager should have direct reward and punishment power (salary, hire, fire, etc.).

5) The project manager should at least be able to influence salary and other rewards.

6) The project manager should stress to his personnel that he has this direct or indirect reward power.

7) The project manager should be able to influence promotion of project personnel.

8) The project manager should let his project personnel know about his power to penalize them, if necessary (e.g., discharge from project, negative feedback to functional organization, influence performance appraisal, etc.).

Style II

The following statements describe individually derived influence sources, characteristic of a team-centered approach to management, classified as style II.

1) The project manager should find out what work assignments interest who in his project organization, and make an effort to divide the work between his project personnel, accordingly.

2) The project manager should make an effort to provide work continuity between projects.

3) The project manager should help his personnel in their career development.

4) The project manager should have a good track record for managing projects successfully.

5) The project manager should be a technical expert in as many disciplines of his work as possible.

6) The project manager should be alert to potential problems and arrange timely assistance.

7) The project manager should have good rapport with top management and elicit help when needed.

8) The project manager should establish friendship ties with his personnel.

III. ASSESSMENT OF PROJECT MANAGERIAL EFFECTIVENESS

A questionnaire with two evaluation scales was used to measure the effectiveness of project managers in two areas: a) their ability to resolve conflict, and b) their overall project performance. The superiors of the project managers in this survey were asked to provide the rating relative to other project managers reporting to those superiors. The specific questions asked and their scales are shown above (Fig. 9).

How would you rate this project manager relative to his peers in your group or department with regard to some performance criteria?

ACKNOWLEDGMENT

The authors acknowledge the helpful assistance given by R. Ratan in evaluating the research data.

REFERENCES

[1] For representative articles which deal with these issues: J. M. Stewart, "Making project management work," *Business Horizons,* vol. 8, 1965; I. Avots, "Why does project management fail," *California Management Review,* Fall, 1969; J. J. Hansen, "The case of the precarious program," *Harvard Business Review,* Jan.–Feb., 1968; P. R. Lawrence and J. W. Lorsch, "New management job: The integrator," *Harvard Business Review,* Nov.–Dec. 1967; A. G. Butler, "Project management: A study in organizational conflict," *Academy of Management Journal,* Fall, 1970; H. J. Thamhain and D. L. Wilemon, "Conflict management in project-oriented work environments," *Proceedings of the Project Management Institute,* Sept. 1974; G. R. Gemmill and H. J. Thamhain, "The power styles of project managers: Some efficiency correlates," presented at the 20th Annual Joint Engineering Management Conference, Oct. 1972; D. H. Morton, "Project manager, catalyst to constant change," *Project Management Quarterly,* vol. VI, no. 1, 1975.

[2] This issue was discussed by Douglas McGregor, *The Human Side of Enterprise.* New York: McGraw-Hill, as early as 1960.

[3] F. E. Fiedler, "A Contingency Model for the Prediction of Leadership Effectiveness," Group Effectiveness Research Laboratory, Dep. of Psychology, University of Illinois, Evanston, IL, 1963; F. E. Fiedler, *A Theory of Leadership Effectiveness.* New York: McGraw-Hill, 1967.

[4] For specific discussions leading to the current research study: H. J. Thamhain and D. L. Wilemon, "Conflict management in project-oriented work environments," in *Proceedings of the Sixth International Meeting of the Project Management Institute,* Sept. 1974; "Conflict management in project life cycles," *Sloan Management Review,* Spring, 1965.

[5] (R. Likert shows that the work environment of an enterprise can be characterized with a relatively small number of key variables. For this study the originally suggested variables have been modified to focus on the project environment.) R. Likert, "Human resource accounting," Personnel, May–June 1973.

[6] J. R. P. French, Jr. and B. Raven, "The basis of social power," in *Studies in Social Power,* D. Cartwright, Ed. Ann Arbor, Michigan: Research Center for Group Dynamics, 1959. For a detailed discussion of the questionnaire and survey technique used in more recent power style studies: G. R. Gemmill and H. J. Thamhain, "Influence styles of project managers: Some project performance correlates," *Academy of Management Journal,* vol. 17, no.2, pp. 216–224, June 1974.

[7] G. R. Gemmill and D. L. Wilemon, "The power spectrum in project management," *Sloan Management Review,* Fall, 1970; G. R. Gemmill and H. J. Thamhain, "Influence styles of project managers: Some performance correlates," *Academy of Management Journal,* June 1974.

[8] Y. K. Shetly aptly discusses the need for flexibility in leadership patterns in "Leadership and organizational character," *Personnel Administration,* p. 20, July–Aug. 1969, as follows: The successful manager is neither an autocrat, nor a complete democrat, rather one who integrates the forces operating in relation to the particular situation in question. The behavior of an effective leader under specific technological considerations may lead to failure under other technological situations. The leadership appropriate in one organizational system may be irrelevant or even dysfunctional in another system.

[9] This conclusion is supported by findings from other studies such as F. E. Fiedler, "Engineer the job to fit the manager," *Harvard Business Review,* p. 119, Sept.–Oct., 1965; D. G. Marquis and D. M. Straight, *Organizational Factors in Project Performance.* Washington, DC: National Aeronautics and Space Administration, July 25, 1965; R. M. Godgetts, "Leadership techniques in the project organization," *Academy of Management Journal,* vol. 11, pp. 211–219, 1968; C. Reeser, "Some potential human problems of the project form of organization," *Academy of Management Journal,* p. 467, Dec. 1969; G. R. Gemmilll and D. L. Wilemon, "The power spectrum in project management," *Sloan Management Review,* pp. 15–25, Fall, 1970; G. R. Gemmill and H. J. Thamhain, "Influence styles of project managers: Some project performance correlates," *Academy of Management Journal,* pp. 216–224, June 1974; D. C. Murphy, B. N. Baker, and D. Fisher, *Determinants of Project Success.* Springfield, VA: National Technical Information Services, Accession Number N-74-30392, 1974; H. J. Thamhain and D. L. Wilemon, "Conflict management in project-organized work environments," *ChemTech Magazine,* June 1975.

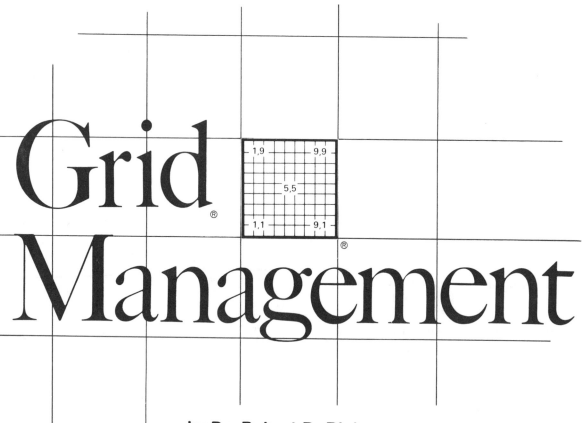

Grid Management

by Dr. Robert R. Blake, Dr. Jane S. Mouton and William R. Taggart

The scene is all-too-familiar. A bright, young employee just out of school is handed a challenging data processing assignment. When the young person tries to explain that there might be a better way of getting the job done, the boss replies, "Your suggestion may look good on the surface," or, "sounds good in school, but around here, we do it like so."

And the way work gets done might be because of any number of factors:

> Traditions and precedents.
>
> What the boss wants.
>
> What gets the manager through the day.
>
> Whatever fixes the problem.
>
> What keeps employees out of trouble.

Even so, some people believe other possibilities exist—different ways of doing business that are better than current procedures. Unfortunately, without an approach that objectively describes how the work is completed now, it's almost impossible to communicate the other possibilities that exist.

Early "people problem" signs

A large-scale computer system, for example, is constantly monitored for peak efficiency. Unused capacity is tapped. Software options are experimented with, results and logs of performance are studied. Signs of early problems with communications lines are surfaced and recognized. Finally, future plans for growth and improvement are developed.

But what useful reference base exists to objectively measure how managers manage and how people operate within an organization?

The Grid

Both research and experience have shown that the Managerial Grid can fill this management vacuum and serve as a problem-solving tool and framework for studying the management/staff interface. The Grid is a tested theory based on broad behavioral science principles. It has been used in the business world since the early 1960s. This same theory serves as the starting point and is used as a model for

272

organizations that engage in Grid Organization Development. This is a six-phase organization change model that helps autonomous organizational units systematically plan for how to most effectively use resources for the best possible long-term profitability and growth.

Polarities for managers

The Grid deals with two basic concerns that always seem to be pulling in opposite directions within an organization. First, is the concern for production, whether measured in units produced, software systems completed, conversions finished or simply return on investment. The degree to which a manager is concerned with production, output and performance applies to the DP industry as easily as it applies to a manufacturing operation.

The second concern is for people —subordinates and colleagues. Putting these two "opposing" concerns together results in the Grid, with the two concerns scaled from 1 to 9, using the horizontal axis for concern for production and the vertical axis for concern for people. Although 81 possible coordinates are possible, five definable and distinct managerial styles predominate (See Figure 1).

In the lower left-hand corner of the Grid is 1,1: Minimal concern for people and production. This individual does just enough to get by and no more. A subordinate walking into this manager's office with a technical question about a data processing project or assignment may get a response like this:

> "I don't really know; why don't you check one of the reference manuals."

> "Your guess is as good as mine; they didn't tell me why the print-out has to be this way."

> "It doesn't matter anyway. Nobody will make much real use of this system. The old way was really better."

The 1,1-oriented manager figures that he or she can hold on just by exerting the minimum amount of effort required to get by—no more, no less.

Results oriented manager

The 9,1-oriented style is characterized by the person who says: "Results are what count—it's the bottom line that's important."

Whereas the 1,1-oriented manager avoids conflict like the plague, the 9,1-oriented person jumps right in and even promotes it—as long as everything goes the way this individual planned it. If the subordinate didn't hear the first time, it is repeated, just so it is understood who is right.

The 9,1-oriented route to success is through control and mastery over others. Failure is avoided at all cost since that is tantamount to admitting defeat. The 9,1-oriented approach to a subordinate concerned about meeting a project due date might be:

> "Deadlines are there to be met."

> "If you can't get it done on time, then next time I will use someone with more experience."

> "What's the matter, aren't you interested in seeing us be successful on this one?"

The 9,1-oriented approach assumes that the staff works best when told what to do. If something doesn't go right, then, "You can be assured I'll find out who's at fault."

Win/lose attitude

Another example of the 9,1 approach might appear in a review meeting with the vendor's field engineering staff over a recurring system problem. While the recognized objective of the meeting is to work together in a problem-solving relationship, an attitude of win-lose often develops.

Both sides see the other as the antagonist, and stereotypical attitudes begin to take over. Attacks and counter-attacks occur and neither side wants to be second best. "After all, the vendor should realize who pays the bills around here, and we have put up with enough inconvenience already. The problem had better be fixed by tonight, or else, and don't expect us to hand over the system to you until we're good and ready. You will probably only make things worse anyway."

Figure 1. The Managerial Grid

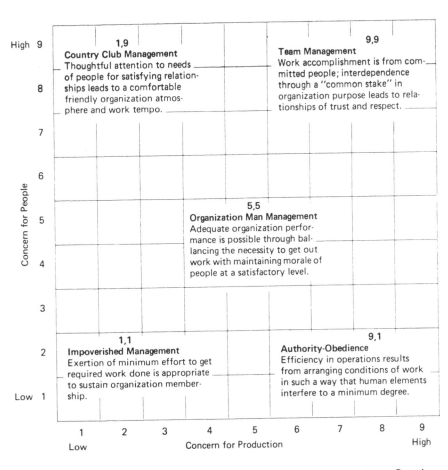

Source: The New Managerial Grid, by Robert R. Blake and Jane Srygley Mouton. Houston: Gulf Publishing Company, 1978. Not to be reproduced without permission of the authors.

Nine principles of effective behavior

1. Informed free choice is the basis for personal action rather than enforced compliance.
2. Active participation in problem solving and decision making is the basis of growth and development rather than passively accepting instructions as to what to do or inactivity reinforced by social isolation.
3. Mutual trust and respect is the basis for sound human relationships rather than suspiciousness and defensiveness.
4. Open communication gives mutual understanding in contrast with one-way, hidden, closed or Machiavellian communication that increases barriers to understanding.
5. Activities are carried out within a framework of goals and objectives for self-direction rather than direction from outside.
6. Conflict resolution is by direct problem-solving confrontation rather than by other ways (suppression, smoothing, withdrawing, compromising or manipulation).
7. One is responsible for one's own actions rather than being responsible to someone else.
8. Critique is used to learn from experience rather than repeating one's mistakes because experience is not studied.
9. A person is engaging in complex work activities or a variety of activities in contrast with engaging in simple ones or in repetitions of the same activity.

The 1,9-oriented individual, on the other hand, sees things quite the opposite from the 9,1-oriented manager. This person views people as the lifeblood of the company. To him or her nothing is more important than ensuring that everyone gets along. The 1,9 approach, with its maximum concern for people and minimum for production, assumes that work will take care of itself if workers operate in harmony.

Keep differences under cover

When dealing with conflict, the 1,9 approach is to smooth over differences and keep them under cover. The best of all worlds is when there is a sense of warmth and friendship.

For example, in a meeting with internal staff and a vendor, there is conflict over whether the problem is hardware or software. The 1,9-oriented manager is likely to react as follows:

> *"The two sides are really saying the same thing. I see a lot of similarity in the two points of view."*
>
> *"Let's move on to the next topic and perhaps this one will work itself out without getting everyone's hackles up."*
>
> *"Hey, let's be friends here. We can't get anything done if we don't get along, and we want to preserve our good relationships."*
>
> *"That reminds me of the one about..."*

The 1,9-oriented manager truly wants to be liked by subordinates and peers and believes that helpfulness results in a harmonious shop and that production will take care of itself because employees work as one big happy family.

Middle of the road

The 5,5-oriented middle-of-the-road manager views a person with a 1,9 orientation as definitely too soft, but sees the opposite—a 9,1 orientation—as surely too hard. There must be a middle ground. The 5,5-oriented person is the manager who calls for compromise and the splitting of differences in order to achieve workable solutions to problems. A decision reached by the majority is seen as a good decision. The manager concentrates on working with what is available and doing what was done yesterday, but just a *little* better. For example, when faced with a difference of opinion as to whether or not to purchase a new peripheral, the 5,5-oriented manager proposes the following:

> *"Perhaps we can test both pieces of equipment. How do the rest of you feel about this?"*

> *"What does the boss think about this vendor? Will we get in trouble if it doesn't work?"*
>
> *"Can we trade off a little complexity in return for a better installation date?"*
>
> *"Just to play it safe, perhaps we should lease for a while before buying."*

The 5,5-oriented manager acts in ways that are consistent with organization traditions and stays within bounds. An experimental approach is confused with going out on a limb, which could invite trouble and censure from above. At the same time, he or she maintains a moderate concern for production. This is a safe way of managing, firmly rooted in precedent and tradition.

Best possible solutions

The 9,9-oriented manager, in contrast, is concerned not with the safe way, or with "my" way, or with a way that everyone can agree to, but with the *best* way. In other words, what should be done that is truly in the best interests of both people *and* production is the overriding objective.

The 9,9-oriented manager realizes that people contribute best when they are involved and when their contribution is honestly valued. Communication is open, direct and

---

The 9,9 manager feels open, direct communication is of great value.

---

forthright. Conflict is brought into the open and dealt with, managed and resolved in a way that shows respect for each party. Meetings with users are not seen as win/lose contests or as negotiation sessions where trade-offs are the rule of the road.

Working toward common goal

The objective of the 9,9-oriented manger is to work toward a solution that is above each person's own vested interest, and consequently represents a solution that each can support more strongly than an original position.

A 9,9-oriented manager, faced with resolving the problem of an employee's continual lateness works with the person involved to find a solution that would be consistent with the following nine principles of effective behavior. (See *The New Managerial Grid*, by Robert R. Blake and Jane S. Mouton. Houston: Gulf Publishing Co., 1978.)

After most DP managers read the five different thumbnail descriptions, most found subordinates in the 1,1, 1,9 and 5,5 positions on the Grid; or perhaps your boss was in the 9,1 corner. However, most managers probably didn't locate themselves until the 9,9 orientation was described. This is an interesting phenomenon that has been researched and measured:

Before learning Grid theory, most managers tend to see themselves as dominantly 9,9 in the way they work on the job. But after a week of intensive study and work in a Grid Seminar with other managers, the percentage that see themselves as working in a 9,9 orientation falls from 70 percent to 20 percent.

Self-deception is destructive

It is clear that learning the theory base as a starting point is only useful if self-deception can be dealt with and cleared away. After all, for any organization, change is possible only if clear differences are seen between the way things are being done now and the way things should be handled. When managers realize this, systematic steps can be taken to close the gap between actual management style and what style truly is sound.

When managers and staff begin to ask the question, "Why do we do it this way?", then problems can be addressed openly and underlying barriers can be identified. Managers take a big step forward when they realize that sound principles of behavior can be applied to the work environment by using a common theory.

Real-world DP uses

The value of any theory, however, lies in how well it can be applied to real-world management/organizational issues. Organizations have put the Grid to work in a variety of ways, but with the same purpose in mind: "How can we do a better job in order to increase both satisfaction *and* productivity?"

How Grid is used

One study team, for example, determined that centralized software support for computer systems at four different locations would result in considerable cost reductions without sacrificing system availability time or risking failure to meet critical deadlines. Team support was far superior to each location continuing to do their own thing.

Another management group realized that restructuring several departmental units was the best way to best take advantage of a new communications and data entry system. The key difference here was getting the involvement and support of the data entry personnel and supervisors instead of just handing down a decision as to how the structural changes were to be implemented.

A large Canadian bank is using the Grid to simply improve inter-data center teamwork and communication. With each site using the same management reference base, it was possible to remove a whole host of barriers that had been impeding progress and cooperation.

A manufacturer of microcomputer systems for industrial applications is using the Grid to help manage the transition from an entrepreneurial based organization to one that uses an integrated management structure with clearly defined responsibilities and financial objectives. The manufacturer is currently working through the fourth of the six-phase Grid OD model.

Another Grid success involved a large division of a Fortune 100 company. They've used the Grid technology to implement a large scale cost-estimating system for use throughout all parts of the organization. Managers, salespeople, engineers and all users learn the system by studying prework first, and then by working on several learning instruments in a team setting.

Change

It is possible to change an organization's culture, but the process must be approached in a systematic and deliberate manner. Research conducted by Scientific Methods, for example, has shown that certain conditions promote good, solid change.

- Get everyone on board by using the Grid as a common theory base.

- Strip away self-deception as to how managers are approaching problems now.

- Recognize the need for systematically examining why the organization operates the way it does.

- Map plans and strategies for moving from the current culture to one that has been designed to be soundest for optimum productivity, profit and satisfaction.

- Ensure that leadership of change starts at the top of the unit and that it is a do-it-yourself effort instead of relying on outsiders.

When these conditions are recognized and agreed to, the "That's not the way we do it here," attitude disappears and is replaced by a quest for excellence that taps human energies and resources to work toward the best possible management solutions. ∎

About the authors

The Grid grew out of consulting work and experimentation that Drs. Robert Blake and Jane Mouton were involved in during the late 1950s at The University of Texas at Austin. This involved consulting studies of managerial problems within several different types of organizations. Shortly afterward, Scientific Methods, Inc., Austin, TX, was formed and is actively engaged in client work throughout the world. Blake and Mouton continue to be active with the company and devote most of their time and energy to research and development activities. Taggart manages the Pittsburgh office of Scientific Methods, Inc. and works closely with organizations exploring and actively engaged in Grid development activities. He is a former operations vice president with the Federal Reserve Bank in Pittsburgh and began his professional career in the data processing field as a programmer and systems analyst. For information on Grid Seminars, contact Scientific Methods, Inc., Box 195, Austin, TX 78767 (512)477-5781.—Ed.

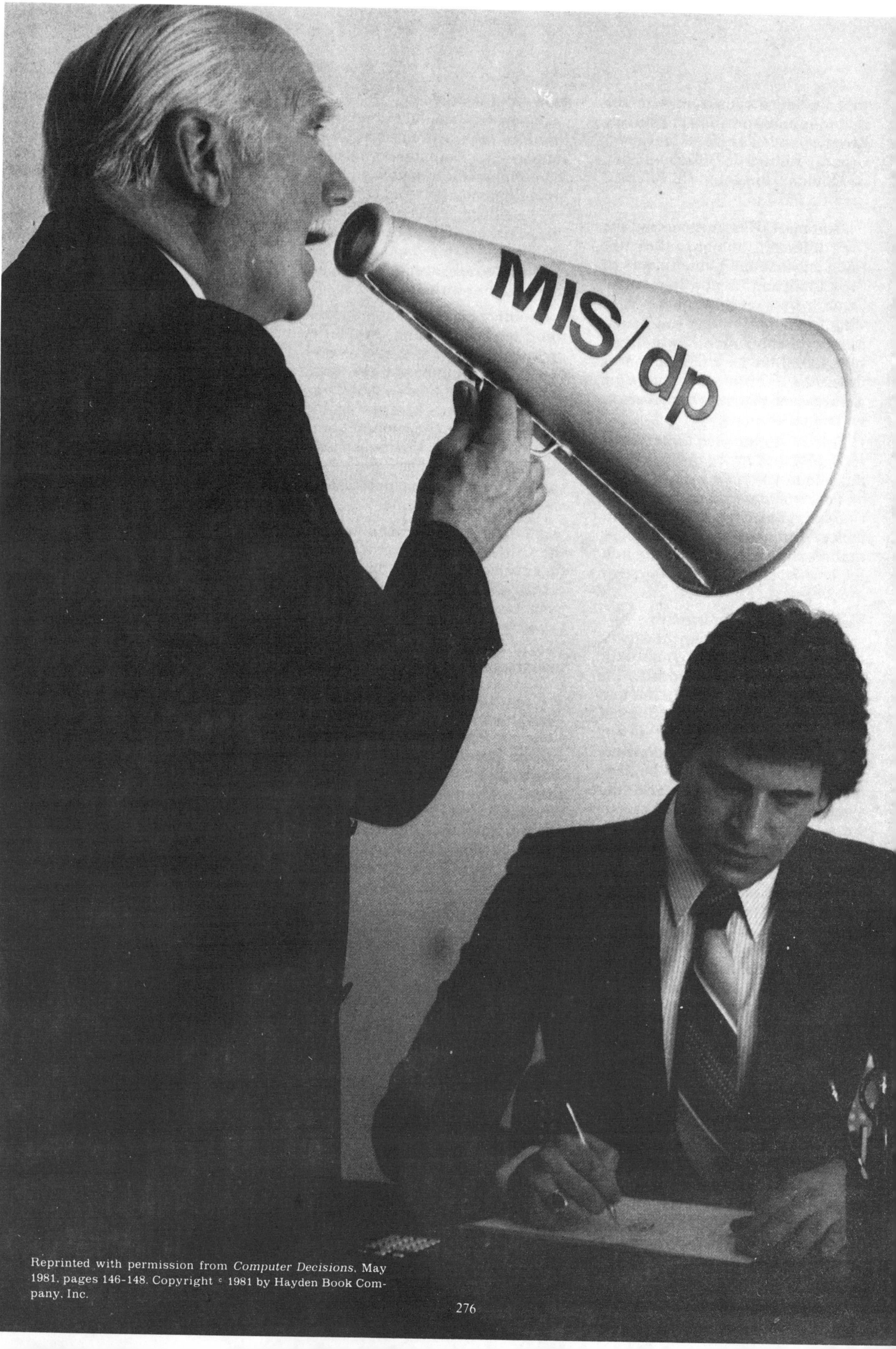
MIS/dp

Are You Getting Through To Your Staff?

Communication is vital to effective management, but it's an art that's too often neglected.

by Eugene Raudsepp

To be a good manager, you must communicate with your subordinates. As obvious as this may seem, inability to get through to fellow employees has destroyed many a promising career. Waste, inefficiency, frustration, and misunderstanding are the fruits of poor interpersonal communications. Yet, as important as good communications are to the smooth functioning of any group, most managers are left to their own devices in this key function.

The basic barrier: Misunderstanding

Why is it that something as simple as communicating with other human beings is so often nearly impossible to accomplish? The major factors, assuming that all parties speak and understand the same language, can be laid to simple misunderstanding.

Distorting information: One serious barrier to effective communication is distortion or omission of information. In transmitting messages, distortion and omission can be reduced by
- Keeping the number of items in the message to a minimum
- Using sketches and other visual aids to reinforce the message
- Itemizing points in a logical sequence
- Underscoring important points
- Using associations to make the message more vivid

On the receiving end, the listener can reduce distortion by freely asking questions and by taking notes.

Converting inferences into fact: An inference represents only a degree of probability. It goes beyond what one is actually observing; it is a conclusion, not necessarily true. Inferences that are turned into facts during transmission can generate false rumors that spread throughout an organization.

Confusion over word meanings: To reduce confusion over the real meaning of words, the listener should try to interpret them from the speaker's perspective, rather than his own. Words, by themselves, are only "pointers." Their true meaning depends on the speaker's feelings, background, knowledge, and conditioning.

In this connection, it is often useful to restate another speaker's position in your words so that he (or she) agrees that you understand him correctly. This is not as easy as it sounds. But once you've succeeded, you will often find that you have a better understanding of why the speaker at first seemed so unreasonable. This is a big step toward a meeting of minds.

Another common error is the tendency to impose a nonexistent precision on a speaker's statement. It's easy to forget that many people think aloud and grope toward their meaning. More often than not, an initial statement is only a first approximation of what a person means. I know an executive who sometimes takes one position at the outset and may completely reverse himself by the time he finishes talking—he thinks aloud.

Asking the wrong questions: The way questions are asked can either impede or help communications. For example, consider a manager who begins a conversation with a subordinate by asking how far along he is with Project X. Chances are the subordinate will become guarded and defensive; he does not know what the manager is after.

Suppose, on the other hand, the manager begins by explaining that the department has been given a high-priority project that must be completed in six months; at the same time, there must not be any overruns. He thus encourages a cooperative, problem-solving attitude in the subordinate.

Substituting argument for dialog: Consider this exchange: "I think we ought to try this approach because it's more efficient."

"Maybe so, but it's too expensive."

"But we'll save in the long run."

"Yes, but it will cause a lot of trouble."

"Not if we introduce it properly."

"There are too many places it can go wrong." *(Continued)*

The author, president of Princeton Creative Research, Inc., Princeton, NJ, was the author of "Delegate your way to success," in the March issue of Computer Decisions.

Getting Through

This interchange could go on endlessly. It boils down to a "yes it is, no it isn't" exchange, accomplishing nothing.

Executive isolation

As a manager rises in the hierarchy, he or she is increasingly likely to become isolated from subordinates. The result is a breakdown in the flow of information he needs.

The first step in eliminating executive isolation is to define specifically the functions you want to be informed about. You cannot allow yourself to be occupied only with those matters that others decide to bring to your attention. You must take the initiative.

The open-door policy: Allowing unlimited access to your office presents difficulties, as any executive who has tried it knows. The telephone rings constantly. Schedules must often be rearranged.

But the inconvenience is far outweighed by the advantages. You can keep tabs on how the organization is faring through the people you see or talk to. You can settle matters quickly and efficiently on a person-to-person basis rather than through a cumbersome exchange of memos. You can encourage and listen to new ideas that might otherwise never come to your attention.

To avoid being swamped by visitors, you must set up guidelines for what should be taken up with you and what shouldn't. Don't let people use you to make decisions they should be making themselves. Equally important, you can't let an open-door policy become an access to idle chatter. Learn to define the matter to be discussed, get the facts, discuss the pros and cons, make the decision, and end the conversation.

Many executives find that too many memos and formal meetings create a barrier between themselves and their subordinates. They prefer to visit a subordinate in his or her office, where that person can feel more relaxed.

How to reduce isolation: One way to reduce executive isolation is to

issue a list of "don'ts"; for example:
- Don't try to shield the boss. Many otherwise excellent supervisors think they are doing the boss a favor when they protect him or her from unpleasant news. By acting as censor, they make the boss less effective.
- Don't think you have to have the solution before you discuss a problem. Nobody has all the answers, and talking about a problem with your boss can put it into perspective and give both of you fresh ideas.
- Don't expect a problem to disappear if you don't talk about it. This

Matters can be settled quickly and efficiently on a person-to-person basis rather than through an exchange of memos, says author Raudsepp.

brand of wishful thinking only postpones and compounds trouble.
- Don't overprotect yourself. Occasionally, a supervisor will play down certain facts if he (or she) feels they reflect his own deficiencies. It is usually impossible to conceal trouble for long, and when it does come to light the boss can think, with some justification, that such a supervisor is less interested in doing a competent job than in saving face.
- Don't dismiss a good idea because it won't affect your operation. If you see a way to improve work methods anywhere in the organization, tell your boss about it. Let him take it from there.

Almost every company has at least one information hoarder—a manager who seems dedicated to sharing information with no one. Often, this person finds it hard to cooperate with others in the organization. More often than not, he feels that he is the only one able to handle his job and that the company would go under without him.

Such a manager often is allowed to continue this habit because no one brings the subject up. His superiors may not be aware of the problem. Subordinates, fearing reprisal, don't dare to accuse him of withholding information. Even when his attitude is pointed out to him, he is apt to have ready such plausible excuses as: "This wouldn't be of interest to anyone," or, "It's confidential," or, "Competitors would hear about it."

Because of his mistakenly inflated self-image, the information hoarder is difficult to cure. Only if one day the tables were turned, and he himself were not informed of a vital mater, might he realize his problem. And if you're trying to institute a data-base management system, his hoarding may raise such obstacles that he may have to be forced to cooperate.

The grapevine: Withholding information makes subordinates feel that they're not trusted, or not important enough, to know what's going on. To fill their need to know, they will rely on the world's oldest communication medium, the grapevine. In most organizations, the grapevine carries more information, true or false, than is recognized or acknowledged. Aside from the serious distortions usually inherent in grapevine messages, they also create the impression that some individuals are in the privileged position of having information that has not been disseminated throughout the organization. This can cause tensions, jealousies, and bad faith among the employees who feel that they have been left in the dark.

Aggravating matters further, grapevine explanations usually arrive before the true facts. Thus, they cause subordinates to question officially sanctioned explanations. Promptness in circulating information is the best safeguard.

The ill-kept secret: Even confidential information can seldom be kept secret for long. Many managers delude themsleves into thinking that something is a secret until they decide to let it out. It has been said that no information is private when two people know it. In any organization, almost all information is known to several persons. So there are many possible leaks. And these weak links in security are more likely to fail as the importance of the news builds.

Certain kinds of information cannot be passed along—for example, a major change in policies, plans, operations, or objectives. As a general rule, however, any plan for change ought to be accompanied by plans for communicating it to all concerned, as early as possible.

An early release of information on the broad purpose of a planned change, with general comments on its direction, is better than withholding information until all the details are settled.

When full disclosure can't be made, you should tell your subordinates that the full story can't be

> Learn to define the matter to be discussed, get the facts, discuss the pros and cons, and then make the decision.

told immediately, but that it will be later. If possible, a date should be set when the information will be released. If the information is such that it can never be fully disclosed, it is best for you to say so.

● Make yourself accessible. Hear subordinates out and follow up.

● Encourage frankness. Do everything you can to eliminate fear that speaking up may bring retaliation.

● Welcome new and different ideas. Be willing to listen to all ideas, including those that may seem strange or silly. Dismissing offbeat thinking will lead to closed minds and, possibly, the loss of good ideas—and also the potential loss of productive employees not easily replaced. Openly reward those whose ideas are accepted. This is the strongest encouragement for further ideas from all staff members.

● Listen for the underlying problem. Try to get to what a person is really trying to say. A gripe about working conditions may mask a belief that you don't appreciate the griper's job performance.

● Accept criticism. Regard it as healthy and normal; regard the lack of criticism as dangerous—a sign that subordinates have given up on trying to get through. □

Wendell L. French and
Robert W. Hollmann

Management by Objectives: The Team Approach

Study of the many books, articles, case studies, speeches, and discussions about management by objectives (MBO) indicates that most forms of this approach tend to reinforce a one-to-one leadership style. It is also apparent that MBO efforts vary from being highly autocratic to highly participative among organizations and even within some organizations. In this article we present a case and strategy for *collaborative* management by objectives (CMBO), a participative, team-centered approach. This approach has a number of unique features that will minimize some of the deficiencies in more traditional versions, but as we shall see, the skills involved and the organizational climate required for its optimal effectiveness may not come easily.

One-to-One MBO

Let us first compare the autocratic and participative characteristics of one-to-one versions of MBO. Examples 1a through 1d in Table 1 illustrate how this form can differ along the autocratic-participative continuum. In one contemporary version of MBO, the superior prepares a list of objectives and simply passes them down to the subordinate. In a second version, the superior prepares the subordinate's list of objectives and allows him or her ample opportu-

nity for questions and clarification. In a third version, the subordinate prepares his own list of objectives and submits this list to his superior for discussion and subsequent editing and modification by the superior. And in a fourth version, the superior and subordinate independently prepare lists of the subordinate's objectives and then meet to agree upon the final list. Similar degrees of subordinate participation also can occur at other steps in the MBO process (in determination of objective measures of performance and in the end-of-the-period evaluation, for example). Obviously many variations are possible, but the point is that the different versions of one-to-one MBO can fall anywhere along the traditional autocratic-participative continuum.

Deficiencies in One-to-One MBO

Disregarding the likely long-range inadequacies of any autocratic form of MBO, we believe that the one-to-one mode has a number of critical deficiencies. First, one-to-one MBO does not adequately account for the interdependent nature of most jobs, particularly at the managerial and supervisory levels. Second, it does not assure optimal coordination of objectives. And third, it does not always improve superior-subordinate relationships, as is widely claimed by

Table 1. Objective Setting in Different Versions of MBO

Degree of Subordinate Influence on Objectives	Very Little	Some	Moderate	Considerable
Individual Orientation	**1a** Superior prepares list of subordinate's objectives and gives it to subordinate.	**1b** Superior prepares list of subordinate's objectives; allows opportunity for clarification and suggestions.	**1c** Subordinate prepares list of his objectives; superior-subordinate discussion of tentative list is followed by editing, modification, and finalization by superior.	**1d** Superior and subordinate independently prepare list of subordinate's objectives; mutual agreement reached after extensive dialogue.
Team Orientation	**2a** Superior prepares individual lists of various subordinates' objectives; hands out lists in group meeting and explains objectives.	**2b** Superior prepares unit and individual objectives; allows opportunity for questions and suggestions in group meeting.	**2c** Superior prepares list of unit objectives which are discussed in group meeting; superior decides. Subordinates then prepare lists of their objectives, discuss with superior; individuals' objectives discussed in team meeting with modifications made by superior after extensive dialogue.	**2d** Unit objectives, including team effectiveness goals, are developed among superior, subordinates, and peers in a group meeting, usually by consensus; superior and subordinates later independently prepare lists of subordinates' objectives, reach temporary agreement; subordinates' objectives finalized after extensive discussion in team meeting.

MBO proponents (we do not know whether a team approach always will improve relations either, but we are much more optimistic about the latter). These deficiencies pertain to all versions of one-to-one MBO, regardless of how autocratic or participative, although we believe that the deficiencies would be more salient under autocratic supervisory behavior. Let us examine these limitations more closely.

Managerial interdependence. A number of writers have pointed out that one-to-one, superior-subordinate MBO does not recognize the interdependent or complementary nature of managerial jobs.[1] We concur with this criticism and believe that effective implementation of MBO requires a "systems view" of the organization. Each manager functions in a complex network of vertical, horizontal, and diagonal relationships, and his success in achieving his objectives is often (if not always) dependent upon the communication, cooperation, and support of other managers in this network.

Wendell L. French is Professor of Management and Associate Dean, Graduate School of Business Administration, University of Washington. He serves as a consultant in organization development for business, industry, government, and education; his publications include *The Personnel Management Process.*

Robert W. Hollmann is Assistant Professor of Management, College of Business and Public Administration, University of Arizona. He has previously served on the faculties of the University of Washington and DePaul University.

The relevance of managerial interdependence is particularly evident when MBO is used with staff managers. A number of authors have described the difficulties in applying MBO to staff positions.[2] We need not reiterate their ideas here, except to stress the point that the advisory and supportive nature of staff work dictates that a staff manager's objectives be highly interrelated with the activities and objectives of other managers, both line and staff. Furthermore, staff objectives are often more qualitative than quantitative, and therefore more difficult to set and measure. Asking the staff manager to set either qualitative or quantitative objectives in isolation from those upon whom his attainment of these objectives is largely dependent does not make good sense.

An indication of the lack of attention to the interdependent nature of managerial jobs can be found in two recent works, one including descriptions of MBO programs in four British firms,[3] the other including five American companies.[4] Eight of the nine companies require that forms be filled out in the MBO programs, but in only one company's form is there any space for the manager to specify the extent to which his objectives require involvement of other managers.

Coordination of objectives. Another deficiency is associated with this interdependency. One of the highly touted advantages of MBO is that it results in effective coordination of objectives; that is, there is better integration (including minimization of gaps and duplication) of the objectives of all managers in the work unit. While this is certainly a desirable benefit, it must be recognized that one-to-one MBO places the responsibility for such coordination entirely upon the superior, since he is the only person in the MBO process to have formal contact with all subordinate managers. In effect, the superior is required to function as a "central processing center of objectives."

We believe that one-to-one MBO simply does not provide the opportunity for maximum coordination of objectives. The superior may be able to marginally, or even adequately, coordinate the objectives of his immediate subordinates on a one-to-one basis, but this procedure does not really do justice to the subtleties of interdependent relationships. Under such circumstances, except for information transmitted informally and sporadically between peers in on-the-job interaction, subordinate managers have little knowledge or understanding of each other's objectives. On the other hand, if these subordinates were provided with the opportunity for dynamic interactive processes in which their objectives are systematically communicated and adjusted, final objectives probably would be more effectively coordinated.

The deficiency in the coordination of objectives is magnified in cases of managers performing highly interrelated tasks but working in different departments. For example, a sales manager in a marketing division organized along product lines needs to coordinate his objectives with those of the appropriate production manager responsible for manufacturing the product. The sales manager may meet his objective of a 5-percent increase in the sales of product X, but the organization is likely to suffer a loss of future sales and customers if the manufacturing output of product X, which is based upon the production manager's objectives, is inadequate to meet these sales commitments. One-to-one MBO between the sales and production managers and their respective superiors provides no systematic method for integrating their objectives, and accordingly, these two managers must rely entirely upon their own initiative for the development of integrative mechanisms. Quite frankly, we doubt that this haphazard approach results in optimal coordination.

Improved superior-subordinate relationships. The participative, or mutual involvement, form of one-to-one MBO is extolled largely for the improvement in superior-subordinate relationships it is expected to bring about. Not all research supports this claim, however. For example, Tosi and Carroll found that even after an intensive and carefully planned MBO program that stressed subordinate participation, subordinate managers did not feel that the superior-subordinate relationship had improved significantly in terms of helpfulness on the part of the superior.[5] While the researchers offered no specific empirical reasons for this finding, other authors have suggested factors that might provide some explanation.

Kerr believes that the typical organization hierarchy creates a superior-subordinate status differential that acts as a deterrent to the expected improvement in relationships.[6] For instance, when MBO is conducted in a somewhat autocratic manner the status differential inhibits the subordinate from challenging the decisions of his boss or the objectives he has established. Even in cases of greater subordinate involvement, status differences may hinder attainment of the desired ideal mutuality in the MBO process. A similar note is struck by Levinson, who believes that rivalry between a boss and his subordinate can easily impede the creation or maintenance of a positive relationship.[7] It is important to point out that Tosi and Carroll also found that the same MBO program stressing increased subordinate participation resulted in no significant increase in subordinates' perceived influence in the goal-setting process.[8] Perhaps superior-subordinate status differentials or rivalry were operating in this organization.

Incompatibility between the superior's role as a coach and his role as a judge may also hamper the superior-subordinate relationship. Researchers at The General Electric Company concluded that the two primary purposes of performance appraisal (performance improvement and salary adjustment) are in conflict.[9] They suggested that these two purposes could be better accomplished in two separate interviews—a proposal with which we agree. Yet even in this approach, it is easy to see the difficult position in which the superior is placed: prior to and during one interview he is expected to *constructively* evaluate the subordinate's performance and help him formulate plans for improvement, while in the second interview he is expected to *judiciously* evaluate the subordinate's performance in order to make crucial salary recommendations and to inform the subordinate of his decision. Only an exceptionally talented person could shift adroitly between these two roles (especially with the same subordinate), and it is our opinion that most managers have great difficulty doing so. Thus, an MBO program that requires the superior to have complete responsibility in performing these incompatible roles, even in separate interviews, could easily strain rather than improve superior-subordinate relationships.

Team Collaboration in MBO

We believe that MBO could be strengthened considerably by increasing the opportunities for systematic collaboration among managers. Furthermore, MBO programs based on cooperative teamwork and group problem solving would represent a positive step toward rectifying some of the deficiencies found in one-to-one MBO. Ironically, in his original description of MBO, Drucker said, "Right from the start . . . emphasis should be on team-work and team results,"[10] but it doesn't look to us as if the MBO movement has gone this way. A number of other authors have called for group or peer goal setting and evaluation in MBO,[11] but with few exceptions,[12] suggestions for a group approach to MBO generally have not been augmented with systematic guidelines or frameworks for implementation.

MBO programs described in the literature and in operation that *do* acknowledge the collaborative dimension can be classified in three categories. First, there are programs that superficially refer to the need for some sort of collaborative effort during the MBO process. For example, the MBO instruction manual may include a statement such as: "Each manager should exert maximum effort to ensure that his objectives are effectively coordinated with those of other managers in his work group." Under this unsystematic approach, then, collaboration is left entirely to each manager's own initiative.

Second, there are programs that provide some formal means for collaboration (see examples 2b and 2c in Table 1). For instance, Wikstrom describes one company program that includes "cross-checking meetings" in which managers present their tentative goals, check the impact of these goals on one another, and make adjustments before finalizing the goals.[13] In a similar vein, Raia suggests team reviews between the superior and his subordinates.[14] Based upon a joint problem-solving approach, these regular review sessions are intended to measure the team's progress toward its goals and to improve team relationships. Raia also encourages the use of a "responsibility matrix" to identify the degree to which various other management positions are related to the major activities a manager performs to accomplish his specific objectives.[15] In essence, then, programs in this second category include collaboration as a tangential aspect of an essentially one-to-one approach.

Third, there are MBO programs that include systematic collaboration as an integral part of the entire process (see example 2d in Table 1). The three-day team objectives meeting described by Reddin illustrates this approach.[16] In this program each team (superior and his immediate subordinates) concentrates on such matters as team-effectiveness areas, team-improvement objectives, team decision making, optimal team organization, team meeting improvements, team-effectiveness evaluation, and team-member effectiveness. Such collaborative approaches appear to have many features congruent with contemporary organization development (OD) and are qualitatively quite different from one-to-one approaches.

MBO and OD Contrasted

One way to describe how CMBO differs qualitatively from a one-to-one approach is to contrast the one-to-one version with the emerging field of OD, which has a strong emphasis on team collaboration. Organization development, in the behavioral-science meaning of the term,[17] is a broader strategy for organizational improvement than is MBO, but it can include the collaborative version as we shall describe it. For instance, Blake and Mouton's six-phase grid OD program includes teamwork development (phase 2) and intergroup development (phase 3), both of which include collaborative goal setting.[18] In fact, they suggest that MBO can be "introduced as the culminating action of Teamwork Development."[19]

Some of the differences, as we see them, between the traditional one-to-one MBO and OD are shown in Table 2. Traditional MBO concentrates on the individual, on goal setting for the individual, on rationality, and on end results. In contrast, OD focuses on how individuals see the functioning of their teams and the organization, on nonrationality, as well as rationality, and on means as well as ends. In addition, OD has a recurring component of system diagnosis that seems to be minimal or absent from the traditional forms of MBO.

Further, OD efforts usually move toward legitimizing open discussion of individual career and life goals, which most MBO programs largely ignore.

Table 2. Traditional MBO Compared with OD

What Traditional (One-to-One) MBO Seems to Do	What OD Seems to Do
1. Assumes there is a need for more goal emphasis and/or control.	1. Assumes there may be a variety of problems; a need for more goal emphasis and/or control may or may not be a central problem.
2. Has no broad diagnostic strategy.	2. Uses an "action-research" model in which system diagnosis and rediagnosis are major features.
3. Central target of change is the individual.	3. Central target of change is team functioning.
4. Asks organization members to develop objectives for key aspects of thier jobs in terms of quantitative and qualitative statements that can be measured.	4. Asks organization members to provide data regarding their perceptions of functional/dysfunctional aspects of their units and/or the total organization.
5. Emphasizes avoidance of overlap and incongruity of goals. Assumes things will be better if people understand who has what territory.	5. Emphasizes mutual support and help. Assumes that some problems can stem from confusion about who has what responsibilities, but also looks at opportunities for mutual help in the many interdependent components across jobs.
6. Focuses on the "formal" aspects of the organization (goals, planning, control, appraisal).	6. Initially taps into "informal" aspects of the organization (attitudes, feelings, perceptions about both the formal and informal aspects—the total climate of the unit or organization).
7. Focuses on individual performance and emphasizes individual accountability.	7. Focuses on system dynamics that are facilitating or handicapping individual, team, and organizational performance; emphasizes joint accountability.
8. Stresses rationality ("logical" problem solving, man's economic motives).	8. Legitimizes for discussion nonrational aspects (feelings, attitudes, group phenomena) of organization life as well as rationality; frequently legitimizes open exploration of career and life goals.
9. Focuses on organizational end results of the human-social system (particularly as measured by "hard data") such as sales figures, maintenance costs, and so forth.	9. Focuses on both ends and means of the human-social system (leadership style, peer relationships, and decision processes, as well as goals and "hard data").
10. Has little interpersonal-relations "technology" to assist superior and subordinate in the goal-setting and review processes.	10. Has extensive interpersonal relations, group dynamics, and intergroup "technology" for decision making, communications, and group task and maintenance processes.

A Strategy for Collaborative MBO

Contemporary organization-development efforts can provide insights and some of the technology for more widespread emergence of collaborative forms of MBO. We would like to propose a nine-phase strategy for Collaborative MBO. Basically, the essential process is one of overlapping work units interacting with "higher" and "lower" units on overall organizational goals and objectives, unit goals and objectives, and individuals interacting with peers and superiors on role definition and individual goals and objectives.

Phase I: Diagnosis of Organizational Problems. A collaborative organizational diagnosis, by discussions or questionnaires involving a cross-section of organization members, suggests the usefulness of a CMBO effort in solving *identified problems.* It appears to us that MBO, as frequently practiced, is a solution in search of a problem. For a variety of reasons, including the existence of a strong goal emphasis under some other name, overwork of many key people in the organization, or problems requiring other solutions, MBO may not be timely or appropriate.

Phase II: Information and Dialogue. Workshops on the basic purposes and techniques of CMBO are held with top management personnel, followed by workshops at the middle- and lower-management levels. These workshops can be conducted by qualified members of the personnel or training departments, by line managers trained in the approach, or if the organization prefers, by a qualified consultant. Having top-level managers conduct the workshops with middle and lower managers may speed up the process of shifting toward the more supportive climate necessary for CMBO.

Phase III: Diagnosis of Organizational Readiness. This diagnosis, based upon interviews and group meetings, must indicate an interest in and a willingness to use the process on the part of several organizational units, especially those at the top of the organization. Ideally, a number of overlapping units should express a desire to implement CMBO; for example, in addition to the president of a manufacturing firm and his immediate subordinates expressing interest, the manufacturing director and his immediate sub-ordinates may want to be involved, and two of these subordinate managers may wish to start the process with their subordinate teams, and so forth. Favorable interest in CMBO from a few units randomly scattered throughout the organization would probably be inadequate to create enough interaction and momentum to give the approach a fair try. A good deal of diagnosis of organizational readiness will have already occurred in the information-and-dialogue phase. Similarly, diagnosis of organizational readiness may reveal the need for supplemental CMBO workshops for some units or for suspending the CMBO effort.

Phase IV: Goal Setting—Overall Organization Level. Overall organization goals and specific objectives to be achieved within a given time period are defined in team meetings among top executives, largely on the basis of consensus. It is important that this phase be an interactive process with middle and lower levels of the organization; inputs about organization goals and objectives from subordinate managerial and supervisory levels must be obtained during (or before) this phase.

Phase V: Goal Setting—Unit Level. Unit goals and objectives essential to achieving overall organization goals and objectives are defined in team situations, largely by consensus. Again, this is an interactive process between higher units and their respective subordinate units.

Phase VI: Goal Setting—Individual Level. This phase begins with individual managers developing their specific objectives in terms of results to be achieved and appropriate time periods. Personal career and development goals are part of this "package." If desired, the manager's superior may simultaneously develop a list of objectives for the subordinate. The superior and subordinate discuss, modify, and tentatively agree on the subordinate's objectives. These discussions are followed by group meetings in which team members discuss each other's objectives, make suggestions for modification, and agree upon each manager's final list of objectives.

Phase VI assumes that there is agreement on the major responsibilities and parameters of the team members' roles. If major responsibilities need to be reviewed or redefined, the following sequence is used as the preliminary stage of phase VI: (1) individual team members list their major responsibilities; (2) individual team members meet with their superior to discuss, modify, and tentatively agree upon their major responsibilities; and (3) team members discuss and work toward consensus on their major responsibilities in group meetings.

Phase VII: Performance Review. On a continuing basis, either the subordinate or the superior initiates discussion whenever progress toward objectives should be reviewed; matters of team concern are discussed in regularly scheduled team meetings. Particularly relevant at this stage are occasions when internal or external factors suggest the need for revision in the original set of goals and objectives; if appropriate, these revisions should be made in collaborative team meetings.

At the end of the agreed-upon time period, each manager prepares a report on the extent to which his objectives have been achieved and discusses this report in a preliminary meeting with his superior. These reports then are presented by each individual in a group meeting, with the discussion including an analysis of the forces helping and hindering attainment of objectives. This review process occurs at all levels (organization, unit, and individual) and ordinarily would start at the lower levels as a convenient way to collate information.

Phase VIII: Rediagnosis. Diagnosis needs to reoccur, but at this phase it is the CMBO process itself that needs examining, as well as the readiness of additional units to use CMBO. Is the CMBO process helping? hindering? in what way? What is the process doing to the relationships between superiors and subordinates and within teams? Something has gone awry if goal setting and performance review are perfunctory or avoided, if the process seems unattached to the basic processes of getting the work of the organization done, or if relationships are becoming strained. On the other hand, if superiors and subordinates and teams find that the process is challenging and stretches and develops their capabilities, and if they feel good about it, the CMBO process is probably on the right track toward increased organizational effectiveness.

Ideally such diagnosis should be ongoing as the CMBO process evolves.

Phase IX: Recycle. Assuming that rediagnosis has resulted in the decision to continue the CMBO effort, the cycle of phases IV through VIII is repeated, probably once a year at the overall organization level. Ongoing individual and team progress reviews may result in modification of unit- or individual-level goals more often than once a year. Through periodic problem sensing and rediagnosis, the details of the process will undoubtedly be modified to more adequately meet the needs of teams and individuals. The nine-phase strategy for implementing CMBO is presented in Figure 1.

Some Contingencies

CMBO is not likely to be an easy process for many organizations. Initial successes depend

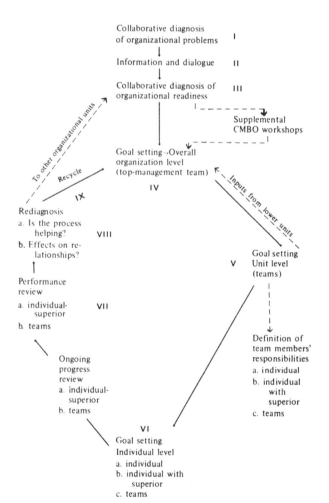

Figure 1. A Strategy for Implementing
Collaborative Management by Objectives

upon a strong desire on the part of the top-management team to cooperate with and help each other. In addition, the process requires some modicum of skill in interpersonal relations and group dynamics. Training in these skills can accompany the CMBO effort, or if an OD effort is under way, such skills will be emerging as part of this broader process.

Proper timing in the introduction of CMBO is also very important. CMBO is by no means a managerial panacea; it should be introduced only when diagnosis suggests its applicability and usefulness as well as organizational readiness. A CMBO effort can be time-consuming, and strong resistance can occur if the process is thoughtlessly superimposed at the wrong time—for example, during a period when people are preoccupied and harried with the annual budgeting process or faced with a major external threat to the organization. It is equally important to recognize that the utility of diagnosing organizational readiness is contingent upon the adequacy of information presented to managers in the CMBO workshops (phase II).

Successful expansion of the process to lower levels of the organization requires commitment to and skills in participative management, as well as a willingness and ability to diagnose the impact of the goal-setting and review processes on organization members and organizational functioning. Such a diagnosis of how things are going might result, for instance, in temporarily postponing phase VI. Successful completion of phases I through V and the appropriate team aspects of phases VII through IX might in itself be a major achievement and a move forward in organizational effectiveness. Developing effective group dynamics takes time and an organization should proceed with caution in this area. A major shift to a collaborative mode cannot be made overnight.

The Merits of CMBO: Research and Practice Clues

There are a number of clues to the merits of a Collaborative MBO approach (that is, the kind that has a team emphasis, is truly collaborative, and exists in a climate of mutual support and help) in research reports and in practice. Likert

cites a study of a sales organization in which salesmen held group meetings at regular intervals to set goals, discuss procedures, and identify results to be achieved before the next group meeting.[20] During these meetings the superior acted as a chairman; he stressed a constructive, problem-solving approach, encouraged high performance, and provided technical advice when necessary. The results of the study showed that salesmen using group meetings had more positive attitudes toward their jobs and sold more on the average than salesmen not using group meetings. According to Likert:

Appreciably poorer results are achieved whenever the manager, himself, analyzes each man's performance and results and sets goals for him. Such man-to-man interactions in the meetings, dominated by the manager, do not create group loyalty and have far less favorable impact upon the salesmen's motivation than do group interaction and decision meetings. Moreover, in the man-to-man interaction little use is made of the sales knowledge and skills of the group.[21]

Another recent study found that managers' perceptions of the supportiveness of the organizational climate and their attitudes toward MBO were significantly related.[22] A supportive climate was viewed in terms of such features as high levels of trust and confidence between superiors and subordinates, multidirectional communication aimed at achieving objectives, cooperative teamwork, subordinate participation in decision making and goal setting, and control conducted close to the point of performance (self-control). Essentially, this climate was seen as comparable to Likert's Participative Group (System 4) management system.[23] The results of the study showed significant ($p < 0.01$) positive correlations between the supportiveness of the climate and how effective managers believed the MBO process to be. Managers' evaluations of MBO effectiveness were assessed in six areas: (1) planning and organizing work, (2) objective evaluation of performance, (3) motivation of the best job performance, (4) coordination of individual and work-group objectives, (5) superior-subordinate communication, and (6) superior-subordinate cooperation. Even more important was the significant ($p < 0.01$) positive correlation between supportiveness of the climate and managers' overall satisfaction with MBO as it related to their jobs.[24]

Holder describes how consensus decision making has been used at Yellow Freight System, Inc. since the early 1950s.[25] Work groups in the firm are organized according to the "linking-pin concept"[26] and decisions, including those dealing with managers' objectives, are made on a consensus basis within each work group. The writer's account is unclear as to whether consensus MBO operates throughout the management hierarchy; however, his description indicates that it extends to as least the regional-manager level. Although Holder provides no objective measure of effectiveness, he suggests that the length of time for which the program has been used attests to its success.

Finally, in explaining a job-enrichment program in a European chemical company, Myers reports: "In 1970, more than 40,000 additional employees conferred in work teams and functional groups to define criteria against which their performance could be measured and to set tangible goals."[27] According to Myers, the program has (a) moved decision making down to the levels where the work is performed, (b) resulted in better integration of individual and organizational goals, (c) required managers to rely upon interpersonal competence rather than official authority to get results, and (d) reduced the traditional barrier between management and nonmanagement. We think this experience is particularly significant; if operative work groups can effectively set objectives in a collaborative environment, it seems reasonable to expect that managers would also be able to do so.

Conclusions

The findings of these studies and organizational programs help confirm our belief that Collaborative Management by Objectives can work. We feel that CMBO, as we have described it, is congruent with a participative, team-leadership style and can avoid many of the dysfunctional spin-offs of the prevailing one-to-one versions of MBO. We do not wish to imply, however, that CMBO will work in all organizations and under any circumstances. Care must be taken to ensure that appropriate conditions are present before and that necessary skills emerge during the implementation of CMBO.

Successful application of CMBO requires that managers be motivated to shift the climate of the organization, or at least the climate of those units using CMBO, in the direction of more teamwork, more cooperation, more joint problem solving, and more support. While a team approach per se would tend to diminish the dysfunctional consequences of status differentials and could shift the locus of commitments among people away from the one-to-one arena toward the lateral or interdependent team arena, a team approach void of mutual support and group skills could create more problems than it would solve. Training of work teams in skills of communication, group processes, and joint problem solving is vital to this shift toward a more supportive climate.

Equally vital to the success of CMBO are skills in diagnosis—both the original diagnosis that identifies the need and readiness for CMBO and the subsequent diagnoses that tune into managers' perceptions of the functional and dysfunctional aspects of the CMBO process and their assessment of the emerging climate. Such continuous "tracking" will be hard work, but the resulting opportunities for modification and other corrective action should make the CMBO process that much more relevant to the needs of the organization and its members.

The nine-phase strategy we have proposed is one way of introducing more systematic collaboration into the MBO process. While it will undoubtedly take considerable effort and attention to make the CMBO strategy work well, this approach can help people, teams, and units become more goal-directed without undermining efforts to maintain or create a participative, responsive team climate in the organization.

REFERENCES

1. See, for example, Gerard F. Carvalho, "Installing Management by Objectives: A New Perspective on Organization Change," *Human Resource Management* (Spring 1972), pp. 23-30; Robert A. Howell, "A Fresh Look at Management by Objectives," *Business Horizons* (Fall 1967), pp. 51-58; Charles L. Hughes, "Assessing the Performance of Key Managers," *Personnel* (January-February 1968), pp. 38-43; Bruce D. Jamieson, "Behavioral Problems with Management by Objectives," *Academy of Management Journal* (September 1973), pp. 496-505; Harold Koontz, "Making Managerial Ap-

praisal Effective," *California Management Review* (Winter 1972), pp. 46-55; and Harry Levinson, "Management by Whose Objectives?" *Harvard Business Review* (July-August 1970), pp. 125-134.

2. See, for example, Thomas P. Kleber, "The Six Hardest Areas to Manage by Objectives," *Personnel Journal* (August 1972), pp. 571-575; Dale D. McConkey, "Staff Objectives Are Different," *Personnel Journal* (July 1972), p. 477ff.; and Burt K. Scanlan, "Quantifying the Qualifiable, or Can Results Management Be Applied to the Staff Man's Job?" *Personnel Journal* (March 1968), p. 162ff.

3. John W. Humble, ed., *Management by Objectives in Action* (New York: McGraw-Hill, 1970).

4. Walter S. Wikstrom, *Managing by- and with-Objectives* (New York: National Industrial Conference Board, 1968).

5. Henry Tosi and Stephen J. Carroll, Jr., "Improving Management by Objectives: A Diagnostic Change Program," *California Management Review* (Fall 1973), pp. 57-66.

6. Steven Kerr, "Some Modifications in MBO as an OD Strategy," *Proceedings, 1972 Annual Meeting,* Academy of Management, 1973, pp. 39-42.

7. Harry Levinson, "Management by Objectives: A Critique," *Training and Development Journal* (April 1972), pp. 3-8; see also Levinson, op. cit.

8. Tosi and Carroll, op. cit.

9. Herbert H. Meyer, Emanual Kay, and John R. P. French, Jr., "Split Roles in Performance Appraisal," *Harvard Business Review* (January-February 1965), pp. 123-129.

10. Peter F. Drucker, *The Practice of Management* (New York: Harper & Bros., 1954), p. 126.

11. See, for example, Carvalho, op. cit.; Wendell French, *The Personnel Management Process: Human Resources Administration,* 3d ed. (Boston: Houghton Mifflin, 1974); Howell, op. cit.; Charles L. Hughes, *Goal Setting* (New York: American Management Association, 1965), p. 123; Jamieson, op. cit.; Kerr, op. cit.; and Levinson, "Management by Whose Objectives?" op. cit.

12. A notable exception is W. J. Reddin, *Effective Management by Objectives: The 3-D Method of MBO* (New York: McGraw-Hill, 1971), chapter 14. Also see Wendell French and Cecil H. Bell, Jr., *Organization Development: Behavioral Science Interventions for Organization Improvement* (Englewood Cliffs, N.J.: Prentice-Hall, 1973), pp. 167-168; and Anthony P. Raia, *Managing by Objectives* (Glenview, Ill.: Scott, Foresman, 1974).

13. Wikstrom, op. cit., pp. 22-23.

14. Raia, op. cit., p. 110.

15. Ibid., pp. 75-78.

16. Reddin, op. cit.

17. French and Bell, op. cit., p. 15.

18. Robert R. Blake and Jane S. Mouton, *Corporate Excellence Through Grid Organization Development* (Houston: Gulf Publishing, 1968); and Robert R. Blake and Jane S. Mouton, *Building a Dynamic Corporation Through Grid Organization Development* (Reading, Mass.: Addison-Wesly, 1969).

19. Blake and Mouton, *Corporate Excellence,* p. 110.

20. Rensis Likert, *The Human Organization* (New York: McGraw-Hill, 1967), pp. 55-59.

21. Ibid., p. 57.

22. Robert W. Hollmann, "A Study of the Relationships Between Organizational Climate and Managerial Assessment of Management by Objectives," unpublished Ph.D. dissertation, University of Washington, 1973.

23. Likert, op. cit.; and Rensis Likert, *New Patterns of Management* (New York: McGraw-Hill, 1961).

24. Hollmann, op. cit.

25. Jack J. Holder, Jr., "Decision Making by Consensus," *Business Horizons* (April 1972), pp. 47-54.

26. Likert, *New Patterns of Management* and *The Human Organization.*

27. M. Scott Myers, "Overcoming Union Opposition to Job Enrichment," *Harvard Business Review* (May-June, 1971), pp. 37-49.

DELEGATE YOUR WAY TO SUCCESS

by Eugene Raudsepp

Most managers accept the premise that the best way to get their work done is to make optimum use of subordinates. Yet most managers admit, when pressed, that they don't delegate as much as they should.

The problem is probably more emotional than procedural. Effective delegation is, admittedly, one of the most difficult managerial tasks. It depends on the finely woven interrelationship between the manager, subordinates, and top management. It depends on the type of company and its goals. It also depends heavily on trust and confidence. But the biggest problem is that many managers, as they climb the executive ladder, continue to feel that if they want a job done right, they have to do it themselves.

A manager who delegates with intelligence and consistent follow-up can accomplish far more than the manager who hugs to his (or her) bosom the tasks his subordinates should be doing. The manager should devote most of his time and energies to planning, supervising, and delegating. That way, he'll contribute more than he might even from a superlative job on tasks that

The author is president of Princeton Creative Research, Inc., Princeton, NJ, and is author of the books Creative Growth Games *and* More Creative Growth Games.

Delegation

his subordinates might not do quite as well. Inadequate delegation limits a manager's effectiveness because he gets bogged down in detail. Carried to its logical extreme, nondelegation can bring operations almost to a standstill.

When a manager delegates successfully, he changes his role from a performer to a trainer, motivator, and evaluator. Through delegation, he develops initiative and self-starting ability in his subordinates. He broadens them on their jobs, increases production, and improves morale. Most employees strive to live up to what is expected of them. They are willing and eager to face challenges, knowing that they are expected to deliver.

What is delegation?

Delegation is simply the passing on, by one person to another, of responsibility for a given task. But effective delegation involves a great deal more.

Delegation is not the abdication of responsibility; it is a continuing process. The manager should always be available to give advice and assistance when needed. He should make sure that needed resources are available, check performance at agreed-upon dates, and generally remain involved as advisor, leader, and sharer of responsibility. He should keep checks and controls on every task he delegates. The degree and kind of control varies, of course, with each subordinate. Some subordinates resent overcontrol and do a good job without frequent checking. Others need the security of formalized periodic reports on their assignments. Either way, there's no excuse for suddenly discovering that a subordinate is not handling his assignment properly.

Effective delegation requires patience and an initial investment of time. "I could have done the job myself twice over for all the time I spent explaining the work to him," is a frequently voiced excuse for not delegating. This may be true, especially with new subordinates. But the time expended is bound to pay off

According to author Eugene Raudsepp, it is important for managers to instruct subordinates to accomplish certain results, rather than to perform certain activities.

in the long run.

Delegation should not be viewed as an opportunity to get rid of unpleasant jobs or those in which the manager is not proficient. Also, it's a mistake to delegate too many meaningless or "make-work" jobs, especially during slack periods. This is a transparent maneuver—one that could lead the subordinate to look on all future delegated tasks as unimportant.

Helps employees develop

Ideally, delegation should help a subordinate develop not only his skills but also his judgment. He must understand what kinds of decisions he has the authority to make. If his authority to make decisions is too restricted, he will infer a lack of confidence in his ability to handle responsibility. If a subordinate is to be held accountable, he or she must have responsibility and authority with a minimum of interference. Effective delegation includes the right to make decisions and mistakes.

Delegation requires meticulous planning, particularly if complex or difficult projects are involved. It entails establishing priorities, setting objectives, and deciding how the project should be accomplished and

by whom, how long it should take, and how well it should be done. This type of planning isn't easy, and some managers tend to avoid it.

There are dozens of reasons why managers do not delegate. Those given here are the most common—but they can be avoided.

Lack of confidence in subordinates. Fearing unsatisfactory results, a manager may reason that a subordinate's judgment might be faulty, or that he will not follow through on his chores. He may feel that the subordinate is too young to command the respect and cooperation of older workers.

Such a manager feels that he must keep track of every detail to get a job done right. He may be a perfectionist who sets high personal standards of performance. He is often tempted to perform a job himself, feeling that he can do the work better and more quickly than his subordinates. Such an attitude must be shunned unless the lack of confidence in a subordinate is based on past experience.

Lack of self-confidence. Many managers, especially those recently promoted or hired, feel insecure in their jobs and in their relationship with their superiors, peers, and subordinates. They may feel overwhelmed by their new duties and responsibilities. As a result, they regress to the pleasant and familiar security and routine of the work they did before they became managers.

Poor definition of duties. A manager must have a clear understanding of his responsibilities and authority. Obviously, he can delegate only those responsibilities that have been assigned to him. If he is unsure of the nature of his own job, he can hardly be expected to delegate properly.

Aversion to risk-taking. Delegation involves making calculated risks. Even with clear communication and instructions, proper controls, and trained subordinates, something will eventually go wrong.

Fear of subordinates as competitors. This frequently leads to open and excessive criticism of a

291

Delegation

subordinate's work, thwarting or playing down his achievements, pitting him against another subordinate to put him in a bad light, ignoring or side-tracking his suggestions and ideas, and concealing his talent or misusing it in low-skill jobs.

An inflated self-image. Some managers believe that they are the pivot upon which all their department's operations turn. This type of manager, as a rule, checks on all details himself. He makes all the decisions, and considers his way of doing things the only right one. He goes to great pains to hire people who reinforce his image of himself. To protect his "kingpin" posture, he makes certain, through selective communication, that only he gets the big picture of what is going on.

The effect that the "indispensable" manager has on his subordinates can be devastating. He fosters only dependence. Whatever self-confidence and individuality his subordinates may have had are soon obliterated; they become automatons who follow only directions and never initiate ideas of their own. Eventually, stronger subordinates become restive. They realize that their growth potential is severely stunted and that the only wise course of action is to resign and go on to someplace where they can grow.

Equating action with productivity. A manager may be hyperactive. Such a person is often afraid that delegation might leave him with nothing to do. Quite commonly, a hyperactive manager complains constantly about overwork, and subordinates have a difficult time getting to see him.

Fear of appearing lazy. Delegation might be construed, by both superiors and subordinates, as trying to avoid working. This can be a sensitive point. A manager, particularly a new one, or one who is unsure of his own talents, can also feel that it is a sign of weakness to need subordinates' help to keep up with workloads.

Poor example. A common reason a manager does not delegate is that his superior did not delegate. The reasoning is "If my boss got to where he is with his style of leadership, why shouldn't I copy him?"

Many young or newly promoted managers who have been held back by their own superiors in the past do not delegate because they want to keep the reins in their own hands, as a protective device.

Analyzing subordinates

A prime requisite for effective delegation is a comprehensive inventory of subordinates' capabilities: skills, qualifications, experience, special talents, interests, motivations, attitude, potential, and limitations.

Such analyses, which should include meetings with subordinates to get their own estimation of their abilities and aspirations, enables the manager to decide to which subordinates he can delegate immediately, and which need further coaching and experience.

Here are a few facts to make delegation easier for all concerned:
- Be sure you and your supervisor agree on what your job is. Take all the initiative you can without encroaching on others' rights. A narrow definition of your job restricts you.
- Be sure your subordinates understand what you expect them to do. The simplest way to delegate is to tell your subordinates what authority you reserve for yourself. It may help to list matters you want discussed with you before any action is taken.
- Prepare written policies your subordinates can use to guide their decisions. A soundly conceived and clearly understood set of policies lets subordinates make decisions and take action with confidence.
- Be humble enough to admit that someone else may be able to do the job as well as you can.
- Make as many subordinates as possible directly responsible to you.

This will help you communicate, make decisions, take action, and exercise control.
- Make subordinates responsible for accomplishing results rather than activities. Once the expected results are spelled out, the subordinate should be able to choose methods he will use in accomplishing them.
- Reward those who get things done. Subordinates will accept responsibility and actively participate in accomplishing objectives only if they feel that rewards go to those who perform. The rewards for being right must always be greater than the penalties for being wrong.
- Distinguish between rush jobs and the less immediate but more important things you have to do; spend more time on the important tasks than the trivial ones.

Self-questioning can ease the decision of what and how much to delegate:
- How important is the decision? Are the stakes so high that a mistake cannot be tolerated? If so, the matter probably cannot be delegated successfully.
- Even though you are more competent than your subordinate, are you as close to the problem? Is your decision more apt to be right?
- Does your failure to delegate mean that you are not giving adequate attention to other more important parts of your job?
- Does your failure to delegate mean you are not developing your subordinates? Are they capable of being developed? If not, can they be transferred or replaced?
- What do top managers really expect of you? Are they measuring you principally by results, so that your decisions must be right? Do they really expect you to develop people?

The art of delegation is a difficult one to learn, but it's a vital management skill. If you do it right, you'll improve employees' morale, get more work done, and ease the burden on yourself. □

How Much Is Enough?

You can get a good idea of whether you are delegating as much as you should by answering the following questions. The more "Yes" answers you give, the more likely it is that you're not delegating enough.

- Do you often work overtime?
- Do you take work home evenings and on weekends?
- Is your pile of unfinished work increasing?
- Do you find that daily operations are so time-consuming that you have little time left over for planning and other important matters?
- Do you feel you have to have close control of every detail to have the job done right?
- Do you frequently find yourself bogged down, trying to cope with the morass of small details?
- Do you frequently have to postpone long-range projects?
- Are you harassed by frequent unexpected emergencies in your department?
- Is a good part of your working day spent on tasks your subordinates could do?
- Do you lack confidence and respect for your subordinates' abilities to shoulder more responsibilities?
- Do you understand what your responsibilities and authority are?

- Do you find yourself irritable and complaining when the work of your group doesn't live up to expectations?
- Do you find that your subordinates never show any initiative?
- Are friction and low morale characteristic of your work group?
- Do your subordinates defer all decisions on problems to you?
- Are policies to guide your subordinates in making decisions ambiguous?
- Do you instruct your subordinates to perform certain activities, rather than to accomplish certain results?
- Have subordinates stopped coming to you to present their ideas?
- Do operations slow down considerably when you are away from your job?
- Do you feel that you're abdicating your role as a manager if you have to ask your subordinates' assistance in order to complete your projects?
- After delegating a project, do you breathe down the subordinate's neck?
- Do you believe that your status and the salary you earn automatically mean that you have to be overworked?

Ichak Adizes

© 1976 by the Regents of the University of California, Reprinted from
CALIFORNIA MANAGEMENT REVIEW, Volume XIX, Number 2, pp.
5-20 by permission of the Regents.

Mismanagement Styles

According to the Peter Principle,[1] individuals in organizations tend to be promoted to their level of incompetence. This means that people mount the ladder of promotion until they fail because they have achieved a position that is beyond their capacities. Yet while author Peter Laurence presents a vivid description of corporate reality, he does not provide a theoretical explanation of this phenomenon. The purpose of this article is to analyze the ways in which some people become managerially incompetent as they climb the organizational ladder and to provide a profile of an effective managerial process.

My research on styles of management shows that four roles must be performed; whenever one of those roles is not performed, a certain style of mismanagement can be observed. It is suggested that the Peter Principle phenomenon occurs because people are promoted on the basis of excellent performances in one or more of these roles, but they become incapable, at a certain stage of their ascent up the hierarchy, of performing the additional roles that are required. As a result they become "organizationally incompetent." They become *mismanagers*.

In this article I will first present the four roles and then describe the several styles of mismanagement that can be discerned in the extreme cases in which one or more, but not all, of the roles is performed. It is my conclusion that managers who excel in all four roles are extremely rare and that this fact accounts for the prevalence of the Peter Principle phenomenon. Several recommendations are made on how to use these findings in organizational staffing and in carrying out organizational change. These recommendations are based on my own experiences, which are reported at the end of this article. This report is based on six years of systematic observations of managerial behavior and experience in effecting organizational change in a variety of organizations and cultures.

The Managerial Function

A manager is one who manages, and managing is getting the job done by working with or through people or by managing the process necessary for accomplishment. Thus, while the production manager is engaged in achieving tangible results working with and through people, the staff specialist can also be considered a manager attending to the intangible processes. This report, however, is concerned only with the managers who work with and through people.

First of all a manager is expected to achieve results equal to or better than those of the competition. The principal qualification for an achiever is the possession of a functional knowledge of his field, whether marketing, engineering, accounting, or any other discipline. But being individually productive, and having the functional knowledge of a particular discipline or technology, does not necessarily enable one to produce commensurate results in working with a group of people.

A manager should thus have more than functional knowledge. He should be more than an individual producer. He should be able to administer the people with whom he works and to see that they also produce results. In this role he schedules, coordinates, controls, and disciplines. He is an implementor: he sees to it that the system works as it was designed to work. "Administration" consists mainly of implementation; "management," on the other hand, entails a higher degree of discretion, as in the setting of goals, strategic planning, and policy making. Discretionary decision making, however, involves entrepreneurship.

In a changing environment a manager must use his judgment and have the discretion to change goals and change the systems by which they are implemented. To perform this role he must be an organizational entrepreneur and an innovator, since, unlike an administrator who is given certain plans to carry out and certain decisions to implement, an entrepreneur has to generate his own plan of action. He has to be a self-starter. A manager who performs the entrepreneurial role has to be sufficiently creative to identify possible courses of action, and he should be willing to take risks. If he is not creative, he will be unable to perceive new possibilities. If he cannot take risks, he may not be able to take advantage of them.

A manager is thus expected to be a producer, for which he must have the functional and technical know-how necessary to turn out maximal results. He is, furthermore, expected to implement

Ichak Adizes is Associate Professor of Managerial Studies in the Graduate School of Management, University of California, Los Angeles. He has served as a consultant to numerous international firms in managerial processes and is president and senior associate of MDOR Institute in Los Angeles.

a system designed to achieve those results in the short run and to initiate new directions whenever opportunities or threats arise in order to maximize those results. He should be a producer (P), an administrator (A), and an entrepreneur (E). The roles that must be performed are those of *producing, implementing,* and *innovating.* But these three roles in combination are also insufficient for adequate managerial functioning. Many an organization that had been managed by an excellent achiever-administrator-entrepreneur (usually their founder) nose-dived when this key individual died or for some reason was replaced. For an organization to be continuously successful, an additional role must be performed.

The fourth essential role of management is that of *integration* (I). This is the process by which individual strategies are merged into a group strategy; individual risks become group risks; individual goals are harmonized into group goals; and ultimately individual entrepreneurship emerges as group entrepreneurship. When a group can operate on its own with a clear direction in mind and can choose its own directions over time without depending on any one individual for its successful operation, then we know that the integrating role has been performed adequately. It requires an individual who is sensitive to people's needs. Such an individual unifies the whole organization behind goals and strategies. If he has been a good integrator, he makes himself dispensable; the strategies which he helped the organization to identify will survive his death. True integrators can thus be measured by the persistence of their unifying process, and this depends on how well they performed the integrating role.

Mismanagement Styles

These four roles of management enable us to construct a typology of incompetence in organizations according to the Peter Principle. Consider, for example, the case of an employee who is a competent individual producer but who, once promoted to a managerial position, fails as a manager because he cannot administer other people. He has difficulty in relating to subordinates; he cannot delegate tasks, coordinate tasks, or follow up on subordinates' accomplishments. Another example is the case of a good technician and administrator who, when further promoted, fails to innovate. He can accomplish what is being delegated to him and he can work with others, but he does not initiate new activity on his own, either because he is not creative or because he is incapable of taking risks. So the entrepreneuring role is not performed, and in the long run the organization stagnates. Even a person who can perform all three of these roles —producer, administrator, entrepreneur—will be an incompetent manager unless he can function as a group integrator and can develop group cohesion around group activity. If he cannot do this, the organization will be too dependent on him; he will be the focal person who makes all crucial decisions by himself and the organization will become too centralized to function well. Also, an organization which has become too dependent on one individual may face major difficulties when that person leaves. Many management-owned companies have failed after the death of the founder because of this deficiency in management.

Let us now describe the styles of mismanagement exhibited in those extreme cases in which a manager (or rather a mismanager) performs only one role, whether that of an individual producer (PXXX), an administrator (XAXX), an entrepreneur (XXEX), or an integrator (XXXI). From these "pure" cases, mixed types of mismanagement can be identified subsequently.

Mismanagement style PXXX: the exclusive producer (the "loner"). The loner is himself very industrious and knowledgeable about his task, but he is neither an administrator, nor an entrepreneur, nor an integrator. He mismanages because he does not administer his staff, initiate systematic change, or mobilize the group with which he works to make the necessary change.

His main fault as a manager is the compulsion to do everything himself. One would think that he carries the whole plan of action in his inner coat pocket, usually on the back of an old envelope. He sees every task as *his* personal responsibility, rather than as the responsibility of his department. He resists delegating authority to his subordinates, even though they may be underutilized, understimulated, and hungry for more responsibility. When he is forced to delegate, he feels highly uncomfortable and quickly finds

reasons to take the authority back into his own hands. He does not allow the delegation process to take root. "They don't do it right" he will say as a pretense for reversing a delegation process or a defense for not performing it.

In an organization that is mismanaged by the loner there is a significant imbalance in the work load; while he is overburdened, the rest of the organization is underworked. In visiting his organization one notices the lack of tension in the atmosphere; people seem to have all the time in the world for the visitor. But when one enters the office of the manager, the contrast is conspicuous. The atmosphere is tense, he speaks rapidly and disjointedly, the phone rings constantly, and secretaries come and go with decisions that have to be implemented. The subordinates are hardly more than spectators to his performance. Still, since he cannot do everything personally, he makes extensive use of "expeditors," persons who assist him with errands or short-term assignments but who have no permanent long-term responsibilities. Most of their time is spent waiting for the next errand or task, which will be assigned in the form of a crisis that should have been handled "yesterday," for which they often have had no previous training, and which is usually presented as a request to "Please help *me*. . . ."

This mismanager does not acknowledge the value of systematic training of subordinates. He prefers the apprenticeship approach, in which they have to learn by actually performing all duties in the organization, and by emulating him. "Why don't they show motivation, take initiative, show me what they can do?" he usually complains. "Who trained me? I learned by myself! Why don't they learn? In this business there are no secrets; just get the job done. . . ."

The loner resents subordinates who do not look industrious and come up with results—he considers it their fault, and he will not listen to their complaints that there was no systematic support for their efforts. Furthermore, he resists advice on how to manage. Consultants who try to change his attitude and behavior are labeled "academicians" who "can't do," and he usually has neither the time nor the patience to listen. "There is too much to do," is his usual defense mechanism. His second line of defense is, "We cannot worry about the long run; if we do not produce results today there might be no tomorrow."

This mismanager is always busy, running from crisis to crisis; his secretary, if he has one, is usually burdened with a work load she cannot meet. But in spite of his constant complaining that he is overburdened, he is happiest when he is busiest. He suffers from anxiety if he does not feel productive and to him being productive does not mean getting others to work, but being personally involved in performing the task. He measures his productivity by how hard *he* works. When you ask him, "Well, how are you doing?" his typical answer will be, "We sold (or produced, or whatever)" or "I am working very hard—I stayed last night until midnight. . . ."

So he usually refuses to accept additional tasks because he always feels he must give the impression that he is overburdened with work. However, when new tasks seem crucial to him he will take them on even though he feels he is already overburdened. When it is suggested that he reduce his work load he has many excuses at hand to show that this would be impossible; it seems that he perceives a reduction in his own work load as a threat to his self-esteem. If he does accept additional tasks, one can safely assume that he will fail in something, since he will try to do everything himself and some tasks will have to be ignored.

In one company I have worked with, one of the vice presidents was a typical loner. He worked longer hours than anyone else; his subordinates were underutilized and undertrained; and he was always immersed in some crisis solution. While I was working on budgetary procedure with one of his subordinates (since he had no time for that), he stuck his head in the door and asked, "So, what are you doing?" "We are preparing a budgetary procedure," we answered, "How about you?" "I was making sales to pay for all of this," he replied sarcastically.

Mismanagement style XAXX: the exclusive administrator implementor (the "bureaucrat"). By the XAXX style of mismanagement I mean the exclusive performance of the implementing role. This manager acts exclusively as an administrator. He is a manager who knows by heart the standard operating procedures in the organization and manages by means of directives that are usually presented in writing. In contrast to the loner, who is a hyperbusy achiever and performer, concerned with *what* is achieved rather than *how* it is achieved, the bureaucratic mismanager spends inordinate amounts of time worrying about administrative details. He is more concerned about *how* things are done than about *what* is being done. He rebukes his subordinates if they do not follow standard operating procedures, even when this was necessary to achieve results; he always has arguments to show why the system must be left intact. His arguments are usually legalistic and unrelated to the missions and objectives of the organization. He considers himself the guardian of the system, rather than of the mission which the system is designed to achieve. His primary and often exclusive commitment is to the implementation of a plan regardless of its wisdom or even its ethics. Over a period of time, the department will perform the same duties, but with more and more complex procedures to assure maximum conformity and minimum uncertainty. This behavior actually hinders changes, because the mushrooming bureaucracy will make change more and more expensive. Thus, both the loner and the bureaucrat inhibit the effective growth of the company. The loner resists new tasks because he accepts only the amount of work *he* can perform alone. The bureaucrat does not allow for effective changes if he perceives them to be a threat to his ability to control.

The bureaucrat abhors ambiguity; he insists that everything be in writing and that all spheres of responsibility be clearly demarcated. He is meticulously organized and has a fantastic memory for details. He is very loyal and does not change organizations easily; he avoids all change as much as possible. His ingenuity in finding reasons to discourage new projects makes him an obstructionist. The organization has to achieve its goals in spite of him, and persons in the organization who are committed to getting things done learn to bypass him.

While the loner evaluates himself by how hard he works, and by the results he achieves, the bureaucrat evaluates himself by *how well he controls* the system and by his success in eliminating digressions from standard procedure and minimizing uncertainty. Because of this, he is prone to the abuse of Parkinson's Law: he gets increasing numbers of subordinates to perform the same job, without achieving any apparent increase in productivity; the only apparent change is that more people are involved in more systems and procedures designed to control even more what appears to be already overcontrolled!

Mismanagement style XXEX: the exclusive entrepreneur (the "crisis maker"). This mismanagement style is exhibited when an individual performs exclusively the innovating role. This person charges ahead at almost any target that appears on his organizational horizon. He attempts to exploit all opportunities simultaneously, whenever they arise, regardless of the repercussions for the organization. He is on several frontiers at the same time, spreading himself thin. He comes into an organization with new ideas and new ways of accomplishing tasks and tries to change the methodology and the tasks simultaneously.

The true entrepreneurial manager must be both a creative person and a risk taker. We can, of course, conceive of both a creative person who does not take risks, and a risk-taking person person who is not creative. Although they are complementary, creativity and risk taking are independent, individual personality characteristics. We maintain that these personality types, by themselves, are less commonly found in managers.

The archetypal creative person is usually treated as a bohemian or reclusive inventor, while the archetypal risk taker is, of course, the compulsive gambler. As a pure type of manager of the entrepreneurial sort, an equal combination of these attributes must be present.

The perspective of the entrepreneur is not limited by the organization with which he is associated. For him creative ideas are as applicable to the problems of the organizations in the environment as they are to those within his organization. This manager is neither local nor cosmopolitan—perhaps he is both.

Subordinates avoid the crisis maker just as they avoid the bureaucrat, but for different reasons. Subordinates of the bureaucrat who wish to be effective avoid him because he is constantly telling them what they should not do, while the subordinates of the crisis maker avoid him because he is always assigning new tasks, forgetting about the old tasks that have been earlier assigned and that already fully occupy the subordinates' time.

The crisis maker has little sense of what people can accomplish. He usually gets upset when objectives are not achieved. He is so excited about his own creative capabilities that he is impatient with limited achievements. He expects instantaneous accomplishment of his ideas and when that is not forthcoming, instead of trying to identify the barriers that prevented effective accomplishment, he changes the assignment altogether and thus ends up loading new assignments on his subordinates. They soon learn not to ask for help.

While the bureaucrat may achieve goals in spite of his mismanagement (because people learn how to bypass him), the harder the crisis maker tries to manage, the further behind he gets; while he is busy making everyone else busy, the organization gets nowhere because he changes directions too often and because his subordinates do not actually cooperate: they always have a reason why tasks couldn't have been done rather than why they shouldn't be done. This behavior might be attributed to their ambiguity as to what to do and how to do it. They have learned that the crisis maker is not to be taken too seriously. No task that he delegates is really intended to be accomplished; in a very short time he will change his mind. But they have also learned not to reject these tasks outright, because the crisis maker identifies himself with the task to the point where rejection of the tasks seems to him a personal rejection. So the subordinate is trapped: on one hand, there is no use in trying to achieve the task since it will be changed; on the other hand, he cannot refuse the task outright. The only way out is to accept the task but to do very little about it and to come up with creative excuses as to why the task could not have been accomplished—to appear cooperative without actually being so.

The crisis maker has many complaints about his subordinates. He keeps them busy, but he complains that they are inefficient. He refuses to see

298

that he is responsible for their ineffectiveness because of his constant changes in goals. As long as they appear to have tried hard to accomplish his plan, however, he is satisfied.

This mismanager has little use for systems. He perceives planning procedures as unwanted constraints because they require him to commit himself to some direction. He likes to change directions. He is an optimist at heart; he believes that there are no barriers to what people can do in spite of the fact that he constantly fails himself and others.

This person is usually very personable and likable, since he is stimulating, enterprising, and full of energy. Working for him can be exciting for a while, until one learns that no matter what one does, the crisis maker will be dissatisfied because he always has new projects and new ideas to achieve before the old ones have been accomplished. He is unrealistic and often vague about his demands; his entrepreneuring, creative mind has no patience for detail.

The crisis maker is not himself a performer. He is not really concerned about results, although he is highly critical of the failures of his subordinates. If the loner appraises himself by how hard he works, and by the results he produces, and the bureaucrat by the control he feels he has, the crisis maker appraises himself by how hard his subordinates *appear* to work. He gets his reinforcement from the appearance of productivity, the beehive atmosphere of activity that attests to the influence of his creative ideas.

The differences among mismanagement styles can be exemplified by describing the different reactions of mismanagers to an office where all subordinates seem to be working peacefully at their desks. The loner, in passing through the office, won't notice it; he is too busy with his own work. The bureaucrat notices it but since no one is asking him to solve any problem he will assume everything is going according to plan and will be satisfied. The crisis maker will be upset; the order, the peacefulness, the lack of tension will disturb him. If there is no crisis in the air, he will produce a new project like a magician in order to prod the organization into frantic activity.

Subsequently, the subordinates of the loner learn that they can take long breaks so long as they are available on short notice to "help get things done." The subordinates of the bureaucrat learn that so long as they come on time, leave on time, comply with all regulations, and don't ask too many questions, their jobs are secure. The subordinates of the crisis maker learn quickly that they have to look busy whenever he is in sight, and preferably pretend to be busy on his latest pet project.

The easiest way to summarize the characteristics of the crisis maker is to present an authentic description of such a mismanager given by one of his subordinates in an interview (somewhat abridged and paraphrased here):

I hate to see him go on vacation, and Monday mornings are just as bad. I know that as soon as he comes back we will have a new set of priorities. . . . We are always in a state of flux. My title, position, and responsibilities change too frequently for me to take hold. If you try to dispute any of his ideas he will produce information, figures, quotes—you name it—to prove he is right. He is a fantastic juggler, throwing out this evidence like a magician to prove that his new pet project is absolutely the best, and that it's your fault if you don't understand how it is related to the previous project. Later on, after we fail, it becomes our fault that we didn't understand him, and before you know it he is presenting all the arguments against it that you presented to him when he first suggested the project. The worst thing that you can do is to remind him that that's what you said in the first place. Even if he doesn't fire you right then, he will keep a grudge. . . . If you suggest a project of your own, he will have a hundred reasons why it cannot be done. But a week later, he will be back with the same idea. This time he will present it as *his*, and as a top priority which should have been done yesterday; he will be angry that no one thought of this before. . . .

He likes to have people around him to listen sympathetically to his ideas, and if they leave he gets hurt. He always has to have an audience, whether it's his secretary or his executive vice-president. He will keep his audience long after the working day is over. This is the price we have to pay to show we take his ideas seriously. Many of his subordinates have gotten divorced or soon will be, because the sort of unequivocal loyalty he demands competes with family life.

Every so often he comes up with five or six new ideas and starts making the rounds of the offices presenting them to people. You have to decide which ones you're going to fight and how. After a while he's left with two ideas, which he pushes through. Then one gets a few memos out to show that one has tried to do something about it, and then one gets ready for the next week and the next bag of ideas. You always have to show token attention and follow-up on his requests. Do not get over-enthusiastic and excited though; when he shows up the next day with the next idea he might be highly upset if he finds that you are too busy to get involved with the latest project.

He is very charismatic. Makes you feel at odds with yourself. If you fail in a task he can show you how you misunderstood his genius. It is always you who were dumb . . . his idea was really so simple.

You must keep him out of details. The details bore him; and if he does make suggestions that he thinks deal with details, he is likely to turn the system upside down . . . you ask him what time it is and he gives you a lecture . . .

You should always tell him about successes. If you tell him you have a problem he will listen, but by the time he is done with helping you out, you will have ten projects ten times more problematic on your hands."

Mismanagement style XXXI: the exclusive integrator (the "superfollower"). By the XXXI style, I mean the mismanager who, while not an entrepreneur or an administrator or an individual producer, is involved in uniting people behind a cause. I call him a superfollower because he tries to find out what plan will be acceptable to the largest number of people and then tries to unite them behind that plan. He has no ideas of his own that he would like to implement. There is nothing he wants to achieve except the position of a conflict resolver. Like the bureaucrat who does not care what he produces as long as it is well implemented, the superfollower is little concerned about what or how he integrates, so long as there is an appearance of consensus, a united front.

This manager is an integrator who deals exclusively with the interactions of others. As such, he is not bound by the limits of his own organization unit. If he is sincerely interested in others, he is likely to exhibit this behavior with others in (and outside) the organization as well as with his own subordinates. On the other hand, if he is a manipulator of others, he is likely to exhibit this kind of behavior outside as well as inside his unit. This type of manager "gets things done through people," whether he cares for people or not. He is not necessarily a local or a cosmopolitan; his perspective is in effect boundless. Like the entrepreneur, we cannot predict from this, his dominant management style, whether or not he will take an open systems perspective.

The superfollower enjoys being instrumental in

solving conflicts; but unfortunately, not all conflict resolutions are functional. A course of action that seems adequate in terms of resolving a short-term need might not be beneficial to the organization in the long run. A consensus among members of an organization at a particular time may satisfy their immediate interest at the expense of the total organization. The total interest of an organization includes groups that are not always represented in its decision-making bodies. While the role of the manager is also to represent future interests, the superfollower is less interested in these than in his immediate constituency.

Short-range interest groups flourish under the superfollower because he does not identify corporate goals for them but rather considers a goal to be that which is desired at a particular moment by a consensus of those participating in the decision-making process. The superfollower does not attempt to lift himself above the temporary interests of the organization and to decide the direction which the organization should take. He will not threaten an already existent consensus. He does not like to confront subordinates. He will not absorb the aggression created when a course of action offends a powerful group. In other words, he does not really lead— he follows. He tries to identify himself *with* a direction which is already acceptable to the organization rather than to identify a direction for the organization which will be the best one to take in the light of all the conditions the organization faces. He is always asking, "What do we agree about. . . ." He hardly ever makes his own suggestions. Instead, he quotes others: "So and so said that . . . and so and so agrees that. . . ."

He will not volunteer to tell you what is going wrong although he is looking for what people worry about in order to work on it. While the loner complains that he never has enough time, the bureaucrat complains that people are late or are spending too much, and the crisis maker complains that nothing ever gets done. If the superfollower complains at all, it is usually that someone did not understand him correctly about something.

The reaction of subordinates to this type of mismanagement is mixed; it can range from enthusiasm through apathy to rebellion. If one happens to belong to a group which gets all it wants from the organization, one will accept him. On the other hand, rebellion can be aroused when the company is following a direction that a minority knows to be disastrous.

In the case of a power struggle among members of the organization this type of mismanager will assess the struggle in order to determine which side is likely to win and then will jump on the bandwagon and try to lead it. He will try to be the focal person who achieves unity by extracting compromising commitments from the various parties involved. He will not mobilize for a controversial alternative, especially not one which requires the dominant group to make concessions, even when such an alternative can provide a unity based on consensus rather than on compromise.

Power struggles under a superfollower can be very dysfunctional. People turn against each other while he maneuvers around them all. Power struggles under the loner are minimal, since most of the time he struggles with himself; and if such struggles exist he is too busy to get involved with them. The crisis maker will manipulate the power struggle, either by introducing it or by channeling it into his latest project. The bureaucrat will fight it zealously if it poses a threat to his control. The superfollower will thrive on it, and never really resolve it. Since he does not present a long-term uplifting and unifying alternative, but advocates the dominant short-term acceptable alternative, people turn against each other rather than uniting against the alternative which the superfollower should have provided if he were capable of entrepreneurial behavior. He does not really unite, but he integrates; and since it is intended only for the short run it provides only an apparent unity. In the long run the group never becomes united. To provide long-term unity we need not only an integrator, but an entrepreneur. The true leader and statesman, who leads rather than follows, is the entrepreneuring integrator: one who can offer alternatives which unite, rather than integrating existing alternatives.

The mismanagement of the superfollower has other long-term repercussions. Since the organization changes directions according to the power shifts within it, it lacks a unified and consistent long-term policy. The organization finds itself oscillating from one direction to another, and these frequent changes are costly.

Mismanagement style XXXX: does not excel in performing any role ("deadwood"). Another pure type of mismanagement is one in which the person in question performs no role well. He is not an integrator because he does not have the social sensitivity and the capacity for communication to perform this function. He cannot perform the entrepreneuring role because he is neither creative nor capable of taking risks. He cannot be an administrator because he is incapable of delegating, coordinating, motivating, or whatever else is necessary in order to carry out a predetermined task. But what is more surprising is that he is not even an individual producer; he is not even technically competent to produce results. He is managerially incompetent, hence I label him deadwood. This type of mismanager can develop when an organization is changing rapidly either in its markets or in its technology. Without an adequate attempt to provide for the development of human resources and to retrain people, the loners of yesterday become the deadwood of today. This can also happen to the bureaucrat and the crisis maker if they lose power because of changes introduced over their heads and if they also lack the psychological energy necessary to reestablish their positions and to perform their roles in a functional way. They accept the enforced change, drift away, and become deadwood.

The deadwood is apathetic. He waits to be told what to do. He does not produce; he does not administer others zealously; he does not worry about power intrigues; and obviously he does not provide sparks like the crisis maker. If he has any "sparking" ideas he keeps them to himself. He is mostly worried about how to survive until retirement and how to keep intact the little he has. In his ample free time he looks for successes that he can take the credit for, a strategy intended to improve his chances of survival. Change is a serious threat to him. He knows that in any change he is the one whose position is most threatened. In order to maximize his chances for organizational survival he resists change, attributes successes to himself, and avoids starting or even joining new projects: his hiring practices also reflect the strategy of survival. He favors the not-so-bright and not-so-aggressive subordinate, the one even less productive than himself, who can pose no threat to him.

He has no complaints about anything. He fears that any complaint will reflect on him; so it is always "Everything is going well, we are making excellent progress," while the company is actually going bankrupt. He trains, but his heart is not in it once he has become deadwood. Why should he train his own replacement? What is the hurry? Hence, he will only go through the motions of training.

This mismanager is afraid of conflict. Conflict may mean change, and change threatens his survival. So he tries to cover up conflicts and explain them away as mere misunderstandings. Planning, organizing, controlling are to him only words that mean more work. Since he is neither a producer, an implementor, an entrepreneur, nor an integrator, the process of management is to him a mere ritual, acted out religiously but only for the sake of survival.

As far as his personality traits are concerned, he might have been any one of the other mismanagers. One can still see, from time to time, traces of the enthusiastic crisis maker or the meticulous bureaucrat that he once was. But by the time he has become deadwood, his main characteristic is a "low metabolism." He smokes or drinks a lot; he coughs, nods, hums, nods his head in agreement; he confides in you about how well he is doing, or did in the past, or will do; but one senses that there is not much to be expected from him.

This person is usually out of the information network. If he does get access to any information he cherishes it and uses it whenever possible, however remotely relevant; this proves to the rest of the organization that he is still plugged in and still kicking.

Comparative Analysis

Identification of mismanagement styles by nature of misinformation. Subordinates, if they misinform a mismanager, will misinform him on different subjects, depending on the type of mismanager he is. The loner will be misinformed about how much free time his subordinates have, the bureaucrat about transgressions and violations in the organization, the crisis maker about the limits to what can be done, for his subordinates will accept any assignment and then come up with excuses for not accomplishing it. But deadwood is not misinformed; he is simply ignored. He is not sufficiently threatening so that anyone has to misinform him so as to protect himself.

Identification of mismanagement by promotion criteria. How do employees get promoted in a mismanaged organization? Under a loner, one must always be present to carry out any errand with minimal fuss. Under a bureaucrat, one must always be organized and informed, and never doubt or question the validity of what is being done and how. Under the crisis maker, the prescription for success is to show enthusiasm, listen carefully, support all the ideas of the boss and agree with all his criticisms of the current situation. With deadwood, there is no sure way to succeed and get promoted. If anyone is really successful, deadwood will be threatened and will find ways to discount the successes of the subordinate and discreetly magnify his own contribution. The only way to succeed is to leave the unit that deadwood mismanages, if possible. Otherwise, all one can do is to lie low and wait for his retirement or replacement, while slowly losing one's own creative capacity.

Identification by creative processes. It is possible to identify the type of mismanagement being practiced by the location of the creative processes in the organization. Under the loner, people can be creative if they have the inclination. He does not feel threatened by it, and he will notice and encourage it if it produces results. The bureaucrat ignores creativity so long as it does not challenge his system of controls. So if there are any creative people they can operate without inhibition. The crisis maker monopolizes creativity. He exhibits anxiety when those around him challenge his creativity with theirs. He could accept them if they would channel their creativity so as to augment his own project, but otherwise he perceives it as a threat. The superfollower does not like creative people who question his leadership either. But in all these cases, creativity is exhibited somewhere. If a creative individual finds himself under the deadwood, he will quit and go elsewhere, or else lose his creative needs because there is no way to express them.

Identification by subordinates' behavior. The kind of dysfunctional behavior exhibited by subordinates of the various kinds of mismanagers also differ. The loner's subordinates learn how to waste time in a creative and enjoyable fashion. Those of the bureaucrat derive their intrinsic rewards from trying to beat the system, and they can be highly creative in thinking of ways to turn the system to their advantage. The subordinates of the crisis maker learn to produce excuses. Those of the deadwood, if they do not leave, find the unchallenging environment congenial, in which case deadwood accumulates. The dysfunctional behavior in this case produces low results, for there will either be high turnover or no turnover at all.

The Mismanagement Mix

Mixed mismanagement style XAEI: the "zealous newcomer." So far we have described and analyzed five pure styles of mismanagers. There are additional styles of mismanagement that are less acute, which occur when more than one role is performed well but still all four are not included. If only one role of management is missing, we can identify a mixed style of mismanagement. Here we will limit ourselves to describing one prominent example of a "mixed" type. The XAEI style, the zealous newcomer, is an individual who is an administrator and an entrepreneur and an integrator, but he is not a producer. An example is the highly respected manager from one industry who is hired by a failing firm in another industry. They expect him to produce instantaneous results. Under pressure he introduces new procedures, penetrates new markets, generates new products, and unifies the organization behind these new directions. He does not exhibit any of the pure styles of mismanagement presented above. He is working hard in "catching up with the industry." He appraises how well he does by "how fast we are moving." If he has any time left he attacks new problem areas; he recognizes the indispensability of change and he hires those who can most quickly bring about change and "get us out of the jam." He is open-minded and does not necessarily hire the people who agree with him. He listens. He acts. He will try to solve conflicts by

providing alternatives of his own and he will take the risk of confronting power centers. Nor is he misinformed. But in time losses start pouring in. The organization and its board of directors realize that crucial mistakes were made; the realities of the market were not properly understood. The mismanager simply did not know the technology and the environment of the organization well enough to be able to innovate successfully and to actually understand what he was told. He did not have enough time to learn all that he had to learn. He was a great administrator, entrepreneur, and integrator; but unfortunately, he just didn't understand what he was doing.

The "textbook manager" (PAEI). How does a manager behave, as opposed to a mismanager? The "textbook manager" is a producer of results, an excellent administrator, entrepreneur, and integrator (PAEI). He initiates action systematically, integrating the human resources to that end. He delegates, develops the organization continuously and systematically in its markets, production facilities, finances, and human resources. Unlike the mismanager, he appraises himself by how well *the group* that he manages performs; by how well, together and individually, they achieve their respective goals, and by how instrumental and supportive he was in facilitating this goal achievement. He listens carefully whenever time allows to what is being said and to what is not being said. He is aware of the need to change. He cautiously, selectively, and systematically introduces it in a planned fashion. In his hiring practices, he is not threatened by a prospective subordinate who is bright and challenging; he looks for potential and is able to identify it. He is sufficiently self-confident and self-realized that he can respect people who act like himself. He manifests anxiety not by complaining but by constructive criticism. He trains systematically. He resolves conflicts in a statesmanlike manner, seeking consensus by elevating people's aspirations and expectations and appealing to their social consciences.

This manager is at once analytic and action-oriented, sensitive but not overly emotional. He seeks maximal integrity in the process, but not at the expense of the necessary short-term results. He does not monopolize information and use it as a source of power. His subordinates are not afraid to report failures; they know that he can be reasonable and supportive. He promotes those with managerial potential and encourages constructive creativity. Overall one finds a well-integrated, goal-seeking organization whose members fully cooperate and fully accept one another and the judgment of their manager. No dysfunctional behavior on the part of subordinates is easily observable. I have labelled this manager the textbook manager because one usually finds him in textbooks; in real life he is rare. The reasons for this rarity will be explained in the following paragraphs.

Is Mismanagement Avoidable?

Does the reader know a manager who fills perfectly all four of these roles and thus exhibits no mismanagement style since he is a manager who is at once an excellent technician, administrator, entrepreneur, and integrator? Probably not. At least such managers are rarely encountered, by comparison with the number of mismanagers. To perform all these roles equally well requires too many different personality traits, some of which are incompatible. To understand why this is so, it is necessary to work out a typology of decision making.

A typology of decision making in management. It is important to realize that the four roles of management involve different kinds of decision-making processes. Producing results and administering involve programmed decisions—those that are made in advance for predetermined cases. Producing is mainly a matter of programmed decisions. Whether the task is producing shoes, making sales, or raising funds, there is a particular sequence that will be most efficient and a particular technology that must be used. There are some nonprogrammed decisions that occur in performing these tasks but management tries to minimize these in order to achieve maximum predictability of outcome. Administrative decisions are also mostly programmed, for the same reasons. Administrators are expected to keep to standard operating procedures as closely as possible.

On the other hand, entrepreneuring and integrating do not involve programmed decisions. There is no program that can tell an integrator or an entrepreneur what to initiate or when and how to do it. One can be taught skills that will be useful for dealing with people, but whether those skills will actually be put into action depends on the individual's personality. Entrepreneuring and integrating are self-starting, discretionary processes which entail creativity and require willingness to take risks.

The four roles of management presented above can be arranged into a hierarchy with the most completely programmable kind of decision-making at the bottom and the least programmable at the top.

Role	Least
Integrating	
Innovating (entrepreneuring)	Decision
Implementing (administering)	Programmability
Producing (doing)	
	Most

The higher one ascends in this hierarchy the more creativity is required, since decisions have to be made from a more diffused and less structured data base. I propose that integrating is less programmable than entrepreneuring because the last does not necessarily deal with people while integrating by my definition involves uniting individuals behind a group decision. If one has to unite a group of individual entrepreneurs, there is a greater degree of creativity required than in making a decision for oneself.

I suggest that in the typical corporate hierarchical organization the higher one ascends, the more nonprogrammed decision making is required and that the Peter Principle phenomenon derives from the fact that at certain levels of promotion the individual finds himself incapable of being as creative as the position requires. Also, entrepreneurship and innovation affect a larger organizational area the higher one moves in the hierarchy; so the higher one ascends, the greater is the risk involved in making decisions. In these circumstances some managers will fail not only because they are deficient in creativity but also because they are unwilling to undertake risk.

Prevalence of mismanagement styles. Since the roles of a manager require both programmed and nonprogrammed decisions, a manager is required to be a "realistic dreamer." He is expected to plan for the future, to initiate change, to take risks; but at the same time he must have both his feet on the ground and must understand the practical consequences of his dreams.

It is hard to find managers who perform all four roles. That requires being highly critical and detail-oriented (administrator) and at the same time highly creative and daring (entrepreneur). Thus qualities that make a manager an outstanding entrepreneur may preclude him from being an outstanding administrator. Furthermore, the qualities that make a good process facilitator and integrator may inhibit entrepreneurship; the entrepreneur is likely to find the process of making plans acceptable to everyone a painful and frustrating one, since it usually involves compromising his own ideas.

Certain characteristics of the individual performer are also incompatible with the other roles of the manager. A manager who is extremely excited about his functional performance might resent being taken away from them in order to administer, innovate and integrate. I have interviewed many artistic directors who would rather direct themselves than hire other directors to do the job. Several architect-partners whom I interviewed expressed to me their anguish that they had no time to design; since the company grew they had to administer, to solicit new projects, and to motivate others to do what they would love to do themselves. The best example is the closest to home: getting to be chairman of one's department in a university is gratifying but it has its costs, and those who love research resent the task and usually mismanage it. On the other hand, those who love administration have "reentry blues" when the mandate expires. They have a very difficult time getting back into research after they have experienced the gratification of administering others.

The most common combinations in my research are the productive entrepreneur (PXEX) (doing and innovating) and the compromising bureaucrat or the nondirective administrator (XAXI) (integrating and administering). These combinations are not "pure," since in these cases the mismanager makes both programmed and nonprogrammed decisions. But he will still mismanage. The PXEX will change directions and try to do everything himself. The XAXI will be a participative administrator but will still provide little direction himself and remain excessively detail-oriented. The combinations most rarely met with are producer-administrator (PAXX), the entrepreneurial-integrator (XXEI), and the producer-administrator-entrepreneur-integrator (the textbook manager) (PAEI).

It does appear that a capacity for one role may inhibit performance in another role. The individual performer who likes functional involvement will resent the time he has to spend in administration. The administrator who feels rewarded by bringing the system under control will feel threatened by change and will therefore not function well as entrepreneur. The innovator's personality traits make him very creative and he is unlikely to cherish the role of integrator, which necessarily means compromising his own ideas to make them acceptable to others.

So it is highly improbable that an individual will have all the qualities that enable him to excel in all four roles. This brings me to the conclusion that most organizations are necessarily somewhat mismanaged. If a manager attempts to perform all four roles by himself, he will probably not excel in any of them.

Certain styles of mismanagement are more prevalent in some types of organization than in others. The loner is prevalent in small, rapidly growing, management-owned companies, and more prevalent in developing countries than in highly industrialized countries. The bureaucrat is prevalent in government agencies and in organizations that operate in secure, noncompetitive environments. The crisis maker is readily found in recently established, owner-managed organizations and in artistic organizations (on the artistic rather than the managerial side, such as the artistic director), while the superfollower is common in political and educational organizations in which decision-making power is vested in the members and the manager is mainly a coordinator. Deadwood can be found in any organization, technology, or culture. What makes it more prevalent in one organization than in others is the rate of change the organization experiences and the capacity of its members to adapt systematically to it. So it appears that organizational goals, technologies, and climates may affect the distribution of these styles; though each style can appear in many different types of organizations.

Mismanagement styles and personality needs. It is important to recognize at this juncture that each of the persons described above mismanages because he is "attuned" only to one type of activity, subordinating any other function to the dominant one.

Role		Primary Orientation
PXXX	=	Achieving
XAXX	=	Controlling
XXEX	=	Innovating
XXXI	=	Integrating

Accordingly, the PXXX integrates all activities for the purpose of achieving results; his total innovating capabilities are oriented only to achieve results. If he controls it is to maximize what he achieves. The XAXX perceives an achievement if he can control more. His innovations are also directed to more control. Any integration done is again for the sake of more control. By the same rationale the primary orientation of XXEX is to innovate. The more he innovates the more he feels he is achieving. He attempts to control maximum variables that will enable him to maximize his creativity and for that purpose he will seek to integrate people exclusively behind his own ideas. The XXXI's achievements are perceived as those of getting along with people. In that direction he puts his creative ideas; he attempts to control what people do.

Similarly, it could be postulated that the PXXX individual has extreme achievement needs (AchN) to the exclusion of other needs. XAXX has extreme power needs, XXEX creative needs, and XXXI affiliation needs. Obviously these assumptions have to be tested.

Degrees of effective management. We have represented the manager who is solely a producer, solely an administrator, solely an entrepreneur and solely an integrator by the notation PXXX, XAXX, XXEX and XXXI, respectively, denoting thereby the unique role performed by the individual in the total composite managerial functional process.

As we have seen, the manager who is mainly an innovator or entrepreneur is the one who possesses the capability of identifying the threats, opportunities and risks in the environment and explores them to the advantage of his organization, whereas, the sole integrator is the manager who has the capabilities for integrating people, whether by his charisma, manipulations or genuine concern. When both the innovating and the integrating capabilities are possessed by one and the same individual, he gives the organization an effective lead—a direction in which to move.

In real-life organizational situations, we see each of the four individual management styles held to a moderate degree by a majority of managers. Cases of total dominance of one role to the complete exclusion of the other three, are rare cases in our experience. The magnitude of the combination of each of the four abilities could be represented by the size of the letters representing the role pattern. For instance, the notation PaEI would denote that the person is primarily a producer, secondly an integrator, thirdly an innovator and lastly an administrator, the implication of which would be that he possesses excellent work and technical skills for the production function; can to a certain extent integrate the people to do the job and can meaningfully translate the innovative ideas of others to the production process, since he is slightly inclined to be an innovator himself; and being very low key in the administration function, he may perhaps be effective in producing without red tape but he does not excel in his systems of implementation either.

As another example, another manager may be denoted by paEI. This person as we noted is an excellent integrator, alert to what goes on in the environment and attuned to the vibrations inside his organization, but he does not excel in the technical knowledge or work ability to produce nor in the administrative skills to do it. Since he has some technical and administrative know-how (having both p and a, instead of X's) his leadership abilities would facilitate his discovering the right person for both the functions, thus getting the job done.

The Manager and the Managerial Process

It is, as I have said, highly improbable that one person can be found to fulfill all four roles

(PAEI), and we cannot rely on such expectations to staff all organizations. Instead, we must normally expect to find *several* types of managers who perform different roles with a sufficient degree of effectiveness and we should integrate their roles in order to provide an adequate managerial process. Thus, to discuss the role of THE manager, as is done in management literature, is not only ethically wrong because of its elitist connotations but a theoretical mistake. *No one manager can manage alone.* It takes several to perform the process adequately, several people who perform roles which seem to be in conflict but really are complementary. There should be individuals who possess the entrepreneurial and integrating qualities which can guide a united organization into new directions. There should be administrators who can translate those new actions into operative systems which produce results. And there should be performers who can put the system into action and set an example for efficient operation. The December 1972 issue of *Fortune* highlights how Arlen Realty has become the biggest real estate company in the nation. Cohen, who formed Arlen Realty and Development, asserts that the organization is by no means a one-man show and he describes the division of labor thus: "My role is where we are going [Entrepreneuring]; Marshall's role is how do we get there [Administering] and Arthur Levine makes sure it works [Producing]."[2] We might presume that the founder is the integrator who brings the group together.

Whenever I come across any manager who presumptuously feels that he can manage it all, I can predic with a high probability that he will be mismanaging. The style of mismanagement will depend on his personality traits. He should possess capabilities in all of the roles; but he must realize that he cannot excel in all of them. A good manager knows himself well; he knows his own capacities and his own weaknesses. Since he cannot perform all the roles, he tries to work with those around him who can complement him. He is perceptive to the needs, styles, and behavior of those with whom he works and he can relate to them and provide support for their roles rather than competing with them. A good manager is humble enough to realize that

he is only part of a highly complex process; he is open-minded enough to accept different roles with different styles and behavioral manifestations; he is willing to give and take, learn and cooperate.

Some executives may have no inclination at all to perform a certain role. They will be mismanaging to some degree in a mixed style; the extent of the mismangement will depend on the manager's rank, responsibility, the importance of the role in question, and the degree of his dereliction.

Any manager who has *no* inclination to perform one of the roles will be a mismanager and be dysfunctional to the total managerial process since he will not be able to cooperate. He will not have the appreciation for the role performed by those in the complementary role positions. Thus instead of a PXXX, one should look for a Paei if one cannot obtain a PaeI or a PAEI.

In a managerial process one seeks a composition of Paei, pAei, paEi, and paeI. Even better will be the composition of PaeI, pAeI, paEI, since all should be interested in integration, assuming that all are working in the same direction. The basic assumption I present hereby is that the more roles a manager excels in performing, or the more complementary the staffing of an organization leading to a staff that in its totality excels in all roles, the more effective and efficient will be the organization and the less will be the dysfunctional mismanagement styles manifested.

If any one of the four roles can be truly indispensable for any executive, it is integration. If an executive does not perform the other roles himself, there may be others to supply them; but he has to be able to integrate in order to allow the other functions to work in a positive fashion. If this function is not fulfilled, the entrepreneur will become a crisis maker, the administrator a bureaucrat, and the producer a loner.

Uses of This Typology in Staffing Decisions and Organizational Change

When dealing with organizations as a consultant, I diagnose the behavior of management according to the essential roles presented here and try to find out whether the organization has individuals in top managerial positions who perform all these roles. Is there an entrepreneur? An integrator? An administrator? A producer or technician? If the top manager actually performs all four roles himself, or if the four roles are divided among different individuals who fully communicate among themselves and share the same values, then I usually find that the managerial process works well. They will check and balance each other. The entrepreneur does not "pull" until the administrator checks the organizational implications and the producer adds his "two bits' worth" on what it takes from a functional or professional point of view to make the entrepreneurial idea a success. The leader is a process facilitator in these discussions: he "keeps the wheels rolling," resolves the conflicts that surface until they all agree on what should be done. Once a decision is made it is well thought out and from an organizational point of view it is as though one excellent manager had done it all by himself. No one of them could have managed well by himself and as a matter of fact, if any one of those managers leaves, a style of mismanagement eventually becomes evident.

When identifying behavioral manifestations of mismanagement I attempt to diagnose them using this typology to isolate management roles that are not being performed. My main therapeutic methodology in this case is one of complementary staffing. The task is to find a manager who possesses those characteristics that enable him to perform the missing role of management. After finding an individual in another organization who has performed well the role that we need, the task is to carry out a successful "organ transplant." I have usually found that there is resistance to those transplants. Bureaucrats like to have people like themselves, and the same holds for other mismanagers. The mismanagers are thus set in their styles and they perceive in the transplant a threat to them. Take, for instance, an organization in which the entrepreneuring role is missing. The bureaucrat will resist the new manager, whom he perceives as a crisis maker who attempts to change things and "mess up" his system. The loner will see in the entrepreneur a source of crisis since the newcomer adds more work to the task he can hardly

perform at present. The superfollower resents the newcomer, since there is a new director who might become a new clique epicenter and compete with him for leadership.

Another example is that of an organization in which the role of administrator is missing. In that case my diagnosis shows me that the organization proceeds from crisis to crisis, and no efficient system of implementation exists. When one tries to transplant an administrator into the system, there is resistance. The entrepreneur fights him because he says he is obstructing new directions, "He has no vision," "He is power hungry," "He is dull," "He does not understand the nature of our markets, we *must* change. . . ."

If a producer is brought into an organization which is mismanaged by a crisis maker, it might be expected that he would be well received; but this is not the case. The achiever is extremely busy getting the job done; he sticks to a task rather than jumping from one to another. The crisis maker gets highly annoyed with this inflexibility and does his best to disrupt him. If on the other hand the achiever is brought into an organization which is mismanaged by a bureaucrat, the bureaucrat also resents the newcomer since the latter is interested in results and starts challenging the system for the sake of achiveing those results.

In transplanting managers from one organization where they perform well their role of management into another where they are needed, it is my job as a consultant to management to see that they are accepted. I act as the agent of change, who monitors the integration of the new individual and backs him up in his new role. To protect him from the mismanagers and to facilitate his entry, I first try to identify his allies, those who want the missing role to be performed. Then I try to put him in a position which enables him to perform his role as fast as possible and in as rewarding a manner as possible. Usually these positions have to be created. I make him chairman of a coordinating or planning committee which I staff with a "critical mass" of the above-mentioned allies. By critical mass I mean that a sufficient number of allies strategically positioned throughout the organization have been identified, organized, and provided with institutional channels to effect change.

If I succeed in finding the manager who is needed in the organization, if I provide him with allies, and if I succeed in protecting him from being fired or made inoperative, then, when after a certain period of monitoring I see that he has been accepted by the rest of the organization, I try to unite the various roles through group interaction. I try to make the entrepreneur more aware of system administration, the administrator more aware of entrepreneuring, and so forth. I found that there is no use in training a mismanager to be something else in the first stage of organizational therapy. He resists it. It goes against his behavior and probably against his personality needs. It's much easier to retrain him after he has seen someone else in the organization who has done an excellent job in that role. Furthermore, if complementary staffing works, the results are much faster; once the organization as a whole is performing well, the positive reinforcement is a stimulus to its members for learning from each other or at least for supporting each other.

Suggestions for Research

I have tried here to identify the various roles of management and the styles of mismanagement which occur when one or more of these roles is not performed. My methodology has been based on observation, in-depth interviews, and action research. It will require further systematic research to determine what affects the prevalence of any one style of mismanagement in any one type of organization and to determine what is needed to treat the pure or mixed types of mismanagement. Furthermore a study can be made to determine what personality needs make one perform one role better than others and which personality needs are truly incompatible. A questionnaire can be drawn up and designed to identify various sets of behavioral manifestations of mismanagement, each set representing a different style according to the perceptions of those surveyed. Once the existence of these styles has been validated, the researcher can proceed to identify which organizational climates each style is most prevalent in, and which climates encourage them. Furthermore, he should identify which personalities are prone to perform which roles better. At a more advanced stage of research we may be able to identify those therapeutic methods that can treat the different styles of mismanagement.

Acknowledgment: I am indebted to my research assistant, J. D. Dawson, for editorial assistance.

REFERENCES

1. Laurence J. Peter and Raymond Hull, *The Peter Principle* (New York: W. Morrow, 1969).
2. *Fortune* (December 1972).

The following article has been further elaborated and additional material edited in a book:

I. Adizes: "How to Solve the Mismanagement Crisis," available from Adizes Institute, 1047 Gayley Avenue, Los Angeles, CA. 90024. The price is $17.35, including tax, postage and handling.

The Advanced Manager

by Gordon Watt

There are always gaps in all management texts. More often these gaps are sensed rather than observed. It should be the objective of an advanced management course to shed light on these areas and to fill them in. The following is an attempt to cover some of this missing material.

1. Don't tell others what you know! Spend a long time on any particular job and make sure no one knows *how* you do something or even *what* you do. Forget job manuals! Destroy any you see on sight! This will ensure that you can always do things your own way as nobody else will know how to do them anyway. It will also increase the firm's hesitancy to replace you as it would take them too long to figure out what you were doing.

4. Use raw fear. Very effective. Eat one employee live each morning. Listen to no suggestions. Brook no disagreement. This will ensure that your directives will never be disregarded nor questioned, as everyone will be too concerned about their own skin.

3. Be attractive to someone higher up the ladder than yourself—a simple ploy, yet effective. If this route is open to you, don't overlook it because it is obvious and basically simple. This is a very strong tactic and is as effective today as it was in Delilah's.

2. Hold meetings. It is always important to remember the conditioning of the masses. The masses are conditioned to view meetings and conferences as important and productive. More importantly, meetings are only held by *important* people. Ipso facto, if you hold meetings you are an important person. A skilled manager can stretch a discourse on the relative merits of square paper clips over an entire morning!

5. Be an authority on all the current management theories: Management By Objectives, Transactional Analysis, Herzberg hygienic theories. Always be the first to attend a management seminar. In this way you will always be able to say, "according to Drucker. . ." You fill in the blanks.

7. Be a womanizer. Probably one of the most intrinsically satisfying pursuits for men in management. Your position can only serve to strengthen your hand here. True, this approach is unlikely to advance your career at all, but while it lasts. . . .

6. Be a "creative" person. Grow a beard. Become an expert in some more or less esoteric area such as human resources or public relations. Strive to create the impression that whatever you do is an art rather than a science. (Remember that this is basically only an illusion and do not fall into the pitfall of believing it yourself!)

8. Play the office politician. This technique contains all these ingredients, and more: danger, excitement, scandal, revenge, and humor. But beyond this, it also offers excellent prospects for advancement. Learn to plant rumors. Stab someone in the back. Divide and conquer. Cultivate the right people.

9. Be indecisive. Spend the whole day pondering the alternatives at hand. Never give in to the impulse to make a decision. If you never make a decision, you can never be blamed for making an incorrect one! Sooner or later the normal course of events will force a decision on you. But statisticians tell us that a good executive need only be right slightly in excess of 50% of the time. And the laws of probability indicate that whatever course of action you take, you will be right in any case 50% of the time. Then too, it is a simple matter to blame any really unfortunate occurrences on someone else. ✲

Part VI: Controlling

"Design engineers will fiddle and tinder forever. If you let them alone, you are guaranteed to have schedule slippages and cost problems. Nothing will come out of the end of the pipe unless you push it out."

—*J. Ronald Fox, Arming America*

Control is the process of making things happen in an orderly fashion, or according to a particular plan. The basic control process involves establishing standards, measuring performance against these standards, and correcting deviations from the standards and plans. Control requires managers to take action at appropriate times so things don't get out of hand. Feedback from the control process points out where action is needed and when there is a need for new or adjusted plans. The nine articles that follow describe the elements of an effective feedback system for software projects.

In "Advanced Project Control," Johnson describes a 10-step procedure that can be used to plan and control any project or subelement of it. The procedure stresses definition of realizable milestones. It also describes when standard management tools (PERT, GANTT, etc.) should be used.

Methodios, in "Internal Controls and Audits," describes various internal control and audit methods that can be employed during development to build into the system the information needed for efficient review by an independent audit group. The reprint also suggests how to organize, staff, and use the audit group effectively.

The next three articles deal with review topics. Weinberg and Freedman, in "Reviews, Walkthroughs and Inspections," summarize the roles of reviews and show how management can use the review's outputs to identify and resolve technical issues. Fagan, in "Design and Code Inspections to Reduce Errors in Program Development," describes how peer reviews and inspections can be used to improve pro-

graming productivity and quality. The article compares inspections with walkthroughs to illustrate the differences between the two. It also provides a set of instructions for completing various reporting forms. Reifer, in "How Do I Know I'm In Trouble: A Review Checklist," finishes the discussion on reviews by providing the reader with a checklist that can be used to keep out of trouble at critical points in the software development life cycle.

Ingrassia, in "The Unit Development Folder (UDF): An Effective Management Tool for Software Development," describes a control technique used throughout industry to keep the individual programer's work visible and to permit control at the unit level.

The next two articles deal with the topics of configuration management and quality control. In "Elements of Software Configuration Management," Bersoff introduces the reader to the important disciplines associated with change control and discusses the constituent parts of an effective configuration management system. In "Assuring Quality: Quality Assurance," Stamm describes what a software quality assurance organization does and when its people get involved in various quality-oriented tasks. He stresses the need for quality planning and provides a good discussion of the issue of organizational accountability.

The final article, "Taking Management's Measure" by Ewers, discusses a method that managers can use to determine how effective their current controls are and where strengthening may be needed.

A ten-step plan to control any
systems project.

BY JAMES R. JOHNSON

Reprinted with permission from *Journal of Systems Management*, May 1977. Copyright © 1977 by The Association for Systems Management.

Advanced

■ Most discussions of project management expand on the major phases of a project: Definition, Design, Programming, System Test, Acceptance Test, and Installation. Within each phase, project management texts describe system tools such as interview questionnaires, input/output layout sheets, control procedures, etc. Most literature also contains advice or suggestions on what to do and what not to do; for example, requiring design signoff is a what to do.

The scope of this project control procedure is limited to the basic concepts. Its content is independent of the project phase and deals with the fundamentals of control. A sports analogy would be a football play where executing the basic functions (blocking and tackling) is independent of the particular play or game. Although a project control procedure is only one of the aspects of project management, it is an essential aspect.

The following procedure lists steps which can be used to plan and monitor a project or any phase of a project. The project control steps are divided into the following segments: planning and monitoring. It is assumed that the scope of the project has previously been defined. Figure 1 shows an illustration of how the 10 step procedure relates to the basic working documents: work plan, PERT chart, and Gantt chart.

Planning a Project

Step 1—Define Tasks—A written description of each task is required. This description provides a common reference point for defining responsibilities. When what has to be done is known, realistic schedules are possible. The ability to define tasks is directly dependent on the nature of the activity. If one-hundred COBOL-F programs have to be converted to COBOL VS, and five have been converted on a pilot basis requiring two man-days each, then the total effort of the project can be defined with a reasonable probability of accuracy.

Conversely, task definition has the highest probability of error at the completion of system design on a large innovative project. For example, assume a management information system (MIS) is proposed for product managers of a large corporation. The MIS objective is to assimilate forecast, production, inventory, cost, and sales data into useful decision making information. For a complex system such as this, it is humanly impossible to complete a realistic final design. The difficulty of identifying useful information prior to physically receiving reports and using the system in a working environment cannot be exaggerated.

System design is not complete at the end of system design. Approval signatures are only an attempt to obtain, but not assurance of, a complete final design. Don't attempt to do all phases of a project at once; add to the programming effort for unanticipated design changes. Be realistic not optimistic. There is no technique available which will identify all required tasks in advance, so allow for the unknown.

Step 2—Estimate Man-days—The accuracy of the man-day estimates is a function of the type of project. For small projects or when in the programming stage on large projects, man-days for specific tasks (ignoring design changes) can be estimated very specifically. However, when performing general system design, the completion of one task may result in the definition of additional tasks. It is a good idea to compensate by doubling the man-days for each task.

Consider that people are actually available for productive work only one-half the time and double the initial estimates. Projects of less than five man-days can be Gantted per week. (See Step 6)

Project Control

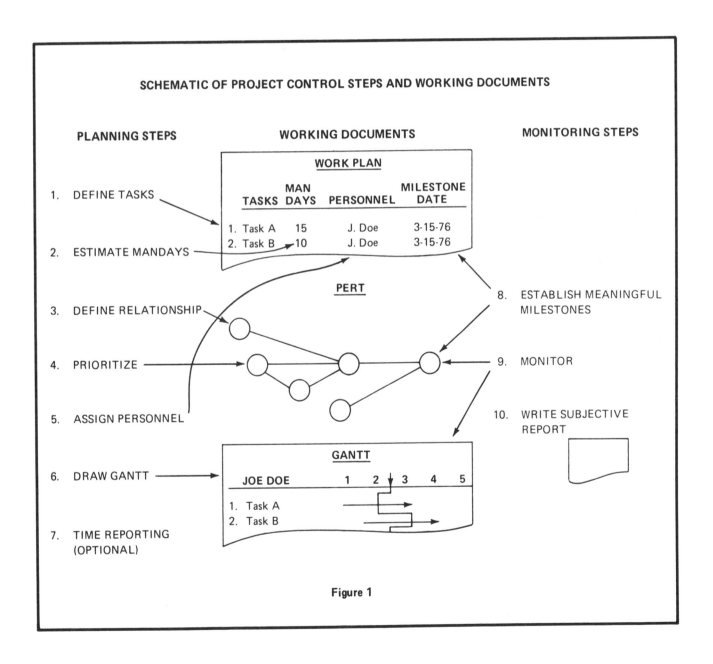

SCHEMATIC OF PROJECT CONTROL STEPS AND WORKING DOCUMENTS

PLANNING STEPS

1. DEFINE TASKS
2. ESTIMATE MANDAYS
3. DEFINE RELATIONSHIP
4. PRIORITIZE
5. ASSIGN PERSONNEL
6. DRAW GANTT
7. TIME REPORTING (OPTIONAL)

WORKING DOCUMENTS

WORK PLAN

TASKS	MAN DAYS	PERSONNEL	MILESTONE DATE
1. Task A	15	J. Doe	3-15-76
2. Task B	10	J. Doe	3-15-76

PERT

GANTT

JOE DOE	1	2	3	4	5
1. Task A					
2. Task B					

MONITORING STEPS

8. ESTABLISH MEANINGFUL MILESTONES
9. MONITOR
10. WRITE SUBJECTIVE REPORT

Figure 1

315

JAMES R. JOHNSON

Mr. Johnson is currently a DP Section Manager at Hallmark Card, Inc., Kansas City, MO. He has an MBA from the University of Iowa and has been published several times in information processing magazines.

The micro approach in estimating involves rolling up a number of detail estimates to obtain the total effort. For programming tasks, the level of detail is at the module level. Analysis of lines of codes by module type can be helpful but this method is burdensome if too much detail is used for input. The macro approach uses the concept of analogy to predict total man-day and elapsed time requirements. To use analogy, project histories must be available for comparisons. Some of the factors used in analogy are: lines of code, number of people assigned to the project, size of project, design innovation, and technology.

Ideally, after man-days have been estimated independently using the micro approach, the total should be compared with the macro results. If allowances for unknown tasks and non-productive time were part of the micro estimating, the two approaches may produce similar results. However, if there are differences which cannot be resolved, the larger estimate is probably correct.

Step 3—Define Tasks Relationship—Define the relationships among tasks. A PERT or CPM diagram may be necessary if there are multiple dependent tasks. The complexity of these relationships might lead one to conclude that some form of automation is required for adequate coordination. There exist many program packages which automate Steps 3-7. Proponents for automated systems, base their arguments on the following: 1) large projects are too complex for manual techniques, and 2) time consuming project control activities should be automated. In response to these contentions, consider the specific activities to be automated. The greatest value of a PERT chart is the planning and thinking required to prepare it. The maximum number of PERT chart events an individual can realistically work with is around 50. Utilizing the concept of modularity, any of the 50 modules can be further sub-PERTed. Thus, complexity results only if a large number of boxes are represented on one page. Most tests on PERT have examples of 300 or more modules in a network. The value of a graphic of this nature is questioned. When segmentation is utilized, the complexity is eliminated.

As for the time consuming argument, there are two considerations. First, manually drawing a PERT network aids the planning process by providing the planners with a more thorough understanding of the relationships. In most cases, modifications do not require re-drawing the chart. A project manager's main concern when deviations occur is correcting the situation. The impact on the schedule is usually obvious. Secondly, automated systems require time and expense: time to learn the conventions, input data, and interpret the results; expense to obtain and run the system. The larger the project the more control is required. Standard techniques for PERT charts are possible with or without an automated system.

Step 4—Prioritize Tasks—Since resources are finite, all tasks cannot be worked concurrently. Thus, priority tasks are those on the critical path or those which may be potential problem areas.

Step 5—Assign Personnel—When assigning personnel to tasks, consideration should be given to experience and talents of individuals. Man-day estimates in Step 3 were made assuming an average experience level. If an inexperienced individual is on the project, man-day estimates should be adjusted. Even for personnel having equivalent experience, productivity can vary substantially. Recent studies have indicated a 10 to 1 productivity ratio for super-programmers.

Time should be allowed for training new personnel on technical skills. Also, a one month project orientation period is generally required. After tasks are assigned, total the man-days for each person. Compare this total to the available days. If an imbalance exists among individuals, tasks should be reassigned. This comparison may appear obvious, but is many times overlooked.

Step 6—Draw Gantt Charts—Gantt tasks in priority order, considering defined relationships among tasks. Since individuals usually work on multiple tasks, elapsed days are greater than task man-day estimates. To assure that available man-days equal Gantted man-days, total the man-days Gantted for a month and compare the result with the available man-days.

Remember, one of the main factors impacting programming tasks is test turnaround time. Poor turnaround time can easily double the elapsed time estimates that were made assuming average turnaround.

Step 7—Automated Time Reporting—Tasks can be loaded into an automated time reporting system if one is available. Do *not* necessarily load the lowest level task since maintenance of the system can become burdensome. Also, the definition of lower level tasks may change as time progresses, especially in general system design.

The purpose of the automated system is to monitor time spent on tasks and provide a historic record of time spent on phases of the project. An automated system should not be used to schedule work.

Step 8—Establish Meaningful Milestones—A meaningful milestone is a point in time when a task or number of tasks can be completed 100 percent, not 95 percent or 98 percent. The following are examples:

1. Report package documentation sign-off
2. Completion of the system test plan
3. Phase I implementation

One important factor, which is often overlooked when milestones are defined, is an explanation of how and who will sign-off on the milestone. For example, in number one above, assume that the group preparing the documentation also decides when it is completed. With this delegation of responsibility, regression to the 98% complete rule in order to stay on schedule, is possible. When milestones are defined, specify how the tasks will be acknowledged complete, and who will sign-off on the completion. An independent individual is the preferred selection for the 'who.'

Step 9—Monitor—There are two types of monitoring which are helpful: individual and project. Individual monitoring is best done by updating Gantt charts with a line showing current status versus expected status at a point in time. Monitoring actual man hours expended versus planned is also possible; however, it does not easily provide an overall visual status as Gantt charts do.

Project monitoring is based on the pre-defined meaningful milestones. It is very important to reconcile variations from each milestone. If the first milestone date is missed by a considerable margin, then there may be good reason to re-evaluate all the remaining projections. This step implies that the project manager: 1) understands the tasks, 2) knows why deviations from the plan occur, and 3) takes appropriate action to correct out-of-control situations.

Extensive project control procedures can have an adverse impact on productivity. Good project control is not elaborate control. When dates slip, there is a tendency to over control and define detailed procedures. For example, instead of monitoring overall progress monthly or weekly, a procedure to monitor progress day-by-day may be implemented. Thus, individuals and the project manager would have to maintain considerable detail data in an attempt to report on a daily basis. Even more important than the extra time required for elaborate controls is the fact

that they can *divert* the attention of a project manager from the relevant issue of finding the real problem.

Success is not dependent on reporting technique. Procedures should not be a burden on a project manager but rather an extension of his control techniques. Assuming the basic steps are followed, there are as many different variations as there are project managers. Some individuals find it difficult to write concise reports, others work effectively with rough Gantt charts and note cards. The point is: a control procedure should not force project managers to standardize all aspects of their jobs. Productivity is greatest when a project manager sticks with the fundamentals and is allowed to function in a manner effective to him.

Step 10—Write Subjective Report—In addition to the objective measures above, a subjective report should be completed periodically by the individual responsible for the project. Numbers and charts do not describe the attitude or motivation of the project team. It has been said that individuals on a successful project always have a 'warm' feeling about the progress. A subjective report represents a personal appraisal of the project status.

Why Projects are Late

The major reason for project lateness involves task definition and man-day assignments and accounts for 80% of the cases. Good project control techniques do not significantly change the amount of resources required to complete a phase. However, by allowing time for unknown tasks and by realistically allowing for non-productive time, the source of estimating errors will be reduced.

The remaining 20% of project lateness cases are caused by not executing a step successfully such as: poorly defined milestones, a missing PERT chart, burdensome control procedures, or poor programming techniques.

Recently the last item listed has received much attention. Structured programming will definitely help minimize this factor.

Summary

The 10 steps, seven for Planning and three for Monitoring, apply to any phase of a project. Obtaining project control is not easy. It requires hard work, involvement, good judgement, and an 'advanced' procedure. 'Advanced' is not synonymous with sophisticated. Proper *execution* of the basic steps, with stress on the fundamentals, is the answer. ●jsm

During the development of a MIS a point is reached where everybody talks about internal controls, audit trails and internal audits. These are the means to maintain accuracy in operations, safeguard the company's assets and assure compliance with existing company policies and procedures.

Reprinted with permission from *Journal of Systems Management*, June 1976. Copyright © 1976 by The Association for Systems Management.

Internal Controls and Audit

BY IOANNIS METHODIOS

■ The Equity Funding[1] scandal was the beginning of a serious and extensive review of the internal controls by all companies. What happened is that 50 percent of the 97,000 policies listed on the books of an Equity Funding life insurance subsidiary were indeed non-existent, and thus the reinsurers who purchased the dummy policies had spent millions of dollars for — quite literally — nothing.

The *Newsweek* magazine, commenting on the above, stated:

Equity Funding executives used company computers as a key tool in the fraud — probably on a grander scale than ever before — and neither standard auditing practices nor Wall Street analysts were sophisticated enough to detect it. Considering that everyone from stockholder to tax collector depends heavily upon audited data, this is a serious problem.[2]

This scandal was the most published case of this kind that ever happened. Although a lot of lower scale frauds have been discovered, they did not have the publicity of the Equity Funding's case. For example, in a U.S. city a man pocketed all the deposit slips at the writing desks of a bank and replaced them with his own electronically coded forms. For three days, every customer who came in without a personal slip and used one of the "blank" forms was actually depositing money into the culprit's account. The thief reappeared, withdrew $100,000 and walked away. He has not yet been found!

In another case, a systems analyst placed orders for expensive appliances and coded them on "special pricing orders." Using his knowledge of the system information flow and procedures, he intercepted the documents as they reached the "special pricing orders" desk. He changed the list price to a nominal price of $6.00 or $7.00 and then put the forged documents back into the regular stream. The appliances were delivered to him and he paid his account promptly. The practice was discovered by systems consultants called in to review the adequacy of the system's internal control procedures.

In all of the mentioned cases we can see a lack of adequate internal controls and security practices and also a lack of comprehensive auditing procedures. The audit, mainly, must prevent the company from fraud or any other kind of damage rather than discovering the happenings afterwards.

Internal Controls

The control function of the management process is the check on current performance to determine if planned goals are being achieved. The control procedure, in general, consists of several steps: (1) the establishment of predetermined goals or standards, (2) the measurement of performance, (3) the comparison of actual performance with the standards, and (4) the making of appropriate control decisions.

To effectively accomplish the above process, we must assume that the computer-produced information that is received is of high quality. For the purpose of our discussion, "quality" is interpreted that, indeed, the information is true and reflects the real situation of the operation(s) that is (are) concerned.

To assure that information is of such quality, an arrangement of internal controls is necessary to evaluate the accuracy of transactions, procedures, methods, and processes that transform a mass of data to what we call management information.

The internal control system, therefore, as defined by D. Sanders,[3] is "the total of all the control arrangements adopted within an organization to (1) check on and maintain the accuracy of business data; (2) safeguard the company assets against fraud and other irregularities; (3) promote operating efficiency; and (4) encourage compliance with existing company policies and procedures."

Weaknesses of the internal control provide opportunities, as we have seen, for defalcations to go undetected. So, one of the first duties of any auditing attempt is to evaluate and review the internal controls system.

Internal Audit

The internal auditor evaluates and reviews the effectiveness and efficiency of the previously defined internal controls.

The Institute of Internal Auditors defines internal audit as: "any independent opinion activity within an organization for the review of operations as a basis for service to management. It is a managerial control which functions by measuring and evaluating the effectiveness of other controls."[4]

The same institution states that:

The objective of internal auditing is to assist all members of management in effective discharge of their responsibilities, by furnishing them with objective analyses, appraisals, recommendations and pertinent comments concerning the activities reviewed. The internal audit is concerned with any phase of business activity where he can be of service to management. This involves going beyond the accounting and financial records to obtain a full understanding of the operations under review.[5]

The term "EDP audit" refers to the evaluation of the internal controls and operations within the EDP department. It covers, with other words, the input, processing and output processes of the data transformation to information and the activities of the DP group. This article is about a comprehensive, companywide audit, which we call "information-systems audit." Put another way, this audit system deals not only with the information-generation process but also with the information flow within the organization and the activities which provide the right person with the right information at the appropriate time and at a reasonable cost to make the right decision. Thus, the EDP audit is a significant part of the whole audit effort regarding the stated purpose.

J. Martin[6] gives an illustration about the duties and responsibilities of the internal audit which is pretty consistent with the stated information-audit. It shows that internal auditors should have a broad DP background and experience to effectively deal with the complex computer systems.

The need for audit specialists is emerging because of the great sophistication of computer systems and applications and the need for accuracy in operations. Also, managers know that a failure will cost so much it is profitable to try and prevent failures.

Expanded Role of Internal Audit

Recently, R. Canning[7] pointed out that there is a need for a broader type of audit and review function — a management-oriented performance review of data processing activity. He insists that, while top management has known how to evaluate the other functions of the enterprise — manufacturing, engineering, marketing and finance, the data processing function is often just a "big, black box." What management seeks is an unbiased means of verifying the performance within the black box, to see if it is satisfactory or if corporate resources are being poorly used. For top management to evaluate the performance of the EDP department and compare it with the outcome of the other divisions of the company, it needs the following controls:[8]

A. Management Control
1. Review performance on a periodic basis — compare development against the formal plans — check functioning of project control systems.
2. Control over the structure that links the responsibility for various departmental decisions to the operations of the users.

B. Resource allocation control

How well the EDP department utilized the resources allocated by the company for its developmental activities and on-going operations. Also, top management needs to know if the department's plans and goals were consistent with the overall company's goals.

C. Technology and operations control

Review the equipment, methods, procedures, and techniques used to track the department's technological growth.

D. Project Management

Top management is interested in evaluating the formal procedures that integrate the EDP project's development and the project's output with the company's standards and also needs to know the formal planning and control tools that are employed.

The internal auditor has to work with the systems designers to establish these internal controls that will give top management this information. The EDP department's performance and "products" are difficult to measure in terms of dollars. Several examples of techniques which have been introduced to successfully overcome that problem. J. Kanter,[9] for example, suggests "return on investment" techniques to solve that problem. The internal audit is done from the executive management's view-point and auditors can help EDP management to meet those expectations.

Difficulties with Computer-Systems Audit

The following problems are common to auditors attempting to audit an information system.
1. Lack of computer experts in the auditing profession.
2. Secrecy and lack of communication in the auditing field compared to the rapid spread of new ideas, techniques, and experiences among computer professionals.
3. Lack of audit research or control and performance standards to help auditors trying to measure DP performance.
4. Lack of high-level management awareness of the potential role of the auditor in control of EDP, and what resources, skills, salary level, and political support are needed to achieve this role.
5. Too narrow interpretation of the auditor's much prized independence, at least for the internal audit function.[12]

Kinds of Internal Controls

The appropriate placement of internal controls is an important part of the overall systems design effort. Logically, these controls must be put at the points which are crucial for the accuracy of the operations, error-sources, or sensitive to any attempt for systems disturbance. There is no one general rule suggesting where exactly to install the internal controls. This is for two reasons:
1. All depends upon the systems designers' perceptions upon what points of the system should be controlled.
2. Control locations are usually kept secret, as much as it is possible.
The usually required internal controls in a company are separated into three categories: organiza-

tional, administrative and procedural controls.

1. **Organizational controls:** These controls fall into two areas: the placement of the EDP function within the organization and the division of duties within the EDP group. An effective EDP group within the organization requires a separation of responsibilities which results in a system of checks and controls throughout the organization. These controls must be flexible enough so that the EDP group retains its service nature to all other functions within the organization. On the other hand, a proper division of duties within the EDP group maximizes the effectiveness of the DP personnel while minimizes, as much as possible, opportunities for manipulation.

2. **Administrative Controls:**

(a) Systems design controls: Systems documentation is the basic of these controls. It provides the means of understanding the system and makes the appropriate corrections whenever it is necessary. Controls of this nature can be systems flow charts, decision tables, systems specifications, etc.

(b) Program documentation: Proper documentation primarily serves the purposes of management, but from an audit standpoint, it is an invaluable part of the review of internal control. Details of record formats, layouts, code structures, program flow charts, etc., assist the auditor in developing meaningful tests of the system — especially if he intends to audit through the computer.

(c) Program testing: Sound programs testing procedures applied to new programs must exist and be followed. The auditor should determine that such procedures are indeed performed and review the procedures in use.

(d) Computer-operation controls:
    (1) use of appropriate manuals
    (2) creation of a data-security program
    (3) control over console intervention
    (4) control over access to the computer site

3. **Procedural controls are separated into:**

(a) Input controls: Are intended to ensure correct input to the computer. Their purpose is to assure that:
    (1) all data are received on time
    (2) all data are converted accurately and completely to a machine-readable language
    (3) all data enter the computer for processing
Such controls, for example, can be: item counts and control totals, number of batches, parity checking, transmission-line error rates, etc.

(b) Computer controls: The purpose of this kind of control is to assure that:

(1) only valid data is processed

(2) unacceptable data is flagged for correction or removal

(3) all data are processed through each program in any application

(4) hardware controls operate satisfactorily (The hardware controls are built into the equipment by the manufacturer. For example, self-checking numbers, comparison check, file identify verification, sequence checks, transaction log, file dump, daily listing, etc.)

(c) Output controls: Controls over distribution of copies and over errors and handling of corrections and resubmission.

(d) Noncomputer controls: There are controls put outside of the DP system because the entire system should be treated as a cohesive entity. So, the noncomputer controls:

(1) promote the effective use of people and equipment and

(2) provide for continuity of operations.

Controls of this kind can be: written, formal procedures for the capture of data, clear-cut documented operator procedures, user special control comparison procedures, etc.

Another type of control is "EDP-progress controls." The purpose of these controls is to provide management with a basis for evaluation of the EDP department's progress within a period of time regarding its outcome, utilization of resources, technological development and project development ability.

The Audit Trail

The audit trail begins with the recording of a transaction, winds through the processing steps and through any intermediate records which may exist and may be affected, and ends with the production of output records and reports. By selecting a representative sample of previously processed source documents and by following the audit trail, the auditor can trace these documents through the data processing systems to their final report or record destinations as a means of testing the adequacy of systems procedures and controls. In a manual system, original transactions may be recorded in one or more books of original entry; from there they may be connected to the final output by means of ledgers, documents, and summary totals. A visual and readily traceable trail is thus created.

In a computer-based system, the form, content, and accessibility of records frequently are such that the auditor is unable to follow a single transaction completely through the system. The audit trail adjusting its nature to the new computerized techniques has been changed from its initial form. Some of the changes in the EDP audit trail which confront the auditor are:

1. Source documents, once transcribed onto a machine-readable input medium, are no longer used in the processing cycle. They may be filed in a manner which makes subsequent access difficult.

2. In some systems, traditional source documents may be eliminated by the use of direct input devices.

3. Ledger summaries may be replaced by master files which do not show the amounts leading up to the summarized values.

4. That data processing cycle does not necessarily provide a transaction listing or journal. To provide such a listing may require a specific action at a reasonable cost.

5. It is sometimes unnecessary to prepare frequent printed output of historical records. Files can be maintained on computer media and reports prepared only for exceptions.

6. Files maintained on a magnetic medium cannot be read except by use of the computer and a computer program.

7. The sequence of records and processing activities is difficult to observe because much of the data and many of the activities are contained within the computer systems.[10]

The audit trail is kept alive by keeping a detailed file of the transactions as they occur. For example, this file can be the input for an audit program, which would extract the transactions for selected accounts and print them in such a way that the accountant or auditor could trace the status of any account, transaction by transaction.

A detailed file of the transactions must be discarded when the cost of keeping it exceeds the probable value of having the data on hand. Application of this general rule is difficult, however, because it is not simple to forecast when and what demands will be made on the files and documents that are saved.

Audit Team

The evaluation of an information system is a team-oriented job rather than a one-man job. There are so many things to look at that it is impossible to have one person with the knowledge covering all areas of concern. The audit team, however, should be kept fairly small to ensure adequate cross-communication and control. The composition and the qualifications of the auditing team will be discussed later.

Planning the Audit

A well structured audit plan is the very first duty of the audit team. The plan should reflect the objectives of the audit and, so, the objectives should be fully defined.

A framework of doing the audit work is very helpful. Usually, the work is divided into several phases such as to assist in the planning and direction of the work and allow each auditor to readily understand how his assigned work is related to the entire audit. The following is a framework applied to a financial-type of audit:

Phase 1: Evaluation of the internal controls: Organization of the company's accounting operations into five functions: Management control, data collection and recording, data conversion, information and/or check distribution, and operation monitoring. During the audit each function is analyzed to the extent necessary to ascertain whether the internal controls were effective for their intended purpose.

Phase 2: Auditing financial transactions: The first step in this phase is to prepare a plan for the selection of the financial transactions to be audited in detail. There are several methods to select a sampling of the financial transactions such as statistical sampling, judgment sampling, etc.

After the sample is obtained, special auditing programs should be developed, in case they are not available, to implement it. The company can buy ready-made "generalized audit programs" from several software houses.

Phase 3: Ascertaining the existence of assets and liabilities: The auditors need to obtain sufficient competent evidential matter through inspection, observation, inquiries, and confirmations to afford a reasonable basis for rendering an opinion as to the existence of the recorded assets and liabilities.

Some other elements of the audit plan should be:

1. Assignment of responsibilities to the individual members of the audit team according to the skills each possesses. Also, assume good cross-communication among the auditors because none of the individualistic responsibilities stands alone but all are interdependent.

2. Close contact must be maintained with the users of the system so that the audit team members can fully understand their needs and requirements.

3. A list of questions should be developed by each auditor in collaboration with users and other team members to explore his responsibility line with the audit objectives at that time. Where possible, quantitative or qualitative limits should be established so that some form of objective measurement of performance can be obtained.

4. A timetable should be established for each phase of the audit.

5. A reporting procedure to keep systems developers and systems users informed of the status of the audit and its findings is extremely important.

Audit Methods

The audit team, to evaluate the computer records and to verify the adequacy of internal controls, must develop a set of disciplines and processing techniques.

Two approaches have been used for the auditing of computer records.

1. Auditing around the computer: It is usually the easiest approach for the auditor. He examines the transactions entering the computer and the outputs generated by computer processing to make sure that all transactions were processed correctly.

Using this method has the advantage of minimizing the interference with the EDP department's day-to-day processing operations and presents no risk of tampering with "live data." This method, also, works well if the system is on a batch processing basis, if transactions are usually recorded manually and if the audit trail is characterized by extensive print-outs. However, as the EDP system becomes more advanced, this auditing method becomes more cumbersome and costly.

2. Auditing through the computer: In this case, the computer is used to obtain information about the operation of the programs and about controls built into the machine itself. An example would be using computer programs to randomly select records from a file to examine or to print information notices, etc.

To achieve these purposes, there are three approaches the auditor can follow:

a. Test-Deck Audit Approach: It is the most economical method of auditing through the computer. In this approach, simulated problems or data using the client's programs and equipment are processed under the auditor's control. Test data are introduced in whatever form is appropriate for the particular system. The auditor must design his test in a manner that will assure him that the system of controls is functioning properly.

The big advantage of the test-deck approach is that program changes are of little concern to the auditor, if the revised programs continue to produce acceptable output from the test data. On the other hand, a test-deck is costly to develop and can be used on only one particular system.

b. "Packaged" Audit Programs: These standardized programs are developed by software houses to audit specific segments of the company's records, such as the securities account, or they are generated sets of audit routines. These packages assume transferrability of audit programs among various EDP installations. The audit packages are really enhanced retrieval packages used to perform functions frequently needed by the auditor. These packages can include test data penetrators (create test cases according to the auditor's criteria), utility packages (create copies of files), and library packages (insure that production programs are controlled, in both their source and object form).

Some of the existing generalized audit packages today are: Audassist, Auditape, Auditpak, Auditronic-16, Ayams, Strata, EDP-Auditor, S/2170, etc. However, differences in equipment and software sometimes make extensive use of packaged audit programs impractical. The trend in equipment manufacture is toward more uniformity in design. Packaged programs, therefore, will likely be much more attractive in the future.

c. Custom Programming: These are programs developed within the company under the internal auditor's guidelines. This presupposes the auditor to have a high level of EDP knowledge, and, ideally, he should write the programs.

Custom programming can be used in combination with a package to provide specific processing that is needed. Also, it will be required for audit routines that are embedded in regular programs, for concurrent auditing.

This approach requires capable programmers to construct the programs and, if the job is to be done efficiently and effectively, the costs will be the least of all the other mentioned methods.

Audit Techniques

Some of the techniques the internal auditors can use to accomplish their job can be:

1. General questioning: The auditor by walking through the facilities and talking to people can ask a variety of "what if . . .?" questions, and often the answers will point out areas where he must ask questions in greater depth. For example, he may ask a file owner what he will do if the file is destroyed, or ask a computer operator what he will do if the machine catches fire.

2. Questions and checklists: Are used to ensure thoroughness and ensure that items to be examined are not forgotten. The items that ought to be on the checklist differ from one organization to another and should be compiled with specific needs in mind. However, as mentioned in the beginning of the paper, there are certain general purpose checklists today which may help the auditor to modify them according to the needs of the particular organization.

3. Spot checks: Are used for such items as the computer operator's log, the record of the Input/Output Control Section, the quality-control reports, logs of security procedural violations, and the tape library

log. The spot checks will ensure that files are being balanced as required and that, in general, the security requirements are not being bypassed.

4. Sampling: The auditor using sampling techniques selects a few transactions and follows what happens to them as far as the process goes. To follow the history of a transaction completely, he may need certain records that might not otherwise be kept in such a way that reference to them is easy. This needs to be done by printing out the items or by punching them into cards and thus leaving an audit trail. Today, given the capability to display records when needed, the audit trail can become a sequence of reference numbers indicating the sequence in which items were posted to the files.

5. Use of erroneous transactions: Are used to see whether the system's validation controls detect them. For example:

a. Quantity invoiced exceeds quantity ordered by 10% but within $300.00.

b. Tool order invoiced although sample tooling has not been approved by receiving inspection.

c. Duplicate payment of invoice paid in same machine run.

6. Attempted security violations: A deliberate and intelligent attempt to violate security can be the best test of the system's security procedures. The auditing group might employ a person who seems to have natural talents in circumventing security procedures. On some systems in which security is of high importance, a "counter-security group" has been employed for an extended period and has proved very effective in finding security loopholes.

7. Test records, pseudo-transactions and a mini-company: Certain records are updated by pseudo-transactions that are entered into the system by the auditors. The fictitious records and transactions are processed by the same programs that process the operational transactions. They are used to check that the programs are functioning currently and have not been tampered with. If actual cash is being balanced to the computer totals, a correction is needed because the false records and transactions will be included in the batch totals and balancing runs.

Some auditors have a collection of records representing a complete system or complete corporation in miniature. This has been referred to as "pilot system" or "mini-company." This technique is particularly important during conversion to a new system. The same records will be retained and the same transactions processed before cutover to ensure that the new system works correctly, and after cutover to ensure that no errors have been introduced.

8. Special programs: Are used in cases of the absence of printed documents to be checked by the auditors. The auditor has to define what he wants to have checked and the programs for performing the checks should, if possible, be written outside the DP department. For example, the programs used may take actions such as the following:

a. Print every 9th record.
b. Print all records who meet certain criteria.
c. Carry out a file balancing operation.

No method or technique can replace the attention, intuition and judgment of an experienced auditor. His experience enables him to quickly evaluate the adequacy of the internal control procedures. His questioning of people leads him to system weaknesses more surely than any automated procedure of fixed-response questionnaire. To a capable auditor a well-run EDP installation looks boring!!!

Organization of the Audit Group

Auditing an information system is a group-oriented process. To effectively evaluate a system, management must assure an unbiased point of view from the audit team. This leads to the conclusion that the internal audit group should be at least independ-ent from the EDP installation and report to another authority outside of the EDP department. The more critical the auditing job is for the company, the higher the position of authority the audit group should possess.

Qualifications of the Audit Members

The internal auditor should obtain knowledge and experience about three basic areas:

1. Knowledge of data processing
2. Knowledge of how to use the computer
3. Understanding of the business operations

Usually, the auditors have a good knowledge of business operations and lack adequate experience and knowledge on DP operations. These disadvantages become greater when an auditor has to deal with advanced computer systems such as real-time, on-line, big data bases, etc.

A very good illustration of the desirable level of computer knowledge expected of an auditor to obtain is provided in Figure 1.

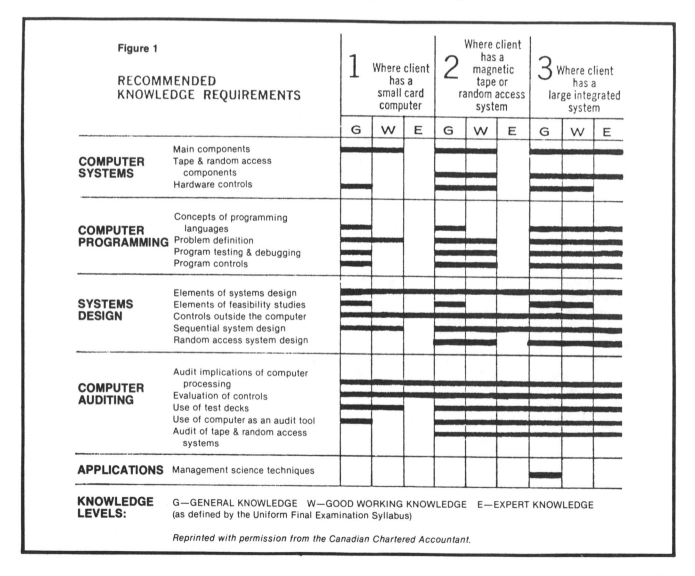

To staff the audit team several different philosophies have been employed:

1. Teach data processing to auditors. The key to success for this approach is the selection and adequate training of the right persons. Its drawback is that this method takes time and costs money.

2. Teach auditing to system analyst/programmers. This approach requires good systems analysts or programmers who are keenly interested in the auditing function and would like to make a career out of auditing.

3. Form audit teams of systems analysts and auditors. This approach integrates the knowledge and experience of two different professional groups.

4. Add programmers to the audit staff. This method makes possible the construction of audit programs by the audit staff. The programmers, however, do not provide technical expertise to the audit staff at a great investment.

5. Contract with outside organization to do the programming. This approach is followed in cases where the audit group does not have programming capabilities.

Role of the Audit Group

The role of the internal audit group is to represent management's viewpoint within the company. To accomplish his duties, the auditor employs tools that assure an objective and unbiased point of view.

A conflict of bias can arise in writing audit programs. The alternatives of writers are (1) the regular application programmers, (2) the new programmers under the auditor's guidelines, (3) the auditor. The third alternative is the ideal solution but is not realistic because a few auditors can write programs by themselves today. Therefore, the audit programs should be written under the close supervision of the auditor.

Another bias can occur in the degree of the auditor's participation in the systems design effort, particularly, in the internal controls design. Since his duty is to evaluate the system, he should participate in the system's design. Non-participation will cause him to spend a lot of time, after the system is ready, to study and understand it. In practice the auditor should follow the system's design process very closely and give guidelines on the ways the internal controls should be designed.

Prerequisites for a Successful Audit Group

A major problem with the internal audit group is how to attract and hold good people. The main difficulties come from the lack of a clear career path for the auditors and from the relatively low salaries paid. However, some EDP auditors are being promoted to supervisory positions in audit, and even to the position of general auditor.

The audit group should be an independent department, getting sufficient resources from management to accomplish its duties. The auditors should be permanent members of the audit staff. Otherwise, the loyalty of auditors "loaned" by other departments will naturally lie with their home departments.

Internal auditors should not design the internal controls, however, they should give guidelines on how the job should be done.

Sufficient training is the critical factor for a successful audit group. The training should be continuous to build competence in the expanding computer technology and to avoid technological obsolescence.

Constructive and sincere cooperation between the auditors and the managers of the organization should be assumed for getting the most beneficial results from an auditing effort.

Finally, top management commitment to support the audit is necessary. This is absolutely necessary in cases where auditors deal with people of higher authority than their own.

Summary

The information systems audit deals with the evaluation of all activities, procedures, methods and techniques involved in a Management Information System. It also informs top management on the progress of the EDP Department.

A series of internal controls and audit trails is built within the system during the systems design effort which gives the auditor the information he wants to accomplish his duties. To get this information, the auditor employs several methods and techniques. To do so, he must possess certain amounts of computer-systems and data processing operations knowledge. Finally, to assure objectivity on his conclusions, the audit group should be independent within the organization and outside of the EDP department.

References

1. R. Dirks, L. Gross, *The Great Wall Street Scandal,* McGraw-Hill, 1974.
2. Editorial-1, *Newsweek,* April 23, 1975.
3. D. Sanders, *Computer and Management in a Changing Society,* McGraw-Hill, 1974.
4. H. Gellman, Using the Computer to Steal, *Journal of Systems Management,* October, 1974.
5. Ibid.
6. J. Martin, *Security, Accuracy, and Privacy in Computer Systems,* Prentice-Hall, 1973.
7. R. Canning, The Internal Auditor and the Computer, *EDP Analyzer,* March, 1975.
8. F. McFarlan, Management Audit for the EDP Department, *Harvard Business Review,* May-June, 1975.
9. J. Kanter, *Management-Oriented MIS,* Prentice-Hall, 1972.
10. G. Davis, *Auditing and EDP,* American Institute of CPA, 1968.

IOANNIS METHODIOS

Ioannis Methodius has a Bachelor of Science degree in Mathematics from the University of Athens, Greece. He is presently a candidate for a Master of Science degree in Technology of Management at The American University, Washington, D. C., and is a member of the Society for Management Information Systems.

Reviews, Walkthroughs, and Inspections

GERALD M. WEINBERG AND DANIEL P. FREEDMAN

Abstract—Formal technical reviews supply the quality measurement to the "cost effectiveness" equation in a project management system. There are several unique formal technical review procedures, each applicable to particular types of technical material and to the particular mix of the Review Committee. All formal technical reviews produce reports on the overall quality for project management, and specific technical information for the producers. These reports also serve as an historic account of the systems development process. Historic origins and future trends of formal and informal technical reviews are discussed.

Index Terms—Project management, software development management, technical reviews.

THE PROBLEM OF CONTROLLING TECHNICAL INFORMATION

ANY CONTROL system requires reliable information. A project management system normally obtains its information by two quite different routes, as indicated in Fig. 1. *Cost and schedule information* comes in channels relatively independent of the producing unit, and can thus be relied upon to detect cost overruns and schedule slippages. *Evaluation of technical output*, however, is often another matter.

If project management is not in a position to evaluate technical output directly, it must rely on the producing unit's own evaluation—a dangerous game if that unit is malfunctioning. If the unit is technically weak in a certain area, the unit's judgment will be weak in the same area. Just where the work is poorest, the evaluation sent to management will be least likely to show the weakness.

But even if the producing unit is not technically weak, the problem of unreliable information persists because of information overload. As a unit overloads, inadequate supervision may affect work quality—while at the same time affecting the quality of the evaluation. The unit *wants* to be done on schedule and *wants* the work to be correct. Under pressure, any human being will see what is wanted instead of what exists. Just when it is needed most, this control system utterly fails.

THE ROLE OF THE FORMAL TECHNICAL REVIEW

Formal technical reviews come in many variations, under many names, but all play the same role in project management, as indicated in Fig. 2. As in Fig. 1, the producing unit controls its own development work, perhaps even conducting informal reviews internally. At the level of the producing unit, in fact, the use of the formal technical review requires no

Manuscript received January 5, 1983.

G. M. Weinberg is with Weinberg and Weinberg, Rural Route Two, Lincoln, NE 68505.

D. P. Freedman is with Ethnotech, Inc., P. O. Box 6627, Lincoln, NE 68506.

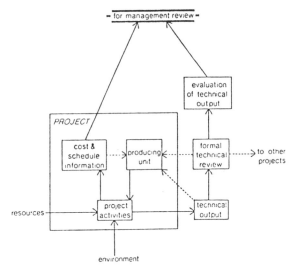

Fig. 1. Management's view of the output of a programming effort.

Fig. 2. The place of the formal technical review.

change, which simplifies its introduction as a project management tool.

As the diagram shows, the formal review is conducted by people who are *not part of that producing unit*. Hopefully, these are people who have no conscious or unconscious reason for favoring or disfavoring the project's work. Moreover, their report—the technical review summary report—goes to management, thus providing *reliable information* to be used in *management reviews* of the project.

MANAGEMENT REVIEWS VERSUS TECHNICAL REVIEWS

Fig. 2 also illustrates the difference between a *technical* review and a *management* review, sometimes called a "project review" or some similar name. The technical review committee is staffed by technical people and studies only technical issues. Its job is to put the evaluation of technical output on the same reliable basis as, say, cost and schedule information to management. Using both sorts of information, management can now make informed judgments of what is to be done in controlling the project.

It should also be noted that most "project control" systems do not concern themselves with the accurate and reliable evaluation of the quality of technical output. Instead, they concern themselves with measuring what can be measured *without* technical review, assuming, more or less, that one module of 300 lines of code is just like any other. If that assumption of quality is correct, then these systems can provide excellent management information for project control.

If that assumption is not correct, however, then only the "cost" side of the "cost effectiveness" ledger has any meaning. Under such conditions, even the best project control systems can provide only an illusion of control. The consequences are familiar enough—missed schedules, cost overruns, unmet specifications, inadequate performance, error-prone production, and huge and never ending maintenance.

REVIEW REPORTS AND PROJECT MANAGEMENT

Whatever goes on *inside* it, the major project control function of *any* review is to provide *management* a reliable answer to the fundamental question:

Does this product do the job it is supposed to do?

Once any piece of work has been reviewed and accepted, it becomes part of the system. Subject to a very small risk factor, it is

1) complete,
2) correct,
3) dependable as a base for related work, and
4) measurable for purposes of tracking progress.

Without reviews, there are no *reliable* methods for measuring the progress of a project. *Sometimes* we get dependable reports from the producers themselves, but *sometimes* is not good enough. No matter how good their *intentions,* producers are simply not in a position to give consistently reliable reports on their own products.

For small, simple objects, with well-intentioned, competent producers, there is some chance of success without reliable progress measures. As projects grow larger and more complex, however, the chance of some self-report being overly optimistic becomes a certainty.

Whatever the system of formal reviews, the review reporting serves as a formal commitment by technically competent and unbiased people that a piece of work is complete, correct, and dependable. The review report states as accurately as possible the completeness and acceptability of a piece of software work, be it specifications, design, code, documentation, test plan, or whatever.

By themselves, these review reports do not guarantee that a project will not end up in crisis or failure. It is up to the management of the project to use the information in the review reports to make management decisions needed to keep the project on track. Well done review reports are not suf-

ficient to make a project succeed, though poorly done reviews, or no reviews at all, are sure to get a project in trouble—no matter how skilled the management or how sophisticated the project management system.

TYPES OF TECHNICAL REVIEW REPORTS

The one report that is always generated by a *formal* review is the *technical review summary report.* This report carries the conclusions of the review to management, and thus is the fundamental link between the review process and the project management system.

Other reports *may* be generated. Issues raised that must be brought to the attention of the producers are placed on a *technical review issues list.*

If issues are raised about something other than the reviewed work itself, a *technical review related issues report* is created for each issue.

On occasion, an organization will institute some *research report,* such as a detailed breakdown of standards used and broken, or a report of hits and misses on a checklist.

Those cases where the review leader has to give a report of a failed review (not a failed product) lead to a *review process report,* the form and content of which will be unique to the situation and organization. For instance, on delicate matters the review process report may be verbal.

Other participants may also report on the process of the review itself. For instance, one or more participants might want to object to the behavior of the review leader.

THE REVIEW SUMMARY REPORT

For effective project management, review summary reports must identify three items:

1) What was reviewed?
2) Who did the reviewing?
3) What was their conclusion?

Fig. 3 shows a widely used format containing these items. Although formats vary, the summary should generally be confined to a single page, lest its conclusion be lost in a forest of words.

THE TECHNICAL REVIEW ISSUES LIST

Whereas the summary report is primarily a report to management, the issues list is primarily a report to the producers. The issues list tells the producers *why* their work was not fully acceptable as is, hopefully in sufficient detail to enable them to remedy the situation.

The issues list is primarily a communication from one technical group to another. It is not intended for nontechnical readers and therefore need not be "translated" for their eyes. Moreover, it is a *transient* communication, in that once the issues are resolved, the list might as well disappear. (We exclude, for the moment, research use of the list). Therefore, the issues list need not be fancy, as long as it is clear.

Practices vary, but among our clients, management does not routinely get the issues list. The summary report already contains, in its assessment of the work, a weighted opinion of the seriousness of the issues, so management need not be burdened with extra paper and technical details.

The issues list need not be *concealed* from management, but when managers routinely receive lists of issues, they naturally try to use the information. For example, they may count issues as a means of evaluating producers or reviewers—a practice which tends to undermine the quality of future reviews.

Another common subversion of the review process is the attempt to make the issues list into a *solutions list*. The job of the review committee is to raise issues; the job of the producing unit is to resolve them. A review committee is generally no better at resolving issues than a producing unit is at raising them. Management may want to see issues lists from time to time to ensure that they are remaining issues lists, rather than solutions lists.

THE TECHNICAL REVIEW RELATED ISSUES REPORT

A related issue is something that comes up in the course of a review that does not happen to be the principal reason for the review. Examples of related issues might be:

1) a typographical error in a related document;

2) a hidden assumption in the specifications that makes part of one module obsolete;

3) a flaw in the original problem statement that makes the entire project plan invalid.

If an organization cannot handle issue 1) without alerting the management chain, it is probably in as bad a shape as an organization that handles issue 3) *without* alerting the manage-

ment chain. The principal project management problem is with middle issues, such as 2). Such issues have always been troublesome to project control systems. When they are detected, the related issue report is a way of notifying *someone* who ought to be in a position to do something about them.

Because a related issue is, by definition, a deviation from smooth product development, there is really no way to develop a standard practice for handling all situations. A related issue report often descends like a bolt from the blue on some people who may not even know that a review is taking place. If it is not communicated in some standard, official form, people may not even recognize it. Therefore, if we want to keep related issue reports from passing directly into the wastebasket, we have got to give them *some* official status.

The mildest approach is to use a standard *transmittal sheet*, identifying the source of the material and attached to the actual communication, which may take any convenient form. Some organizations prefer a formal follow-up system that requires that each related issue report receive a reply within a few days. Another approach is to send the related issue report through the appropriate manager, leaving any action or follow-up decision on the managerial level.

HISTORICAL ANALYSES

Some of the information obtained from an historical analysis of review reports can be extremely specific. For instance, many organizations classify the types of problems turned up in each review and tabulate the frequency of each type. A similar tabulation is made of errors that slip through the review only to be caught at a later stage.

Comparison of these tabulations—in total, by review group, and by producer—provides clear guidance for future educational and reviewing practices. It is essential, however, that this information be used for improvement of project management, not for punishment of individuals, lest the whole scheme backfire and produce better methods of concealing errors and deficiencies.

To illustrate appropriate use of such historical analyses, let us say that most of the flaws detected during code reviews centered around the module interfaces. If this deficiency was project-wide, the training department could set up special training for everyone, guided by the specific types of interfacing errors recorded in the review reports.

Or perhaps the interfacing errors, upon analysis, reveal a weakness in project standards concerning interfaces. Whatever the problem, the historical records should first make it visible, them make it measurable, and finally help narrow it down to its true source.

REVIEWS AND PHASES

Any time after a project begins, an accurate, complete review report history can be compared with the schedule projected at the beginning of the development cycle. In which phases did the estimated time match the actual time? Where did the deviations occur? Were the deviations caused by problems in development? Were they mistakes in the original estimate?

Such historical information is obviously essential if project management is to improve from project to project. Yet such information will be meaningless if the "phases" of the project plan do not correspond to units of work marked at both beginning and end by reviews.

In order for any project control system to work, the system life cycle must be expressed in terms of measurable phases—some meaningful, reviewable product that represents the end of one phase and the beginning of the next. If there is nothing that can be reviewed, then nothing has been produced, and if nothing has been produced, how can it be controlled?

VARIETIES OF REVIEWED MATERIALS

Much of the earliest public discussion of reviews focused on the varieties of *code reviews*, rather than reviews of other materials produced in the life cycle. In the early history of software development, we were primarily concerned with code accuracy, because the coding seemed to be the major stumbling block to reliable product development. As our coding improved, however, we began to see other problems that had been obscured by the tangle of coding errors.

At first we noticed that many of the difficulties were not coding errors but design errors, so more attention was devoted to *design reviews*. As these techniques begin to be effective at clearing up design problems, the whole cycle starts again, for we notice that design is no longer the major hurdle.

In many of these cases, we never clearly understood the problem the design was attempting to solve. We were solving a *situation*, not a problem. Currently, increased emphasis is being placed on the analysis process, which becomes the next area of application of technical reviews—*specification reviews*.

Other types of reviewed material include *documentation*, *test data* and *test plans*, *tools* and *packages*, *training materials*, *procedures* and *standards*, as well as any other "deliverable" used in a system.

Reviews of these materials are conducted not only during development, but also during operation and maintenance of the system.

PRINCIPAL VARIETIES OF REVIEW DISCIPLINES

It is possible to conduct a review without any particular discipline decided in advance, simply adjusting the course of the meeting to the demands of the product under review. Many reviews are conducted in just this way, but over time special disciplines tend to evolve which emphasize certain aspects of reviewing at the expense of others.

For instance, many of the best known review disciplines are attempts to "cover" a greater quantity of material in the review. The "inspection" approach tries to gain efficiency by focusing on a much narrower, much more sharply defined, set of questions. In some cases, an inspection consists of running through a checklist of faults, one after the other, over the entire product. Obviously, one danger of such an approach is from faults that do not appear on the checklist, so effective inspection systems generally evolve methods for augmenting checklists as experience grows.

Another way to try to cover more material is by having the product "walked through" by someone who is very familiar with it—even specially prepared with a more or less formal presentation. Walking through the product, a lot of detail can be skipped—which is good if you are just trying to verify an overall approach or bad if your object is to find errors of detail.

In some cases, the walkthrough is very close to a lecture about the product—which suggests another reason for varying the formal review approach. In some cases, rapid education of large numbers of people may suggest some variation of the formal review.

In a walkthrough, then, the process is driven by the *product being reviewed*. In an inspection, *the list of points to be inspected* determines the sequence. In a plain review, the order is determined by the *flow of the meeting as it unfolds*. In contrast to these types, the various kinds of "round-robin" reviews emphasize a *cycling through the various participants*, with each person taking an equal and similar share of the entire task.

Round-robin reviews are especially useful in situations where the participants are at the same level of knowledge, a level that may not be too high. It ensures that nobody will shrink from participation through lack of confidence, while at the same time guaranteeing a more detailed look at the product, part by part.

REAL VERSUS IDEAL REVIEWS

Although many "pure" review systems have been described, people who observe actual reviews will never find one following all the "rules." By examining some of the real advantages and disadvantages of one of these "pure" systems, we can understand why every real review system involves aspects of all the major varieties. We will use the walkthrough as our example, but any system could be used to illustrate the same points.

With a walkthrough, because of the prior preparation of the presenter, a large amount of material can be moved through rather speedily. Moreover, since the reviews are far more passive than participating, larger numbers of people can become familiar with the walked through material. This larger audience can serve educational purposes, but it also can bring a great number of diverse viewpoints to bear on the presented material. If all in the audience are alert, and if they represent a broad cross section of skills and viewpoints, the walkthrough can give strong statistical assurance that no major oversight lies concealed in the material.

Another advantage of the walkthrough is that it does not make many demands on the participants for preparation in advance. Where there are large numbers of participants, or where the participants come from diverse organizations not under the same operational control, it may prove impossible to get everyone prepared for the review. In such cases, the walkthrough may be the only reasonable way to ensure that all those present have actually looked at the material.

The problems of the walkthrough spring rather directly from its unique advantages. Advance preparation is not required, so each participant may have a different depth of understanding. Those close to the work may be bored and not pay attention. Those who are seeing the work for the first time may not be able to keep up with the pace of presentation. In either case, the ability to raise penetrating issues is lost.

WHY THERE IS SO MUCH VARIETY IN REVIEWS

Although all reviews occupy the same role in project management as a control system, managers are justifiably confused by the great variety found in technical review practices. The practice of technical review differs from place to place for a variety of reasons, the principal ones being:

1) different external requirements, such as government contract provisions;

2) different internal organizations, such as the use or nonuse of teams;

3) continuity with past practices.

Continuity is probably the strongest reason. When it comes to social behavior, people tend to resist changing what they already do, even if it does not seem exceptionally productive in today's environment. In many project management systems, formal technical reviews have been introduced as a new form of some old practice, perhaps because it was easier to introduce reviews in this way.

HOW REVIEWS EVOLVED

The idea of reviews of software is as old as software itself. Every early software developer quickly came to understand that writing completely accurate programs was too great a problem for the unaided human mind—even the mind of a genius. Babbage showed his programs to Ada Lovelace, or to anyone else who would review them. John von Neumann regularly submitted his programs to his colleagues for review.

These reviews, in our terms, were *informal* reviews, because they did not involve formal procedures for connecting the review reports to a project management system. Informal review procedures were passed on from person to person in the general culture of computing for many years before they were acknowledged in print. The need for reviewing was so obvious to the best programmers that they rarely mentioned it in print, while the worst programmers believed they were so good that *their* work did not need reviewing.

Around the end of the 1950's, the creation of some large software projects began to make the need for some form of technical reviewing obvious to management all over the world. Most large projects had some sort of reviewing procedures, which evolved through the 1960's into more formalized ideas.

In the 1970's, publication espousing various review forms began to appear in the literature. For those interested in a history of publication, a bibliography appears in Freedman and Weinberg [1]. Publications, however, tend to conceal the grass-roots origin of reviews, giving the impression that they were "invented" by some person or company at a certain time and place.

WHERE REVIEWS ARE GOING

Today, the evolution of reviewing procedures continues, primarily on an experiential basis within projects. Reviews are a partial formalization of a natural social process, arising from the superhuman need for extreme precision in software. Therefore, the "science" of reviewing is a *social* science, and it is difficult to make general, quantifiable statements that apply to all reviews.

Some experimental work has been done on reviews, but these experiments generally suffer from the following problems:

1) Only one or two narrowly defined review procedures are examined.

2) Reviewers are novices in the procedures used.

3) The environment is significantly different from that of a real software development or maintenance environment.

Field reports overcome items 2) and 3), but introduce the problem of experimental control. Nevertheless, many of these reports indicate that effective project management is not possible without the technical review, in one form or another. These reports are sometimes puzzling to managers in other organizations, who have "tried reviews," but who have failed to overcome some of the human problems of changing entrenched social practices.

The best evidence for the effectiveness of reviews is that their use continues to spread. A body of practical knowledge has grown with this spread, particularly concerning the problems associated with starting a system of reviews. We anticipate that most future development of review technology will arise from such on-the-job experiments, rather than any theoretical or laboratory work.

REFERENCES

[1] D. P. Freedman and G. M. Weinberg, *Handbook of Walkthroughs, Inspections, and Technical Reviews: Evaluating Programs, Projects, and Products,* 3rd ed. Boston, MA: Little, Brown and Company, 1982. (Because this reference contains an extensive bibliography, we are omitting further references here.)

Gerald M. Weinberg, photograph and biography not available at the time of publication.

Daniel P. Freedman, photograph and biography not available at the time of publication.

Substantial net improvements in programming quality and productivity have been obtained through the use of formal inspections of design and of code. Improvements are made possible by a systematic and efficient design and code verification process, with well-defined roles for inspection participants. The manner in which inspection data is categorized and made suitable for process analysis is an important factor in attaining the improvements. It is shown that by using inspection results, a mechanism for initial error reduction followed by ever-improving error rates can be achieved.

Design and code inspections to reduce errors in program development

by M. E. Fagan

Successful management of any process requires planning, measurement, and control. In programming development, these requirements translate into defining the programming process in terms of a series of operations, each operation having its own exit criteria. Next there must be some means of measuring completeness of the product at any point of its development by inspections or testing. And finally, the measured data must be used for controlling the process. This approach is not only conceptually interesting, but has been applied successfully in several programming projects embracing systems and applications programming, both large and small. It has not been found to "get in the way" of programming, but has instead enabled higher predictability than other means, and the use of inspections has improved productivity and product quality. The purpose of this paper is to explain the planning, measurement, and control functions as they are affected by inspections in programming terms.

An ingredient that gives maximum play to the planning, measurement, and control elements is consistent and vigorous *discipline*. Variable rules and conventions are the usual indicators of a lack of discipline. An iron-clad discipline on all rules, which can stifle programming work, is not required but instead there should be a clear understanding of the flexibility (or nonflexibility) of each of the rules applied to various aspects of the project. An example of flexibility may be waiving the rule that all main paths will be tested for the case where repeated testing of a given path will logically do no more than add expense. An example of necessary inflexibility would be that *all* code must be

Figure 1 Programming process

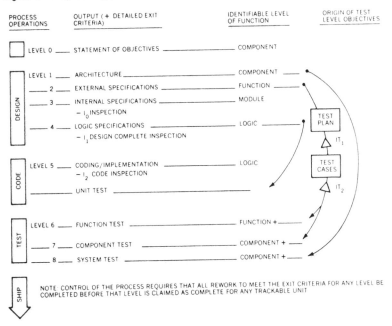

inspected. A clear statement of the project rules and changes to these rules along with faithful adherence to the rules go a long way toward practicing the required project discipline.

A prerequisite of process management is a clearly defined series of operations in the process (Figure 1). The miniprocess within each operation must also be clearly described for closer management. A clear statement of the criteria that must be satisfied to exit each operation is mandatory. This statement and accurate data collection, with the data clearly tied to trackable units of known size and collected from specific points in the process, are some essential constituents of the information required for process management.

In order to move the form of process management from qualitative to more quantitative, process terms must be more specific, data collected must be appropriate, and the limits of accuracy of the data must be known. The effect is to provide more precise information in the correct process context for decision making by the process manager.

In this paper, we first describe the programming process and places at which inspections are important. Then we discuss factors that affect productivity and the operations involved with inspections. Finally, we compare inspections and walk-throughs on process control.

The process

A process may be described as a set of operations occurring in a definite sequence that operates on a given input and converts it to some desired output. A general statement of this kind is sufficient to convey the notion of the process. In a practical application, however, it is necessary to describe the input, output, internal processing, and processing times of a process in very specific terms if the process is to be executed and practical output is to be obtained.

In the programming development process, explicit requirement statements are necessary as input. The series of processing operations that act on this input must be placed in the correct sequence with one another, the output of each operation satisfying the input needs of the next operation. The output of the final operation is, of course, the explicitly required output in the form of a verified program. Thus, the objective of each processing operation is to receive a defined input and to produce a definite output that satisfies a specific set of exit criteria. (It goes without saying that each operation can be considered as a miniprocess itself.) A well-formed process can be thought of as a continuum of processing during which sequential sets of exit criteria are satisfied, the last set in the entire series requiring a well-defined end product. Such a process is not amorphous. It can be measured and controlled.

Unambiguous, explicit, and universally accepted exit criteria would be perfect as process control checkpoints. It is frequently argued that universally agreed upon checkpoints are impossible in programming because all projects are different, etc. However, *all* projects do reach the point at which there is a project checkpoint. As it stands, any trackable unit of code achieving a clean compilation can be said to have satisfied a universal exit criterion or checkpoint in the process. Other checkpoints can also be selected, albeit on more arguable premises, but once the premises are agreed upon, the checkpoints become visible in most, if not all, projects. For example, there is a point at which the design of a program is considered complete. This point may be described as the level of detail to which a unit of design is reduced so that one design statement will materialize in an estimated three to 10 source code instructions (or, if desired, five to 20, for that matter). Whichever particular ratio is selected across a project, it provides a checkpoint for the process control of that project. In this way, suitable checkpoints may be selected throughout the development process and used in process management. (For more specific exit criteria see Reference 1.)

The cost of reworking errors in programs becomes higher the later they are reworked in the process, so every attempt should be made to find and fix errors as early in the process as possible. This cost has led to the use of the inspections described later and to the description of exit criteria which include assuring that all errors known at the end of the inspection of the new "clean-compilation" code, for example, have been correctly fixed. So, rework of all known errors up to a particular point must be complete before the associated checkpoint can be claimed to be met for any piece of code.

Where inspections are not used and errors are found during development or testing, the cost of rework as a fraction of overall development cost can be suprisingly high. For this reason, errors should be found and fixed as close to their place of origin as possible.

Production studies have validated the expected quality and productivity improvements and have provided estimates of standard productivity rates, percentage improvements due to inspections, and percentage improvements in error rates which are applicable in the context of large-scale operating system program production. (The data related to operating system development contained herein reflect results achieved by IBM in applying the subject processes and methods to representative samples. Since the results depend on many factors, they cannot be considered representative of every situation. They are furnished merely for the purpose of illustrating what has been achieved in sample testing.)

The purpose of the test plan inspection IT_1, shown in Figure 1, is to find voids in the functional variation coverage and other discrepancies in the test plan. IT_2, test case inspection of the test cases, which are based on the test plan, finds errors in the test cases. The total effects of IT_1 and IT_2 are to increase the integrity of testing and, hence, the quality of the completed product. And, because there are less errors in the test cases to be debugged during the testing phase, the overall project schedule is also improved.

A process of the kind depicted in Figure 1 installs all the intrinsic programming properties in the product as required in the statement of objectives (Level 0) by the time the coding operation (Level 5) has been completed—except for packaging and publications requirements. With these exceptions, all later work is of a verification nature. This verification of the product provides no contribution to the product during the essential development (Levels 1 to 5); it only adds error detection and elimination (frequently at one half of the development cost). I_0, I_1, and I_2 inspections were developed to measure and influence intrinsic

Figure 2 A study of coding productivity

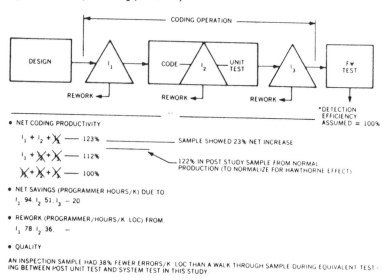

- NET CODING PRODUCTIVITY

$$I_1 + I_2 + \cancel{X} \quad \text{——} \quad 123\%$$ ——————— SAMPLE SHOWED 23% NET INCREASE

$$I_1 + \cancel{X} + \cancel{X} \quad \text{——} \quad 112\%$$ —— 122% IN POST STUDY SAMPLE FROM NORMAL PRODUCTION (TO NORMALIZE FOR HAWTHORNE EFFECT)

$$\cancel{X} + \cancel{X} + \cancel{X} \quad \text{——} \quad 100\%$$

- NET SAVINGS (PROGRAMMER HOURS/K) DUE TO

$$I_1 \ 94, I_2 \ 51, I_3 \ - 20$$

- REWORK (PROGRAMMER/HOURS/K LOC) FROM

$$I_1 \ 78, I_2 \ 36, \quad —$$

- QUALITY

AN INSPECTION SAMPLE HAD 38% FEWER ERRORS/K LOC THAN A WALK THROUGH SAMPLE DURING EQUIVALENT TESTING BETWEEN POST UNIT TEST AND SYSTEM TEST IN THIS STUDY

quality (error content) in the early levels, where error rework can be most economically accomplished. Naturally, the beneficial effect on quality is also felt in later operations of the development process and at the end user's site.

An improvement in productivity is the most immediate effect of purging errors from the product by the I_0, I_1, and I_2 inspections. This purging allows rework of these errors very near their origin, early in the process. Rework done at these levels is 10 to 100 times less expensive than if it is done in the last half of the process. Since rework detracts from productive effort, it reduces productivity in proportion to the time taken to accomplish the rework. It follows, then, that finding errors by inspection and reworking them earlier in the process reduces the overall rework time and increases productivity even within the early operations and even more over the total process. Since less errors ship with the product, the time taken for the user to install programs is less, and his productivity is also increased.

The quality of documentation that describes the program is of as much importance as the program itself for poor quality can mislead the user, causing him to make errors quite as important as errors in the program. For this reason, the quality of program documentation is verified by publications inspections (PI_0, PI_1, and PI_2). Through a reduction of user-encountered errors, these inspections also have the effect of improving user productivity by reducing his rework time.

A study of coding productivity

A piece of the design of a large operating system component (all done in structured programming) was selected as a study sample (Figure 2). The sample was judged to be of moderate complexity. When the piece of design had been reduced to a level of detail sufficient to meet the Design Level 4 exit criteria[2] (a level of detail of design at which one design statement would ultimately appear as three to 10 code instructions), it was submitted to a design-complete inspection (100 percent), I_1. On conclusion of I_1, all error rework resulting from the inspection was completed, and the design was submitted for coding in PL/S. The coding was then done, and when the code was brought to the level of the first clean compilation,[2] it was subjected to a code inspection (100 percent), I_2. The resultant rework was completed and the code was subjected to unit test. After unit test, a unit test inspection, I_3, was done to see that the unit test plan had been fully executed. Some rework was required and the necessary changes were made. This step completed the coding operation. The study sample was then passed on to later process operations consisting of building and testing.

inspection sample

The inspection sample was considered of sufficient size and nature to be representative for study purposes. Three programmers designed it, and it was coded by 13 programmers. The inspection sample was in modular form, was structured, and was judged to be of moderate complexity on average.

coding operation productivity

Because errors were identified and corrected in groups at I_1 and I_2, rather than found one-by-one during subsequent work and handled at the higher cost incumbent in later rework, the overall amount of error rework was minimized, even within the coding operation. Expressed differently, considering the inclusion of *all* I_1 time, I_2 time, and resulting error rework time (with the usual coding and unit test time in the total time to complete the operation), a *net* saving resulted when this figure was compared to the no-inspection case. This net saving translated into a 23 percent increase in the productivity of the coding operation alone. Productivity in later levels was also increased because there was less error rework in these levels due to the effect of inspections, but the increase was not measured directly.

An important aspect to consider in any production experiment involving human beings is the Hawthorne Effect.[3] If this effect is not adequately handled, it is never clear whether the effect observed is due to the human bias of the Hawthorne Effect or due to the newly implemented change in process. In this case a *control sample* was selected at random from many pieces of work *after the I_1 and I_2 inspections were accepted as commonplace.* (Previous experience without I_1 and I_2 approximated the net cod-

337

ing productivity rate of 100 percent datum in Figure 2.) The difference in coding productivity between the experimental sample (with I_1 and I_2 for the first time) and the control sample was 0.9 percent. This difference is not considered significant. Therefore, the measured increase in coding productivity of 23 percent is considered to validly accrue from the only change in the process: addition of I_1 and I_2 inspections.

control sample The control sample was also considered to be of representative size and was from the same operating system component as the study sample. It was designed by four programmers and was coded by seven programmers. And it was considered to be of moderate complexity on average.

net savings Within the coding operation only, the net savings (including inspection and rework time) in programmer hours per 1000 Non-Commentary Source Statements (K.NCSS)[4] were I_1: 94, I_2: 51, and I_3: −20. As a consequence, I_3 is no longer in effect.

If personal fatigue and downtime of 15 percent are allowed in addition to the 145 programmer hours per K.NCSS, the saving approaches one programmer month per K.NCSS (assuming that our sample was truly representative of the rest of the work in the operating system component considered).

error rework The error rework in programmer hours per K.NCSS found in this study due to I_1 was 78, and 36 for I_2 (24 hours for design errors and 12 for code errors). Time for error rework must be specifically scheduled. (For scheduling purposes it is best to develop rework hours per K.NCSS from history depending upon the particular project types and environments, but figures of 20 hours for I_1, and 16 hours for I_2 (*after the learning curve*) may be suitable to start with.)

quality The only comparative measure of quality obtained was a comparison of the inspection study sample with a fully comparable piece of the operating system component that was produced similarly, except that walk-throughs were used in place of the I_1 and I_2 inspections. (Walk-throughs[5] were the practice before implementation of I_1 and I_2 inspections.) The process span in which the quality comparison was made was seven months of testing beyond unit test after which it was judged that both samples had been equally exercised. The results showed the inspection sample to contain 38 percent less errors than the walk-through sample.

Note that up to inspection I_2, no machine time has been used for debugging, and so machine time savings were not mentioned. Although substantial machine time is saved overall since there are less errors to test for in inspected code in later stages of the process, no actual measures were obtained.

Table 1 Error detection efficiency

Process Operations	Errors Found per K.NCSS	Percent of Total Errors Found
Design I₁ inspection ⎤ Coding ⎬ I₂ inspection ⎦	38*	82
Unit test ⎤ Preparation for ⎬ acceptance test ⎦	8	18
Acceptance test	0	
Actual usage (6 mo.)	0	
Total	46	100

*51% were logic errors, most of which were missing rather than due to incorrect design.

In the development of applications, inspections also make a significant impact. For example, an application program of eight modules was written in COBOL by Aetna Corporate Data Processing department, Aetna Life and Casualty, Hartford, Connecticut, in June 1975.[6] Two programmers developed the program. The number of inspection participants ranged between three and five. The only change introduced in the development process was the I_1 and I_2 inspections. The program size was 4,439 Non-Commentary Source Statements.

An automated estimating program, which is used to produce the normal program development time estimates for all the Corporate Data Processing department's projects, predicted that designing, coding, and unit testing this project would require 62 programmer days. In fact, the time actually taken was 46.5 programmer days including inspection meeting time. The resulting saving in programmer resources was 25 percent.

The inspections were obviously very thorough when judged by the inspection error detection efficiency of 82 percent and the later results during testing and usage as shown in Table 1.

The results achieved in Non-Commentary Source Statements per Elapsed Hour are shown in Table 2. These inspection rates are four to six times faster than for systems programming. If these rates are generally applicable, they would have the effect of making the inspection of applications programs much less expensive.

inspections in applications development

Table 2 Inspection rates in NCSS per hour

Operations	I_1	I_2
Preparation	898	709
Inspection	652	539

Inspections

Inspections are a *formal*, *efficient*, and *economical* method of finding errors in design and code. All instructions are addressed

Table 3. Inspection process and rate of progress

Process operations	Rate of progress*(loc/hr) Design I_1	Code I_2	Objectives of the operation
1. Overview	500	not necessary	Communication education
2. Preparation	100	125	Education
3. Inspection	130	150	Find errors
4. Rework	20 hrs/K.NCSS	16 hrs/K.NCSS	Rework and resolve errors found by inspection
5. Follow-up	–	–	See that all errors, problems, and concerns have been resolved

* These notes apply to systems programming and are conservative. Comparable rates for applications programming are much higher. Initial schedules may be started with these numbers and as project history that is keyed to unique environments evolves. the historical data may be used for future scheduling algorithms.

at least once in the conduct of inspections. Key aspects of inspections are exposed in the following text through describing the I_1 and I_2 inspection conduct and process. I_0, IT_1, IT_2, PI_0, PI_1, and PI_2 inspections retain the same essential properties as the I_1 and I_2 inspections but differ in materials inspected, number of participants, and some other minor points.

the people involved

The inspection team is best served when its members play their particular roles, assuming the particular vantage point of those roles. These roles are described below:

1. *Moderator*—The *key person* in a successful inspection. He must be a competent programmer but need *not* be a technical expert on the program being inspected. To preserve objectivity and to increase the integrity of the inspection, it is usually advantageous to use a moderator from an unrelated project. The moderator must manage the inspection team and offer leadership. Hence, he must use personal sensitivity, tact, and drive in balanced measure. His use of the strengths of team members should produce a synergistic effect larger than their number; in other words, *he is the coach*. The duties of moderator also include scheduling suitable meeting places, reporting inspection results within one day, and follow-up on rework. *For best results the moderator should be specially trained.* (This training is brief but very advantageous.)
2. *Designer*—The programmer responsible for producing the program design.
3. *Coder/Implementor*—The programmer responsible for translating the design into code.
4. *Tester*—The programmer responsible for writing and/or executing test cases or otherwise testing the product of the designer and coder.

If the coder of a piece of code also designed it, he will function in the designer role for the inspection process; a coder from some related or similar program will perform the role of the coder. If the same person designs, codes, and tests the product code, the coder role should be filled as described above, and another coder—preferably with testing experience—should fill the role of tester.

Four people constitute a good-sized inspection team, although circumstances may dictate otherwise. The team size should not be artificially increased over four, but if the subject code is involved in a number of interfaces, the programmers of code related to these interfaces may profitably be involved in inspection. Table 3 indicates the inspection process and rate of progress.

scheduling inspections and rework

The total time to complete the inspection process from overview through follow-up for I_1 or I_2 inspections with four people involved takes about 90 to 100 people-hours for systems programming. Again, these figures may be considered conservative but they will serve as a starting point. Comparable figures for applications programming tend to be much lower, implying lower cost per K.NCSS.

Because the error detection efficiency of most inspection teams tends to dwindle after two hours of inspection but then picks up after a period of different activity, it is advisable to schedule inspection sessions of no more than two hours at a time. Two two-hour sessions per day are acceptable.

The time to do inspections and resulting rework must be scheduled and managed with the same attention as other important project activities. (After all, as is noted later, for one case at least, it is possible to find approximately two thirds of the errors reported during an inspection.) If this is not done, the immediate work pressure has a tendency to push the inspections and/or rework into the background, postponing them or avoiding them altogether. The result of this short-term respite will obviously have a much more dramatic long-term negative effect since the finding and fixing of errors is delayed until later in the process (and after turnover to the user). Usually, the result of postponing early error detection is a lengthening of the overall schedule and increased product cost.

Scheduling inspection time for modified code may be based on the algorithms in Table 3 *and on judgment.*

I₁ inspection process

Keeping the objective of each operation in the forefront of team activity is of paramount importance. Here is presented an outline of the I_1 inspection process operations.

VP	Individual Name	Inspection file Missing	Wrong	Extra	Errors	Error %
CD	CB Definition	16	2		18	3.5 ⎫ 10.4
CU	CB Usage	18	17	1	36	6.9 ⎭
FS	FPFS	1			1	.2
IC	Interconnect Calls	18	9		27	5.2
IR	Interconnect Reqts	4	5	2	11	2.1
LO	Logic	126	57	24	207	39.8 ⬅
L3	Higher Lvl Docu	1		1	2	.4
MA	Mod Attributes	1			1	.2
MD	More Detail	24	6	2	32	6.2
MN	Maintainability	8	5	3	16	3.1
OT	Other	15	10	10	35	6.7
PD	Pass Data Areas		1		1	.2
PE	Performance	1	2	3	6	1.2
PR	Prologue/Prose	44	38	7	89	17.1 ⬅
RM	Return Code/Msg	5	7	2	14	2.7
RU	Register Usage	1	2		3	.6
ST	Standards					
TB	Test & Branch	12	7	2	21	4.0
		295	168	57	520	100.0
		57%	32%	11%		

Figure 4 Summary of code inspections by error type

VP	Individual Name	Inspection file Missing	Wrong	Extra	Errors	Error %
CC	Code Comments	5	17	1	23	6.6
CU	CB Usage	3	21	1	25	7.2
DE	Design Error	31	32	14	77	22.1 ⬅
FI			8		8	2.3
IR	Interconnect Calls	7	9	3	19	5.5
LO	Logic	33	49	10	92	26.4 ⬅
MN	Maintainability	5	7	2	14	4.0
OT	Other					
PE	Performance	3	2	5	10	2.9
PR	Prologue/Prose	25	24	3	52	14.9 ⬅
PU	PL/S or BAL Use	4	9	1	14	4.0
RU	Register Usage	4	2		6	1.7
SU	Storage Usage	1			1	.3
TB	Test & Branch	2	5		7	2.0
		123	185	40	348	100.0

1. *Overview* (whole team) — The designer first describes the overall area being addressed and then the specific area he has designed in detail — logic, paths, dependencies, etc. Documentation of design is distributed to all inspection participants on conclusion of the overview. (For an I_2 inspection, no overview is necessary, but the participants should remain the same. Preparation, inspection, and follow-up proceed as for I_1 but, of course, using code listings *and* design specifications

as inspection materials. Also, at I_2 the moderator should flag for special scrutiny those areas that were reworked since I_1 errors were found *and other design changes* made.)

2. *Preparation* (individual) — Participants, using the design documentation, literally do their homework to try to understand the design, its intent and logic. (Sometimes flagrant errors are found during this operation, but in general, the number of errors found is not nearly as high as in the inspection operation.) To increase their error detection in the inspection, the inspection team should first study the ranked distributions of error types found by recent inspections. This study will prompt them to concentrate on the most fruitful areas. (See examples in Figures 3 and 4.) Checklists of clues on finding these errors should also be studied. (See partial examples of these lists in Figures 5 and 6 and complete examples for I_0 in Reference 1 and for I_1 and I_2 in Reference 7.)

3. *Inspection* (whole team) — A "reader" chosen by the moderator (usually the coder) describes how he will implement the design. He is expected to paraphrase the design as expressed by the designer. Every piece of logic is covered at least once, and every branch is taken at least once. All higher-level documentation, high-level design specifications, logic specifications, etc., and macro and control block listings at I_2 must be available and present during the inspection.

Now that the design is understood, *the objective is to find errors*. (Note that an error is defined as any condition that causes malfunction or that precludes the attainment of expected or previously specified results. Thus, deviations from specifications are clearly termed errors.) The finding of errors is actually done during the implementor/coder's discourse. Questions raised are pursued only to the point at which an error is recognized. It is noted by the moderator; its type is classified; severity (major or minor) is identified, and the inspection is continued. Often the solution of a problem is obvious. If so, it is noted, but no specific solution hunting is to take place during inspection. (The inspection is *not* intended to redesign, evaluate alternate design solutions, or to find solutions to errors; it is intended just to find errors!) A team is most effective if it operates with only one objective at a time.

Within one day of conclusion of the inspection, the moderator should produce a written report of the inspection and its findings to ensure that all issues raised in the inspection will be addressed in the rework and follow-up operations. Examples of these reports are given as Figures 7A, 7B, and 7C.

Figure 5 Examples of what to examine when looking for errors at I₁

I₁ Logic

Missing

1. Are All Constants Defined?
2. Are All Unique Values Explicitly Tested on Input Parameters?
3. Are Values Stored after They Are Calculated?
4. Are All Defaults Checked Explicitly Tested on Input Parameters?
5. If Character Strings Are Created Are They Complete. Are All Delimiters Shown?
6. If a Keyword Has Many Unique Values, Are They All Checked?
7. If a Queue Is Being Manipulated. Can the Execution Be Interrupted; If So, Is Queue Protected by a Locking Structure; Can Queue Be Destroyed Over an Interrupt?
8. Are Registers Being Restored on Exits?
9. In Queuing/Dequeuing Should Any Value Be Decremented/Incremented?
10. Are All Keywords Tested in Macro?
11. Are All Keyword Related Parameters Tested in Service Routine?
12. Are Queues Being Held in Isolation So That Subsequent Interrupting Requestors Are Receiving Spurious Returns Regarding the Held Queue?
13. Should any Registers Be Saved on Entry?
14. Are All Increment Counts Properly Initialized (0 or 1)?

Wrong

1. Are Absolutes Shown Where There Should Be Symbolics?
2. On Comparison of Two Bytes, Should All Bits Be Compared?
3. On Built Data Strings, Should They Be Character or Hex?
4. Are Internal Variables Unique or Confusing If Concatenated?

Extra

1. Are All Blocks Shown in Design Necessary or Are They Extraneous?

4. *Rework* — All errors or problems noted in the inspection report are resolved by the designer or coder/implementor.

5. *Follow-Up* — It is imperative that every issue, concern, and error be entirely resolved at this level, or errors that result can be 10 to 100 times more expensive to fix if found later in the process (programmer time only, machine time not included). It is the responsibility of the moderator to see that all issues, problems, and concerns discovered in the inspection operation have been resolved by the designer in the case of I₁, or the coder/implementor for I₂ inspections. If more than five percent of the material has been reworked, the team should reconvene and carry out a 100 percent reinspection. Where less than five percent of the material has been reworked, the moderator at his discretion may verify the quality of the rework himself or reconvene the team to reinspect either the complete work or just the rework.

commencing inspections

In Operation 3 above, it is one thing to direct people to find errors in design or code. It is quite another problem for them to find errors. Numerous experiences have shown that people have to be taught or prompted to find errors effectively. Therefore, it

Figure 6 Examples of what to examine when looking for errors at I_2

INSPECTION SPECIFICATION

I_2 *Test Branch*
Is Correct Condition Tested (If X = ON vs. IF X = OFF)?
Is (Are) Correct Variable(s) Used for Test
(If X = ON vs. If Y = ON)?
Are Null THENs/ELSEs Included as Appropriate?
Is Each Branch Target Correct?
Is the Most Frequently Exercised Test Leg the THEN Clause?

I_2 *Interconnection (or Linkage) Calls*
For Each Interconnection Call to Either a Macro, SVC or Another Module:
Are All Required Parameters Passed Set Correctly?
If Register Parameters Are Used, Is the Correct Register Number Specified?
If Interconnection Is a Macro,
Does the Inline Expansion Contain All Required Code?
No Register or Storage Conflicts between Macro and Calling Module?
If the Interconnection Returns, Do All Returned Parameters Get Processed
Correctly?

is prudent to condition them to seek the high-occurrence, high-cost error types (see example in Figures 3 and 4), and then describe the clues that usually betray the presence of each error type (see examples in Figures 5 and 6).

One approach to getting started may be to make a preliminary inspection of a design or code that is felt to be representative of the program to be inspected. Obtain a suitable quantity of errors, and analyze them by type and origin, cause, and salient indicative clues. With this information, an inspection specification may be constructed. This specification can be amended and improved in light of new experience and serve as an on-going directive to focus the attention and conduct of inspection teams. The objective of an inspection specification is to help maximize and make more consistent the error detection efficiency of inspections where

Error detection efficiency

$$= \frac{\text{Errors found by an inspection}}{\text{Total errors in the product before inspection}} \times 100$$

reporting inspection results

The reporting forms and form completion instructions shown in the Appendix may be used for I_1 and I_2 inspections. Although these forms were constructed for use in systems programming development, they may be used for applications programming development with minor modification to suit particular environments.

The moderator will make hand-written notes recording errors found during inspection meetings. He will categorize the errors

345

Figure 7A Error list

1. PR/M/MIN   Line 3:   the statement of the prologue in the REMARKS section needs expansion.
2. DA/W/MAJ   Line 123:   ERR – RECORD – TYPE is out of sequence.
3. PU/W/MAJ   Line 147:   the wrong bytes of an 8-byte field (current – data) are moved into the 2-byte field (this year).
4. LO/W/MAJ   Line 169:   while counting the number of leading spaces in NAME, the wrong variable (1) is used to calculate "J".
5. LO/W/MAJ   Line 172:   NAME – CHECK is PERFORMED one time too few.
6. PU/E/MIN   Line 175:   In NAME – CHECK, the check for SPACE is redundant.
7. DE/W/MIN   Line 175:   the design should allow for the occurrence of a period in a last name.

Figure 7B Example of module detail report

DATE_____

CODE INSPECTION REPORT

MODULE DETAIL

MOD/MAC ____CHECKER_____ SUBCOMPONENT/APPLICATION_____

SEE NOTE BELOW

PROBLEM TYPE	MAJOR*			MINOR		
	M	W	E	M	W	E
LO LOGIC		9			1	
TB TEST AND BRANCH						
EL EXTERNAL LINKAGES						
RU REGISTER USAGE						
SU STORAGE USAGE						
DA DATA AREA USAGE		2				
PU PROGRAM LANGUAGE		2				1
PE PERFORMANCE						
MN MAINTAINABILITY					1	
DE DESIGN ERROR					1	
PR PROLOGUE				1		
CC CODE COMMENTS						
OT OTHER						
TOTAL	13			5		

REINSPECTION REQUIRED? ___Y_____

*A PROBLEM WHICH WOULD CAUSE THE PROGRAM TO MALFUNCTION A BUG M = MISSING, W = WRONG, E = EXTRA
NOTE   FOR MODIFIED MODULES, PROBLEMS IN THE CHANGED PORTION VERSUS PROBLEMS IN THE BASE SHOULD BE SHOWN IN THIS MANNER 3/(2) WHERE 3
        IS THE NUMBER OF PROBLEMS IN THE CHANGED PORTION AND 2 IS THE NUMBER OF PROBLEMS IN THE BASE

and then transcribe counts of the errors, by type, to the module detail form. By maintaining cumulative totals of the counts by error type, and dividing by the number of projected executable source lines of code inspected to date, he will be able to establish installation averages within a short time.

Figures 7A, 7B, and 7C are an example of a set of code inspection reports. Figure 7A is a partial list of errors found in code inspection. Notice that errors are described in detail and are classified by error type, whether due to something being missing,

346

Figure 7C Example of code inspection summary report

CODE INSPECTION REPORT
SUMMARY
Date___11 20 -___

To: Design Manager_____KRAUSS_____Development Manager___GIOTTI___
Subject: Inspection Report for_____CHECKER_____Inspection date___11 19 -___
System/Application_____Release_____Build_____
Component_____Subcomponents(s)_____

Mod/Mac Name	New or Mod	Full or Part Insp	Programmer	Tester	ELOC Added, Modified, Deleted										Inspection People-hours (X.X)				Sub-component
					Pre-insp			Est Post			Rework			Prep	Insp Meetg	Re-work	Follow-up	
					A	M	D	A	M	D	A	M	D						
	N		McGINLEY	HALE	348			400			50			9.0	8.8	8.0	1.5	
				Totals														

Reinspection required?___YES___ Length of inspection (clock hours and tenths)___2.2___
Reinspection by (date)___11/25/-___ Additional modules/macros?___NO___
DCR #'s written___C-2___
Problem summary: Major___13___ Minor___5___ Total___18___
Errors in changed code Major_____Minor_____Errors in base code: Major_____Minor_____

___LARSON___   ___McGINLEY___   ___HALE___
Initial Desr   Detailed Dr   Programmer   Team Leader   Other   Moderator's Signature

---

wrong, or extra as the cause, and according to major or minor severity. Figure 7B is a module level summary of the errors contained in the entire error list represented by Figure 7A. The code inspection summary report in Figure 7C is a summary of inspection results obtained on all modules inspected in a particular inspection session or in a subcomponent or application.

inspections and languages

Inspections have been successfully applied to designs that are specified in English prose, flowcharts, HIPO, (Hierarchy plus Input-Process-Output) and PIDGEON (an English prose-like meta language).

The first code inspections were conducted on PL/S and Assembler. Now, prompting checklists for inspections of Assembler, COBOL, FORTRAN, and PL/1 code are available.[7]

personnel considerations

One of the most significant benefits of inspections is the detailed feedback of results on a relatively real-time basis. The programmer finds out what error types he is most prone to make and their quantity and how to find them. This feedback takes place within a few days of writing the program. Because he gets early indications from the first few units of his work inspected, he is able to show improvement, and usually does, on later work even during the same project. In this way, feedback of results from inspections must be counted for the programmer's use and benefit: *they should not under any circumstances be used for programmer performance appraisal.*

Skeptics may argue that once inspection results are obtained, they will or even must count in performance appraisals, or at

Figure 8 Example of most error-prone modules based on I_1 and I_2

Module name	Number of errors	Lines of code	Error density, Errors/K. Loc
Echo	4	128	31
Zulu	10	323	31
Foxtrot	3	71	28
Alpha	7	264	27 ←Average
Lima	2	106	19 Error
Delta	3	195	15 Rate
.	.	.	.
.	.	.	.
	67		

least cause strong bias in the appraisal process. The author can offer in response that inspections have been conducted over the past three years involving diverse projects and locations, hundreds of experienced programmers and tens of managers, and so far he has found no case in which inspection results have been used negatively against programmers. Evidently no manager has tried to "kill the goose that lays the golden eggs."

A preinspection opinion of some programmers is that they do not see the value of inspections because they have managed very well up to now, or because their projects are too small or somehow different. This opinion usually changes after a few inspections to a position of acceptance. The quality of acceptance is related to the success of the inspections they have experienced, the *conduct of the trained moderator*, and the *attitude demonstrated by management*. The acceptance of inspections by programmers and managers as a beneficial step in making programs is well-established amongst those who have tried them.

Process control using inspection and testing results

Obviously, the range of analysis possible using inspection results is enormous. Therefore, only a few aspects will be treated here, and they are elementary expositions.

most error-prone modules

A listing of either I_1, I_2, or combined $I_1 + I_2$ data as in Figure 8 immediately highlights which modules contained the highest error density on inspection. If the error detection efficiency of each of the inspections was fairly constant, the ranking of error-prone modules holds. Thus if the error detection efficiency of inspection is 50 percent, and the inspection found 10 errors in a

Figure 9   Example of distribution of error types

	Number of errors	%	Normal/usual distribution, %
Logic	23	35	44
Interconnection/Linkage (Internal)	21	31 ?	18
Control Blocks	6	9	13
—	·	8	10
—	·	7	7
—	·	6	6
—	·	4	2
		100%	100%

module, then it can be estimated that there are 10 errors remaining in the module. This information can prompt many actions to control the process. For instance, in Figure 8, it may be decided to reinspect module "Echo" or to redesign and recode it entirely. Or, less drastically, it may be decided to test it "harder" than other modules and look especially for errors of the type found in the inspections.

If a ranked distribution of error types is obtained for a group of "error-prone modules" (Figure 9), which were produced from the same Process A, for example, it is a short step to comparing this distribution with a "Normal/Usual Percentage Distribution." Large disparities between the sample and "standard" will lead to questions on why Process A, say, yields nearly twice as many internal interconnection errors as the "standard" process. If this analysis is done promptly on the first five percent of production, it may be possible to remedy the problem (if it is a problem) on the remaining 95 percent of modules for a particular shipment. Provision can be made to test the first five percent of the modules to remove the unusually high incidence of internal interconnection problems.

distribution of error types

Analysis of the testing results, commencing as soon as testing errors are evident, is a vital step in controlling the process since future testing can be guided by early results.

inspecting error-prone code

Where testing reveals excessively error-prone code, it may be more economical and saving of schedule to select the most error-prone code and inspect it before continuing testing. (The business case will likely differ from project to project and case to case, but in many instances inspection will be indicated). The selection of the most error-prone code may be made with two considerations uppermost:

349

Table 4. Inspection and walk-through processes and objectives

Inspection		Walk-through	
Process Operations	*Objectives*	*Process Operations*	*Objectives*
1. Overview	Education (Group)	—	—
2. Preparation	Education (Individual)	1. Preparation	Education (Individual)
3. Inspection	Find errors! (Group)	2. Walk-through	Education (Group) Discuss design alternatives Find errors
4. Rework	Fix problems	—	
5. Follow-up	Ensure all fixes correctly installed	—	

Note the separation of objectives in the inspection process.

Table 5 Comparison of key properties of inspections and walk-throughs

Properties	*Inspection*	*Walk-Through*
1. Formal moderator training	Yes	No
2. Definite participant roles	Yes	No
3. Who "drives" the inspection or walk-through	Moderator	Owner of material (Designer or coder)
4. Use "How To Find Errors" checklists	Yes	No
5. Use distribution of error types to look for	Yes	No
6. Follow-up to reduce bad fixes	Yes	No
7. Less future errors because of detailed error feedback to individual programmer	Yes	Incidental
8. Improve inspection efficiency from analysis of results	Yes	No
9. Analysis of data → process problems → improvements	Yes	No

1. Which modules head a ranked list when the modules are rated by test errors per K.NCSS?
2. In the parts of the program in which test coverage is low, which modules or parts of modules are most suspect based on $(I_1 + I_2)$ errors per K.NCSS and programmer judgment?

From a condensed table of ranked "most error-prone" modules, a selection of modules to be inspected (or reinspected) may be made. Knowledge of the error types already found in these modules will better prepare an inspection team.

The reinspection itself should conform with the I_2 process, except that an overview may be necessary if the original overview was held too long ago or if new project members are involved.

Inspections and walk-throughs

Walk-throughs (or walk-thrus) are practiced in many different ways in different places, with varying regularity and thoroughness. This inconsistency causes the results of walk-throughs to vary widely and to be nonrepeatable. Inspections, however, having an established process and a formal procedure, tend to vary less and produce more repeatable results. Because of the variation in walk-throughs, a comparison between them and inspections is not simple. However, from Reference 8 and the walk-through procedures witnessed by the author and described to him by walk-through participants, as well as the inspection process described previously and in References 1 and 9, the comparison in Tables 4 and 5 is drawn.

Figure 10A describes the process in which a walk-through is applied. Clearly, the purging of errors from the product as it passes through the walk-through between Operations 1 and 2 is very beneficial to the product. In Figure 10B, the inspection process (and its feedback, feed-forward, and self-improvement) replaces the walk-through. The notes on the figure are self-explanatory.

effects on development process

Inspections are also an excellent means of measuring completeness of work against the exit criteria which must be satisfied to complete project checkpoints. (Each checkpoint should have a clearly defined set of exit criteria. Without exit criteria, a checkpoint is too negotiable to be useful for process control).

Inspections and process management

The most marked effects of inspections on the development process is to change the old adage that, "design is not complete until testing is completed," to a position where a very great deal must be known about the design before even the coding is begun. Although great discretion is still required in code implementation, more predictability and improvements in schedule, cost, and quality accrue. The old adage still holds true if one regards inspection as much a means of verification as testing.

Observations in one case in systems programming show that approximately two thirds of all errors reported during development are found by I_1 and I_2 inspections prior to machine testing.

percent of errors found

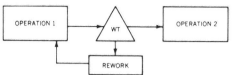

Figure 10 (A) Walk-through process, (B) Inspection process

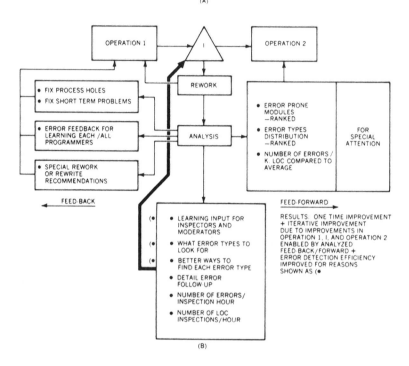

RESULT: ONE-TIME IMPROVEMENT DUE TO ERROR REMOVAL IN PROPORTION TO ERROR DETECTION EFFICIENCY OF WALK-THROUGH

(A)

(B)

The error detection efficiencies of the I_1 and I_2 inspections separately are, of course, less than 66 percent. A similar observation of an application program development indicated an 82 percent find (Table 1). As more is learned and the error detection efficiency of inspection is increased, the burden of debugging on testing operations will be reduced, and testing will be more able to fulfill its prime objective of verifying quality.

effect on cost and schedule
Comparing the "old" and "new" (with inspections) approaches to process management in Figure 11, we can see clearly that with the use of inspection results, error rework (which is a very significant variable in product cost) tends to be managed more during the first half of the schedule. This results in much lower cost than in the "old" approach, where the cost of error rework was 10 to 100 times higher and was accomplished in large part during the last half of the schedule.

process tracking
Inserting the I_1 and I_2 checkpoints in the development process enables assessment of project completeness and quality to be

Figure 11 Effect of inspection on process management

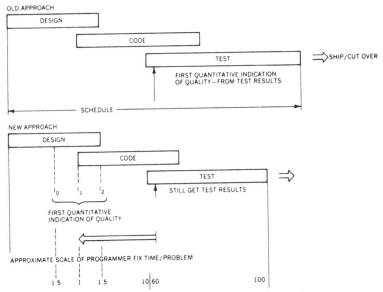

- POINT OF MANAGEMENT CONTROL OVER QUALITY IS MOVED UP MUCH EARLIER IN SCHEDULE.
- ERROR REWORK AT THIS LEVEL IS 1/10 AS EXPENSIVE.

made early in the process (during the first half of the project instead of the latter half of the schedule, when recovery may be impossible without adjustments in schedule and cost). Since individually trackable modules of reasonably well-known size can be counted as they pass through each of these checkpoints, the percentage completion of the project against schedule can be continuously and easily tracked.

effect on product knowledge

The overview, preparation, and inspection sequence of the operations of the inspection process give the inspection participants a high degree of product knowledge in a very short time. This important side benefit results in the participants being able to handle later development and testing with more certainty and less false starts. Naturally, this also contributes to productivity improvement.

An interesting sidelight is that because designers are asked at pre-I_1 inspection time for estimates of the number of lines of code (NCSS) that their designs will create, and they are present to count for themselves the actual lines of code at the I_2 inspection, the accuracy of design estimates has shown substantial improvement.

For this reason, an inspection is frequently a required event where responsibility for design or code is being transferred from one programmer to another. The complete inspection team is convened for such an inspection. (One-on-one reviews such as desk debugging are certainly worthwhile but do not approach the effectiveness of formal inspection.) Usually the side benefit of finding errors more than justifies the transfer inspection.

inspecting modified code Code that is changed in, or inserted in, an existing module either in replacement of deleted code or simply inserted in the module is considered modified code. By this definition, a very large part of programming effort is devoted to modifying code. (The addition of entirely new modules to a system count as new, not modified, code.)

Some observations of errors per K.NCSS of modified code show its error rate to be considerably higher than is found in new code; (i.e., if 10.NCSS are replaced in a 100.NCSS module and errors against the 10.NCSS are counted, the error rate is described as number of errors per 10.NCSS, not number of errors per 100.NCSS). Obviously, if the number of errors in modified code are used to derive an error rate per K.NCSS for the whole module that was modified, this rate would be largely dependent upon the percentage of the module that is modified: this would provide a meaningless ratio. A useful measure is the number of errors per K.NCSS (modified) in which the higher error rates have been observed.

Since most modifications are small (e.g., 1 to 25 instructions), they are often erroneously regarded as trivially simple and are handled accordingly; the error rate goes up, and control is lost. In the author's experience, *all* modifications are well worth inspecting from an economic and a quality standpoint. A convenient method of handling changes is to group them to a module or set of modules and convene the inspection team to inspect as many changes as possible. But all changes must be inspected!

Inspections of modifications can range from inspecting the modified instructions and the surrounding instructions connecting it with its host module, to an inspection of the entire module. The choice of extent of inspection coverage is dependent upon the percentage of modification, pervasiveness of the modification, etc.

bad fixes A very serious problem is the inclusion in the product of bad fixes. Human tendency is to consider the "fix," or correction, to a problem to be error-free itself. Unfortunately, this is all too frequently untrue in the case of fixes to errors found by inspections and by testing. The inspection process clearly has an operation called Follow-Up to try and minimize the bad-fix problem, but the fix process of testing errors very rarely requires scrutiny of fix quality before the fix is inserted. Then, if the fix is bad, the whole elaborate process of going from source fix to link edit, to test the fix, to regression test must be repeated at needlessly high cost. The number of bad fixes can be economically reduced by some simple inspection after clean compilation of the fix.

Summary

We can summarize the discussion of design and code inspections and process control in developing programs as follows:

1. Describe the program development process in terms of operations, and define exit criteria which must be satisfied for completion of each operation.
2. Separate the objectives of the inspection process operations to keep the inspection team focused on one objective at a time.:

Operation	Objective
Overview	Communications/education
Preparation	Education
Inspection	Find errors
Rework	Fix errors
Follow-up	Ensure all fixes are applied correctly

3. Classify errors by type, and rank frequency of occurrence of types. Identify *which types* to spend most time looking for in the inspection.
4. Describe *how* to look for presence of error types.
5. Analyze inspection results and use for constant process improvement (until process averages are reached and then use for process control).

Some applications of inspections include function level inspections I_0, design-complete inspections I_1, code inspections I_2, test plan inspections IT_1, test case inspections IT_2, interconnections inspections IF, inspection of fixes/changes, inspection of publications, etc., and post testing inspection. Inspections can be applied to the development of system control programs, applications programs, and microcode in hardware.

We can conclude from experience that inspections increase productivity and improve final program quality. Furthermore, improvements in process control and project management are enabled by inspections.

ACKNOWLEDGMENTS
The author acknowledges, with thanks, the work of Mr. O. R. Kohli and Mr. R. A. Radice, who made considerable contributions in the development of inspection techniques applied to program design and code, and Mr. R. R. Larson, who adapted inspections to program testing.

Figure 12   Design inspection module detail form

DATE _____

DETAILED DESIGN INSPECTION REPORT

MODULE DETAIL

MOD/MAC _____ SUBCOMPONENT/APPLICATION _____

SEE NOTE BELOW

PROBLEM TYPE:	MAJOR*			MINOR		
	M	W	E	M	W	E
LO: LOGIC						
TB: TEST AND BRANCH						
DA: DATA AREA USAGE						
RM: RETURN CODES/MESSAGES						
RU: REGISTER USAGE						
MA: MODULE ATTRIBUTES						
EL: EXTERNAL LINKAGES						
MD: MORE DETAIL						
ST: STANDARDS						
PR: PROLOGUE OR PROSE						
HL: HIGHER LEVEL DESIGN DOC						
US: USER SPEC						
MN: MAINTAINABILITY						
PE: PERFORMANCE						
OT: OTHER						
TOTAL						

REINSPECTION REQUIRED? _____

*A PROBLEM WHICH WOULD CAUSE THE PROGRAM TO MALFUNCTION A BUG. M = MISSING, W = WRONG, E = EXTRA
NOTE: FOR MODIFIED MODULES, PROBLEMS IN THE CHANGED PORTION VERSUS PROBLEMS IN THE BASE SHOULD BE SHOWN IN THIS MANNER: 3(2) WHERE 3
IS THE NUMBER OF PROBLEMS IN THE CHANGED PORTION AND 2 IS THE NUMBER OF PROBLEMS IN THE BASE.

CITED REFERENCES AND FOOTNOTES

1. O. R. Kohli, *High-Level Design Inspection Specification*, Technical Report TR 21.601, IBM Corporation, Kingston, New York (July 21, 1975).
2. It should be noted that the exit criteria for I_1 (design complete where one design statement is estimated to represent 3 to 10 code instructions) and I_2 (first clean code compilations) are checkpoints in the development process through which every programming project must pass.
3. The Hawthorne Effect is a psychological phenomenon usually experienced in human-involved productivity studies. The effect is manifested by participants producing above normal because they know they are being studied.
4. NCSS (Non-Commentary Source Statements), also referred to as "Lines of Code," are the sum of executable code instructions and declaratives. Instructions that invoke macros are counted once only. Expanded macroinstructions are also counted only once. Comments are not included.
5. Basically in a walk-through, program design or code is reviewed by a group of people gathered together at a structured meeting in which errors/issues pertaining to the material and proposed by the participants may be discussed in an effort to find errors. The group may consist of various participants but always includes the originator of the material being reviewed who usually plans the meeting and is responsible for correcting the errors. How it differs from an inspection is pointed out in Tables 2 and 3.
6. *Marketing Newsletter*, Cross Application Systems Marketing, "Program inspections at Aetna," MS-76-006, S2, IBM Corporation, Data Processing Division, White Plains, New York (March 29, 1976).

7. J. Ascoly, M. J. Cafferty, S. J. Gruen, and O. R. Kohli, *Code Inspection Specification*, Technical Report TR 21.630, IBM Corporation, Kingston, New York (1976).

8. N. S. Waldstein, *The Walk-Thru—A Method of Specification, Design and Review*, Technical Report TR 00.2536, IBM Corporation, Poughkeepsie, New York (June 4, 1974).

9. Independent study programs: *IBM Structured Programming Textbook*, SR20-7149-1, *IBM Structured Programming Workbook*, SR20-7150-0, IBM Corporation, Data Processing Division, White Plains, New York.

GENERAL REFERENCES

1. J. D. Aron, *The Program Development Process: Part 1: The Individual Programmer*, Structured Programs, 137–141, Addison-Wesley Publishing Co., Reading, Massachusetts (1974).

2. M. E. Fagan, *Design and Code Inspections and Process Control in the Development of Programs*, Technical Report TR 00.2763, IBM Corporation, Poughkeepsie, New York (June 10, 1976). This report is a revision of the author's *Design and Code Inspections and Process Control in the Development of Programs*, Technical Report TR 21.572, IBM Corporation, Kingston, New York (December 17, 1974).

3. O. R. Kohli and R. A. Radice, *Low-Level Design Inspection Specification*, Technical Report TR 21.629, IBM Corporation, Kingston, New York (1976).

4. R. R. Larson, *Test Plan and Test Case Inspection Specifications*, Technical Report TR 21.586, IBM Corporation, Kingston, New York (April 4, 1975).

Appendix: Reporting forms and form completion instructions

Instructions for Completing Design Inspection Module Detail Form

This form (Figure 12) should be completed for each module/macro that has valid problems against it. The problem-type information gathered in this report is important because a history of problem-type experience points out high-occurrence types. This knowledge can then be conveyed to inspectors so that they can concentrate on seeking the higher-occurrence types of problems.

1. MOD/MAC: The module or macro name.
2. SUBCOMPONENT: The associated subcomponent.
3. PROBLEM TYPE: Summarize the number of problems by type (logic, etc.), severity (major/minor), and by category (missing, wrong, or extra). For modified modules, detail the number of problems in the changed design versus the number in the base design. (Problem types were developed in a systems programming environment. Appropriate changes, if desired, could be made for application development.)

Figure 13   Design inspection summary form

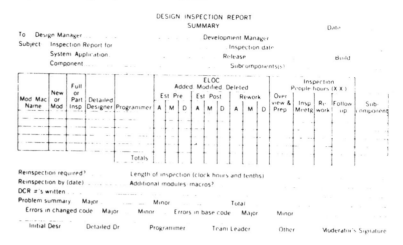

4. REINSPECTION REQUIRED?: Indicate whether the module/
   macro requires a reinspection.

All valid problems found in the inspection should be listed and
attached to the report. A brief description of each problem, its
error type, and the rework time to fix it should be given (see
Figure 7A, which describes errors in similar detail to that required but is at a coding level).

Instructions for Completing Design Inspection Summary Form

Following are detailed instructions for completing the form in
Figure 13.

1. TO: The report is addressed to the respective design and
   development managers.
2. SUBJECT: The unit being inspected is identified.
3. MOD/MAC NAME: The name of each module and macro as it
   resides on the source library.
4. NEW OR MOD: "N" if the module is new; "M" if the module
   is modified.
5. FULL OR PART INSP: If the module/macro is "modified,"
   indicate "F" if the module/macro was fully inspected or "P"
   if partially inspected.
6. DETAILED DESIGNER: and PROGRAMMER: Identification of
   originators.
7. PRE-INSP EST ELOC: The estimated executable source lines
   of code (added, modified, deleted). Estimate made prior to
   the inspection by the designer.

Figure 14   Code inspection module detail form

DATE_____

CODE INSPECTION REPORT

MODULE DETAIL

MOD/MAC _____   SUBCOMPONENT/APPLICATION _____

SEE NOTE BELOW

PROBLEM TYPE	MAJOR*			MINOR		
	M	W	E	M	W	E
LO: LOGIC						
TB: TEST AND BRANCH						
EL: EXTERNAL LINKAGES						
RU: REGISTER USAGE						
SU: STORAGE USAGE						
DA: DATA AREA USAGE						
PU: PROGRAM LANGUAGE						
PE: PERFORMANCE						
MN: MAINTAINABILITY						
DE: DESIGN ERROR						
PR: PROLOGUE						
CC: CODE COMMENTS						
OT: OTHER						
TOTAL:						

REINSPECTION REQUIRED? _____

*A PROBLEM WHICH WOULD CAUSE THE PROGRAM TO MALFUNCTION. A BUG M = MISSING, W = WRONG, E = EXTRA
NOTE   FOR MODIFIED MODULES PROBLEMS IN THE CHANGED PORTION VERSUS PROBLEMS IN THE BASE SHOULD BE SHOWN IN THIS MANNER 3(2), WHERE 3
        IS THE NUMBER OF PROBLEMS IN THE CHANGED PORTION AND 2 IS THE NUMBER OF PROBLEMS IN THE BASE

8. POST-INSP EST ELOC: The estimated executable source lines of code. Estimate made after the inspection.

9. REWORK ELOC: The estimated executable source lines of code in rework as a result of the inspection.

10. OVERVIEW AND PREP: The number of people-hours (in tenths of hours) spent in preparing for the overview, in the overview meeting itself, and in preparing for the inspection meeting.

11. INSPECTION MEETING: The number of people-hours spent on the inspection meeting.

12. REWORK: The estimated number of people-hours spent to fix the problems found during the inspection.

13. FOLLOW-UP: The estimated number of people-hours spent by the moderator (and others if necessary) in verifying the correctness of changes made by the author as a result of the inspection.

14. SUBCOMPONENT: The subcomponent of which the module/macro is a part.

15. REINSPECTION REQUIRED?: Yes or no.

16. LENGTH OF INSPECTION: Clock hours spent in the inspection meeting.

17. REINSPECTION BY (DATE): Latest acceptable date for reinspection.

Figure 15 Code inspection summary form

CODE INSPECTION REPORT
SUMMARY   Date

To   Design Manager   Development Manager
Subject   Inspection Report for   Inspection date
           System Application   Release   Build
           Component   Subcomponents(s)

Mod Mac Name	New or Mod	Full or Part Insp	Programmer	Tester	ELOC Added Modified Deleted									Inspection People hours (X X)				Sub component
					Pre-insp			Est Post			Rework			Prep	Insp Meetg	Re work	Follow up	
					A	M	D	A	M	D	A	M	D					
				Totals														

Reinspection required?   Length of inspection (clock hours and tenths)
Reinspection by (date)   Additional modules macros?
DCR = s written
Problem summary   Major   Minor   Total
  Errors in changed code Major   Minor   Errors in base code   Major   Minor

Initial Desr   Detailed Dr   Programmer   Team Leader   Other   Moderators Signature

18. ADDITIONAL MODULES/MACROS?: For these subcomponents, are additional modules/macros yet to be inspected?

19. DCR #'S WRITTEN: The identification of Design Change Requests, DCR(s), written to cover problems in rework.

20. PROBLEM SUMMARY: Totals taken from Module Detail forms(s).

21. INITIAL DESIGNER. DETAILED DESIGNER, etc.: Identification of members of the inspection team.

Instructions for Completing Code Inspection Module Detail Form

This form (Figure 14) should be completed according to the instructions for completing the design inspection module detail form.

Instructions for Completing Code Inspection Summary Form

This form (Figure 15) should be completed according to the instructions for the design inspection summary form except for the following items.

1. PROGRAMMER AND TESTER: Identifications of original participants involved with code.

2. PRE-INSP. ELOC: The noncommentary source lines of code (added, modified, deleted). Count made prior to the inspection by the programmer.

3. POST-INSP EST ELOC: The estimated noncommentary source lines of code. Estimate made after the inspection.

4. REWORK ELOC: The estimated noncommentary source lines of code in rework as a result of the inspection.

5. PREP: The number of people hours (in tenths of hours) spent in preparing for the inspection meeting.

Reprint Order No. G321-5033.

How Do I Know I'm
in Trouble: A Review Checklist

November 1, 1985

Prepared By:

Donald J. Reifer

Prepared For:

Texas Instruments, Inc.
Lewisville, Texas 75067
Purchase Order #W1853969

Acknowledgment

The author acknowledges that he built upon work he accomplished while affiliated with the Aerospace Corporation to prepare this checklist[1]. He acknowledges Mr. Richard Marshall's contributions to this previous work. He also acknowledges the valuable inputs given by Ms. P. Moore and the rest of the RCI and Texas Instrument's review team.

Purpose

The purpose of this guide is to provide the reader with a set of checklists for use at the five major software reviews illustrated in Figure 1. Each of these reviews is held at a strategic point during the software product development cycle. Each of these reviews is held primarily to assess risk and determine whether or not the project should move into the next phase of development. Such reviews provide management with the opportunity to accomplish the following:

- Ensure that the developers have not misinterpreted or misunderstood the customer's requirements as scoped by contractual specifications.

[1]D.J. Reifer, "The Software Engineering Checklist," *Proceedings AIAA Computers in Aerospace Conference*, 1977.

- Identify major problems (both technical and managerial) and direct the developer to take action to correct them before they get out of control.

- Provide technical direction and manage the timely delivery of quality software products.

- Close out the project by obtaining formal approval and acceptance of the final product and its accompanying documentation.

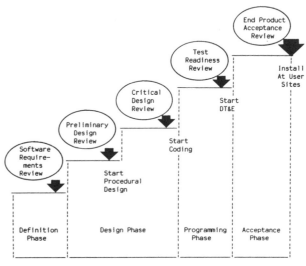

Figure 1: Major Life Cycle Reviews

For those interested in a look at the software product life cycle and its associated work activities, we refer you to our report entitled "What Software People Do: A Work Breakdown Structure (RCI-TR-013)".

Scope

The review checklists contained within this guide are applicable to medium to large scale software projects (over 10,000 lines and 10 people). They are responsive to current Department of Defense regulations and represent what many in industry feel are good practices. They are generic in nature and can be tailored for use on most projects. RCI believes they can be utilized profitably on most any type of application to identify risks that impede the successful delivery of an acceptable software product on-time and within budget.

The checklists contained within this guide are intended for use by management. Their primary purpose is to identify risk. They are not intended to be used to determine whether or not the product is technically correct. Instead, they should be used to identify problems so that management can direct actions to overcome them.

Review Checklists

How do I know I'm in trouble checklists for the following five major software product life cycle reviews are provided as subsequent charts:

- *Software Requirements Review* — held to assess the risks associated with plans and requirements.

- *Preliminary Design Review* — held to assess the risks associated with design and test approaches.

- *Critical Design Review* — held to assess the risks associated with committing to code.

- *Test Readiness Review* — held to assess the risks associated with starting software development test and evaluation (DT&E).

- *End-Product Acceptance Review* — held to certify that the software end-items have been produced, delivered and meet the specified acceptance criteria.

Checklists are provided in question and answer form. If the answer to the question posed is "yes", then place a check in the corresponding box. After you complete each checklist, review those items with no check to determine what action, if any, is needed to remedy the situation. Risk determination is judgmental, so use common sense when you decide which of your problems requires action.

Software Requirements Review

[ ] Have the following documents been provided in an acceptable form:
    [ ] Software Development Plan?
    [ ] Software Configuration Management Plan?
    [ ] Software Quality Assurance Plan?
    [ ] Software Requirements Specification(s)?
    [ ] Draft User's Manual?
    [ ] Draft Acceptance Test Plan?

[ ] Have the issues associated with the timely delivery of software been factored into the following analyses:
    [ ] Functional Analysis?
    [ ] Logistics Support?
    [ ] Reliability Engineering?
    [ ] Systems Safety?
    [ ] Life Cycle Cost?
    [ ] Security?

[ ] Have the system engineering activities resulting in the allocation of functions to hardware, firmware and software been reviewed for technical and economic feasibility? Do they make sense?

[ ] Are the Software Requirements Specifications complete, consistent, feasible, testable and traceable?

[ ] Do the Software Requirements Specifications identify functional, performance, interface and test requirements and are these requirements presented in an understandable way?

[ ] Have the trade-off and design studies that have applicability for decisions relating to the following been completed and reviewed:
    [ ] Computer instruction set selection?
    [ ] Programming language selection?
    [ ] Sizing and timing budget establishment?
    [ ] Design methods and tool selection?
    [ ] Programming standards and conventions establishment?
    [ ] Data base design (conceptual)?

[ ] Have all computer programs required by the project been identified and are their development schedules compatible?

[ ] Have the management methods and controls to be used during design and development been identified?

[ ] Are schedules for the development of all computer programs (deliverable and non-deliverable) and the procedures for monitoring and reporting their status sufficiently detailed?

[ ] Are milestones verifiable and achievable?

[ ] Have technical performance measures been established for software?

[ ] Are personnel resources identified to include numbers, names, duration of assignment and required skills?

[ ] Are organizational responsibilities and interfaces workable?

[ ] Has a risk analysis been conducted to identify those factors that impact the chances of realizing cost, schedule and technical goals and has a risk management plan been formulated to deal with them?

[ ] Has a procedure for monitoring and reporting sizing and timing data and data base storage requirements been approved?

[ ] Is the quality assurance organizations structured to have an independent reporting relationship outside of the development group?

[ ] Are all four functions of configuration management adequately addressed in the development plans (i.e., configuration identification, change control, status accounting and configuration audit)?

Preliminary Design Review

[ ] Have the following documents been provided in an acceptable form:
    [ ] Baselined Software Requirements Specification(s)?
    [ ] Software Design Architectural Specification?
    [ ] Software Integration & Test Plan?
    [ ] Software Development Test & Evaluation Plan?
    [ ] Updated Software Development Plan?
    [ ] Software Practices & Procedures Manual?
    [ ] Data Dictionary Document (Optional)?

[ ] Have the following analyses been performed in conjunction with the top-level architectural design:
    [ ] Partitioning Analysis (Modularity)?
    [ ] Executive Control and Start/Recovery?
    [ ] Data Flow Analysis?
    [ ] Control Flow Analysis?

[ ] Have storage allocation charts been developed and allocated to each software component in the design architecture?

[ ] Are the engineering equations mature?

[ ] Have the results of prototyping been factored into the architectural design?

[ ] Have critical components been identified and has trial coding been scheduled for them?

[ ] Have the human engineering aspects of the design been treated and are solutions acceptable to the potential user?

[ ] Are the developmental tools and facility requirements identified and have plans been made and actions taken to insure their availability when needed?

[ ] Has an acceptable test & integration approach been formulated for software?

[ ] Are the test tools and facility requirements identified and have plans been made and actions taken to insure their availability when needed?

[ ] Has the test group participated in the requirements and design analysis?

[ ] Have security and supportability requirements been factored into the design?

[ ] Have plans, schedules and budgets been updated and has a cost-to-complete estimate been developed?

[ ] Has the risk analysis been updated and has an acceptable risk management plan been formulated?

[ ] Has progress been measured quantifiably and has the work-in-progress monitoring system been demonstrated as meeting expectations?

[ ] Have procedures and tools been developed for mechanizing management and configuration management plans?

[ ] Is a Configuration Control Board established for software and are change control procedures working?

[ ] Is the configuration management system understood by those who will have to use it?

[ ] Is a library established for storing, controlling and distributing software products and are the library procedures understood and working?

[ ] Has an independent software quality assurance group been formed and is it contributing as a team member to the design and test activities?

[ ] Are interdisciplinary teams working those design issues that cross system component boundaries (i.e., software, hardware, etc.)?

Critical Design Review

[ ] Have the following documents been provided in an acceptable form:
    [ ] Software Detailed Design Specification(s)?
    [ ] Unit Test Plan?
    [ ] Programmer's Notebook?
    [ ] Draft Program Maintenance Manual?
    [ ] Updated Test & Management Plans?
    [ ] Updated Specifications (Requirements & Design)?

[ ] Have the following analyses been performed in conjunction with the detailed design:
    [ ] Algorithm Accuracy?
    [ ] Critical Timing & Sequence Control?
    [ ] Dimensional Analysis?
    [ ] Singularity Analysis?
    [ ] Undesired Event Handling?

[ ] Have detailed timing and storage allocation statistics been compiled?

[ ] Are the algorithms sufficient to realize the requirements of the engineering equation formulation?

[ ] Has trial code been analyzed and designs modified accordingly?

[ ] Have peer reviews been held for each software unit and has the rework identified been accomplished?

[ ] If the software is being developed top-down, have units comprising each build been completed, reviewed and placed under change control?

[ ] Are the tools (both hardware and software) needed for software implementation completed, qualified, installed and accepted and has the team been trained in their use?

[ ] Are the facilities needed for software implementation in-place, operating and ready for use?

[ ] If a new compiler is to be used, has it been validated and does it produce acceptable object code for the target machine?

[ ] Have plans, schedules and budgets been updated and has a cost-to- complete estimate been developed?

[ ] Are staffing-up problems being addressed and are contingency plans in place to deal with the problems associated with getting people to do the job?

[ ] Has the risk analysis been updated and has an acceptable risk management plan been formulated?

[ ] Are the management procedures and tools developed for measuring and reporting progress working?

[ ] Are the procedures established for configuration management working and is product integrity being preserved?

[ ] Are the procedures established for software quality assurance working and is quality an integral part of the product being produced?

[ ] Is the test group up-to-speed and will they be ready to evaluate the code once it is produced using their facilities and tools?

[ ] Has everything possible been done to insure that if you commit to coding your risks will become manageable?

Test Readiness Review

[ ] Have the following documents been provided in an acceptable form:
   [ ] Baselined Software Requirements Specifications?
   [ ] Software Design Specification(s)?
   [ ] Unit Test Plan/Report?
   [ ] Software Integration & Test Plan/Report?
   [ ] Software Development Test & Evaluation Plan?
   [ ] User's Manual?
   [ ] Operation Manual?
   [ ] Draft Program Maintenance Manual?

[ ] Have the following evaluations been performed in conjunction with unit testing:
   [ ] Verification of computation using nominal data?
   [ ] Verification of computation using stress data?
   [ ] Verification of data output options and formats?
   [ ] Exercise of all executable statements in a unit at least once?

   [ ] Test of options at each branch point?
   [ ] Standards compliance confirmation?

[ ] Have the following evaluations been performed in conjunction with software integration and test:
   [ ] Verification of computation throughout the anticipated range of operating conditions including nominal, abnormal, failure and degraded mode situations?
   [ ] Verification of performance throughout the anticipated range of operating conditions including nominal, abnormal, failure and degraded mode situations?
   [ ] Verification of performance throughout the anticipated range of operating conditions as various strings of units are linked together and various modes are exercised?
   [ ] Verification of end-to-end functional flows and data base linkages?
   [ ] Exercise of all logic switching and executive control options at least once?

[ ] Are the facilities and tools needed for software development test and evaluation (DT&E) ready, qualified and available for operational use?

[ ] Are the test teams adequately staffed and does this staff have the prerequisite familiarity with the test facilities and operational software to do their job?

[ ] Have master schedules for software DT&E been established and are they reasonable based upon the results of unit and software integration testing?

[ ] Have the data bases to be used for software DT&E testing been created and validated?

[ ] Has a test case structure been established that identifies for each test:
   [ ] The software requirement(s) to be demonstrated?
   [ ] Required inputs?
   [ ] Facility and test tool requirements?
   [ ] Expected outputs and analysis methods?
   [ ] Major software entitles to be exercised by the test?

   ] Has a test network showing the interdependencies among test events and the planned time deviations for these activities been prepared?

[ ] Have user-defined scenarios been developed to test interactive or operator-oriented software?

End-Product Acceptance Review

[ ] Have the following deliverable documents been provided in a form that meets company standards and/or the requirements of the contract:
   [ ] Software Requirements Specification(s)?
   [ ] Software Design Specification(s)?
   [ ] Unit Test Plan/Report?
   [ ] Software Integration & Test Plan/Report?

[ ] Software Development Test & Evaluation Plan/Report?

[ ] User's Manual?

[ ] Operation Manual?

[ ] Program Maintenance Manual?

[ ] Configuration Index?

[ ] Version Description Document?

[ ] Project Post-Mortem Report?

[ ] Are all deliverable computer programs free of rework and/or liens and are they provided in the form and on the media required by company standards and the requirements of the contract?

[ ] Have all acceptance criteria been concurred with and has the instrument of acceptance been signed-off (DD250?)?

[ ] Has test data been provided to substantiate that the computer program being delivered is actually the computer program that was subjected to test?

[ ] Have all action items been closed out to the satisfaction of the customer?

[ ] Have all approved changes been incorporated and is the computer program and its documentation of the latest version?

[ ] Is the code patch-free?

[ ] Has the computer program been delivered with sufficient memory, speed and input/output capacity in reserve?

[ ] Has the computer program been installed on the target computer and does it execute and produce acceptable results?

[ ] Can representative users operate the computer program easily and with minimum coaching?

[ ] Is the documentation sufficient to allow the software maintenance organization to easily repair an/or modify the computer program?

[ ] Will we be embarrassed if we prematurely release this product?

References

1. DOD, *UDRSS Software Quality Assurance Plan*, 25 February 1981.

2. George Neil, *Software Acquisition Management Guidebook: Reviews And Audits*, ESD-TR-78-17, November 1977.

3. Donald Reifer, "The Software Engineering Checklist," *Proceedings Computers in Aerospace Conference*, 1977.

4. TRW, *Airborne Systems Software Acquisition Engineering Guidebook for Reviews And Audits*, Report No. 30323-6006-TU-OO, November 1977.

5. USAF, *Technical Reviews and Audits For Systems, Equipments and Computer Programs*, MIL-STD-1521A, 1 June 1976.

TRW-SS-76-11

THE UNIT DEVELOPMENT FOLDER (UDF): AN EFFECTIVE MANAGEMENT TOOL FOR SOFTWARE DEVELOPMENT

Prepared by
Frank S. Ingrassia

October 1976

DEFENSE AND SPACE SYSTEMS GROUP

SYSTEMS ENGINEERING AND INTEGRATION DIVISION

ONE SPACE PARK, REDONDO BEACH, CALIFORNIA 90278

ABSTRACT

This paper describes the content and application of the Unit Development Folder, a structured mechanism for organizing and collecting software development products (requirements, design, code, test plans/data) as they become available. Properly applied, the Unit Development Folder is an important part of an orderly development environment in which unit-level schedules and responsibilities are clearly delineated and their step-by-step accomplishment made visible to management. Unit Development Folders have been used on a number of projects at TRW and have been shown to reduce many of the problems associated with the development of software.

THE UNIT DEVELOPMENT FOLDER (UDF): AN EFFECTIVE MANAGEMENT TOOL FOR SOFTWARE DEVELOPMENT

One of the main side effects resulting from the invention of computers has been the creation of a new class of frustrated and harried managers responsible for software development. The frustration is a result of missed schedules, cost overruns, inadequate implementation and design, high operational error rates and poor maintainability, which have historically characterized software development. In the early days of computer programming, these problems were often excused by the novelty of this unique endeavor and obscured by the language and experience gap that frequently existed between developers and managers. Today's maturity and the succession of computer-wise people to management positions does not appear to have reduced the frustration level in the industry. We are still making the same mistakes and getting into the same predicaments. The science of managing software development is still in its infancy and the lack of a good clear set of principles is apparent.

The problems associated with developing software are too numerous and too complex for anyone to pretend to have solved them, and this paper makes no such pretensions. The discussion that follows describes a simple but effective management tool which, when properly used, can reduce the chaos and alleviate many of the problems common to software development. The tool described in this paper is called the Unit Development Folder (UDF) and is being used at TRW in software development and management.

What is a UDF? Simply stated, it is a specific form of development notebook which has proven useful and effective in collecting and organizing software products as they are produced. In essence, however, it is much more; it is a means of imposing a management philosophy and a development methodology on an activity that is often chaotic. In physical appearance, a UDF is merely a three-ring binder containing a cover sheet and is organized into several predefined sections which are common to each UDF. The ultimate objectives that the content and format of the UDF must satisfy are to:

(1) Provide an orderly and consistent approach in the development of each of the units of a program or project

(2) Provide a uniform and visible collection point for all unit documentation and code

(3) Aid individual discipline in the establishment and attainment of scheduled unit-level milestones

(4) Provide low-level management visibility and control over the development process

Figure 1 illustrates the role of the UDF in the total software development process.

If one follows a fairly standard design approach, the completion of the preliminary design activity marks the point at which UDFs are created and initiated for all units comprising the total product to be designed and coded. Therefore, the first question to be answered is, "What is a unit?" It was found that, for the purpose of implementing a practical and effective software development methodology to meet the management objectives stated earlier, a unique element of software architecture needed to be defined. This basic functional element is designated a "unit" of software and is defined independently of the language or type of application. Experience has indicated that it is unwise to attempt a simple-minded definition which will be useful and effective in all situations. What can be done is to bound the problem by means of some general considerations and delegate the specific implementation to management judgment for each particular application.

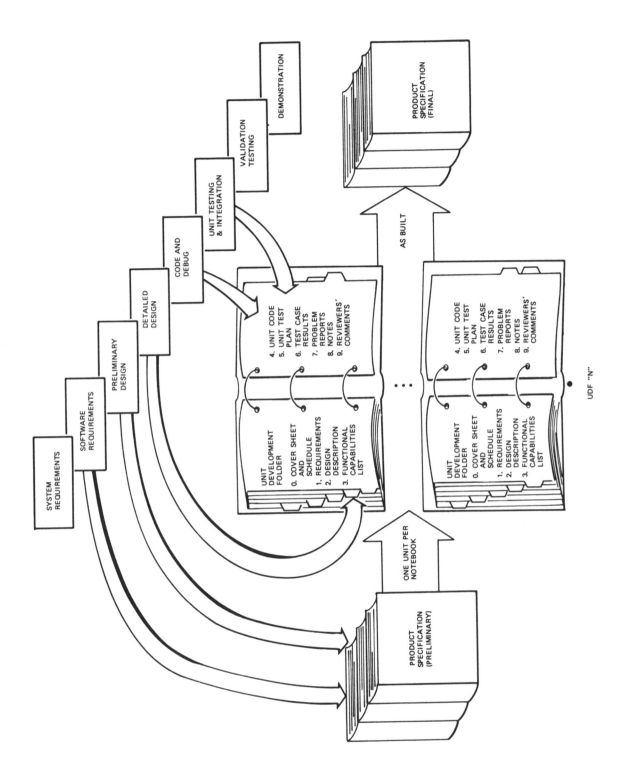

Figure 1. The UDF in the Development Process

At the lower end of the scale a "unit" can be defined to be a single routine or subroutine. At the upper end of the scale a "unit" may contain several routines comprising a subprogram or module. However it is defined, a unit of software should possess the following characteristics:

(1) It performs a specific defined function

(2) It is amenable to development by one person within the assigned schedule

(3) It is a level of software to which the satisfaction of requirements can be traced

(4) It is amenable to thorough testing in a disciplined environment.

The key word in the concept is manageability — in design, development, testing and comprehension.

A natural question that may arise at this point is, "Why should a unit contain more than one routine?" The assumption for this proviso is that the design and development standards impose both size and functional modularity. Since functional modularity can be defined at various levels, the concept can become meaningless if it is not accompanied by a reasonable restriction of size. Consequently, the maximum size constraint on routines may sometimes result in multiple-routine units.

The organization and content of a UDF can be adapted to reflect local conditions or individual project requirements. The important considerations in the structuring of a UDF are:

(1) The number of subdivisions is not so large as to be confusing or unmanageable

(2) Each of the sections contributes to the management and visibility of the development process

(3) The content and format of each section are adequately and unambiguously defined

(4) The subdivisions are sufficiently flexible to be applicable to a variety of software types

(5) The individual sections are chronologically ordered as nearly as possible.

The last item is very important since it is this aspect of the UDF that relates it to the development schedule and creates an auditable management instrument. An example of a typical cover sheet for a UDF is shown in Figure 2; the contents of each section will be briefly described in subsequent paragraphs.

The UDF is initiated when requirements are allocated to the unit level and at the onset of preliminary design. At this point it exists in the skeletal form of a binder with a cover sheet (indicating the unit name and responsible custodian) and a set of section separators. The first step in the process is for the responsible work area manager to integrate the development schedules and responsibilities for each of his UDFs into the overall schedule and milestones of the project. A due date is generated for the completion of each section and the responsibility for each section is assigned. The originators should participate in establishing their interim schedules within the constraints of the dictated end dates.

The organization and subdivisions of the UDF are such that the UDF can accommodate a variety of development plans and approaches; it can be used in a situation where one person has total responsibility, or in the extreme where specialists are assigned to the particular sections. However, in the one-man approach it is still desirable that certain sections, indicated in the following discussion, be assigned to other individuals to gain the benefits of unbiased reviews and assessments.

The development of the UDF is geared to proceed logically and sequentially, and each section should be as complete as possible before proceeding to the next section. This is not always possible, and software development is usually an iterative rather than a linear process. These situations only serve to reinforce the need for an ordered process that can be understood and tracked even under adverse conditions.

Once a specific outline and UDF cover sheet have been established, it is imperative that the format and content of each section be clearly and completely defined as part of the project/company standards to avoid ambiguity and maintain consistency in the products. The following discussion expands and describes the contents of the UDF typified by the cover sheet shown in Figure 2.

Section 0. COVER SHEET AND SCHEDULE

This section contains the cover sheet for the unit, which identifies the routines included in the UDF and which delineates, for each of the sections, the scheduled due dates, actual completion dates, assigned originators and provides space for reviewer sign-offs and dates. In the case of multiple-routine units, it may be advisable to include a one-page composite schedule illustrating the section schedules of each item for easy check-off and monitoring. Following each cover sheet, a UDF Change Log should be included to document all UDF changes subsequent to the time when the initial development is completed and the unit is put into a controlled test or maintenance environment. Figure 3 illustrates a typical UDF Change Log.

Section 1. REQUIREMENTS

This section identifies the baseline requirements specification and enumerates the requirements which are allocated for implementation in the specific unit of software. A mapping to the system requirements specification (by paragraph number) should be made and, where practical, the statement of each requirement should be given. Any assumptions, ambiguities, deferrals or conflicts concerning the requirements and their impact on the design and development of the unit should be stated, and any design problem reports or deviations or waivers against the requirements should be indicated. In addition, if a requirement is only partially satisfied by this unit it will be so noted along with the unit(s) which share the responsibility for satisfaction of the requirement.

Section 2. DESIGN DESCRIPTION

This section contains the current design description for each of the routines included in the UDF. For multiple routine units, tabbed subsection separators are used for handy

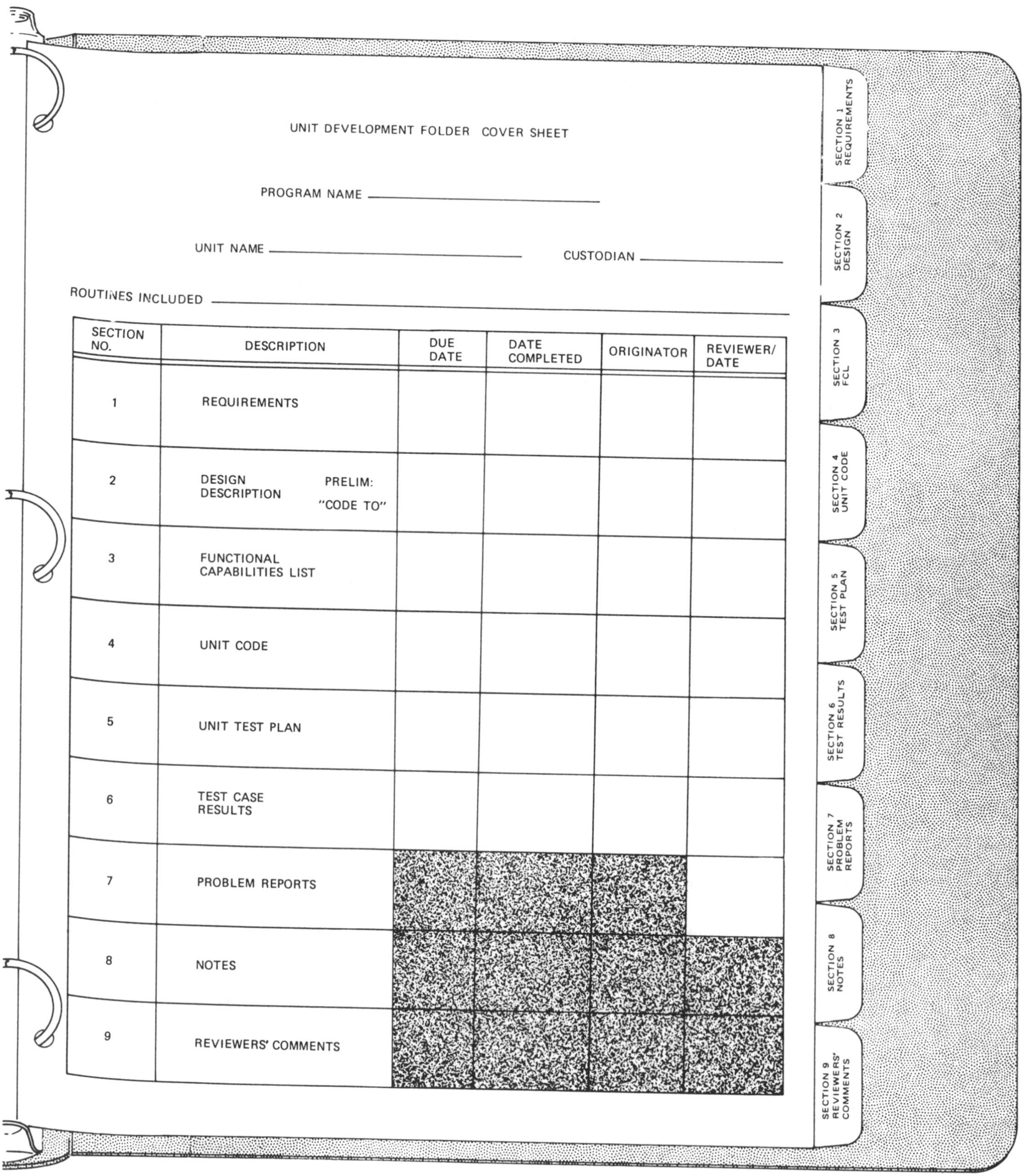

UNIT DEVELOPMENT FOLDER COVER SHEET

PROGRAM NAME _____

UNIT NAME _____   CUSTODIAN _____

ROUTINES INCLUDED _____

SECTION NO.	DESCRIPTION	DUE DATE	DATE COMPLETED	ORIGINATOR	REVIEWER/ DATE
1	REQUIREMENTS				
2	DESIGN DESCRIPTION PRELIM: "CODE TO"				
3	FUNCTIONAL CAPABILITIES LIST				
4	UNIT CODE				
5	UNIT TEST PLAN				
6	TEST CASE RESULTS				
7	PROBLEM REPORTS				
8	NOTES				
9	REVIEWERS' COMMENTS				

SECTION 1 REQUIREMENTS

SECTION 2 DESIGN

SECTION 3 FCL

SECTION 4 UNIT CODE

SECTION 5 TEST PLAN

SECTION 6 TEST RESULTS

SECTION 7 PROBLEM REPORTS

SECTION 8 NOTES

SECTION 9 REVIEWERS' COMMENTS

Figure 2. UDF Cover Sheet and Layout

UDF CHANGE LOG

UNIT NAME _____ VERSION _____ CUSTODIAN _____

DATE	DPR/DR Number	Section(s) Affected and Page Numbers	Retest Method	Mod No.

NOTE: This revision change log is to be used for all changes made in the UDF after internal baseline (i.e., subsequent to mod number assignment). It is inserted immediately after the coversheet.

Figure 3. Example of a UDF Change Log

indexing. A preliminary design description may be included if available; however, the end item for this section is detailed design documentation for the unit, suitable to become (part of) a "code to" specification. The format and content of this section should conform to established documentation standards and should be suitable for direct inclusion into the appropriate detailed design specification (Figure 1). Throughout the development process this section represents the current, working version of the design and, therefore, must be maintained and annotated as changes occur to the initial design. A flowchart is generally included as an inherent part of the design documentation. Flowcharts should be generated in accordance with clear established standards for content, format and symbol usage.

When the initial detailed design is completed and ready to be coded, a design walk-through may be held with one or more interested and knowledgeable co-workers. If such a walk-through is required, the completion of this section may be predicated on the successful completion of the design walk-through.

Section 3. FUNCTIONAL CAPABILITIES LIST

This section contains a Functional Capabilities List (FCL) for the unit of software addressed by the UDF. An FCL is a list of the testable functions performed by the unit; i.e., it describes what a particular unit of software does, preferably in sequential order. The FCL is generated from the requirements and detailed design prior to development of the unit test plan. Its level of detail should correspond to the unit in question but, as a minimum, reflect the major segments of the code and the decisions which are being made. It is preferred that, whenever possible, functional capabilities be expressed in terms of the unit requirements (i.e., the functional capability is a requirement from Section 1 of the UDF). Requirements allocated to be tested at the unit level shall be included in the FCL. The FCL provides a vector from which the TEST CASE/REQUIREMENTS/FCL matrix (Figure 4) is generated. The FCL should be reviewed and addressed as part of the test plan review process.

The rationale for Functional Capabilities Lists is as follows:

(1) They provide the basis for planned and controlled unit-level testing (i.e., a means for determining and organizing a set of test cases which will test all requirements/functional capabilities and all branches and transfers).

(2) They provide a consistent approach to testing which can be reviewed, audited, and understood by an outsider. When mapped to the test cases, they provide the rationale for each test case.

(3) They encourage another look at the design at a level where the "what if" questions can become apparent.

Section 4. UNIT CODE

This section contains the current source code listings for each of the routines included in the unit. Indexed subsection separators are used for multiple routine units. The completion date for this section is the scheduled date for the first error-free compilation or assembly when the code is ready for unit-level testing. Where code listings or other

TEST CASE/REQUIREMENTS/FCL MATRIX

REQUIREMENTS DOCUMENT _____

DATE _____

Req'ts Paragraph Number	FCL NO.	TEST CASE NUMBER										OTHER ROUTINES
		1	2	3	4	5	6	7	8	9	0	

INSTRUCTIONS: Mark an X in the appropriate box when a particular test case fully tests a particular requirement. Mark a "P" when a test partially tests a requirement. If a requirement is partially tested in another routine, mark a "P" in the "other routines" column. If more space is required, attach additional copies of this figure.

Figure 4. Example Test Case/Requirements/FCL Matrix

relevant computer output are too large or bulky to be contained in a normal three-ring binder, this material may be placed in a separate companion binder of appropriate size which is clearly identified with the associated UDF. In this event, the relevant sections of the UDF will contain a reference and identification of the binder with a history log of post-baselined updates. Figure 5 illustrates a typical reference form.

An independent review of the code may be optional; however, for time-critical or other technically important units, a code walk–through or review is recommended.

Section 5. UNIT TEST PLAN

This section contains a description of the overall testing approach for the unit along with a description of each test case to be employed in testing the unit. The description must identify any test tools or drivers used, a listing of all required test inputs to the unit and their values, and the expected output and acceptance criteria, including numerical outputs and other demonstrable results. Test cases shall address the functional capabilities of the unit, and a matrix shall be placed into this section which correlates requirements and functional capabilities to test cases. This matrix will be used to demonstrate that all requirements, partial requirements, and FCLs of the unit have been tested. An example of the test case matrix is shown in Figure 4. Check marks are placed in the appropriate squares to correlate test cases with the capabilities tested. Sufficient detail should be provided in the test definition so that the test approach and objectives will be clear to an independent reviewer.

The primary criteria for the independent review will be to ascertain that the unit development test cases adequately test branch conditions, logic paths, input and output, error handling, a reasonable range of values and will perform as stipulated by the requirements. This review should occur prior to the start of unit testing.

Section 6. TEST CASE RESULTS

This section contains a compilation of all current successful test case results and analyses necessary to demonstrate that the unit has been tested as described in the test plan. Test output should be identified by test case number and listings clearly annotated to facilitate necessary reviews of these results by other qualified individuals. Revision status of test drivers, test tools, data bases and unit code should be shown to facilitate retesting. This material may also be placed in the separate companion binder to the UDF.

Section 7. PROBLEM REPORTS

This section contains status logs and copies of all Design Problem Reports, Design Analysis Reports and Discrepancy Reports (as required) which document all design and code problems and changes experienced by the unit subsequent to baselining. This ensures a clear and documented traceability for all problems and changes incurred. There should be separate subsections for each type of report with individual status logs that summarize the actions and dispositions made.

LISTINGS/TEST RESULTS

SEE SEPARATE NYLON PRONG BINDER IDENTIFIED AS

_____ FOR CODE LISTINGS

OR TEST RESULTS.

HISTORY LOG

CODE MOD NUMBER	DATE	REVIEWED BY
_____	_____	_____
_____	_____	_____
_____	_____	_____
_____	_____	_____
_____	_____	_____
_____	_____	_____
_____	_____	_____
_____	_____	_____
_____	_____	_____
_____	_____	_____
_____	_____	_____

Figure 5. Example Reference Log for Separately-Bound Material

Section 8. NOTES

This section contains any memos, notes, reports, etc., which expand on the contents of the unit or are related to problems and issues involved.

Section 9. REVIEWERS' COMMENTS

This section contains a record of reviewers' comments (if any) on this UDF, which have resulted from the section-by-section review and sign-off, and from scheduled independent audits. These reviewers' comments are also usually provided to the project and line management supervisors responsible for development of the unit.

SUMMARY

The UDF concept has evolved into a practical, effective and valuable tool not only for the management of software development but also for imposing a structured approach on the total software development process. The structure and content of the UDF are designed to create a series of self-contained systems at the unit level, each of which can be easily observed and reviewed. The UDF approach has been employed on several software projects at TRW and continues to win converts from the ranks of the initiated. The concept has proved particularly effective when used in conjunction with good programming standards, documentation standards, a test discipline and an independent quality assurance activity.

The principal merits of the UDF concept are:

(1) It imposes a development sequence on each unit and clearly establishes the responsibility for each step. Thus the reduction of the software development process into discrete activities is logically extended downward to the unit level.

(2) It establishes a clearly-discernible timeline for the development of each unit and provides low-level management visibility into schedule problems. The status of the development effort becomes more visible and measurable.

(3) It creates an open and auditable software development environment and removes some of the mystery often associated with this activity. The UDFs are normally kept "on the shelf" and open to inspection at any time.

(4) It assures that the documentation is accomplished and maintained concurrent with development activities. The problem of emerging from the development tunnel with little or inadequate documentation is considerably reduced.

(5) It reduces the problems associated with programmer turnover. The discipline and organization inherent in the approach simplifies the substitution of personnel at any point in the process without a significant loss of effort.

(6) It supports the principles of modularity. The guidelines given for establishing the unit boundaries assure that at least a minimum level of modularity will result.

(7) It can accommodate a variety of development plans and approaches. All UDF sections may be assigned to one performer, or different sections can be assigned to different specialists. The various sections contained in the UDF may also be expanded, contracted or even resequenced to better suit specific situations.

As a final comment, it must be emphasized that no device or approach can be effective without a strong management commitment to see it through. Every level of management needs to be supportive and aware of its responsibilities. Once the method is established it also needs to be audited for proper implementation and problem resolution. An independent software quality assurance activity can be a valuable asset in helping to define, audit and enforce management requirements.

Elements of Software Configuration Management

EDWARD H. BERSOFF, SENIOR MEMBER, IEEE

Abstract—Software configuration management (SCM) is one of the disciplines of the 1980's which grew in response to the many failures of the software industry throughout the 1970's. Over the last ten years, computers have been applied to the solution of so many complex problems that our ability to manage these applications has all too frequently failed. This has resulted in the development of a series of "new" disciplines intended to help control the software process.

This paper will focus on the discipline of SCM by first placing it in its proper context with respect to the rest of the software development process, as well as to the goals of that process. It will examine the constituent components of SCM, dwelling at some length on one of those components, configuration control. It will conclude with a look at what the 1980's might have in store.

Index Terms—Configuration management, management, product assurance, software.

INTRODUCTION

SOFTWARE configuration management (SCM) is one of the disciplines of the 1980's which grew in response to the many failures of our industry throughout the 1970's. Over the last ten years, computers have been applied to the solution of so many complex problems that our ability to manage these applications in the "traditional" way has all too frequently failed. Of course, tradition in the software business began only 30 years ago or less, but even new habits are difficult to break. In the 1970's we learned the hard way that the tasks involved in managing a software project were not linearly dependent on the number of lines of code produced. The relationship was, in fact, highly exponential. As the decade closed, we looked back on our failures [1], [2] trying to understand what went wrong and how we could correct it. We began to dissect the software development process [3], [4] and to define techniques by which it could be effectively managed [5]-[8]. This self-examination by some of the most talented and experienced members of the software community led to the development of a series of "new" disciplines intended to help control the software process.

While this paper will focus on the particular discipline of SCM, we will first place it in its proper context with respect to the rest of the software development process, as well as to the goals of that process. We will examine the constituent components of SCM, dwelling at some length on one of those components, configuration control. Once we have woven our way through all the trees, we will once again stand back and take a brief look at the forest and see what the 1980's might have in store.

Manuscript received April 15, 1982; revised December 1, 1982 and October 18, 1983.

The author is with BTG, Inc., 1945 Gallows Rd., Vienna, VA 22180.

SCM IN CONTEXT

It has been said that if you do not know where you are going, any road will get you there. In order to properly understand the role that SCM plays in the software development process, we must first understand what the goal of that process is, i.e., where we are going. For now, and perhaps for some time to come, software developers are people, people who respond to the needs of another set of people creating computer programs designed to satisfy those needs. These computer programs are the tangible output of a thought process—the conversion of a thought process into a product. The goal of the software developer is, or should be, the construction of a product which closely matches the real needs of the set of people for whom the software is developed. We call this goal the achievement of "product integrity." More formally stated, product integrity (depicted in Fig. 1) is defined to be the intrinsic set of attributes that characterize a product [9]:

- that fulfills user functional needs;
- that can easily and completely be traced through its life cycle;
- that meets specified performance criteria;
- whose cost expectations are met;
- whose delivery expectations are met.

The above definition is pragmatically based. It demands that product integrity be a measure of the satisfaction of the real needs and expectations of the software user. It places the burden for achieving the software goal, product integrity, squarely on the shoulders of the developer, for it is he alone who is in control of the development process. While, as we shall see, the user can establish safeguards and checkpoints to gain visibility into the development process, the prime responsibility for software success is the developer's. So our goal is now clear; we want to build software which exhibits all the characteristics of product integrity. Let us make sure that we all understand, however, what this thing called software really is. We have learned in recent times that equating the terms "software" and "computer programs" improperly restricts our view of software. Software is much more. A definition which can be used to focus the discussion in this paper is that software is information that is:

- structured with logical and functional properties;
- created and maintained in various forms and representations during the life cycle;
- tailored for machine processing in its fully developed state.

So by our definition, software is not simply a set of computer programs, but includes the documentation required to define, develop, and maintain these programs. While this notion is not very new, it still frequently escapes the software

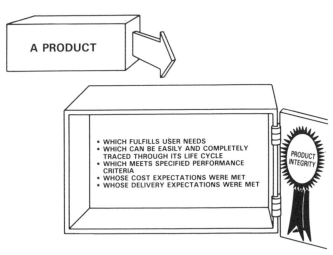

Fig. 1. Product integrity.

development manager who assumes that controlling a software product is the same as controlling computer code.

Now that we more fully appreciate what we are after, i.e., to build a software product with integrity, let us look at the one road which might get us there. We have, until now, used the term "developer" to characterize the organizational unit responsible for converting the software idea into a software product. But developers are, in reality, a complex set of interacting organizational entities. When undertaking a software project, most developers structure themselves into three basic discipline sets which include:

- project management,
- development, and
- product assurance.

Project management disciplines are both inwardly and outwardly directed. They support general management's need to see what is going on in a project and to ensure that the parent or host organization consistently develops products with integrity. At the same time, these disciplines look inside a project in support of the assignment, allocation, and control of all project resources. In that capacity, project management determines the relative allocation of resources to the set of development and product assurance disciplines. It is management's prerogative to specify the extent to which a given discipline will be applied to a given project. Historically, management has often been handicapped when it came to deciding how much of the product assurance disciplines were required. This was a result of both inexperience and organizational immaturity.

The development disciplines represent those traditionally applied to a software project. They include:

- analysis,
- design,
- engineering,
- production (coding),
- test (unit/subsystem),
- installation,
- documentation,
- training, and
- maintenance.

In the broadest sense, these are the disciplines required to take a system concept from its beginning through the development life cycle. It takes a well-structured, rigorous technical approach to system development, along with the right mix of development disciplines to attain product integrity, especially for software. The concept of an ordered, procedurally disciplined approach to system development is fundamental to product integrity. Such an approach provides successive development plateaus, each of which is an identifiable measure of progress which forms a part of the total foundation supporting the final product. Going sequentially from one baseline (plateau) to another with high probability of success, necessitates the use of the right development disciplines at precisely the right time.

The product assurance disciplines which are used by project management to gain visibility into the development process include:

- configuration management,
- quality assurance,
- validation and verification, and
- test and evaluation.

Proper employment of these product assurance disciplines by the project manager is basic to the success of a project since they provide the technical checks and balances over the product being developed. Fig. 2 represents the relationship among the management, development, and product assurance disciplines. Let us look at each of the product assurance disciplines briefly, in turn, before we explore the details of SCM.

Configuration management (CM) is the discipline of identifying the configuration of a system at discrete points in time for the purpose of systematically controlling changes to the configuration and maintaining the integrity and traceability of the configuration throughout the system life cycle. Software configuration management (SCM) is simply configuration management tailored to systems, or portions of systems, that are comprised predominantly of software. Thus, SCM does not differ substantially from the CM of hardware-oriented systems, which is generally well understood and effectively practiced. However, attempts to implement SCM have often failed because the particulars of SCM do not follow by direct analogy from the particulars of hardware CM and because SCM is a less mature discipline than that of hardware CM. We will return to this subject shortly.

Quality assurance (QA) as a discipline is commonly invoked throughout government and industry organizations with reasonable standardization when applied to systems comprised only of hardware. But there is enormous variation in thinking and practice when the QA discipline is invoked for a software development or for a system containing software components. QA has a long history, and much like CM, it has been largely developed and practiced on hardware projects. It is therefore mature, in that sense, as a discipline. Like CM, however, it is relatively immature when applied to software development. We define QA as consisting of the procedures, techniques, and tools applied by professionals to insure that a product meets or exceeds prespecified standards during a product's development cycle; and without specific prescribed standards, QA entails insuring that a product meets or

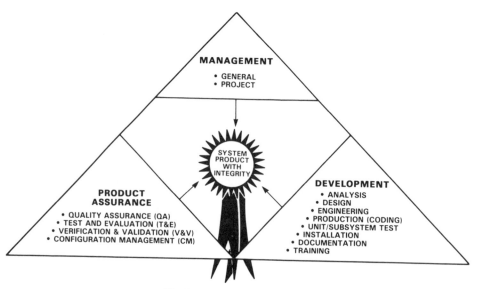

Fig. 2. The discipline triangle.

exceeds a minimum industrial and/or commercially acceptable level of excellence.

The QA discipline has not been uniformly treated, practiced or invoked relative to software development. First, very few organizations have software design and development standards that compare in any way with hardware standards for detail and completeness. Second, it takes a high level of software expertise to assess whether a software product meets prescribed standards. Third, few buyer organizations have provided for or have developed the capability to impose and then monitor software QA endeavors on seller organizations. Finally, few organizations have been concerned over precisely defining the difference between QA and other product assurance disciplines, CM often being subservient to QA or vice versa in a given development organization. Our definition of software given earlier suggests still another reason for the software QA discipline being in the same state as SCM so far as its universal application within the user, buyer, and seller communities. Software, as a form of information, cannot be standardized; only structures for defining/documenting software can be standardized. It follows that software development techniques can only be meaningfully standardized in relation to information structures, not information content.

The third of the four product assurance disciplines is validation and verification (V&V). Unlike CM and QA, V&V has come into being expressly for the purpose of coping with software and its development. Unlike QA, which prinicpally deals with the problem of a product's adherence to pre-established standards, V&V deals with the issue of how well software fulfills functional and performance requirements and the assurance that specified requirements are indeed stated and interpreted correctly. The verification part of V&V assures that a product meets its prescribed goals as defined through baseline documentation. That is, verification is a discipline imposed to ascertain that a product is what it was intended to be relative to its preceding baseline. The validation part of V&V, by contrast, is levied as a discipline to assure that a product not only meets the objectives specified through baseline documentation, but in addition, does the right job.

Stated another way, the validation discipline is invoked to insure that the end-user gets the right product. A buyer or seller may have misinterpreted user requirements or, perhaps, requirements have changed, or the user gets to know more about what he needs, or early specifications of requirements were wrong or incomplete or in a state of flux. The validation process serves to assure that such problems do not persist among the user, buyer, and seller. To enhance objectivity, it is often desirable to have an independent organization, from outside the developing organization, perform the V&V function.

The fourth of the product assurance disciplines is test and evaluation (T&E), perhaps the discipline most understood, and yet paradoxically, least practiced with uniformity. T&E is defined as the discipline imposed outside the development project organization to independently assess whether a product fulfills objectives. T&E does this through the execution of a set of test plans and procedures. Specifically in support of the end user, T&E entails evaluating product performance in a live or near-live environment. Frequently, particularly within the miliatry arena, T&E is a major undertaking involving one or more systems which are to operate together, but which have been individually developed and accepted as stand-alone items. Some organizations formally turn over T&E responsibility to a group outside the development project organization after the product reaches a certain stage of development, their philosophy being that developers cannot be objective to the point of fully testing/evaluating what they have produced.

The definitions given for CM, QA, V&V, and T&E suggest some overlap in required skills and functions to be performed in order to invoke these disciplines collectively for product assurance purposes. Depending on many factors, the actual overlap may be significant or little. In fact, there are those who would argue that V&V and T&E are but subset functions of QA. But the contesting argument is that V&V and T&E have come into being as separate disciplines because conventional QA methods and techniques have failed to do an adequate job with respect to providing product assurance, particularly for computer-centered systems with software components. Management must be concerned with minimizing the application of excessive and redundant resources to address the overlap of these disciplines. What is important is that all the functions defined above are performed, not what they are called or who carries them out.

THE ELEMENTS OF SCM

When the need for the discipline of configuration management finally achieved widespread recognition within the software engineering community, the question arose as to how closely the software CM discipline ought to parallel the extant hardware practice of configuration management. Early SCM authors and practitioners [10] wisely chose the path of commonality with the hardware world, at least at the highest level. Of course, hardware engineering is different from software engineering, but broad similarities do exist and terms applied to one segment of the engineering community can easily be applied to another, even if the specific meanings of those terms differ significantly in detail. For that reason, the elements of SCM were chosen to be the same as those for hardware CM. As for hardware, the four components of SCM are:

- identification,
- control,
- auditing, and
- status accounting.

Let us examine each one in turn.

Software Configuration Identification: Effective management of the development of a system requires careful definition of its baseline components; changes to these components also need to be defined since these changes, together with the baselines, specify the system evolution. A system baseline is like a snapshot of the aggregate of system components as they exist at a given point in time; updates to this baseline are like frames in a movie strip of the system life cycle. The role of software configuration identification in the SCM process is to provide labels for these snapshots and the movie strip.

A baseline can be characterized by two labels. One label identifies the baseline itself, while the second label identifies an update to a particular baseline. An update to a baseline represents a baseline plus a set of changes that have been incorporated into it. Each of the baselines established during a software system's life cycle controls subsequent system development. At the time it is first established a software baseline embodies the actual software in its most recent state. When changes are made to the most recently established baseline, then, from the viewpoint of the software configuration manager, this baseline and these changes embody the actual software in its most recent state (although, from the viewpoint of the software developer, the actual software may be in a more advanced state).

The most elementary entity in the software configuration identification labeling mechanism is the software configuration item (SCI). Viewed from an SCM perspective, a software baseline appears as a set of SCI's. The SCI's within a baseline are related to one another via a tree-like hierarchy. As the software system evolves through its life cycle, the number of

branches in this hierarchy generally increases; the first baseline may consist of no more than one SCI. The lowest level SCI's in the tree hierarchy may still be under development and not yet under SCM control. These entities are termed design objects or computer program components (see Fig. 3). Each baseline and each member in the associated family of updates will exist in one or more forms, such as a design document, source code on a disk, or executing object code.

In performing the identification function, the software configuration manager is, in effect, taking snapshots of the SCI's. Each baseline and its associated updates collectively represents the evolution of the software during each of its life cycle stages. These stages are staggered with respect to one another. Thus, the collection of life cycle stages looks like a collection of staggered and overlapping sequences of snapshots of SCI trees. Let us now imagine that this collection of snapshot sequences is threaded, in chronological order, onto a strip of movie film as in Fig. 4. Let us further imagine that the strip of movie film is run through a projector. Then we would see a history of the evolution of the software. Consequently, the identification of baselines and updates provides an explicit documentation trail linking all stages of the software life cycle. With the aid of this documentation trail, the software developer can assess the integrity of his product, and the software buyer can assess the integrity of the product he is paying for.

Software Configuration Control: The evolution of a software system is, in the language of SCM, the development of baselines and the incorporation of a series of changes into the baselines. In addition to these changes that explicitly affect existing baselines, there are changes that occur during early stages of the system life cycle that may affect baselines that do not yet exist. For example, some time before software coding begins (i.e., some time prior to the establishment of a design baseline), a contract may be modified to include a software warranty provision such as: system downtime due to software failures shall not exceed 30 minutes per day. This warranty provision will generally affect subsequent baselines but in a manner that cannot be explicitly determined *a priori*. One role of software configuration control is to provide the administrative mechanism for precipitating, preparing, evaluating, and approving or disapproving all change proposals throughout the system life cycle.

We have said that software, for configuration management purposes, is a collection of SCI's that are related to one another in a well-defined way. In early baselines and their associated updates, SCI's are specification documents (one or more volumes of text for each baseline or associated update); in later baselines and their associated updates, each SCI may manifest itself in any or all of the various software representations. Software configuration control focuses on managing changes to SCI's (existing or to be developed) in all of their representations. This process involves three basic ingredients.

1) Documentation (such as administrative forms and supporting technical and administrative material) for formally precipitating and defining a proposed change to a software system.

2) An organizational body for formally evaluating and

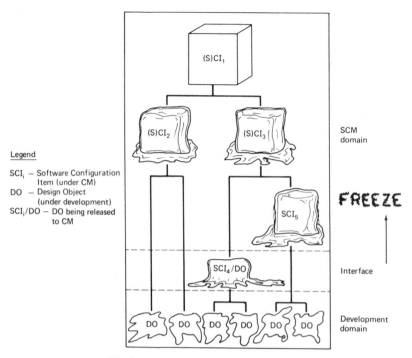

Fig. 3. The development/SCM interface.

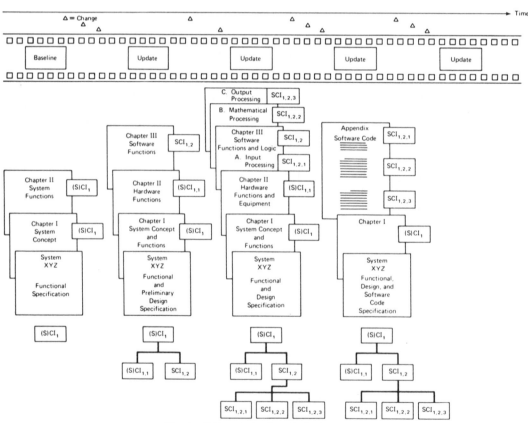

Fig. 4. SCI evolution in a single document.

approving or disapproving a proposed change to a software system (the Configuration Control Board).

3) Procedures for controlling changes to a software system.

The Engineering Change Proposal (ECP), a major control document, contains information such as a description of the proposed change, identification of the originating organization, rationale for the change, identification of affected baselines and SCI's (if appropriate), and specification of cost and schedule impacts. ECP's are reviewed and coordinated by the CCB, which is typically a body representing all organizational units which have a vested interest in proposed changes.

Fig. 5 depicts the software configuration control process.

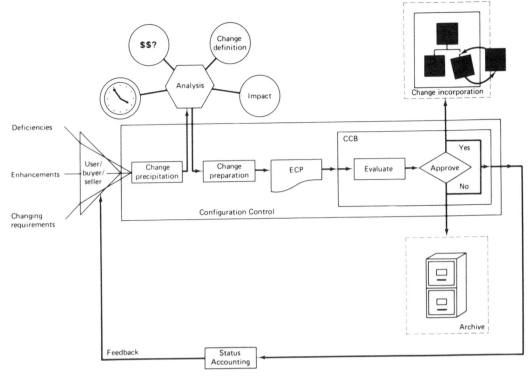

Fig. 5. The control process.

As the figure suggests, change incorporation is not an SCM function, but monitoring the change implementation process resulting in change incorporation is. Fig. 5 also emphasizes that the analysis that may be required to prepare an ECP is also outside the SCM purview. Note also from the figure how ECP's not approved by the CCB are not simply discarded but are archived for possible future reference.

Many automated tools support the control process. The major ones aid in controlling software change once the coding stage has been reached, and are generically referred to as program support libraries (PSL's). The level of support provided by PSL's, however, varies greatly. As a minimum, a PSL should provide a centralized and readily available repository for authoritative versions of each component of a software system. It should contain the data necessary for the orderly development and control of each SCI. Automation of other functions, such as library access control, software and document version maintenance, change recording, and document reconstruction, greatly enhance both the control and maintenance processes. These capabilities are currently available in systems such as SOFTOOL's change and configuration control environment (CCC).

A PSL supports a developmental approach in which project personnel work on a common visible product rather than on independent components. In those PSL's which include access controls, project personnel can be separately assigned read/write access to each software document/component, from programs to lines of code. Thus, all project personnel are assured ready access to the critical interface information necessary for effective software development. At the same time, modifications to various software components, whether sanctioned baselines or modules under development, can be closely controlled.

Under the PSL concept, the programmer operates under a well-defined set of parameters and exercises a narrower span of detailed control. This minimizes the need for explicit communication between analysts and programmers and makes the inclusion of new project personnel less traumatic since interface requirements are well documented. It also minimizes the preparation effort for technical audits.

Responsibility for maintenance of the PSL data varies depending on the level of automation provided. For those systems which provide only a repository for data, a secretary/librarian is usually responsible for maintaining the notebooks which will contain the data developed and used by project personnel and for maintenance of the PSL archives. More advanced PSL systems provide real time, on-line access to data and programs and automatically create the records necessary to fully trace the history of the development. In either case the PSL provides standardization of project recordkeeping, ensures that system documentation corresponds to the current system configuration, and guarantees the existence of adequate documentation of previous versions.

A PSL should support three main activities: code development, software management, and configuration control. Support to the development process includes support to design, coding, testing, documentation, and program maintenance along with associated database schema and subschema. A PSL provides this support through:

- storage and maintenance of software documentation and code,
- support to program compilation/testing,
- support for the generation of program/system documentation.

Support to the management of the software development process involves the storage and output of programming data such as:

- collection and automatic reporting of management data related to program development,

- control over the integrity and security of the data in the PSL,
- separation of the clerical activity related to the programming process.

PSL's provide support to the configuration control process through:

- access and change authorization control for all data in the library,
  - control of software code releases,
  - automatic program and document reconstruction,
  - automatic change tracking and reporting,
  - assurance of the consistency between documentation, code, and listings.

A PSL has four major components: internal libraries in machine-readable form, external libraries in hardcopy form, computer procedures, and office procedures. The components of a PSL system are interlocked to establish an exact correspondence between the internal units of code and external versions (such as listings) of the developing systems. This continuous correspondence is the characteristic of a PSL that guarantees ongoing visibility and identification of the developing system.

Different PSL implementations exist for various system environments with the specifics of the implementation dependent upon the hardware, software, user, and operating environment. The fundamental correspondence between the internal and external libraries in each environment, however, is established by the PSL librarian and computer procedures. The office procedures are specified in a project CM Plan so that the format of the external libraries is standard across software projects, and internal and external libraries are easily maintainable.

Newer PSL systems minimize the need for both office and computer procedures through the implementation of extensive management functionality. This functionality provides significant flexibility in controlling the access to data and allocating change authority, while providing a variety of status reporting capabilities. The availability of management information, such as a list of all the software structures changed to solve a particular Software Trouble Report or the details on the latest changes to a particular software document, provides a means for the control function to effectively operate without burdening the development team with cumbersome procedures and administrative paperwork. Current efforts in PSL refinement/development are aimed at linking support of the development environment with that of the configuration control environment. The goal of such systems is to provide an integrated environment where control and management information is generated automatically as a part of a fully supported design and development process.

Software Configuration Auditing: Software configuration auditing provides the mechanism for determining the degree to which the current state of the software system mirrors the software system pictured in baseline and requirements documentation. It also provides the mechanism for formally establishing a baseline. A baseline in its formative stages (for example, a draft specification document that appears prior to the existence of the functional baseline) is referred to as a "to-be-established" baseline; the final state of the auditing process conducted on a to-be-established baseline is a sanctioned baseline. The same may be said about baseline updates.

Software configuration auditing serves two purposes, configuration verification and configuration validation. Verification ensures that what is intended for each software configuration item as specified in one baseline or update is actually achieved in the succeeding baseline or update; validation ensures that the SCI configuration solves the right problem (i.e., that customer needs are satisfied). Software configuration auditing is applied to each baseline (and corresponding update) in its to-be-established state. An auditing process common to all baselines is the determination that an SCI structure exists and that its contents are based on all available information.

Software auditing is intended to increase software visibility and to establish traceability throughout the life cycle of the software product. Of course, this visibility and traceability are not achieved without cost. Software auditing costs time and money. But the judicious investment of time and money, particularly in the early stages of a project, pays dividends in the latter stages. These dividends include the avoidance of costly retrofits resulting from problems such as the sudden appearance of new requirements and the discovery of major design flaws. Conversely, failing to perform auditing, or constraining it to the later stages of the software life cycle, can jeopardize successful software development. Often in such cases, by the time discrepancies are discovered (if they are), the software cannot be easily or economically modified to rectify the discrepancies. The result is often a dissatisfied customer, large cost overruns, slipped schedules, or cancelled projects.

Software auditing makes visible to management the current status of the software in the life cycle product audited. It also reveals whether the project requirements are being satisfied and whether the intent of the preceding baseline has been fulfilled. With this visibility, project management can evaluate the integrity of the software product being developed, resolve issues that may have been raised by the audit, and correct defects in the development process. The visibility afforded by the software audit also provides a basis for the establishment of the audited life cycle product as a new baseline.

Software auditing provides traceability between a software life cycle product and the requirements for that product. Thus, as life cycle products are audited and baselines established, every requirement is traced successively from baseline to baseline. Disconnects are also made visible during the establishment of traceability. These disconnects include requirements not satisfied in the audited product and extraneous features observed in the product (i.e., features for which no stated requirement exists).

With the different point of view made possible by the visibility and traceability achieved in the software audit, management can make better decisions and exercise more incisive control over the software development process. The result of a software audit may be the establishment of a baseline, the redirection of project tasking, or an adjustment of applied project resources.

The responsibility for a successful software development project is shared by the buyer, seller, and user. Software auditing uniquely benefits each of these project participants. Appropriate auditing by each party provides checks and balances over the development effort. The scope and depth of the audits undertaken by the three parties may vary greatly. However, the purposes of these differing forms of software audit remain the same: to provide visibility and to establish traceability of the software life cycle products. An excellent overview of the software audit process, from which some of the above discussion has been extracted, appears in [11].

Software Configuration Status Accounting: A decision to make a change is generally followed by a time delay before the change is actually made, and changes to baselines generally occur over a protracted period of time before they are incorporated into baselines as updates. A mechanism is therefore needed for maintaining a record of how the system has evolved and where the system is at any time relative to what appears in published baseline documentation and written agreements. Software configuration status accounting provides this mechanism. Status accounting is the administrative tracking and reporting of all software items formally identified and controlled. It also involves the maintenance of records to support software configuration auditing. Thus, software configuration status accounting records the activity associated with the other three SCM functions and therefore provides the means by which the history of the software system life cycle can be traced.

Although administrative in nature, status accounting is a function that increases in complexity as the system life cycle progresses because of the multiple software representations that emerge with later baselines. This complexity generally results in large amounts of data to be recorded and reported. In particular, the scope of software configuration status accounting encompasses the recording and reporting of:

1) the time at which each representation of a baseline and update came into being;

2) the time at which each software configuration item came into being;

3) descriptive information about each SCI;

4) engineering change proposal status (approved, disapproved, awaiting action);

5) descriptive information about each ECP;

6) change status;

7) descriptive information about each change;

8) status of technical and administrative documentation associated with a baseline or update (such as a plan prescribing tests to be performed on a baseline for updating purposes);

9) deficiencies in a to-be-established baseline uncovered during a configuration audit.

Software configuration status accounting, because of its large data input and output requirements, is generally supported in part by automated processes such as the PSL described earlier. Data are collected and organized for input to a computer and reports giving the status of entities are compiled and generated by the computer.

The Management Dilemma

As we mentioned at the beginning of this paper, SCM and many of the other product assurance disciplines grew up in the 1970's in response to software failure. The new disciplines were designed to achieve visibility into the software engineering process and thereby exercise some measure of control over that process. Students of mathematical control theory are taught early in their studies a simple example of the control process. Consider being confronted with a cup of hot coffee, filled to the top, which you are expected to carry from the kitchen counter to the kitchen table. It is easily verified that if you watch the cup as you carry it, you are likely to spill more coffee than if you were to keep your head turned away from the cup. The problem with looking at the cup is one of overcompensation. As you observe slight deviations from the straight-and-level, you adjust, but often you adjust too much. To compensate for that overadjustment, you tend to overadjust again, with the result being hot coffee on your floor.

This little diversion from our main topic of SCM has an obvious moral. There is a fundamental propensity on the part of the practitioners of the product assurance disciplines to overadjust, to overcompensate for the failures of the development disciplines. There is one sure way to eliminate failure completely from the software development process, and that is to stop it completely. The software project manager must learn how to apply his resources intelligently. He must achieve visibility and control, but he must not so encumber the developer so as to bring progress to a virtual halt. The product assurers have a virtuous perspective. They strive for perfection and point out when and where perfection has not been achieved. We seem to have a binary attitude about software; it is either correct or it is not. That is perhaps true, but we cannot expect anyone to deliver perfect software in any reasonable time period or for a reasonable sum of money. What we need to develop is software that is good enough. Some of the controls that we have placed on the developer have the deleterious effect of increasing costs and expanding schedules rather than shrinking them.

The dilemma to management is real. We must have the visibility and control that the product assurance disciplines have the capacity to provide. But we must be careful not to overcompensate and overcontrol. This is the fine line which will distinguish the successful software managers of the 1980's from the rest of the software engineering community.

Acknowledgment

The author wishes to acknowledge the contribution of B. J. Gregor to the preparation and critique of the final manuscript.

References

[1] "Contracting for computer software development—Serious problems require management attention to avoid wasting additional millions," General Accounting Office, Rep. FGMSD 80-4, Nov. 9, 1979.

[2] D. M. Weiss, "The MUDD report: A case study of Navy software development practices," Naval Res. Lab., Rep. 7909, May 21, 1975.

[3] B. W. Boehm, "Software engineering," *IEEE Trans. Comput.,* vol. C-25, pp. 1226–1241, Dec. 1976.

[4] *Proc. IEEE* (Special Issue on Software Engineering), vol. 68, Sept. 1980.

[5] E. Bersoff, V. Henderson, and S. Siegel, "Attaining software product integrity," *Tutorial: Software Configuration Management,* W. Bryan, C. Chadbourne, and S. Siegel, Eds., Los Alamitos, CA, IEEE Comput. Soc., Cat. EHO-169-3, 1981.

[6] B. W. Boehm *et al., Characteristics of Software Quality, TRW Series of Software Technology,* vol. 1. New York: North-Holland, 1978.

[7] T. A. Thayer, *et al., Software Reliability, TRW Series of Software Technology,* vol. 2. New York: North-Holland, 1978.

[8]   D. J. Reifer, Ed., *Tutorial: Automated Tools for Software Eng.*, Los Alamitos, CA, IEEE Comput. Soc., Cat. EHO-169-3, 1979.

[9]   E. Bersoff, V. Henderson, and S. Siegel, *Software Configuration Management*. Englewood Cliffs, NJ: Prentice-Hall, 1980.

[10]   ——, "Software configuration management: A tutorial," *Computer*, vol. 12, pp. 6–14, Jan. 1979.

[11]   W. Bryan, S. Siegel, and G. Whiteleather, "Auditing throughout the software life cycle: A primer," *Computer*, vol. 15, pp. 56–67, Mar. 1982.

[12]   "Software configuration management," Naval Elec. Syst. Command, Software Management Guidebooks, vol. 2, undated.

Edward H. Bersoff (M'75–SM'78) received the A.B., M.S., and Ph.D. degrees in mathematics from New York University, New York.

He is President and Founder of BTG, Inc., a high technology, Washington, DC area based, systems analysis and engineering firm. In addition to his corporate responsibilities, he directs the company's research in software engineering, product assurance, and software management. BTG specializes in the application of modern systems engineering principles to the computer based system development process. At BTG, he has been actively involved in the FAA's Advanced Automation Program where he is focusing on software management and software configuration management issues on this extremely complex program. He also participates in the company's activities within the Naval Intelligence community, providing senior consulting services to a wide variety of system development efforts. He was previously President of CTEC, Inc. where he directed the concept formulation and development of the Navy Command and Control System (NCCS), Ocean Surveillance Information System (OSIS) Baseline now installed at all U.S. Navy Ocean Surveillance Centers. He also served as Experiment Director for the Joint ARPA, Navy, CINCPAC Military Message Experiment. This test was designed to examine the usefulness of secure, automated message processing systems in an operational military environment and to develop design criteria for future military message processing systems. Prior to joining CTEC, Inc., he was Manager of Engineering Operations and Manager of FAA Operations for Logicon, Inc.'s Process Systems Division. He joined Logicon from the NASA Electronics Research Center. He has taught mathematics at universities in Boston, New York, and Washington, DC. His technical contributions to the fields of software requirements and design range from early publications in computer architecture, reliability and programming languages, to more recent publications in software quality and configuration management. A textbook entitled *Software Configuration Management* (Prentice-Hall) represents the product of three years of research in the field by Dr. Bersoff and his colleagues.

Dr. Bersoff is a member of AFCEA, American Management Association, MENSA, and the Young Presidents' Organization.

Transforming "show biz" into real project payoffs.

ASSURING QUALITY QUALITY ASSURANCE

by Stephen L. Stamm

The concept of software quality assurance (SQA) has reached maturity over the past decade, although not without difficulty. There is a widespread opinion that the payoff on most SQA programs is marginal at best and that quality assurance is really a form of "show biz," and certainly not worth much of an investment.

Since 1978, the software quality assurance program outlined here has been in active use for military programs at GE's Space Div. The principles of SQA, however, are broadly applicable, and an SQA program drawn up for the commercial sector or for dealing with small projects would have functional similarities throughout. In the past, SQA programs have been accepted only because they were part of the contract. Also, with the science of measuring software still in its infancy, it is sometimes difficult to determine the effectiveness of an SQA program. The guidelines and philosophy expressed in this article show a user how to get something for his money without going over the funding estimates given.

The primary purpose of the SQA program is to assure that the delivered software meets all the requirements of the contract or end user. And, to help secure contracts, its secondary purpose is to define and implement specific measures which will assure that the delivered software is a high quality product; e.g., that it incorporates the features necessary to achieve testability, maintainability, reliability, etc. In the typical organization, this responsibility is given to an SQA group which, working with 3% to 5% of the project funding, is expected to perform independently. It is unrealistic to expect anything other than superficial results from this approach.

An independent audit of the software at any point in the development cycle must be conducted in depth. But this capability requires a resource which is a significant fraction of the development effort itself. No project can afford this either in the expenditure of funds or in the utilization of technical personnel. A person who is capable of performing a good in-depth audit is willing to do this occasionally, but doesn't want to make a career of it—he'd rather be developing his own software. Another negative aspect of an SQA group working on a project as an independent entity is that it is likely to suffer from an outsider image and be viewed as an enemy that doesn't really understand the problem. The atmosphere created is hardly conducive to achieving an effective SQA program.

The practical approach to achieving viable SQA is to make it a part of everybody's job. Each element of the software development process involves QA aspects with which each member of the development team must identify to obtain the desired high quality product. Quality can't get added to the "recipe" by someone else later on in the process; it has to be included at each step. In this approach, the primary job of the SQA group is to produce the SQA plan and then to manage it. Managing does not require high level software developmen expertise, and becomes far less difficult and costly to staff properly than previously described methods. The typical elements of the "SQA is Everybody's Job" approach are shown in the table, which presents the specific SQA roles of each of the generic performing organizations spread over the duration of the project in terms of the development cycle phases.

THE SQA PLAN

The first order of business is for the SQA group to define its requirements by preparing the project SQA plan. The presentation of all QA aspects of the development process in a single plan assures an integrated approach (e.g., design practices) and complementary rather than conflicting QA features in the test program and the configuration management system. The SQA plan must include at least the following topics:

- *Organization*: the organizational approach to implementing the SQA program includes the definition of the roles and responsibilities of each group in the project organization. The independence of the SQA group must be clearly established.
- *Requirement Traceability*: this defines the methodology to assure that all requirements in top level specifications are satisfied in the lower-tier specifications, and sets up the verification of all requirements through traceability to test plans.
- *Documentation*: the documentation to be produced must be defined to assure formal, controlled communication among the project organizational elements; standards for the preparation of the documentation; and the measures to be applied to assure compliance with the standards.
- *Software Engineering Methodology*: the application of the quality-related software engineering methodology on the project must be defined (e.g., structured walk-throughs, software development folders), and provisions for monitoring compliance must be set forth.
- *Training*: the requirements for certifying the software development personnel's knowledge of the QA measures to be applied to the project must be defined.
- *Formal Reviews*: a definition of the reviews to be conducted and the methodology to be applied must be made to assure readiness, smooth interface with the customer, and maximization of the benefits to be derived from each review.
- *Test Program*: as the keystone of SQA, the SQA plan must specifically define the measures for technical review of the test plan/procedures and compliance with prescribed testing standards; the role of the SQA group in conducting the tests and certification of the results; the system for reporting test discrepancies; the "requirement for retest" decision process; measures to assure control of special test software; and measures to assure control of hardware used to test the software.
- *Configuration Management*: the QA considerations that place requirements on the project configuration management system include a software library with control procedures to assure unambiguous identification of the products and prevention of unauthorized modifications; definition of procedures for the generation, disposition, tracking and closeout of design and test discrepancies; and a configuration audit prior to delivery of the products.

**The practical approach to achieving viable software
quality assurance is to make it part of everybody's job.**

THE PROJECT ORGANIZATIONS' ROLES IN THE SOFTWARE QUALITY ASSURANCE PROGRAM

DEVELOPMENT CYCLE PHASE	SYSTEM ENGINEERING	SOFTWARE DEVELOPMENT	PROJECT ORGANIZATION — TEST AND INTEGRATION
Requirements Definition	• Requirements traceability • Technical review of specs • Prepare SW Rqt's Rev. (SRR)	• Prepare Programming Standard Document (PSD) • Develop/Implement Programmer Training Plan	
Preliminary Design	• Requirements traceability analysis • Technical review of specs and Interface Control Documents (ICD) • Technical Review of PDR material	• Complete PSD • Initiate SW Development Folders (SDF) • Prepare Prelim. Design Review (PDR)	• Trace test requirements to test plans
Detail Design and Code	• Technical review of specs and ICDs • Technical review of test plans • Tech. Rev. of CDR Mat'l	• Trace requirements to design implementation • Conduct structured walk-throughs • Prepare Critical Design Review (CDR) • Maintain SDFs	
Test and Operations	• Technical review of test procedures • Prepare Discrepancy Reports (DR)	• Technical review of test procedures • Prepare DRs	• Trace test plans to test procedures • Conduct test readiness meetings • Conduct post-test meetings • Prepare DRs

Production of a high quality product must start at the front end of the development process. The precise definition of the software system requirements in terms of the functions to be provided, together with related performance parameters (e.g., timing and sizing), is absolutely essential. Quality will be judged by the user after delivery, so there must be no uncertainty or ambiguity about what he will get: user disappointment is tantamount to poor quality. During the requirement definition phase, the primary contribution to producing a high quality product is a strong system engineering group. It must work with less easily defined requirements, such as portability and reliability, which might subsequently result in specific design standards.

The quality mechanism used to assure that the requirements have been met is a formal software requirements review (SRR). This mechanism is especially rewarding because it is self-stimulating and self-motivating. Few people want to make fools of themselves in public. However, the review can be no better than the capabilities of the reviewers, and the SQA group must assure adequate participation in and preparation for the review. It is especially important that the eventual operators of the system participate in all such reviews and that appropriate action items are formulated during the presentation.

During the requirement definition phase, it is important to put into place the means for producing the high quality product (code, database, and documentation). Primarily, this requires two things: the definition of what high product quality is, and programmers who understand and are capable of working to these definitions. Each programmer must be provided with a copy of a programming standards document (PSD). But then, with strong management support, the software development group must run training sessions on the content and application of the PSD. The SQA group, for its part, must certify that each programmer participates in this training activity.

As the project moves on to product design, a large contribution to assuring the quality of the end product is made during the preliminary design phase. Before the detail design of a software module is begun, each programmer must have a precise and detailed

PROJECT MANAGEMENT	QUALITY ASSURANCE
	• Prepare Project SCA Plan • Audit traceability analysis accomplishment • Audit spec review accomplishment • Review spec compliance to documentation standards • Review PSD scope for completeness • Review training plan for scope • Audit training attendance
• Conduct SRR • Prepare Configuration Management Plan (CMP)	• Assure SRR action item closure • Assure proper participation • Review for compliance with SQA plan
	• Audit traceability analysis accomplishment • Audit spec and ICD review accomplishment • Review compliance to documentation standards • Review PSD for completion
• Establish engineering review/change control board	• Audit Implementation of board • Audit existence/completeness of SDFs • Audit traceability analysis accomplishment
• Conduct PDR	• Assure PDR action item closure
	• Audit traceability analysis accomplishment • Audit spec and ICD review accomplishment • Review compliance to documentation standards • Audit walk-through accomplishment • Audit Test Plan review accomplishment
• Conduct CDR	• Assure CDR action item closure • Audit SDF's maintenance
	• Audit traceability analysis accomplishment • Audit meeting accomplishment and procedures • Audit test proc review accomplishment • Review compliance to documentation stds. • Certify test results and reports
• Prepare preship audit • ERB/CCB DR disposition	• Conduct preship audit • Monitor/expedite DR closure • Prepare statistical report on DR activity

definition of what the module is to do, how well it must perform, the environment in which it must operate, and its external interfaces. During the preliminary design phase, the focus of the SQA program is to assure that this will happen.

The detail requirements/environment/interface definition is performed by the software development group. To evaluate the quality of this activity, considerable technical expertise and an intimate understanding of the system level requirements are needed. The only practical approach is to apply the system engineering group to this task. It has defined the top level requirements and must now evaluate the software development group's response to these requirements, resolving any difficulties arising from interpretation and intent.

The quality of the software product is strongly dependent on the ability to test it, and during the development process it is necessary to look ahead a bit and assure testability. The test group must trace the module requirements into the preliminary test plans it is preparing, and then feed back any special design requirements needed to implement the test plan. Its contribution to product quality starts much earlier in the development cycle than is commonly acknowledged.

We have found that an effective mechanism to establish the desired clear communication with the programmer is the software development folder (SDF). The SDF documents the life history of a module from the time its requirements are defined until it is released to the test group. It is initiated in this phase by the cognizant programmer, and one of the first things to be included are the module requirements/environment/interfaces. So, the SDF provides a specific mechanism to assure that the required communcation has been achieved at this very personal level. The SQA group audits the SDF initiation when it actually occurs.

At the start of the preliminary design phase, the top-level specs assume a degree of sacredness, and a formal change control procedure must be established. This is done best by having program management create a board to rule on changes, called either the engineering review board (ERB) or the change control board (CCB). The board must provide the means for making rational and integrated change decisions and not degenerate into an administrative function—a change-processing paper mill. Quality objectives will be met only if program management creates a real working board consisting of top-level organizational representation, a board that actually makes changes rather than just record decisions made elsewhere in an undisciplined and invisible fashion.

The preliminary design phase ends with another formal review, the preliminary design review (PDR), which has the same objectives as the software requirements review described previously.

"Quality must be built in; it can't be tested in" is an overworked cliché but nonetheless true. This next phase is a critical period in the development cycle, yet it is the most difficult time to apply specific quality measures. The detail design and code phase should be met with the application of a combination of quality-oriented mechanisms.

Because they are so complex, we have learned that special attention must be given to the development of software interfaces. The bulk of this work must be done by the software development group, but to assure a sharp focus on this activity, the responsibility for the interface control documents (ICD) is placed in the system engineering group. In this way, at least two people are working toward the timely and complete definition of the interface details with the system engineers and are providing an in-depth review function on a continual basis.

When the software design is complete, another formal review must be conducted and successfully completed before huge amounts of resources are committed to the subsequent coding and testing efforts—the critical design review (CDR). This review assures that there is a well-defined design in place, with a minimum risk of subsequent redesign or inefficient application of the expanding programming team. The CDR achieves a top-level review of the product's quality at this point in the development cycle, e.g., the completeness of the documentation,

MARCH 1981

The quality of the software product is strongly dependent on the ability to test it.

adherence to the more easily audited standards, and traceability of functional requirements to the design implementation. The CDR, however, is not a suitable mechanism for reviewing the lowest-level detail of the design, which is where the quality must be built in. To achieve this, the structured walk-through has been found to be very effective. In this informal (typically around a table) minireview setting, the programmer can lead several reviewers through the complete design, making it possible to evaluate testability, operability, maintainability, transportability, etc. The vital task of the SQA group is to prepare the plan for this activity (module, date, participants) and to make sure that it is performed. Otherwise, the informality of the process can slip into lip service exercises or into continual rescheduling—finally past the date of product delivery.

The process of code-and-debug is not usually amenable to close scrutiny or audit. Because of the softness of the software, management visibility can become completely lost and product quality can suffer. Special measures must be employed to avert this situation and to assure that the programmer does not work in isolation. The structured walk-through technique is employed again after successful compilation has been achieved. This means a line-by-line review, the only way to check for adherence to coding and code documentation standards. The experience of senior people and the fresh approach and more recent academic training of the junior staff members can be used very

profitably at this point.

During this code-and-debug period the software development folder (SDF) should also be maintained, even if it is a very difficult discipline to impose on the typical programmer. But the SDF is the best management defense against the "trust me" syndrome and forms the basis for the subsequent preparation of the formal test procedures and users' manuals. Without good source material in the SDF, there is seldom the time or the inclination for high quality in subsequent documentation.

COMPLETE REVIEW OF SDF

The SDF must always be available for review and audit. Prior to turnover of a module to the test group for formal testing, a complete review of the SDF is conducted by the software development group supervisor and the SQA representative. The goal here is to provide documented evidence that the module is adequately debugged before the turnover occurs. After the SDF is certified complete, it is placed in the software library.

The design of the test program is finalized during this phase. The system engineering group has the responsibility of reviewing these plans and assuring that the test program will indeed verify all the software functional and performance requirements. The SQA group audits this review and any discrepancies that are to be resolved.

Software quality assurance must involve, of course, much more than testing, and

the SQA group must not be a part of the test group, which is a separate organizational entity. As we now describe the elements of the SQA program used during the test phase of the development cycle, we will further note that the SQA role in actual testing is minor. This arises again from the fundamental differences between hardware and software, i.e., the "softness" of test items. In software testing there are no gauges to monitor or traces on a scope to analyze; there isn't even any noise! The quiescent atmosphere of the software test is not the place to expect much in the way of SQA activity. The significant SQA tasks are performed before and after the test is run. This realization, that SQA has very little to do with the actual testing of the product, is fundamental to implementing an SQA program that really works. Unlike hardware QA, a successful software QA program must focus on methods and techniques that contribute to the software quality rather than on conducting the test.

The first important SQA measure in the test process is to identify what is being tested and to define precisely the test environment. These are configuration management (CM) functions. The project management must include these SQA requirements in the CM system. This is usually achieved by establishing a controlled software library, and all software test articles (code and database) with appropriate version identification are drawn from this library. Formal testing of other than controlled software is meaningless.

The next SQA measure is to define the test precisely before it is run, especially the success/failure criteria, and to achieve a prior agreement by all interested parties, including the end user. This is done by having the test director from the test and evaluation group conduct a pretest readiness meeting, at which the test procedures are modified to become the agreed-upon procedures that will be used in the test, and subsequently controlled as a part of the CM system.

The SQA function during the test is to make sure the procedure is being followed precisely or that changes are documented properly. After completion of the test, the test director conducts a post-test meeting and the SQA representative assigned to the test certifies the correctness of the test report, which includes the discrepancy reports (DRs) resulting from the test. At this meeting, each DR is assigned to the proper individual for resolution and subsequent reports to the ERB/CCB. The SQA representative monitors DR closure activity.

The discrepancy reports provide one excellent measure of the product quality, and it is the responsibility of the SQA group to analyze this data and prepare statistical reports. Examples of product quality data that might be used by management to identify weak

"And that's my philosophy of life. . . . go with the flow."

© DATAMATION

The key to a successful software quality assurance program is to assign a realistic role to the SQA group.

spots in the software implementation process are the number of DRs, the frequency distribution of DRs by type, the mean time of closure, and the DR rate as a function of product life. The analysis of DRs continues while the product is being used in its operational environment. This information is especially useful for the definition of subsequent product improvements or the design of new products.

A further measure of product quality is simply the extent to which specific code has been exercised. Tools are available to analyze the frequency with which paths are executed. The most important result of these analyses is to uncover code in the final product that has never been executed in the formal test program. It must then be determined if there is a hole in the test program, a flaw in the design, or simply some superfluous code that is about to be delivered. The SQA program should require the application of code analysis tools which support the measurement of the software quality as part of the test program.

The major SQA milestone during the test phase is a configuration audit conducted by the SQA group prior to shipment of the product from the factory. Through this audit, the company management and the customer are provided data to decide if the software is of sufficient quality to ship to the operational site. Specifically, the configuration audit accomplishes the following: 1) the product to be shipped is compared with the documented configuration identification represented by the applicable specifications and manuals; 2) the test results and DR dispositions are reviewed to verify that the product meets its specified performance requirements; 3) the product to be shipped is compared with the tested configuration; 4) any requirement not verified by testing is verified by comparison with appropriate detail/design documentation; and 5) all open items that are to be resolved after field installation are identified.

WINNING SQA PROGRAM

Software quality assurance can be made a useful ingredient of a software development project. The elements needed to achieve a successful SQA program must include the following:

• An SQA plan that has high project visibility, that specifically defines the SQA program at a level of detail suitable for implementation, and that has the wholehearted support of project and company management.

• A project organization that distributes the SQA program responsibility, placing the SQA tasks where the capability really exists.

• The application by the programming staff of special software engineering techniques specifically targeted at enhancing product quality.

• Measurement of the effectiveness of the SQA program and, if possible, of the quality of the product.

• Finally, SQA personnel as an integral part of the project team (dispel the "outsider" image). Even if they are assigned to the project by a boss who has an independent line of communication to top-level company management, quality compromises can be resolved prudently.

The key to a successful SQA program is to assign a realistic role to the SQA group. They first define the project's SQA program and then they manage its implementation. But they do not create quality in the product —that's a part of everybody's job.　　✳

Stephen L. Stamm is manager of software productivity programs at GE's Space Div. in King of Prussia, Pa.

Using this method, a manager can get an accurate picture of how his shop measures up in terms of management effectiveness.

TAKING MANAGEMENT'S MEASURE

by Jack Ewers

Some dp shops seem to have everything under control. Work is done logically, at the proper time and in the right sequence. In other shops, everything seems to be going on at once. Nothing is planned or integrated, and users and dp personnel are equally frustrated.

Managers usually make some comparisons of their shops against other shops. The comparisons provide a hazy idea of strengths and weaknesses but are not a formal evaluation technique. A better measure of the effectiveness of dp management is required. A method is needed to produce a documented measure of current performance and a means to plan and track improvements. Finally, the method should allow a manager to measure his *own* effectiveness and plan for his *own* improvements independent of assistance from internal or external auditors.

The effectiveness of dp management can be measured against the following major functions:
- Organization
  How well are people resources organized and managed?
- Management planning and control
  How well is the *work* of the department managed?
- Accountability
  How well are the results geared to the needs of the organization?
- Security
  How well are physical assets managed?

The first major management function is organization. This function is made up of the following elements:
- Mission statement
  Does the department understand what its role is?
- Department structure
  Are people correctly organized to carry out the department's assigned missions?
- Personnel management
  How well are the people managed?

Mission Statement. The first requirement of organization is a clear understanding of the organizational role of the dp department. This understanding is expressed in a mission statement. The mission of the dp department should be written and clearly defined. It must be approved by higher management (does management agree?) and it should be well understood by all users and dp department personnel (is department authority/responsibility clear to all employees?). In addition, the mission should be reviewed periodically to determine if it should be changed.

Agreement among all interested parties on the mission of the department is critical so that management and users know what to expect from the department, dp has a clear understanding of its role in the organization, and meaningful audits can be conducted to determine if the mission is being accomplished.

Department Structure. Second is a well-defined department structure. Limits of authority and responsibility within the department should be evident so that dp personnel are aware of the authority and responsibility of their position, understand their reporting relationships, and are able to work with the rest of the department.

Clear lines of authority and responsibility help management and users to understand the department and work effectively with it.

An organization chart is a good vehicle for displaying the department structure. It should be complete and current. The department must have a structure appropriate to its defined mission.

Personnel Management. The third requirement of proper organization is personnel management. Here are some of the indicators of the quality of that management.

Job descriptions. A job description should be written and approved for each position in the department. Well-developed sets of job descriptions offer the following advantages:
- Allow dp personnel to understand the content of their job.
- Outline a step-by-step advancement process, recognizing that there are degrees of knowledge, authority and responsibility that must be traversed. The employee then knows that he is not expected to comprehend all facets of dp in the early years of his career.
- Provide career paths so that employees can look forward to recognized advancement steps.
- Allow jobs to be slotted into a salary scale consistent with the organization and dp market.

PERFORMANCE REVIEWS

A manager must know the quality of the resources available to perform the department's mission. Periodic performance reviews provide a formal, rational, structured method for making that assessment. Informal appraisals are often based more on emotion and personality than on a careful analysis of the facts.

Performance reviews also make employees aware of how their performance is viewed. They provide a basis for equating pay and performance, and provide an opportunity for managers to help employees improve their performance and career development.

Finally, reviews establish a documented history of performance for use by appropriate organizational managers.

Short-term objectives. Short-term direction is needed to ensure that sufficient effort is applied to stated goals. Short-term objectives are continual reminders of what is important and keep the department on track.

Quarterly reviews are appropriate for managers and supervisory personnel. Analysts and programmers should have a monthly review of objectives since their jobs tend to last less than a month. Certain situations may dictate weekly reviews.

Short-term objective reviews establish agreement on what can be accomplished in the time frame under consideration, answer the question "Are people working on the right things?" and keep managers informed

A manager must know the quality of the resources available to perform the department's mission.

of progress, slippages and problems.

Training. A training program should be developed yearly and kept current with on-going project requirements. It should support the technical needs of projects and personnel needs identified in the long-range plan. A training history by employee and subject should be maintained. Proper training also ensures that new, effective technology is introduced into the organization and that costly redesigns, reprogramming, extensive debugging, testing, and inefficient systems do not come about because of a lack of technical knowledge.

Training is also needed to introduce more efficient methods, e.g., on-line program development, structured analysis and programming, into the dp department.

Turnover. Turnover can be an indicator of the quality of management. An excessively high turnover may indicate poor personnel management. High turnover is costly because of the retraining required and lessens productive effort while training is taking place.

Contract employees. The number of contract employees may be another indicator of the quality of department personnel management. A consistently high level may mean that more attention should be paid to increasing head count. The hourly rate for contract people is usually higher than in-house rates, and contract people charge a premium rate for overtime. In-house overtime is available at a lesser rate.

Technological and application experience gained by contract people is lost when their work is completed. In-house people must learn how the new system operates.

No use of contract resources, however, may indicate a lack of flexibility; i.e., head count is kept high to accommodate project peaks.

MANAGE-MENT PLANNING

The second major function against which management effectiveness is measured is management planning and control. This function is concerned with how the *work* of the department is managed.

Dp Long-Range Plan. The first element of management planning and control is a long-range plan. A long-range (three-year) plan should be developed and updated yearly. Any complex, meaningful action requires a plan, and the direction of an dp department is no exception. A formal, approved plan is necessary to ensure that department efforts will support organizational goals (how do I coordinate departmental goals and organizational goals?) and to ensure that resources will be available when needed. (What resources are needed and when?)

An effective plan helps to guarantee that scarce resources will be committed to the most productive actions. (What are the most productive actions? Why? What resources do they require?)

A long-range dp plan should be developed in concert with user department plans so that it will support user plans and also aid user participation in decisions regarding the allocation of dp resources. (What are user department plans/goals? How can dp help?)

The plan must be approved by management so that it agrees with the allocation of resources. (What does management expect dp to be doing?)

It must be rewritten, or updated, year-ly to adapt to changing requirements and interface with yearly budget planning (will the dp budget support the plan?) and it must indicate how transitions to new technology will be made. (When will the upgrade occur? How long will it take? What will it cost? What is the best way to do it?)

The long-range plan should include the following elements:

- Organizational and user department goals and strategies
- Strategy for transition to new equipment
- Master event schedule for all major projects
- Forecasted operating costs
- Forecasted personnel requirements
- Hardware inventory, present and planned
- Software and operating system requirements
- Data transmission requirements
- Forecast of educational requirements
- Resources required to change computer facilities
- Personnel requirements by application
- Personnel requirements summary

The long-range plan should also report current year actual accomplishment against last year's plan.

Management Control. Management control means that a manager is in control of the resources at his disposal and can measure their performance. Control of the resources implies that the manager is aware of how the resources are being consumed (what are the people and machines doing?) and that the work of the department is directed towards departmental goals (are they doing the right things?).

Control also implies that plan can be compared to actual (are we on schedule?) and that plans and resources can be shifted prior to disaster (should I put more people on project X?). Finally, control means that the effect of resource shifts can be predicted. (Should I move employee A or B to project X? What will be the effect of either move?)

Project control, the first requirement of management control, implies that projects are properly selected, developed and managed. Projects should be selected and given priorities in a rational, formal, documented manner. They should support organizational and user department goals. The project selection process answers the following question: "How do I know that the right project and priorities are selected?"

An independent evaluation of the relative and absolute value of projects by those who benefit from and pay for the projects is an excellent method of selection. The group must be able to make informed decisions. Establishing the group at a high level can be risky.

"In most large organizations, top management, top user management, steering

"If you don't mind, I'd like to get a second opinion."

©DATAMATION

Projects should be selected and given priorities in a rational, formal, documented manner.

committees, and such groups are so far removed, in sheer organizational distance, from the specifics of any proposed project or operation that they are effectively prohibited from applying analytical criteria to the edp decisions they must make.

"The sheer technical merits of the project have little relevance at this point, since neither time nor expertise is ordinarily available at these levels for such considerations. This clearly suggests that the guts of the resource-allocation process cannot be managed just by assigning responsibility for it to decision-making groups at the top of a company.

"But it does suggest that these groups must pay attention to the process by which new project ideas are generated at the technical levels of the organization. They should carefully consider this question respecting lower organizational levels.

"Does the planning process adequately involve the people who have sufficient understanding and credibility to both develop a new dp application idea and evaluate its worth?"[1]

The council should meet often enough to deal with new projects and changing requirements.

OTHER METHODS

Other methods of project selection make use of cost/benefit criteria. Whatever method is used, no project should proceed until it has written user approval.

Project development process. Each project should proceed through an orderly development process. A standard development process should be in place so that efforts can be concentrated on the problem, not on the method. The development process should include a formal project request. The request should include objectives, benefits and user signature.

A phased approach to development is essential. Responsibilities and documentation for each phase should be spelled out, review points should be established, written user approval should be required before each major phase is started, and costs and schedules should be recalculated at the end of each major phase. Programming and documentation standards and an abbreviated process for small and/or maintenance projects also should be established.

Project planning and control system. A major part of the mission of the dp department is the development and enhancement of application systems. The dp manager must know how this responsibility is being carried out.

Systems development and enhancement also represents a major commitment of

edp resource. These resources need to be planned, monitored, and controlled. A project planning and control system is a vehicle for evaluating dp's performance in application development and for planning, monitoring and controlling the resources committed to this function.

The project planning and control system should ease the matching of requirements and available resources.

The system should simplify shifting of resources and development of new plans. (What would happen if I moved analyst A and programmers C and D to project X in February? What is the completion date for project X if I assign only programmer E based on his current assignments? What other resources are available in February?)

A project planning and control system should enhance the planning, scheduling, and monitoring of numerous activities within one project (what are the dependencies? What is the critical path? If activity A is delayed one month, what effect will it have on the rest of the project?) and should assist in the measurement of cost vs. plan, and milestone accomplishment vs. schedule. It should also contribute positively to project reviews and critiques, and finally, should identify expected resources. The project control system should be integrated with the time reporting and computer utilization systems.

Operational control, the second requirement of management control, is part of the dp mission and is the stewardship of the production environment, i.e., the timely, accurate, and efficient handling of those systems in a production status. User operations depend on these systems and so the dp manager must have effective control of this environment.

Operational control includes application maintenance, computer operations, data entry, and output distribution. These activities should be controlled through standard instructions, run books, etc. (How does the operator initiate/run this job? What input does it require? Who should receive the output? What control totals should be logged/analyzed? What should be done if the job aborts?)

Weekly and daily schedules should be a standard operational tool. (When should this job be run? What are the relationships to other systems? What is the data entry cutoff time? What is the effect of a rerun?)

Another requirement of good operational control is an ongoing analysis of schedule vs. capacity (will everything get done on-time? If not, what schedule adjustments must be made? Do we need more capacity? When? How much?) as well as a forecast of load vs. capacity.

Operational control also implies an analysis of machine downtime (should some

hardware be replaced/repaired? Is downtime excessive? Should maintenance policies be revised?) and measurement of operations performance (are schedules met? Are reports delivered on time? How productive is the operations environment? What standards are used to measure productivity?).

The following operational questions should be asked:

"Is there a concise, objective performance reporting system that embraces turn-round time, rerun time, hardware-software component utilization, and user complaints in such a way as to permit both senior dp management and top management, itself, to quantitatively monitor performance?

"Have the scheduling and control procedures been modified to become consistent with the technical options made possible by the most recent generation or machines acquired by the department?

"Does the manager of computer operations have commensurate salary, management, and technical background with the manager of systems and programming?

"Is there a managerial career path with an opportunity for advancement in operations which is commensurate with that in systems and programming?"[2]

Budget, another measure of control within the edp department, is a formal method of planning and controlling costs. Good control over costs is indicated by adherence to budget. Budget reports should:
- accurately reflect costs
- measure actual vs. planned costs
- be published at least monthly

ACCOUNT-ABILITY

The dp manager is responsible for a large expenditure of funds. He should account for the use of those funds. Accountability has two basic elements: identification of expenditures by source, e.g., manufacturing or order entry, and allocation of those expenditures according to some rational basis.

Chargeout system. A chargeout system is a key element in establishing accountability for the dp function.

"Concern for the 'chargeout issue' signals the transition from informal to formal data processing management control. Chargeout usually spearheads the data processing management control program, and is used to bring users/managers into the control realm. Since it introduces user/manager to formal accountability for data processing, it is often met with volatile reactions."[3]

In another view,[4] "If one compares the arguments for overhead accounting and

1. McFarlan, Warren F., "Management Audit of the EDP Department, *Harvard Business Review*, May-June 1973.

2. McFarlan, op. cit.
3. Nolan, Richard L., *Management Accounting and Control of Data Processing*, July 1976.
4. McFarlan, op. cit.

HOW TO GRADE
THE MANAGEMENT TEST

The scorecard below can be used to compute a reasonable estimate of dp management effectiveness and to plan and track improvements. A rough "grade" can be calculated by using the formula:

TOTAL YES ANSWERS
67 (total possible answers)

Percentage		
93 - 100	= EXCELLENT	- don't mess with it
85 - 92	= ABOVE AVERAGE	- improvement needed but not critical
77 - 84	= AVERAGE	- allocate resources for improvement in next year's budget
69 - 76	= BELOW AVERAGE	- lay out improvement plans now
below 69	= NOT ADEQUATE	- improvement plan should start with a new manager

DP MANAGEMENT EFFECTIVENESS SCORECARD

Organization
Mission Statement
- written — YES NO
- approved — YES NO
- understood — YES NO
- reviewed — YES NO

Department Structure
- organization chart
  - complete — YES NO
  - current — YES NO
- appropriate for mission — YES NO

Personnel Management

Job Descriptions
- written — YES NO
- approved — YES NO
- complete set — YES NO

Performance Reviews
- periodic — YES NO
- formal — YES NO
- documented — YES NO

Short-term objectives
- M.B.O. for managers and supervisory — YES NO
- monthly objectives for analysts and programmers — YES NO

Training
- yearly forecast — YES NO
- support planned projects — YES NO
- history by subject and employee — YES NO

Turnover
- appropriate (10%) — YES NO

Contract Employees
- moderate usage — YES NO

Management Planning and Control
Dp Long Range Plan
- yearly — YES NO
- support organizational/user dept. goals — YES NO
- approved — YES NO
- feedback on last year's plan — YES NO
- complete — YES NO

Management Control

Project Control

Project Selection

User/Management Council
- appropriate management level — YES NO
- timely meetings — YES NO

Other Selection Methods — YES NO

Project Development Process
- standard development process — YES NO
- project request — YES NO
- phased approach — YES NO
- review points — YES NO
- phased user approval — YES NO
- phased cost/schedule calculations — YES NO
- program and documentation standards — YES NO
- appreviated for small projects — YES NO
- maintenance projects — YES NO

Project Planning and Control System
- match requirements and resources — YES NO
- shift resources and develop new plans — YES NO
- coordinate project activities — YES NO
- predict problems — YES NO
- measure — YES NO
  - cost vs. plan — YES NO
  - accomplishment vs. schedule — YES NO
- project reviews/critiques — YES NO
- identification of resources expended — YES NO

Operational Control
- standard instructions, run books — YES NO
- weekly/daily schedules — YES NO
- analysis of schedule vs. capacity — YES NO
- forecast of load vs. capacity — YES NO
- analysis of machine downtime — YES NO
- measurement of operational performance — YES NO

Budget
- accurate — YES NO
- actual vs. planned — YES NO
- monthly — YES NO

Accountability
Chargeout System
- accurate accumulation — YES NO
- rational allocation basis — YES NO
- accurate allocation — YES NO
- understood by users — YES NO
- allows acquisition of new hardware — YES NO

User Requirements
- user satisfaction — YES NO
- project backlog — YES NO

Security
- policy statement — YES NO
- risk analysis — YES NO
- responsibility assigned — YES NO
- contingency plan — YES NO
- physical/logical security — YES NO
- off-site storage — YES NO

TOTAL YES ANSWERS ÷ 67 = SCORE

MAY 1980

A measure of accountability for dp expenditures is how well user requirements are being met.

those for chargeout accounting, it is clear that chargeout frequently offers the more significant advantages where management is vigorous or the edp department is becoming mature.''

A chargeout system should accurately accumulate all resources consumed; e.g., disk space, core, programer time, data entry time, and have a rational basis for allocation of costs. The system may be changed to promote different objectives. For example, production, maintenance, or new systems development can be encouraged or discouraged through adjustments in the chargeout system. New systems development may be partly or wholly subsidized, charged on a fixed cost basis, or charged for resources consumed.

The chargeout system must accurately allocate costs according to an approved method, be understood by users, and adequately provide for the acquisition of new hardware.

User requirements. Another measure of accountability for dp expenditures is how well user requirements are being met. The dp department exists to service users. If user requirements are not being met, the dp department is not fulfilling its mission.

Here are some indicators of how well users are being served:

● User satisfaction. How do major users rate dp service in terms of cost (production systems, new development), time performance (production systems, new development) and quality (maintenance, new development)?

"Are users satisfied with speed and quality of service? If not, why not? If they are, have operations procedures and capacities been studied to ensure that this is not being achieved through highly inefficient procedures which are hidden by the existence of excessive computer manpower and machine resources?"[5]

● Project backlog

Security. The dp department is responsible for the security of the hardware and information entrusted to it. This program should include a general policy statement outlining the objectives and scope of the security program and an analysis of risks and exposures to determine the position of the dp facility regarding security. Overall responsibility for the security program should be assigned to one person.

Development of a contingency plan

on how to respond to and recover from emergency situations should also be a part of the security program.   ✸

5. Ibid.

JACK EWERS

Mr. Ewers is a senior staff specialist and application consultant in Honeywell's Corporate Computer Operations in Minneapolis, Minn. He provides consulting services for Honeywell on data processing technology and management and office automation. He is currently chairman of a special interest group on programmer productivity at the University of Minnesota Management Information Systems Research Center.

Part VII: Management and Productivity

"Exact scientific knowledge and methods are everywhere, sooner or later to replace rule-of-thumb,"

—Fredrick Taylor

Software technology is in a state of rapid development. Advanced concepts like Ada™, fourth-generation languages, modern software engineering environments, and rapid prototyping fill the literature and offer a glimmer of hope to those trying to improve the productivity of their organizations. Yet, it is a fact that most software shops do not use the state-of-the-art in their current state-of-the-practice. Because technology insertion is capital intensive and time is of the essence, it often takes years to transition something new into a production organization. How can management make better use of the software technology at their disposal? What can they do to quicken the transfer of technology into practice in their shops? What are the costs and the ramifications of establishing corporate programs committed to improving productivity and quality? These and other similar questions are addressed in the five articles reprinted in this section.

In "Managing Change," Braverman describes steps that can be taken by managers to anticipate and control change. He argues that there will always be change and that the manager must be ready to handle it. My own experience confirms that he is right. The difference between a good manager and a mediocre one is the person's ability to cope with change.

In "Software Engineering Practices in the US and Japan," Zelkowitz et al. investigate the topic of software technology transfer by surveying development practices of 30 companies in the United States and Japan. They make comparisons between the two countries and provide several recommendations for improving software productivity in their conclusions.

The next three articles deal with the issues and experiences associated with productivity and quality management. In "Managing Software Development Projects for Maximum Productivity," Howes discusses the complex subject of productivity measurement and then proposes a simple measurement scheme and relates it to the standard tools a manager uses to plan and control a project. In "Building Quality and Productivity into a Large Software System," Prell and Sheng describe the approaches they used to improve the way AT&T Bell Laboratories managed the people and information associated with the development of 5ESS switching system. Metrics are discussed as they relate how their strategy worked in practice on this large development. In "Software Engineering with GTE," Griffin discusses the steps GTE took to deal with the issues of technology transfer and standardization. This discussion provides pointers to diversified organizations trying to figure out how to use the technology base to improve their productivity.

Managing Change

by Philip H. Braverman

Some changes are unavoidable. Some are desirable. Some come down as edicts; others just sneak in. Set up ways to handle them before they happen.

Most project managers would agree that "change" is the major factor influencing the success or failure of a dp development project. It's as simple as this: Changes that occur during the course of a project are not only unavoidable, but are often desirable if the application produced is not to be obsolete or irrelevant by the time it is installed. Uncontrolled changes, on the other hand may adversely affect schedules, costs, productivity, rework and morale.

> Observe always that everything is the result of a change and get used to thinking that there is nothing Nature loves so well as to change existing forms and to make new ones like them.
>
> Marcus Aurelius, *Meditations*

Change must be an orderly, controlled process if project disasters are to be averted. This requires a fundamental understanding of the origin of change and some tools and techniques to assist project management. A procedure for controlling change must be a formal part of every project plan, and an accepted standard in the organization's dp user management system.

Let's define what we mean by "change" in the context of a dp development project:

• Change is any event, action, or edict which may affect the scope of a project, the schedule of a project, or the resources planned for the project.

• The net effect of the change to the scope, schedule or resources could be zero—but that is usually not the case.

• The normal case is that the change will add more function, lengthen the project schedule, and cost more. Changes are, therefore, the enemy of those who get committed to a project with fixed schedules and resources, in an environment where change can foster defensive behavior and reduce cooperation between the users and dp.

> He that will not apply new remedies must expect new evils.
>
> Bacon

Change is usually described as stemming from "internal" or "external" forces.

Internal changes are derived from events such as:

reorganizations

new products to be produced

policy of business practice changes

requirements for new information

misunderstood requirements

departmental cutbacks

External changes may come from:

competitive pressures for increased service

federal or local legislation

union contract conditions

changes in capability or availability of hardware or software

Any of these (and this is by no means an exhaustive list) can have an effect on the project—usually a substantial effect. And of course, the longer the project, the more likely that these events will occur.

Any one of them may be a showstopper and wreak havoc on a project at any stage, causing a major change of direction or even the demise of the project. However, these sources of change are usually not very subtle. They come crashing down, often as not, as directives or edicts. They are widely known and easily explained to executive management and to the users, who may not like the effects on the costs or schedules, but can at least understand why things have changed.

A project change control system should be able to handle these situations nicely so that resulting changes to the job definition schedule and resources will be tolerated by management. It's not all that easy. You still have to know what you are doing and have some procedural tools to deal with change. Unfortunately, few projects or installations have an adequate way to control project change.

Project assumptions and management and user expectations are much more subtle and difficult kinds of "change" to deal with, ones that can cause the most aggravation and frequently can cause unpleasant surprises toward the end of the project.

Assumptions and expectations —"theirs" and "ours"

As project managers and good estimators we build a set of plans for each subphase of the development process. Besides the overall detailed work plans and schedules there are plans for: testing, training, documentation, conversion, financial reviews, project reviews and more. Each plan is based on a certain set of assumptions which incorporated the best (at the time) knowledge available.

Plan assumptions fix such project variables as resources, skill levels, productivity, decision and approval times, available hardware, test time, systems programming support and dozens more. That's what goes into the project plans. Our expected output is what we assumed about the product we produce: the functions that are implemented, the quality of the documentation, ease of use, amount of implementation support required, reliability of the code, system performance, and so forth.

Now the problem is that unless all of the plan assumptions are quantified and well documented at the beginning of the project, there may be little basis for empathy and a lot of nonproductive explaining to do when a schedule slips or a cost overrun occurs because an assumption turned out to be miles off. For example, test time requirements should have been specifically set as a plan assumption, such as "two turnarounds per day per programmer during prime working hours and an overnight shot." If you were counting on decisions being made within "five working days" by the users, this should have been documented. If a certain release of a systems software product was "needed prior to systems test entry," that milestone should have been built into the project plan and put on the critical path.

The list of plan assumptions, which is really a list of dependencies for a successful project, must also be subject to change control. Unless the assumptions are well documented to begin with, there are no formal reference points from which to measure changes. The project manager has to rely on memory and often vague commitments, "but I thought that was your responsibility." Or, "Well, I really didn't actually commit that resource, I thought it was still an open issue."

Is it possible to "manage" management and user expectations? Controlling change becomes difficult, to say the least, if management and the users had widely differing expectations from the project manager in the first place. If there is no uniform basis of understanding, there really is no baseline from which to measure change and the project may have very little chance for success. How often have you heard comments like these from users well into a project?

I thought that transaction would be in the system!

Everyone knows it should work this way.

You should have known we can't go on-line in that month.

I thought you got all the bugs out while you were testing!

My people weren't consulted before you made that change.

What do you mean my data files need cleaning?

I expected response time to be much faster than that.

These examples may reopen old wounds for many of us. Unfortunately they occur much too often in developing complex on-line application systems. Now expectations are not 100% manageable, but here are some ideas which may be useful:

Management and user expectations should be fully understood before the start of the project. This can be accomplished with pre-project reviews of the project goals, project plans and assumptions. The project planners should educate the users and management as to what the product will look like, how it will be developed, and when it will be installed and tuned. Differences in perception about the project or the system should be sought out and promptly resolved. When management and user goals are aligned with the project team goals, you can proceed with more confidence.

The outcome of these sessions should be documented to reflect a common understanding of the major schedule milestones and assumptions. Feasibility studies or other project documentation generated thus far should be updated. A simple example might be the preparation and distribution of a list of functions to be included in the system and specifying also the function that will not be included in the first version. (If this sounds like I am suggesting user-oriented requirements and general design documentation, I certainly am.)

The system performance issue should also be addressed at an early stage. Even though there may be little basis for precise performance statements at this time, project management should understand what the user requires and what he perceives to be "good" or "bad" response time. Early user education is required regarding

PROJECT CHANGE REQUEST

PROJECT TITLE_____ PCR NUMBER_____

INITIATED BY _____ DATE SUBMITTED_____

DESCRIPTION OF THE CHANGE (Add Attachments if necessary)_____

FUNCTIONS, PROGRAMS OF FILES AFFECTED_____

DOCUMENTATION AFFECTED_____

HARDWARE OR SYSTEMS SOFTWARE IMPACT_____

CHANGES TO BE IMPLEMENTED BY_____

PLANNED START_____ PLANNED COMPLETION_____

APPROVED BY_____ TITLE_____ DATE_____

RESOURCES AFFECTED   YES   NO   SUMMARY OF EFFECT
MANPOWER   ___   ___
SCHEDULE   ___   ___
OTHER   ___   ___

ADDITIONAL APPROVALS   APPROVED BY_____ DATE_____
                       APPROVED BY_____ DATE_____

A change request form is first submitted to the project manager for evaluation and approval. If no resources are affected, the approved form may be used to communicate the change and initiate the work. If the change impacts resources, additional approvals may be required from management, the users, or a change board.

the factors that affect system performance, as many are user influenced design alternatives as well as management hardware expenditure decisions.

A lack of a clear definition of the user and management responsibilities during the project causes many project

---

*. . . especially for **small** projects, where sometimes the effects of change are felt more violently . . .*

---

problems. The user must be told to expect that he will have to fund and provide the resources for such tasks as design reviews, file cleaning, training, and methods and procedures if those were the plan assumptions. A project manager needs a firm commitment for these resources before the project starts —rather than waiting until the last minute and invariably being caught short.

To summarize, managing project changes that will ultimately affect the original expectations of the users and management can only be accomplished if there is a baseline of understanding and assumptions, documented and free of technical jargon, to which normal change control procedures can be applied.

Necessary, nice to have, and "nonsense"

Proper management of change requires a written, widely understood, enforceable change control standard or procedure. A procedure once developed and proven workable should become the standard for all projects and one that management expects will be applied consistently. Vital components of a procedure for controlling change include:

- a way to detect change—what is under change control?
- initiation of a request for a change
- a change evolution scheme
- a management decision process
- incorporation of the change into the project plan

As a project manager, I tend to hold every member of the project team responsible for an awareness and feedback to me of any event or problem that may impact our schedule, workscope or resource requirements. Ultimately, I suppose, the project manager bears this burden, but everyone on the project should be properly educated and motivated to contribute. In order to help the project manager, the team must be thoroughly familiar with those items under change control such as: the requirements and design documentation, the project plans, estimates, assumptions, personnel assignments

and commitments. That puts the team in an excellent position to detect subtle changes, and the side benefits of this level of orientation are obvious.

If you can create an environment in which each team member understands the reason for controlling change and is motivated to use your change control procedures, you have a much better chance of making your project a success.

A useful mechanism for introducing a change into your change control system is a Project Change Request notifier (see Fig. 1). The request can be filled out by anyone associated with the project including the user groups. It is a project management control document, not a technical document. It should contain a certain minimum amount of information:

- statement of a problem or a need to change a specification
- some priority indication of importance or business impact
- the date requested or required for the change to be incorporated

When the change request is given to the project manager, it should be logged and the originator given some idea as to when the change will be evaluated. The originator may be asked to provide further information or clarification which will assist the personnel who are assigned to evaluate the change.

Changes fall rather neatly into three categories: necessary, nice to have, and nonsense. Then there is a time dimension—whether to make the change immediately or perhaps in a later version of the system. If the change evaluation committee (or change review board) has a good mix of users and technical people, management ought to receive a sound recommendation as to the importance of the change and the probable effect on workscope schedule and project resources.

Somebody in the management system must then make a decision. Often top management is involved if the change is of sufficient magnitude or highly controversial. But probably most changes will be approved or disapproved, depending upon some predetermined criteria, by the project manager and his user counterpart. The recommendations of any change evaluation, however brief, should become a part of the ongoing project documentation.

If approved, the new effort must be incorporated into the project plans and schedules. This is a crucial step which should be done promptly, and even for small changes. Otherwise the sum total of a lot of small changes may look like a large overrun by the end of the project. The old saw that projects slip a

day at a time is mostly a reflection of project changes of many varieties that just didn't get properly documented when they occurred.

Project personnel must be made aware of approved changes and adjust their schedules and priorities accordingly. In fact, change control is an excellent tool to communicate new information to the project team. It's what can keep everyone working to common goals and eliminate expensive misunderstandings. By the way, don't forget to include some time in the original project estimate for change evaluation. On a long, large project, this task can consume a substantial number of man-weeks. The results of change control activities should be reported upward on a regular basis along with other aspects of concern to management and the users.

A "must" for management

A system for managing change is a "must" for project management, *especially* for small projects, where sometimes the effects of change are felt more violently than on projects of greater size. A good system can help a project stay on course and provide an audit trail of all the events and decisions that may have caused changes to the schedules and resource requirements over the life of the project. (Changes weren't just allowed to "happen," they were always under control.) However, to control change, you must establish and maintain a base from which to measure change. This means good documentation of: system requirements, specifications, and system design, as well as project plans and estimates, assumptions, and expectations. Get started! Good management control of change will begin with change request #001. ✳

Mr. Braverman is manager of San Francisco area projects for IBM's dp services organization, a contract programming group. For the past six years he has been responsible for numerous dp development projects in San Francisco and in Havant, England. Prior to entering project management, he was district education manager for IBM in San Francisco.

This in-depth survey of 30 companies reveals actual goings-on in software production. Results show that, while practice is 10 years behind research, we have the tools to narrow the gap.

Software Engineering Practices in the US and Japan

Marvin V. Zelkowitz, Raymond T. Yeh, Richard G. Hamlet, John D. Gannon, and Victor R. Basili,
University of Maryland

The term *software engineering* first appeared in the late 1960's to describe ways to develop, manage, and maintain software so that resulting products are reliable, correct, efficient, and flexible. [1] The 15 years of software engineering study by the computer science community has created a need to assess the impact that numerous advances have had on actual software production. To address this need, IBM asked the University of Maryland to conduct a survey of different program development environments in industry to determine the state of the art in software development and to ascertain which software engineering techniques are most effective. Unlike other surveys, such as the recent one on Japanese technology, [2] we were less interested in recent research topics. Journals, such as the *IEEE Transactions on Software Engineering* adequately report such developments; we were more interested in discovering which methods and tools are actually being used by industry today. [3] This report contains the results of that survey.

The goal of this project, which began in spring 1981 and continued through summer 1983, was to sample about 20 organizations, including IBM, and study their development practices. We contacted major hardware vendors in the US, and most agreed to participate. Several other software companies and other "high-technology" companies were contacted and agreed to participate. While we acknowledge that this survey was not all inclusive, we did study each company in depth, and based on discussions with others in the field, we believe that what we found was typical.

We were not interested in R&D activities in these companies. Most had individuals engaged in interesting developments, and most knew what was current in the field. Our primary concern was what the average programmers in these companies did to develop software projects.

Data was collected in a two-step process. A detailed survey form was sent to each participating company. When the form was returned, a follow-up visit was made to clarify the answers given. We believe that this process, although limiting the number of places surveyed, allowed us to present more accurate information than if we had relied on the returned forms alone.

Each survey form contained two parts. Section one asked for general comments on software development for the organization as a whole. The information typically represented the *standards and practices* document for the organization. In addition, several recently completed projects within each company were studied. Each project leader completed the second section of the survey form, which described the tools and techniques used on that project.

Several companies were concerned that the projects we were looking at were not typical of them. (Interestingly, very few companies claimed to be doing typical software.) However, since the companies selected the projects they described on the form, we believe we saw the better developed projects—if there is any bias to our report, it is that the average industry project is probably worse than what we describe here.

Thirty organizations in both the US and Japan participated in the study: five IBM divisions, 12 other US companies, and 13 Japanese companies. About half the Japanese companies were not interviewed, while the other half were interviewed to varying degrees of detail. All US companies were interviewed. The "Acknowledgments" section at the end of this article lists the US participants. Some of the Japanese participants never responded to our request for permission to use their names, so only a few Japanese companies are listed.

Table 1 characterizes the companies visited, divisions within a company, and the projects studied, arbitrarily

Reprinted from *Computer*, June 1984, pages 57-66. Copyright 1984 by The Institute of Electrical and Electronics Engineers, Inc.

classifying projects and teams into four groups according to sizes: small, medium, large, and very large. Projects are classified according to the number of staff-months needed to complete them, and teams according to the number of members. All companies listed with zero projects were Japanese companies that submitted part one of our form only. We interviewed at least one manager in depth in all surveyed US companies, in addition to general project management personnel.

After reviewing the basic data, we recognized the following three software development environments:

(1) *contract software*. Department of Defense and NASA aerospace systems;
(2) *data processing applications*. Software produced by an organization for its own internal business use; and

(3) *systems software*. Operating system support software produced by a hardware vendor as part of a total hardware-software package of products for a given operating system.

A single company might have projects in more than one of these categories. For example, one aerospace company was involved in several DoD-related projects and one internal data processing application.

General observations

This article is a series of general observations about each environment. Two of our first observations were that the data collected by each organization is insufficient and interpretations for similar concepts (e.g., phases of the life cycle, job descriptions from similar sounding titles, what certain automated tools should or did do, etc.) differ. We could have generated a survey consisting of 50 to 100 techniques and proceeded to tabulate them in a report. However, as we found out, the detailed interview process was much more informative. In addition, we would not want others quoting such numbers, since they would be subjective and imprecise. We believe that the structure we chose gives a better idea of software development today.

Every company had either written guidelines or unwritten folklore as to how software was developed, and major deviations were rare. Differences in projects within a company were less than the differences in projects among companies. But more significant was the wide gulf between practices in industry and those documented in current software engineering literature.

The literature contains many references to software engineering methodology, including tool support throughout the life cycle, specification and design languages, test data generators and coverage metrics, measurement and management practices, and other techniques. We found surprisingly little use of software engineering practices across all companies. No organization fully tries to use the available technology. Although some companies had stronger management practices than others, none used tools to support these practices in any significant way.

We are not implying that the companies do not have talented personnel. Most have individual projects that try to keep abreast of current technology, but within each company these projects are relatively rare, and the resulting experience is rarely applied to a different project.

Table 1. Companies surveyed. The size of the project is in staff-months where (S)mall = < 10, (M)edium = 10-100, (L)arge = 100-1000, and (V)ery (L)arge = > 1000. Team size is in staff members where S = < 10, M = 10-25, L = 25-50, and VL = > 50.

CODE	NO. OF DIVISIONS	NO. OF PROJECTS	INTERVIEWED	PROJECT SIZE	TEAM SIZE
A	2	3	Yes	L	L
B	2	7	Yes	VL	VL
C	1	1	No	S	M
D	1	3	Yes	L	L
E	3	4	Yes	VL	VL
F	1	3	Yes	VL	VL
G	1	2	Yes	L	L
H	1	7	Yes	L	M
I	1	9	Yes	VL	VL
J	1	4	Yes	L	VL
K	1	8	Yes	VL	M
L	1	1	Yes	L	VL
M	1	3	Yes	M	VL
N	1	2	No	S	S
O	1	1	Yes	VL	VL
P	1	1	No	M	-
Q	2	0	No	M	L
R	1	0	No	-	-
S	1	1	Yes	M	S
T	1	4	Yes	VL	VL
U	1	0	Yes	L	VL
V	1	1	Yes	M	S
W	1	1	Yes	L	S
X	1	1	No	L	S
Y	1	1	No	L	-
Z	1	2	Yes	M	S
AA	2	5	Yes	VL	VL
BB	1	1	Yes	M	S
CC	1	1	Yes	L	S
DD	1	7	Yes	VL	VL

Organizational structure. Most companies had an organizational structure similar to the one in Figure 1. The software technology group typically has one to five individuals collecting data, modeling resource usage, and generating standards and practices documents. However, this group has no direct authority to mandate software engineering practices even within a single division. As a result, standards often vary within a single organization.

We believe that this structure explains a current anomaly in the use of software engineering techniques. Developers of real products often think that members of the software technology (research) group (who attend na-

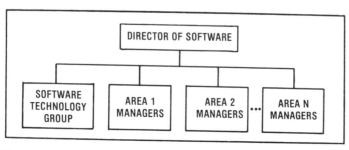

Figure 1. Typical organization structure.

tional conferences and write most of the research papers) are too optimistic about the effects of these techniques, since they have not applied them to software products. Managers know their personnel often lack the education and experience needed to apply these techniques successfully. Even techniques that have been adopted are frequently misused. For example, although many companies used the term *chief programmer* to describe their programming team organizations, most descriptions bore little resemblance to the technique outlined in the literature. Many projects had two to three levels of managers who handled staff and resource acquisition but did not actively participate in system design.

A further problem in many organizations is that generally no one person is the Director of Software (see Figure 1), responsible for making software decisions. In some companies, software activities span several divisions. So even if such a person exists in each division, standards vary across the company. Interestingly, organizations often have one person making hardware decisions.

Tool use. Tools are not widely used in the industry. Not too surprisingly, the use of tools varies inversely from how far the tools are from the code development phase. Tools are most frequently used during the code and unit test phase of software development (e.g., compilers, code auditors, test coverage monitors, etc.). Tools are less frequently used in the adjacent phases of the software life cycle—design and integration (e.g., PDL processors and source code control systems). Few requirements or maintenance tools are used. Table 2 gives some indication of which techniques and tools are used. In classifying companies, we were somewhat subjective because we counted tools used on most projects, but not necesarily all, within a company. For example, every company used high-level languages on some projects, but they also used assembly language quite frequently.

Companies tend to adopt methods relatively early because their "capitalization" cost is relatively low, but tool use takes longer, since development or purchase costs are higher.

Although the percentages in Table 2 are not exact, the trends seem clear. Tool use generally has the flavor of vintage-1970 timesharing. Jobs have a batch flavor in that runs are built and then compiled. Tool support is minimal—mostly compilers and simple editors.

Timesharing computer systems and compiler writing became practical in the late 1960's and early 1970's; thus, on-line access and high-level languages can probably be labeled the successes of the 1960's. Similarly, since reviews and pseudocode or program design language (PDL) were so widely used, we can call them the successes of the 1970's. It is disappointing that few other tools have been adopted by industry. Testing tools are used by only 27 percent of the companies, and most are simply test-data generators. Only two companies used any form of unit test tool to measure test-case coverage. In a few cases, tools were developed but deemed too expensive to use. In one company, the quality assurance group had developed a testing tool and was trying to get it used on various projects. However, each project manager with whom we spoke

praised the tool but claimed it was too expensive to run, increased the size of the system too much, etc.

PDL is frequently used, but it is not automated. Some PDL processors are simply manual formatters, while some do a pretty print and indent the code. Often the PDL is only a coding standard and not enforced by any tool. Only one location had a PDL processor that checked interfaces and definition/use patterns for variables.

Our sample identified two general classes of companies. One class had strong management control over development with little tool support, while the other had relatively lax control over programmers, who generally built their own tools. In one extreme case, three project managers we interviewed expounded the virtues of their individual text editors.

The problems in using tools can be attributed to several factors. Corporate management, particularly of hardware vendors, tends to have an engineering background. Managers have little, if any, software background and are not sympathetic with the need for tools. No separate corporate entity exists whose charter includes tools, so we have no focal point for tool selection, deployment, and evaluation. Tools must be funded from project development budgets, so there is a fair amount of risk and expenditure for a project manager to adopt a new tool and train people to use it. Since project management is rated according to whether current costs and schedules are met, tool use must be amortized across several projects to be effective. Consequently, a project manager building and using a new tool will almost always stand out as unproductive. Companies often work on different hardware, so tools are not transportable, limiting their scope and their perceived advantage. The most striking example of this handicap was one system in which one million dollars was spent building a database, yet no one ever thought of using that database on another system. The need to maintain large existing products (written in the past in assembly code) makes it hard to introduce a new tool that processes a new higher level langauge. Finally, many of the tools are incomplete and poorly documented. Because such tools fail to live up to promises, project managers are justifiably reluctant to adopt them or consider subsequently developed tools.

Review process. At the end of each phase, the evolving software product is subject to a review process to try to uncover problems as soon as possible. A review might be either an *inspection* or a *walk-through,* without regard to the distinctions made in the software engineering

Table 2. Method or tool use.

METHOD OR TOOL	PERCENTAGE OF COMPANIES
High-level languages	100
On-line access	93
Reviews	73
Program design languages	63
Some formal methodology	41
Some test tools	27
Code auditors	18
Chief programmer team	7
Any formal verification	0
Formal requirements or specifications	0

literature.[4] Nearly everyone agrees that reviews work, and nearly everyone uses them, but the ways reviews are conducted differ greatly. Most agree that software projects can be routinely completed within time and budget constraints that only a few years ago could be managed only by luck and sweat. Reviews were instituted first for code, then extended to design. Extensions to requirements and test-case design are not universal, and some feel that the technique may have been pushed beyond it usefulness. Managers would like to extend the review process, while the technical people are more inclined to limit it to the best understood phases of development.

Two aspects of reviews must be separated: managerial control and technical utility. Managers must be concerned with both aspects, but technical success cannot be assured by insisting that certain forms be completed. If the tasks assigned to the reviewers are ill-defined, or the form of the product reviewed inappropriate, the review will waste the time of valuable people. Lower level managers prefer to use reviews only when they think reviews are appropriate.

The technical success of the review process rests on the expertise and interest of the people conducting the review, not on the mechanism itself. The review process must be continually changed to reflect past successes and failures, and much of this information is subjective, implicitly known to experienced participants. Some historical information is encoded in review checklists, which newcomers can be trained to use. However, subjective items like the *completeness* of requirements are of little help to a novice.

New and old companies differed considerably in their approaches to reviews. New companies were less committed to reviews, treating code reviews as training exercises for junior employees or as verification aids for particularly difficult modules. Since the newer companies did not have a large existing software base, they emphasized rapid development rather than maintenance. However, as companies grew and aged, accumulating software, reviews seemed to take on added significance as an important verification aid.

Data collection. Every company collects some data, but not much of it becomes part of the corporate memory to be used beyond the project on which it was collected. Data generally belongs to individual managers, and they decide what to do with it. Data is rarely evaluated and used in an analysis to see if the process could have been improved. The opposite is true in Japanese companies in which "postmortem" analysis is frequently performed.

Several companies are experimenting with resource models, such as Price S. Slim.[5,6] No company seems to trust any model enough to use it extensively; instead the models are used to check manual estimates. Figure 2 shows that little data is being collected across all companies. The levels of Figure 2 are somewhat arbitrary; *high* represents the amount of data collected by the NASA Software Engineering Laboratory (resource use by programmer in each module, detailed error reports including causes, etc.), while *low* represents a minimal amount of data (e.g., the number of major and minor errors detected in reviews, outstanding error reports per time period, etc.).[7] In general, more error data than resource data is collected, and resource data is typically limited to hours spent by each programmer on the project to facilitate project billing.

It is extremely difficult to compare data across companies. First of all, quantitative data is quite rare within most companies. Error data is rarely tied to causes of errors, and the process of counting errors is never fed back into the development process. Knowing how many errors occurred does not necessarily improve the programming process if you don't know why they occurred. To keep the review process open, results are sometimes limited to the review group and the quality assurance manager. In addition each company has different definitions for most of the measured quantities, such as

- *lines of code,* which is defined as source lines, comment lines, with or without data declarations, executable lines or generated lines;
- *milestone dates,* which depend on the local software life cycle used by the company (whether requirements, specification, or maintenance data are included will significantly affect the results);
- *personnel,* which might include programmers, analysts, typists, librarians, or managers.

The differing definitions prevent any meaningful comparison. It is quite evident that the computer industry needs more work on the standardization of terms before it can address these quantitative issues. Also, it is not clear that management believes in a need for such data except for budgeting, so it is rarely collected.

Software development environments in the US

In describing the general characteristics of software environments, we limit discussion, for the most part, to the 13 companies in the US where we made site visits to over 20 different locations and interviewed approximately 60 project managers. Comments on Japanese software develop-

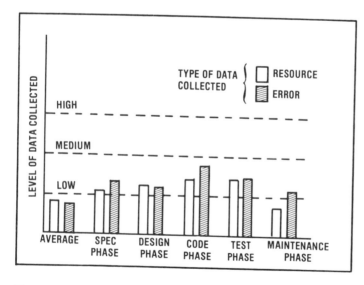

Figure 2. Amount and type of data collected.

ment and comparisons with the techniques used in the US are presented in the subsequent section.

General life cycle. The life cycle of a project consists of the requirements and specification phase, the design phase, the code and unit test phase, and the integration test phase.

Requirements and specification phase. At all places contacted, requirements were in natural language text. Some projects had requirements documents that could be processed by machine, but tool support was limited to screen-oriented text editors. No analysis tools (like SREM and PSL/PSA were used except on toy projects.[8,9] Projects were either too small to justify the use of a processor or too large to make such use economical.

Reviews determine if the system architecture is complete, if the specifications are complete, the internal and external interfaces are defined, and the system can be implemented. These reviews are the most difficult to perform, and their results depend greatly on the quality of people doing the review because the specifications are not formal. There is little traceability between specifications and designs.

Design phase. Most designs are expressed in some form of PDL or pseudocode, which makes design reviews effective. Tools that manipulate PDL vary from editors to simple text formatters. Only one company extended its PDL processor to analyze interfaces and the data flow in the resulting design.

While the use of PDL seems to be accepted practice, its use is not particularly effective. For example, we consider the expansion of PDL to code a reasonable measure of the detail in a design. A PDL-to-source-code expansion ratio of 1:1 may indicate that the design has the same detail as its eventual code. With design and code being separate tasks, this expansion indicates that the two concepts are not separated. The expansion ratios of PDL to source code were 1:5-10 at one location, 1:3-10 at another, and 1:1.5(!!)-3 at a third. Customer involvement with design varied greatly even within installations. Some produced volumes of PDL with an attitude similar to that for older projects that produced many detailed flowcharts: Nobody cares, but it's in the contract.

Code and unit test phase. Most code was in higher level languages—Fortran for scientific applications or some local variation of C, Pascal or PL/1 for systems work. In the aerospace industry, Fortran was the predominant language. People who normally worked in assembly language thought that Fortran and PL/1 signficantly enhanced their productivity. Historical studies have shown that programmers produce an average of one line of debugged source code per hour regardless of the language. (Brooks contains a concise review of this work.[10])

Despite claims that they used chief programmer teams in development, very few first- or second-line managers ever wrote any PDL or code themselves. We heard complaints that chief programmer teams worked well only with small groups, six to nine people, and on projects in

which a person's responsibility was not divided among different groups.

Much of the code and unit test phase lacks proper machine support. Code auditors could greatly enhance the code review process. We studied one code review form and found that 13 of 32 checks could be automated. Manual checks are currently performed for proper indentation of the source code, initialization of variables, interface consistency between the calling and called modules, etc.

Most unit testing could be called *adversary* testing. The programmer claims to have tested a module and the manager either does or doesn't believe the programmer. Almost no unit test tools are used to measure how effectively the tests devised by a programmer exercise the source code. While a test coverage measure like statement or branch coverage is nominally required during the review of unit test, mechanisms are rarely available to ensure that such criteria have been met.

Integration test phase. Integration testing is mostly stress testing—running the product on as much real or simulated data as is possible. The data processing environment had the highest level of stress testing during integration testing. Testing in the systems software environment was not as rigorous compared to integration testing in the data processing environment.

Resources. Office space for programmers varied from one to two programmers sharing a Santa-Teresa style office with a terminal to large bullpens divided by low, movable partitions.[11] Terminals were the dominant mode for computer access. Some sites had terminals in offices, while others had large terminal rooms. The current average seems to be about two to seven programmers per terminal. Newer companies had two terminals per programmer and some were replacing terminals with personal computers. Within the last two years most companies have realized the cost-effectiveness of giving programmers adequate computer access via terminals but have still not provided adequate response time. A response time of 10 to 20 seconds was considered good at some places, where a subsecond response time was possible.[12]

Most companies are willing to invest in hardware, such as terminals, to assist their programmers but are reluctant to invest in software that might be as beneficial.

Education. Most companies have agreements with a local university to send employees for advanced training, and have their own seminar series. However, there is little training for project management. Only one company has a fairly extensive training policy for all software personnel.

Many companies had two problems with their educational program: (1) Programmers were sent to courses with

Table 3. Six lines of source code per staff-month.

LINES OF CODE	APPLICATION AND LANGUAGE
75	OS in Assembly
91	I/O controller in HLL
142-167	OS in HLL
182-280	Assembly applications

little or no follow-up experience, so what they learned was rarely put into practice and often forgotten; and (2) Some sites were far away from any quality university, and the isolation caused problems.

Data collection efforts. The data typically collected on projects includes the number of lines of PDL for each level of design, the number of lines of source code produced per staff-month, the number and kinds of errors found in reviews, and a variety of measures on program trouble reports. As Table 3 shows, the range in productivity was from 75 to 280 lines of code per month for different products using relatively similar development methods. This discrepancy illustrates that using lines of code as a measure of productivity is unwise and that more refined productivity measures are needed. Because of the differing application areas, we cannot really compare numbers in Table 3. However, it does seem obvious that the difficulty of the application area has more impact on productivity than the implementation language used (operating systems and other real-time programs being the most difficult).

One location reported that two major and five minor errors per 1000 lines were found during reviews in the design phase, and five major and eight minor errors per 1000 lines

---

US software developers are primarily producing applications, systems, or data processing software.

---

were found during reviews in the code phase. Realistically, though, the classification of errors into categories like *major* and *minor* may be useful for quality control in product distribution, but it sheds little light on the causes and possible treatments of these errors and their prevention in future systems.

Development environments. The development environments centered on three types of projects: applications software, systems software, and data processing.

Applications software. We studied 13 projects in four companies that produce applications software. In this area, software is contracted from the organization by a Federal agency, typically the Department of Defense or NASA. Software is developed and "thrown over the wall" to the agency for operation and maintenance. Typically, none of the organizations we surveyed were interested in maintenance activities. All believed that the payoff in maintenance was too low and that smaller software houses could do whatever maintenance was necessary.

Since contracts are awarded after a competitive bidding cycle initiated by a "Request for Proposal," and requirements analysis is typically charged against company overhead, analysis is kept to a minimum before the contract is awarded. Requirements are written in English, and no formal tool is used. In addition, since the goal is to win a contract, there is a clear distinction between cost and price. *Cost* is the amount needed to build a product—a technical process that most companies feel capable of

handling. On the other hand, *price* is a marketing strategy needed to win a bid. The price has to be low enough to win, but not so low that either money will be lost on the project or the company will be deemed "not responsive" to the requirements of the RFP. Thus, many ideas of software engineering developed during the 1970's on resource estimation and workload characterization are not meaningful in this environment because of the competitive process of winning bids.

In addition, two distinct types of companies emerged within this group—system developers and software developers. The system developers would package both hardware and software for a government agency into products such as a communications network. In this case, most of the costs were for hardware, and software was not considered significant. On the other hand, the software developers simply built systems on existing hardware systems. DEC's PDP/11 series seemed to be the most popular with system builders that were not hardware vendors.

All companies surveyed had a methodology manual; however, they were either out of date, or were just in the process of being updated. In this environment, Department of Defense MIL specifications were a dominant driving force, and most standards were oriented to government policies. The methodology manuals were often policy documents outlining the type of information to be produced by a project but not how to obtain that information.

Tool use was relatively sparse. Fortran was the dominant programming language. Two tools did seem to be used. In compliance with DoD specifications, most had some sort of management reporting forms on resource utilization. However, these generally did not report on programmer activities. PDL was the one programming tool that many companies did depend on, probably because the cost was low.

Staff turnover was uniformly low, generally five to 10 percent a year. Space for programmers seemed adequate, with one to two per office being typical. All locations except one used terminals for all computer access, and that one site had a pilot project to build private offices connected to a local minicomputer.

Systems software. We studied 18 projects produced by 11 vendors. Most of the projects were for large machines although some projects for microprocessors were included. Operating systems for those machines were the most important projects studied. The other projects, mostly compilers and utilities, did not follow the development rules for operating systems projects because the other projects were considered small, and hence their designs would be well understood.

Many companies are heading towards a policy of never building a large product. Development effort is limited to no more than two years and 10 programmers on any particular product. A great deal of effort is expended in the design of traditionally large pieces of software like operating systems to segment them into pieces of this size. Japanese companies also seem quite proficient at designing and assembling small projects only.

Software is generally written on hardware similar to the target machine. Terminals are universally used and the ratio of programmers to terminals varies from 1:2 to 3:1. Getting a terminal is frequently less of a problem than getting CPU cycles to do development.

In most places, software support is generally limited to text editors and interactive compilers. High-level development languages exist, and in most cases, the policy is that they be used; however, a substantial portion of operating systems remains in assembly language (20 to 90 percent depending on the company). The reasons are partly good (such as the prior existence of assembly code) and partly the usual: alternatives have never been considered at the technical level. Text formatting programs are in wide use, but analysis of machine-readable text other than source code is virtually nonexistent.

We studied 18 projects produced by 11 vendors. Most of these were for large machines, with operating systems being the major product.

Most testing is considered part of the development effort. There may be a separate test group, but it reports to the development managers. Only a final field test may be under the control of an independent quality control group. One company assigned the quality control person directly to the development group, but group members believed that the independence of that individual in testing the system had been compromised as a result.

Maintenance is usually handled by the development staff. A field support group obtains trouble reports from the field and forwards them to the development organization for correction. In most cases, the developers, even if working on a new project, handle errors.

Programmers are usually organized into small teams by project, and usually stick with a project until it is completed. The term *chief programmer team* is used incorrectly to describe conventional organizations: a chain of managers (the number depends on project size) who do not program, and small groups of programmers with little responsibility for organization.

Staff turnover is relatively high (up to 20 percent per year) compared with that in the applications software area. Most programmers typically have private cubicles parceled out of large open areas. The lack of privacy is often stated as a negative factor.

Software engineering practices vary widely among the projects we investigated. Not surprisingly, the older the system, the fewer software engineering techniques used.

Data processing. We studied seven data processing projects at five locations, although every location had some data processing activities for internal use. Most data processing software that we studied was developed in Cobol, although some systems were written in Fortran. There is a need to maintain the code throughout the life cycle.

Requirements were mostly in English and unstructured, although one company structured specifications by user function. Designs, especially for terminal-oriented products, were similar—a prototype set of simulated screen displays and menus to which the user could respond. The most striking difference in the data processing environment was the heavy involvement of users in the two development steps. The success of the project depended on how much the user was involved *before* integration testing. One site clearly had a success and a failure on two different projects that used the same methodology. The company directly attributed the success to the high level of interest on the part of the user assigned to the team during development.

All data processing was done at terminals. Office space was more varied than in the other two environments we observed. Some places used one- and two-person offices, while others partitioned large open areas into cubicles. Stress was often high in that overtime was more common, and turnover was the highest in this environment—often up to 30 percent per year. One location had a low turnover rate, which they attributed to their salaries being higher than those offered by comparable companies.

Data processing environments often use a phased approach to development, and quality control is especially important. One company, which had had numerous failures, attributed its recent successes to never attempting any development that would require more than 18 months. Since these systems often managed the company's finances, the need for reliability was most critical, and stress testing was higher than in other areas.

Japan and US comparisons

Unlike the recent survey by Kim[2] which emphasized the integrated tool sets and artificial intelligence techniques being employed by Japanese industry, we found the level of technology used by the Japanese to be similar to US practices, but with some important differences. Programmers in both countries complain about the amount of money going toward hardware development and the lack of resources for software. However, we found that Japanese companies typically optimize resources across the company rather than within a single project. One effect of this policy is that tools become a capitalized investment paid for or developed out of company overhead rather than project funds. The cost of tools is spread among more projects, knowledge about tools is known to more in the company, and project management is more willing to use tools since the risk is lower. Thus, tool development and use is more widespread in Japan. Our survey does reinforce some of the conclusions of the earlier survey, namely:

(1) Japanese often use techniques developed in the US or Europe;
(2) Emphasis seems to be on practical tools.

Two successful techniques used by the Japanese are keeping projects small and relating failures to their causes through postmortem analyses of error data.

Improving software development in the US

While tool use is important for software development, the most important factor that we saw was the quality of the personnel on various projects. We firmly believe that tools cannot replace good people or good methods for software production. However, tool use *can* help a good programmer be even better.

Some very small changes can improve productivity in many installations. While there is no empirical evidence that will permit us to forecast gains, there is a general consensus in the software community (like that for the use of high-level languages) that supports these ideas.

- *More and better computer resources should be made available for development.* The computer systems being used for development are comparable to those available in the late 1960's or early 1970's providing timesharing on large machines. The use of screen editors at some locations has been a major improvement, but other tools seem limited to batch compilers and primitive debugging systems. Response time seems to be a major complaint at many development installations.

- *Methods and tools should be evaluated.* A separate organization with this charter should be established. As of now, it does not appear that any one group in most companies has the responsibility to study the research literature and try promising techniques. Since the most successful tools have been high-level-language compilers, the first tools to be developed should be integrated into compilers. Thus, these tools should concentrate on the design and unit test phases of development, which have formal languages and relatively straightforward compiler extensions. This organization could both acquire and evaluate the tools by looking at case studies and/or conducting experiments.

- *Tool support should be built for a common high-level language.* The tools we would pick first include a PDL processor, a syntax-directed editor—an editor that knows the underlying language syntax and prevents such errors from entering the program [13]—a code auditor, and a unit test coverage monitor. The PDL processor should at least check interfaces. Unfortunately, commercially available processors do little more than format a listing; however, interface checking is nothing more than 20-year-old compiler technology. The processor should also construct graphs of data flow through the design and extract PDL from source code so that while both are maintained together they can be viewed separately. Code auditors can be used to check that source code meets accepted standards and practices. Many checks, such as those to verify whether begin-end blocks are aligned, are boring to perform manually and are therefore error prone. Unit testing tools can evaluate how thoroughly a program has been exercised. These tools are easy to build and should be accepted quickly, since many managers require statement or branch coverage during unit test.

- *PDL processors should support an automated set of metrics that cover the design and coding process.* The metrics in turn can monitor progress; characterize the intermediate products, such as design and source code; and attempt to predict the characteristics of the next phase of development. Possible metrics include design change counts, control and data complexity metrics for source code, and structural coverage metrics for test data. [14]

- *In syntax-directed editors, the grammar of the underlying language is built in, so the programmer needs to include only valid constructs at any point in the program.* Such systems facilitate top-down program development and often permit interactive context switching between program editing and program execution. [13,15] The programmer can then think more about algorithm design than keyboarding the program text.

- *The review process should be improved.* Reviews or inspections are a strong part of current methodology. The review process can be strengthened by the tools mentioned earlier. Manual labor in design and code reviews could be reduced with more effective tools. Such tools would permit reviewers to spend more time on the major purpose of the review—the detection of logical errors—and avoid the distractions of formatting or syntactic anomalies.

- *Incremental development such as iterative enhancement should be used.* [16] Many successful companies limited development to under two years and 10 people. One data processing company, after repeatedly failing to deliver software, decided never to build anything that required more than 18 staff-months. Since then they have been successful. Several other companies reported similar experiences. Large projects tend to have several layers of management and their success seems to depend on a stronger review process that comprises requirements, design, and code reviews. Smaller projects need less management and can succeed with only design reviews.

- *Data should be collected and analyzed.* Most of the data being collected now is used primarily to schedule work assignments. Measurement data can be used to classify projects, evaluate methods and tools, and provide feedback to project managers. Data should be collected across projects to evaluate and help predict the productivity and quality of software. The kind of data collected and the analysis performed should be driven by a set of questions that need answers rather than by what is convenient to collect and analyze. For example, classifying errors into major and minor categories does not shed any light on development activities. A more detailed examination of error data can determine the causes of common errors, many of which may have remedies. Project postmortems should be conducted.

Observations

We identified several approaches for improving software productivity although they are not strictly supported (or contradicted) by the data we collected. We offer these to stimulate discussion on this important topic.

- *Maintain compiler technology.* Many companies seem to contract out compiler development to smaller software houses because the nature of building most compilers is pedestrian. While compiler technology is relatively straightforward and perhaps cheaper to contract to a software house, the implications are far reaching. Software research is heading toward an integrated environment that covers the entire life cycle of software development. Research papers are being written about requirements and specification languages, design languages, program complexity measurement, knowledge-based Japanese fifth-generation languages, etc.[17] All of these depend on mundane compiler technology as their base.

- *Try prototyping.* Prototyping is one of the hot topics in software engineering literature today.[18] It is also crucial for all other engineering disciplines, but it was never mentioned on any survey form or during our visits. A form of prototyping in building data processing application software was common: the creation of screen displays during the design process. This technique and others should be expanded.

- *Develop a test and evaluation methodology.* Test data has to be designed and evaluated. While the current software development process provides for the design of test data in conjunction with the design of software, there is little tool support for this effort. As a result, almost every project builds its own test data generator, and a few even build test evaluators. Concepts like attribute grammars may provide the basis for a tool to support test data generation.[19]

- *Examine the maintenance process.* Surprisingly, maintenance was rarely mentioned in our interview process, even though it is an expensive activity that most companies engage in. A Japanese project is to build maintenance workstations; their view is that development is a subset of maintenance. This implies that the successful methods and tools used in development should be adapted for use in this stage of the process.

- *Encourage innovation.* Experimental software development facilities are needed. Management should be encouraged to use new techniques on small funded-risk projects.

In preparing this article for publication, we were grateful for the thoughtful insights and comments from the reviewers. However, two issues kept on creeping into their reviews, and we suspect that the reader might have similar opinions.

(1) The comment was made that the reviewer (or his colleagues) used more or better tools, thus the survey was not representative. However, as we stated at the beginning, the goal was to look at production programmers—not research laboratories. We suspect that most reviewers and probably many readers of *Computer* also represent the research category.

(2) Names were sometimes given to demonstrate that industry is doing something about the problem. However, every person mentioned by the reviewers was interviewed by us and is included in this article. They either represent a research environment, and are not involved in "revenue-producing" software, or are considered an anomaly within their own company.

We are not saying here that software practices are dismal in the US. Technology transfer takes time, and it appears that the current level in industry represents the research environment of the mid-1970's—a delay of only 10 years. However, certain practices we mentioned do hinder technology transfer. We hope that this article is an impetus to address those issues so that discussions can start within companies to improve the process and shorten—still further—the time it will take to adopt good practices in industry. ✱

Acknowledgments

This project was sponsored by the IBM Corporation. We also acknowledge the cooperation of the following organizations for allowing us to survey their development activities: Bankers Trust Company, AT&T Bell Telephone Laboratories, Digital Equipment Corporation, Hewlett-Packard, Honeywell Large Information Systems Division, Kozo Keikaku Kenkyujo, Japan Information Processing Service, Microsoft, Nomura Computer Systems Ltd., Software Research Associates (Japan), Sperry Univac, System Development Corporation, Tandem Computers, Tokyo Electric Power Company, Toshiba Corporation, TRW, Wang Laboratories, and Xerox Corporation. Several Japanese companies did not respond to our request to use their names, so they are not listed here. This project would not have been possible without the help of all these companies.

References

1. *Software Engineering,* P. Naur and B. Randell, eds., NATO Scientific Affairs Division, Brussels, 1969.

2. K. H. Kim, "A Look at Japan's Development of Software Engineering Technology," *Computer,* Vol. 16, No. 5, May 1983. pp. 26-37.

3. R. C. Houghton, "Software Development Tools: A Profile," *Computer,* Vol. 16, No. 5, May 1983, pp. 63-70.

4. M. E. Fagan, "Design and Code Inspections to Reduce Errors in Program Development," *IBM Systems J.,* Vol. 15, No. 3, Mar. 1976, pp. 182-211.

5. F. Freiman and Park, *PRICE Software Model Overview,* RCA, *Cherry Hill, N.J.,* Feb. 1979.

6. L. Putnam, "SLIM Software Life Cycle Management Estimating Model: User's Guide," *Quantitative Software Management,* (July 1979).

7. *Collected Papers: Volume 1,* tech. report 82-005, NASA Goddard Space Flight Center, Software Engineering Laboratory, Code 582.1, Greenbelt, Md., 1982.

8. M. W. Alford, "A Requirements Engineering Methodology for Real-time Processing Requirements," *IEEE Trans. Software Engineering,* Vol. SE-3, No. 1, Jan. 1977, pp. 60-69.

9. D. Teichroew and E. A. Hersey III, "PSL/PSA: A Computer-Aided Technique for Structured Documentation and Analysis of Information Processing Systems," *IEEE Trans. Software Engineering,* Vol. SE-3, No. 1, Jan. 1977, pp. 41-48.

10. F. P. Brooks, Jr., *The Mythical Man-Month.,* Addison-Wesley, Reading, Mass., 1975.

11. G. M. McCue, "IBM's Santa Teresa Laboratory—Architectural Design for Program Development," *IBM Systems J.,* Vol. 17, No. 1, Jan. 1978, pp. 4-25.

12. A. J. Thadani, "Interactive User Productivity," *IBM Systems J.,* Vol. 20, No. 4, Apr. 1981, pp. 407-423.

13. T. Teitelbaum and T. Reps, "CPS—The Cornell Program Synthesizer," *Comm. ACM,* Vol. 24, No. 9, Sept. 1981, pp. 563-573.

14. V. R. Basili, *Models and Metrics for Software Management and Engineering,* IEEE-CS Press, Los Alamitos, Calif. 1980.

15. M. V. Zelkowitz, "A Small Contribution to Editing with a Syntax-Directed Editor," *Proc. ACM Sigsoft Symp. Practical Software Development Environments,* Apr. 1984, pp. 1-6.

16. V. R. Basili and A. J. Turner, "Iterative Enhancement: A Practical Technique for Software Development," *IEEE Trans. Software Engineering,* Vol. SE-1, No. 4, Dec. 1975, pp. 390-396.

17. H. Karatsu, "What Is Required of the Fifth Generation Computer—Social Needs and Its Impact," *Fifth Generation Computer Systems,* North-Holland, Amsterdam, 1982.

18. "ACM SIGSOFT Software Engineering Symposium: Workshop on Rapid Prototyping," *ACM Sigsoft Software Engineering Notes,* Vol. 7, No. 5, Dec. 1982.

19. A. Duncan and J. Hutchinson, "Using Attributed Grammars To Test Design and Implementation," *Proc. IEEE Fifth Int'l Conf. Software Engineering,* 1981, pp. 170-178.

Raymond T. Yeh is professor of computer sciences at the University of Maryland. He has served as chairman of the Computer Science Departments at the Universities of Maryland and Texas at Austin. He was also director of the Center for Information Sciences Research at Maryland. Yeh received a BS in electrical engineering, an MA in mathematics, and a PhD in mathematics from the University of Illinois. He is the founding editor-in-chief of *IEEE Transactions on Software Engineering.*

Richard G. Hamlet has been with the University of Maryland since 1971 and is now associate professor. He will move to the Oregon Graduate Center in July 1984. His research interests include computability theory, programming languages, and software engineering, particularly testing theory. Hamlet received a BS in electrical engineering in 1959 from the University of Wisconsin in Madison, an MS in engineering physics in 1964 from Cornell University, and a PhD in computer science in 1971 from the University of Washington in Seattle.

John D. Gannon has been with the University of Maryland since 1975 and is now associate professor. His research interests include human-factors approaches to programming language design, formal specification and validation, and distributed computing. Gannon received an AB in mathematical economics in 1970 and an MS in computer science in 1972 from Brown University in Providence, R.I., and a PhD in computer science in 1975 from the University of Toronto.

Martin V. Zelkowitz has been with the Computer Science Department of the University of Maryland since 1971 where he is an associate professor and, since August 1982, an associate chairman for education. His research interests include compiler and language design and the building of integrated tools for software development. He has also worked with the Institute for Computer Sciences and Technology of the National Bureau of Standards since 1976 and is the chairman of the Computer Society's Technical Committee on Software Engineering. He is past chairman of ACM Sigsoft and is now on the Sigsoft Executive Committee.

He received a BS in mathematics from Rensselaer Polytechnic Institute in 1967 and an MS and PhD in computer science from Cornell University in 1969 and 1971.

Victor R. Basili is professor and chairman of the Computer Science Department at the University of Maryland in College Park, where he has been involved in the design and development of several software projects, including the SIMPL family of programming languages. He is currently measuring and evaluating software development in industrial settings and has consulted with many agencies and organizations, including IBM, GE, CSC, Naval Research Laboratory, Naval Surface Weapons Center, and NASA. Basili has published over 50 papers on the methodology, the quantitative analysis, and the evaluation of the software development process and product. In 1982, he received the Outstanding Paper Award from *IEEE Transactions on Software Engineering.* He serves on the editorial boards of the *Journal of Systems and Software* and *IEEE Transactions on Software Engineering.* He is a member of the ACM and the IEEE-CS Executive Committee of the Technical Committee on Software Engineering.

Managing Software Development Projects for Maximum Productivity

NORMAN R. HOWES

Abstract—In the area of software development, data processing management often focuses more on coding techniques and system architecture than on how to manage the development. In recent years, "structured programming" and "structured analysis" have received more attention than the techniques software managers employ to manage. Moreover, these coding and architectural considerations are often advanced as the key to a smooth running, well managed project.

This paper documents a philosophy for software development and the tools used to support it. Those management techniques deal with quantifying such abstract terms as "productivity," "performance," and "progress," and with measuring these quantities and applying management controls to maximize them. The paper also documents the application of these techniques on a major software development effort.

Index Terms—Performance evaluation, productivity analysis, progress measurement, software development methodologies, work breakdown structure.

I. INTRODUCTION

IN 1977 we began developing a Project Management System to support worldwide operations. It was designed to assist with the day to day management of large engineering and construction jobs. As a management information system, it was necessary to interface with the company's financial and materials management systems. The result was that these systems had to be totally redesigned to support this new Project Management System.

The overall effort took about two million man-hours. The development of this system called BRICS (Brown & Root Integrated Control System) was managed using the system being developed but in a manual rather than automated mode. The key management concepts used to control this development effort; namely, performance evaluation, multibudgeting, and forecasting with the "variance" technique were documented in [1].

In order to give a complete self-contained treatment of these concepts, the scope of the paper was limited to these (somewhat technical) topics. This necessitated omitting the discussion of other BRICS capabilities such as productivity evaluation. Moreover the successful management of a large-scale software development project involves more than applying techniques such as these. An experienced software development manager has a fixed idea (philosophy) of how software development should be managed. If such a philosophy is a successful one it will automatically tend to maximize productivity and keep the work progressing as planned.

The purpose of this paper is to document such a philosophy,

Manuscript received January 12, 1983.

The author is with Brown & Root, Inc., P. O. Box 3, Houston, TX 77001.

to show the principle techniques necessary to support it, and to point out some common pitfalls that experience teaches one to avoid.

II. HOW ONE VIEWS SOFTWARE DEVELOPMENT

Scientists know that the way you "look at" a problem often influences whether you can solve it or not. Similarly, your viewpoint influences your ability to manage a software development project efficiently. The author has found it helpful to think of software development management as consisting of two separate but related parts: project planning and project execution. Both parts have five components. The planning components are:

subdivision of work
quantification
sequencing of work
budgeting
scheduling.

Subdivision of work is the decomposition of a job into manageable pieces which will be referred to as "work packages." This is sometimes called "packaging the work." Work packages should consist of one generic type of work, should be of short duration, should be logically related to how the work is to be performed, and it should be possible to assign responsibility for the completion of a given work package to one person.

Normally the subdivision of work is arrived at through a series of decompositions based on how the work will be performed. An example of this process is given in Fig. 1. Here, the job of developing the BRICS system was first decomposed into several major components such as developing a requirements specification, translating the requirements into a functional design, expanding the functional design into a technical design, implementing the design (coding), integration testing, acceptance testing, etc.

This is the first level of decomposition. Level 1 components are further subdivided as shown in Fig. 1 to product components at level 2. For example, the technical design component is subdivided into detailed design of processing modules, detailed design of data management modules, calculation of system timings, etc. These level 2 components are further decomposed into level 3 components and so on until the total effort has been subdivided into manageable components (work packages). When the work has been divided in this fashion, the resultant hierarchy is called a "work breakdown structure" (WBS).

Once the work has been subdivided, it can be quantified. Quantification is that component of planning which deter-

Reprinted from *IEEE Transactions on Software Engineering*, Volume SE-10, Number 1, January 1984, pages 27-35. Copyright © 1984 by The Institute of Electrical and Electronics Engineers, Inc.

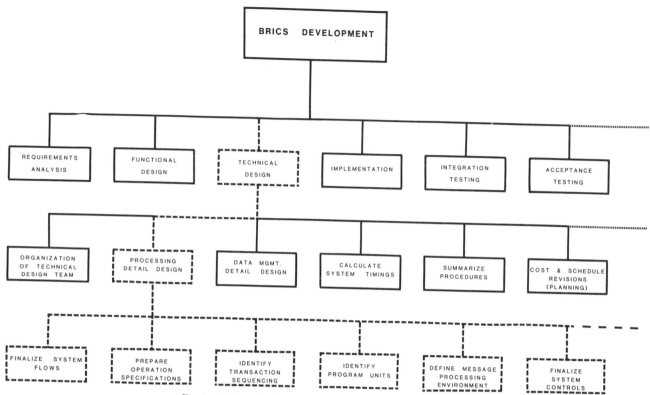

Fig. 1. System development work breakdown structure (WBS).

mines the amount of work (man-hours), overhead, and computer resources required for each work package in the work breakdown structure. The estimated cost for each work package is based on this infomation.

Fig. 2 shows a copy of the "detailed estimate worksheet" used for quantifying and budgeting work packages for the BRICS software development effort. Note that BRICS work packages were referred to as "control packages" (a departure from standard WBS terminology peculiar to this project). The first step in quantification is to list the activities in each work package and their "unit of measure." The example shown in Fig. 2 is for the FINALIZE SYSTEM FLOWS work package shown in Fig. 1. The unit of measure for activities 2.2.20.1 and 2.2.20.2 is flowcharts. The unit of measure for activities 2.2.20.3 and 2.2.20.4 is reports.

The next step in quantification is to assign quantities to each activity (in the activity's unit of measure). How this was done for work package 2.2.20 (FINALIZE SYSTEM FLOWS) is shown in Fig. 2. The final step in the quantification process is to record the number of man-hours necessary to accomplish each activity in each work package. Depending on who you talk to, the man-hours may be considered as part of the quantification or part of the estimate. For the purposes of this paper it will be considered part of the quantification.

After the work packages have been quantified, the sequence in which the work packages are to be executed needs to be determined. This sequence of work provides the software development manager with an understanding of the order in which the work is to proceed. As the sequence of work is developed, the work breakdown structure needs to be reviewed to ensure that the subdivision of work is compatible with the sequence in which the work is to be completed. This may lead

DETAILED ESTIMATE WORKSHEET

PROJECT BRICS   PAGE 1 OF 1

PREPARED BY ____   CONTROL PACKAGE 2.2.20   DATE 9-19-79

ACTIVITY	DESCRIPTION	UNITS	QTY	MHRS	$	REF
2.2.20.1	Prepare Final Batch Flowcharts	Charts	60	720		101
2.2.20.2	Prepare Final On-Line Flowcharts	Charts	30	360		102
2.2.20.3	Prepare Batch Flow Narratives	Reports	60	360		
2.2.20.4	Prepare On-Line Flow Narratives	Reports	30	240		
	Total			1680		

Fig. 2. Detailed estimate worksheet.

to changes in the work breakdown structure such as changing or creating new work packages to better define the manner and order in which the work is to be accomplished.

After the work packages have been quantified and sequenced, they must be estimated. The estimate for each work package will specify the planned cost to complete the work in the work package. After the estimates are approved by manage-

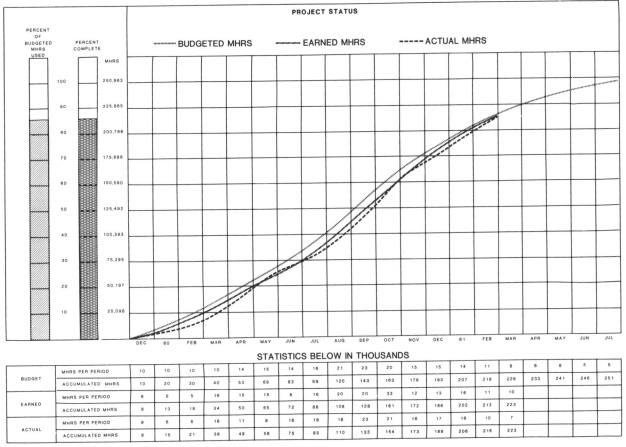

Fig. 3.   Project status summary.

		DEC 80		FEB	MAR	APR	MAY	JUN	JUL	AUG	SEP	OCT	NOV	DEC 81	FEB	MAR	APR	MAY	JUN	JUL
BUDGET	MHRS PER PERIOD	10	10	10	10	14	15	14	16	21	23	20	15	15	14	11	8	8	8	5	5
	ACCUMULATED MHRS	10	20	30	40	53	69	83	99	120	143	163	178	193	207	218	226	233	241	246	251
EARNED	MHRS PER PERIOD	6	5	5	16	15	15	6	16	20	20	33	12	13	16	11	10				
	ACCUMULATED MHRS	8	13	18	34	50	65	72	88	108	128	161	172	186	202	213	223				
ACTUAL	MHRS PER PERIOD	9	6	6	16	11	9	18	18	18	23	21	18	17	16	10	7				
	ACCUMULATED MHRS	9	15	21	38	49	58	75	93	110	133	154	173	189	206	216	223				

STATISTICS BELOW IN THOUSANDS

ment they will be called "budgets." The man-hours for a given work package are the "man-hour budget" for the package. The terms "work package budget" and "work package man-hour budget" imply a management allocation of resources in terms of cost and man-hours to complete the work package.

Finally, the work packages need to be scheduled to complete the planning process. The purpose of scheduling is not only to predict when a job can be completed given the sequence of work and the resources available but also to establish start and end dates for each work package. The software manager uses these scheduled dates for the work packages to control the work and communicate progress of the work.

III. The Project Plan

The budget for your software development effort is the composite of all the budgets for all the work packages in your WBS and the schedule for your project is the composite of all work package schedules. Together the budget and the schedule are referred to as the "plan" or the "baseline."

Again, it is important how this plan is visualized. It is helpful to see an integrated picture of the budget and the schedule components of the plan. This is achieved by using the schedule to "time-phase" the budget. Time phasing shows graphically how the budget is to be expended over time. Fig. 3 shows the time phasing of the manhour budget for the TECHNICAL DESIGN and IMPLEMENTATION branches of the BRICS WBS hierarchy shown in Fig. 1.

The algorithm for time phasing the budget with the schedule is documented in [1]. It can be done manually, but if the number of work packages in your WBS exceeds 100 it becomes fairly difficult. One of the things BRICS does is to automatically produce time phasing graphs for work breakdown structures of any size whose budget and schedule have been entered into the system.

IV. Project Execution

Basically, the software manager's job is to control the development effort in accordance with the project plan discussed above. The five components of project control are:

accumulation of actual expenditures
progress measurement
performance evaluation
productivity measurement
change control and forecasting.

The activities of project control allow the software manager to monitor progress; anticipate and rectify problems; and to continue the "communication" established by the plan to meet requirements, cost objectives and the schedule.

Classical cost accounting methods are used to accumulate actual expenditures of manhours and costs. Each work package is considered as a ledger account and each expenditure incurred for each work package is posted to the appropriate account as it is incurred. Man-hour expenditures should be posted weekly to accommodate the productivity reporting discussed in a later section. Costs can be posted weekly or monthly. For plotting purposes it is advisable to maintain a historical record of the actual expenditure of man-hours for each work package at the end of each reporting period.

Collecting expenditures at the work package level allows for computing the actual expenditure for any element in the WBS at any level simply by summing. A plot of the actual expenditures against the baseline during the technical design and implementation of BRICS is also given in Fig. 3.

Progress measurement is that element of control that is involved with periodically (usually weekly) determining the status of each work package. Status is measured in percent complete. Usually the best method for measuring percent complete is to compare the actual number of units completed for each activity in a work package with the "budgeted quantity" (quantity shown on the detailed estimate worksheet) for that activity. The ratio obtained is the percent complete for the activity. Percent complete for the work package is computed using the formula

WP % comp

$$= \frac{\sum (\text{activity \% complete}) (\text{activity man-hour budget})}{\text{work package man-hour budget}}$$

where the summation is taken over all activities in the work package. It is the responsibility of the software manager to insure this data is collected periodically as it is the basis for the calculations used in performance evaluation.

V. PERFORMANCE EVALUATION

Performance evaluation is that element of control which compares actual progress and expenditures to the project plan, identifies deviations from the plan and determines solutions to correct for these deviations. Actual expenditures and the baseline are expressed in terms of manhours spread over time as shown in Fig. 3. But progress is measured in percent complete. In order to measure progress in the same units as the budget and expenditures so a comparison can be made one uses the concept of "earned value" (earned man-hours). Earned value (EV) for a work package is defined as

EV = (work package man-hour budger) (work package % complete).

Conceptually, earned value represents the (man-hour) value of work accomplished relative to the (manhour) budget. By computing earned value at the work package level it can be obtained for any element in the WBS hierarchy by summing the earned value for all work packages under the given hierarchy element.

A plot of earned value and actual manhour expenditure against the baseline for the BRICS technical design and implementation is given in Fig. 3. This plot is the software manager's principle performance evaluation tool. A detailed discussion of how to interpret such an earned value graph is given in [1]. Basically, if the earned value "curve" is tracking the baseline curve closely, work is progressing as planned and if it is tracking the actual expenditure curve closely, productivity is as planned.

VI. PRODUCTIVITY MEASUREMENT

If the earned value curve deviates significantly from either the baseline or the actual man-hour curve, or both there is reason for concern. It is the responsibility of the software manager to take steps to rectify the problem but before this can be done the problem must first be isolated.

Suppose the earned value curve is tracking the baseline closely but deviates sharply from the actual expenditure curve with the "actuals" curve running "above" the earned value curve. This means the work content is being executed as planned (as scheduled) but the cost in man-hours is significantly more than planned. The obvious conclusion is low productivity. In order to know which work packages are experiencing low productivity, the software manager needs a weekly productivity report.

The calculation of productivity for a work package is as follows: first, the work package is assigned a unit of measure just like the activities in the work package. Each activity in the package may have a different unit of measure and it is not necessary that the work package unit of measure be the same as any of its activities. For instance, the unit of measure for work package 2.2.20 shown in Fig. 2 could be documents and its quantity could be 180.

The work package man-hour budget is obtained by summing the man-hours for each activity in the package. In this case it is 1680 man-hours. Dividing 1680 man-hours by 180 units gives 9.33 man-hours per unit or man-hours per document. This ratio will be referred to as the "budgeted cost per unit" or simply the "budgeted unit rate." Productivity is defined as output per man-hour. Consequently, the unit rate is the reciprocal of productivity since it is measured in terms of man-hours per unit (output).

The "actual unit rate" for an activity in the work package could be determined by dividing the actual manhour expenditure for the activity by the actual number of units completed on the activity. But to collect costs and compute unit rates for each activity would lead to far too much detail. This is the reason for "packaging" the work in the first place so it can be treated as manageable pieces instead of a mass of detail. What is desired is an actual unit rate for the work package. It is obtained using the formula

work package actual unit rate

$$= \frac{\text{work package actual man-hour expenditure}}{(\text{work pkg. \% complete}) (\text{work pkg. quantity})}$$

where the formula for work package % complete was given in Section IV. Similarly, budgeted unit rates and actual unit rates can be computed at summary levels of your work breakdown structure by assigning a quantity and unit of measure to each summary level WBS element and using the formulas

WBS element budgeted unit rate

$$= \frac{\text{WBS element man-hour budget}}{\text{WBS element quantity}}$$

WBS element actual unit rate

$$= \frac{\text{WBS element actual man-hour expenditure}}{(\text{WBS element \% comp.}) (\text{WBS element quantity})}$$

where the WBS element man-hour budget and the WBS

HIERARCHY	DESCRIPTION	UOM	QUANTITIES CONTROL BUDGET	ACTUAL	% CMP	FORECAST	MANHOURS CONTROL BUDGET	ACTUAL	% BUD	FORECAST	MANHOURS PER UNIT CONTROL BUDGET	ACTUAL	FORECAST
TECH DSGN 2.2	TECHNICAL DESIGN	DOC	6214	138	2	6214	93210	1662	2	93210	15.00	12.04	15.00
PROC DSGN	PROCESS. DETAIL DSGN	DOC	1688	138	6	1688	25151	1662	7	2515	14.90	12.04	14.90
2.2.20	FINALIZE SYST FLOWS	DOC	180	138		178	1680	1662	99	1966	9.33	12.04	11.04
2.2.20.1	BATCH FLOWCHARTS	CHT	60	58	100	58	720	752	100	752	12.00	12.97	12.97
2.2.20.2	ON-LINE FLOWCHARTS	CHT	30	31	100	58	360	480	100	480	12.00	15.48	15.48
2.2.20.3	BATCH NARRATIVES	REP	60	29	50	58	360	232	64	464	6.00	8.00	8.00
2.2.20.4	ON-LINE NARRATIVES	REP	30	20	67	31	240	198	83	296	8.00	9.00	9.90
2.2.22	OPERATION SPECS.	DOC	32	0	0	32	628	0	0	628	19.63		19.63
2.2.22.1	LIST JOB STREAMS	LST	16	0	0	16	124	0	0	124	7.75		7.75
2.2.22.2	PRELIM OPER SPECS	SPC	16	0	0	16	384	0	0	384	24.00		24.00
2.2.22.3	REVIEW WITH OPS MGMT	RVW	5	0	0	5	120	0	0	120	24.00		24.00
2.2.24	IDENT TRANS SEQUENCE	DOC	33	0	0	33	552	0	0	552	16.73		16.73
2.2.24.1	TRANS SEQ WORKSHEETS	WKS	33	0	0	33	528	0	0	528	16.00		16.00
2.2.24.2	TEAM REVIEW OF WKSTS	RVW	1	0	0	1	24	0	0	24	24.00		24.00
2.2.25	IDENTIFY PRGM UNITS	DOC	734	0	0	734	11684	0	0	11684	15.92		15.92
2.2.25.1	PREPARE PRGM CHARTS	CHT	398	0	0	398	6368	0	0	6368	16.00		16.00
2.2.25.2	PREPARE PSB WKSHEETS	WKS	104	0	0	104	1132	0	0	1132	10.88		10.88
2.2.25.3	PREPARE DLI CALL PTN	PTN	104	0	0	104	1132	0	0	1132	10.88		10.88
2.2.25.4	PREPARE ON-LINE HIER	HIR	128	0	0	128	3052	0	0	3052	23.84		23.84

Fig. 4.   Productivity report.

element actual man-hour expenditure are obtained by summing the work package man-hour budgets and actual man-hour expenditures for all the work packages under the given WBS element in the work breakdown structure hierarchy, and where the WBS % complete is given by

$$\text{WBS element \% complete} = \frac{\sum (\text{work pkg. \% comp.})(\text{work pkg. man-hour budget})}{\text{WBS element man-hour budget}}$$

where the summation is taken over all work packages under the given WBS element in the hierarchy.

An example of such a productivity report is given in Fig. 4. The software manager uses the performance report of Fig. 3 together with the productivity report to spot trends and isolate problem work packages. It is also necessary to consult the project schedule to spot problems. Even though productivity is satisfactory, work packages may not be starting or finishing as planned. Such a case would lead to the earned value curve tracking the actual curve closely but deviating significantly from the baseline curve on the performance report.

There are three reasons why software development work does not progress in accordance with the plan. They are:

1) changes in the scope of work,
2) quantity deviations, and
3) productivity deviations.

Changes in the scope of work are redefinitions of the original requirement. Their basis can range from a change in the user procedures to a better design alternative. Quantity deviations arise from errors in the quantification process and productivity deviation arise from not accomplishing the work at the planned unit rate.

It is important for the software manager to distinguish among these three types of deviations. If work is not progressing as planned because of low productivity, pressure can be applied to increase productivity. Normally, the visibility given to productivity by this management approach tends to stimulate productivity. Applying pressure when productivity meets or exceeds planned unit rates may be counterproductive. Programmers and analysts need to be rewarded for exceeding planned productivity estimates even though the work is not progressing as planned for other reasons. Failure to do so may well introduce productivity problems where you did not have them before.

VII. Change Control and Forecasting

It is also important for the software manager to distinguish among the types of deviations in order to "keep the baseline current." This means providing for an up-to-date account of the scope of work and an audit trail of how the original budget evolved into the current baseline. If the baseline is not kept current, the percent complete and earned value computations will not be correct as will be seen in what follows.

A "variance" will denote the documentation of a deviation from the baseline. A "change order" is a variance that represents an agreed upon change in the scope of work. If the development is being done for a client, a change order will be a client approved variance and may result in a change to the contract. Then the original contract together with all change orders represents the current contractual environment under which the work is performed. The original budget for a work package together with all change orders affecting the package is the "client budget" (called control budget in [1]) for the package. The client budget for the project is the sum of the client budgets for all work packages.

Variances other than change orders will be designated as quantity or productivity variances depending on whether they arose as the result of a (current or projected) quantity or productivity deviation. Sometimes an observed deviation will have both a quantity and productivity component. It is important that the distinction be made and a separate variance be used to document each component. This is because quantity variances will be used to update the baseline whereas productivity variances will only update the forecast.

The client budget for a work package together with all quantity variances that affect the package is the "control budget" (called target budget in [1]) for the package. The control budget for the project is the sum of the control budgets for all work packages. It represents the real scope of work as currently understood and consequently is the true baseline to measure progress against. This is the budget the software manager uses to control the work and consequently this the budget used for calculating earned value.

The control budget for a work package together with all the productivity variances affecting the package is the "forecast" for the package. By constructing the forecast from the budget in this way the difference between the forecast and the budget is automatically quantified and estimated since each variance must be quantified and estimated. A comparison of the budgets and the forecast for a hypothetical development effort is given in Fig. 5.

One of the functional capabilities of BRICS is to provide the user with a means of storing his original quantifications and budgets in the computer and then as time progresses to enter expenditures as they are incurred, progress (percent complete) as it is measured and variances as they are recognized and quantified. BRICS then automatically produces plots of the earned value against the baseline and the "actuals," productivity reports, and an audit trail of how the budgets and the forecast evolved.

As a result the forecast should have more credibility than many of the "subjective guess" forecasts that occur on many software projects. Moreover, the contributions from scope changes, quantification errors, and productivity deviations can be determined. It is impractical to attempt tracking every single deviation from the plan. In practice one relies on the "Law of Compensating Error" to balance out small or insignificant variances and concentrates on tracking the significant ones.

Which variances to track is a matter of judgment, but normally enough of them should be tracked to ensure the forecast is accurate to a tolerance of approximately 5 percent. Also, it is more important to track quantity variances than productivity variances as they affect the baseline. All change orders should be tracked.

VIII. SELECTING AN APPROPRIATE WBS

There are several software development methodologies on the market. Most of them are in essence a work breakdown structure for software development even though they may not be presented in that format. In any event, they are at least a subdivision of work in that they divide the software development process up into tasks that can be assigned to the analysts and programmers.

Which methodology to choose is probably less important than having a proven methodology and recognizing it for what it is. Many software development projects use these methodologies but few of them use them as the basis for deriving a project plan as described above. It is important that the tasks in the methodology either become the work packages in your subdivision of work or that they be packaged together to form work packages.

These work packages then need to be quantified, sequenced, budgeted, and scheduled as described above. The project plan (baseline) is then produced from this data. During execution of the plan, expenditures need to be accumulated, progress needs to be measured, and variances need to be posted against these work packages. Furthermore, a manual or automated system is needed to produce performance evaluation and productivity reports from these data.

The author has a software development WBS that will be discussed briefly in the next section. However, the BRICS development effort was managed using another methodology. The reader may be interested in the experience and it may shed some light on the problem of selecting an appropriate WBS for your job.

In 1978 Brown & Root purchased a software development methodology called SPECTRUM which is marketed by J. Toellner & Associates. SPECTRUM was used on a small to medium sized application prior to beginning the functional design of BRICS. From what the author could learn from some of those associated with the project, SPECTRUM worked as it was supposed to but the effort required to complete all the SPECTRUM forms was greater than the development effort itself. It may be that this methodology is targeted at larger development efforts and the "overhead" was too great for a smaller project.

So as not to lose their investment but in order to have a more streamlined methodology, Brown & Root undertook to rewrite SPECTRUM. At this time Brown & Root was employing a number of Arthur Andersen consultants and that firm had their own methodology. Both Arthur Andersen and Brown & Root personnel participated in the rewrite. The result was a mixture of SPECTRUM, Arthur Andersen's methodology and Brown & Root experience. This new methodology became the standard for use on the BRICS project. It was now small enough to fit in two rather large ring binders and became known as the "Black Book" methodology (a name derived from its black binders). Since that time Brown & Root has written a much small methodology called PROMPT for small to medium sized software projects. The WBS shown in Fig. 1 was extracted from the Black Book Methodology.

The author's experience with the Black Book methodology was that it was still too cumbersome. Many of the tasks were unnecessary and most of them required too elaborate forms that were never used again. The extensive documentation

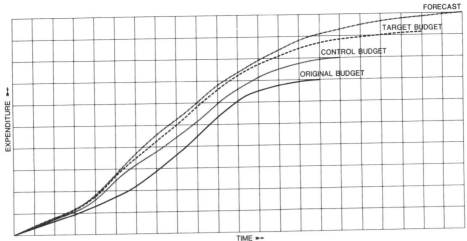

Fig. 5. Budget and forecast comparison.

tended to mask the reason for the individual tasks which often resulted in mechanical completion of forms in order to get a task over with rather than designing the system.

We partially circumvented the problem by distributing the author's methodology to development team members. When tasks were encountered that did not relate to the system being developed, they were "interpreted" in terms of the author's methodology and in several cases management granted permission to substitute other documents for the forms in the Black Book methodology. Proceeding in this manner we managed to finish the technical design phase exactly on schedule and 8 percent under the original estimate. Previously the functional design phase had exceeded the original estimate by 12 percent. In total the project succeeded in completing the design work at a tiny margin under the original estimate and on schedule. Even after acceptance testing the project was less than 6 weeks behind schedule after 4 years development.

IX. A Proposed Methodology

The author's methodology is a simple one. The document distributed to team members was only 20 pages. In the face of current thinking in the software engineering field it may seem old fashioned. It is based on the fundamentals of "top-down" architecture but pays little attention to structured programming or some of the activities referred to as structured analysis.

In summary the methodology works like this. First you determine what the system is to do. This is normally documented in something called a requirements specification. It can range from a list of report formats to be produced to satisy a business application to a formal analysis of how the system is to behave in a real-time environment as, for instance, in an air-defense system. How such a specification was developed for a military command and control system was documented in [2].

From here on the methodology centers around constructing something called a "system flowchart." A system flowchart is no ordinary flowchart like one used to describe a program. The system flowchart is constructed in a series of "levels." In fact, it is not a single chart but a family of charts.

The level 1 system flowchart is constrained to have no more than 6 "boxes" not counting the symbols for inputs, screens, files, and reports. The figure of 6 may seem arbitrary and is.

Another number could be used without altering the structure, but experience has shown 6 to be a good number. The boxes represent processing of some sort. At the first level the boxes usually represent subsystems. The level 1 system flowchart is a "first-cut" at visualizing how the system will be organized at the highest level.

At this point 6 catalogs are begun. These are the component catalog, the input catalog, the report catalog, the screen catalog, the file catalog, and the interface catalog. If a database management system is being used the file catalog may be named something more appropriate like a segment catalog. Each symbol on the level 1 flowchart is assigned an identifier. If the symbol represents a screen the identifier is logged in the screen catalog; if it represents a file it is logged in the file catalog, etc.

Even though the component catalog is limited to 6 components at level 1, the other catalogs are not. As many files, reports, etc. that can be defined at this level should be. The intent is that the level 1 system flowchart should be logically complete and as many files, screens, etc. as are needed to accomplish this is permissable. Also, at this time every member of each catalog must be documented as clearly as possible at this level of detail.

Finally, one normally begins drawing a system hierarchy showing how the components are decomposed at this point. The hierarchy is a shorthand notation for the system flowchart and is valuable for communicating system concepts where the detail of the system flowchart is not necessary.

Next, the level 1 system flowchart is expanded to level 2. Each level 1 component is decomposed into no more than 6 level 2 components. The flowchart is redrawn to reflect the new interfaces among the various level 2 components and new files to accommodate these interfaces, to handle temporary storage, etc. As the flowchart expands, each new interface, each new file and each new component needs to be labeled and cataloged. Just as with level 1, each item in each catalog needs to be documented as clearly and completely as is possible at this level of detail.

This decomposition process continues level by level until you reach components that are too small to decompose further. A general rule of thumb is if a component can be coded with no more that 200 lines of executable code (200 line of code in the procedure division for Cobol programs) that it is unnecessary to decompose it further. These low level compo-

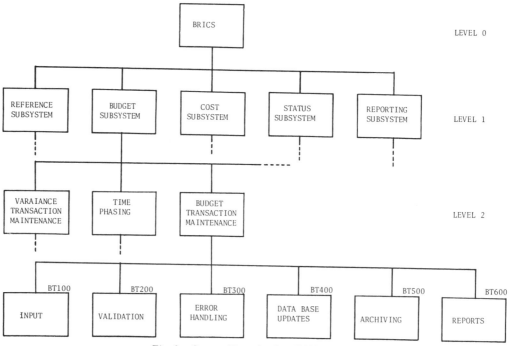

Fig. 6. System hierarchy for BRICS Project.

nents are called modules and eventually become the programs in your system. Figs. 6 and 7 show a simplified level 3 system hierarchy and flowchart, respectively.

When there is no longer anything left to decompose you are through with the design. Detail program specifications remain to be written for each module. Whether these modules adhere to the principles of structured programming or not is of less consequence than the structure induced on the system by this decomposition process. Care should be taken to document each program thoroughly by the liberal use of comment statements.

Modifications to this outline of a methodology will have to be made to accommodate special system requirements such as security, real-time operation, large database requirements, etc. This can be done by adding appropriate work packages to your work breakdown structure.

The Black Book methodology WBS shown in outline in Fig. 1 called for level 1 elements titled functional design, technical design, implementation, etc. Functional design corresponded roughly to developing the system flowchart down to level 2 in the author's methodology. At this point one of the hardest tasks is definition of the interfaces especially when interfacing with systems whose development or maintenance is outside your realm of responsibility.

Technical design corresponded roughly to developing the system flowchart down to level 4, but the parallel was imperfect. The Black Book methodology did not provide for the maintenance of the catalogs of the author's methodology and permitted substituting the system hierarchy diagrams for the system flowcharts. Moreover it possessed many forms to be filled out that were not relevant to the author's methodology.

The BRICS development was accomplished by adding those work packages from the authors methodology needed to develop the system flowchart to the Black Book methodology. The result was satisfactory. Other systems interfacing with BRICS and being developed concurrently used only the Black Book methodology and used only the system hierarchy diagrams. These projects had difficulty with the methodology and eventually abandoned it.

X. PITFALLS TO AVOID

The advice given in this section is likely to be at odds with the advice you may receive from other quarters. It is only the author's opinion and the only thing the author has to recommend it is that it has worked for the author.

First, do not embark on a large software development project without a proven methodology. It is more important to have a methodology and stick with it than not to use a methodology because of a perceived shortcoming with it. Do not be afraid to modify a methodology to meet your individual requirements. No methodology is universal. A methodology may work well in the hands of its author but not make sense to you. In this regard use common sense. Do not try to use something you do not understand.

Use the methodology to build a work breakdown structure. Base your estimates and schedule on this WBS. Use these to produce a project plan (baseline) and measure performance against it as was discussed in previous sections.

Avoid methodologies that avoid flowcharting. People with nontechnical backgrounds tend to have difficulty with flowcharting and consequently there has been a trend toward replacing them with various hierarchical diagramming schemes. Hierarchical diagrams appeal to our logical intuition whereas flowcharts appeal to our geometrical intuition. They give us a means of visualizing what the system is doing. It is important that the analysts designing the system have a highly developed visualization of the system under development just as an architect can visualize the structure he is designing.

Beware of advice from individuals who tell you that software development is intrinsically different from the development of "tangible" products and as such cannot be quantified and estimated accurately. This usually means they have little experience in the tasks to be estimated. Quantification and estimating may not be easy but they are "do-able."

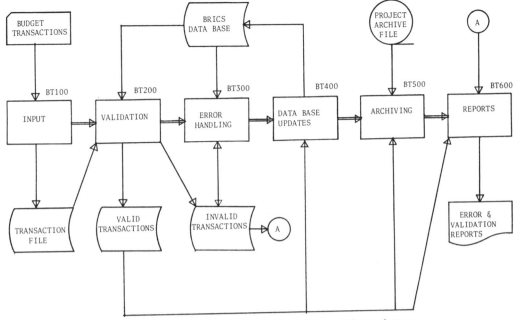

Fig. 7. Level 3 system flowchart for budget transaction maintenance
subsystem.

It is true that during quantification and estimating some estimating assumptions may need to be documented as explained in [1, p. 247]. Furthermore, an estimating assumption may prove to be inaccurate at a later date causing a variance to be entered against the baseline. The quantity and criticality of these estimating assumptions will determine the amount of "contingency" built into the estimate, and there is no substitute for experience in correlating cost risk with your estimating assumptions. But the need for estimating assumptions is no reason to discard quantification and estimating as unrealistic.

Furthermore, the vast majority of software development is for products similar in nature to products that already exist, but reflecting the individual requirements of a certain organization. Thousands of multimillion dollar financial systems have been developed in the past and thousands more will be developed in the future. Beware of the one who tries to convince you that the system under consideration is uniquely different from anything in existence. The problem is in matching experience to the work at hand and often those responsible for making DP decisions do not have the background to discern whether the proposed software manager has the experience or not.

Management's need for a reasonably accurate assessment of the cost of development of a new product before deciding to undertake development is universally understood. But in the software development field, software managers frequently encourage general management to undertake risks they do not understand by failing to develop estimates based on detailed quantification.

Finally, avoid the temptation to begin coding before the detailed program specifications have been written for all the modules. Once programming gets underway, maintaining complete documentation will become more difficult. It is best to begin the programming effort with an accurate roadmap. Make implementation a summary level WBS element at a high level. This isolates coding work packages from design work packages.

Think of software as hardware. The modules should become as "chips" or IC's in your mind. Modularity is more important that structured programming. Enforce the limit on the number of lines of code in a module. Each module should be independent of other modules. The goal is to be able to change out modules without affecting other modules just as one changes out a character generator chip to produce a different type font on the screen. This is not a perfect analogy because some of the modules of a software system always correspond to the CPU chip of a computer. Nonetheless, this should be your viewpoint and goal.

You can gain a great deal of insight and advise from others about software development by reading the book containing [3].

REFERENCES

[1] N. R. Howes, "Project management systems," *Inform. & Management,* vol. 5, pp. 243–258, Dec. 1982.
[2] ——, "Development of effective command and control systems," *Signal Mag. (J. Armed Forces Commun. Electron. Ass.)* pp. 44–48, Feb. 1977.
[3] J. I. Schwartz, "Construction of software, problems and practicalities," in *1974 U.S.C. Seminar: Modern Techniques for the Design and Construction of Reliable Software.* Reading, MA: Addison-Wesley, 1975, pp. 15–54.

Norman R. Howes was born in Kansas City in 1939. He graduated from Eastern New Mexico University, Portales, in 1964 and received the Ph.D. degree in mathematics from Texas Christian University, Fort Worth, in 1968.

He is currently Project Manager for the BRICS project within Land Operations Group at Brown & Root, Inc., Houston, TX. He began his professional career at Texas Instruments in 1966 where he was Head of the Optronics Technical Staff and member of the Computer Advisory Board. He has authored several papers in the areas of mathematics, physics, and computer science and was a member of the Faculties of TCU and the University of Dallas between 1968 and 1971. Thereafter, he was Vice President of Alpha Systems, Inc. In 1973 he joined E-Systems, Inc. as Staff Scientist and later became Computer Consultant to Chief of Defense Denmark. He joined Brown and Root, Inc. in 1978.

Building Quality and Productivity into a Large Software System

Edward M. Prell and Alan P. Sheng
Bell Laboratories

The key to developing larger and more complex software systems is to improve the way we manage people and information.

As the cost of computer hardware continues to drop, larger and more complex computer systems become economically feasible; hence our ability to design large, complex software systems of high quality becomes more important. So it is not surprising that the demand for software and competent software designers has increased dramatically over the last two decades, to the extent that today we are outstripping our supply of trained talent and our current development methodologies.

These shortfalls are particularly apparent in large software development efforts (those requiring more than 100K source lines or 50 staff-years). In such projects, complexity seems to increase in nonlinear fashion both within the software itself and the structure of the organization charged with its development.

Nowhere is this complexity more intensely felt than in the debugging phase. Indeed, it is here that software developers have come to realize that we can no longer afford to rely on debugging as a means of assuring software quality. Rather, quality must be built into the software throughout the design and implementation process.

In our work at AT&T Bell Laboratories, we participated in the development of the computer-controlled 5ESS switching system.[1] Early in the project, we realized that the challenge of large-scale software development could only be met by creating increasingly sophisticated procedures. Although our own software needs were more extensive than those of many others, we feel our experience is applicable to most projects.

The 5ESS system is a time-division switch utilizing state-of-the-art technologies in both hardware and software. Its distributed modular architecture allows one system design to service a wide range of applications covering the needs of rural, suburban, and metropolitan areas (from fewer than 1000 to more than 100,000 telephone lines). As a second-generation digital switching system, the 5ESS required creating new hardware, software, and support capabilities. The first three generic releases of the software showed that we achieved significant increases in productivity and quality simultaneously by improving our management techniques and our methodology.[2]

Management approach

To improve quality and productivity and reduce development time, the management team established a project structure wherein work assignments and staff responsibilities logically reflected one another. Clear and effective lines of communications were established with well-understood goals, responsibilities, and expectations. Management also fostered a team spirit requiring strong, positive work attitudes and firm commitments toward our goals by the entire organization. A formal, rigorous development methodology was implemented to provide a uniform structure to the development process and to assure a high level of

Reprinted from *IEEE Software*, July 1984, pages 47-54. Copyright ©1984 by The Institute of Electrical and Electronics Engineers, Inc.

designed-in quality. Metrics were established and data collected during the entire development cycle to monitor progress, productivity, and quality.

Figure 1 demonstrates the results of the above approach on productivity and quality. It is based on the data from the development of three 5ESS generic releases which showed an increase in both productivity and quality. The curves show that there was a relationship between productivity and quality and that it was not necessary to sacrifice one for the other. Increases in productivity and quality could be achieved simultaneously if the environment or the methodology/technology is improved, resulting in higher operating regions as depicted.

Project structure

This project involved simultaneous development of several generic releases. The development encompassed several hundred staff years (software alone), more than 500,000 new or modified non-commentary source lines, and one to two years of development time. Therefore it was critically important that both the organizational responsibilities and the components of the development structure be clearly defined and easily understood by everyone.

Structured development decomposition. Figure 2 shows that the generic was hierarchically decomposed into capabilities, design units, and program functions. A capability was defined as a logical grouping of externally demonstrable functions. For example, in Figure 2 the ability to provide three-way calling service to a customer is externally demonstrable and is, therefore, a capability. Other examples of capabilities are other custom calling features, system initialization, and maintenance and recovery of specific hardware complexes. The implementation of a capability required the development of many functions which were used internally within the programs and were not visible to the user. These were called design units and were defined by the types of functions they performed. The example in Figure 2 shows digit analysis, data-base management, hardware control, etc., as design units. Together they provided the necessary functions needed by a capability. The design units were in turn decomposed into program functions which were written in the C language. Typically a function consists of 50 to 100 C statements. Today there are over 10,000 functions in a typical 5ESS generic, with many of the functions and primitives being reused in various design units.

Management and staff responsibilities. The responsibilities of the levels of management and staff reflected a data-driven, bottom-up development process with a top-down supported methodology. Figure 3 shows the levels of accountability and the corresponding areas of responsibility. The executive director and the directors were responsible for the overall project, made project-level decisions, and set project directions and goals. The department heads (second-level management) were responsible for the deployment of resources to ensure the quality of the capabilities and their scheduled completions. The supervisors had direct developmental responsibility for the capabilities and design units. In addition, each capability was assigned a capability manager—a supervisor—with overall responsibility for the development of the capability even though many of its components (design units) were developed by other supervisory groups. The capability manager had to make sure the design units were properly integrated into the capability before it was delivered to the separate system testing organization. Technical staff members had the direct responsibility for the design and implementation work assigned to them. In addition, they were charged with the responsibility of building in the desired quality by serving as formal reviewers or inspectors of the work of their peers.

Development Methodology

The software of the 5ESS switching system was developed using the phased validation technique. This approach was essential to uncover problems early and to build in the desired quality during all phases of development. A critical attribute of a good methodology is to maximize the

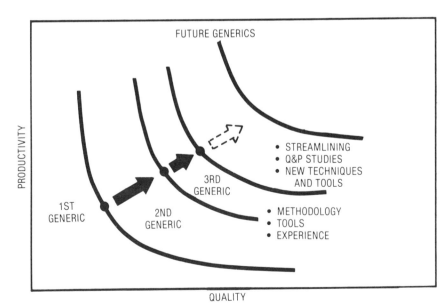

Figure 1. Productivity and quality.

number of problems found and corrected in the same development phase as they occur. Thus requirements problems were to be discovered and resolved during the requirements phase, design problems in the design phase, etc. The methodology also provided natural and visible benchmarks to monitor development progress easily and effectively. Although the methodology was strongly supported by the management of the project, many of its basic ideas and improvements originated at the engineering level.

The validation methodology broke down the development process into the following phases:

(1) architecture,
(2) capability requirements,
(3) capability design,
(4) design unit design,
(5) coding,
(6) unit test,
(7) capability test,
(8) system test, and
(9) site/acceptance test.

Figure 4 shows the overall development process as specified by the methodology. Each development phase had a visible output. The work accomplished in each phase was validated through formal peer reviews, code inspections, or test executions. The successful completion of each phase was a prerequisite to the start of the next phase. All completions were further reviewed by a supervisory committee, whose main charter was to assure the technical quality of the work by making sure that effective technical validations were conducted and that the issues uncovered had been satisfactorily resolved. The completed benchmarks as approved by this committee were then recorded in a project management tracking system which supported the development methodology. The reports and summaries from this project management database were available for review by all members of the project team.

Visible outputs. Each of these phases had visible output—formal

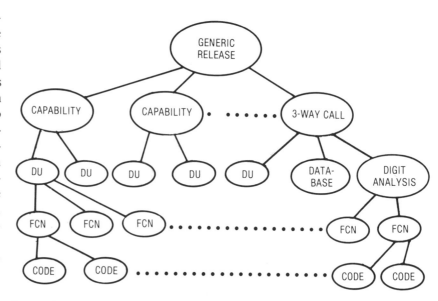

Figure 2. Hierarchical structure.

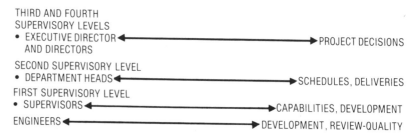

Figure 3. Accountability.

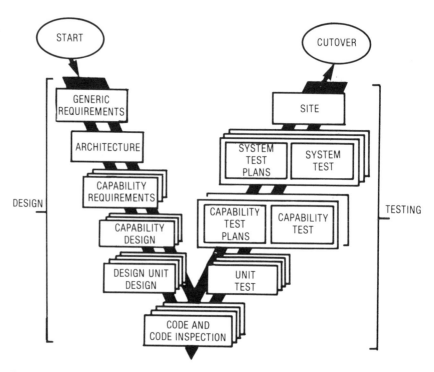

Figure 4. Development process.

design documents, well documented program code, or detailed test scripts and test results. The design documents included not only design specifications, but also design requirements and test plans. The methodology provided specific guidelines for the development of each type of design document associated with the various development phases. It defined a uniform outline and fixed format for each document type. This ensured that all the important aspects of the system, such as global interfaces, recovery functions, resource objectives, and usage, were appropriately addressed by every capability and design unit during all phases of development. In addition, formal interface specifications were required in all the documents. The level of details in the specifications and the documenation expanded as we proceeded through the development phases.

The main bodies of the design documents were written in English. Tools and aids such as pseudo-code, structure charts, cause and effect charts, and formal test scripts were used in the detailed specifications. A formal requirements or design language may help to improve the quality of the documentation in the future. But we believe that the difficult task is the thought process and the engineering judgments that go into a design. Therefore, the language used should not divert the current focus of the methodology from the engineering aspects of design.

The design documents were internally released after being formally reviewed and approved by the supervisory committee. At this point they were frozen and put under change control. Further changes or additions were made through addenda or reissues of the documents. These corrections were subject to the same validation process as the original documents.

Validation process. Our technical review process sought to uncover technical problems and areas of concern and to achieve and ratify a collective agreement on the technical work described in the documents. It

is well known that the cost of finding and correcting software faults in a large project increases dramatically during the later phases of development.[3] The reviews were an effective way of discovering problems during the earlier phases, where corrections could be made easily without affecting the rest of the system and using expensive resources such as the test laboratories.

The reviewers were selected from specific organizations or technical areas, including the system/site testers, that would eventually test the specific capability. The reviewers were not only expected to bring expertise from their own areas but also to understand the entire design document and to participate throughout the review. The reviewers were as responsible as the original authors for the quality of the document. Using a five-point rating scheme, each reviewer selected a disposition varying from accepting the document as it was to rejecting the entire document and demanding a new start. All the reviewers had to be satisfied before the review was approved. The consensus was usually accomplished by follow-up meetings between the author(s) and the reviewer(s). The project viewed the work of the reviewers as essential for a high-quality product, and the most qualified reviewers were in demand.

All the program code was formally inspected before the testing phases started. Code was also inspected at the peer level using a formalized process with well defined entry and exit criteria. We looked for the proper implementation of the design, the correctness of the logic, and the conformance to the established coding style of the project. We also used a rating scheme similar to the one used in the review process. To ensure effective inspection with uniform standards, the entire development organization was trained in a two-day code inspection course. Inspections proved to be an efficient way to discover program bugs. Inspections were not only less expensive than testing, they also un-

covered certain problems that are very difficult to find systematically during testing.

The testing phases were complete when the test plans and scripts were successfully executed. The design units had to meet the requirements set forth in the capability design and the design unit documents. Unit testing was generally performed using an "execution environment"[4] on a general-purpose computer. Then the design units were integrated into the corresponding capability by using the capability test plan. When capability testing was complete, the unit was formally delivered to the independent system test organization. The delivery required formal documentation of the test plan execution indicating mutual agreement on the merits of the results and any defects requiring correction after delivery. The system testers then executed the system test plan, which focused on system-level interactions, anomalies, and behavior under stress conditions. Both capability tests and system tests were executed on the target machine, the 5ESS system. Only after successful execution of all the planned system tests was the generic ready for release to the field. A few remaining defects were negotiated with the user.

Independent audits. To further assure system quality, our corporate Quality Assurance Center performed technical audits on selected documentation, including all the capability requirements documents, the user-level manuals, and the development methodology itself. Conducting audits as part of the development process assisted the designers in designing-in quality and finding problems during the phases where they occurred. The auditors thoroughly reviewed all the documentation, attended many review meetings, and interviewed many developers and users of the manuals. They not only addressed technical issues but also such matters as style, clarity, and preciseness. The audit results were carefully reviewed by the authors and designers, and actual problems were corrected.

The audits were especially effective in providing feedback on the clarity, organization, and style of the documents. By improving the language of the documentation the Quality Assurance Center had a direct impact on the development methodology. The preciseness of the documentation not only focused the energies of the project members but also inspired them with confidence in the quality of the design.

Metrics

To monitor development progress, software quality, and project productivity, we collected appropriate development data and established meaningful metrics. We needed not only quantitative measurements, but also clearly defined goals. Since a large software system is highly complex and many aspects must be considered when assessing progress, quality, and productivity,[5] we can only cover some of the metrics that were used on the 5ESS system project.

Development progress metrics. We measured the overall project by monitoring the progress of capabilities and design units through their appropriate phases. Management understood that coding was a relatively minor part of the total task. They did not use code counting as a metric of progress. Instead, they measured detailed development progress by the completion of planned benchmarks, and they monitored progress of the capabilities and design units individually through all the development phases. If a capability or design unit benchmark was expected to be more than one week late, the responsible supervisor documented an action plan. This provided a mechanism for the management team to redirect resources and to resolve problems blocking progress.

We also combined the capability benchmarks for each development phase to establish overall progress metrics and goals for that phase. Figure 5 shows the planned and the actual progress curves for capability requirements, designs, and test plans. These metrics provided a clear proj-

ect view of the progress of each development phase at the capability level. To obtain a more detailed view at the design unit level, we established similar curves using design unit, code inspection, and unit test benchmarks and used these curves to monitor actual progress.

To measure development progress, we established an additional metric—equivalent source lines. Although this was not a direct measure, we found that it accurately reflected overall development progress. The metric was based on a good understanding of what percentage of total job went into each development phase. This approach provided a common metric for the products of the various development phases. It accounted for the progress of the entire project rather than just the coding phase, which was a very small portion of the job.

We obtained the equivalent source lines by using the following percentages:

Requirements	10%
Capability design	20%
Design unit	20%

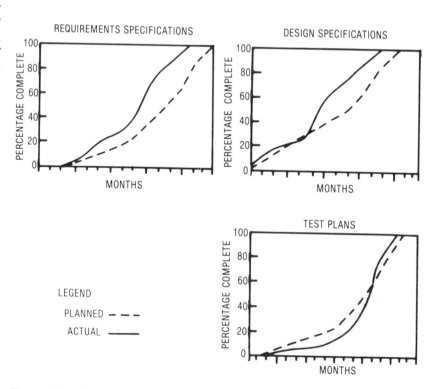

Figure 5. Development progress metrics—capability level (dotted lines, planned; solid lines, actual).

Code	10%
Test	25%
System test support	15%

These percentages were derived using special time cards from our engineers and are based upon our actual earlier experience. For example, a capability with a code size of 1000 source lines would translate into 100 equivalent source lines for the requirements work, 200 for capability design, 200 for design unit work, 100 for code, 250 for capability testing, and 150 for supporting the work of system testing. Using this metric, we tracked the progress of the entire project by summing the equivalent source lines attributed to the completed development phases of all the capabilities (Figure 6).

The management team now had a clear and current view of where the project was and what the problem areas might be. We updated these metrics once a week and supplemented them at the twice-weekly meetings in which the supervisors made their progress reports. In these meetings we identified our common problems and assigned corrective actions. It was important to track the timely resolution of these action items. Crisp reporting was necessary, and the meetings emphasized accomplishments as well as problems. Our main concern was how to jointly solve the identified problems as expeditiously as possible.

Quality metrics. A wide array of standard metrics is available to evaluate quality.[6] The 5ESS system project used a number of these, including metrics for fault density, fault discovery and correction rates, the number of open problems and their severities, etc.[7] Let us now discuss some of the specific project-dependent metrics which we used.

=====

The most important aspect of quality is the performance of the system as perceived by the user.

=====

The most important aspect of quality is the performance of the system as perceived by the user. For switching systems this means the capacity to switch phone calls, the reliability of the system to provide continuing service, the percentage of calls completed, the frequency and duration of recovery actions due to software or hardware faults, the response time to the commands input by the telephone company craft personnel, etc. During the capability and system testing phases we routinely operated the system in simulated field environments over durations of several days. We kept accurate data and computed metrics for all the performance characteristics of the sys-

tem. We established a priori objectives in terms of all the performance metrics. Figure 7 shows the call completion rate as an example of these metrics. During the early stages of development a large percentage of the calls were not properly completed due to either hardware or software problems. As development progressed and the system approached field quality, the completion rate improved to over 99.99 percent. These metrics provided direct measures of the system performance and were major considerations in assessing overall system quality.

To assure that the computing capacity and memory requirements of the system were successfully achieved, we established allocations for each function and program segment early in development. These allocations were based on system performance objectives and available resources. Actual usages were then measured and monitored constantly as development progressed. In this way we avoided the frequent pitfall of discovering a computing capacity or memory usage problem late in the development cycle. The resulting system performance exceeded the original goals.

Productivity metrics. We also used several productivity metrics on the project. These included the number of source lines, number of program functions, and pages of associated documentation generated per staff-year. The ideal software productivity metric, however, is yet to be established. The "product" used in computing this ideal metric should be directly related to the value of the software. In spite of the efforts of many, there is not now a commonly applicable metric for the software product, due to the wide variability of software applications even within similar industries. The most practical and widely used metrics are still based on the line count of the software. One drawback of these metrics, however, is that they can only be used after development is complete or almost complete.

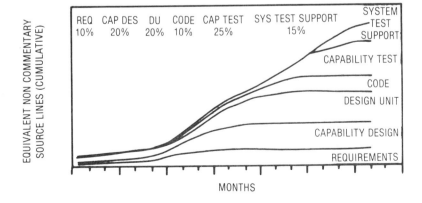

Figure 6. Development progress metric – overall progress.

We again used equivalent source lines for the latest 5ESS generic. This time we used it as a measure of productivity during the course of development before all (or any) source lines had been written. The product of each development phase was characterized by the equivalent source lines computed from the estimated code size. By using equivalent source lines as a common product for all the development phases, we could add the products of each phase and compute and compare the productivity. In Figure 6 the slope of the curve represents the productivity of the entire organization and could be easily normalized to a per-staff-year basis. The curve could also be extrapolated, based on the calculated productivity and the staffing level, to estimate project progress and completion.

each level. Lines deleted at one level are generally replaced by new lines that are counted as lines written at the next higher level. The shapes of the distributions (the size of the tail region) indicate that program module B was implemented more productively (lower levels) than program module A. Also, the ratio of the number of lines of code kept to the total lines of code written measures the productivity in generating correct source code.

Efforts for further improvement

We are maintaining a productivity and methodology group to find new approaches to further improve our development process and our work environment. In addition, productivity and quality circles[8] have been

---

The most practical and widely used metrics are still based on the line count of the software.

Another aspect of productivity is efficiency in generating source code. We established a metric called "change level" that measured the change frequency of the source lines. We defined the source lines that were initially written following the program design as level one lines. The change level was increased by one every time one or more source lines at a certain level were changed or replaced. Therefore, the change level measured the iterations required to correct the program. Clearly, productivity is strongly correlated to the number of levels of changes needed (iterations) before a program is correct.

Figure 8 shows typical distributions of change levels for the source lines of two program modules. In Figure 8 the change levels are plotted horizontally. The vertical bars show the total lines of source code written (entire bar), lines of source code deleted (black), and lines of source code that are unchanged (white), at

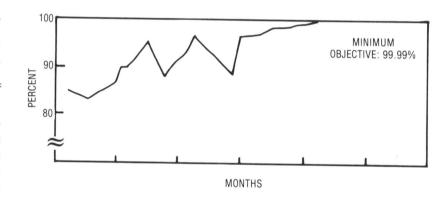

Figure 7. Call completion rate.

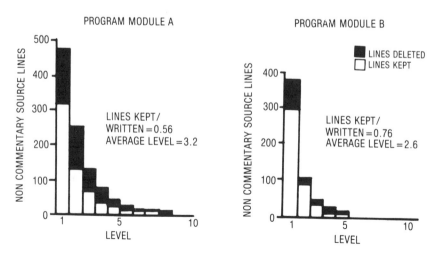

Figure 8. Productivity metric—change level examples.

formed within the development organization. These circles are based on the precept that nobody knows more about how to improve the productivity and quality of his work than the worker himself.[9] The circle members are all staff volunteers who are highly motivated and innovative. The circle discussions are brainstorming sessions, usually without any particular formal structure. The sessions have been very productive in identifying areas for improvements; their suggestions range from simple procedural modifications to sophisticated tools improvements, and from straightforward ideas with immediate applicability to proposals for technological breakthroughs with potentially high payoffs. Management considers all ideas and suggestions seriously. A work list of over 100 items spanning 10 different categories now exists as a result of the ongoing circle discussions. Using the Pareto principle of "the vital few and the trivial many,"[10] we identify those suggestions that would result in the greatest improvement in quality and productivity. We have already implemented an appreciable portion of these suggestions and we are actively pursuing more. There is no doubt that the circle activities are contributing substantially to the productivity and quality of the project as well as to improvements in the entire work environment.

From our experiences in developing three large software releases of the 5ESS system, we believe a number of management and methodology innovations were the key contributors to improving software quality and productivity.

Primarily, we had a well-defined development structure that corresponded to a clear set of responsibilities and goals for all levels of management and staff. Our goals and achievements for progress, quality, and productivity in development were quantified and made visible to gain common project recognition and support. A formal development methodology, fully supported by management, proved to be indispensable; it provided a uniform development process that supported the concept of built-in quality.

Management also demonstrated a true concern for its people, especially their development as individuals. They emphasized personal successes and provided numerous opportunities to demonstrate them. Here again, the quantization of tasks provided by a good development methodology made it much easier to perceive and appraise the contributions and growth of individual people.

In the end, what made the difference was the whole organization's commitment to the use and continuous improvement of its development methodology. We are sure that similar methodologies can work; that high quality and high productivity go hand in hand; and that people and their faithful execution of methodology make a significant positive difference in the results. ∎

References

1. F. T. Andrews and W. B. Smith, "No. 5 ESS—Overview," *Proc. 10th International Switching Symposium,* Mar. 1981, pp. 3.1.1-3.1.6.

2. H. L. Bosco et al., "Managing a Very Large Software Switching Project," *Proc. Int'l Conf. Software for Telecommunication Switching Systems,* July 1983, pp. 116-120.

3. B. W. Boehm, "Software Engineering," *IEEE Trans. Computers,* Vol. C-25, No. 12, Dec. 1976, pp. 1226-1241.

4. P. D. Mandigo and G. L. Miller, "5 EES Switch-Simulation Environment," *Bell System Technical Journal* (to be published).

5. A. J. Perils and F. G. Sayward, *Software Metrics,* MIT Press (1981).

6. B. W. Boehm, J. R. Brown, and M. Lipow, "Quantitative Evaluation of Software Quality," *Proc. Second Int'l. Conf. Software Engineering,* Oct. 1976, pp. 592-605.

7. Z. Jelinski and P. B. Moranda, "Software Reliability Research," *Statistical Computer Performance Evaluation,* 1972, pp. 465-484.

8. S. Ingle, *Quality Circles Master Guide,* Prentice-Hall, Englewood Cliffs, N.J., 1982.

9. W. Ouchi, *Theory Z,* Addison-Wesley, Reading, Mass., 1981.

10. J. M. Juran, *Mangerial Breakthrough,* McGraw-Hill, Hightstown, N.J., 1964.

Edward M. Prell is the director of the 5ESS System Software Laboratory at AT&T Bell Laboratories in Naperville, Illinois. His organization is responsible for the development of the base software of the 5ESS. Since 1962, he has worked on and managed various hardware and software projects at AT&T Bell Laboratories. He received a BSEE from the University of Kentucky, an MSEE from Columbia University, and an MS degree in management science from the Stevens Institute of Technology.

Alan P. Sheng is the supervisor of the Software Productivity and Design Methods Group at AT&T Bell Laboratories in Naperville, Illinois. His group is responsible for the software development methodology used in developing the 5ESS switching system. Sheng is developing a knowledge-based system for software design and program generation. He received a BS degree in physics from the University of California at Berkeley and a PhD in physics from MIT.

The authors' address is AT&T Bell Laboratories, 1200 E. Warrensville Rd., Naperville, IL 60566.

Software Engineering in GTE

William G. Griffin, GTE Laboratories

Efficient software development within a diverse corporation requires a common methodology and an accommodation of rapidly evolving technologies.

In 1983, GTE spent approximately $475 million on company and customer-supported research and development conducted by more than 4700 scientists and engineers at 38 business-unit technology centers. The largest component of this R&D investment was related to software in embedded real-time products—central office systems, communication command and control, and PBX systems—and network-based information services, such as GTE Telenet.

GTE is a decentralized corporation, and each business unit is responsible for its own technology needs. Therefore, there are many different software development styles within the corporation, each oriented toward different market needs. In addition, GTE has a multimillion-dollar investment in management information systems for the operation of the corporation's business. This article presents the management perspective on the GTE software engineering culture—methodology, environment, and tools as well as the problems of new technology transfer.

A corporate approach to software engineering

During the mid-70's, several of GTE's senior software engineering managers met informally to discuss the future of software within the corporation. They recognized the need for a forum to share information and address issues for what was beginning to be a rapidly expanding technology within GTE. They created the Software Steering Committee and gave it

responsibility for interbusiness-unit communications on software engineering issues. This committee reports to the Engineering Council, which is composed of the vice presidents of engineering from each business unit.

The primary SSC focus was software engineering for embedded real-time systems, like switching systems, command and control systems, and networking. The management information system organizations, which were not concerned with the hardware resource or time constraints, did not participate. An SSC management subgroup was formed to study software engineering and management issues and to manage the SSC itself, which had grown too large to function as a single working body. Initially, the SSC met four times a year to examine the diverse software activities within the corporation and to share experiences and software engineering tools.

By 1980, the SSC had published *GTE Corporate Software Development Methodology* and specifications for an integrated software development environment. Since the primary technical goals of the committee had been met, the SSC meet less frequently after 1980, but its management subgroup continued regular meetings. By 1982, it had evolved into a committee of senior software engineering managers from each business unit conducting software R&D.

As management information systems became more real-time oriented

This article is an expanded version of the presentation made by Griffin as a member of the keynote panel at Compsac 83, November 9, 1983, in Chicago.

430

Reprinted from *Computer*, November 1984, pages 66-72. Copyright © 1984 by The Institute of Electrical and Electronics Engineers, Inc.

and more important to the deregulated telephone business, GTE Data Services, the group responsible for telephone information systems and services, became an active participant in the SSC. Significantly, software engineering for embedded systems became increasingly concerned with database technology for MIS.

Also in 1982, the SSC created peripheral special interest groups in areas where there was sufficient interest or a known corporate need. Members of these interest groups—software engineers and managers—meet as often as necessary to conduct business and prepare semiannual reports for the SSC.

The SSC continues to function as a forum for sharing knowledge and software among the different business units' software engineering management staff. The committee also brings issues to the attention of senior corporate engineering management for action. It currently meets quarterly, and its annual conference attracts a broad attendance from the GTE software engineering community. This conference features internal technical papers, as well as presentations by leading scholars and consultants.

The SSC relation to some of the special interest groups is illustrated in Figure 1. The Special Interest Group for High-Level Languages has existed for many years and sponsors its own annual conference. Major Sighill discussion topics are Pascal, Chill and Ada compilers, fourth-generation programming languages, language standards, and innovative language applications. The Special Interest Group for Networking has established a logical network for technical computing centers within GTE. A few years ago, the primary Signet focus was X.25 interfaces on host computers. Today, operational issues of technical computing and local area networks are the primary concern. The Special Interest Group for Tools has established a relational database that describes all software engineering, artificial intelligence, and CAD tools available within GTE.

Software methodology

In 1979, when the *GTE Corporate Software Development Methodology* was in the final stages of preparation, it was expected that GTE business units would adopt it as the corporation standard for the development of software for embedded systems and the development of tools for this type of software development environment. This methodology, the result of several years of extensive work by the SSC, consists of four major parts:

- A software architecture for all systems. It is represented as a hierarchy of logical components, each level of the hierarchy being a decomposition of the preceding higher level (see Figure 2). The message class handles all communications between classes;
- A detailed description of the development process based on the software life-cycle model;
- A description of the necessary aspects of configuration management; and

- A list of the necessary documentation for each phase of the development process.

To this original methodology document was appended a glossary of terms and prescribed structure-chart symbols.

A major advantage of a company-wide methodology has been that software engineers and managers have been able to communicate through the use of common terms (see box on p. 69 for examples).

The 1979 corporate methodology brought together existing methodologies used in several GTE divisions, incorporating the ideas of Warnier,[1] Yourdon,[2] and Jackson.[3] It contained common, state-of-the-art ideas and was probably not unique to GTE. Noted consultants, both in and out of academia, reviewed it before it was approved by the SSC and senior engineering management.

As a practical matter, compliance with the methodology depends on the

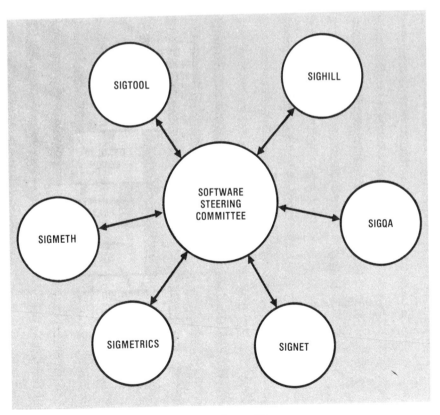

Figure 1. The GTE Software Steering Committee.

perseverance of the first two levels of management. GTE's software development methodology has been endorsed by senior levels of management. The rigor of adherence to the methodology varies somewhat across the business units. Business units that develop software for the Department of Defense have adhered most faithfully, but other business units have also used it successfully.

The project best documented for general reference is the GTD-5 EAX Digital Central Office Switching System. The GTD-5 EAX can support 10,000 to 150,000 voice lines in many configurations, ranging from those of small rural communities to large metropolitan areas. The system and support software contain over 1 million lines of Pascal code in a distributed

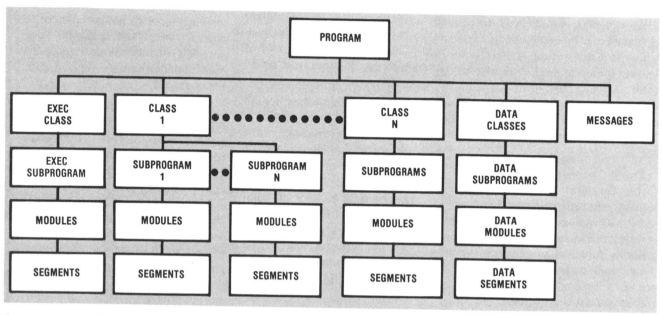

Figure 2. Hierarchy of logical components in GTE software architecture.

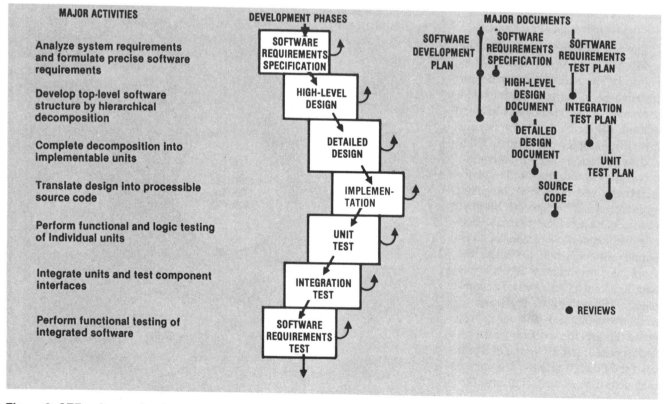

Figure 3. GTE software development process.

network of microprocessors. Vanderlei[4] has described the use of the *GTE Corporate Software Development Methodology* on this ambitious product development.

By 1983, the SSC felt that the methodology was evolving and should be reviewed. The committee directed the Special Interest Group for Methodology to update the methodology document to accommodate experiences of software developers and new technologies. The updated methodology recognizes that movement from one phase of the life cycle to another is often a more iterative process than previously documented and that it includes alternate styles of software development for well-understood information-processing applications, such as end-user written prototype systems that use fourth-generation languages. Other major modifications to the methodology are

- Greater emphasis on testing during earlier phases of the software life cycle,
- A dynamic, rather than static, interpretation of the hierarchy of logical components, and
- A uniform standard to be tailored to individual organizations and their specific environments.

Figure 3 describes the activities, phases, and documentation of the revised software development process.

Software tool development

Software engineering methodologies and tools are not necessarily closely coupled. Nevertheless, six years ago the SSC wrote the requirements specification for an integrated software engineering environment in order to mechanize GTE's software methodology. This specification, known as the "Structured Techniques of Engineering Projects," or STEP, was implemented by a software engineering group at GTE Government Systems in Needham, Massachusetts.[5] The high-level STEP architecture is described in Figure 4. Implemented in Pascal, it has these major features:

- Enforces a set of standards throughout the development; for example, the software hierarchy and its development process of GTE's software methodology;
- Provides an integrated tool set built around a portable data management system for configuration management;
- Ensures that documentation is current;
- Provides relatively easy transportation across operating systems; and
- Provides management reports on project status.

STEP was particularly portable from Tops20 to MVS to VMS. It has also been effective in military system projects, where precision has the highest priority. STEP failed, how-

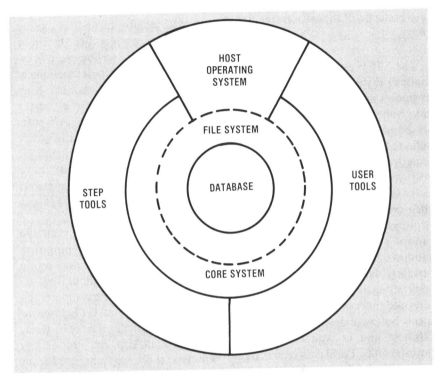

Figure 4. The STEP architecture.

Terminology from the *GTE Corporate Software Development Methodology*

Subprogram:	The name given to the level of problem decomposition immediately subordinate to the class; a set of modules. Typically no greater than 5,000 lines of code.
Module:	The name given to the hierarchical level of problem decomposition immediately subordinate to the subprogram; a compilable set of software logic which is the largest subdivision of the subprogram; a set of segments. Typically no greater than 500 lines of code.
Segment:	A logic entity created during detailed design; that which is implemented; a set of software logic which is a subdivision of a module. A segment has one entry point and one exit point. Usually restricted by project standards to one page of design language, code of flowchart. Typically no greater than 50 lines of code.

ever, to gain wide acceptance in GTE, where engineers preferred more familiar tools. Its major technical problem has been performance. Like other tools written as application programs with their own data management system (for easy portability), STEP performs less well than tools integrated with the data management services of a specific operating system. Some of the commercial business units of GTE rejected STEP because of this performance penalty and its narrow interpretation of the software methodology.

The STEP experience revealed the cultural differences among software engineers in a large, diverse corporation with a tradition of autonomy for its businesses. These differences are reflected in management style, staff experience, computer environments, software engineering tools, and products. GTE businesses generally have their own software tool development groups. These local software tool groups are free to acquire software products from GTE Laboratories or vendors, develop their own software engineering tools where necessary, and integrate them into the local environment. Software developed within one business unit is available to other business units. Local data centers may have difficulty, however, in maintaining the numerous tools available and

purging those that have become obsolete.

GTE business units have generally targeted tools for the operating system level. Unix, MVS, VMS, and Tops20 are the operating systems most frequently used in the corporation for software development. The software environment and tools for GTD-5 EAX product development have been documented by Rice.[6] They cover all phases of the software life cycle and are supported on a distributed Unix and MVS environment that can be characterized as a modified version of the programmers workbench. It is interesting to note that tools functionally equivalent to Unix tools have been provided to developers under MVS/TSO. The GTD-5 EAX software development tools, which, except for code generators and testing tools, are application-independent, have evolved continuously from previous product developments over the past 15 years.

GTE Laboratories serve all the business units by prototyping new state-of-the-art software engineering techniques, with heavy input from academia. As a result, the computer science environment at GTE Laboratories includes many flavors of Unix, Interlisp, Zeta Lisp, etc. Proprietary, prototype tools are transferred from GTE Laboratories to the local tool groups for development into produc-

tion-quality tools. GTE has invested most heavily in the development of compilers, configuration management tools, and testing tools, with increasing investment in tools for the pre-implementation phases of the software life cycle.

We recognize that it is easiest to change software engineering tools and environments prior to the start of a new product development. For economic reasons, however, tools must span product lifetimes, possibly seeing more than a decade of use. Therefore, the acceptance of new software engineering tools may be slower than the development of new software technology.

Technology transfer

The transfer of technology from the research phase to use in systems development is very slow. James documented the problems in software technology transfer in industry.[7] We agree with him that the success of software technology transfer requires the recipients' cooperation. For some years, GTE Laboratories have had a business advocate system to assist in the technology transfer to the business units. The business advocate coordinates GTE Laboratories' technology transfer plans with the business units' technology development plans.

We also recognize that economic need influences the enthusiasm for technology transfer between business units. Engineers are likely to be more receptive to new technologies if their project requires those technologies. In situations where a software technology, such as a particular programming language, is specified in the delivered product or development process, technology transfer may be easier.

Software technology suffers, however, from its abstract quality—the lack of specific metrics describing its value. It is abstract because there is no generally accepted method for evaluating computing environments or software engineering tools. Consequently, the cost of integrating new tools into product development is difficult to

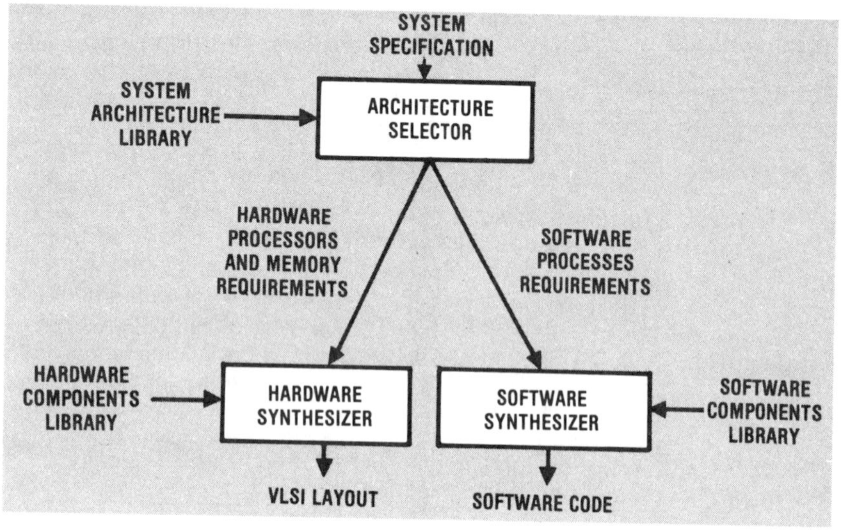

Figure 5. A system compiler.

justify, particularly when considerable training may be required before engineers are able to use the new tools. We believe new software technology requires extensive experimentation to assist the technology transfer process.

Within GTE, the formation of a central software tool development and maintenance group has been frequently discussed. This group would create a basic tool set by integrating tools available from many sources, including subcontracts to local tool groups. The central group would also perform the productization of technology transferred from GTE Laboratories into usable tools. There are pro and con arguments on whether GTE needs such a central tool group, given its decentralized business culture. Of greatest concern is whether the central service organization could react to rapid changes in business unit needs.

The future

GTE has been investing heavily in R&D to improve software quality and development productivity. Over the next five years, however, it is likely that the major influence on the software development will *not* be new software technology. Rather, it will be high-performance, robust personal computers used as software engineering workstations. These distributed development environments will present great challenges in configuration management for large product developments.

We see a trend towards the Unix operating system within GTE for embedded systems. It is portable across the complete hierarchy of computers used for development of real-time systems, and it may become the de facto standard software engineering operating system within GTE for DEC and IBM computers and for the coming software engineering workstations. The layered versions of Unix on top of other operating systems, such as VMS and VM, will encourage this migration. GTE recently announced product support for a version of Unix System III as the operating system

used by the Omni-Action Office System, our shared logic, multifunctional workstation with voice, data, text, and graphics capabilities.

The MVS operating system will probably continue to be used for mainframe information processing applications. Fourth-generation prototyping tools will continue their rapid acceptance for use in the development of mainframe- and personal computer-based information systems. GTE is already using Ada for several projects and will be using Ada Programming Support Environments as they mature. It is likely that the potential for reuse of software tools and application designs will encourage further use of APSE and perhaps Ada for development of embedded systems and data-processing applications beyond those required by the government.

Future methodology and support tools will put more emphasis on the early phases of the software life cycle. GTE business units are currently evaluating the GTE Laboratories' Requirements Processing System and the Test Plan Generator.[8] These tools allow checking for consistency and completeness of the real-time system requirements and allow for automatic generation of test plans from the requirements specification. Later this year, GTE will put in service a compiler-based environment, the General-Purpose Compiling System, which has evolved from the GTE Laboratories Chill Compiling System.[9] The CCS was a bootstrap testbed for an innovative compiling-system architecture and compiler-based tools. It has language-dependent front ends, multiple-target, machine-code generators, and the capability of language-to-language translation for one class of block-structured languages. We are also seeing the use of fourth-generation languages in real-time system development.[10] Other software technologies, like relational database management systems originally developed for management information systems application, will be used on real-time product developments once performance constraint obstacles are overcome.

Current computer-science research within GTE supports the evolution of the software life-cycle paradigm suggested by Wirth.[11] This evolutionary view of methodology and tools emphasizes reuse, higher level languages, and sharing, as suggested by Boehm and Standish.[12] Other research activity at GTE Laboratories indicates that some products with programmable microprocessors will revert to hard-wired custom logic. Silicon compilers in VLSI design and rapid microfabrication will eliminate software in some systems where speed is a concern.[13]

In 1983, Dasarathy, Prerau, and Vellenga[14] of GTE Laboratories described a hypothetical system compiler (Figure 5). They projected that integrated, intelligent tools would synthesize optimal system designs and automate the decomposition into software and optimal integrated-circuit designs from a requirements specification. In order to achieve this utopian automation, new paradigms of software engineering such as those described by Balzer, Cheatham, and Green[15] are necessary. Consequently, the dominant software engineering research themes at GTE Laboratories will be specification, integrated environments, reusable software components, and the application of knowledge-based systems to the software development process. In short, we expect today's software development methodology and software engineering tools to evolve rapidly and improve product quality and development productivity, and we realize that the software engineering management process must also evolve to make this technology a reality. □

Acknowledgments

I wish to thank the members of the GTE Software Steering Committee who provided input to this article. I also thank B. Dasarathy, C. McGowan, and R. Wirth from the Computer Science Laboratory, who assisted in reviewing the final draft of this article.

Part VIII: Case Studies

"The most frustrating thing is that we know how we ought to manage . . . and we refuse to change . . . ."

—David Packard

Case studies can be used to communicate experiences and lessons learned to managers quickly and in an understandable manner. Each of the seven cases in this section has been selected because it provides a meaningful message that could help our readers be better managers and supervisors.

The first case deals with the Multics project at the Massachusetts Institute of Technology. Corbato and Clingen provide an interesting and revealing disclosure of the real problems experienced in the commercial development of a large, time-sharing utility by several organizations. The message of this case study is that incremental, evolutionary development should be planned for in new undertakings so that the software and system can mature naturally over time.

The development of Apple's Macintosh computer and its associated software serves as our next case study. Guterl describes the flow of events, the management decisions, and the approaches taken to develop a commercial product whose success or failure revolved around delivery of user-friendly software for a highly volatile and competitive marketplace. The message of this case is that success can be realized in a relatively unstructured setting if innovation and personnel initiative are rewarded.

The Galileo project is an ongoing project that serves as our next case study. Barry and Reifer discuss the approach being used by NASA/Jet Propulsion Laboratory to manage the development of a complement of instruments in a geographically dispersed environment where autonomy is preserved. The message of this case is that geographical dispersion can be managed when a suitable framework reinforced by standards and tempered by discretion is employed.

The Army's Safeguard ballistic missile defense project is our next case study. Stephenson details the magnitude of the effort and the many factors that affected its conduct. Key messages of this case are that a considerable percentage of staff resources on a large project was not directly involved with the software developmental activities and that care must be exercised to account for all facets of the software production job.

The final case study is a revealing parody of the practices used by the Navy to develop its tactical software. Weiss chronicles the development of a fictional system whose requirements are typical of Navy tactical systems currently operational or under development. He used information gathered by interviewing responsible Navy individuals as the basis of the report, which includes recommendations on how to avoid common pitfalls in such developments.

4. A MANAGERIAL VIEW OF
THE MULTICS SYSTEM DEVELOPMENT[1]

F. J. Corbato
Massachusetts Institute of Technology
C. T. Clingen
Honeywell Information Systems, Inc., Cambridge

1. Introduction

A reasonable question of a software manager might be "What possible insight can I gain from the agonies of someone else's project?" Of course, not much if one takes too literally from another's experience every problem and his reaction to it. But one of the attributes of a shrewd manager is to abstract from the circumstances of others those aspects of a previous episode which are germane to his own. Moreover, successful large-scale software development efforts are sufficiently rare that their chronicles may still be viewed with the curiosity accorded a traveler to a distant land.

An objection to the study of large-scale projects which is often raised is that the only difficulty is in the word "large." If only one could do it with a small team, so the reasoning goes, one's difficulties would vanish. Such an argument ignores completely those systems which have such vast scope or construction deadlines that they exceed the capacity or technical knowledge of a small group. With time, of course, formerly large efforts become more modest in scale as the sophistication, tools, and engineering knowledge improve, but there will always be externally-set pressures to engineer ever more ambitious systems.

The present paper is a case-history look at the development of the Multics System from a management point of view. The goals and features of the Multics System have already been described at length [1-6] and a summary of the technical experience of the project has been presented elsewhere [7]. Further, there have been several books published that address the internal structure and organization of the system [8,9,10].

Thus, for the present purposes only a brief recapitulation is in order. The system planning, begun in 1964, was for a new computer system which could serve as a prototype of a computer utility. Although Multics is now offered as a standard product by Honeywell Information Systems Inc., the system planning

---

1. This research was supported by the Advanced Research Projects Agency of the Department of Defense and was monitored by the Office of Naval Research under contract number N00014-70-A-0362-0006.

and development was a cooperative effort involving three separate organizations: the computer department of the General Electric Company (since acquired by Honeywell Information Systems Inc.), the Bell Telephone Laboratories (1965 to 1969) and Project MAC of M.I.T. (since renamed the M.I.T. Laboratory for Computer Science).

The design goals were many but included:

1. Convenient remote terminal use

2. Continuous operation (i.e., without shutdown) analogous to power and telephone companies

3. A wide range of configuration capacity which could be dynamically varied without system or user program reorganization

4. An internal file system with apparent reliability high enough for users to entrust their only copies of programs and data to it

5. The ability of users to share selectively information among themselves

6. The ability to store and create hierarchical structures of information for purposes of system administration and decentralization of user activities

7. The ability to support a wide range of applications ranging from heavy numerical production calculations to interactive time-sharing users without inordinate inefficiency

8. The ability to allow a multiplicity of programming environments and human interfaces within the same system

9. The ability to evolve the system both with changes in technology and in user aspirations.

The above goals were ambitious ones, not because of any one particular idea, but because they had never been tied together in a single comprehensive system. Moreover, to achieve the goals, many novel techniques were proposed.

The importance of the above list of goals from a management viewpoint is that it clearly signalled a strong research and development effort added to the ordinary problems of building a large software complex. Not only had an implementation of the goals not been successfully achieved before, but there were large knowledge gaps in the likely behavior of both system and users. In particular, the behavior of the system required extrapolating user attitudes to the domain of rapid-access large-memory computing, presuming what typical programming practices would be, and making assumptions of the behavorial properties of virtual memory systems.

Perhaps it is the normal naivete of those beginning a large project -- most of those on the project had never done anything like it before and the average age was less than 30 -- but everyone seemed to assume that those aspects of the system development they were not responsible for would be implemented in an orderly, straightforward, clear way, without schedule slippage or serious debugging difficulties. Still, there were many major problems which were perceived from the beginning and others which only became apparent with time. To structure the presentation we will take in order sections on the problems perceived early, the problems detected later, a discussion of the various tools which were used, and finally some general observations of software development management.

2. Problems Perceived in the Project

As already mentioned, the project goals were ambitious and in turn led to technical challenges in three major areas: hardware, languages, and general software ideas. Let us take these topics up.

2.1. Hardware

The basic hardware system chosen was the newly marketed GE 635 which allowed both multiple processors and multiple memory modules. However, to support the fundamental ideas of controlled information sharing and large-memory management at the user level, it was necessary to design rather radical changes in the processor architecture which allowed addressing suitable for segmentation of the memory. Moreover, to relieve the user of managing the multiple levels of the physical storage hierarchy, further processor modifications had to be introduced to support the management of paging by the supervisor. In addition, processor architectural changes were required for the hardware access control mechanisms so that the supervisor could properly control access to all information in the system. To support the supervisor functions, both an interrupt clock and a nonrepeating calendar clock had to be designed. To support the projected large number of communication lines to terminals, it was necessary to design a special purpose input-output controller. Finally, the requirements of information storage also dictated the design of a high-transfer rate drum as a second-level paging buffer and the design of an ultra-high performance disk.

One property of hardware design is that it must usually be done first and yet hardware problems are the most difficult to correct or change. This results partly from the rigidity of the engineering practices and procedures which must support the maintenance of the hardware and partly from the large fan-out of design decisions which are a consequence of the basic hardware architecture. This property which emphasizes prudence, along with the number of design problems listed above, had the result of producing unforeseen delay in hardware delivery schedules. Not only was the design time prolonged by careful checking for consistency and coherence, but the unfamiliarity of the new ideas often led to communication difficulties among hardware and software designers.

Another cause of delay was confusion over reliability specifications of hardware. Often those responsible for software would expect hardware when delivered to be at the ultimate reliability level; conversely, hardware engineers would expect reliability to follow a learning-time experience curve and reach the final specifications only asymptotically after an extended period of time. The result was unanticipated delay when unreliability seriously hampered the system debugging process. Moreover, a large amount of unanticipated software effort was expended in developing software programs to recover from transient hardware failures.

These learning-time difficulties were particularly apparent in the information storage parts of the system and affected the core memories, the paging drum and the disks. In the first two cases the difficulties were eventually overcome but in the case of the disk design, several unplanned substitutions became necessary using later technologies.

Further complications arose from the specialized input-output controller which, while effective, was unusual in design and intricate in operation. This resulted in an inordinate amount of hardware and software design time and a substantial engineering burden to support its relatively unique properties. Later in the project as the overall system design became streamlined and simplified, the controller was replaced by a more conventional one which was fabricated using a later technology.

The significance of the above hardware problems, typical of the industry at the time, lies in their cumulative impact upon the project. In fact the overall set of design problems was anticipated; but it is also fair to say that it was not properly appreciated then how many things could go wrong -- or in effect -- how much the state-of-the-art was being pushed. In retrospect, the major miscalculation was not to have anticipated the normal unreliability of newly-developed hardware, for if there had been better prediction, there could have been better planning. The result, of course, was delay in the evolution of the project and delay in the discovery of other problem areas.

2.2. Languages

An immediate consequence of a significant departure from previous system design is the obsolescence of all previous software. Not only is an assembler not available, but the usual compilers and general software aids and debugging tools are also missing. Partly because the construction of assemblers was felt to be understood, several false steps were taken. Initial attempts to patch over an assembler from the related GE 635 were finally abandoned when the cumulative magnitude of the system architectural changes began to be appreciated. A second effort to develop an elaborate macroassembler was also abandoned in the face of unexpected difficulties which produced an ever-receding completion date. Finally a primitive assembler was built to serve both the purpose of direct coding and as a final pass of a compiler. As with many other activities, the simplest form survived.

As unexpected as the assembler difficulty was, it was dwarfed by the problem that arose out of the compiler implementation. Most of the system software was to be programmed in the compiler language and as a result there was a strong interest in choosing one which was advanced and comprehensive in its design. The language chosen was PL/1 partly because of the richness of its constructs and partly because of the enthusiasm of those planning to implement the compiler. The difficulties in carrying out this implementation are described in great detail elsewhere [11], but one can summarize by noting that the language implementation became an inadvertent research project. Not only were efficient mechanisms unknown for many of the language constructs, partly because of the consequences of their interaction, but major interfacing also had to be designed to the supporting system environment which itself was under development. One compiler version, to be built by a vendor, never became operational when it belatedly became clear that typical Fortran compiler construction techniques did not extrapolate well. There was no contingency plan for this disaster and massive efforts were required to patch a "quick and dirty" compiler into a usable tool. Only several years after the start of the project was a compiler of the quality anticipated by the PL/1 designers finally produced.

It is now obvious that the Multics development would have been much easier if a simpler language had been chosen for implementation. In choosing another language there would still have been a very difficult compromise to make in choosing one of those existent in 1965. Alternatively developing a new language (or subsetting PL/1) would have required a firmness and dogmatism that was incommensurate with the structure of the project organization. Nevertheless, in hindsight, it is believed that one of the two latter courses would have been the more effective development path. However, having been successfully developed, PL/l is now one of the strengths of the system.

2.3. New Software Ideas

In order to implement the system goals described earlier, a variety of new software techniques were needed. Notions of user management of memory and storage spaces were to be approached with the technique of using segments. Each segment would represent a user-named region of memory which would maintain its identity even while a part of the user's active memory address space. Further, the sharing of information, data, and programs would be done by the user specifying for every segment a list of those allowed each of several classes of access. These lists themselves could be varied by a user at any time. Segments themselves were to be stored in a physically multilevel and logically hierarchical file system which each user could name and structure to suit his filing needs. Both the segmentation and file system were to be supported by system-mediated paging which would dynamically and automatically move information among the physical memory levels in response to execution demands and the duration of reference inactivity. This virtual memory system was to be unique in that the entire file system was to be included in the one-level store that the processes acted upon.

Finally, the user environment would include conventions which would allow all procedures to be possibly recursive, to be pure (i.e., not self-modifying), to allow automatic retrieval and binding of subprograms only upon execution demand, and to support rings of protection as a generalization of the user-supervisor relationship. Most of these ideas were individually understood but never before had there been an attempt to synthesize a coherent system containing all of them.

It was in the software synthesis area where the difficulties were best anticipated -- probably because new ground obviously had to be broken. Nevertheless, it is fair to say that the iterative nature of the design process was not sufficently appreciated. The need for iteration develops in part because of the magnitude of the effort and the inability of a single individual to comprehend the effect of a particular module design on the system behavior as a whole. Not only does he usually not know the expected usage pattern of his software path, but it is hard to estimate the impact on the system performance of an occasional exercising of it. A straightforward approach is to create a perhaps crude and incomplete system, begin to use it and to observe the behavior. Then on the basis of the observed difficulties, one simplifies, redesigns and refines the system. In the case of Multics, most areas of the system were redesigned as much as half a dozen times in as many years.

Such a redesign is done with hardware where breadboarding and test machines are common occurrences. There it is assumed that design iteration will occur and no one expects to go into production using a prototype design. It is only in recent years that it has begun to be recognized that software designing is similar.

A second reason for underestimating the need for iteration is that systems with unknown behavioral properties require the implementation of iterations which are intrinsic to the design process but which are normally hidden from view. Certainly when a solution to a well-understood problem is synthesized, weak designs are mentally rejected by a competent designer in a matter of moments. On larger or more complicated efforts, alternative designs must be explicitly and iteratively implemented. The designers, perhaps out of vanity, often are at pains to hide the many versions which were abandoned, and if absolute failure occurs, of course one hears nothing. Thus the topic of design iteration is rarely discussed. Perhaps we should not be surprised to see this phenomenon with software, for it is a rare author indeed who publicizes the amount of editing or the number of drafts he took to produce a manuscript.

It is important to recognize too that "state-of-the-art" is to be measured with respect to the experience of the team actually doing the work. Thus, even though a particular design already may have been implemented successfully somewhere, a team with little background related to that design should recognize that their activities will contain a large component of uncertainty due to the research they must do to get up to speed. Overlooking this "locality of expertise" can lead to the misjudgement that a task is a routine engineering effort rather than the more realistic characterization as a research and development project.

In summary, with the inevitable design indeterminancy characteristic of a large, state-of-the-art system when coupled with inexperienced project management can lead to severe schedule underestimation. Even with management experience, scheduling will always be a problem since predicting the pace of research is, at best, an educated guess. Planning explicitly for at least one complete design and implementation iteration may lead to some apparently extravagant schedules, but for those developments where the solutions are poorly understood such planning usually proves to be realistic, if not optimistic.

2.4. Geographical Separation

Geographical separation (Massachusetts, New Jersey, Arizona) was an obvious difficulty in pursuing the development of a system, yet one that was felt to be outweighed by the strengths that each organization brought to the project. On a project with a strong developmental flavor it is hard to eliminate a need to interact with fellow designers and implementors on an impromptu basis. Three types of technology were employed but the communication obstacles were never completely overcome. These technologies were the telephone, the airplane, and the xerographic copying machine. The role of the telephone which included transmission of programs and data was clearly important as was the availability of good one-day airline service between two of the sites. Not so obvious was the importance of the modern copying machine industry which just came to maturity as the project began. The ability to disseminate rapidly memoranda describing prototype designs was vital to the success of the project; design interactions proceeded in parallel and at an enlivened pace while ideas were fresh in the heads of the authors and readers. Moreover, by allowing the fast distribution of definitive design memoranda, technical control of the project was greatly enhanced. The key point is that early capture in written form of design descriptions is vital for orderly development, and one must be careful not to let formal publication mechanisms be a hindrance.

2.5. Three-Organization Cooperation

The reasons for wanting multiple organization participation were strong. Each organization had unique ingredients contributing to the ambitious project goals. The computer manufacturing, marketing and maintenance could best be done by a company dedicated to that business. The computational expectations and requirements of a diverse company with needs ranging from engineering to business management could clearly be supplied by the Bell Laboratories. Moreover, they had special competence in the communication area and had shown themselves to be inventive and sophisticated users of previous computer systems. Lastly the university, often a source of innovation, could be expected to approach problems without being constrained by past solutions; certainly several years of pioneering development of time-sharing systems gave evidence of this.

And yet, there were problems too. Most important was that the project remained a cooperative since none of the organizations felt able to accept the ascendancy of the others. The effect was that of a three-cornered marriage where success depended on each party wanting to make the arrangement work. Such an arrangement was obviously organizationally weak. Decision-making depended on tacit agreements of leadership responsibility and more importantly on a consensus by the half-dozen or so major technical leaders in the three organizations.

Diffuse responsibility along with intra-organizational allegiances required diplomacy and tact. More significantly, though, a loose organizational structure made ruthless decisions difficult and encouraged design by aggregation. These problems were recognized and consciously fought but decisions to kill a design, or more frequently an implementation, were often postponed until negative evidence was nearly overwhelming. As a result of this rejection mechanism weakness, schedules inevitably became prolonged.

3. Problems Which Became Apparent Later

One distinction between those problems just described and those which developed later is that the latter are more systemic in character. Many of these problems were a result of the project stresses produced by the delays resulting from the first set of problems.

3.1. Different Organizational Goals

It is of course unrealistic to expect every organization involved in a project to have the same objectives. In the initial enthusiasm of a project it is easy to ignore differences. In the case of the Multics project, the three organizations attached different levels of importance to 1) research and development in computer science, 2) development of a commercial product, and 3) useful computational service in the short term. The inclusion of several objectives, in turn, left unresolved priorities of time, money, or concept demonstration. The default effect was to favor concept demonstration but not without great stress because of the unplanned delay which resulted.

3.2. A More Than Two-Year Project

As soon as a project extends beyond a couple of years, several new needs gradually appear. Foremost is that turnover of highly trained and specialized staff develops. Although the reasons for departure were usually unrelated to the project, nevertheless replacements had to be recruited and trained. Because of the highly developmental character of the project, bringing a new person "up to speed" usually took 6 to 9 months. More importantly to maintain this training process, a generous portion of the project personnel resources had to be directed towards documentation and education.

One might argue staff turnover is an obvious consequence of delay in a large project. Not so obvious, however, is sponsor turnover. In some form, every project has at least one sponsor, and in the case of Multics there were three. The initial sponsors were enthusiastic supporters of the project (or it never would have started!) but also had many other responsibilities. With time, promotions, changes and reorganizations are inevitable and executive replacements are made. There then develops the need to repersuade key persons that project concepts and goals are both desirable and feasible. Such repersuasion represents an overhead requiring the very best project personnel since the life of the project depends upon successfully educating and communicating. One can only conclude that long projects are especially hazardous because of the mandatory success of this "reselling" requirement. Obviously any project segmentation into useful subprojects enhances the likelihood of success since periodic exhibits of progress are more easily demonstrated to sponsors.

A long project also has to address the need for evolution. Fortunately the Multics projects had as one of its goals such a requirement and evolution became a major factor in the survival of the project. Not only were there changes in the level of technology, e.g., from transistors to integrated circuits, from drums to large memories, but also there were changes in the relative importance of conceptual objectives and the techniques used to achieve them. The burden which evolution requirements place upon a system are many but include: 1) careful design of functionally modular domains and procedures within them, 2) argument passing and control transfer conventions which are fail-safe, 3) enforcement of programming standards, and 4) in general a vigorous adherence to good software engineering practices. Such practices on a first attempt are frequently less effective than artful but gimmicky short-cuts. Moreover it is important to recognize that there is a design time overhead associated with the discovery of general, but effective, techniques. Nevertheless, if evolution is to be achieved, this design investment cannot be avoided.

3.3. Misestimated Schedules

Almost all large projects face the difficulty of schedule slippage. Partly the difficulty is inexperience in following an unknown path. Some of the trouble is that individuals are often unconsciously wishful. Usually there is no realistic penalty for a slipped schedule and this encourages optimism. Partly too, there is miscommunication of the significance of milestones. For example, software modules said to be complete may still have serious bugs that produce system "crashes". Occasionally also, individuals estimate too conservatively either out of personal reluctance to follow a particular design strategy or because of an overzealous desire for a "safe" schedule. The Multics project had all of these problems but in the latter phases, as individuals and managers became more experienced, schedule estimations became more and more reliable. No panacea was ever discovered except that of better familiarity with the tasks to be accomplished.

3.4. Imbalanced Resources

Perhaps it was a carryover from the early computer system days when successful production of hardware was the primary problem, but the development of Multics software was hampered by a shortage of computer time. This shortage was in part due to unanticipated delays generating a sudden need for more help; clearly, system programmers were available on a shorter time scale than hardware so the response was to increase the programming staff. However, these programmers in turn created more demand for computer resources and greater communication and coordination problems. Thus for short-term reasons, some long-term delay was probably introduced [12]. More importantly, because the budgets for personnel and for equipment were handled differently, a nonoptimum mix of resources was applied. In retrospect, it would have been better to add more hardware even at the expense of reducing the programming staff.

3.5. Unnecessary Generality

Because a major requirement of the system design was that it achieve a consensus endorsement, it was always easier to design for generality. Some of these design efforts were so expansive they bordered on the grandiose and were easily detected, but far more designs suffered from the more subtle problem of merely taking on too many requirements at once. Here the judgment was a pragmatic one, namely, that the resultant mechanisms were either too complicated or too ineffective. Ponderous mechanisms after programming were often allowed to go into the debugging phase only to be scrapped later when their ineffectiveness became more obvious; hindsight suggests it would have been better to budget in advance the amount of program that a set of ideas was deemed to be worth and to make their initial implementation be as lean as possible.

4. Management Tools and Their Effectiveness

Although system developers often bemoaned the lack of tools for development and management often suspected excessive tool building, it is probably true that most projects could benefit from more attention to the methodology of design, construction, and production. The Multics development was no exception. However, during the history of the project, a significant number of techniques and ideas were used. A list of the more important ideas with some brief remarks is:

A.   High-Level System Programming Language: The best comment that can be made is that the system would never have been completed without the use of a high-level language for most of the system programming [11].

Although not without problems, the use of the high-level language made each programmer a factor of 5 to 10 more productive in a coding sense and more concerned with the semantics than the syntax of modules.

B.   Structured Programming: Although the phrase had not been coined, structured programming principles were used under the guise of "good engineering practice". The use of the language PL/1, the establishment of call/return conventions, and argument passing and intermodule communications were all aspects of this usage. The model of hardware design and engineering served as a major inspiration. Although good engineering practices can never be a complete solution since they only describe a style, they imposed an order to the project that was a strong sinew of strength.

C.   Design Review: Perhaps the most difficult problem in designing a complex system is assigning the right person to the right job. Prior experience is not always a good indication of how a person will perform in a new situation. Youth and immaturity make judgment suspect. Thus the design process must be approached warily. In the case of Multics, the general strategy was to let design leadership be exposed rather than imposed. Potential designers were first asked to write position papers describing the design problems, their scope, and realistic solutions. If these position papers were persuasive, a design document was next initiated which proposed a particular mechanism (and omitted alternative designs). If after a review of the document by his technical peers, a consensus was reached, a set of module designs was prepared by the designer. In turn, the same designer was then expected to implement and debug his ideas, perhaps with assistance but without loss of responsibility.

The above process, although not flawless, was very effective in forcing ideas into written form suitable for design review. By coupling design with implementation responsibility, communication problems were minimized. And the written design document became a part of the vital System Programmers' Manual which was the definitive description of the system. This manual became a crucial educational tool when staff turnover developed in the later phases of the project.

The above design process was carefully applied in the early design stages but in retrospect could have been carried further. In particular, a rigorous review after programming but <u>before</u> debugging can be of immense value in minimizing waste effort and debugging time. Such a review should include mandatory reading of all code by at least one other peer. One should expect a scrutiny of style, logic, and the overall algorithmic behavior. On those occasions when such practices were applied, either major improvements usually occurred, or in other instances entire design strategies were revised. The principal obstacles to universal application were the absence of a disciplined design tradition among programmers and the occasional unwillingness by managers "to waste two men on the same job."

D. Test Environments: In at least two instances, the file system and the communication system with terminals; it was possible to isolate and simulate the input-output behavior of a section of the system. Such isolation was of immense value when the system was being upgraded since it decoupled the debugging of major areas. Not only did such decoupling reduce the number of system integration bugs but it significantly reduced the total debugging time since integration bugs were usually the most difficult to analyze.

E. Production Techniques: Most important of all the software tools used for development was the system itself. The rate of system improvement went up dramatically after it was possible to do all software development in a compatible, self-consistent environment. The development use of the system for itself was not possible until a period of over four years after the beginning of the project. The long delay period strongly suggests that more effort should have been applied to establishing a sub-design of a skeletal subsystem which could have been placed in operation sooner and then evolved into more complete form.

A consequence of using the system itself for development, and of the design goals of easy maintenance and evolution, was the option of rapid system changes. Mechanically, changes to some parts of the system could be made literally in seconds while more central changes might require 10 minutes. It was rapidly found that the principal obstacle to change was the ability to update and propagate the system documentation information. Gradually a pattern developed where a new system was installed once or twice a week under the direction of a single person acting as an editor (in the magazine sense) who also was accountable for any reliability problems that developed. Gradually, too, the process of submitting and assembling systems was made more and more automatic, thus lessening the chance of human error. The ability to make system changes without long delays was especially efficient since it allowed the consequences of module changes to develop while the details were still fresh in programmers' minds.

F.   Management and Performance Tools: Already described elsewhere [13] are various tools which were used in evaluating system performance. Perhaps the most fundamental idea was the decoupling of the gathering of event information from its presentation. Thus, module writers were encouraged to record significant events in single memory cell counters; it was then possible later to write programs which would analyze the raw data into more meaningful form.

PERT charts were attempted in early stages of the project, but with very mixed results. The difficulty was that the relational structure of the chart would drastically change from month to month as a result of unexpected delays or failures in key tasks. However, the exercise of preparing the chart was effective in forcing designers to think through better the problems of system integration and planning.

Inventories of completed modules, their sizes and the status of their debugging were kept, especially in the early stages. The contribution they made was more valuable in demonstrating lack of progress than in telling how nearly accomplished a task was. Perhaps the most effective way to view an inventory is as a lower bound of the work to be performed.

An over-all comment applies to the above list. It was found that the importance of the various tools changed considerably during the different phases of the project. The lesson we draw is that one must avoid management rigidity by frequently examining the effectiveness of the tools currently in place and altering them as needed.

5. General Observations

Although comments have been made throughout, there are further observations possible regarding the over-all problems of software development management.

5.1. Size is a Liability

Traditionally, the best software has been produced by individuals and not teams. Not the least of the reasons for this phenomenon is the need to communicate among the team members. Clearly, if a project is totally disorganized, an n person team needs on the order of a $n^2/2$ communication links. If a full hierarchical structure is assumed one only needs a bit more than n links. The rub is that if one assumes a reporting fan-out of say, six, one also has introduced on the order of $\log_6 n$ levels to the team and a new danger of managerial isolation. Because individuals when reporting upwards in a managerial frame often filter out bad news for fear failure will be equated with incompetence, it is necessary to conclude that "perfect" hierarchies are especially dangerous in technical management. What is being observed here is not that n should be 1, but rather that enlarging the number of personnel on a project should be viewed as a major management decision.

5.2. Inhomogeneity of Technical Understanding

The ultimate limitations to the complexity of a large system are the resources required for its fabrication and widespread understanding of how it should function. In an overly ambitious project, managers who do not understand the details of what they are managing are easily blustered and misled by subordinates. Conversely, low-level staff may be unable to appreciate the significance of details and fail to report serious problems. At the least, such confusion generates extra design iterations, and at the worst, eventual project disasters result.

Inhomogeneity of system knowledge is hard to quantify but a useful test is to consider how interchangeable all the personnel on a project are. To the extent that each manager cannot program the lowliest module and the most junior programmer does not understand the strategic system objectives, the system design process is vulnerable to mishaps of misunderstanding. Of course the converse does not guarantee success, but the likelihood of detecting problems at an early stage is certainly higher.

5.3. Decision Costs

Inevitably in building a large-scale system, many decisions must be made on the basis of very incomplete information and one might wish to consider contingency planning. Unfortunately contingency planning, if it is done with complete redundancy, is particularly costly both in requiring major budgeting and in the use of key leadership. Moreover, even the most disciplined professional engineer may have serious ego problems when the subproject he has worked on for many months is deemed second best and scrapped. One can endure these problems on projects of great national importance such as the NASA program placing men on the moon or the war-time Manhattan Project developing nuclear weapons, but ordinarily major contingency planning is not available as a realistic hedge for decisions.

If only partial contingency planning is done, there will be increased project complexity. Moreover, unexpected events or developments will inevitably occur.

As a result, a great deal of the success of a project will depend upon the improvisational skill and the resources available to the technical managers. The perils of insufficient effort being devoted to decision making are obvious, but it is argued that there is a balance between the extreme of "overdeciding" and maintaining the flexibility to react to the unforeseen.

Not all decisions are equally important and deciding the relative importance of a decision is one of the more critical tasks a manager faces. Clearly the impact of some decisions such as the choice of a brand of computer or a particular programming language can permeate a project completely. Not so obvious is the more subtle effect of software conventions such as the choice of a character set or a module interface. Again, design understanding can only reinforce the decision-making process with the likelihood of wiser choices.

5.4. Psychology

There are several places where psychological issues enter into software projects. In contrast to many engineering projects, one cannot readily "see" progress on a software system. This intangible aspect dictates that a more expert means must be employed to gauge the level of project accomplishment. In such a situation, the selection of frequent "milestones" becomes an important management consideration. It is especially important that two properties are met: 1) there is an unequivocal understanding of when the milestone is passed, and 2) the significance of the milestone relative to the final project objective is comprehensible to all levels of personnel.

A second area where psychology enters into a software project is that of the programming staff. Frequently programming teams are composed of imaginative, energetic young staff members who all too often are inexperienced with large projects (not many persons today have worked on two!), naive in a broad sense, and sometimes simply irresponsible. One might wonder why one assigns them to tasks at all. Unfortunately, because of the immaturity of the software profession, the alternative of staffing with older, more mature programmers can just as easily be worse. Too often the field has evolved faster than the ability of individuals to grow technically. As a result, excessive inflexibility and dogmatism are frequently observed traits of older programmers, many of whom appear to be trying to relive some programming triumph of a decade ago.

One consequence of a professionally immature staff is that attempts by management to monitor individual performance are frequently resented. This monitoring problem is believed to be easing as it becomes clearer what standards of professional performance are. Today most programmers consider it reasonable that their programs be audited for quality before acceptance whereas only a decade ago such an inspection often precipitated a personnel crisis.

Part of the immaturity problem faced by large projects is traceable to the rapid development of the computer field and the consequent shortage of good programmers. But another part has a more insidious reason. As a project evolves into new areas of development and accomplishment, it is inevitable that individuals will develop key knowledge and become genuine experts in subcomponents of the effort. Such key knowledge or "know-how" is not rapidly transferred and may require six to twelve months of effort even with highly qualified and competent programmers. In a highly structured and intricate project, knowledge compartmentalization can lead to serious project difficulties if managers are inhibited (even unconsciously) from exercising effective control over a key person for fear that he may quit. With time the professional expectations of a programmer are rising, so this problem should ease in the future. Nevertheless, it will probably always be true that the only prudent course a software manager can take is to have considerable personnel redundancy in all critical knowledge areas. In this way one can keep the project vulnerability to intimidation at an acceptable level, and one also has insurance against accidents incapacitating those playing pivotal roles.

5.5. Evaluation of Progress

One of the more unsatisfying areas in discussions of large software projects is that of evaluating progress. Clearly one can set schedules for major milestones with experienced estimation (and often a good deal of guessing and hedging). And it is easy enough to monitor progress and even debate the reasonableness of such items as only one week for debugging a particular module or two weeks to integrate a pair of large subsystems. What is hard, however, is to prejudge the over-all performance and acceptability of the result. Frequently software specifications are diffuse and incomplete (e.g., make the module easy to maintain) and implementations of subsystems can unexpectedly resemble the seaweed in the Sargasso Sea.

Simulation is often suggested as an answer for performance questions but with large software systems, the difficulty of correctly modeling the system is commensurate with that of building the system itself. Just because the performance evaluation question is hard, does not mean one should behave in ostrich fashion and ignore it. Rather the emphasis should be on developing crude, quickly evaluated system models and measures that allow one to make rough predictions of system performance.

For example, there should be an expectation for the amount of program required to implement the functions of every subsystem so that the input-output and primary memory impact can be computed. Critical software paths should be counted out instruction-by-instruction to get lower bounds of performance. Worst-case timing and capacity estimates should be developed. The important thing is that all the models and calculations be kept simple enough so that they can be frequently recomputed as better information develops.

An oversimplified modeling and estimation approach can easily be off by 25 to 50%. However, large software projects usually have not failed by these amounts, large as they are, but rather have foundered on orders-of-magnitude miscalculations.

But if the above is the case, of what value can an earlier prediction of the disaster have? The answer lies in that with early warning, one has the chance of redirecting a project without fatal compromise of the objectives. Necessity is a great stimulus to seeking out more effective solutions, especially when the survival of the project is at stake. Further, there is a process of trading off performance with features. Just as an experienced hiker, when filling his backpack, may start with a large number of almost "essential" items, then reevaluate their importance and discard some of them as he begins to weigh the total load, so too can the essentialness of program features be reevaluated. Thus, the real importance of early performance warnings is that they can not only save people time and computer time, but they may even allow a project redirection from a disastrous course.

6. Conclusions

If one observed a long, involved military engagement, one would not be inclined to form a single conclusion. And so it is with our experiences with the Multics system development. One can observe, though, that despite the unexpectedly large technological jump that was undertaken, the development effort did succeed, and today the system has become a viable commercial product.

There are four major reasons we can single out for the successful development. These are:

1)   The system was built to evolve. Without this property, one has a ship without a rudder. With it one can revise one's course as the unexpected is encountered or as one's destination changes.

2)   The system goals were articulated in an extensive body of papers and memoranda. As personnel changes inevitably occurred, the transmittal

of philosophical ideas was possible without distraction of the more important team members.

3) The system was implemented in a higher-level language so that the effectiveness of each programmer was amplified and the project size minimized.

4) The system was implemented by a development team whose members were extraordinarily loyal and dedicated to the project goals. By conventional practice, the project management should not have been able to function effectively because of its loose structure. The organizational weakness was overcome by the collective determination of the individual team members who wanted the project to succeed.

Of the above reasons, the first, evolvability, is the most important technically. But one cannot discount the last, which one might label inspiration. For without it, no really difficult project can succeed.

References

1. Corbato, F. J. and V. A. Vyssotsky, "Introduction and overview of the Multics system," AFIPS Conf. Proc. 27, 1965, FJCC Spartan Books, Washington, D. C., 1965, pp. 185-196.
2. Glaser, E. L., J. F. Couleur, and G. A. Oliver, "System design of a computer for time-sharing application," AFIPS Conf. Proc. 27, 1965, FJCC Spartan Books, Washington, D. C., 1965, pp. 197-202.
3. Vyssotsky, V. A., F. J. Corbato, and R. M. Graham, "Structure of the Multics Supervisor," AFIPS Conf. Proc. 27, 1965, FJCC Spartan Books, Washington, D. C., 1965, pp. 203-212.
4. Daley, R. C., and P. G. Neumann, "A general-purpose file system for secondary storage," AFIPS Conf. Proc. 27, 1965, FJCC Spartan Books, Washington, D. C., 1965, pp. 213-229.
5. Ossanna, J. F., L. Mikus, and S. D. Dunten, "Communication and input/output switching in a multiplex computing system," AFIPS Conf. Proc. 27, 1965, FJCC Spartan Books, Washington, D. C., 1965, pp. 231-241.
6. David, E. E., Jr., and R. M. Fano, "Some thoughts about the social implications of accessible computing," AFIPS Conf. Proc. 27, 1965, FJCC Spartan Books, Washington, D. C., 1965, pp. 243-247.
7. Corbato, F. J., C. T. Clingen, and J. H. Saltzer, "Multics -- the first seven years," Proceedings of the SJCC, May 1972, pp. 571-583.
8. Organick, E. I., The Multics System: An Examination of its Structure, MIT Press, Cambridge, Massachusetts and London, England, 1972.

9. Watson, R. W., Timesharing System Design Concepts, McGraw-Hill Book Company, New York, New York, 1970.

10. Ikeda, Katsuo, Structure of a Computer Utility: Anatomy of Multics (in Japanese), Shokoda Co. Ltd., Tokyo, Japan, 1974; second edition, 1976.

11. Corbato, F. J., "PL/1 as a tool for system programming," Datamation 15, May 6, 1969, pp. 68-76.

12. Brooks, Frederick P., Jr., The Mythical Man-Month -- Essays on Software Engineering, Addison-Wesley Publishing Company, Reading, Massachusetts, 1975. (See Chapter 2 especially.)

13. Saltzer, J. H., and J. W. Gintell, "The Instrumentation of Multics," Communications of the ACM, Vol. 13, no. 8, Aug. 1970, pp. 495-500.

Design case history: Apple's Macintosh

A small team of little-known designers, challenged to produce a low-cost, exceptionally easy-to-use personal computer, turns out a technical milestone

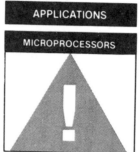

In 1979 the Macintosh personal computer existed only as the pet idea of Jef Raskin, a veteran of the Apple II team, who had proposed that Apple Computer Inc. make a low-cost "appliance"-type computer that would be as easy to use as a toaster. Mr. Raskin believed the computer he envisioned, which he called Macintosh, could sell for $1000 if it was manufactured in high volume and used a powerful microprocessor executing tightly written software.

Mr. Raskin's proposal did not impress anyone at Apple Computer enough to bring much money from the board of directors or much respect from Apple engineers. The company had more pressing concerns at the time: the major Lisa workstation project was getting under way, and there were problems with the reliability of the Apple III, the revamped version of the highly successful Apple II.

Although the odds seemed against it in 1979, the Macintosh, designed by a handful of inexperienced engineers and programmers, is now recognized as a technical milestone in personal computers. Essentially a slimmed-down version of the Lisa workstation with many of its software features, the Macintosh sold for $2495 at its introduction in early 1984; the Lisa initially sold for $10 000. Despite criticism of the Macintosh—that it lacks networking capabilities adequate for business applications and is awkward to use for some tasks—the computer is considered by Apple to be its most important weapon in the war with IBM for survival in the personal-computer business.

From the beginning, the Macintosh project was powered by the dedicated drive of two key players on the project team. For Burrell Smith, who designed the Macintosh digital hardware, the project represented an opportunity for a relative unknown to demonstrate outstanding technical talents. For Steven Jobs, the 29-year-old chairman of Apple and the Macintosh project's director, it offered a chance to prove himself in the corporate world after a temporary setback: although he cofounded Apple Computer, the company had declined to let him manage the Lisa project. Mr. Jobs contributed relatively little to the technical design of the Macintosh, but he had a clear vision of the product from the beginning. He challenged the project team to design the best product possible and encouraged the team by shielding them from bureaucratic pressures within the company.

The early design

Mr. Smith, who was a repairman in the Apple II maintenance department in 1979, had become hooked on microprocessors several years earlier during a visit to the electronics-industry area south of San Francisco known as Silicon Valley. He dropped out of liberal-arts studies at the Junior College of Albany, New York, to pursue the possibilities of microprocessors—there isn't anything you can't do with those things, he thought. Mr. Smith later became a repairman at Apple Computer, in Cupertino, Calif.,

Fred Guterl   Associate Editor

where he spent much time studying the cryptic logic-circuitry of the Apple II, designed by company cofounder Steven Wozniak.

Mr. Smith's dexterity in the shop impressed Bill Atkinson, one of the Lisa designers, who introduced him to Mr. Raskin as "the man who's going to design your Macintosh." Mr. Raskin replied noncommittally, "We'll see about that."

However, Mr. Smith managed to learn enough about Mr. Raskin's conception of the Macintosh to whip up a makeshift prototype using a Motorola 6809 microprocessor, a television monitor, and an Apple II. He showed it to Mr. Raskin, who was impressed enough to make him the second member of the Macintosh team.

But the fledgling Macintosh project was in trouble. The Apple board of directors wanted to cancel the project in September

---

Defining terms

Backplane: an electrical connection common to two or more printed-circuit boards.

Bit-mapped graphics: a method of representing data in a computer for display in which each dot on the screen is mapped to a unit of data in memory.

Buffers: computer memory for holding data temporarily between processes.

Direct-memory access: a mechanism in a computer that bypasses the central processing unit to gain access to memory. It is often used when large blocks of data are transferred from memory to a peripheral.

Icons: small graphic images on a computer screen that represent functions or programs; for example, a wastebasket designates a delete operation.

Memory management: a mechanism in a computer for allocating internal memory among different programs, especially in multitasking systems.

Mouse: a box the size of a cigarette pack used to move a cursor on a computer screen. The movement of the cursor matches the movement of the mouse. The mouse also may have one or more buttons for selecting commands on a menu.

Multitasking: the simultaneous execution of two or more applications programs in a computer (also known as concurrency).

Operating system: a computer program that performs basic operations, such as governing the allocation of memory, accepting interrupts from peripherals, and opening and closing files.

Programmable-array logic: an array of logic elements that are mass-produced without interconnections and that are interconnected at the specification of the user at the time of purchase.

Subroutines: a section of a computer code that is represented symbolically in a program.

Window: a rectangularly shaped image on a computer screen within which the user writes and reads data, representing a program in the computer.

Reprinted from *IEEE Spectrum*, December 1984, pages 34-43. Copyright ©1984 by The Institute of Electlrical and Electronics Engineers, Inc.

1980 to concentrate on more important projects, but Mr. Raskin was able to win a three-month reprieve.

Meanwhile Steve Jobs, then vice president of Apple, was having trouble with his own credibility within the company. Though he had sought to manage the Lisa computer project, the other Apple executives saw him as too inexperienced and eccentric to entrust him with such a major undertaking, and he had no formal business education. After this rejection, "he didn't like the lack of control he had," noted one Apple executive. "He was looking for his niche."

Mr. Jobs became interested in the Macintosh project, and, possibly because few in the company thought the project had a future, Mr. Jobs was made its manager. Under his direction, the design team became as compact and efficient as the Macintosh was to be—a group of engineers working at a distance from all the meetings and paper-pushing of the corporate mainstream. Mr. Jobs, in recruiting the other members of the Macintosh team, lured some from other companies with promises of potentially lucrative stock options.

With Mr. Jobs at the helm, the project gained some credibility among the board of directors—but not much. According to one team member, it was known in the company as "Steve's folly." But Mr. Jobs lobbied for a bigger budget for the project and got it. The Macintosh team grew to 20 by early 1981.

The decision on what form the Macintosh would take was left largely to the design group. At first the members had only the basic principles set forth by Mr. Raskin and Mr. Jobs to guide them, as well as the example set by the Lisa project. The new machine was to be easy to use and inexpensive to manufacture. Mr. Jobs wanted to commit enough money to build an automated factory that would produce about 300 000 computers a year. So one key challenge for the design group was to use inexpensive parts and to keep the parts count low.

Making the computer easy to use required considerable software for the user-computer interface. The model was, of course, the Lisa workstation with its graphic "windows" to display simultaneously many different programs. "Icons," or little pictures, were used instead of cryptic computer terms to represent a selection of programs on the screen; by moving a "mouse," a box the size of a pack of cigarettes, the user manipulated a cursor on the screen. The Macintosh team redesigned the software of the Lisa from scratch to make it operate more efficiently, since the Macintosh was to have far less memory than the 1 million bytes of the Lisa. But the Macintosh software was also required to operate quicker than the Lisa software, which had been criticized for being slow.

A free hand to explore

The lack of a precise definition for the Macintosh project was not a problem. Many of the designers preferred to define the computer as they went along. "Steve allowed us to crystallize the problem and the solution simultaneously," recalled Mr. Smith. The method put strain on the design team, since they were continually evaluating design alternatives. "We were swamped in detail," Mr. Smith said. But this way of working also led to a better product, the designers said, because they had the freedom to seize opportunities during the design stage to enhance the product.

Such freedom would not have been possible had the Macintosh project been structured in the conventional way at Apple, according to several of the designers. "No one tried to control us," said one. "Some managers like to take control, and though that may be good for mundane engineers, it isn't good if you are self-motivated."

Central to the success of this method was the small, closely knit nature of the design group, with each member being responsible for a relatively large portion of the total design and free to consult other members of the team when considering alternatives. For example, Mr. Smith, who was well acquainted with the price of electronic components from his early work on reducing the cost of the Apple II, made many decisions about the economics of Macintosh hardware without time-consuming consultations with purchasing agents. Because communication among team members was good, the designers shared their areas of expertise by advising each other in the working stages, rather than waiting for a final evaluation from a group of manufacturing engineers.

Housing all members of the design team in one small office made communicating easier. For example, it was simple for Mr. Smith to consult a purchasing agent about the price of parts if he needed to, because the purchasing agent worked in the same building.

Andy Hertzfeld, who transferred from the Apple II software group to design the Macintosh operating software, noted, "In lots of other projects at Apple, people argue about ideas. But sometimes bright people think a little differently. Somebody like

The influence of Steven Jobs, chairman of Apple Computer Inc. (center), on the Macintosh personal computer project was crucial, if sometimes idiosyncratic. Here he tells designers Andy Hertzfeld (left) and Burrell Smith on a Friday afternoon how urgent it is to write software for the sound generator: "If I don't hear sound out of that thing by Monday morning, we're ripping out the amplifier."

Burrell Smith would design a computer on paper and people would say, 'It'll never work.' So instead Burrell builds it lightning fast and has it working before the guy can say anything.''

The closeness of the Macintosh group enabled it to make design tradeoffs that would not have been possible in a large organization, the team members contended. The interplay between hardware and software was crucial to the success of the Macintosh design, using a limited memory and few electronic parts to perform complex operations. Mr. Smith, who was in charge of the computer's entire digital-hardware design, and Mr. Hertzfeld became close friends and often collaborated. "When you have one person designing the whole computer," Mr. Hertzfeld observed, "he knows that a little leftover gate in one part may be used in another part."

To promote interaction among the designers, one of the first things that Mr. Jobs did in taking over the Macintosh project was to arrange special office space for the team. In contrast to Apple's corporate headquarters, identified by the company logo on a sign on its well-trimmed lawn, the team's new quarters, behind a Texaco service station, had no sign to identify them and no listing in the company telephone directory. The office, dubbed Texaco Towers, was an upstairs, low-rent, plasterboard-walled, "tacky-carpeted" place, "the kind you'd find at a small law outfit," according to Chris Espinosa, a veteran of the original Apple design team and an early Macintosh draftee. It resembled a house more than an office, having a communal area much like a living room, with smaller rooms off to the side for more privacy in working or talking. The decor was part college dormitory, part electronics repair shop: art posters, bean-bag chairs, coffee machines, stereo systems, and electronic equipment of all sorts scattered about.

There were no set work hours and initially not even a schedule for the development of the Macintosh. Each week, if Mr. Jobs was in town (often he was not), he would hold a meeting at which the team members would report what they had done the previous week. One of the designers' sidelines was to dissect the products of their competitors. "Whenever a competitor came out with a product, we would buy and dismantle it, and it would kick around the office," recalled Mr. Espinosa.

In this way, they learned what they did not want their product to be. In their competitors' products, Mr. Smith saw a propensity

A challenge in building the Macintosh was to offer sophisticated software using the fewest and least-expensive parts.

for using connectors and slots for inserting printed-circuit boards —a slot for the video circuitry, a slot for the keyboard circuitry, a slot for the disk drives, and memory slots. Behind each slot were buffers to allow signals to pass onto and off the printed-circuit board properly. The buffers meant delays in the computers' operations, since several boards shared a backplane, and the huge capacitance required for multiple PC boards slowed the backplane. The number of parts required made the competitors' computers hard to manufacture, costly, and less reliable. The Macintosh team resolved that their PC would have but two printed-circuit boards and no slots, buffers, or backplane.

To squeeze the needed components onto the board, Mr. Smith planned the Macintosh to perform specific functions rather than operate as a flexible computer that could be tailored by programmers for a wide variety of applications. By rigidly defining the configuration of the Macintosh and the functions it would perform, he eliminated much circuitry. Instead of providing slots into which the user could insert printed-circuit boards with such hardware as memory or coprocessors, the designers decided to incorporate many of the basic functions of the computer in read-only memory, which is more reliable. The computer would be expanded not by slots, but through a high-speed serial port.

Simplifying the software

The software designers were faced in the beginning with often-unrealistic schedules. "We looked for any place where we could beg, borrow, or steal code," Mr. Hertzfeld recalled. The obvious place for them to look was the Lisa workstation.The Macintosh team wanted to borrow some of the Lisa's software for drawing graphics on the bit-mapped display. In 1981, Bill Atkinson was refining the Lisa graphics software, called Quickdraw, and began to work part-time implementing it for the Macintosh.

Quickdraw was a scheme for manipulating bit maps to enable applications programmers to construct images easily on the Macintosh bit-mapped display. The Quickdraw program allows the programmer to define and manipulate a region—a software representation of an arbitrarily shaped area of the screen. One such region is a rectangular window with rounded corners, used throughout the Macintosh software. Quickdraw also allows the programmer to keep images within defined boundaries, which makes the windows in the Macintosh software appear to hold data. The programmer can unite two regions, subtract one from the other, or intersect them.

In Macintosh, the Quickdraw program was to be tightly written in assembly-level code and etched permanently in ROM. It would serve as a foundation for higher-level software to make use of graphics.

Quickdraw was "an amazing graphics package," Mr. Hertzfeld noted, but it would have strained the capabilities of the 6809 microprocessor, the heart of the early Macintosh prototype. Motorola Corp. announced in late 1980 that the 68000 microprocessor was available, but that chip was new and unproven in the field, and at $200 apiece it was also expensive. Reasoning that the price of the chip would come down before Apple was ready to start mass-producing the Macintosh, the Macintosh designers decided to gamble on the Motorola chip.

Another early design question for the Macintosh was whether to use the Lisa operating system. Since the Lisa was still in the early stages of design, considerable development would have been required to tailor its operating system for the Macintosh. Even if the Lisa had been completed, rewriting its software in assembly code would have been required for the far smaller memory of the Macintosh. In addition, the Lisa was to have a multi-tasking operating system, using complex circuitry and software to run more than one computer program at the same time, which would have been too expensive for the Macintosh. Thus the decision was made to write a Macintosh operating system from scratch, working from the basic concepts of the Lisa. Simplifying the Macintosh operating system posed the delicate problem of restricting the computer's memory capacity enough to keep it inex-

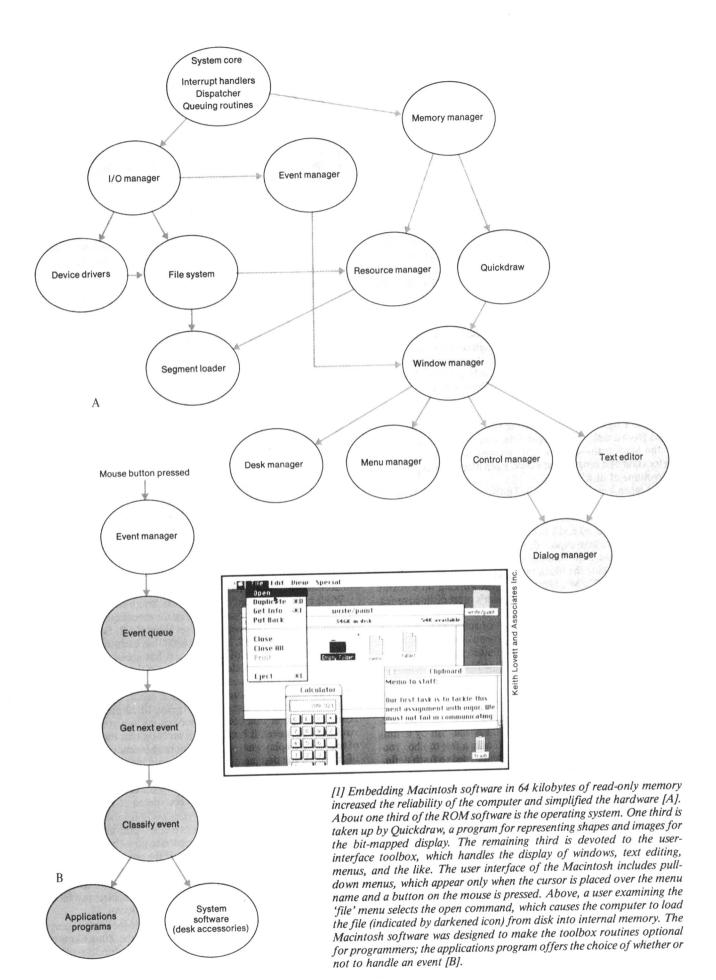

A

Mouse button pressed

Event manager

Event queue

Get next event

Classify event

B

Applications programs

System software (desk accessories)

System core

Interrupt handlers
Dispatcher
Queuing routines

Memory manager

I/O manager

Event manager

Device drivers

File system

Resource manager

Quickdraw

Segment loader

Window manager

Desk manager

Menu manager

Control manager

Text editor

Dialog manager

Keith Lovett and Associates Inc.

[1] Embedding Macintosh software in 64 kilobytes of read-only memory increased the reliability of the computer and simplified the hardware [A]. About one third of the ROM software is the operating system. One third is taken up by Quickdraw, a program for representing shapes and images for the bit-mapped display. The remaining third is devoted to the user-interface toolbox, which handles the display of windows, text editing, menus, and the like. The user interface of the Macintosh includes pull-down menus, which appear only when the cursor is placed over the menu name and a button on the mouse is pressed. Above, a user examining the 'file' menu selects the open command, which causes the computer to load the file (indicated by darkened icon) from disk into internal memory. The Macintosh software was designed to make the toolbox routines optional for programmers; the applications program offers the choice of whether or not to handle an event [B].

461

pensive but not so much as to make it inflexible.

The Macintosh would have no multitasking capability but would execute only one applications program at a time. Generally, a multitasking operating system tracks the progress of each of the programs it is running and then stores the entire state of each program—the values of its variables, the location of the program counter, and so on. This complex operation requires more memory and hardware than the Macintosh designers could afford. However, the illusion of multitasking was created by small programs built into the Macintosh system software. Since these small programs—such as one that creates the images of a calculator on the screen and does simple arithmetic—operate in areas of memory separate from applications, they can run simultaneously with applications programs [Fig. 1].

Since the Macintosh used a memory-mapped scheme, the 68000 microprocessor required no memory management, simplifying both the hardware and the software. For example, the 68000 has two modes of operation: a user mode, which is restricted so that a programmer cannot inadvertently upset the memory-management scheme; and a supervisor mode, which allows unrestricted access to all of the 68000's commands. Each mode uses its own stack of pointers to blocks of memory. The 68000 was rigged to run only in the supervisor mode, eliminating the need for the additional stack. Although seven levels of interrupts were available for the 68000, only three were used.

Another simplification was made in the Macintosh's file structure, exploiting the small disk space with only one or two floppy-disk drives. In the Lisa and most other operating systems, two indexes access a program on floppy disk, using up precious random-access memory and increasing the delay in fetching programs from a disk. The designers decided to use only one index for the Macintosh—a block map, located in RAM, to indicate the location of a program on a disk. Each block map represented one volume of disk space.

This scheme ran into unexpected difficulties and may be modified in future versions of the Macintosh, Mr. Hertzfeld said. Initially, the Macintosh was not intended for business users, but as the design progressed and it became apparent that the Macintosh would cost more than expected, Apple shifted its marketing plan to target business users. Many of them add hard disk drives to the Macintosh, making the block-map scheme unwieldy.

By January 1982, Mr. Hertzfeld began working on software for the Macintosh, perhaps the computer's most distinctive feature, which he called the user-interface toolbox.

The toolbox was envisioned as a set of software routines for constructing the windows, pull-down menus, scroll bars, icons, and other graphic objects in the Macintosh operating system. Since RAM space would be scarce on the Macintosh (it initially was to have only 64 kilobytes), the toolbox routines were to be a part of the Macintosh's operating software; they would use the Quickdraw routines and operate in ROM.

It was important, however, not to handicap applications programmers—who could boost sales of the Macintosh by writing programs for it—by restricting them to only a few toolbox routines in ROM. So the toolbox code was designed to fetch definition functions—routines that use Quickdraw to create a graphic image such as a window—from either the systems disk or an applications disk. In this way, an applications programmer could add definition functions for a program, which Apple could incorporate in later versions of the Macintosh by modifying the system disk. "We were nervous about putting [the toolbox] in ROM," recalled Mr. Hertzfeld, "We knew that after the Macintosh was out, programmers would want to add to the toolbox routines."

Although the user could operate only one applications program at a time, he could transfer text or graphics from one applications program to another with a toolbox routine called scrapbook. Since the scrapbook and the rest of the toolbox routines were located in ROM, they could run along with applications programs, giving the illusion of multitasking. The user would cut

text from one program into the scrapbook, close the program, open another, and paste the text from the scrapbook. Other routines in the toolbox, such as the calculator, could also operate simultaneously with applications programs.

Late in the design of the Macintosh software, the designers realized that, to market the Macintosh in non–English-speaking countries, an easy way of translating text in programs into foreign languages was needed. Thus computer code and data were separated in the software to allow translation without unraveling a complex computer program, by scanning the data portion of a program. No programmer would be needed for translation.

Gambling on the 68000

The 68000, with a 16-bit data bus and 32-bit internal registers and a 7.83-megahertz clock, could grab data in relatively large chunks. Mr. Smith dispensed with separate controllers for the mouse, the disk drives, and other peripheral functions. "We were able to leverage off slave devices," Mr. Smith explained, "and we had enough throughput to deal with those devices in a way that appeared concurrent to the user."

When Mr. Smith suggested implementing the mouse without a separate controller, several members of the design team argued that if the main microprocessor was interrupted each time the mouse was moved, the movement of the cursor on the screen would always lag. Only when Mr. Smith got the prototype up and running were they convinced it would work.

Likewise, in the second prototype, the disk drives were controlled by the main microprocessor. "In other computers," Mr. Smith noted, "the disk controller is a brick wall between the disk and the CPU, and you end up with a poor-performance, expensive disk that you can lose control of. It's like buying a brand new car complete with a chauffeur who insists on driving everywhere."

The 68000 was assigned many duties of the disk controller and was linked with a disk-controller circuit built by Mr. Wozniak for the Apple II. "Instead of a wimpy little 8-bit microprocessor out there, we have this incredible 68000—it's the world's best disk controller," Mr. Smith said.

Direct-memory-access circuitry was designed to allow the video screen to share RAM with the 68000. Thus the 68000 would have access to RAM at half speed during the live portion of the horizontal line of the video screen and at full speed during the horizontal and vertical retrace [Fig. 2].

While building the next prototype, Mr. Smith saw several ways to save on digital circuitry and increase the execution speed of the Macintosh. The 68000 instruction set allowed Mr. Smith to embed subroutines in ROM. Since the 68000 has exclusive use of the address and data buses of the ROM, it has access to the ROM routines at up to the full clock speed. The ROM serves somewhat as a high-speed cache memory.

The next major revision in the original concept of the Macintosh was made in the computer's display. Mr. Raskin had proposed a computer that could be hooked up to a standard television set. However, it became clear early on that the resolution of television display was too coarse for the Macintosh. After a bit of research, the designers found they could increase the display resolution from 256 by 256 dots to 384 by 256 dots by including a display with the computer. This added to the estimated price of the Macintosh, but the designers considered it a reasonable tradeoff.

To keep the parts count low, the two input/output ports of the Macintosh were to be serial. The decision to go with this was a serious one, since the future usefulness of the computer depended largely on its efficiency when hooked up to printers, local-area networks, and other peripherals. In the early stages of development, the Macintosh was not intended to be a business product, which would have made networking a high priority.

The key factor in the decision to use one high-speed serial port was the introduction in the spring of 1981 of the Zilog Corp.'s 85530 serial-communications controller, a single chip to replace two less expensive conventional parts—"vanilla" chips—in the

Macintosh. The risks in using the Zilog chip were that it had not been proven in the field and it was expensive, almost $9 apiece. In addition Apple had a hard time convincing Zilog that it seriously intended to order the part in high volumes for the Macintosh.

"We had an image problem," explained Mr. Espinosa. "We wore T-shirts and blue jeans with holes in the knees, and we had a maniacal conviction that we were right about the Macintosh, and that put some people off. Also, Apple hadn't yet sold a million Apple IIs. How were we to convince them that we would sell a million Macs?"

In the end, Apple got a commitment from Zilog to supply the part, which Mr. Espinosa attributes to the negotiating talents of

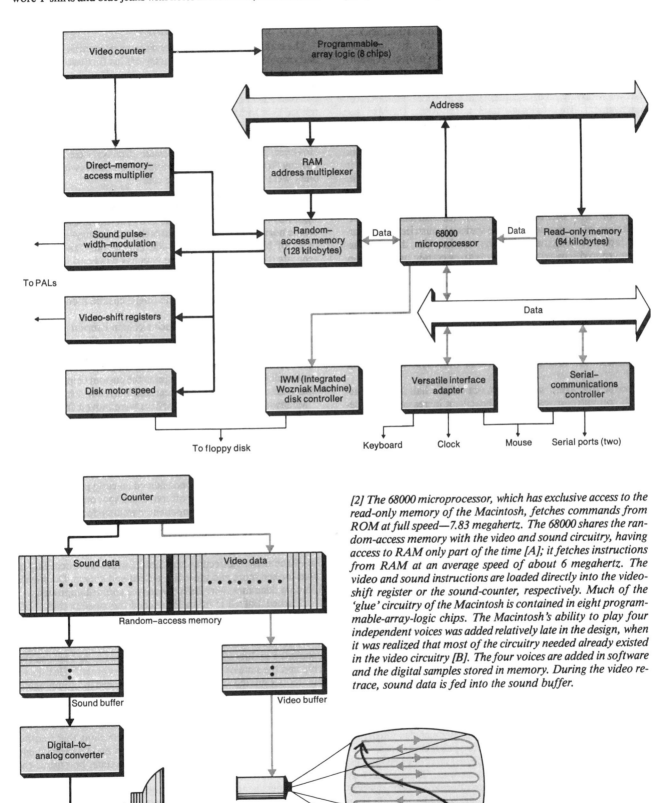

[2] The 68000 microprocessor, which has exclusive access to the read-only memory of the Macintosh, fetches commands from ROM at full speed—7.83 megahertz. The 68000 shares the random-access memory with the video and sound circuitry, having access to RAM only part of the time [A]; it fetches instructions from RAM at an average speed of about 6 megahertz. The video and sound instructions are loaded directly into the video-shift register or the sound-counter, respectively. Much of the 'glue' circuitry of the Macintosh is contained in eight programmable-array-logic chips. The Macintosh's ability to play four independent voices was added relatively late in the design, when it was realized that most of the circuitry needed already existed in the video circuitry [B]. The four voices are added in software and the digital samples stored in memory. During the video retrace, sound data is fed into the sound buffer.

Mr. Jobs. The serial input/output ports "gave us essentially the same bandwidth that a memory-mapped parallel port would," Mr. Smith said. Peripherals were connected to serial ports in a daisy-chain configuration with the Applebus network.

Designing a factory without a product

In the fall of 1981, as Mr. Smith worked on the fourth Macintosh prototype, the design for the Macintosh factory was getting under way. Mr. Jobs hired Debi Coleman, who was then working as financial manager at Hewlett-Packard Co. in Cupertino, Calif., to handle the finances of the Macintosh project. A graduate of Stanford University with a master's degree in business administration, Ms. Coleman was a member of a task force at HP that was studying factories, quality management, and inventory management. This was good training for Apple, for Mr. Jobs was intent on using such concepts to build a highly automated manufacturing plant for the Macintosh in the United States. Briefly he considered building the plant in Texas, but since the designers were to work closely with the manufacturing team in the later stages of the Macintosh design, he decided to locate the plant at Freemont, Calif., less than a half-hour's drive from Apple's Cupertino headquarters.

Mr. Jobs and other members of the Macintosh team made frequent tours of automated plants in various industries, particularly in Japan. At long meetings held after the visits, the manufacturing group discussed whether to borrow certain methods they had observed.

The Macintosh factory design was based on two major concepts. The first was "just-in-time" inventory, calling for vendors to deliver parts for the Macintosh frequently, in small lots, to avoid excessive handling of components at the factory and reduce damage and storage costs. The second concept was zero-defect parts, with any defect on the manufacturing line immediately traced to its source and rectified to prevent recurrence of the error.

The factory, which was to churn out about a half million Macintosh computers a year (the number kept increasing), was designed to be built in three stages: first, equipped with stations for workers to insert some Macintosh components, delivered to them by simple robots; second, with robots to insert components instead of workers; and third, many years in the future, with "integrated" automation, requiring virtually no human operators.

In building the factory, "Steve was willing to chuck all the traditional ideas about manufacturing and the relationship between design and manufacturing," Ms. Coleman noted. "He was willing to spend whatever it cost to experiment in this factory. We planned to have a major revision every two years."

By late 1982, before Mr. Smith had designed the final Macintosh prototype, the designs of most of the factory's major subassemblies were frozen, and the assembly stations could be designed. About 85 percent of the components on the digital-logic printed-circuit board were to be inserted automatically [Fig. 3], and the remaining 15 percent were to be surface-mounted devices inserted manually at first and by robots in the second stage of the factory. The production lines for automatic insertion were laid out to be flexible; the number of stations was not defined until trial runs were made. The materials-delivery system, designed with the help of engineers recruited from Texas Instruments in Dallas, Texas, divided small and large parts between receiving doors at the materials distribution center. The finished Macintoshes coming down the conveyor belt were to be wrapped in plastic and stuffed into boxes using equipment adapted from machines used in the wine industry for packaging bottles.

As factory construction progressed, pressure built on the Macintosh design team to deliver a final prototype. The designers had been working long hours but with no deadline set for the computer's introduction. That changed in the middle of 1981, after Mr. Jobs imposed a tough and sometimes unrealistic schedule, reminding the team repeatedly that "real artists ship" a finished product. In late 1981, when IBM announced its personal computer, the Macintosh marketing staff began to refer to a "window of opportunity" that made it urgent to get the Macintosh to customers.

"We had been saying, 'We're going to finish in six months' for two years," Mr. Hertzfeld recalled.

The new urgency led to a series of design problems that seemed to threaten the Macintosh dream.

Facing impossible deadlines

The computer's circuit density was one bottleneck. Mr. Smith had trouble paring enough circuitry off his first two prototypes to squeeze them onto one logic board. In addition he needed faster circuitry for the Macintosh display. The horizontal resolution was only 384 dots—not enough room for the 80 characters of text needed for the Macintosh to compete as a word processor. One suggested solution was to use the word-processing software to allow an 80-character line to be seen by horizontal scrolling. However, most standard computer displays were capable of holding 80 characters, and the portable computers with less capability were very inconvenient to use.

Another problem with the Macintosh display was its limited dot density. Although the analog circuitry, which was being designed by Apple engineer George Crow, accommodated 512 dots on the horizontal axis, Mr. Smith's digital circuitry—which consisted of bipolar logic arrays—did not operate fast enough to generate the dots. Faster bipolar circuitry was considered but rejected because of its high power dissipation and its cost. Mr. Smith could think of but one alternative: combine the video and other miscellaneous circuitry on a single custom n-channel MOS chip.

Mr. Smith began designing such a chip in February 1982. During the next six months the size of the hypothetical chip kept growing. Mr. Jobs set a shipping target of May 1983 for the Macintosh but, with a backlog of other design problems, Burrell Smith still had not finished designing the custom chip, which was named after him: the IBM (Integrated Burrell Machine) chip.

Meanwhile, the Macintosh offices were moved from Texaco Towers to more spacious quarters at the Apple headquarters, since the Macintosh staff had swelled to about 40. One of the new employees was Robert Belleville, whose previous employer was the Xerox Palo Alto Research Corp. At Xerox he had designed the hardware for the Star workstation—which, with its windows, icons, and mouse, might be considered an early prototype of the Macintosh. When Mr. Jobs offered him a spot on the Macintosh team, Mr. Belleville was impatiently waiting for authorization from Xerox to proceed on a project he had proposed that was similar to the Macintosh—a low-cost version of the Star.

As the new head of the Macintosh engineering, Mr. Belleville faced the task of directing Mr. Smith, who was proceeding on what looked more and more like a dead-end course. Despite the looming deadlines, Mr. Belleville tried a soft-sell approach.

"I asked Burrell if he really needed the custom chip," Mr. Belleville recalled. "He said yes. I told him to think about trying something else."

After thinking about the problem for three months, Mr. Smith concluded in July 1982 that "the difference in size between this chip and the state of Rhode Island is not very great." He then set out to design the circuitry with higher-speed programmable-array logic—as he had started to do six months earlier. He had assumed that higher resolution in the horizontal video required a faster clock speed. But he realized that he could achieve the same effect with clever use of faster bipolar-logic chips that had become available only a few months earlier. By adding several high-speed logic circuits and a few ordinary circuits, he pushed the resolution up to 512 dots.

Another advantage was that the PALs were a mature technology and their electrical parameters could tolerate large variations from the specified values, making the Macintosh more stable and more reliable—important characteristics for a so-called appliance product. Since the electrical characteristics of each integrated circuit may vary from those of other ICs made in different batches, the sum of the variances of 50 or so components in a computer may be large enough to threaten the system's integrity.

Even as late as the summer of 1982, with one deadline after another blown, the Macintosh designers were finding ways of adding features to the computer. After the team disagreed over the choice of a white background for the video with black characters or the more typical white-on-black, it was suggested that both options be made available to the user through a switch on the back of the Macintosh. But this compromise led to debates about other questions.

"It became an intense and almost religious argument," recalled Mr. Espinosa, "about the purity of the system's design versus the user's freedom to configure the system as he liked. We had weeks of argument over whether to add a few pennies to the cost of the machine."

Improvements through competition

The designers, being committed to the Macintosh, often worked long hours to refine the system. A programmer might spend many night hours to reduce the time needed to format a disk from three minutes to one. The reasoning was that expenditure of a Macintosh programmer's time amounted to little in comparison with a reduction of two minutes in the formatting time. "If you take two extra minutes per user, times a million people, times 50 disks to format, that's a lot of the world's time," Mr. Espinosa explained.

But if the group's commitment to refinements often kept them from meeting deadlines, it paid off in tangible design improvements. "There was a lot of competition for doing something very bright and creative and amazing," said Mr. Espinosa. "People were so bright that it became a contest to astonish them."

The Macintosh team's approach to working—"like a chautauqua, with daylong affairs where people would sit and talk about how they were going to do this or that"—sparked creative thinking about the Macintosh's capabilities. When a programmer and a hardware designer started to discuss how to implement the sound generator, for instance, they were joined by one of several nontechnical members of the team—marketing staff, finance specialists, secretaries—who remarked how much fun it would be if the Macintosh could sound four distinct voices at once so the user could program it to play music. That possibility excited the programmer and the hardware engineer enough to spend extra hours in designing a sound generator with four voices.

The payoff of such discussions with nontechnical team members, Mr. Espinosa said, "was coming up with all those glaringly evident things that only somebody completely ignorant could come up with. If you immerse yourself in a group that doesn't know the technical limitations, then you get a group mania to try and deny those limitations. You start trying to do the impossible—and once in a while succeeding."

The sound generator in the original Macintosh was quite simple—a one-bit register connected to a speaker. To vibrate the speaker, the programmer wrote a software loop that changed the value of the register from one to zero repeatedly. Nobody had even considered designing a four-voice generator—that is, not until "group mania" set in.

Mr. Smith was pondering this problem when he noticed that the video circuitry was very similar to the sound-generator circuitry. Since the video was bit-mapped, a bit of memory represented one dot on the video screen. The bits that made up a complete video image were held in a block of RAM and fetched by a scanning circuit to generate the image. Sound circuitry required similar scanning, with data in memory corresponding to the am-

I. Macintosh prototypes

	Date	Selling price, dollars	Description
1.	December 1979	500	Based on the Motorola 6809 microprocessor, with 64 kilobytes of random-access memory, using television display with a resolution of 256 by 256 dots
2.	January 1981	1000	Changed to the 68000 microprocessor; increased resolution to 356 by 256 dots by incorporating a CRT
3.	June 1981		Added Zilog high-speed serial port
4.	February 1982		Redesigned computer around custom CMOS chip
5.	July 1982	2000	Redesigned computer with programmable-logic arrays; increased screen resolution to 512 by 256 dots
6.	September 1982	2000	Modified design for 5¼-inch disk drive
7.	July 1983	2495	Modified for 3½-inch disk drive

II. Three generations of personal computers

	Star	Lisa	Macintosh
Date of introduction	April 1981	January 1983	February 1984
Initial price, dollars	15 055	9995	2495
Current price, dollars	8995	5995	2195
Microprocessor	Proprietary	68000	68000
Random-access memory, kilobytes	768	1000	128
Display resolution, dots	1024 by 808	720 by 364	512 by 342

plitude and frequency of the sound emanating from the speaker.

Mr. Smith reasoned that by adding a pulse-width–modulator circuit, the video circuitry could be used to generate sound during the last microsecond of the horizontal retrace—the time it took the electron beam in the cathode-ray tube of the display to move from the last dot on each line to the first dot of the next line. During the retrace the video-scanning circuitry jumped to a block of memory earmarked for the amplitude value of the sound wave, fetched bytes, deposited them in a buffer that fed the sound generator, and then jumped back to the video memory in time for the next trace. The sound generator was simply a digital-to-analog converter connected to a linear amplifier.

To enable the sound generator to produce four distinct voices, software routines were written and embedded in ROM to accept values representing four separate sound waves and convert them into one complex wave. Thus a programmer writing applications programs for the Macintosh could specify separately each voice without being concerned about the nature of the complex wave.

Gearing up for production

In the fall of 1982, as the factory was being built and the design of the Macintosh was approaching its final form, Mr. Jobs began to play a greater role in the day-to-day activities of the designers. Although the hardware for the sound generator had been designed, the software to enable the computer to make sounds had not yet been written by Mr. Hertzfeld, who considered other parts of the Macintosh software more urgent. Mr. Jobs had been told that the sound generator would be impressive, with the analog circuitry and the speaker having been upgraded to accommodate four voices. But since this was an additional hardware expense, with no audible results at that point, one Friday Mr. Jobs issued an ultimatum: "If I don't hear sound out of this thing by Monday morning, we're ripping out the amplifier."

That motivation sent Mr. Hertzfeld to the office during the weekend to write the software. By Sunday afternoon only three voices were working. He telephoned his colleague Mr. Smith and asked him to stop by and help optimize the software.

"Do you mean to tell me you're using subroutines!" Mr. Smith exclaimed after examining the problem. "No wonder you can't get four voices. Subroutines are much too slow."

By Monday morning, the pair had written the microcode programs to produce results that satisfied Mr. Jobs.

Although Mr. Jobs's input was sometimes hard to define, his instinct for defining the Macintosh as a product was important to its success, according to the designers. "He would say, 'This isn't what I want. I don't know what I want, but this isn't it.' " Mr. Smith said.

"He knows what great products are," noted Mr. Hertzfeld. "He intuitively knows what people want."

One example was the design of the Macintosh casing, when clay models were made to demonstrate various possibilities. "I could hardly tell the difference between two models," Mr. Hertzfeld said. "Steve would walk in and say, 'This one stinks and this one is great.' And he was usually right."

Because Mr. Jobs placed great emphasis on packaging the Macintosh to occupy little space on a desk, a vertical design was used, with the disk drive placed underneath the CRT.

Mr. Jobs also decreed that the Macintosh contain no fans, which he had tried to eliminate from the original Apple computer. A vent was added to the Macintosh casing to allow cool air to enter and absorb heat from the vertical power supply, with hot air escaping at the top. The logic board was horizontally positioned.

Mr. Jobs, however, at times gave unworkable orders. When he demanded that the designers reposition the RAM chips on an early printed-circuit board because they were too close together, "most people chortled," one designer said. The board was redesigned with the chips farther apart, but it did not work because the signals from the chips took too long to propagate over the increased distance. The board was redesigned again to move the chips back to their original position.

A problem in radiation

When the design group started to concentrate on manufacturing, the most imposing task was preventing radiation from leaking from the Macintosh's plastic casing. At one time the fate of the Apple II had hung in the balance as its designers tried unsuc-

[3] Most of the discrete components in the Macintosh are inserted automatically into the printed-circuit boards.

cessfully to meet the emissions standards of the Federal Communications Commission. "I quickly saw the number of Apple II components double when several inductors and about 50 capacitors were added to the printed-circuit boards," Mr. Smith recalled. With the Macintosh, however, he continued, "we eliminated all of the discrete electronics by going to a connectorless and solderless design; we had had our noses rubbed in the FCC regulations, and we knew how important that was." The high-speed serial I/O ports caused little interference because they were easy to shield.

Another question that arose toward the end of the design was the means of testing the Macintosh. In line with the zero-defect concept, the Macintosh team devised software for factory workers to use in debugging faults in the printed-circuit boards, as well as self-testing routines for the Macintosh itself.

The disk controller is tested with the video circuits. Video signals sent into the disk controller are read by the microprocessor. "We can display on the screen the pattern we were supposed to receive and the pattern we did receive when reading off the disk," Mr. Smith explained, "and other kinds of prepared information about errors and where they occurred on the disk."

To test the printed-circuit boards in the factory, the Macintosh engineers designed software for a custom bed-of-nails tester that checks each computer in only a few seconds, faster than off-the-shelf testers. If a board fails when a factory worker places it on the tester, the board is handed to another worker who runs a diagnostic test on it. A third worker repairs the board and returns it to the production line.

When Apple completed building the Macintosh factory, at an investment of $20 million, the design team spent most of its time there, helping the manufacturing engineers get the production lines moving. Problems with the disk drives in the middle of 1983 required Mr. Smith to redesign his final prototype twice.

Some of the plans for the factory proved troublesome, according to Ms. Coleman. The automatic insertion scheme for discrete components was unexpectedly difficult to implement. Many of the precise specifications for the geometric and electrical properties of the parts had to be reworked several times. Machines proved to be needed to align many of the parts before they were inserted. Although the machines, at $2000 apiece, were not expensive, they were a last-minute requirement.

The factory had few major difficulties with its first experimental run in December 1983, although the project had slipped from its May 1983 deadline. Often the factory would stop completely while engineers busily traced the faults to the sources—part of the zero-defect approach. Mr. Smith and the other design engineers virtually lived in the factory that December.

In January 1984 the first salable Macintosh computer rolled off the line. Although the production rate was erratic at first, it has since settled at one Macintosh every 27 seconds—about a half million a year.

Creating the 'shelf space' for sales

The marketing of the Macintosh shaped up much like the marketing of a new shampoo or soft drink, according to Mike Murray, who was hired in 1982 as the third member of the Macintosh marketing staff. "If Pepsi has two times more shelf space than Coke," he explained, "you will sell more Pepsi. We want to create shelf space in your mind for the Macintosh."

To create that space on a shelf already crowded by IBM, Tandy, and other computer companies, Apple launched an aggressive advertising campaign—its most expensive ever.

Mr. Murray proposed the first formal marketing budget for the Macintosh in late 1983: he asked for $40 million. "People literally laughed at me," he recalled. "They said, 'What kind of a yo-yo is this guy?' " He didn't get his $40 million budget, but he got close to it—$30 million.

The marketing campaign started before the Macintosh was introduced. Television viewers watching the Super Bowl football game in January 1984 saw a commercial with the Macintosh over-

466

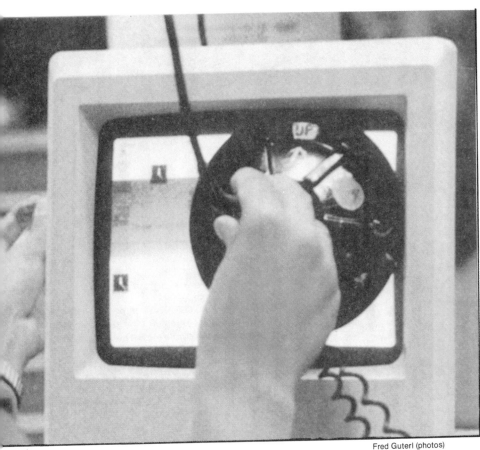

The Macintosh factory borrowed assembly ideas from other computer plants and other industries. A method of testing the brightness of cathode-ray tubes was borrowed from television manufacturers.

Each Macintosh is burned in—that is, turned on and heated—to detect the potential for early failures before shipping, thus increasing the reliability of the computers that are in fact shipped.

Fred Guterl (photos)

coming Orwell's nightmare vision of 1984.

Other television advertisements, as well as magazine and billboard ads, depicted the Macintosh as being easy to learn to use. In some ads, the Mac was positioned directly alongside IBM's personal computer. Elaborate color foldouts in major magazines pictured the Macintosh and members of the design team.

"The interesting thing about this business," mused Mr. Murray, "is that there is no history. The best way is to come in really smart, really understand the fundamentals of the technology and how the software dealers work, and then run as fast as you can."

The future challenge

"We've established a beachhead with the Macintosh," explained Mr. Murray. "We're on the beach. If IBM knew in their heart of hearts how aggressive and driven we are, they would push us off the beach right now, and I think they're trying. The next 18 to 24 months is do-or-die time for us."

With sales of the Lisa workstation disappointing, Apple is counting on the Macintosh to survive. The ability to bring out a successful family of products is seen as a key to that goal, and the company is working on a series of Macintosh peripherals—printers, local-area networks, and the like. This, too, is proving both a technical and organizational challenge.

"Once you go from a stand-alone system to a networked one, the complexity increases enormously," noted Mr. Murray. "We cannot throw it all out into the market and let people tell us what is wrong with it. We have to walk before we can run."

Only two software programs were written by Apple for the Macintosh—Macpaint, which allows users to draw pictures with the mouse, and Macwrite, a word-processing program. Apple is counting on independent software vendors to write and market applications programs for the Macintosh that will make it a more attractive product for potential customers. The company is also modifying some Lisa software for use on Macintosh and making versions of the Macintosh software to run on the Lisa.

Meanwhile the small, coherent Macintosh design team is no longer. "Nowadays we're a large company," Mr. Smith remarked.

"The pendulum of the project swings," explained Mr. Hertzfeld, who has taken a leave of absence from Apple. "Now the company is a more mainstream organization, with managers who have managers working for them. That's why I'm not there, because I got spoiled" working on the Macintosh design team.

To probe further

This article is part of a design-case-history series appearing periodically in *Spectrum*. The previous installment was "The Atari video computer system" [March 1983, p. 45].

A description of the Macintosh hardware and software can be found in the February 1984 issue of *Byte* magazine (McGraw-Hill Publications, New York), including articles by Mr. Smith and Mr. Hertzfeld.

For information on Apple Computer Inc.'s Lisa workstation, see "Personal computers" in the January 1984 *Spectrum* [p. 41]. The Xerox Star workstation was discussed in "Chips oust clips" [April 1983, p. 42].

For product information about the Macintosh, write to Apple Computer Inc., 20525 Mariani Ave., Cupertino, Calif. 95014; telephone 408-996-1010. ◆

GALILEO FLIGHT SOFTWARE MANAGEMENT - THE SCIENCE INSTRUMENTS*

R. C. Barry
Jet Propulsion Laboratory
Pasadena, California

and

D. J. Reifer
Software Management Consultants
Torrance, California

Abstract

The approach JPL is employing to manage instrument flight software development in a distributed environment is described. The software management approach needed to handle the development of each of these instruments by geographically-dispersed institutions was a major challenge because of the autonomy of each developer. The vehicle used to meet this challenge was the Instrument Software Management Plan. The Plan is described and one instrument is used as an example. Current status and an evaluation of the approach is presented.

Introduction

In 1984, the Galileo Orbiter spacecraft will be launched beginning a four-year mission to explore Jupiter and its four Galilean satellites as described in Reference 1. This paper describes and evaluates the software management approach developed at the Jet Propulsion Laboratory (JPL) to manage the flight software development for eight microprocessor-based science instruments. Several other recent papers [2,3,4] and [5] describe various aspects of the overall Galileo Project software development and management practices.

This introduction presents the background for the instrument software study. For a more complete introduction to the Galileo Project and its software task, see Reifer's introduction.[2] The challenges are defined, and the instrument software management objectives presented. Next, the science instruments software management approach is described. The contents of the required Science Instrument Software Management Plan and its relationship to other project plans are discussed. The section "Lessons Learned" gives the current status of the software as of this writing, assesses its perceived strengths and weaknesses and identifies those challenges that remain. The domain of applicability of the material presented is defined, and the paper ends with a set of conclusions that should be valuable to software managers or software system engineers faced with exercising management control over

sets of small, loosely linked, but highly reliable software built in a distributed environment where autonomy and isolation are the rule.

Background

The literature contains many references on managing large-scale software development. While some of these deal specifically with small, real-time, or process-control systems, most address the problems of large projects.[6] There are a number of good references introducing various other aspects of designing and developing microprocessor-based systems[7,8,9,10,11], but little source material can be found that addresses the management of software development for distributed microprocessor systems. Yet, the management problems in using networks of microprocessors interconnected to satisfy advanced applications (from autos to spacecraft) are being faced by many organizations. These problems are profound by nature and are the subject of this paper.

Table 1 names the nine science instruments aboard the orbiter spacecraft. The maximum output data rate and memory size is given for each instrument. This data is presented to contrast the rather small size of the data systems to the relatively larger task of managing this software as part of the integrated project software.

The complex management structure required by a large project places a heavy interface burden on the subsystem. The management structure for Galileo is divided into three general areas. A relatively small (approximately 10-man) Project Office has primary budget and schedule responsibility. The JPL technical divisions provide staffing for about 10 positions that require direct instrument interfacing. These technical divisions have the primary task of providing technical expertise, manpower, and line management as needed to carry out the requirements definition and interface control for all sciences. For the JPL instruments (NIMS, SSI) the instrument development is managed from within one of the technical divisions. The Science Instrument Organization is responsible for the detailed instrument design and development. For a typical instrument, there are approximately 10 people involved in the management, design, development, and testing of instrument software. Instrument software funding is

---

*This work was performed for the Jet Propulsion Laboratory, California Institute of Technology, sponsored by the National Aeronautics and Space Administration under Contract No. NAS7-100.

Table 1. Galileo Science Instrument Summary

Instrument	Maximum Data Rate, bits/s	Memory Size, kbytes	
		ROM	RAM
Solid state imaging (SSI)	768.	3	3.5
Near infrared mapping spectrometer (NIMS)	11.52	3	1.75
Photopolarimeter radiometer (PPR)	0.18	4	0.25
Ultraviolet spectrometer (UVS)	1.0	–	0.75
Energetic particle detector (EPD)	0.92	6	3
Plasma subsystem (PLS)	0.60	8	8
Magnetometer (MAG)	0.24	4	4
Dust detector subsystem (DDS)	0.024	3	2
Plasma wave subsystem (PWS) (contains no microprocessor)	645.	–	0.25

provided through a different project office than that for other Galileo software. The bottom line to this discussion is that the one or two individuals developing instrument flight software spend much of their effort on nonprogramming tasks.

Problem Definition

The Galileo Software Management Plan applies to all project funded software. However, the plan recognizes the special circumstances and unique character of the science instrument flight software development, and allows flexibility in how they are to be managed. This section describes the unique features surrounding the management of this software, and summarizes the spacecraft system level requirements on the software.

Instrument Management Philosophy

On past projects, JPL has assigned a Cognizant Engineer (CE) and a staff of system engineers (from 1 to 5, depending upon the project phase and instrument complexity) to each science instrument. This staff was responsible to the project for such items as interface control, subcontract management, compliance with project design standards, scheduling, status reporting, and funds control. The Galileo Project has reduced its direct management and control of the instruments. Rather than a single JPL CE per instrument, there is an Instrument Coordinator (IC), typically responsible for two instruments. The IC is supported by a smaller staff (0 to 2 individuals dependent upon project phase). The instrument Principal Investigator (PI) has been given a more complete responsibility and control over the instrument management and design. The primary JPL interest is now concentrated on defining system level requirements and interfaces and coordinating the procurement of JPL-supplied parts. The IC is principally responsible for verifying instrument compliance at the interfaces. This policy was, in the early project phases, referred to as the "Black Box Science" approach. In both the hardware and software areas, it has proven difficult to clearly define the separation of control and responsibility between the PI and the project. This has resulted in a kind of "Gray Box" approach where project authority encroaches upon some areas of instrument management and upon the design of some of the internal instrument hardware and software. Since this is the first JPL mission containing microprocessors and software within the instruments, it has been necessary to incorporate a new factor — software development and management — into the project philosophy. The remainder of this paper will concentrate on the software related issues.

System Level Requirements

The items discussed below had the largest effect on increasing the range of the software management beyond that originally anticipated. These and other software requirements are documented in the Galileo Orbiter Functional Requirements Book.[12]

Read Only Memory. Very early in the project, mask-defined Read Only Memory (ROM) was recommended for primary instrument program storage. It has the advantage of minimum mass and power, and would add stability to the instrument software design.

Reliability. Traditionally, because of mass and power constraints, JPL-flown science instruments have not been allowed the luxury of block redundancy for failure protection. However, standards for parts reliability, screening, qualification and design have always been applied equally to the spacecraft systems and the instruments. The effect on instrument reliability of adding a microprocessor and its associated software required additional study to assure that total subsystem reliability was not degraded.

Interface Design and Verification. The spacecraft data system design is heavily dependent upon a high-speed bus communication interface with an extremely low-error specification.

Flexibility. Because of the change dynamics inherent in a large project that spreads design and test over a multiyear period, it is required to design each subsystem with as large a measure of flexibility as is feasible within cost constraints.

Reprogrammability. A limited reprogrammability capability has been required of the science instruments. It is required that all code (including that in ROM) be modularized to the 256-byte level, that linkage be provided for patching, and that 512 bytes of RAM margin be provided.

<u>Telemetry Formats</u>. More detailed requirements have been placed on the instruments, reducing the freedom they have, relative to past JPL missions, for independently defining formats.

<u>Command Data</u>. The use of a Data System Bus (DSB) communication network has increased both the flexibility, power, and complexity of the instrument command interface.

<u>Cultural Shock of Software</u>. LSI microprocessor-based hardware and software design is new to most of the instrument teams. They are confronted with new capabilities and new constraints, and are required to find software solutions to problems for which they previously relied with confidence on hardware solutions backed by direct experience.

Galileo Science Instrument Software Management Approach

General Approach and Documentation Requirements

The Galileo Project Software Management Plan[13] is the central and controlling software management document. Volume I describes the management and technical approach and Volume II contains the more detailed Software Technical and Administrative Procedures (STAPS), which define each of the milestones and/or documents required by the plan. This project plan recognizes that the instruments' software will be managed more loosely than other project software. There are five deliverables required of each instrument: an Instrument Software Management Plan (ISMP), a Software Requirements Document (SRD), a Software Interface Specification (SIS), a Software Test Plan (STP), and the Software Delivery, which includes software and supporting documentation. STAPs define these deliverable requirements in more detail. In addition, the Galileo Orbiter Functional Requirements Book[12] contains a Level 4 Functional Requirement (FR) for each instrument that contains hardware/software partitioning at a high level. The ISMP is the key element upon which the detailed management of each instrument is based.

Instrument Software Management Plan Objectives

The objectives of the Galileo Orbiter ISMP are enumerated below:

1. It acts as a planning tool for the instrument software developers to use in laying out a systematic approach to the design, development, implementation, and testing of the software.

2. It provides visibility required by the Project Galileo software management staff, which will review and concur in the plan to ensure that appropriate design considerations are developed, and to assure minimal system level risk of hazard to the spacecraft or to the accomplishment of successful data return.

3. It is used by both the Science Instrument Development Team and the project staff to assure orderly transition between the subsystem development and testing and its integration and testing at the system level.

4. It provides a structure that allows maximum instrument autonomy within the guidelines of project requirements and constraints. The objective is to implement these capabilities in such a manner as to place the smallest reasonable overhead on the instrument teams in producing documentation and following the strict JPL large project software standards.

Plan Contents

Each team is required to define a plan that meets the general project requirements, but that is compatible with the needs, environment, and capabilities unique to the instruments' home organization. The ISMP is modeled after the Project Plan, but scaled down to the barest essentials. Most plans are from 10 to 15 pages long. STAP 3.1[14] describes the contents required. Sections of the Plan are:

1. <u>Instrument Overview and Software Sizing</u>.

2. <u>Development Team Organization and Structure</u>. Organization charts with named personnel for project management and interfaces (about 20 people) and instrument management and software ware personnel (typically 5 to 10 people) are included.

3. <u>Software Design and Development Process</u>. This section defines the development process and milestones, and gives a brief description of each item. A Development Flowchart is required, as is a Milestone Table that defines accomplishment responsibility, review type and attendance, approvals and concurrences required, and change control for each milestone. The flow and table are simplifications of corresponding items in the project's Software Management Plan. A software schedule that places emphasis upon reporting the project deliverables, and on identification of all critical interfaces is required. Those hardware elements that require close coordination (such as ROM procurement, support equipment, and instrument bread board, etc.) are included in the development flow and schedule.

4. <u>Resource Requirements</u>. Definition of the overall manpower requirements for software, and identification of other resources needed in the development are included in this section. Manpower is presented as a distribution of personnel requirements over calendar time. Most instruments peak at 2 or 3 full-time software personnel, and accumulate a total of 2 or 3 man years of effort during the prelaunch period.

5. <u>Reprogramming Plans</u>. The general instrument strategy with respect to pre- and postlaunch reprogramming is defined in this section.

Lessons Learned

Current Status

Since this is the first experience in microprocessor software management for most of the parties involved, the lessons learned will be presented as a loosely connected collection of positive and negative observations. Only the ultimate success in delivering operable and flexible software on schedule and without significant cost overrun will determine the final validity of the conclusions that were based on these observations.

It should be noted that the dates given below reflect the recent two-year Galileo launch delay. One instrument team completed its Engineering Model ROM definition in February 1980. Several others have complete, or nearly complete software operating in instrument breadboard hardware. Others have initial coding complete and are in the early testing phases. One instrument has just begun coding. Flight ROM definition cut off will be April 1981, initial spacecraft interface testing is scheduled for May 1981, and instrument delivery to JPL for spacecraft integration and system test will be October 1982.

As of this writing, instrument software has progressed close to the planned schedule, and has caused no subsystem schedule slips. Total manpower expended has averaged about 30% above the original estimates, but this has not been a significant cost factor overall.

Strong Points

Science Instrument Software System Engineer. The creation of the position of Science Instrument Software System Engineer (SISSE) to supplement the efforts of the Spacecraft Software System Engineer (S/C SSE), and filling it with a technically competent, dedicated individual is considered a primary strong point. Because of the extensive differences in team organizations, environment, location, and application, the tasks of managing the instrument flight software requires more attention than can be shared with the task of managing the larger, but more centralized engineering systems. In addition, the objectives of the instrument data systems are significantly different from others on the spacecraft, and an individual with direct experience in flight project science instrument areas can be applied effectively to the task. It is clear that this full-time position has paid for itself in defining the detailed instrument software procedures (STAPS), generating and negotiating the approval of the Software Interface Specifications, and reviewing the individual Instrument Software Management Plans to obtain approaches that are acceptable to the project and the teams. The SISSE has also identified a number of potential instrument problem areas and taken a leadership role in identifying options for corrective action. It has also been the project focal point for clarification of project instrument software requirements. Finally, the detailed understanding of each instrument gained during the flight software development phases should prove to be valuable in other Galileo instrument software areas (such as telemetry processing, data analysis, sequence generation software, and in flight operations).

Software Requirements in Spacecraft Design Book. The inclusion of functional software requirements in the Galileo Orbiter Functional Requirements Book is considered a qualified

success. The Level 4 (subsystem level) requirements[12] each contain a description of the software at a level that is comparable to the subsystem hardware description. This requirement was made only after the original drafts had been completed, and the software addition clearly complements and clarifies the hardware-orient descriptions, generally enhancing the value of the documents. Also, as the lack of a high-level software specification has been especially prevalent in embedded computer applications, it is felt that the step achieved here may lead to better system design in the future.

Data Bus Interface Definition. The implementation of microprocessor-controlled instruments in the Galileo spacecraft was significantly complicated by the distributed nature of the spacecraft data system. The design of the spacecraft data system bus was new, and significantly different from ground-based standards. It was necessary to define a conservative, yet flexible and efficient protocol for hardware and software. A Level 3 Spacecraft Design Book Functional Requirements FR)[15] was generated very early in the project. This FR contained provisions for a separate section to document the details of negotiated implementations selected by each bus user. These sections have now been completed and in use for approximately 9 months. The detailed information contained in them has proven highly useful to the spacecraft engineering subsystem designers, the instrument team, and the early Mission Operations System (MOS) design personnel.

Management Flexibility. Management flexibility is considered essential to successful management of the instrument software. Projects frequently fall prey to the ill of establishing admirable management policies that prove too expensive and inflexible to implement. The result is usually no control whatsoever, since the written policies cannot be followed. The Galileo Project has been relatively successful in establishing general policies and guidelines early and then providing more detailed definition and interpretation as the development approaches new phases. While this has proven a very difficult task, and at times modification of goals was required to be consistent with work that had progressed too far to change in its entirety, it was possible to negotiate deviations from the general goals and policies for each significant case as it appeared. The result of this policy of give-and-take is that the project has maintained an understanding of the individual instrument software development processes and has retained control in approval and/or concurrence of the negotiated acceptable development milestones. This process also provides the project with a valid set of milestones to monitor, and the set of instrument-defined criteria to assess successful milestone completion.

Influence of Spacecraft Design. There has also been some limited success in influencing the spacecraft design and development processes to take into account the flight software design, and of influencing software design to be spacecraft system compatible. Traditionally, JPL deep-space spacecraft design has been highly constrained by the requirements to optimize hardware for minimum mass and power and maximum utilization of the available telemetry downlink bandwidth. This has placed considerable restrictions upon software design, both flight and ground. The Galileo End-to-End Information System (EEIS) has set general mission requirements to attempt to optimize the cost of effective data return across a broader set of criteria, which includes spacecraft operability, Mission Operations System cost, and programming cost. These requirements have been folded back into the science software design and development, and have resulted in such activities as: Project funding of improved subsystem software development tools; a requirement on instrument design for inflight reprogrammability and memory margin (along with suggested implementation options); hardware support for reduction of power management problems by employing RAM memory keep-alive power; techniques for minimization of long ROM turnaround times (along with identification of alternative design options like pulsed-circuit PROMS on the spacecraft and EPROM and/or RAM replacement for ground based testing); definition of highly autonomous instrument modes and functional-level commanding; and standardization of telemetry formats in areas related to ground processing and spacecraft real-time operations monitoring.

Weak Points

The following is an enumeration of problem areas and goals that we feel were not properly achieved. Again, final judgement as to the importance of these issues must be reserved until they can be projected against their role in the ultimate success of the mission.

Requirements Specification. It is felt that considerable improvement is needed in the area of requirements specification. The organization and content of the Orbiter System Functional Requirements, the Policies and Requirements for Orbiter Science Instruments,[16] and the guidelines for preparation and evaluation of science instrument proposals should be redefined to account for the increased utilization of software in instrument design. It is felt that these documents do not adequately address the issues of functional commanding, spacecraft-versus-ground data processing, the software development and testing environment, and the Mission Operations Support environment.

Data System Hardware/Software Design Tradeoffs. Several areas of data system hardware design and hardware/software tradeoffs were constrained by study time and experience limitations and should be reevaluated on future projects. These include data bus hardware and software design and protocol, the bus adapter design (reconsider hybrid circuits or a smart interface processor), early establishment of adequate memory margin, memory maintenance power, and a reassessment of the decision to use mask programmable ROM as the primary nonvolatile memory element in the science instruments.

Timely Schedule Generation and Review Cycles. The next two items appear mundane and old-hat; however, better planning in these areas would have increased the effectiveness of the software management task. Firm project-reported schedules and

milestones were not established early in the development cycle. The five ISMP deliverable milestones should have been reported as primary subsystem milestones from the start. This would have been helpful in prioritizing the production of subsequent detailed STAPS and requirements. As it happened, the review of the ISMP was delayed. This resulted in the necessity of accepting more deviations from the plans as described in the STAP because some of the work was already done before the plans were reviewed. Several alternatives could have been employed to avoid this problem: peakload management help could have been acquired, or a quicker response could have been made by limiting the depth of the review, or a preliminary document review could have been held with the instrument author presenting the plan. All of these approaches would have resulted in more timely identification of obvious problem areas.

Future Challenges

The Galileo Orbiter science instruments are still 12 months away from initial spacecraft interface testing. Another 5 years will be spent in system test and interplanetary cruise prior to Jupiter Orbital Operations. While it is not possible to predict all the software difficulties that might be experienced in this period, some challenging tasks can surely be seen ahead. These will include:

Interface Verification of ROM. Interface verification of ROM based code will be required. Since this code is mostly assembly-language generated, and I/O oriented for a rather difficult-to-program microprocessor, it is not now clear how to provide an adequate verification without the high cost of detailed analysis or emulation. The planned focus is on code and data segments for each of the interface functions as documented in the communication protocol specification.[15] A set of operational scenarios will be generated for which the program designers (or an independent reviewer) will respond with a code walkthrough.

Software System Level Integration. The spacecraft system level integration testing will include software requirement and interface verification and validation. The distributed spacecraft data system and rather large total memory size (360 kbytes) will make this a very difficult task. Early establishment of the overall approach to software integration is required. Then, each subsystem will be required to generate an integration test segment that can be executed in the subsystem environment. This same test sequence and the subsystem generated test data will be used for initial integration testing, and will become a part of the regression test baseline.

Documentation Completion and Adequacy. The generation of complete and adequate documentation is critically important for the science instruments. Instrument teams are very small, with typically only one or two individuals involved in software generation. The long life time of the project combined with the need for in-flight anomaly workarounds and science data acquisition optimization requires the project to generate and maintain documentation adequate to allow reprogramming in the face of significant personnel turnover. The contents and completeness of all essential instrument documentation is being reviewed as part of the finalization of the Instrument Software Management Plans. Delivery of this documentation is required with delivery of the instrument code. Changes to the instrument software will be the responsibility of the instrument team, but the project change control board will require change justification, interface verification, presentation of validation test data (from ground-based breadboard or engineering model), and documentation updates before the change is accepted for uplink to the spacecraft.

Domain of Applicability

The discussion prsented in this paper should apply most directly to the development of embedded software systems utilizing a general-purpose microprocessor as a part of a large project. Table 1 summarizes the Galileo instrument data systems sizes and complexities. These instruments were developed within a complex management structure that required multiple interfaces at several levels of management and design. The instrument design was done at more than a dozen locations, from Santa Barbara, California, to Munich, West Germany.

Conclusions

The authors believe that the Galileo Project is well on its way to achieving its goals in managing the science instrument flight software. Adequate visibility into the team's software design and development has been maintained to insure general compliance to the project software requirements. By utilizing separate team-generated instrument software management plans, this has been accomplished in a manner that allows extensive flexibility in accommodating the diverse differences in instrument software design and in instrument software development approaches. Table 2 summarizes the lessons that have been learned in the process of defining and applying the instrument flight software management. Among the strong points were assignment of a fulltime Science Instrument Software System Engineer, complete interface definition, and management flexibility. Additional work is recommended in the area of requirements specification, hardware design influence, and timely scheduling and review. The success of future challenges in the area of interface verification, software integration and testing, documentation adequacy, and control of reprogramming will be based upon the groundwork described in this paper. The fruition of these efforts will be seen as a measure of the successful data acquisition and optimization in the environs of Jupiter beginning in 1986.

References

1. JPL Internal Project Document 625-200, Project Galileo Mission Plan Document, 15 May 1979.

2. D. J. Reifer, R. C. Barry, B. T. Larman, and P. M. Molko, "Lessons Learned From the Galileo Project — Introduction," IEEE COMPSAC 80.

3. P. M. Molko, "SAMS: Addressing Managers' Needs," IEEE, COMPSAC 80.

4. B. T. Larman, "Flight Software: New Challenges and New Approaches," IEEE, COMPSAC 80.

5. R. E. Loesh, B. T. Larman, P. M. Molko, and D. J. Reifer, "Implementing A Software Management Discipline," submitted for consideration to the Fifth International Conference on Software Engineering, February 1981.

6. D. J. Reifer, Tutorial, Software Management, IEEE, 1979.

7. S. Magers, "Managing Software Development in Microprocessor Projects," Computer, IEEE, June 1978.

8. P. Heckel, "Developing Software for Microprocessor-Based Products," Mini-Micro Systems, February 1980.

9. J. G. Posa, "Programming Microcomputer Systems with High-Level Languages," Electronics, January 18, 1979.

10. M. Schindler, "Can One μC Development System be 200 Times More Powerful than Another? Shop and See," Electronic Design, December 6, 1978.

11. W. W. Lattin, et al., "Special Issue on Microprocessor Applications," Proceedings of the IEEE, February 1978.

12. JPL Internal Project Document 625-205, Galileo Orbiter Functional Requirements Book,
    Level 1: Introduction
    Level 2: Orbiter Design Criteria
    Level 3: Orbiter System Functional Requirements
    Level 4: Orbiter Subsystem Functional Requirements, sections separately dated.

13. JPL Internal Project Document 625-510, Project Galileo Software Management Plan, Volume I: Technical Development and Management Policies and Approach, Revision C, June 10, 1980.

14. JPL Internal Project Document 625-510, Volume II, STAP 3.1, Science Instrument Software Management Plan Procedure, Dec. 20, 1979.

15. JPL Internal Project Document 625-205, GLL-3-270, Functional Requirement, Galileo Orbiter Data System Intercommunication Requirements, 10 October 1978.

16. JPL Internal Project Document 625-52, Project Galileo Policies and Requirements for Orbiter Science Instruments, 12 August 1978.

Table 2. Summary of Software Management Feature Effectiveness

Software Management Task or Feature	Value to Project Management	Implementation Ease	Introduction Timeliness	Changes Since Introduction	Overall Value, Comments
Creation of SISSE	High	Good	Good	No	A strong point
Instrument software mgmt plans	High	Good	Some late	No	A strong point
High-level software reqmts Level 1, 2; policies	Med	Fair	Some late	Yes	A weak point
Level 3 (3-310) software requirements	Med	Fair	Some late	Yes	Not used to full potential
Level 3 (3-270) interface protocol	High	Good	Good	No	A strong point
Level 3 (3-280, -290) telemetry, command	High	Fair	Some late	Yes	Necessary, but awkward structure
Level 4 subsystem functional requirements	Med	Fair	Some late	Yes	Necessary, but awkward structure
Project visibility	Med	Difficult	Good	No	Adequate
System level design feedback	Low	Fair	Too late	No	High potential value
Project Software Mgmt Plan and STAPS	High	Fair	Some late	No	Good, but difficult to prepare
Interface verification	High	Unknown	–	Yes	A future challenge
Instrument SRD	High	Mixed	Some late	Yes	Value TBD
Instrument test plan	Med	Unknown	Too late	No	Should ease integration task
Instrument software delivery pkg and procedure	Med	Unknown	Good	Yes	To project software library
Inflight reprogramming preparation	Med	Unknown	Too late	Yes	Unknown
Software mgmt contribution to increased operability	High	Difficult	Good	No	A new attempt
Change control	High	Unknown	Good	No	Value TBD
Review effectiveness	Med	Difficult	Fair	No	Fair
Schedule visibility and control	High	Moderate	Poor	Yes	A weak point
1802 user consultant	Low	Moderate	Good	Yes	Not utilized effectively

AN ANALYSIS OF THE RESOURCES USED IN THE
SAFEGUARD SYSTEM SOFTWARE DEVELOPMENT

W. E. Stephenson
Bell Laboratories

Reprinted from *Proceedings, Second International Conference on Software Engineering*, 1976, pages 312-321. Copyright © 1976 by The Institute of Electrical and Electronics Engineers, Inc.

The SAFEGUARD System represents the development of one of the largest, most complex software systems ever undertaken. Various types of software were developed, including real time applications, support, and hardware installation and maintenance. Two million instructions were developed at a cost of approximately five thousand staff years of effort. The objective of this paper is to document the staff resources utilized in this development. The actual development rates for the different types of software and the various factors affecting those rates are analyzed. Software productivity is shown to be a function of the type of software - logical, algorithmic, man machine, etc. Emphasis is placed upon total project productivity. The allocation of staff resources for the systems engineering, design, code and unit test, and integration activities, which had an approximate percentage distribution of 20, 20, 17, 43, is analyzed and characterized.

I. Introduction

SAFEGUARD was a Ballistic Missile Defense (BMD) system primarily designed to respond to attacks by intercontinental ballistic missiles.[1] It was composed of three major subsystems: missiles, radars, and data processing and control. Incoming missiles, after being detected and tracked by the radars, were to be intercepted and destroyed by defensive missiles. The radars and missiles were controlled by the data processing system.

There were three types of sites in the SAFEGUARD System: Perimeter Acquisition Radar (PAR), (the long range radar site), Missile Direction Center (MDC), and Ballistic Missile Defense Center (BMDC), (the Command Center site). Although several PAR and MDC sites were planned, only one of each was deployed. The long-range radar, or PAR, site utilized a single-faced, phased-array radar to provide early detection and trajectory data on threatening missiles. Functions of this site included long-range surveillance, detection, tracking, and target classification of threatening objects in support of long-range defensive missile intercepts.

The PAR target trajectory and classification data was supplied to the Missile Direction Center site. This site provided additional surveillance and target tracking and also performed the functions of track, battle planning, and guidance for short and long-range defensive missiles. Both the long-range radar (PAR) and Missile Direction Center (MDC) sites reported to the Ballistic Missile Defense Center (BMDC), a central command center. The BMDC provided a command interface with other military systems and a means of disseminating command directives and controls.

The PAR and MDC radars were controlled by the data processing systems, collocated with the radars. At the PAR and MDC sites, application programs performed several functions, such as surveillance, tracking, target classification, radar management and testing, intersite communication, and console display functions. Additional application programs at the MDC supported the battle management and defensive missile guidance functions. The BMDC data processing system primarily contained display and command/control programs. All application programs were executed in real-time (deadlines on the order of milliseconds) and were implemented on a special purpose multi-processor computer with a throughput in excess of 10 million instructions/second. The software systems contained at each of these sites were called processes. A process is a collection of all of the real-time application software and the operating system which are required to perform a design mission on one computer at one site. The long-range radar and Missile Direction Center sites each contained two processes, the tactical process and an exercise process. The exercise process was used to test the tactical process. At the Command and Control site the tactical and exercise functions were contained in a single process.

Each of the processes contained several different functions. A function performed one general task, while a process contained many interactive functions with many diverse roles, such as radar management and intersite communications.

The development and deployment of the SAFEGUARD System entailed the development of one of the largest, most complex software systems ever undertaken. One of the initial problems associated with this software development was how to accurately forecast the resource requirements for the total software development. Available forecasting algorithms focused primarily on the in-line development effort (software design-code-test) of the delivered product, without addressing support functions such as simulation development, data reduction, hardware installation and maintenance, etc. These activities had to be accounted for primarily through judgment and management experience. Being now in a position to view the total software development effort on SAFEGUARD in retrospect, the actual resource expenditures can be assessed and characterized.

This report will address the total complement of software developed for the SAFEGUARD project, the deliverable product as well as the support functions, and identify the staff year resources expended. Although some detailed example cases will be presented, in general the report will concentrate on project level resources, rather than individual program development areas. These project level areas include requirements development and evaluation, design, code, test, and support activities. As a result of this approach, the productivity rates presented, in terms of instructions per staff year, are lower than those usually quoted for software development. The data does, however, accurately reflect the _total_ resources expended in the software development cycle.

To gain a better appreciation of what drove the resource expenditures, a discussion of the factors affecting software development productivity is included. Many factors, some of them unique to a project like SAFEGUARD, had a profound effect on the project productivity rate.

A number of different resource utilization data points will be presented. The two major ones are the total productivity rate for the development of all SAFEGUARD software and the productivity rate for the development of the deliverable product, i.e., the real-time software. These two data points, based upon the total project staff are:

Total Software Development -
418 instructions/staff year

Real-time Software Development -
146 instructions/staff year

The allocation of staff resources in the development of the real-time applications software was:

Systems Engineering - 20 percent
Design   - 20 percent
Code and Unit Test - 17 percent
Integration Testing - 43 percent

Some general guidelines for forecasting software development resource requirements, based upon SAFEGUARD experience, will be presented. Briefly, these lessons were learned:

- All elements of software development must be taken into account. Forecasting must include, in addition to the deliverable software package, support software, requirements development, evaluation, simulations, documentation, data reduction, adequate testing, etc.

- Develop procedures to monitor detailed resource allocation across all elements of the project from the beginning of the development effort.

- Software development and resource forecasting are, today, not well defined procedures. Judgment must be exercised as to how the results of other projects, such as those presented here for SAFEGUARD, apply.

- As a project matures and a more structured approach to development evolves, the productivity rate increases. This is particularly true of a first-time large-scale system development effort.

II. Objectives

The primary objective of this paper is to identify the staff resources utilized in the development of the software for the SAFEGUARD System. Emphasis is placed upon the productivity, in terms of instructions

developed per staff year, that was experienced in this development. The myriad of factors which had a substantial effect on the software development in SAFEGUARD, such as state of the art design, false starts, design changes, etc., will be highlighted. (An attempt has been made, using example cases, to eliminate the effect of these factors and identify the costs for a mature program development.) The data presented addresses total system software development as opposed to individual programmer or even group productivity levels. The reasons for this distinction are several:

- The objective of the paper is to present the resource expenditures for the development of a large software system, not individual components or programs.

- The interdependence of actual coding and testing of programs upon the many other activities, such as system requirements generation and design, required in the SAFEGUARD development make it difficult and of questionable value to isolate to a unit or program level.

- Code and unit test algorithms for individual programmer production can be very misleading, since this activity was probably the easiest and most straightforward in the entire SAFEGUARD development. A moderately good programmer can produce code at a very high rate, but without correct requirements, design, and testing that code is worthless.

Thus, what will be presented is project productivity data which will encompass all the people involved in the development of all the software produced. It is hoped that by presenting the data in this manner, potential pitfalls in applying these data to future development algorithms can be avoided. These include overlooking support software and support facilities which are required for the development of the deliverable software or overlooking essential non-software producing activities such as requirements specification, evaluation, documentation, etc.

III. Productivity Factors

This section presents a very critical element in the discussion of software productivity and the resources expended for SAFEGUARD -- what factors had a substantial effect on the resource utilization in the development of SAFEGUARD software.

A. _Nature of the System._ The factor which had the greatest effect on the development of SAFEGUARD software, which made the development, if not unique, certainly greatly separated from a "nominal" software system development project, was the nature of the system itself. The project dealt with state of the art system requirements and design. This type and size system had never been developed before, and, indeed there was considerable opinion that it could not be done. This factor greatly influenced the resources required in software development, and had various ramifications throughout the development process utilized in software development. Most software systems will not face this magnitude of design problem, and hence will not require the resources expended in SAFEGUARD to overcome them.

B. _State of the Software Development Process._ A significant factor in the development of the SAFEGUARD software was the state of the software development process. At the time SAFEGUARD development commenced, and to a large extent even today, the software development process had not achieved the maturity of a true engineering discipline, such as achieved by the corresponding hardware development process. The process was, for the most part, not well structured. No one methodology or approach was uniformly accepted as a standard or even as better than another. As a result, the evolution of a software engineering discipline, well matched to the needs of the project, was a continuous one. This necessitated a learning experience for all members of the project, from programmers to upper management. The development of a disciplined approach required time to identify, understand, and develop methods to cope with fundamental problems associated with the development process. Initially, there was some over-emphasis on some apparently critical activities which in retrospect turned out to be of lesser importance. An example of this was an early emphasis on producing code at the expense of shortening the design interval. This resulted in an initial product which was not always adequate. It is almost impossible to quantify the effect this total learning experience had upon the software productivity rate. But it is clear that as the organization matured and a more structured development approach evolved, the corresponding productivity rates increased. This phenomenon is not unique to SAFEGUARD, and in fact is probably characteristic of any first-time large-scale system development effort. Although its impact is difficult to explicitly quantify, its effect is implicit in the productivity rate data.

C. System Engineering. The systems engineering effort on SAFEGUARD was a critical element in the development of the system. This effort produced the operational requirements for all of the real-time applications software. The requirements were issued in preliminary form as soon as possible, so that actual software development could get the earliest possible start. An obvious effect on this preliminary issue is the subsequent modification of requirements following preliminary system design and evaluation reviews. Additional modifications were required due to necessary customer injected changes to the system objectives. The value of this early start on software design far outweighed the impact of subsequent requirements modifications and design changes in that it permitted detailed development planning and preliminary design to proceed. The effect of these evolving requirements upon SAFEGUARD development was, however, much more severe than would be expected on systems which do not challenge the state of the art. A considerable "learning curve" resulted in which requirements were evaluated, updated, and modified, resulting design changes incorporated, simulations revamped to reflect the changes, and results of the simulations analyzed to evaluate performance. This sequence of events was repeated many times as more understanding of the many unique characteristics of the system was developed. While this learning curve was expensive, in terms of both resources and schedule, the enhancements to system performance, both corrections to errors and improvements to working products, were invaluable. The effects of this learning curve were not, however, unexpected. The impact of the nature of the system, the state of the art design required, and the resulting "false starts" were accounted for in system scheduling and resource planning. As a result, although there were resource impacts due to the factors outlined here and below, the system was developed on schedule, within predicted costs, and with its required capabilities.

Thus, with fairly periodic modifications occurring in the system requirements and design, some isolated and some with widespread effects throughout the system, the "learning curve" period on SAFEGUARD for the development of stable requirements, design, and at least preliminary code extended two to three years into the development cycle.

Another systems engineering activity, which was not direct in-line support of SAFEGUARD, was long-range planning and future system design. This activity accounted for approximately 20 percent of the systems engineering effort shown in Section V.

D. Design. Much of the previous discussion of the nature of the SAFEGUARD System and its impact on requirements development and stability also applies, as noted previously, to software design. However, in addition to impacts on design due to the modifications in requirements and system objectives, state of the art design itself was a significant factor.

Given satisfactory requirements, methods had to be devised in program and algorithm design to implement those requirements. Great emphasis was placed upon system simulations and data from the prototype (Meck Island) system. This procedure, however, implied a period of modification until satisfactory results were obtained from a set of candidate designs and simulation results. Major changes in some of the basic algorithmic design to meet modified system objectives and to incorporate results derived from the prototype system were made as late as fifteen months before the deployment of the system, more than five years into the development cycle.

E. Testing/Integration. The most obvious factor affecting resource utilization in the unit, element, and integration testing, i.e., process and system testing, phases of the software development was the sheer size of the real-time system, approximately 789,000 instructions, 450,000 64 bit words of data, and 50,000 64 bit words per second of real-time input/output. Experience in software development has indicated that productivity rates decrease as the size of the software package increases.[2] Experience on SAFEGUARD tends to support this hypothesis. Perhaps the primary factor affecting the rate of testing and integration of the system was again the nature of the system itself. The real-time software was composed of three applications processes and two exerciser processes, with a common operating system contained within each process. Each of these applications processes was highly interactive (1) within itself, (2) with its exercise system, and (3) with the other applications processes. The processing of the system was highly parallel, rather than serial, in nature. Program bugs in one function were often manifested only in the operations of an entirely different process. This characteristic of the overall system made the integration of the several processes difficult and time consuming.

F. Hardware Systems. Another aspect of the SAFEGUARD System which made it somewhat unique was that most of the hardware was designed specifically for SAFEGUARD. The main computer, and all the peripheral hardware units other than tape and disk units, printers, and card readers were in this category. This affected the resource expenditure in the development of SAFEGUARD software.

First, as the hardware was developed by separate organizations geographically removed from the software development, communication between the two areas was primarily via design documentation. Many problems were encountered during the early design phase of the software because the documentation simply did not reflect the hardware design.

Secondly, the new hardware components, including

the real-time computer, were still in their own debugging state when software testing and integration utilizing these components were underway. Considerable time was expended during the early software testing cycle correcting latent hardware design deficiencies. The impacts on the amount of time required to test and integrate the software are obvious.

G. Product Quality. It is, of course, the goal of every software development project to develop a high quality product. This was particularly the case on SAFEGUARD, since the software was contained in a nuclear weapon defense system. There could not be any design defects or program bugs which prevented the deployed system from performing its design function. A set of five very comprehensive contractor demonstration tests had to be passed before the system was accepted by the government. These factors led to a development program designed and implemented to assure the absence of program defects or design errors which would prevent the system from performing its mission. The implication of this approach was that a great deal of staff and time was spent in integration testing to insure that the system design and operation was of high quality, i.e., that it would work as required.

The success of this approach was demonstrated in a program conducted after the deployment of the system. A set of 57 tests, called dispersion tests, were conducted at the development site. The purpose of this program was (1) to determine the adequacy of the integration testing activities conducted on SAFEGUARD and (2) to characterize the robustness of the system against a broad spectrum of attack patterns. The program was highly successful, with all tests being satisfactorily completed. Only one software design problem affecting the primary performance objective of the system was detected. This contrasts to approximately five thousand such problems which were identified and corrected prior to the activation of the system. The success of this program verified the system integration approach taken on SAFEGUARD and showed the high quality of the software system. While the software development was costly, the system worked as predicted in test situations.

H. Impact of Factors Affecting Productivity. The impact of the several factors discussed above upon the development of the real-time applications software for SAFEGUARD was quite substantial. Programs, functions, and in some cases major portions of entire processes went through one or more false starts during their development. However, the efforts expended during these early developments were not entirely wasted, for many valuable lessons were learned. Nevertheless, design, coding, and testing of various components of the system went through several iterations. While these impacts were costly, they had been, as noted above, accounted for in the early development planning.

An incremental approach in software development and testing was fundamental to SAFEGUARD. This procedure led to multiple versions of functions being developed and delivered incrementally to the test groups. Each version added capabilities not required, or desired due to their complexity, for initial test activities. However, in addition to these scheduled redeliveries, additional versions had to be developed to incorporate modifications in requirements, design, and redirection of overall system objectives. Code had to be modified or redone to reflect changes in functions or hardware which interfaced with that particular function.

On the average, there were five to six versions or releases of each real-time applications function

delivered to integration testing. An estimated average of 1.5 of these versions were redone as a result of false starts.

IV. Software Developed for SAFEGUARD

The various types of software developed on the SAFEGUARD project will now be described in very general terms. It is not intended to give detailed functional descriptions of the software, but rather to give a generic description of the different types and sizes of functions produced.

A. Real-Time Software. The heart of the project was of course the real-time software which executed on the main computer and was deployed on site. There were two general types of real-time software, applications and support. All of this software was developed in a high level language, similar to PL1, developed uniquely for SAFEGUARD, although the sizes have been shown in terms of assembly language instructions (since this is the most accurate basis for sizing the functions).

Applications Software. The applications software was composed of two types, the tactical and exercise software which resided at each of three distinct types of sites.

Missile Direction Center (MDC) Real-Time Process. This software process controlled the operation of the MDC site. The primary functions included the detection, tracking, and classification of offensive missiles and the battle planning, launch, and guidance to intercept of defensive missiles, in addition to a large collection of hardware test programs. This process was the most complex of the application processes. It was composed of 317,000 assembly language instructions, exclusive of the operating system.

Long Range Radar Real-Time Process. The long range radar real-time process had a primary role of long range detection, track, and classification of offensive missile systems. It also contained a large collection of hardware test programs. It was composed of 221,000 assembly language instructions, exclusive of the operating system.

Exercise Real-Time Processes. The exercise processes for these two sites contained functions which simulated offensive and defensive missile environments for the testing of the tactical processes. These two exercisers contained a total of 70,000 assembly language instructions, exclusive of the operating system.

Command and Control Site Real-Time Process. The Command and Control tactical process had a primary role of supplying command and control functions to personnel for the overall control of the SAFEGUARD System. This process did not control a radar. Also, the exercise software was contained within the tactical process as part of one software system. This process contained a total of 81,000 assembly language instructions, exclusive of the operating system.

Tactical Computer Operating System. A unique operating system was developed for SAFEGUARD. The same operating system, with minor modifications, supported all of the applications processes. While most of this software was executed in real-time, some of the support utilities were non-real-time. It contained a total of 100,000 assembly language instructions.

B. Non-Real-Time Software. A large amount of software was developed to support the development and operation of the real-time code. This software operated on a variety of computers, including the real-time computer, GE635 and various models of IBM 360 and 370 computers.

Development Support. Several software facilities were developed to support the development and testing of software operating on the real-time computer. These facilities included the compilers, loaders, binders, test processes for the real-time support software, libraries for the development and control of software, data reduction, exercise simulation support, and a simulation of the real-time computer for testing purposes. Included in the category were various support activities such as the development of configuration management procedures, management reporting systems, and documentation. This total package of support software contained 632,000 instructions, primarily PL1 statements.

Hardware Installation & Maintenance. Since most of the hardware utilized in SAFEGUARD was developed for the system, hardware installation and maintenance software packages had to be developed, primarily for the radars and the data processing system. A total of 840,000 assembly language instructions were contained in these functions.

C. Total Software Size. The following numbers reflect the totals of the above three major categories.

Real-Time Software	789,000 instructions
Support Software	632,000 instructions
Installation and Maintenance Software	840,000 instructions
TOTAL	2,261,000 instructions

V. Resources Utilized

This section will present the staff resources utilized in the development of SAFEGUARD software. It does not include, nor does this report address, resources for hardware development or the R&D project which preceded SAFEGUARD. This is, to some extent, misleading in that much value was gained from the R&D effort. In particular, the development and verification of tracking and guidance algorithms in the R&D project proved absolutely essential to SAFEGUARD development. However, this algorithm development was so complex and unique to this particular system that ignoring the resources expended in the R&D effort to support SAFEGUARD should not affect the application of this study to other, less unique, system developments, but rather should make the results more applicable.

Table 1 contains the number of staff years expended in the development of each of the software products defined in Section IV plus the systems engineering effort previously discussed. The experience and educational background of the staff varied widely across the project, from essentially zero experience to ten or more years and associate degrees to doctorates. The average for the project was approximately four years experience and a bachelors degree. The figures for calendar year 1969 begin on July 1, while the figures for 1975 terminate on April 1, the activation date of the SAFEGUARD system.

The Missile Direction Center software was the largest single software process and, by far, the most complex. This is reflected in the number of staff years expended on this process in relation to the other functions. The development of Missile Direction Center software, which represented 14 percent of the total number of instructions developed, required 24 percent of the staff.

The staff resources were divided among the major categories of software and systems engineering as follows:

Real-Time Applications - 46 percent
Tactical Computer Operating System - 5 percent
Development Support - 24 percent
Hardware Installation and Maintenance - 12 percent
Systems Engineering - 13 percent

VI. Software Productivity Data Points

A number of different data points based upon SAFEGUARD software development experience will be presented in this section. This will allow the effects of the many different types and complexity of software to be highlighted. The data points will be expressed in terms of number of assembly language instructions developed per staff year.

A. Real-Time Software. What is perhaps the most meaningful data point presented is the number of staff years required for the entire project to produce the real-time software, both applications and the operating system, which was deployed on site. The total size of these software processes was 789,000 instructions. The total amount of effort expended in SAFEGUARD software development, as shown in Table 1, was 5407 staff years. This yields a productivity rate of 146 instructions per staff year. (If the hardware installation and maintenance software development resources are excluded, the productivity rate becomes 165 instructions per staff year.)

To better characterize the resource utilization in software production on SAFEGUARD, perhaps it is useful to examine other statistics which can be derived. If one looks at the real-time code, again 789,000 instructions, and only the staff dedicated to those functions, the following data results:

789,000 instructions/2765 staff years
= 285 instructions/staff year

This data point gives a better picture of the cost of "pure" project level software development without the systems engineering and support functions included.

B. Total SAFEGUARD Software. Having examined the data depicting the development of the application software for SAFEGUARD, i.e., the real-time software, the production rate for all SAFEGUARD software will now be presented.

The size of the total set of SAFEGUARD software, as described in Section IV, was 2,261,000 instructions. The total number of staff years expended in the effort, as shown in Table 1, was 5407. This yields a total development rate of

418 instructions/staff year

C. Individual Software Processes. A compilation of each of the SAFEGUARD software processes, its size, the number of staff years expended, and the resulting number of instructions per staff year is contained in Table 2. As is readily noticeable, there is a wide dispersion in the productivity rate across these different software functions. This is, of course,

TABLE 1

STAFF YEARS/FUNCTION

	1969	1970	1971	1972	1973	1974	1975	TOTAL
Real-Time Applications								
Missile Direction Center (MDC)	42	160	249	293	303	198	53	1298
Long Range Radar	18	70	135	168	213	161	33	798
Command Center	–	–	32	48	46	36	5	167
Exercisers	11	42	62	67	39	7	1	229
SUBTOTAL	71	272	478	576	601	402	92	2492
Tactical Computer Operating System	11	44	56	60	47	47	8	273
Development Support	40	142	306	298	251	194	62	1293
Hardware Installation & Maintenance	33	129	168	162	99	32	2	625
Systems Engineering	33	112	167	165	115	105	27	724
	188	699	1175	1261	1113	780	191	5407

TABLE 2

FUNCTION	INSTRUCTIONS SIZE	STAFF YEARS	INST./STAFF YEAR
Real-Time Applications			
Missile Direction Center (MDC)	317,000	1298	244
Long Range Radar	221,000	798	277
Command Center	81,000	167	485
Exercisers	70,000	229	306
Tactical Computer Operating System	100,000	273	366
Development Support	532,000	1293	411
Hardware Installation & Maintenance	840,000	625	1344
Systems Engineering			
A. Simulations	100,000	157	637
B. Analysis & Design	--	567	--
TOTAL	2,261,000	5407	418

primarily due to the wide disparity in the nature and complexity of the functions.

The real-time code was, for the most part, the most complex and had, by far, the most stringent requirements. It is this code which contained the state of the art design and the complications which arose from that design. The productivity rate for the real-time software, 285 instructions per staff year, therefore, reflected this higher degree of difficulty. In order to obtain a better feel for the types of software and their comparative rates of production, Table 3 contains some example subsets of the Table 2 software functions, grouped more generically as to function and type of code.

TABLE 3

SOFTWARE TYPE	SIZE (INSTRUCTIONS)	INSTRUCTIONS/ STAFF YEAR
Real-Time (Total)	789,000	285
Real-Time Process (Logical)	81,000	485
Real-Time Function (Logical)	67,300	974
Real-Time Process (Algorithmic/Logical)	317,000	244
Real-time Function (Algorithmic/Logical)	23,000	438
Hardware Installation	350,000	1097
Hardware M&D	490,000	1601

The total real-time software has already been discussed. The process level real-time logical code example refers to the Command Center process. The primary function of the software was data communication and the command and control interface with operating personnel. It did not contain any complex algorithms. The nature of this code resulted in the highest real-time process productivity rate, 485 instructions per staff year. This was the composite rate for the design, code, unit test, element test, and system integration phases of the development. The real-time function level logical code example refers to the function within the Missile Direction Center which performed essentially the same function as the Command Center. Further, it reflects the final version of this code development, following false starts incurred due to requirements instability. This example more clearly shows the development of a "mature" function of primarily logical code. This maturity is reflected in a productivity rate twice that of process example. However, the productivity rate for this function and for the real-time function level algorithmic/ logical example below do not include integration resources while the process examples do.

The real-time algorithmic/logical process example is the Missile Direction Center (MDC) process. Although the MDC contained a large amount of primarily logical code, including the function quite similar to the Command Center, it also contained a considerable amount of highly complex algorithmic code. This resulted in the lowest rate, 244 instructions per staff year, of all the software developed on SAFEGUARD. The real-time function level algorithmic/logical example

is of the tracking function within the MDC. This example also highlights the development of a "mature" function in that it was the second version of this function. Hence the effects of false starts experienced previously have been eliminated. The track function development is further examined in Section VII. The hardware installation code reflects software developed primarily from hardware specifications and requirements. While algorithmic code was included in these functions, these algorithms were essentially defined by the hardware design and hence were not nearly as complex as those contained in the Missile Direction Center. This much greater simplicity and stability is reflected in the much higher productivity rate. The hardware maintenance and diagnostic (M&D) software was of a nature similar to the installation software, only more straightforward. The functions required were defined by the hardware design. The particular interface capabilities and requirements of the hardware in essence dictated the capabilities and functional requirements of the software. The uniqueness of this type of software is reflected in the relatively high productivity rate of 1601 instructions per staff year, and is therefore misleading when compared to a process like the Missile Direction Center.

VII. Example Cases

Having discussed the software development on SAFEGUARD in total project terms, it will be useful to examine some example cases dealing with the development of "partial processes" or functions within the processes described previously. The example cases deal with code developed during the middle or latter portions of the total project development, and therefore reflect a much more stable requirements and design environment. In fact, two of these examples reflect the second and fourth versions of code, which were done due to revisions in requirements and design and lessons learned during the previous developments. These example cases, therefore, eliminate some of the factors which had a tremendous impact upon SAFEGUARD overall development, e.g., the state of the art design.

A. Missile Direction Center (MDC) Track Function (Version 2). Tracking was the function within the MDC tactical process which contained the search and offensive target track functions. This function was probably the most complex within the SAFEGUARD System, due to the highly sophisticated tracking algorithms contained within it. It was within this function that much of the state of the art design and iterative simulation and evaluation efforts were expended.

The total development cycle for this version of the track function, from design to delivery to integration, spanned 11 months. The design and architecture required a total of 315 staff months. The code and unit test interval spanned four months, with 190 staff months expended here. Element tests, tests of several units together which formed a software path through the function, had an expenditure of 125 staff months. The effort also included all the documentation, from design specifications to detailed test specifications, required to produce this software package.

The track function contained 23,000 instructions, which yields the following development productivity rates:

Design - 876 inst./staff year
Code and Unit Test - 1452 inst./staff year
Element Test - 2208 inst./staff year
Total development - 438 inst./staff year

Since tracking was but a small part of the total MDC process, 23,000 out of 317,000 instructions, it is not possible to determine the number of staff months expended in the integration of the track function with the rest of the process. As mentioned previously, the system processing was parallel rather than serial in nature and all elements were highly interactive. It is, therefore, impossible to identify a portion of the integration effort as being devoted to one of the many functions.

B. Long Range Radar Real-Time Process. Portions of the long range radar process were redone during the period January 1, 1973 through September 1, 1973. This new version, however, had changes in all major software functions within the process. A total of 36,000 new instructions were developed for this version out of a total of 221,000 instructions in the process.

The design of the modifications required a total of 300 staff months. Code and unit testing and element testing overlapped in time, since the different functions within the process being modified were delivered incrementally. A total of 350 staff months were expended on code and unit testing, and 150 on element testing, yielding the following productivity rates:

Design - 1440 inst./staff year
Code and Unit Test - 1234 inst./staff year
Element Test - 2880 inst./staff year
Total development - 540 inst./staff year

The overall development rate was higher than that of the MDC track function, but 11,000 of the instructions developed for this process were for functions that were not algorithmic in nature, e.g., communication and display functions quite similar to the Command Center process. Hence, one would expect a higher rate of development. As in the case of the MDC track function it is not possible to separate the integration effort for this code from the rest of the system. However, the next example deals with process and system integration.

C. Integration Testing. The integration rates, covering both process integration and netted system integration, for both long range radar and Missile Direction Center processes will now be developed.

Long Range Radar Process Integration Testing. The period of integration that will be covered is from September 1, 1973 through January 1, 1975, the shipment date of the final process to site. During this time period a total of 383 staff years were expended on the integration of this process. Of this total, 120 staff years were charged directly to the integration task and the remaining 263 staff years were integration support people, i.e., the designers and coders of the functions within the process who were called upon to correct any problems found by the integration team. This effort also included the exercise process since it was integrated with the tactical process. This yields the following integration rate:

246,000 instructions/383 staff years
= 642 instructions/staff year

The total staff expended on these two processes was 883 staff years. Hence, the integration activity represented approximately 43 percent of the total staff resources directly expended in the two areas, excluding systems engineering.

Missile Direction Center (MDC) Integration. The

time period covered by the integration of the MDC process ran from September 1, 1972 through January 1, 1975. The longer integration interval of the MDC reflects the additional complexity of this process with respect to the long range radar process plus the earlier availability of the prime functions within the MDC, e.g., the track function as opposed to the final version of the long range radar process.

During this time period a total of 734 staff years were expended on the integration of the MDC. Of this total, 215 staff years were charged directly to the integration task, while the remaining 519 staff years were involved in a support role. Also, as in the previous example, the integration numbers include the exercise process.

The integration rate for the MDC and its exercise process was:

362,000 inst./734 staff years
= 493 inst./staff year

The total staff expended was 1442 staff years, hence integration represented approximately 51 percent of the direct total development effort, excluding systems engineering.

The higher percentage expenditure of resources, and hence lower productivity rate, in the integration of the Missile Direction Center (MDC) as compared to the long range radar process can be attributed to several factors.

First, as noted several times previously, the Missile Direction Center (MDC) was the most complex and largest software process in the SAFEGUARD System, and the rate of development was a function of both factors. Second, the later start date for long range radar process integration, while correctly reflecting the useful software integration period, does not include the substantial personnel learning curve achieved in prior efforts. This learning curve is partially reflected in the MDC numbers, with its year head start. (However, some integration occurred on earlier versions). Third, the responsibility for netted system integration, i.e., the integration of both tactical processes (and exercise processes), rested with the MDC integration team. Hence, for the period of netted integration, the MDC team was performing two roles, one process testing and the other system testing.

D. Program Conversion. During the latter part of the development cycle of SAFEGUARD, it was decided to modify a portion of the data reduction package which executed on an off-line computer for operation on the real-time computer. This is an example of a development with very detailed and stable requirements, conversion of a set of already existing non-real-time programs for execution by the real-time operating system, and reprogramming from PL1 to assembly language.

The design phase of the development required four staff months. The total code and unit test interval lasted for 10.5 months. However, the first month and half was primarily a learning period in the programming language and no code was developed. A total of 66 staff months were expanded in this interval. The reduction system contained 22,200 instructions, which yields the following productivity rates:

. Design - 66,600 inst./staff year
. Code and Unit Test - 4032 inst./staff year

The only design effort necessary was conversion of the system to a real-time operating structure, hence the large productivity. The code and unit test figures represent what was done when clear, detailed, and stable requirements existed and the only "problem" was converting those requirements into tested code. This was obviously not the environment for most of the SAFEGUARD development.

VIII. Allocation of Resources

This section addresses the allocation of staff resources in the development of the SAFEGUARD real-time applications software. This data will be presented for the four major activities in software development: systems engineering, design, code and unit test, and integration testing. The integration data includes element testing, testing of several units together which formed a software path through a function, and process and system integration. The process/system integration figures are split between the direct test personnel and support activities, such as the design effort required to analyze and correct problems identified by the test effort. The staff figures reflect the data shown in Table 1 for the real-time applications software and the systems engineering effort. The total effort for these two areas was 3216 staff years. In addition 317 staff years of integration support from the design support area are included in the integration staff figures. Hence the total effort was 3533 staff years.

The Missile Direction Center (MDC) track function and long range radar process examples in Section VII yield data points for design, code and unit test, and element test. The integration examples, together with the integration expenditure of the Command Center, 50 staff years, provide the data points for process/system integration. Utilizing the project systems engineering data and the track function integration examples yields the following staff allocations:

Systems Engineering	–	20 percent
Design	–	23 percent
Code and Unit Test	–	14 percent
Integration Testing	–	43 percent
. Element	–	9 percent
. Process/System	–	34 percent
. Direct	– 11 percent	
. Support	– 23 percent	

Replacing the track function data points with those of the long range radar example yield the following changes:

Design	– 17 percent
Code and Unit Test	– 20 percent

The systems engineering, element test, process/system integration data do not change.

The higher software design costs for the track function example reflect the complexity of this function. The nature of this function made its design more difficult than the actual coding and testing. The "problem" was slightly different for the long range radar process. A portion of the changes made were quite analogous to the track function example. As noted in Section VII, however, a large portion of this software package was made up of logical code of a much simpler nature than the track example or the total applications software package. Therefore, the design activities were not nearly as complex. A considerable portion of the design, primarily of the

logical code, was done by the programmers themselves. Hence, the higher code and unit test figures. Most of this data is, however, based upon two isolated example cases. Experience in the development of the remaining applications software indicates that these two examples in staff allocation tend to bound the division of resources. Extrapolation of these data points and data from the remaining applications software provides the following "best estimate" of the staff resource allocation for the applications software development:

Systems Engineering	–	20 percent
Design	–	20 percent
Code and Unit Test	–	17 percent
Integration Testing	–	43 percent
. Element	–	9 percent
. Process/System	–	34 percent
. Direct	– 11 percent	
. Support	– 23 percent	

Eliminating systems engineering from the development effort data may give a better feel for the allocation of "pure" software development resources:

Design	– 25 percent
Code and Unit Test	– 21 percent
Integration	– 54 percent

The above sets of allocation figures are by no means precise. This is due to the nature of software development itself and to the total accuracy and availability of resource data. They are, however, quite representative of the SAFEGUARD development as a whole and of the variability existing between different types of software.

IX. Summary

This report has presented a set of software development resource expenditures as experienced in the development of the SAFEGUARD System. A number of different data points have been examined, ranging from example cases of individual functions to the entire SAFEGUARD software package. The different types of software and their basic characteristics have been highlighted. The major factors which had a significant effect upon the resource expenditures in the development of the software have been explored. In many cases these factors, due to the state of the art nature of the SAFEGUARD System, made the software development quite costly in comparison with other systems of a not so unique nature.

It is perhaps worthwhile to reiterate the major points of the report to again put the data presented in perspective.

The resources presented include all the activities required in the software development effort, from requirements to simulations to hardware installation and maintenance. The data presented does not in any way address the number of instructions that were produced by a programmer. What it does address is the resources required on SAFEGUARD to deliver a software system.

As noted above, a number of factors had a profound effect on the resources required for the SAFEGUARD System development. The very nature of the system, being a state of the art design, led to a considerable instability in requirements and design. Changes in system objectives also had major impacts. These factors led to false starts and major system design changes, which, although predicted and accounted for in SAFEGUARD planning, nevertheless had a significant impact on the resources required. The impact of these various factors is implicitly included in the resources presented and should be recognized as such.

For the reasons cited above, the numbers contained in this paper should not be considered without including the various components of the numbers and the factors affecting them. The productivity rates presented and the differences between them are highly dependent upon the different types of software and their development environments. Recognizing these guidelines, the major data points presented in the paper were:

> Total Software Developed –
> 2,261,000 instructions
>
> Total Real-Time Software Developed –
> 789,000 instructions
>
> Total Project Staff –
> 5407 staff years
>
> Total Software Productivity Rate –
> 418 instructions/staff year
>
> Real-Time Software Productivity Rate –
> 146 instructions/staff year
>
> Real-Time Software Allocation of Resources –
>
> System Engineering – 20 percent
> Design   – 20 percent
> Code and Unit Test – 17 percent
> Integration Testing – 43 percent

The lessons learned in the development of the SAFEGUARD System are numerous. Among them are some general recommendations which may prove useful in attempting to forecast software development resources for future software systems.

First, as has been stressed several times, care must be exercised to account for all facets of the development job. The many varied support tasks and software packages which are required for the development of a deliverable system can amount to considerable resource expenditures.

As can be seen from SAFEGUARD experience, 49 percent of the staff resources were not _directly_ involved in the development of the deliverable real-time software. These support activities, including requirements definition, evaluation, simulation development, and data reduction, must be accounted for and, obviously, performed in order to successfully develop a system.

Second, procedures should be developed to accurately monitor the resource allocation across the project throughout the development cycle. This will allow management to actively monitor the allocation of resources across the project, compare these allocations with planning algorithms, and update their algorithms and/or schedules as required. Reallocations of resources can be made, based upon these reports, when it becomes obvious that the correct resource balance has not been achieved. More detailed monitoring of this data should have been performed for SAFEGUARD. This would have permitted a more detailed analysis of the SAFEGUARD development process.

Third, a learning period and its associated training costs will probably be required across the

project, for programmers through upper management. This is particularly true for a first-time large-scale development project. As a result of this learning process, productivity rates will probably increase as project maturity increases.

Fourth, a very important factor to keep in mind is that neither software development nor forecasting software development resources are well defined procedures. Since there is no "standard" procedure for developing software, the resource expenditures for one project probably will not be directly applicable to another. Therefore, the information presented here must be applied cautiously to other development projects. Hopefully, the maintenance of detailed resource expenditures, as suggested above, across development projects will help make the process of forecasting for future projects more of a science than an art.

References

1. SAFEGUARD Data-Processing System, The Bell System Technical Journal, 1975 Special Supplement.

2. F. P. Brooks, _The Mythical Man Month_, Essays on Software Engineering, Addison, 1975.

NRL Report 7909

The MUDD Report: A Case Study
of Navy Software Development Practices

DAVID M. WEISS

Information Systems Staff
Communications Sciences Division

May 21, 1975

NAVAL RESEARCH LABORATORY
Washington, D.C.

PREFACE

This report is one result of a year-long investigation into Navy software problems. During this investigation the author talked to many people associated with Navy software development. All of these people, from contracting personnel to program managers to programmers, were keenly interested in finding ways to improve software quality. Although it is not yet possible to give an algorithm for producing reliable software, many mistakes can be avoided by staying aware of problems encountered in the past. The purpose here is to describe some of these problems in a context familiar to Navy software developers in the hope that they can recognize and avoid similar errors in the future.

This report chronicles the development of a mythical software system and describes where and how the developers went awry. The report is based on more than 30 interviews with people responsible for development of various kinds of Navy software in more than ten Navy activities. The pitfalls described typify problems which actually occurred in software development efforts, but all persons and situations described in this report are fictional.

The report is organized into five sections. The first section is a brief introduction. The second section is a chronicle of system development. The reader is urged to try to estimate the effect of the decisions described as he reads about them. The third section is an analysis of the mistakes made by the people who developed the system. The fourth section contains some conclusions about the system development under discussion. The fifth section contains some recommendations which will be helpful to program managers in avoiding the pitfalls described in the second and third sections.

THE MUDD REPORT:
A CASE STUDY OF NAVY SOFTWARE DEVELOPMENT PRACTICES

GLOSSARY

ANSI	American National Standards Institute
ASWCCS	Antisubmarine Warfare Command and Control System
CDBDD	Common Data Base Design Document
CDR	Critical Design Review
CONTAC	Consolidation of Tactical Data
CPDS	Computer Program Design Specification
CPPS	Computer Program Performance Specification
CPTP	Computer Program Test Plan
CPTPR	Computer Program Test Procedures
CSDD	Computer Subprogram Design Document
DROWN	Defense Related Ocean Warning Network
DUMS	Data Use and Maintenance System
FOC	Final Operational Capability
FTAC	Fleet Tactical Analysis Center
FTIC	Fleet Tactical Intelligence Center
FTOE	Fleet Tactical Operational Evaluation
FTOSA	Fleet Tactical Operational Support Agency
GECOS	General Comprehensive Operating System
IOC	Initial Operating Capability
JCS	Joint Chiefs of Staff

MUDD	Multisource Unified Data Distribution
NERL	Naval Electronics Research Laboratory
NOISY	Naval Office of Intelligence Systems
NPA	Naval Programming Activity
ODORS	Office for the Determination of Ocean Reconnaissance Strategy
OSIS	Ocean Surveillance Information System
PMAS	Program Modification Authorization System
PTA	Proposed Technical Approach
SCS	Super Computing Systems
SDS	Ship Data Source
SIPS	Ships Information Processing System
SOR	Specific Operational Requirements
TSOR	Temporary Specific Operational Requirements
WWMCCS	Worldwide Military Command and Control System

INTRODUCTION

This report is an analysis of the major problems encountered in developing the Multi-source Unified Data Distribution (MUDD) system. The emphasis is on the difficulties which caused schedule slippage and cost overruns. It is not the intention to provide here a full-scale evaluation of the system but rather to engender understanding of the pitfalls that can occur during the course of a Navy software development effort.

HISTORY

The MUDD effort began in the late 1960's. At that time a number of manual and semiautomated data collection and distribution systems existed. The purpose of these systems was to maintain a data base of items of tactical and intelligence interest. The usual procedure for obtaining an item of information from these systems (for example, the number of U.S. intelligence-gathering ships in the Atlantic during October 1965) was as follows:

1. Find someone with a list of all such systems and the people who maintained them;

2. Ca¹ ꞏ꞉ꞏ ꞏ of these people to discover whether their data base had a list of U.S. intelligence gathering ships in the Atlantic;

3. Get them to extract the necessary data from their data base;

4. Compare all lists so obtained and resolve contradictions by some (usually ad hoc) method.

People with unusual fortitude sometimes repeated steps 3 and 4 several times.

Need for MUDD

The events leading to the birth of the MUDD system occurred one summer when a submarine was reported missing in an area thought to be free of hostile forces. In the course of reacting to this report, the disposition of all forces, U.S. and otherwise, in the area of interest was requested. In addition, because of unreliable communications in the area caused by weather conditions, a request was made for the location of all ships in nearby areas that might serve as communication relays. Retrieval of the additional information took much too long. When a communication link into the area was finally established, all the procedures associated with command and control, such as briefings, transmission of tactical data, and coordination of search plans, had to be accomplished. There was much confusion and further delay. If the submarine had been under attack or in serious trouble, by the time command and control functions were established and operating, it would long have been lost.

Later investigations of this incident disclosed other cases in which retrieval and dissemination of data was delayed past the time when it was needed. A notorious example was the request made by Rear Adm. Sealey concerning the number of intelligence ships used in a certain area during the previous year. Several weeks were required to obtain the requested data. The admiral's staff found that of the four systems which had the necessary information, one was a manual system and could possibly retrieve the data from deep storage in 6 months, one automated system was down for 2 months while a new computer was being installed, with the estimated conversion time to the new computer for the necessary programs being 6 months after installation, another automated system could provide the information as soon as their lead programmer recovered from a nervous breakdown and wrote the programs, in an estimated time of 3 months and yet another automated system offered to provide the data within 2 weeks but accidentally erased the primary tape containing the information while debugging the necessary program, and the backup tape proved to be unreadable.

After the investigation, the Joint Chiefs of Staff (JCS) directed Rear Adm. Sealey to find means for quickly and efficiently retrieving and disseminating tactical data. The admiral then directed that a committee be formed to consider ways of consolidating the collection and distribution of tactical information. This committee became known as the Consolidation of Tactical Data (CONTAC) committee.

The CONTAC committee initially met in November 1968 and was composed of representatives from the Fleet Tactical Intelligence Center (FTIC), the Fleet Tactical Analysis Center (FTAC), and Fleet Tactical Operational Evaluation (FTOE).

Initial Operational Requirements

After several months of study the CONTAC committee produced a Temporary Specific Operational Requirements (TSOR) document for MUDD. A part of a transcription of a tape recording of the meeting of 18 February 1969 of the Committee, at which an outline for the TSOR was approved, is as follows:

> *Capt. J. McGork (FTOE)*: Let me review the reasoning behind Ed's [E. Wood] presentation to see if I understand it. Our ships collect an enormous amount of tactical information on a continuing basis. Most of this information is either lost or takes so long to process that it's worthless by the time we see it. Why not install an information-gathering facility on our ships which can communicate in a timely way with a central land-based computer? This computer can keep all that tactical data stored away, cross-index it, and produce it on demand. The information-gathering facility on each ship can be the same, since they're all getting the same kind of information. We could install a standard computer, like that new UYK-7, with a standard program in it to collect information. The information stored on the ship can be periodically transmitted to the computer on the shore, and vice versa. Since we're standardizing all the computers and their programs, we can keep development costs down. The only difference will be in the shore-based computer, which can be the same as the others but needs a different program. Finally, all aspects of gathering and disseminating the information will be under our control, and we can change them as we like. Now does that summarize the case pretty well?

> *Mr. E. Wood (FTAC)*: Yes sir, that's a good summary.

> *Mr. A. Corde (FTOE)*: I'd like to point out, Captain, that although conceptually the programs used to gather data on board the ships will be the same, there may be some variation in the programs from ship to ship because the ships themselves are not identical. This might be a problem, but we think we know how to handle it.

> *Capt. McGork (FOTE)*: Well, wouldn't the differences in the program be minor?

> *Mr. Corde (FTOE)*: Yes, probably.

> *Capt. McGork (FTOE)*: I don't see how that would be a real problem then.

Cdr. T. Sharp (FTIC): I don't think we should ignore the intelligence aspects here. Why restrict the material collected to tactical information? I think the system should deal with both tactical and intelligence information.

Capt. McGork (FTOE): Good point. When the final TSOR is written, let's emphasize both the tactical and intelligence aspects of this thing. We may be able to open more funding channels that way.

By the end of March 1969 the TSOR describing MUDD was written. It depicted a system in which ships at sea gather various kinds of tactical and intelligence data, store the data in an on-board computer, and transmit it periodically to a shore-based computer. The shore-based computer maintains the data it receives in a large data base and provides facilities for data analysis and transmittal back to the ships. The computer simultaneously operates in batch, time-shared, and communication modes so that it can output data on a terminal display for the benefit of intelligence analysts or a line printer and so that it can maintain communications with its data sources.

While the TSOR was being written, the Navy intelligence community heard of the plans for the proposed MUDD system. Realizing the potential of the MUDD system as a data source, intelligence was interested in contributing to the development of MUDD and using the system when it became operational.

Specific Operational Requirements

Between March and June 1969 the CONTAC committee met several more times and was expanded to include members of the Navy intelligence community. Representatives of the Naval Office of Intelligence Systems (NOISY), the Office for the Determination of Ocean Reconnaissance Strategy (ODORS), and the Defense Related Ocean Warning Network (DROWN) were added to the committee. Based on the influence of the additional committee members, the original MUDD concept was expanded and Specific Operational Requirements (SOR), along with a Proposal Technical Approach (PTA), were written. The MUDD concept, as expressed in the SOR, is to provide a system for rapid collection, correlation, and distribution of tactical and intelligence data gathered by various classes of ships at sea. Each ship designated as a MUDD source establishes a data base of tactical and intelligence data. This data base is transmitted either directly or via a relay station (perhaps a satellite) to a land-based computer. The land-based computer maintains a central data base containing all data received from ships, provides a facility for correlating and analyzing the data, and transmits relevant data back to the ships and to various interested intelligence systems. The shipborne part of the system described in the SOR was unchanged from the TSOR. The land-based system now had the additional burden of communicating with intelligence systems, some still in the predevelopment stage, such as OSIS and ASWCCS.

Before disbanding, the CONTAC committee had one major decision left to make: the assignment of responsibility for the development of MUDD. The committee debated this question over the course of several months and finally came to an impasse, as indicated by the following excerpt from the minutes of an October 1969 meeting which summarizes the nature of the dispute:

> Capt. McGork (FTOE) presented a summary of the discussion to date on the question of system development responsibility. He mentioned that each activity represented here has made a case for obtaining development responsibility. FTOE has the most experience in fleet operations and their evaluation. FTIC is the only agency represented here that combines fleet operational and intelligence experience. FTAC argues that the most important aspect of the system is tactical and therefore it should get the responsibility. NOISY has the most experience with intelligence systems and their development. DROWN claims the highest priority based on national defense and its needs. ODORS believes it has the best overall grasp of the relationship between fleet strategical operations and intelligence needs. Mr. Smith (NOISY), on behalf of Mr. Jones (ODORS), Mr. Brown (DROWN), and himself, suggested a compromise whereby the intelligence activities would assume joint responsibility for system development. This was rejected by the fleet activities. Cdr. Sharp (FTIC) then suggested, on behalf of the fleet activities, that a coalition of the fleet activities do the development. This was rejected by the intelligence activities. Mr. Wood (FTAC) proposed that the question, along with the various alternative solutions suggested be submitted to Rear Adm. Sealey for arbitration. The proposal was accepted, and Mr. Wood was directed to write a memo to the admiral explaining the situation.

Rear Adm. Sealey met with the CONTAC committee on 4 December 1969, discussed the situation with them, and informed them of the decision he had made. A transcription of a portion of that meeting is as follows:

> *Rear Adm. Sealey*: Gentlemen, this reminds me of one of the problems facing Solomon, and I plan to solve it in the same way he proposed to solve that one. You seem to have divided yourselves into two groups—the fleet activities and the intelligence activities. This system also divides naturally into two parts: an information gathering part and an information distribution part. OK. To me that means that one of the fleet activities should assume responsibility for the information gathering part, which is mostly concerned with fleet operations, and that one of the intelligence activities should assume responsibility for the information distribution part. FTOE will develop everything that's needed for gathering information on board ship and transmitting it to the central computer. NOISY will develop everything else. FTIC and FTAC will consult with FTOE, and ODORS and DROWN

will consult with NOISY. FTOE will also take responsibility for coordinating the two efforts. Capt. McGork, I want to see two PTA's, one for each part of this system, within 8 weeks. Any questions?

Initial Operating Capability of MUDD

Once the question of development responsibility for MUDD was settled, progress through the design stage of the development cycle was rapid. By mid-1970 an initial operating capability (IOC), along with cost and time estimates, had been defined, the computers and programming languages to be used were established, and the agencies to do the software development work were selected. Estimated completion time for the IOC was 18 months. Because of its proposed role as the standard Navy computer, the AN/UYK-7 was chosen for use by the MUDD system for both ship- and shore-based facilities. The Naval Electronics Research Laboratory (NERL) was chosen to develop the software for the shore-based subsystem by NOISY, ODORS, and DROWN because of the extensive experience NERL had in developing intelligence systems. The fleet activities selected the Fleet Tactical Operations Support Agency (FTOSA) to develop the software for the ship-based subsystem. FTOSA at that time was also simultaneously developing several other shipboard systems using AN/UYK-7 computers and was experienced in software development for shipboard computers.

Both NERL and FTOSA decided to use the CMS-2 programming language to develop their subsystems. The basis for the choice of CMS-2 is contained in a memorandum of 15 June 1970 from Lt. Cdr. Swift of FTOSA to Capt. McGork entitled "Selection of a programming language for the ship-based MUDD subsystem," part of which follows:

1. Candidate languages for programming the shipboard MUDD subsystem fall into two categories: assembly language and high-level languages. Examples of possible high-level languages are CMS-2, FORTRAN, COBOL, ALGOL, and PL/I.

2. Assembly language provides the required speed but is expensive in terms of development time and cost and maintenance cost. In addition, assembly-language programs are difficult to modify. For these and other reasons, current programming trends in the naval, commercial, and academic worlds favor high-level languages over assembly languages.

3. High-level languages such as FORTRAN, COBOL, ALGOL, and PL/I provide many advantages in terms of programming and computational power, ease of development and maintenance, modularity, and modifiability. The only high-level-language compilers available for the AN/UYK-7 computer are for CMS-2. Use of any other high-level language would require a high initial investment in funds and time to write a compiler.

4. Until recently CS-1 was the standard Navy tactical programming language. It has now been superseded by CMS-2. The CMS-2 language embodies a high degree of machine independence, contains a definitional facility for high-level constructs, and provides extension capabilities.

5. OPNAVINST 03500.27A of 6 March 1969 designates CMS-2 as the standard high-level language to be employed in the production of operational processor programs for tactical data systems.

6. It is recommended that the CMS-2 language be used for development of the ship-based MUDD subsystem.

Development

During the time MUDD was under development, the documentation standard Weapons Specification WS-8506, revision 1, was published and established as a Navy standard. The original MUDD specifications did not conform to WS-8506 because the standard did not exist when the specifications were written. Later revisions of the specifications, and all MUDD documentation written after WS-8506 was published, were written to conform to WS-8506. The documents mentioned here are those required by WS-8506.

The first step in the development was to produce the Computer Program Performance Specification (CPPS). Three variations of this document were eventually produced; one version for the entire MUDD system, one for the ship-based subsystem, and one for the shore-based subsystem. Events in the development followed the pattern established by splitting the software development responsibility and producing separate CPPS documents.

Prior to the start of system design, a simulation program for the shore-based system was developed. (The developers of the ship-based system never attempted a simulation.) This program began as a high-level functional simulation to gather statistics on system capability and was initially used to demonstrate the feasibility of using a UYK-7 computer for the shore-based system. An early attempt was made to use this simulator as a system simulator for use in program checkout but was later abandoned because of the effort involved in keeping it up to date.

FTOSA and NERL proceeded to design the ship- and shore-based subsystems independently of each other with occasional coordination meetings to discuss communications between the two subsystems. A Computer Program Design Specification (CPDS), Computer Subprogram Design Document (CSDD), Common Data Base Design Document (CDBDD), Computer Program Test Plan (CPTP), and Computer Program Test Procedures (CPTPR) were produced for each subsystem. A Critical Design Review (CDR) for each subsystem was then held.

Before the CPDS, CSDD, CDBDD, CPTP and CPTPR documents were produced, only the project sponsor and small system design groups at NERL and FTOSA saw the proposed designs. Neither design groups included an operational commander, intelligence analyst, or maintenance programmer.

Critical Design Reviews

The two CDR's followed essentially the same course with the same results: the two designs were approved and coding began. Only the CDR for the shore-based system is discussed here.

The CDR was held on 31 October 1970, approximately 5 months after definition of the IOC. One copy of the CPPS was delivered to NERL by its software contractor, Super Computing Systems (SCS), on 30 September 1970, 1 month prior to the CDR. One copy each of the CPDS, CSDD, CDBDD, CPTP, and CPTPR was delivered to NERL 2 weeks prior to the review. (NERL then distributed copies of these documents to all CDR attendees and to all potential users of the system.) The total amount of documentation was 723 pages. The program manager found the documents to be quite thorough and detailed. Attending the review were representatives of FTOE, NOISY, ODORS, DROWN, NERL, and SCS. With the exception of the NERL and SCS people, these representatives were only recently introduced to MUDD. The original CONTAC committee members played a role in the MUDD project for 2 years (until September 1970), but by the time of the CDR all of them had been reassigned to other projects. The description of the CDR presented here is taken from an interview with one of the attendees.

> The CDR took about 3 hours. We spent the first hour and a half listening to a presentation made by someone from SCS. He talked about the functions of the system, the computer configuration, and all of the software modules. As I recall, there was something like four modules, one for each system function like message processing, display handling, data analysis, and correlation. He went through a flowchart of each module, showing all of its submodules and their purposes. I think he would have gone into more detail, but there seemed to be a lot of questions from the management people on exactly what the system, and each of its modules, was supposed to do. Then he gave us a detailed breakdown of all the milestones for each part of the development cycle. After that he went into the reporting procedures they were going to use, the weekly and monthly meetings, and that kind of thing. After he finished, we had a question-and-answer session, mostly about backup procedures, operator interface, and printout formats. They had samples of every kind of output or input the system could handle. It was a pretty good review. They had detailed answers for everything and covered the whole system pretty thoroughly. By the end of the review, everyone was satisfied with the design.

Since there were no objections to the design at or after the CDR's, work proceeded on both subsystems. By December 1970, 2 months after the CDR's, coding of both subsystems was well started. From this time until total system integration the two software development efforts proceeded independently, except for the communication modules. The only interface between the subsystems was the messages they exchanged; hence this was the only topic the two developers discussed jointly. The history of the two development projects, up to system integration, will be discussed separately here.

DUMS Development

The shore-based subsystem was known as the Data Use and Maintenance System (DUMS). DUMS was functionally partitioned into four areas: communications, message processing, data base update and maintenance, and on-line user interaction.

Since DUMS was required to handle data of varying security classifications, it was partitioned into two separate subsystems. One subsystem, known as the high-level system, processed all data at the Top Secret level. Data at the Secret level and below was handled by the other subsystem, known as the low-level system. The requirements for the high-level system included the capability for sanitization and transmission of data to the low-level system. By using what were essentially duplicate subsystems, the DUMS developers hoped to prevent, or at least make extremely expensive, unauthorized access to highly sensitive data.

Development activity for DUMS was apportioned as follows: 30% of the time was allowed for design, 40% for coding, and 30% for checkout. A multiprocessor UYK-7 configuration was selected to provide the required computing power. Prior to MUDD few tactical or intelligence systems used multiprocessors. The DUMS designers, aware that memory sharing in computer systems often caused memory utilization problems in the software, took measures to prevent memory conflicts between programs. The design called for all references to shared memory to be processed by a special module.

The development was contracted to SCS and monitored by NERL. Between the CDR and the beginning of test and evaluation the only people aware of the specifics of development progress and the detailed workings of DUMS were the contractor personnel working on the system, the technical montors at NERL, and a few people at NOISY.

DUMS Coding

Coding of DUMS proceeded smoothly, and coding milestones were easily met. Approximately halfway through coding, a major change occurred in the DUMS system. A hardware change from the UYK-7 to a WWMCCS Honeywell computer was forced on the developers of DUMS. The results of this change were numerous and included the following:

- All code written up to this point had to be discarded because of the lack of a CMS-2 compiler for the Honeywell machine;

- Large parts of the system had to be redesigned for compatibility with GECOS, the Honeywell operating system;

- Programming personnel had to be either retrained or replaced;

- Estimated cost of the shore subsystem was increased by about 50% (part of this increase was due to initial underestimation; experience with system development enabled a more accurate estimate to be made the second time);

- Estimated system completion time was increased by 9 months (as with cost, part of this increase was also due to more accurate estimating).

Coding of DUMS was declared complete within 2 weeks of the revised estimated completion time, about 1 year after coding started. Checkout of the system took far longer than estimated however. The initial estimate for the checkout period was 30% of the development cycle, or about 5 months. The actual checkout period took about 8 months, or about 60% longer than estimated.

Many of the errors found during checkout were concentrated in mathematical subroutines. Inaccuracies in ship tracking, which were eventually traced to a position-determination routine in which the programmer used 22/7 as an approximation for π, is one example.

Another source of problems was the message-processing routines. The formats of incoming and outgoing messages, especially to and from other intelligence systems, were found to be different than expected. Modifying the system to accommodate unexpected changes to message formats was a problem that plagued the developers and continues to plague the maintainers of DUMS.

A third set of problems occurred when new versions of the GECOS operating system and FORTRAN and COBOL compilers were released partway through the checkout period. A number of new bugs appeared when the new versions went into use. One module, for example, had to be rewritten when there was a change in the meaning of the status bits returned to it by the operating system after a certain executive function was invoked. The change was undocumented, unexpected, and difficult to discover. Several weeks were required to find the resultant bug, which suddenly appeared, intermittently, after the new executive version was released. As with the previous problem, program modification to solve this type of problem has been a continual source of annoyance during the lifetime of DUMS.

In June 1972, more than 1-1/2 years after coding started, DUMS was deemed ready for system integration by NERL. The DUMS developers were somewhat surprised to find that the ship-based subsystem was not quite ready for integration at this point. In fact system integration did not start until September 1972, almost 2 years after the critical design reviews.

SIPS Development

The ship-based subsystem was known as the Ship Information Processing System (SIPS). The strategy used to develop SIPS was dictated by the number of different versions of the subsystem needed. The development of this strategy was explained in an interview with Donald Dosier, FTOSA project manager for the first year of the development effort:

> Our approach to developing the system was worked out in a series of meetings we had with the contractor. The problem was that although we had a general design which specified what modules were required

for an SDS [each shipboard system was known as a Ship Data Source],
and we had the specific requirements for each ship type that was
included in the IOC, we had no plan for going from the general design
to a specific version for a specific ship type. We considered two
approaches: one was to write a generalized system and then modify
it for each version we needed, and the other was to write one
specific version for some ship type and then modify it to fit other
ship types. The generalized system idea had the advantages that
all the common code could be immediately identified and easily
changed as functional requirements changed, a baseline system for
reference purposes would always exist, and we could control the
modification process easily so we would always know exactly what
was being modified. The disadvantage was that we would not have a
demonstrable system that could actually be installed and tested on a
ship for a long time. On the other hand, if we built a specific version
to start with, we could install it on a ship and test it while the other
versions were being derived from it. The disadvantage was that we
might not end up with as much common code as the other way, since
the programmers would be free to modify anything they thought needed
modification. The final decision rested with me, and frankly I wasn't sure
exactly what to do. The contractor finally convinced me that the two
approaches really weren't very dissimilar and that if we produced a
specific version first, we could always use it as a baseline. So we
picked the largest of the ship classes that were included in the IOC
and started to write an SDS system for that class on the theory that
since it had more functional requirements than any of the other classes,
its SDS system would be the most general.

As with DUMS, the details of development of SIPS were known to only a few people,
none of whom were to be involved in its use or maintenance.

SIPS Coding

Progress on the baseline SDS was quite good. By April 1971, approximately 7 months
after the CDR, coding was completed and testing had been started. By mid-June the
developers had enough confidence in the system to start several parallel efforts to modify
the baseline SDS to fit other ship classes. At this point in the development cycle the contractor apparently started having personnel problems. The contractor was originally chosen
by a low-bidder procedure which selected the (technically qualified) contractor with the
lowest average cost rate per programmer. Discussions with the contracting officer have
since revealed that the contractor maintained his low rates by hiring three experienced
programmer-designers at high salaries and a number of inexperienced programmers at low
salaries. Of the experienced personnel, one left the company and one was transferred at the
end of checkout of the baseline SDS. The third remained with the project and was promoted
to a managerial position several months after modification of the baseline SDS began.
Their positions were all filled by internal promotions, two from within the project and one
(the most senior) from elsewhere in the contractor's organization. The average turnover

rate of contractor personnel for the SDS project was quite high during the entire development cycle.

By October 1971, about 1 year after the start of coding, it was apparent that SIPS was far behind schedule. Milestones were slipped by an average of 12 weeks. More programmers were brought onto the project to start other parallel development efforts to modify the baseline SDS system. This was an attempt to have an SDS system ready for each class of ship in the IOC by the start of system integration. As development continued, the number of versions of SDS modules became quite large. There was a different version of every major module in the system for each ship class under development. In addition each module under development for each SDS had several versions corresponding to different progress levels and different sets of requirements, since system requirements were occasionally changed. Finally, each module had its own set of documentation. The proliferation of different versions of modules required the establishment of a strict system of controls over the coding process. A Program Modification Authorization System (PMAS) was installed in December 1971, more than a year after the start of coding. PMAS was a manual system which required a programmer to obtain approval for starting a new version of a module. All requests for new module versions, along with justification and a description of the difference between the baseline module and the new version, were kept in a single book. This book was searched for duplicate module versions before any module modification was approved. Despite these measures, SIPS was not ready for system integration until September 1972, almost 2 years after the CDR.

One more problem, not specific to MUDD, relates to the coding phase of the software development. The monitoring procedures used to assess development progress included a percent-completed estimate for each module in the system on a weekly basis. These estimates were prepared by the programmers and were often wildly inaccurate. Many programmers had a tendency to report a module as 75% complete at the end of coding. Data compiled from other system development efforts typically show that 40% to 50% of the development effort is spent in testing and debugging. Examination of MUDD progress reports shows some modules, on which work was continuing, as 90% complete for as long as 6 weeks.

MUDD Integration

System integration proceeded smoothly, in fact better than expected. The interface between the two subsystems consisted of the communication link and the messages transmitted over it. The communication programs for each subsystem were checked out by sending test messages from one subsystem to the other. System integration consisted of sending, receiving, and processing these same test messages. Both subsystems used the same test messages during checkout.

MUDD Test and Evaluation

The MUDD system was ready for test and evaluation by the beginning of December 1972, approximately 2-1/2 years after the IOC was defined and about 1 year after the initial estimated completion date for the IOC. During the initial stages of test and evaluation it became clear that many bugs were left in the system and that it worked to no one's satisfaction. One problem was that few people could agree on evaluation criteria. As specified in WS-8506, a CPTP and CPTPR were written (one for each subsystem). These were written early in the development cycle, however, and requirements and specifications, particularly for the shore-based subsystem, had undergone many changes. In addition the end users of the system (who had not been consulted since the CDR's), now that they had a chance to observe the system in operation, wanted it modified. The end users with the most complaints generally were either intelligence analysts or operational commanders. Both analysts and commanders had similar complaints: They were not receiving the data they needed, and the system was too inflexible for their requirements. For example, an operational commander could easily obtain a list of all hostile ships which entered or left a given area within the last week but could not obtain a list of hostile ships currently in his area. The existence of two independent developers complicated matters. There was much finger-pointing, cursing, and threatening. A compromise arrangement, involving rewrites of the CPTP and CPTPR (as specified in WS-8506) for each subsystem, was reached. This created further delay in system delivery.

The IOC for MUDD was delivered and turned over to the Naval Programming Activity (NPA) for maintenance in June 1973, 3 years after initiation of development and 1-1/2 years late.

In the hardware world, maintenance means the prevention and detection of component failure caused by aging and/or physical abuse. Since programs do not age or wear out, maintenance in the software world is often a euphemism for continued test and debug, and modification to meet changing requirements. This was certainly true for the MUDD system. Maintenance was especially difficult and costly because of the large number of modules in the ship subsystem. One example was the time of 3 weeks and the cost of $3000 to change a conversion constant from six-place to seven-place accuracy. Most of the cost was absorbed by documentation changes and the time needed to ferret out all modules in which the change had to be made. Most modifications were larger than this and involved changes required by the users.

One requested modification was rejected because it involved a change in formats of messages received by the SDS systems. The reason was that all modules within the system that referenced message components did so by using the disk addresses of the components. The proposed change in the format of the messages would have required a change in the way the messages were stored on the disk. The disk addresses used in all modules which referenced messages would then have had to be changed. The only way to be sure of locating all sections of code using these addresses was to read through all the programs in each SDS system. Reading through all the programs was deemed to be too expensive and time consuming just to change a message format. Somewhat later a conversion module was added which allowed the new format at the expense of translation between old and new formats.

The level of effort required for MUDD maintenance, considering programmers and analysts only, started at about 50% of the level of effort during the coding phase of the development cycle. After about 4 months the level of effort dropped to about 30% of the level during coding and has remained there since.

Final Operational Capability of MUDD

In view of the 100% time overrun and 150% cost overrun incurred by MUDD, the definition of the Final Operating Capability (FOC) was postponed several times. As of the beginning of 1974 the FOC was still not clearly defined, although several sets of requirements had been written for it. Budgetary constraints have prevented the implementation of a set of requirements satisfactory to all agencies involved in the development and use of the system. Much of the wrangling involved has been similar to the arguments over development responsibility in the original CONTAC committee.

ANALYSIS

It would be desirable to give an algorithm for the proper development of systems such as MUDD and then compare it with the process actually used by the developers. Unfortunately the art of software development has yet to be reduced to an engineering discipline, and no such algorithm is known. The best that can be done is to use hindsight-aided perception to point out the kinds of decisions that adversely affected MUDD development. Some of these decisions were external to MUDD, some were the best of several bad alternatives, and all seemed quite logical to the people who made them at the time they were made. Each contributed in some measure to increased cost and decreased performance of the MUDD system.

This section analyzes the effect on MUDD software of various development decisions. Most MUDD software problems were not the result of a single decision; hence references to the same problem appear in several different places. Similarly, references to suggested remedies appear in several different places.

Consequence of System Configuration Choice

A major consequence of deciding to install MUDD systems on ships of different classes is that the software will vary somewhat from ship to ship. This is because different ships have different equipment, have different onboard computer configurations, and collect somewhat different data. There are two ways of developing software under these conditions. One way is to develop one set of code for all ships and never vary it. The other way is to develop modules which support different requirements. All modules which support the requirements of a particular ship can then be combined to produce the system for that ship.

If one set of code is developed for all ships, different ship configurations can be represented by different sets of initialization data, and there is then only one set of code to maintain for all ships. The feasibility of this approach depends on how great the difference in shipboard equipment configurations are. (Talks with MUDD maintenance programmers indicate that this technique was not feasible for MUDD because of the large variation in shipboard equipment.) However, it seems that this sort of approach was never even considered by the designers, even though it had been successfully used in other programs, such as the fire-control software for the Talos and Terrier missiles.

If the modular approach is used, then unless the software is organized in such a way as to minimize the number of modules that change from one configuration to another, large amounts of software have to be customized for each ship. The results are increased development costs because of the extra software that must be written, inability of project management to keep track of software development, voluminous amounts of documentation to chronicle differences in different ships' systems, and a nightmare job of testing, debugging, evaluating, and modifying the software. The software design for the MUDD system becomes doubly difficult: the designers must take into account not only the effectiveness of the design for any given ship, but must also consider the effect of the design on total system development. In other words a good design for a one-ship MUDD system may be a poor design in terms of the amount of code that must be changed to fit it into a multiship system. The key consideration in the software design can be expressed as follows: Each module in the system must provide ways of using some facility of the system without revealing the method used to implement that facility. This idea is known as information hiding. A system designed with information hiding in mind allows one module to be modified without causing modifications in other modules. Such a design may be quite difficult to accomplish and may seem unnatural to a designer who considers the most important considerations to be efficiency in time and space. One example of the use of information hiding is that the module which accepts input data need not know the details of how and where this data is stored in the data base. Otherwise, when the data base format is changed, the input module must be changed also.

In view of their problems in producing SDS systems, the most important design question confronting the SIPS designers was how to partition the system in such a way that it would be easy to modify. This question was never asked, let alone answered. The interview with the FTOSA project manager concerning development strategy shows a lack of awareness of the key issues involved in partitioning software.

Rigorous application of the information-hiding principle in conjunction with a modular development approach could be expected to have yielded the following benefits to the ship-based subsystem developers.

- Production of different SDS systems could proceed on a module-by-module rather than system-by-system basis; that is, a programmer modifying a module would not have to worry about the effects on other modules of his changes.

- Programmers need not understand the entire system before starting work on any particular module. The effects of high programmer turnover rates are thereby minimized.

- A library of modules sharable among SDS systems could be established.

- Design review documents would be readable, and design decisions could be evaluated.

The designers of the ship-based subsystem did in fact use a modularized design but did not design or implement the modules according to the information-hiding principle. Most modules in each SDS system took advantage of specific implementation details of other

502

modules in the interest of efficiency. The result was that a change in one module set off a chain reaction of changes in other modules, with some of the changed modules not even referencing the module originally changed. In such a situation, adding programmers to a project can be more hindrance than help. The imposition of PMAS was an attempt to control the module explosion which resulted from the poor design technique used. Two results of PMAS were an increase in documentation and a decrease in programmer productivity; programmers waited until approval was granted for each module before coding it. Naturally system development time and cost were both increased.

Another effect of module proliferation manifested itself as difficulty in estimating system progress. Completing a set of modifications to a module yielded little information concerning progress in modifying an SDS system to fit a different ship class because of the chain reaction effect.

As we shall see later, the effects of the multiship configuration decision combined with the bad modularization strategy adopted by the SIPS developers continue to plague the MUDD system.

External Interfaces

One requirement imposed on MUDD early by the CONTAC committee was that MUDD exchange data with various intelligence systems. As a result the shore-based subsystem was continually plagued by changes in data formats required for communication with other systems such as OSIS and ASWCCS. Data interfaces were defined by negotiation between representatives of the systems. Seemingly arbitrary interface changes occurred often, sometimes unheralded by documentation and in spite of negotiations. There were (and are) no standard data formats for transferring data between computers and no agency for arbitrating disputes over where the responsibility lies for providing various types of data. Software designers must accept the uncertainties inherent in communicating with systems beyond their control as a fact of life and design accordingly. The principle of information hiding may be applied in this situation. If knowledge of the data formats used in communicating with another system are confined to a single module, only that module need be changed when the formats change. The same concept applies to communications with the operating system. Some of the errors most difficult to find in DUMS were caused by operating-system changes. Finding and correcting these errors would have been easier if they had been confined to a single module.

System Development Split

Another early MUDD decision that had significant effects on the cost of the system was Rear Adm. Sealey's compromise. Both DUMS and SIPS performed many similar functions on the same data, and many opportunities for sharing programs were not exploited. Besides design and coding, many other duplicate efforts could have been avoided by a unified development effort. Examples are critical design reviews and documentation. A more specific example is the communication subsystems. Both the ship- and shore-based subsystems had to transmit and receive messages in the same format. A common design would have allowed sharing of code and documentation. Not only the development task would have been simplified but also checkout and maintenance.

In addition to software considerations, dividing the developers into tactical and intelligence groups affected the type and format of data received by the end users. Operational commanders using an SDS received data from DUMS, whose developers were mainly interested in the intelligence considerations. The reverse was true for intelligence analysts using DUMS. The effect of this conflict of interest did not manifest itself until test and evaluation, after the software was developed and when it was hardest to modify.

Coordination with Users and Maintainers

Once the software-development phase of a system is declared complete, remaining problems are often left to be worked out between the users and the maintainers of the system. Often, neither of these groups has participated in system development. With one exception the MUDD developers did their best to maintain this tradition. The only opportunity given to end users of MUDD to comment on the system design occurred just prior to the CDR's, when they received a copy of the design documents. The maintainers did not see MUDD until after it was accepted. As a result many changes to the system were requested after it was delivered. Because it took the maintenance programmers time to learn the system, initial modifications were accomplished slowly.

In addition to the preceding problems, partitioning the life-cycle support of software among different activities can prevent the designers of a system from receiving feedback from the users concerning design mistakes made. Later systems designed by the same design group will then have the same design errors.

Choice of Computer, Language, and Support Software

Most of the decisions discussed so far had far-reaching effects on software design, coding, checkout, maintenance, and documentation; most were made without serious consideration of these effects. The choices of computer hardware, programming language, and support software to be used were made with consideration of their effects on software as the prime motivation. Unfortunately all of the choices had adverse software effects. The principle of standardizing the computers to be used was based on the idea of obtaining the capability to transport software and data unchanged from one computer to another. The idea was (and is) a good one. Since the Navy standard computer was a UYK-7, it was the necessary choice for the computer. Unfortunately the available software for UYK-7 computers was limited. The only high-level programming language available for the UYK-7 was CMS-2, a new language for which little support software had been developed. There was no operating system (either time-sharing or batch), text editor, linkage-editor, utility library, or reliable compiler available for CMS-2 on the UYK-7. Any of these would have been invaluable in developing, modifying, and testing the modules for the SDS systems. In addition CMS-2 was not well suited for producing large software systems. For example it was difficult to create and manipulate complex data structures in CMS-2. This may be one reason the disk addresses of message components were known to any program module that needed to manipulate parts of messages. Furthermore, although CMS-2 was supposed to be the standard Navy tactical programming language, as many as five versions of the language existed when MUDD development started.

Several alternatives were available to the MUDD developers at the time they decided to use CMS-2. The major ones were:

1. Develop a set of good support software for CMS-2 and the UYK-7;

2. Develop a compiler for CMS-2 on a computer with good support software and require that this compiler generate code for the UYK-7;

3. Develop a compiler for ANSI standard FORTRAN or COBOL, ALGOL, or some other "standard" high-level language for the UYK-7. Then do all software development in that language on a computer with good support software. As programs are developed, transport their high-level-language source code to the UYK-7 for use with its compiler.

With the aid of hindsight the viability of some of these approaches can be established. From the point of view of a system developer, alternatives 2 and 3 are least expensive, with 3 somewhat more attractive, since one result will be a compiler for a "standard commercial" language for the UYK-7. All programs which conform to the standards adopted for the language will then be available for use on the UYK-7. The disadvantage of this approach is that the high-level language may be inappropriate for tactical, real-time programming. In that case alternative 2 could be considered. We can estimate the cost of alternative 2 or 3 as less than 3 man-years for development of the compiler. Standard compiler development techniques are well known, and such a compiler could be written in less than 1 year, especially for a language such as ALGOL or FORTRAN.

Coding of the ship-based subsystem took about 8 months longer than expected. The corresponding cost overrun was more than 10 man-years. It is not possible to say how much time would have been saved if alternative 2 or 3 were used, but the difference between the cost overrun and the compiler development cost is more than 7 man-years. Additional benefits could have been gained using alternative 3 when DUMS was forced to a WWMCCS computer. Since WWMCCS supports ANSI standard FORTRAN and COBOL, some code might have been salvaged in the change of computers.

From the point of view of the Navy, alternative 1 is probably the least expensive, since good support software will be reusable by many system-development efforts.

Critical Design Reviews

The most significant events of the design part of the development cycle were the CDR's. The MUDD CDR's were no more than tutorials on the design of the subsystems and their expected courses of development. This was unfortunate, since the CDR's represented the last chance for detecting design flaws and estimating potential problems before the start of coding. We can point to three factors that prevented the DUMS CDR from being effective:

- It was impossible for anyone to read and analyze the massive amount of documentation within the 1 week allowed for its review before the CDR.

- The change in upper-level management before the CDR insured that none of the upper-level managers would fully comprehend the MUDD system. These managers turned the CDR's into tutorials to aid their understanding of MUDD.

- The amount of time allotted for the CDR was insufficient. A week might have been adequate but not 3 hours.

The CDR for SIPS suffered from essentially the same problems as the DUMS CDR. Because the CDR's were ineffective, no critical analysis of the design of either MUDD subsystem was ever done. An example of the type of design weakness that should have been detected at the DUMS CDR is the constraint placed on shared memory references. The constraint was imposed to prevent possible memory deadlocks between programs. The results were increased software complexity, increased software size, and increased run time of processes using shared memory. One way of looking at the design is that complexity and efficiency in space and time were traded off in fear of a ghost problem. This tradeoff was unnecessary. Other real-time systems under development at the same time as MUDD solved the problems of sharing memory without imposing any special constraints.

It is significant that FTOSA and NERL were each excluded from the other's CDR, since each would probably have been the best critic of the other's design.

Simulation

The MUDD software was required to handle data from communication lines and sensors and to deal interactively with humans. Simulators are particularly useful in supporting experimental checkout of this type of software.

A simple simulator was written and used for DUMS, but only to establish that the hardware would meet MUDD needs. The attempt to modify this simulator into a development tool failed because no one was willing to expend the effort needed to keep it up to date. This was unfortunate, since simulation can be a powerful aid in developing and maintaining a reliable system.

Documentation

Both the development programmers and the maintenance programmers at NPA could have been helped considerably by a good set of documentation. Although the set of documents specified in WS-8506 were produced for each MUDD subsystem, they often contributed to development errors and were not of much help in modifying the programs.

The numerous errors found in mathematical subroutines, such as the use of 22/7 for π, appear to be partly the result of subprogram specifications that were not written precisely; hence programmers could not understand all the desired effects of the subprograms they were writing. Another way of viewing this is that all the assumptions made by subprograms which called a particular subprogram were not explicitly specified; that is, programmers were given too much design latitude in a programming task.

Good comprehensible documentation whose structure paralleled the structure of the system would have reduced the learning time for new programmers. This was an important consideration for MUDD because of the high turnover rate among programmers who worked on the system.

The documentation, especially for SIPS, was often out of date. This became more and more true as maintenance proceeded, both because of the expense involved in changing documentation for all of the SDS systems when a change common to all of them was made and because of the patches inserted by shipboard programmers. Even had the documentation been current, it would not have helped significantly. One reason is that the motivations for implementation decisions were rarely discussed. This contributed to the fear-of-deletion syndrome to be mentioned in the maintenance subsection. In addition potentially useful flowcharts were often ambiguous or accompanied by cryptic explanations. A simple example of an ambiguous flowchart is shown in Fig. 1. The result of execution of the algorithm given in this flowchart depends on the direction of shift used in the loop. The documenter apparently felt that this was a trivial detail and specified it nowhere.

The dilemma of providing documentation which accurately reflects the current state of a system is difficult to solve. The solution probably does not lie in establishing a rigid, problem-independent documentation standard.

Development Procedures

Many of the MUDD development problems were either directly attributable to or compounded by bad software design decisions and external influences on the system. Other factors adversely influenced the development, however. One factor was that the programmers used by the contractors to do the coding either had little programming experience or were simply bad programmers. Another was the high turnover rate of contractor personnel. New programmers entering the project had to go through a learning process before they understood the requirements of their part of the system (if they ever did). A possible explanation of these two factors is that the contractor was specified in a low-bidder procedure which selected the (technically qualified) contractor with the lowest paid programmers and designers. A third factor was the dependence on programmer estimates of completion, expressed as percentages, for monitoring progress. Well-defined, demonstrable milestones would have provided a better measure.

Although coding of DUMS was completed within 2 weeks of the (revised) estimated completion date, checkout took about 3 months longer than expected. This apparently was because the computer was changed after some coding had been done. The experience gained by comparing the actual coding time to the estimated coding time was used to

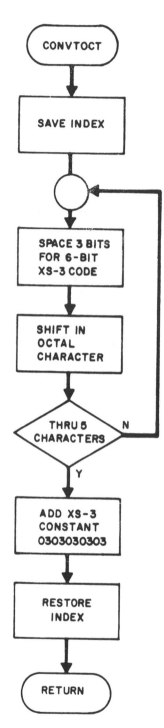

Fig. 1 — Sample MUDD flowchart

forecast accurately the time needed for coding the system on the new computer. No such experience existed for checkout however. Data compiled from other system-development efforts typically show that 40% to 50% of the development effort is spent in testing and debugging. The initial estimate for checkout of DUMS was 5 months, or 30% of the time, and the revised estimate was also 5 months.

DUMS Hardware Change

The largest disaster that befell the DUMS developers was the hardware change forced upon them. Since the developers had no control over this change, we will not discuss the reason for it. Instead we will discuss why this change was so disastrous.

The largest parts of the cost of the change were associated with redesigning the interface between the software and the computer system and recoding all programs already written. (A side issue associated with the hardware change was whether the cost of the change should be charged to hardware, software, or some combination of the two.) Redesign could not be avoided, but recoding costs associated with retraining of programmers could have been minimized if DUMS had been written in a commercially available high-level language or if a CMS-2 compiler had been available for the new computer. Another effect of using WWMCCS equipment was that the system was now subject to external influences over which the developers had little or no control. New versions of the operating system, compilers, assembler, and other support software were released and old ones discarded, with no approval by the DUMS developers required. As mentioned previously, good software partitioning would have reduced this problem. Some benefits were gleaned from the change of computer. Honeywell support software was somewhat better than UYK-7 support software, and this eased the rewrite task.

MUDD Integration Procedures

System integration of the ship- and shore-based subsystems proceeded smoothly. One might expect this, since the only point of contact between the two involved communications, and the communication specifications were jointly developed. The remainder of each subsystem was independent of the other and had already undergone checkout prior to system integration. In addition the data used to perform integration tests were mostly the same as the data used to check out the subsystems. This was probably because generation of test data was not easy, partly owing to the lack of a simulator.

MUDD Test and Evaluation Procedures

It is not surprising that MUDD test and evaluation did not proceed smoothly. The project was conceived in 1969 and did not undergo any evaluation until 1973. During that interval system requirements changed significantly without corresponding changes of the evaluation criteria or the test plan. Moreover, after critical design reviews, the users of the system were not consulted concerning their needs. Finally, as was noted, system integration procedures did not thoroughly test the entire system. Consequently, when real data were used during operational test and evaluation, many bugs appeared for the first time. Attempts to locate the cause of errors were complicated by lack of trust between the developers. Each contractor tried to fix the blame for programming problems on the other contractor.

Conflicts between intelligence and tactical requirements appeared during test and evaluation. Many requests for system modifications, caused by these conflicts, were made during this time. The example given previously, wherein an operational commander wanted position reports on hostile ships in his area, while the intelligence analyst was mainly interested in the sailing patterns of the ships, is typical. DUMS maintained the sailing patterns and some sighting data on a tape file that was updated once a week in a batch mode. To send tracking data to an SDS on a daily basis required that the data be kept in an online file, which meant either adding it to a new file or fitting it into the data base kept by DUMS. Since there were a number of requests like this, a redesign of the data base was required. Since the format of the data base was known and used by many DUMS routines, the proposed redesign would have been costly and lengthly and was postponed until the "maintenance" stage. The effects of many of the early MUDD decisions, such as splitting the development effort, not continually consulting the users, and not using a good software partitioning strategy, were clearly apparent here.

Because of the many changes to MUDD, both proposed and actual, since its inception, the question of what was an acceptable system was open to much discussion. One possible hindsight-aided solution to this problem is to have had a careful definition of acceptance requirements, with allowances for change, written into development contracts. At least this would have provided firm grounds for acceptance, nonacceptance, or negotiation.

MUDD Maintenance

The accumulation of many of the problems from the test and evaluation procedure descended on the heads of the maintenance programmmers. Since NPA had no hand in designing, developing, testing, or using MUDD, it took the NPA programmers some time to understand the system. Talks with NPA programmers indicate that they were appalled at the job of modifying and debugging MUDD, especially the ship-based subsystem. One fear ever-present in their minds was that they could never detect all the side effects of deleting a section of code. Consequently they never deleted any sections of code. They effected modifications by jumping around sections of code that they suspected were no longer needed. Unfortunately they could not be sure that a section of code was unneeded without an inordinate amount of effort. Of course this made the program more difficult for the next programmer to modify. The amount of code in the system continued (and continues) slowly to grow as modifications are made. The cost of modifying MUDD also continues to grow as it becomes harder and harder to understand any part of the system.

The maintenance programmers were plagued with an additional major problem. Since the lead time for modifying programs was long, shipboard personnel sometimes inserted corrections, known as patches, directly into the shipboard SDS computers. These patches were often passed from one ship to another. Soon a library of patches was circulating among SDS ships. A maintenance programmer trying to modify or correct an SDS program was unaware of some of the code in the shipboard system; hence his changes often would not work. Maintenance on MUDD was frustrating.

As is true in many Navy systems, the separation of maintenance programmers from software developers prevented the developers from becoming aware of the problems some of their decisions caused. This may lead to a repetition of these problems when later systems are developed.

CONCLUSIONS

This report shows the kinds of bad decisions, both internal and external to MUDD, which adversely affected MUDD development. Usually the adverse effects were not immediately obvious and generally depended on hidden assumptions that the decision makers were not aware of. Unfortunately consequences of many of these decisions troubled the project throughout its development and continue to trouble it. In a report of this kind it is easy to pint out and even deride such decisions. It should be remembered, however, that the MUDD developers were trying to produce a system of a type which had not been produced previously and which used new hardware (the UYK-7) and new software (CMS-2) at the same time. Consequently a model of the development process was not available to the system developers. It is hoped that anyone who undertakes development of a similar system will use MUDD as a source of synthetic experience which will help to avoid similar errors.

RECOMMENDATIONS

Although there is no known algorithm for proper software development, it is possible to avoid many of the kinds of pitfalls described in this MUDD report. The list of recommendations given below are designed to help those responsible for the creation and support of Navy software systems. Most of the recommendations in one way or another are concerned with interfaces: interfaces between and within systems, interfaces between people, interfaces between the Navy and its contractors, interfaces within the Navy, etc. Each recommendation is as specific as possible, with an attached set of problems, usually drawn from the MUDD report, which the recommendation should help avoid.

- *Unify life-cycle control of software.* Development responsibility for a system should not be split, and maintenance activity should not be independent of development activity. In particular, system maintainers should participate in the development cycle from requirements definitions to delivery. Separation of control over software during its lifetime leads to additional interfaces and inhibits feedback useful for preventing repetition of errors.

- *Require the participation of experienced software engineers in all system decisions.* The effect of early decisions such as determination of system configuration, assignment of development responsibility, and choice of support software on system software is not always obvious.

- *Require the participantion of system users in the development cycle from the time requirements are established until the time the system is delivered.* MUDD users never saw the system until operational test and evaluation. Many of the modifications they then requested could not be implemented because the changes were too costly. Changes which are inexpensive and easy at system design time are often extremely expensive and difficult after the software has been written.

- *Write acceptance criteria into software development contracts.* Both the contracting agency and the contractor then have a clear idea of the requirements the system must meet to be accepted. If the criteria are not clearly established in the contract, there may be misunderstanding and a protracted delay for negotiation before the system is delivered.

- *Develop software on a system that provides good support facilities.* If necessary, consider developing support software prior to or in conjunction with system development. Most support software is a good example of sharable software. The DUMS developers were considerably aided by the presence of support software, and the SDS developers were sorely in need of it. Support software includes, among others, assemblers, compilers, operating system, text editors, and management information systems.

- *Design software for maximum compatibility and reusability.* Design decisions that cause one system to be distinguished from another should be delayed as long as possible in the design process. If MUDD had been designed in this way, there would have been little difference between DUMS and SIPS. The differences that existed would have been isolated and easily traceable to a few design decisions.

- *Allocate development time properly among design, coding, and checkout.* Software-development experience indicates that *rough* estimates for these phases are 40% for design, 20% for coding, and 40% for checkout. Some of the variables involved are the nature of the project, the design models available for the project, and the experience of the designers. All developers should keep a file of past experience in this area for future guidance. Since manpower-allocation estimates are based in part on the time estimates for the different phases of development, improper estimation can be quite expensive.

- *List, in advance of design, all areas in which requirements are likely to change.* This can be done at the time requirements are stated and will help the designer to partition the software. The responsibility for identifying all areas where requirement changes are most likely to occur lies with the program manager. He must specify these areas as early as possible to all concerned, including contractors, developing agencies, and system designers.

● *Use state-of-the-art design principles, such as information hiding.* Large systems, such as the ship-based subsystem of MUDD, must be designed using principles that optimize the chances for producing reliable, inexpensive, maintainable software. The resulting design may even seem unnatural to designers accustomed to optimizing for efficiency. Ignorance of information hiding helped produce a MUDD system that was expensive, late, unreliable, and difficult (and sometimes impossible) to improve or maintain. The basic problem in MUDD was that each module took advantage of implementation decisions made in other modules. A change to one module then started a chain reaction of changes in other modules. Naturally, the larger the number of changes required, the lower the probability and the higher the expense of correctly implementing a modification to the system.

The software design should isolate and insulate all areas where requirements are most likely to change. In particular all interfaces with other systems over which the developers and users have no control should be transparent to the rest of the system. Data obtained from other systems can change in format in unpredicted and unheralded ways. Often the only recourse in such situations is to change the module which inputs the data. A change of this nature should not require a change to more than one module. This is an important instance of the need for information hiding.

● *Critical design reviews should be active reviews and not passive tutorials.* Sufficient time must be allowed to read design documents before the review, and the documents must be readable. Alternative design decisions and the reasons for eliminating them should be discussed. In addition no code should be written until the design is approved. The critical design review is the last and most important time to catch errors before coding starts. Once code has been written, any design change involves at least examining all existing code for the impact of the change and may involve discarding and modifying code. System progress is delayed during this process. Consequently the cost of a design change during coding may be 2 or 3 times the cost of the change before coding. The multiplier becomes larger the farther the system progresses in the development cycle.

● *Do not depend on progress reports to know the state of the system.* Progress reports ultimately depend on the programmer's estimate of his progress. Programmers are notoriously optimistic concerning the state of their programs. There is always "just one bug left." Rather than progress reports, milestones can be used as an indication of development progress.

● *Require executable milestones that can be satisfactorily demonstrated.* Without demonstration of soundness, major design decisions may be left untested until it is too late to change them at reasonable cost. Milestones demonstrating system capabilities that will rest on major design decisions should be written into development contracts.

- *Ensure that a proper variety of test data is used.* The differing MUDD experience between system integration and test and evaluation is indicative of some of the problems that arise when a system is incompletely tested. Support software capable of monitoring system tests and reporting on failure and on what code has and has not been tested is now coming into use. Generation of test data can be facilitated by the use of a simulator. Although testing cannot by itself be used to guarantee reliability, it will probably remain for some time to come as the basis for finding errors and inspiring confidence in systems.

- *Maintain current, complete documentation.* Documentation is an often neglected part of software development. In many systems it is done on an after-the-fact basis and rarely updated. This may be because no one knows how to do it properly. Unreliable documentation forces the maintenance programmer to rely on nothing but code reading, a long and tedious process, for his understanding of the system. Well-written documentation will have few redundancies and many cross-references; it will be tailored to suit the system being documented. One sure sign of danger is when coders use unofficial documents and produce the official ones only because of contract requirements.

ACKNOWLEDGMENTS

Although this report purports to be the work of a single author, it is his expression of the accumulated software experiences of many people. Thanks are owed to all of those who patiently endured the questions of the author and thereby contributed their time and some part of their experience. Significant contributions were also made by Frank Manola, Dr. David Parnas and Dr. John Shore, all of whom helped clarify many sections of this report. Thanks are also owed to Georgine Spisak, who patiently typed and retyped many early drafts.

CITED REFERENCES

1.   Alvin Toffler, *Future Shock*, Random House, New York, 1970.

2.   C. E. Garrison, "Technological Progress in Electronic Components, A Life Cycle Support Problem," *Defense Systems Management Review, 1 (1): 25-38 (1976).*

3.   "Worldwide Electronics Market," *Electronics Magazine,* 50 (1):   81-82 (1976).

4.   "Memories," *Electronics Magazine,* 50 (3):   46-48 (1977).

5.   Phillip J. Klass, "Chip Carriers Offer Microcircuit Gains," *Aviation Week and Space Technology,* 106 (4):   49-51 (1977).

Part IX: Annotated Software Management Bibliography

This short bibliography provides the reader with a list of references on software management-related topics. Entries selected are to be used by the practicing manager; therefore, readability and practicality were the primary criteria used in preparing this list. The intention of this list is to provide the entry-level reader with a number of useful references. Thus, theoretical and/or philosophical considerations were somewhat sacrificed.

1. B. Abramson and R.D. Kennedy, *Managing Small Projects, TRW Technical Report TRW-SS-69-02,* Redondo Beach, Calif., January 1969.

This well-written, humorous book condenses some hard lessons learned in project management and communicates them in a style that is extremely readable. The book stresses the planning and review processes and provides practical hints on how-to do it.

2. L.J. Arthur, *Programmer Productivity: Myths, Methods and Murphology,* John Wiley & Sons, New York, 1983.

This book relates metrics to the software life cycle and advances approaches to use software engineering technology to improve organizational productivity and quality. The book has some good ideas and is worthwhile reading for managers trying to understand how to use the technology base to help themselves manage new developments.

3. E.H. Bersoff, V.D. Henderson, and S.G. Siegel, *Software Configuration Management: An Investment in Product Integrity,* Prentice-Hall, Englewood Cliffs, N.J., 1980.

This book provides a comprehensive and complete discussion of the subject of software configuration management. The topics of configuration identification, configuration controls, configuration auditing, and status accounting are developed simply and with insight into potential problem areas.

4. B.W. Boehm, *Software Engineering Economics,* Prentice-Hall, Englewood Cliffs, N.J., 1981.

This classic text discusses the issues, experiences, and approaches associated with software cost estimation and life cycle management and describes the COnstructive COst MOdel (COCOMO) software cost and schedule estimation model and the factors, constraints, and mathematical formulas upon which it is based. It shows how the model can be used to help managers better plan and control their projects so acceptable projects will be delivered on-time and within budget.

5. D.H. Brandon, *Data Processing Organization and Manpower Planning,* Petrocelli, New York, N.Y., 1974.

This book concentrates on people issues in data processing and discusses functions performed, organizational options, job families, personnel selection criteria, training, and the like. The book is very useful to those who are planning to start an organization and define its job descriptions and career paths.

6. F.P. Brooks, Jr., *The Mythical Man-Month: Essays on Software Engineering,* Addison-Wesley, Reading, Mass., 1975.

This well-written monograph discusses the problems and pitfalls that beset the author as he managed the development of the IBM 360 operating system. Well illustrated, readable, and full of sagacious advice.

7. J.D. Cooper and M.J. Fisher, *Software Quality Management,* Petrocelli, New York, N.Y., 1979.

This excellent collection of papers treats all aspects of software quality management from metrics through tools and techniques. Although dated, it is probably the best work on quality available today.

8. J.D. Couger and R.A. Zawacki, *Motivating and Managing Computer Personnel,* Wiley-Interscience, New York, N.Y., 1980.

This book discusses what interests data processing people in their work environment. Concentration is placed on understanding one's self and one's subordinates.

9. Defense Systems Management School, *System Engineering Management Guide,* available from Fort Belvoir, Virginia, 1983.

This guidebook was developed to establish a framework for managing the development of complex, large-scale weapons system projects. The guide discusses tools and techniques used to define a systems requirements, configure the system, manage its development, and verify the capability of its design. Interesting sections on technical performance achievement and risk management are included in the text.

10. T. DeMarco, *Controlling Software Projects,* Yourdon Press, New York, N.Y., 1982.

This book's message is that measurement is an inseparable part of the planning and control process and stresses the need to establish metrics. The book advocates that the measurement system used for project control be established as the estimates for it are generated.

11. J.R. Distaso, B.F. Kohl, K.W. Krause, J.W. Shively, E.D. Stuckle, J.T. Ulmer, and L.R. Valembois, *Developing Large-Scale, Real-Time Software: The BMD-STP Experience, TRW Technical Report TRW-SS-79-01,* Redondo Beach, Calif., February 1979.

A hard-hitting post mortem that describes the software engineering techniques used and the lessons learned during the development of the very large, real-time, anti-missile defense system, the System Technology Program.

12. P.F. Drucker, *Management: Tasks, Responsibilities, Practices,* Harper and Row, New York, 1974.

Peter Drucker writes books on management that read like novels. His insight, knowledge, and keen presentation skill are communicated in this classic text, which touches on many aspects of management that a data processing executive needs to know.

13. M. Dyer, "The Management of Software Engineering, Part IV: Software Development Practices," *IBM Systems Journal,* Vol. 19, No. 4, 1980, pages 451-465.

This fourth article in the *IBM Systems Journal* series discusses coding, testing, and integration technology and their relationship with IBM's life-cycle software engineering and management practices and details the practices used to manage code and ensure its correctness.

14. M.W. Evans, P. Piazza, and J.B. Dolkas, *Principles of Productive Software Management,* John Wiley & Sons, New York, 1983.

This well-written text attempts to resolve issues in software management by describing techniques that can be integrated to help project leaders to plan and control the process and products of software development. The book, which also contains an excellent discussion on the topic of test management, relates support disciplines like configuration management to the process and shows how they can be used to reduce risk.

15. D.P. Freedman and G.M. Weinberg, *Handbook of Walkthroughs, Inspections and Technical Reviews,* (Third Edition), Little, Brown and Company, Boston, Mass., 1982.

This handbook discusses the subject of technical reviews and the mechanics of successfully holding them and provides answers to the questions "How do I structure the review environment?" "How do I conduct a review?" and "How do I report the results?." The book is well written, easy to use, and insightful.

16. H. Dines Hanson, *Up and Running,* Yourdon press, New York, N.Y., 1984.

This book describes how structured techniques were used to make an electronic bond system project a success and shows how good software engineering and management methods can be combined to create a framework that allows a manager to assist both the progress of the project and quality of the products during the development of the system.

17. P.L. Hunsaker and A.J. Alessandra, *The Art of Managing People,* Prentice-Hall, Englewood Cliffs, N.J., 1980.

This book describes how to deal with people and emphasizes the need for interaction and discusses techniques for effective listening, questioning, projecting and problem solving. The book is simple to understand and has some very profound messages.

18. H. Koontz and C. O'Donnell, *Principles of Management: An Analysis of Managerial Functions,* McGraw-Hill, New York, 1972.

This is one of the classic textbooks in management and is recommended to all those who wish to broaden their viewpoint into management realms. Each of the five functions of management are detailed, as are the principles that govern their effective use.

19. R.C. Linger, "The Management of Software Engineering, Part III: Software Design Practices," *IBM Systems Journal,* Vol. 19. No. 4, 1980, pages 432-450.

This third article in the *IBM Systems Journal* series discusses software design technology and its relationship with IBM life-cycle software engineering practices and procedures and details the design practices used to develop correct software on time and within budget.

20. D. McGregor, *The Human Side of Enterprise,* McGraw-Hill, New York, 1960.

Another of the classic textbooks in management. This readable text discusses the Theory X versus the Theory Y manager, which is important to understand because it serves as a basis for understanding what can be used to motivate programing professionals.

21. H.D. Mills, "The Management of Software Engineering, Part I: Principles of Software Engineering," *IBM Systems Journal*, Vol. 19, No. 4, 1980, pages 415-420.

This introductory article defines what software engineering is and discusses its relationship to software management. It is the first part of a five-part discussion on the subject of the practices used to manage software engineering at IBM Federal Systems Division.

22. P.W. Metzger, *Managing a Programming Project,* Second Edition, Prentice-Hall, Englewood Cliffs, N.J., 1981.

This textbook describes how project management techniques can be related to the software life cycle to produce visible products that satisfy user requirements. Tasks and products are described in detail and related to project management techniques in this easy to read volume.

23. D. O'Neill, "The Management of Software Engineering, Part II: Software Engineering Program," *IBM System Journal,* Vol. 19, No. 4, 1980, pages 421-431.

This article describes the software life cycle and related software engineering technical interfaces and defines skills needed and describes the IBM training approach used to develop these skills.

24. W. Ouchi, *Theory Z: How American Business Can Meet the Japanese Challenge,* Addison Wesley, Reading, Mass., 1981.

This book discusses how American firms could learn from the Japanese to make their work environments more socially attractive and to motivate their employees to greater productivity. The book compares U.S. and Japanese employer/employee roles and attitudes and shows how they can be combined to create a humanistic philosophy of management directed toward mutually beneficial common goals. The book demonstrates its hypotheses by describing how several firms like Hewlett Packard have put similar management styles into practice over the last decade.

25. A. Perlis, F. Sayward, and M. Shaw (Editors), *Software Metrics: An Analysis and Evaluation*, The MIT Press, Cambridge, Mass., 1981.

This collection of papers discusses metrics and its role during the life cycle. From a managerial viewpoint, much of what is described is very theoretical. Review of the volume can yield some useful insights into how to employ the technology as a control tool.

26. T.J. Peters and R.H. Waterman, Jr., *In Search of Excellence*, Harper & Row, New York, N.Y., 1982.

This management classic, which advocates a return to the basics of management, advances strategies that companies can follow to be successful. Some of its messages to managers include: have a bias for action; be close to your customer; use a simple and lean staff; employ a hands-on, value-driven style; and achieve productivity through people management.

27. N.H. Prentiss, Jr., *Viking Software Data, RADC-TR-77-168*, Rome, N.Y., May 1977.

A post mortem of the Viking project that discusses problems encountered, their solutions, and major lessons learned. Interesting reading for all those venturing into project management.

28. R.E. Quinnan, "The Management of Software Engineering, Part V: Software Enginering Management Practices," *IBM Systems Journal*, Vol. 19, No. 4, 1980, pages 451-465.

This article discusses the software management practices used by IBM to manage its software engineering program. Documentation, reviews, cost management, and program management practices are discussed.

29. D.J. Reifer, "Contracting for Software Quality Assurance," *Proceedings of the 13th Hawaii International Conference on System Science*, University of Hawaii, Honolulu, Hawaii, January 1980.

This paper discusses contractual strategies for acquiring quality software. Incentives (both positive and negative) are discussed and examples provided to show that the approach works in the real world.

30. T.A. Rullo, *Advances in Computer Programming Management*, Volume 1, Heyden & Sons, Hasbrouck Heights, N.J., 1980.

Another collection of papers that discusses the many aspects of software engineering management. Unfortunately, it does so in somewhat of an ad hoc manner. Many of the papers tend toward the theoretical, although they seem full of common sense.

31. P.C. Semprevivo, *Teams in Information Systems Development*, Yourdon Press, New York, N.Y., 1980.

This monograph presents a comprehensive approach to organizing, evaluating, and improving team performance when building effective information systems. Guidelines are presented in a form that allows them to be used almost immediately.

32. B. Shneiderman, *Software Psychology*, Winthrop, New York, N.Y., 1980.

This text discusses the team approach to programing and provides insights into its positive and negative attributes. Some criteria for selection are described, as are the problems in putting the approach into action. Programing as human performance is also discussed.

33. H.F. Spirer and D.J. Reifer, *Successful Management of Software Projects*, the MGI Management Institute, available from the Association for Computing Machinery, New York, N.Y., 1980.

This two-volume, self-study course provides skill development in the rudiments of the five aspects of software management: planning, organizing, staffing, directing, and controlling. Useful for the new manager trying to figure out what to do.

34. R.C. Tausworthe, *Standardized Development of Computer Software*, Part I: *Methods, Report SP43-29*, Jet Propulsion Laboratory, Pasadena, Calif., July 1976.

This monograph discusses various methods used in the development of software and describes how they can be integrated together to form a consistent and disciplined methodology. Excellent book on the interface between software engineering and management.

35. R.C. Tausworthe, *Standardized Development of Computer Software, Part II: Standards, Report SP43-29*, Jet Propulsion Laboratory, Pasadena, Calif., August 1978.

This monograph establishes the detailed rules used for software implementation on the Deep Space Network project. Standards described include those for requirements, design, coding, testing, quality assurance, and documentation.

36. R. Thomsett, *People and Project Management*, Yourdon Press, New York, N.Y., 1980.

This monograph is a well-written, nicely illustrated treatise on the interface between people and methods in a project management environment. Good reading, but too short and with too little detail to put the concepts into practice.

37. W.S. Turner III, *Project Auditing Methodology*, North-Holland, Amsterdam, The Netherlands, 1980.

This book provides the reader with an in-depth coverage of audits. It begins by describing the principles behind audits and what they are really trying to achieve and then discusses audit concepts, procedures, and reporting, emphasizing what is needed to make them work for you instead of against you. It also provides lessons learned to help the reader avoid mistakes commonly made by non practitioners.

38. P. Wegner (Editor), *Research Directions in Software Technology,* The MIT Press, Cambridge, Mass., 1979.

This book provides the reader with an understandable but nontrivial description of concepts and research issues associated with software technology. The problems in large system development are identified, and methods to deal with them are discussed. Good book for gaining insight into technological risks and what is being done to handle them.

39. G. Weinberg, *The Psychology of Computer Programming,* Van Nostrant Reinhold, New York, N.Y. 1971.

This is indeed one of the classics in the field. Weinberg provides advice and insight into the psychological considerations of programing. The egoless programing approach recommended is as applicable today as it was a decade ago.